# SOURCE READINGS
# IN ANCIENT HISTORY

## *The Ancient Near East*
## *and Greece*

# SOURCE READINGS IN ANCIENT HISTORY

## The Ancient Near East and Greece

❁❁❁❁❁

### LOUIS COHN-HAFT

*Smith College*

THOMAS Y. CROWELL COMPANY

*New York · Established 1834*

*To*

HERA, TONY, MARIO

First Printing, June, 1965
Second Printing, September, 1967

# PREFACE

THIS collection of source readings stems from the experience of over a decade of teaching at Smith College, where an introductory course in ancient history has been given annually to about a hundred students. In this enterprise over the years my colleagues and I eliminated first the textbooks, and then gradually all but the smallest vestiges of reading in modern works in favor of required reading exclusively in the sources. We cannot claim that this is the best, or even the only good way to teach ancient history, but we have been gratified by the results.

The remarkable and heartening growth in the availability of translations of classical literature in inexpensive paperback books has been a boon to us, as no doubt it has been to all who teach ancient history. Nevertheless, the variety of material wanted for a course in ancient history is such as to make a "reader" highly desirable. My purpose has accordingly been to compile an anthology substantial enough to suffice as the only required reading for the course, and the generosity of a brave publisher has indeed made it possible to include in this volume a far greater extent and variety of sources than are to be found in other currently available collections. Even so, any anthology is only a sampling. A word is therefore in order about the principles that guided the selection.

An attempt has been made to give some idea of the variety that exists in the accessible texts. At least one example has been included of nearly every kind of source: papyri, inscriptions, literary works of all sorts, and official documents both public and private. Equal treatment, however, has not been aimed at; rather the effort has been (on pedagogical grounds) to emphasize readings that are not mere fragments or snippets but those long enough and intrinsically engaging enough to be, if not in every case positively pleasurable, at any rate readable. There are included, therefore, many more literary sources—substantial passages and in many instances complete texts—than the usually briefer and thornier nonliterary documents. (For this distinction, as well as other technical matters regarding the ancient texts, the reader should consult the introductory essay on "The Sources for Ancient History.") Among the literary sources themselves, particular effort

[ v ]

has been made to present lesser known authors and works. The celebrated authors have not been neglected, but the primary criterion for selection has been the value of the passage to the student of history rather than its literary importance. The humbler authors have thus received far more space than is usually their lot, for in many instances they are of great significance to the historian, although little prized by the literary critic.

Another emphasis has been that placed on particular topics. Negatively, the most striking example of this is in the important topic of ancient religion. I have omitted even the most famous of the hymns and prayers that occupy so large a place in the sources for the Near East. These pieces, while sometimes quite beautiful, are suited rather to such specialized studies as theology and poetic imagery. They do not in my experience yield much to the student of general history, and the nature of religion and the imposing role played by it among the peoples of the ancient Near East are, I believe, sufficiently attested in practically every other kind of source. On the positive side, the most conspicuous topical emphasis is that given to law, legal institutions, and law courts. The sources for almost all the ancient peoples are exceptionally rich in this sort of material. Also, the law codes and judicial proceedings deal with a very wide range of customs, institutions, attitudes, ideas, and people—and further, they are usually found in documents that are both extensive and intrinsically interesting.

On one matter a customary apology is demanded: the spelling of proper names. Complete consistency is impossible short of such grotesqueries as Sokrates, Platon, Aristoteles, Thoukydides, and so forth. Similarly with the Near East, and especially Egypt, where to use spellings refined by the latest scholarship (as, for instance, in the late Sir Alan Gardiner's *Egypt of the Pharaohs,* 1961) would be to load the text with accents, breathings, and other phonetic markings. To add to the difficulties, in the translations I have used, the translators often follow differing conventions. I have chosen to leave the spellings of proper names as I found them, except in a few cases where it appeared confusion might result. In this I have been comforted by the knowledge that the ancients themselves cared little for orthographic consistency and are thus the more faithfully represented by a modest anarchy in this respect. No serious reader is likely, I believe, to be bothered by such interchangeable spellings as: Amon–Amun–Amen, Ellil–Enlil, Athena–Athene, Peiraeus–Piraeus. Another kind of inconsistency may seem less justifiable to some. Many of the translators are English, and I have left in their texts such Anglicisms as *-ise* (e.g., realise) and the ubiquitous *-our* (e.g., honour), where an American writes *-ize* and or.

Explanatory notes have been kept to a minimum for two reasons: first, I believe the impact of source readings to be greater when they are read without intrusions; second, the student ought, I think, to be encouraged to deduce everything he can from the text itself and then learn to seek further needed information for himself. On the other hand, the student is not an expert, and footnotes have been used where it seemed nothing was to be gained by forcing him to seek highly specialized and perhaps inaccessible data. A glossary of technical terms, especially units of currency and weights and measures, is printed at the end of the volume, along with an index of sources, and these should satisfactorily supplement the material found in the footnotes and in the introductions to individual selections.

For a book such as this, the customary expressions of gratitude are inevitably inadequate since most of the book is patently the work of others. Aside from the translators and publishers, who are credited individually in the appropriate places, there are persons to whom I owe a special acknowledgment for making this collection possible. My wife, Athena Capraro Cohn-Haft, in reading, advising, typing, and proofreading, has worked as hard on the book as I have. My colleagues in the teaching of History 12, Nina G. Garsoïan, Helen Stokes Greven, Nelly S. Hoyt, Charles W. MacSherry, and Max Salvadori, have helped more perhaps than they know, in giving me the benefit of their experiences in the course. Kathleen J. Lord not only typed substantial portions of the book, but while I was on a lengthy stay abroad did much of the arduous and sometimes vexing labor of obtaining the necessary permissions to reprint copyrighted translations. The librarians of the William Allan Neilson Library of Smith College were, as always, devoted, skilled, and gracious in tracking down the obscure information and frequently even more obscure texts I sought. Finally, I owe much to the several people at the Thomas Y. Crowell Company whom I can now claim as friends: especially John T. Hawes, whose idea it was to produce the book; and Philip Winsor, whose editorial pencil and never-failing patience and courtesy contributed decisively to steering the work to completion.

LOUIS COHN-HAFT

*Northampton, Massachusetts*
*April, 1965*

# CONTENTS

# II

# PEOPLES OF THE
# EARLY IRON AGE

# Contents

# III

# THE CLASSICAL AGE

# OF GREECE

# IV

## ASPECTS OF CLASSICAL GREEK CULTURE

# CONTENTS

# THE SOURCES FOR
# ANCIENT HISTORY

## WHAT IS A "SOURCE"?

IN the modern study of history a continually increasing emphasis has been placed upon "letting the past speak for itself"—in short, upon the sources. A book like this one is a reflection of this tendency to introduce the student directly to the voice of the past rather than to have him know it only through the interpretations of present-day historians. A historical "source" may be readily defined as *anything* that has been preserved that was contemporary with the period under study: a thought, a voice, a building, a poem, a dish, a laundry bill. Some of these potential sources are by their nature not preservable; others, such as voices or moving images, have only been susceptible of preservation in very recent times; many others that might have been preserved have been lost through indifference, accident, or deliberate destruction.

## ARCHAEOLOGY

From the distant period called "antiquity" relatively little has survived, and it is therefore all the more fitting that great stress be placed upon the sources as the meager materials from which we try to understand the remote past. In the last hundred years these slender remains have been notably augmented by archaeologists who literally dig up the past. In the process not only have important additions to existing areas of knowledge been made, but whole epochs of history, hitherto completely lost, have been opened to study.

What the archaeologist finds are, of course, material objects, and these range from such glamorous items as the treasure buried with the Egyptian king Tut-ankh-Amon to more prosaic (and more abundant) finds of broken pottery. Most of the sources uncovered are non-written sources, but some are objects on which writing is found, and it is to written sources alone that, for evident practical reasons, the present volumes are restricted.

## WRITING MATERIALS

In the selection and exploitation of materials on which and with which to write, great variety exists, and human ingenuity has been bounded only by custom and by available natural resources. In the first part of this book the two major geographical areas studied are Mesopotamia and Egypt. In Mesopotamia and the lands of Hither Asia to which Mesopotamian influence spread, the availability of clay from the muddy riverbanks led to its use as the main material on which writing was done. A few very important public documents (like Selection 5, the Law Code of Hammurabi) were carved on stone, but the overwhelming mass of written material from this area is found on tablets of clay. When dried, these tablets became very hard; and in archaeological excavations in Mesopotamia and the adjoining lands such inscribed clay tablets are regularly found, frequently in great quantity. In Egypt stone is plentiful and it was regularly used as a writing material, but the great Egyptian contribution was writing in ink on paper manufactured from the pulp of the papyrus plant, which grows in profusion along the banks of the Nile River. In the extremely dry climate this rugged paper resisted rot, and tens of thousands of papyrus documents from all epochs of ancient Egyptian history have been found. Clay, papyrus, and stone are the chief materials on which the ancients wrote, but they are not the only ones, and writings are also discovered on parchment (sheepskin) and metals (especially bronze), and occasionally on wood, wax, leather, and gems.

## KINDS OF SCRIPT

To some extent materials determine the way people write. The most convenient way of writing on wet clay was by impressing marks with a stylus. The cuneiform (wedge-shaped) signs thus produced are so characteristic of the civilization that originated in Mesopotamia that modern scholars refer to "the cuneiform world." Similarly, carving in a hard substance like stone lends itself to a rigid, stylized form of writing such as the Egyptian hieroglyphs or the block letters of our own script, derived from the stone carving of ancient Greece and Rome. Writing with a quill pen on paper, on the other hand, allows for a cursive script and the phenomenon of distinctive individual handwriting.

More important, however, than the way of writing is the type of script used. The fully developed cuneiform script was a phonetic syllabary, that is, each separate sign represented a syllabic sound. When the system was adopted by newly literate peoples of the Near East—and numerous peoples did adopt it—all they needed to do was to learn the signs and their sounds, and to combine them in ways that made sense in their own languages. In Egypt a different system was used. Originally ideographic—that is, each sign representing a word—the Egyptian writing added signs to denote grammatical functions, and it evolved in the direction of a phonetic script. Eventually the hieroglyphs (holy markings) became a complicated system in which there were ideographic signs and signs that stood for phonetic syllables. In addition there were signs that represented individual separate sounds. In this last type the Egyptians are thought to have paved the way that led to the invention of the alphabet.

### THE ALPHABET

The kinds of script already described—ideographic signs and signs denoting phonetic syllables—are capable of putting into writing the widest range of human expression, but they are not the simplest and most efficient way of doing it. An ideographic script needs as many signs as there are words, an extremely difficult task to learn. The Chinese script, the last major script in use today that is primarily ideographic, is so great a barrier to communication in a civilization that aims at universal literacy that the present Chinese government is making strenuous efforts to break with a tradition going back more than two thousand years and to supplant the characters with an easier script. A phonetic syllabic script reduces the number of signs very considerably, but still leaves enough of them to make literacy a difficult acquisition. The simplest form of writing is a phonetic alphabet (so called from the first two letters, *alpha* and *beta,* of the Greek script), that is, a system in which each sign represents a single sound. (To the English-speaking reader the full simplicity of a phonetic alphabet is perhaps not immediately clear, since the proverbial difficulty of English spelling results from the failure of English to exploit fully the *phonetic* aspect of the alphabet. In English a given sound may be denoted by a number of different letters or combinations of letters. Therefore, knowing the sound of an English word does not guarantee to a literate person the knowledge of how to write that word, nor can he necessarily tell how to pronounce a word simply from having seen it written. As an example: in the first sentence of this parenthesis I count ninety-seven places in which there is possible confusion as to the proper pronunciation of the written letters! In this regard Italian, for example, in which language a strict relation exists between sound and written sign, illustrates far better than does English the value of the phonetic alphabet. In it one can pronounce correctly a word read for the first time, and write correctly a word heard for the first time.) Although there is a wide range of possible sounds that can be made by the human vocal apparatus, no single language actually uses very many of them. Only a quite modest number of signs therefore needs to be learned.

The invention of the alphabet, one of the great technological triumphs of antiquity, is now believed to have occurred in about the nineteenth century B.C. among a people speaking a Semitic language who worked in the Egyptian copper mines of the Sinai Peninsula. Their efforts were taken up by kindred people along the Syria-Palestine coast, the group of people known collectively as the Canaanites. At the Canaanite city of Ugarit (modern Ras Shamra) a French archaeological expedition in the late 1920's and early 1930's unearthed the remains of a flourishing trading city dating about 1500 B.C. The large number of clay tablets found at Ugarit proved to be of extraordinary importance, for in them the standard signs of the syllabic cuneiform script had been adapted to create a phonetic alphabet of about thirty characters. By 1000 B.C. the descendants of the Canaanites, the Phoenicians, had perfected and standardized this alphabet, converting the complex cuneiform characters into simple, stylized letters easily used for writing with pen and ink on papyrus. In the eighth century B.C. the Greeks learned the Phoenician alphabet and adapted it to their own tastes and needs, passing it on to the Romans and ultimately to all of the modern peoples of Europe.

## NONLITERARY AND LITERARY SOURCES

A division of written sources used for convenience by scholars is that of nonliterary and literary sources. Although there are, of course, border-line cases, the distinction is generally clear. A nonliterary source is one that served some specific practical purpose; it is usually brief and not intrinsically entertaining. Public documents of all sorts—decrees, laws, dedications, tax records, treaties, and so forth—all come under this heading. In the same category are private documents such as wills, marriage contracts, and business agreements of all kinds. A literary source is a written work that is primarily a finished literary composition. Whatever additional practical purpose it may once have had, it is a work that can be read simply as a piece of literature, entertaining (or not) in its own terms. Poems, plays, hymns, stories, historical narratives, speeches, philosophical treatises—all these fall willy-nilly into the category of literary sources.

In the study of antiquity, literary works play a far greater role as sources than they do for modern history. The reason is obvious: the overall poverty of the historian of antiquity in source material constrains him to use whatever he can grasp, however unsuitable it may appear on the surface. Thus for example, a historian of American politics would not be likely to use a play or a poem or a work of prose fiction as his source of information on any given problem, but rather would examine a vast array of statistical data, official records, and the like. The historian of ancient politics, however, does not enjoy the luxury of having at his disposal official archives or statistical data of any kind, and he may find that an allusion in a play or a poem happens to offer him the only information available about a particular political institution or event.

All of the source material for the cuneiform world and for Egypt has been found and read in modern times—within the last century and a quarter—and it is predominantly nonliterary. For the ancient Hebrews non-literary evidence has been found in recent times (e.g., Selections 25 and 33), but the major source is still the single collection of literary works that we know as the Old Testament (Selections 26, 28, and 31), a book that has not had to be rediscovered but has, of course, been read and copied continuously into our own day. The Persians, too, had a holy book, the Zend-Avesta, which has survived the millennia, but the nature of that work is such that it does not offer much precise information of the kind the historian seeks (see Selection 35). The modern finds, mainly of non-literary material, therefore loom larger with respect to our knowledge of the Persians than to that of the Hebrews. For the Greeks and the Romans there is also a continuous literary tradition that has preserved through the ages numerous works of literature, a far greater body of material than the single books of the Hebrews and the Persians. The works of ancient Greek and Latin literature, the "classics," are the major source for Greek and Roman history, but they too have been importantly supplemented, especially for certain periods of time and for particular topics, by modern finds mostly of a nonliterary sort—most frequently inscriptions on stone (e.g., Selections 50 and 51).

## FRAGMENTARY CONDITION OF
## THE ANCIENT SOURCES

One may say that almost *all* the written sources for ancient history are of a fragmentary and uncertain nature. Papyri are torn or have wormholes, and even clay tablets are frequently chipped and broken; inscriptions on stone have been worn by weather or smashed by earthquake, vandalism, and war.

The literary works, too, inevitably underwent alterations as they were copied by hand through the centuries, and missing pages, transposed paragraphs, and unintelligible or patently erroneous words and phrases are not infrequent. The techniques and the standards of modern scholarship have introduced order into this chaos. A rigorous system of notation has been developed whereby lacunae, doubtful readings, scribal errors, and the like are identified in the publishing of ancient texts. In the present book this elaborate apparatus has been omitted in the interest of legibility, and only an occasional note or indication of a break in the text has been inserted where it seemed desirable.

## IDENTIFYING OF PASSAGES

Since ancient writings are subjected to minute examination by scholars, a method of citing particular sections of a work, sentences, even lines is necessary. In the publication of papyri and inscriptions the lines of the original are marked and numbered. The same is done for poetry. For the longer prose works of Greek and Latin literature the system for identifying specific passages that was developed in late antiquity has been maintained by modern scholars. Thus in a work such as Herodotus' *History of the Persian Wars,* for example, the division into nine "books" represents the original papyrus rolls (*volumina*); the subdivision into "chapters" corresponds roughly to paragraphs. In some works a further subdivision into sentences is utilized. Hence a reference, for example, to "Book I, 13, 4" (or "I xiii, 4" or most simply "1.13.4") of a given work is to the first major division, the thirteenth paragraph, the fourth sentence in the original text. Titles, incidentally, are frequently only modern conventions; ancient literary works, especially prose, were often known by the author's name alone, with the addition of a descriptive word or phrase where necessary to avoid confusion.

## USE OF SOURCES

For the historian the value of a source lies in the information he can gain from it. When applied to sublime works of literature this may seem a Philistine approach, but the historian, however responsive he may be to literature, when he is using it as a source must examine it microscopically, seeking to draw from it every bit of knowledge or insight that he can. He need not, of course, be insensitive to its intrinsic merit, but aesthetic pleasure is not his aim. From some sources he may get general impressions, the "feel" of the past. From most, however, he derives highly specific and detailed information. The student of history will not have the skill of the professional historian, but he may be surprised—and pleased—to find how much he can infer from even the briefest and most unpromising sources. He may also be surprised, if he is using a textbook in ancient history along with the present work, at how often the information and even the very words he finds in the sources are echoed in his textbook. It is not after all too surprising, for the writer of the textbook got his knowledge too from the sources.

# I

# BRONZE AGE CIVILIZATION IN THE ANCIENT NEAR EAST

*The most spectacular event in modern historical study is the discovery of two thousand five hundred years of history, the history of what is conventionally called the ancient Near East. To appreciate what this has meant for our awareness of man's journey through time, one need only note that the twenty-five hundred years from Classical Greece to the present—the only period for which a history was known until less than a century ago—has been doubled, and we now trace civilization back in an unbroken line to about 3000 B.C. It is to the development of scientific archaeology and linguistic studies in the nineteenth century that the debt is owed for revealing to us this vast extent of human experience.*

*The evolution of the human race is, of course, much further back in time. The oldest known "human" skull, from the Olduvai Gorge in Tanganyika, has recently (1961) been estimated to be that of a man who lived a million years ago. The evolution of* homo sapiens, *the species to which belongs every person who has lived on earth in historical times, took a long time after that. Some scholars believe that there is no sure evidence of modern man,* homo sapiens, *earlier than twenty-five thousand years ago.*

*Man's progress has been rapid, judged by the standards of geological* time, in which the age of the earth is now reckoned at something between two and four billion years, or by comparison with the time needed for animal evolution, in which the earliest known fossil of a primate is dated to sixty million years ago. Within a few thousands of years man emerged from the caves or from the nomadic life in which he was always at the mercy of nature's whims in acquiring his food. In a few favorable locations, settled village life began. Two fundamental, revolutionary discoveries had made this possible: the domestication of animals and the cultivation of plants. These revolutionary events occurred about eight to ten thousand years ago; man had taken his single most decisive step in freeing himself from his environment, in exercising control over nature.

The new way of life ushered in at that time is known as the Neolithic (New Stone Age) Revolution, and it occurred in several places, principally along the banks of rivers, where the crucial problem of a dependable water supply was easily solved. Thereafter, change was speedy. Communities increased in size; social organization became complex; new techniques, new tools and weapons were invented. By about five thousand years ago two conditions were realized which warrant speaking of the organization of human life as being "civilized." The scale and nature of community life had made cities, and the art of writing had been invented.

It is at this point that "prehistory" gives way to "history," the chronicle of man's civilized experience, known to us from written records as well as from material remains. At about the same time, stone was supplanted by metal as the chief material out of which tools and weapons were made: at first copper was used, but shortly after 3000 B.C. copper was joined with tin to form bronze. This earliest epoch of civilization is called by archaeologists the Bronze Age. The main centers where civilization was invented and where the earliest of the Bronze Age peoples began the historical adventure of mankind are two: Mesopotamia, the land between the Tigris and Euphrates Rivers; and Egypt, the narrow strip of desert watered by the Nile River.

# MESOPOTAMIA

IT IS not necessary to engage in the specialists' argument over whether Mesopotamia or Egypt should receive priority. The earliest records of both cultures are approximately contemporaneous; they are sufficiently similar to indicate that each met like problems in somewhat the same way, and they are sufficiently different to justify for each a claim to originality and independence.

The early history of Mesopotamia is complex. It is a story of small warring states, of the spreading of civilization to different peoples, of conquests, of empires. The people who invented civilization in Mesopotamia were the Sumerians, who occupied a small amount of territory in the lower part of the Tigris-Euphrates and had ports on the Persian Gulf. Who they were, where they came from are still puzzles. Their language belongs to none of the well-known language groups. Ultimately they were so thoroughly assimilated by their neighbors that their language disappeared and the very memory of their name was lost, to be rediscovered only in modern times. Before they succumbed, however, they had developed between 3000 and 1700 B.C. a lofty civilization: literature, techniques of political and economic administration, religious institutions, art, law, and a method of writing—all of which they passed on to the neighboring peoples who supplanted them. One important aspect of the highly organized civilization of Sumer was the keeping of elaborate records of all kinds. These include detailed accounts of the management of temple estates; private contracts of sale, rent, loan, marriage; annalistic—and frequently legendarily boastful—narratives of royal dynasties and their exploits. This last type and its more purely literary counterparts form the elements out of which modern researchers are able to reconstruct the chronology and the major events of this remote period.

Sumer was organized into a number of independent city-states, each with its king (*lugal*) and its temple administration (in the hands of an *ensi* or *patesi*). The rivalries among the separate cities were intense and took the form of chronic warfare in which the royal lines were perpetually attempting to extend control over their neighbors. During the period down to about 2250 B.C. the city that had the greatest eminence and came closest to conquering and uniting the whole land of Sumer was Ur. The disaster of conquest, with its attendant miseries of humiliation and destruction, was of frequent occurrence, and such events are commemorated in poems which modern scholars, mindful of their Biblical echoes, have called "lamentations." For the nature of daily life, for private persons and their thoughts and experiences, our sources are fragmentary and impressionistic. Much information comes from poems and religious documents, hymns and prayers and legends of the gods. The most important comes from legal documents, for these throw light on Mesopotamian society, its class divisions, its personal relations, its standards of behavior, and show the adaptation of Sumerian life and thought to the traditions of the Semitic-speaking peoples who came under the cultural sway of Sumer.

# 1 *The Epic of Gilgamesh*

*Gilgamesh* has been called the first major work in literature. The text of the poem as we have it dates from about 700 B.C., but the original source is perhaps a thousand years earlier—nearly a thousand years before the *Iliad* and *Odyssey* and most of the books of the Old Testament. More important to the historian than its age, however, is the immense influence that the poem exerted. Originally a Sumerian folk epic and only one of a number of epic tales about a hero and his adventures, in its finished form *Gilgamesh* became a work known to the whole world of the ancient Near East. Just as the sacred book of the Hebrews and the Homeric poems of the Greeks are known in translation all over the Western world today, so *Gilgamesh* became the admired possession of the "cuneiform world," the area stretching from the Iranian plateau in the east to the Syrian coast and Asia Minor in the west, where the distinctive script of the Sumerians was adopted by a score or more of peoples for writing their languages. The major part of the text that we have is written in the Akkadian language, on twelve fragmentary tablets found in the ruins of the library of an Assyrian monarch. Fragments of the text are known in the Hittite and Hurrian tongues as well as in Sumerian. All indications are that the original Sumerian story was reworked or translated by peoples all over the Near East, who thus claimed the Sumerian folk hero as their own.

SOURCE: *Gilgamesh, Epic of Old Babylonia* by William Ellery Leonard. Copyright 1934 by William Ellery Leonard, R 1962 by Barbara A. Hayward. Reprinted by permission of The Viking Press, Inc.

However one feels about its literary merits, the poem is to the historian a great treasury of information about early attitudes, ideas, and traditions. In addition to the miraculous adventures of the hero, the poem contains impressive passages on love, friendship, and the nature of the gods. The theme of the latter part of the poem is the hero's search for eternal life after the shock of his friend's death, and the section which immediately strikes most readers is the narrative of the Great Flood, with its close parallel to the Biblical story of Noah.

The text that follows is complete as we have it. Breaks represent lacunae in the tablets. Summary bridge passages are those of the translator, William Ellery Leonard.

❀❀❀❀❀

TABLET I

All things he saw, even to the ends of the earth,
He underwent all, learned to know all,
He peered through all secrets,
Through wisdom's mantle that veileth all.
What was hidden he saw,
What was covered he undid;
Of times before the stormflood he brought report.
He went on a long far way,
Giving himself toil and distress;
Wrote then on a stone-tablet the whole of his labour.
He built the walls of ramparted Uruk,
He laid the foundations, steadfast as bronze,
Of holy Eanna, the pure temple . . .

Two thirds of him is god,
One third of him is man,
There's none can match the form of his body . . .

[*The inhabitants of Uruk call upon the gods for help:*]

"Gilgamesh keeps the son from the father,
Building the walls through the day, through the night.
He is herdsman of ramparted Uruk,

[ 13 ]

He is herdsman and lord of his folk,
Strong and splendid, knowing wisdom.
Gilgamesh keeps the lover from the maiden,
The daughter of a hero,
The chosen of a noble!"
The great gods heard their outcries.
The gods of heaven called the lord Anu:
"Was he not of thy making, this almighty wild bull,
This hero Gilgamesh?
He hath not his like in the whole land . . .
Gilgamesh keeps the son from the father,
Building the walls through the day, through the night.
He is herdsman of ramparted Uruk,
He is herdsman and lord of his folk,
Strong and splendid,
Knowing wisdom.
Gilgamesh keeps the lover from the maiden,
The daughter of a hero,
The chosen of a noble!"

The great god Anu lent ear to their cries.
Aruru was summoned, she the great goddess:
"Thou, Aruru, madest Gilgamesh;
Now make another like unto him.
So long as he pleases
Let him come at Gilgamesh.
Let them contend together,
That Uruk may have peace."

As Aruru this heard,
She shaped in her heart a warrior of Anu.
Aruru washed her hands,
She pinched up some clay and spat on it.
She moulded Engidu,
Fashioned a hero, a glorious scion,
A fighter of Ninurta's.
His whole body was shaggy with hair,
Hair he bore on his head like a woman,
The plenty of his hair sprouted like grain.

[ 14 ]

He knew naught of land and people,
He was clothed like the god of the herds
With the gazelles he eats the plants,
With the wild beasts he drinks at the watering-place,
With the throng at the water he makes glad his heart.

He walked to the watering-place
Toward a hunter, a stalker of wild beasts;
On one day, on a second, and a third,
Toward the hunter he walked to the watering-place.
The hunter saw him, the hunter's face grew troubled.
Without his quarry he turned back to his house.
He was down-cast, troubled; he shrieked.
His heart was afraid and his face was dark.
Grief made way into his heart,
And he looked like a wanderer of far ways.

The hunter opened his mouth,
Speaks, and says to his father:
"My father, a man that came from the hills
Hath become strong indeed in the land,
Mighty in power like a fighter of Anu's.
Ever he goeth along on the hills,
He is ever beside the wild beasts,
Ever are his feet at the watering-place.
I am afraid, I cannot go near to him.
He hath filled my pits which I dug;
My traps which I laid
He hath destroyed.
So from my hands he let my quarry get away,
The throngs of the fields;
No catch he allows me."

The father opened his mouth,
Speaks, and says to the hunter:
"Seek out Gilgamesh, the lord of Uruk . . .
Beg for a priestess¹ and lead her back with thee . . .
When the wild beasts come to the watering-place,

1.   One of the sacred prostitutes at the temple of Ishtar (Astarte).

[ 15 ]

Then let her cast her garment off,
That he may take his fill of her.
When he sees her, he will draw near;
Then will he become a stranger to his wild beasts,
Who on his own steppes grew up with him."

The hunter heard the counsel of his father . . .
He started on the way, he entered into Uruk.
He goes to Gilgamesh, and to him he says:
"A man that came from the hills
Hath become strong indeed in the land.
Mighty in power like a fighter of Anu's.
Ever he goeth along on the hills,
He is ever beside the wild beasts,
Ever are his feet at the watering-place.
I am afraid, I cannot go near to him.
He hath filled my pits which I dug;
My traps which I laid
He hath destroyed.
So from my hands he let my quarry get away,
The throngs of the fields;
No catch he allows me."

Gilgamesh says to him, to the hunter:
"Go, my hunter, and get thee a priestess.
When the wild beasts come to the watering-place,
Then let her cast her garment off,
That he may take his fill of her.
When he sees her, he will draw near;
Then will he become a stranger to his wild beasts,
Who on his own steppes grew up with him."

The hunter went yonder and got him a priestess.
They made themselves ready, went forth straight on.
On the third day they came to their goal:
The hunter and the priestess sat themselves down.
One day, a second day, they sat by the watering-place.
The wild beasts come along and drink at the watering-place.
Glad is the throng of the flood.

[ 16 ]

So too comes he, Engidu . . .
With the gazelles he eats the plants,
With the beasts he drinks at the watering-place,
His heart is happy with the throng of the flood.
Then the priestess saw him, the great strong one,
The wild fellow, the man of the steppes:
"There he is, woman!
Loosen thy buckle,
Unveil thy delight,
That he may take his fill of thee!
Hang not back, take up his lust!
When he sees thee, he will draw near.
Open thy robe that he may rest upon thee!
Arouse in him rapture, the work of woman.
Then will he become a stranger to his wild beasts,
Who on his own steppes grew up with him.
His bosom will press against thee."
Then the priestess loosened her buckle,
Unveiled her delight,
For him to take his fill of her.
She hung not back, she took up his lust,
She opened her robe that he rest upon her.
She aroused in him rapture, the work of woman.
His bosom pressed against her.
Engidu forgot where he was born.
For six days and seven nights
Was Engidu given over to love with the priestess.
When he had sated himself with the fill of her,
He raised up his face to his wild ones:
At sight of Engidu, the gazelles flee away,
The wild of the fields shrink back before him.
Then Engidu marvelled,
His body stood as in a spell,
His knees quivered, because his wild ran off . . .
The speed of his onset is not what it was.
He hearkens and opens his ear:
He turns about and sits down at the feet of the priestess.
He looks the priestess in the face,
And to what the priestess now speaks
His ears give heed.

The priestess says to him, to Engidu:
"Engidu, how beautiful thou, how like a god!
Why must thou rush with animals over the steppes?
Come, I will lead thee into ramparted Uruk,
To a pure house, the dwelling of Anu and Ishtar,
Where Gilgamesh lives, matchless in might,
And like a wild bull lords it over the folk" . . .
She talks to him, till he likes her words.
Knowing his own heart, he seeketh a friend.
Engidu says to her, to the priestess:
"Woman, go to! Lead me to the pure, the holy house,
The dwelling of Anu and Ishtar,
Where Gilgamesh lives, matchless in might,
And like a wild bull lords it over the folk.
I will challenge him to a fight.
I will call the strong one.
I will call out in Uruk:
'I too am a strong one!'
I alone can alter fate,
I, born on the steppes, matchless in might.
O Gilgamesh, may I behold thy face!
Well I know what the outcome will be."
Then she stripped off the one of her robes,
And clothed him therewith;
In the other robe she herself remained clad.
She took him by the hand
And led him like a bridegroom
To a festal meal at a pinfold,
And the shepherds foregathered around him.
But Engidu, born in the steppes,
Was wont to eat only plants with the gazelles,
Only to drink water with the wild,
Only to be glad with the throng of the flood,
Only to suck the milk of the wild creatures.
Then they set bread before him.
He was bewildered, and looked on it, and marvelled.
Engidu understood not how to eat bread,
To drink wine he had not learned.
Then the priestess opens her mouth and says to Engidu:
"Eat bread, Engidu, the glory of life,

Drink wine, Engidu, the custom of the land."
Then Engidu ate bread till he was full,
Then he drank wine, seven beakers.
His spirit loosed itself, he grew merry,
His heart rejoiced and his face glowed . . .
He anointed himself with oil, and became like a noble,
He put on a robe and was then as a bridegroom.
He took his weapon, he attacked lions,
So that the great shepherds found rest at night,
For Engidu was their safeguard . . .

Engidu and the priestess
Arrived at ramparted Uruk.
They found the people adorned with fillets,
Day and night they were keeping a feast . . .
The priestess says to him, to Engidu:
"Engidu . . . I will show thee Gilgamesh . . .
Thou shalt look upon him and behold his face.
His whole body is filled with strength,
His power is greater than thine.
He goes not to rest by day and by night . . .
Shamash loves Gilgamesh,
Anu, Ellil, and Ea made him wise.
Ere thou camest hither from the hills,
Did Gilgamesh in Uruk behold thee in dreams.
Gilgamesh rose up, and told his dreams,
And says to his mother:
'My mother, this night I saw a dream:
The stars stood in heaven,
Then there fell from on high
An image as of Anu upon me.
I sought to lift it up, it was too heavy for me;
I sought to shake it off,
I could not shake it off.
The folk of Uruk assembled before it . . .
And the warriors kissed its feet.
I gathered it close in my arms like a woman,
And threw it at thy feet,
And thou didst liken it to me.'
The lady Ninsun, who knows all things,

Says to her lord,
The lady Ninsun, who knows all, says to Gilgamesh:
'Gilgamesh, if the stars stood in heaven,
And there fell upon thee an image as of Anu,
And thou soughtest to lift it up, but it was too heavy for thee,
And thou soughtest to shake it off,
But thou couldst not shake it off,
And thou threwest it at my feet,
And I did liken it to thee . . .
Verily, that is one as thou, Gilgamesh,
Who was born in the steppes,
And whom the hills reared.
Thou wilt see him and fight with him.
The warriors will kiss his feet.
Thou wilt spare him and lead him to me.'


Gilgamesh lay down and saw a second dream,
And told it to his mother:
'My mother, I saw a second dream:
I walked on the street of Uruk,
An axe lay there, and the people assembled around it.
The axe, strange was its shape.
Upon it I looked and was glad.
I gathered it close in my arms like a woman,
And threw it at thy feet,
And thou didst liken it to me.'


The lady Ninsun, who knows all things,
Says to her son,
The lady Ninsun, who knows all, says to Gilgamesh:
'Gilgamesh, if thou saw'st an axe,
If thou gather'dst it close in thine arms like a woman,
And I likened it unto thee,
That meaneth a strong man,
A comrade, who rescues his friend.
His power will be strong in the land,
And mighty as an axe will be his strength' . . .
These, Engidu, were the dreams of Gilgamesh."

Thuswise the priestess talks to Engidu.
They go together to seek out Gilgamesh.


### TABLET II

[*The beginning is lacking.*]

Engidu goes along the market-street
Of ramparted Uruk.
Marvelling he looks at the mighty work;
He bars the way of the warriors of Uruk;
Then the folk of Uruk crowd against him,
The land is assembled . . .
But in fear the folk turn away.
They fall down . . . like a weak child . . .
The couch had been spread for goddess Ishtar . . .
At the gates of her house
Engidu barred the going-to,
Allowed not Gilgamesh that he enter in.
They grappled each other at the gates of her house.
They fought in the street . . .
That the doorposts quaked and the wall swayed . . .
Gilgamesh crumpled his leg to the ground,
His anger softened, he checked his onset.
When he had checked his onset,
Says Engidu to him, to Gilgamesh:
"Thee, as one matchless, thy mother bore,
The wild cow of the fold, the goddess Ninsun.
Over all men is thy head lifted up,
Ellil to thee hath allotted
The kingdom over mankind!"

[*What follows here is damaged. The two enemies straightway become friends. Gilgamesh challenges Engidu to go forth with him against the monster Khumbaba, who lives in the distant cedar-forest, but Engidu replies:*]

"In the hills, my friend, I found it out,

[ 21 ]

As I roamed with the wild beasts.
Hither and thither ten thousand miles
Stretches that forest.
Who could dare enter therein?
Khumbaba's bellow is a stormwind,
His mouth is fire, his snort is death!
Whence came thy resolve to dare this,
A battle without its like on earth,
The conquest of Khumbaba?"

Gilgamesh opened his mouth and says to Engidu:
". . . My heart hath its longing
To conquer Khumbaba."
Engidu opened his mouth and says to Gilgamesh:
"How against Khumbaba
Can we make way to the cedar-forest?
Its keeper, Gilgamesh, is a mighty hero . . .
Ellil hath set him therein,
To the terror of men, for warding the cedars.
And whoso enters his forest
Is suddenly faint."

Gilgamesh opened his mouth and says to Engidu:
"Who, my friend, is so exalted . . .
That he should ascend on high
And dwell for ever with Shamash?
The days of men are numbered,
Whatever they do is empty wind."[2]
"My friend, he to whom we go is fearful,
Khumbaba to whom we go
Is of power almighty."

Gilgamesh speaks to Engidu:
"My friend,
We both will strive against Khumbaba.
Thou art now afeared of death, and thy power is gone.
I will go on before thee . . .
If I fall, I will make myself a name.

2. Compare introduction to Selection 79.

'Gilgamesh,' so men will say,
'Hath gone forth against the almighty Khumbaba.'
Verily, I will make myself a name.
My friend, let us call the handworkers;
In our sight shall they cast us hatchets."

They went and called the handworkers.
There sit the masters, setting the right time:
They cast hatchets,
They cast heavy axes,
They cast great daggers . . .

*[What follows is damaged. Gilgamesh takes leave of the elders of Uruk:]*

"Khumbaba, of whom men tell, will I see,
Whose name fills the lands.
I will overcome him in the cedar-forest.
I will let the land hear
How strong is the scion of Uruk.
I will set my hand to it and fell the cedars,
I will make myself a sounding name."

The elders of Uruk answered Gilgamesh:
"Thou art yet young, Gilgamesh,
And thy valour runs away with thee.
What thou willest to do, knowest thou not.
We hear that Khumbaba is frightful to look on.
Who, then, would wish to encounter his weapons?
Hither and thither ten thousand miles
Stretches that forest.
Khumbaba's bellow is a stormwind,
His mouth is fire, his snort is death!
Whence came thy resolve to dare this,
A battle without its like on earth,
The conquest of Khumbaba?"
Gilgamesh heard the speech of his counsellors
He looked yonder and called to his friend:
"Now, my friend, so will I do!" . . .

[ 23 ]

*[What follows is partly destroyed. Gilgamesh prays to Shamash, the sungod, and then arms himself for the expedition against Khumbaba. On his departure the elders give Gilgamesh their blessing:]*

"Gilgamesh, trust not in thy powers . . .
He who goeth to vanward, wardeth his comrade,
He who knoweth the way wardeth his companion.
Let Engidu go on before thee,
He knoweth the way to the cedar-forest.
He is wise in fight, he understandeth combats.
May Engidu save the friend,
May he ward the comrade . . .
May Shamash fulfil thee thy longing,
May he let thine eye see what thy mouth hath spoken.
May he open for thee the barred path,
Unclose for thy steps the way,
Unclose the mountain for thy feet!
May the night bring thee nothing but joy,
May Lugalmaradda fulfil thy longing . . .
Like a child mayst thou get what thou long'st for.
In the stream of Khumbaba, whither thy desire is,
Mayst thou bathe thy feet! . . .
Ever clear be the water in thy waterskin!
Unto Shamash make libations of water,
And at thine offering be mindful of Lugalmaradda."

Engidu opened his mouth and spake to Gilgamesh:
. . . "Now start on thy way!
Be thy heart fearless! Fix eye upon me!—
We will win against Khumbaba."


TABLET III

*[The beginning is destroyed.]*

Gilgamesh opened his mouth and speaks,
Says to Engidu:
"My friend, let us go to the splendid palace

And stand before Ninsun, the great queen:
The lady Ninsun, who knoweth all things,
Will lend goodspeed to our footsteps."
They took each other by the hand;
Gilgamesh and Engidu went to the splendid palace,
And stood before Ninsun, the great queen . . .

Ninsun arose, adorned her body,
Sprinkled the ground, mounted up to the roof;
She mounted up unto Shamash,
Laid frankincense before him,
Laid down a holy gift;
Unto Shamash she lifted her arms:
"Why hast thou for my son Gilgamesh
Provided a heart
Whose stormy unrest findeth no peace?
Even now thou hast driven him
To start on a far way
To the dwelling-place of Khumbaba.
He will meet with a fight such as he knows not yet,
He will wander a way that he knows not:
So, from the day of his going,
Till the day of his coming home,
Till he reaches the cedar-forest,
Till he throws Khumbaba, the strong, to the ground,
And hath destroyed from out the land
All evil which thou hatest . . .
As often as thou yearnest for Aja, thy belovèd,
May she not wend unto thee;
Aja, thy belovèd,
May she give thee to ponder thereon!" . . .

She burnt much incense,
She called Engidu and says to him:
"Engidu, thou strong one, thou alone art my comfort;
Shelter for me now Gilgamesh, my son! . . .
From the day of his going,
Till the day of his coming home,
Till he reaches the cedar-forest,

[ 25 ]

Be it a month . . . be it a year . . .
Yield not from his side!"


TABLET IV

[*The first part is lacking. Where the text begins again, the two friends
are already climbing the cedar-mountain, which takes several days. They
rest during the nights. One morning Gilgamesh had told his friend a
dream, which has not been preserved for us. On the morning of the
next day Gilgamesh says to Engidu:*]

"My friend, I had a second dream,
And the dream which I saw was horrible:
On the top of a mountain we two were standing,
When the mountain caved in." . . .
Then said Engidu to his friend:
"The dream thou hadst is good,
The dream thou saw'st is fine . . .
My friend, the mountain thou saw'st
Is the cedar-mountain!
We are going to seize Khumbaba and kill,
And cast his corpse into the plain!" . . .
After twenty miles they ate a little,
After thirty miles they rested for the night . . .

Gilgamesh sank on his knee,
And planted his elbow.
A sleep, such as is shed upon mankind,
Overtook him.
At midnight he ended his sleep.
He stood up and says to his friend:
"My friend, didst thou not call me?
Why am I awake?
Didst thou not touch me?
Why am I so startled?
Did not some god go by?
Why are my limbs so lamed?
My friend, I saw a third dream,
And the dream which I saw was horrible:

[ 26 ]

The heavens shrieked,
The earth bellowed,
A storm gathered,
Darkness came forth,
A flash flamed,
A fire shot up,
The clouds thickened,
It rained death.
Then the brightness vanished, the fire went out,
The blaze that had fallen turned to ashes.
Let us climb down,
That we may take counsel on the plain."

*[What follows here is badly damaged. We gather that Engidu persuades Gilgamesh in spite of his dream to press on to the mountain-peak where lies the cedar-forest. Before the magic gate in the great palisade which surrounds the forest, the watchman of Khumbaba, clothed in seven magic mantles, receives the two friends. But they succeed in overpowering him. Yet the instant Engidu, in his amazement, touches the gleaming portal, he is seized with a mysterious faintness.]*

Engidu opened his mouth and speaks,
Says to Gilgamesh:
"My friend, let us not enter the forest;
. . . my hands are lamed!"
Gilgamesh opened his mouth and speaks,
Says to Engidu:
"My friend,
Thou shalt not act like a weakling! . . .
Art thou not wise in fight? . . .
Forget death! Then ours will be the outcome . . .
The laming of thy hands will be over,
And thy faintness pass off! . . .
Let us enter, my friend,
Let us fight side by side—
Did not thine own heart urge to the fight?"
Then the twain got into the cedar-forest.
Their words stood still,
And they themselves stopped and stood.

## TABLET V

They took their stand and gaze at the forest,
They survey the height of the cedars,
They survey the entrance to the forest,
Where Khumbaba goes about, roving along.
Roads had been laid out, a path been well builded.
They see the cedar-mountain, the abode of the gods,
The holy temple of Irnini.
On the mountain the cedars uplift their abundance.
Their shadow is beautiful, is all delight.
Thistles hide thereunder, and the dark prick-thorn,
Sweet-smelling flowers hide under the cedars.

[*The rest is for the most part destroyed. With the help of the sungod the friends succeed in slaying Khumbaba, and return home to Uruk victorious.*]

## TABLET VI

Gilgamesh washed his weapons, he cleansed his weapons,
Let his hair fall down on the nape of his neck,
Threw off his unclean garments,
And put on clean raiment . . .
Gilgamesh set his crown on . . .
Then Ishtar, sublime one,
Lifted her eyes to the beauty of Gilgamesh:
"Go to, Gilgamesh, be my consort,
Spend thy love, spend thy love upon me.
Be thou my husband, be I thy wife!
I will have a chariot harnessed for thee
Of lapislazuli and of gold;
Its wheels are golden,
Its horns of precious stones.
Daily shalt thou have a span of strong mules.
Under the fragrance of the cedars, O enter my house!
When thou hast entered our house, shall they
Who sit upon thrones kiss thy feet,
And kings, lords, and princes

Shall bow down before thee.
The treasure of the hills and the land
Shall they bring thee as tribute.
Thy goats and sheep shall cast twins.
With heavy ladings shall thy mules come,
Gloriously shall thy runners rush along by the chariot,
Thy mule in the yoke
Shall not have his like upon earth" . . .

Gilgamesh opened his mouth and speaks,
Says to Ishtar, sublime one:
"Keep thy gifts to thyself! . . .
My fare and nourishing is good enough.
Have I not food as befits a god,
Have I not drink as is due a king?
Thou art like a back-door
Which keeps not the storm out,
Like a palace which slayeth the heroes,
Like an elephant who shakes off his carpet,
Like pitch which weighs down its bearer,
Like the skin-bottle that burdens its bearer,
Like the mortar of lime
That holds not the stone-wall fast,
Like a shoe that pinches its wearer!
For which of thy consorts has thy love lasted?
Which of thy shepherds could bind thee for ever?
Go to, I will count off all thy paramours,
I will hold a reckoning with thee:
Tammuz, the lover of thy youth,
Hast thou year after year made to wail.
Thou fellest in love with the dappled shepherd-bird;
Thou smotest him and brakest his wings.
Now he stands in the woods and cries 'Kappi' (my wing)!
Thou fellest in love with the lion, the puissant;
Seven and again seven pitfalls
Thou duggest for him.
Thou fellest in love with the horse, the joyous in battle;
But whip, spur, and goad
Ordainedst thou him,

Seven miles to gallop onward ordainedst thou him,
To drink muddied waters ordainedst thou him,
His mother Silili thou madest to wail.
Thou fellest in love with the herdsman, the keeper,
Who ever scattered the grain for thee,
And daily slaughtered a kid for thee;
Thou smotest him,
Turnèdst him into a wolf,
And his own shepherd-boys give him chase,
And his dogs bite-up his shanks.
Thou fellest in love with Ishullanu,
The gardener of thy father,
Who ever brought thee nosegays,
And daily decked thy table;
Thou liftedst thine eyes to him and lurèdst him:
'Dear Ishullanu, let us enjoy love together' . . .
Ishullanu spake to thee:
'What wilt thou of me?
Hath my mother not baked,
And have I not eaten,
That I should eat dishes
Of evil deeds and of curses,
Dishes that become thorns and thistles to me?'
As thou heardest this his talking,
Thou smotest him,
And turnèdst him into a bat . . .
And now hast thou fallen in love with me,
And wilt treat me as them."

As Ishtar this heard,
Ishtar was wroth and mounted to heaven.
Ishtar stepped up to Anu, her father;
To Antu, her mother, she went, and she spake:
"My father, Gilgamesh hath curst me,
Gilgamesh hath tallied up my evil deeds,
My evil deeds and my curses!"
Anu opened his mouth and speaks,
Says to Ishtar, sublime one:
"And thou hast besought his love,
And Gilgamesh hath tallied off thy evil deeds,

Thy evil deeds and thy curses?"
Ishtar opened her mouth and speaks,
Says to Anu, her father:
"My father, do thou create a bull-of-heaven.
That he may butt Gilgamesh down,
And do thou fill the bull's body with fire!
If thou wilt not listen to me, I descend
And shatter the gates of the underworld . . .
Then will I lead up the dead,
That they may eat those who are alive—
Then the dead shall outnumber the living."
Anu opened his mouth and speaks,
Says to Ishtar, sublime one:
"My daughter, what wilt thou of me?
Then will there come seven years of barren straw.
Hast thou gathered-in the grain for men?
Hast thou seen to a growth of green herbs for the cattle?"
Ishtar opened her mouth and speaks,
Says to Anu, her father:
"Enough grain for men have I stored away,
Fodder enough for the cattle have I seen to.
These seven years of barren straw—
Let them come!" . . .

Anu lent ear to her words,
Let a bull-of-heaven descend
And come unto Uruk . . .
At his first snort he kills
Three hundred warriors.
And Engidu grasped the bull-of-heaven
By his horns.
At his second snort
Two hundred warriors he knocks over.
At his third snort
Engidu stalks up to him,
Leaps on his back,
And grasps him by the thick of the tail . . .
Then Engidu opened his mouth and speaks,
Says to Gilgamesh:
"My friend,

We have made our name glorious" . . .
And Gilgamesh, like a huntsman,
Thrusts his sword between nape and horns.
When they had laid low the bull-of-heaven,
Their heart had peace . . .
And in front of Shamash they sat down to their rest,
Both of the brothers.

Then Ishtar mounted the walls of ramparted Uruk,
Sprang on the battlements and shrieked down:
"Woe unto Gilgamesh who affronted me,
Who killed the bull-of-heaven."
As Engidu heard these words of Ishtar,
He tore loose a thigh-bone from the bull-of-heaven,
And flung it into her face:
"Could I but get hold of thee,
I would do unto thee as unto him!
Round thy neck would I hang his entrails!"
Then Ishtar assembled the damsels of the temple,
The harlots and the priestesses;
Over the thigh-bone of the bull-of-heaven
They wailed a chant . . .
Gilgamesh called the masters, the handworkers all.
The masters praise the thickness of the horns;
Thirty pounds of lapislazuli was the weight of each.
Two fingers thick was their shell.
Six measures of oil (as much as both horns held)
Did he pour, as oil of anointing,
To his god, Lugalmaradda;
Brought the horns to his god's temple,
And fastened them on his throne.
Then they washed their hands in the Euphrates,
Start off and wander along
On the market-street of Uruk.
The people of Uruk stand assembled
And gaze upon them.

Gilgamesh speaks thus
To the maid-servants of his palace:

"Who is the most beautiful among the heroes?
Who is the mightiest among men?"

"Gilgamesh is the most beautiful among the heroes!
Gilgamesh is the mightiest among men!" . . .
Then Gilgamesh makes in his palace
A feast of rejoicing.

The warriors rest in their beds of night.
Also Engidu rests, beholding dreams.
Then Engidu rose up,
Tells the dreams, and speaks to his friend:
"My friend,
Wherefore have the great gods been in council?" . . .


### TABLET VII

[*The beginning is badly damaged. Engidu takes sick and speaks in his feverish dreams to the gate in the palisade of the cedar-forest.*]

He talks to the door as to a human being:
"Thou door of the forest . . .
Who hast no understanding,
From twenty miles away did I marvel at thy wood . . .
Till I saw the lofty cedar . . .
Its wood is not thy strange wood . . .
Two and seventy ells is thy height,
Four and twenty ells is they breadth . . .
A prince in Nippur built thee . . .
Had I known, thou door,
That this would come to pass,
And that beauty would bring this disaster,
I had lifted the axe
And shattered thee all!" . . .

[*Engidu curses the hunter and calls to Shamash:*]

"Shamash, punish the hunter!
Destroy his wealth!
Make less his power! . . .
May serpents go on before him!" . . .

So curses he the hunter;
The fullness of his heart goads him.
Then it goads him to beshrew the woman:
"Woman, I will appoint thee thy fate;
It shall cease not in the land
For ever and for ever.
I will curse thee with a great cursing,
My cursings shall reach unto thee . . .
Be the street thy dwelling,
In the shadow of the wall shalt thou house.
Be thy feet ever weary,
May the outcast and the despoiled
Smite thee on the cheeks . . .
Because thou didst lure me away from my fields."

Shamash heard the speech of his mouth.
Forthwith he calls to Engidu from heaven:
"Why, O Engidu, beshrewest thou the priestess?
She who gave thee dishes to eat
Such as beseem a god only?
She who gave thee wine to drink
Such as beseems a king only?
She who clothed thee in a gorgeous robe,
And gave thee the glorious Gilgamesh for friend?
For Gilgamesh is thy nearest friend . . .
He maketh thee to rest on a bed well-prepared,
To dwell in a quiet dwelling-place . . .
The princes of the earth kiss thy feet.
He maketh for thee
The people of ramparted Uruk to weep,
To sorrow for thee.
Much people he maketh to serve thee.
Himself after thy death will put on mourning,
Will clothe himself in the skins of lions,
And haste away over the steppes."
Engidu heard the word of the hero Shamash . . .
And his angry heart grew quiet.

[*But Engidu's sufferings set in anew. He recounts to his friend what oppresses him.*]

[ 34 ]

"Gilgamesh, my friend,
I beheld dreams this last night:
The heavens called, the earth answered.
In the dark night am I standing there alone,
I see a man with forbidding face . . .
He is hideous to look on,
His nails are eagle-talons . . .
He made my arms into wings like a bird's:
'Descend, descend, I say, into the house of darkness,
To the dwelling of Irkalla,
To the house
Which none leave again who have betrodden it,
To a way whose road turneth not,
To the house whose inhabitants do without light,
Where dust is their nourishment and clay their food.
They are as birds clothed with wings,
They see not the light,
They dwell in the darkness.'
In the house of dust which I entered . . .
Are kings' crowns bowed down.
There do dwell the mighty ones
Who from the days of old ruled the land . . .
In the house of dust which I entered
Dwell priest-prince and wailing-priests,
Dwell the conjurers and the rapt seers,
Dwell the high-priests of the great gods . . .
Dwells the queen of the earth, Eresh-Kigal.
Belit-Seri, she the scribe of the earth,
Standeth bowed before her . . .
And readeth to her aloud.
Then she raised her head and saw me,
She stretched out her hand and took me to herself" . . .


[*Then Gilgamesh moaned and said:*]


"My friend,
Who with me hast ranged through all hardships . . .
My friend, the dream comes true!" . . .

[ 35 ]

On the day when he saw the dream
His fate was fulfilled.
Engidu lies stricken,
For one day,
For a second day,
Engidu suffers pain in his bed.
For a third day, and a fourth,
Engidu lies stricken.
For a fifth, a sixth, and a seventh,
For an eighth, a ninth, and a tenth day.
Engidu's pain grows great.
For an eleventh and a twelfth day,
Engidu lies in his bed . . .
He calls Gilgamesh and speaks:
"A god hath cursed me, my friend.
Not like one wounded in battle
Is it mine to die.
I once feared the fight . . .
But, my friend,
He who falls in the fight is happy.
As to me, I must die in my bed. . . ."


TABLET VIII

Then Gilgamesh assembles his nobles and says:
"Hear me, ye elders, look upon me!
For Engidu, for my friend, I weep.
Like a wailing woman I cry bitterly.
The axe on my side,
The lance in my hand,
The sword in my girdle,
The joys of my eyes,
My festal robe that decks my strength,
What is it to me?—
An evil spirit hath risen up
And cast me down into ruin." . . .

[*And Gilgamesh returns to Engidu's bed and speaks:*]

"Engidu, my young friend,
Thou panther of the steppes,
Who couldst do all things,
So that we climbed the mountain,
Overthrew Khumbaba,
Who housed in the cedar-forest,
So that we seized and slew the bull-of-heaven,
What kind of sleep is this
That hath now seized upon thee?
Dark is thy look,
And thine ears take not my voice!"
But he lifts up his eyes no more.
Gilgamesh touched him on the heart,
But the heart beats no more.
Then he covered up his friend like a bride.

Like as a lion, Gilgamesh raised his voice,
Like as a lioness, he roared out.
He turns round to his friend,
He tears his hair and strews it forth . . .
Soon as beamed the first shimmer of morning,
Gilgamesh raised a new cry:
"I made thee to rest on a bed well-prepared,
I made thee to dwell in a quiet dwelling-place . . .
I made princes of the earth kiss thy feet.
Now will I make the people of ramparted Uruk
Beweep thee and sorrow for thee;
Much people will I make to serve thee,
And I will myself put on mourning for thee,
Will clothe myself in a lion's skin,
And haste away over the steppes." . . .

[*Gilgamesh is in mourning for his friend six days and six nights, and
then leaves Uruk and hastens into the steppes.*]


TABLET IX


Gilgamesh weeps bitterly

[ 37 ]

For his friend Engidu,
And hastes away over the steppes:

"Will I too not die as Engidu?
Grief has made way into my heart,
I have gotten the fear of death.
Therefore do I haste away over the steppes.
To Utnapishtim, son of Ubara-Tutu,
I take the way with all haste.

"When by night I come
To the ravines of the mountains
And see lions,
I now grow afraid.
I lift my head and beseech Sin, the moongod.
Unto Ishtar, the strong goddess,
Press upward my prayers:
Protect me, ye gods!" . . .

[*After long wanderings Gilgamesh reaches the mountain Mashu at the earth's end.*]

As he got to the mountain Mashu,
He beheld the twain
Who day by day keep the watch
Over the rising and setting of the sun.
Above them is the dike of heaven . . .
Their breast below reaches the underworld.
Scorpion-men are they
Who keep the watch at their gate,
And their monstrousness is terror,
And their glance is death,
And horrible the fierce sheen of them
Overspreading the hills.
At its rising, at its setting,
They keep the watch of the sun.

Gilgamesh beheld them,
And for fear and fright his visage darkened,

With a wildered heart he bowed unto them.
The scorpion-man calls to his wife:
"He who here comes to us
Hath a body like the gods!"
To the scorpion-man his wife replies:
"Two thirds of him is god,
One third of him is man."

The scorpion-man, the male, calls;
To Gilgamesh, image of the gods,
He says the word:
"Thou hast fared a long journey
Till thou camest to us,
To the mountains that are hard to pass through.
Give me tidings,
I will know thy journey . . .
The goal of thy faring will I know." . . .

Gilgamesh gave answer to him,
To the scorpion-man:
"To Utnapishtim, my forefather,
Will I go,
To him who entered the assembly of the gods
And looked upon life;
Him would I ask about death and life."
The scorpion-man opened his mouth, speaks,
And says to Gilgamesh:
"Never was there, Gilgamesh, a way thither,
And no one hath found
A path through the mountains.
Twelve miles wide is the inside of the mountains,
Thick is the darkness, light is there none." . . .

[*There is a large gap in the text. Gilgamesh will not be dissuaded and
receives finally the permission to pass through the inside of the mountain of Mashu, at whose gate the scorpion-men keep the watch.*]

As Gilgamesh this heard,
He started on his road,

After the bidding of the scorpion-men.
Along the road of the sun went Gilgamesh.

One mile he completed,
Thick was the darkness, light was there none.
In this dusk he can see not
What lies behind him.

Two miles he completed,
Thick was the darkness, light was there none.
In this dusk he can see not
What lies behind him.

Three miles he completed,
Thick was the darkness, light was there none.
In this dusk he can see not
What lies behind him.

Four miles he completed,
Thick was the darkness, light was there none.
In this dusk he can see not
What lies behind him.

Five miles he completed,
Thick was the darkness, light was there none.
In this dusk he can see not
What lies behind him.

Six miles he completed,
Thick was the darkness, light was there none.
In this dusk he can see not
What lies behind him.

Seven miles he completed,
Thick was the darkness, light was there none.
In this dusk he can see not
What lies behind him.

Eight miles he completed,
Then cries he aloud.

Thick was the darkness, light was there none.
In this dusk he can see not
What lies behind him.

Nine miles he completed,
Then feels he the northwind.
His face is headed forwards.
Thick was the darkness, light was there none.
In this dusk he can see not
What lies behind him.

Ten miles he completed,
And now was he near to
The end of the mountain.

Eleven miles he completed,
Then he sees a shimmer of the sun.

Twelve miles he completed,
And then it grew bright.

Before him lay a grove of the gods;
As he saw it, he drew nigh unto it.
It bears rubies for fruit,
Hung with grape-clusters, lovely to look on.
Lapislazuli are its branches,
It bears fruit, desirable to see . . .
Gilgamesh stopped in his wandering,
And lifted up his eyes
Unto that grove of the gods.


### TABLET X

Siduri, she the divine cup-bearer,
Sits there by the rim of the sea.
Sits there and looks afar off . . .
She is wrapped in a shawl . . .
Gilgamesh ran thither and drew nigh unto her.
He is clad in skins,

His shape is awesome,
His body godlike,
Woe is in his heart.
He is like a wanderer of far ways.
The face of her, the cup-bearer, looks afar off,
She talks to herself and says the word,
Takes counsel in her heart:
"Is he yonder one who deviseth ill?
Whither is he going in the wrath of his heart?"
As Siduri saw him, she locked her gate,
Locked her portal, locked her chamber . . .

Gilgamesh says to her, to the cup-bearer:
"Cup-bearer, what ails thee,
That thou lockest thy gate,
Lockest thy portal,
Lockest thy chamber?
I will crash the door, I will break the lock." . . .

The cup-bearer says to him, to Gilgamesh:
"Why are thy cheeks so wasted,
Thy visage so sunken,
Thy heart so sad,
Thy shape so undone?
Why is woe in thy heart?
Why art thou like a wanderer of far ways?
Why is thy countenance
So destroyed with grief and pain?
Why hast thou from wide-away
Made haste over the steppes?"

Gilgamesh says to her, to the cup-bearer:
"Why should my cheeks not be so wasted,
My visage so sunken,
My heart so sad,
My shape so undone?
How should woe not be in my heart?
Why should I not be like
A wanderer of far ways?

Why should not my countenance
Be destroyed with grief and pain?
Why should I not to the far-away
Make haste over the steppes?
My belovèd friend, the panther of the steppes,
Engidu, my belovèd friend,
The panther of the steppes who could do all things,
So that we climbed the mountain,
Overthrew Khumbaba,
Who housed in the cedar-forest,
So that we seized and slew the bull-of-heaven,
So that we laid lions low
In the ravines of the mountain,
My friend,
Who with me ranged through all hardships,
Engidu, my friend, who killed lions with me,
Who with me ranged through all hardships,
Him hath the fate of mankind overtaken.
Six days and six nights have I wept over him,
Until the seventh day
Would I not have him buried.
Then I began to be afraid . . .
Fear of death seized upon me.
Therefore I make away over the steppes.
The fate of my friend weighs me down.
Therefore I make haste
On a far way over the steppes.
The fate of Engidu, my friend,
Weigheth me down.
Therefore I make haste on a long road over the steppes.
Why should I be silent thereon?
Why should I not cry it forth?
My friend, whom I love,
Hath turned into earth.
Must not I too, as he,
Lay me down
And rise not up again
For ever and for ever?—
Ever since he is gone, I cannot find Life,

And rove, like a hunter, round over the fields.
Cup-bearer, now I behold thy face;
But Death, whom I fear, I would not behold."

The cup-bearer, she says to him, to Gilgamesh:
"Gilgamesh, whither runnest thou?
Life, which thou seekest, thou wilt not find.
When the gods created mankind,
They allotted to mankind Death,
But Life they withheld in their hands.
So, Gilgamesh, fill thy body,
Make merry by day and night,
Keep each day a feast of rejoicing!
Day and night leap and have thy delight!
Put on clean raiment,
Wash thy head and bathe thee in water,
Look cheerily at the child who holdeth thy hand,
And may thy wife have joy in thy arms!"

Gilgamesh says again to her, to the cup-bearer:
"Go to, cup-bearer!
Where is the way to Utnapishtim?
What is his sign? Give it to me!
If it can be done,
I will pass over the sea;
If it cannot be done,
I will make away over the steppes."

The cup-bearer she says to him, to Gilgamesh:
"Never, Gilgamesh, was there a place of crossing,
And no one who came since the days of old
Could pass over that sea.
Only Shamash, the hero,
Hath passed over that sea.
But who except Shamash can pass over it?
There is no getting to the place of crossing,
Toilsome the way thereunto,
The waters of death are deep
That lie there to thwart thee.

[ 44 ]

Where wilt thou, Gilgamesh, pass over that sea?
When thou comest to the waters of death,
What, then, wilt thou do?
Gilgamesh, Ur-Shanabi is there,
The shipman of Utnapishtim,
Who hath with him coffers of stone.
He picks plants in the forest.
Him do thou seek out.
If it can be done, fare across with him;
If it cannot be done, turn again back."

[*What follows is badly damaged. Gilgamesh seeks for Ur-Shanabi, but finds at first only his stone coffers, which he breaks to pieces in his anger. Then suddenly he beholds Ur-Shanabi.*]

Ur-Shanabi says to him, to Gilgamesh:
"What is thy name? Say forth!
I am Ur-Shanabi,
Man-servant of Utnapishtim, the far one."

Gilgamesh speaks to him, to Ur-Shanabi:
"My name is Gilgamesh,
I have come from long away . . .
At last, Ur-Shanabi, I behold thy face.
Let me look on Utnapishtim, the far one."

Ur-Shanabi says to him, to Gilgamesh:
"Why are thy cheeks so wasted,
Thy visage so sunken,
Thy heart so sad,
Thy shape so undone?
Why is woe in thy heart?
Why art thou like a wanderer of far ways?
Why is thy countenance
So destroyed with grief and pain?
Why hast thou from long away
Come ahaste over the steppes?"

Gilgamesh says to him,

[ 45 ]

To Ur-Shanabi, the shipman:
"Why should my cheeks not be so wasted,
My visage so sunken,
My heart so sad,
My shape so undone?
Why should woe not be in my heart?
Why should I not be like
A wanderer of far ways?
Why should not my countenance
Be destroyed with grief and pain?
Why should I not from long away
Come ahaste over the steppes?
My belovèd friend, the panther of the steppes,
Engidu, my belovèd friend,
The panther of the steppes, who could do all things,
So that we climbed the mountain,
Overthrew Khumbaba,
Who housed in the cedar-forest,
So that we seized and slew the bull-of-heaven,
So that we laid lions low
In the ravines of the mountain,
My friend,
Who with me ranged through all hardships,
Engidu, my friend,
Who with me laid lions low,
Who ranged through all hardships with me,
Him hath the fate of mankind overtaken.
Six days and six nights have I wept over him;
Until the seventh day
Would I not have him buried.
Then I began to be afraid . . .
Fear of death seized upon me.
Therefore I make away over the steppes.
The fate of my friend weigheth me down;
Therefore I make haste
On a far way over the steppes.
The fate of Engidu, my friend,
Weigheth me down.
Therefore I make haste on a long road over the steppes.

Why should I be silent thereon?
Why should I not cry it forth?
My friend, whom I love,
Hath turned into earth.
Engidu, my friend, whom I love,
Hath turned into earth.
Must not I too, as he,
Lay me down,
And rise not up again
For ever and for ever?"

And Gilgamesh says again to him,
To Ur-Shanabi, the shipman:
"Come, Ur-Shanabi, where is the way to Utnapishtim?
What is his sign? Give it to me!
Give me, give me his sign!
If it can be done,
I will pass over the sea;
If it cannot be done,
I will make away over the steppes."

Ur-Shanabi says to him, to Gilgamesh:
"Thy hands, O Gilgamesh,
Have hindered a landing.
Thou brakest to pieces the coffers of stone,
The coffers of stone are to-broken;
And so I cannot ferry thee over.
Gilgamesh, take the axe in thy arm,
Go down to the forest,
Cut poles of length sixty ells,
Smear them with pitch and bear them to me."

As Gilgamesh this heard,
He took the axe in his arm,
Drew the sword from his girdle,
Went down to the forest,
And cut poles of length sixty ells,
Smeared them with pitch . . .
And brought them to Ur-Shanabi.

Gilgamesh and Ur-Shanabi boarded the ship,
They headed the ship into the flood,
And sailed forth,
A way of one month and fifteen days.
As he took his bearings on the third day,
Ur-Shanabi had reached the waters of death.
Ur-Shanabi says to him, to Gilgamesh:
"Quick, Gilgamesh, take a pole!
For thy hands must not touch
The waters of death.
A second, a third, a fourth pole,
Take, Gilgamesh!
A fifth, a sixth, a seventh pole,
Take, Gilgamesh!
An eighth, a ninth, a tenth pole,
Take, Gilgamesh!
An eleventh, a twelfth pole,
Take, Gilgamesh!"

At a hundred and twenty
Gilgamesh had used up the poles.
Now he made his hips free . . .
Gilgamesh stripped off his garment,
And with his hands made high the mast.
Utnapishtim descrieth his face afar;
Talks to himself and saith the word,
Takes counsel in his heart:
"Why are the stone-coffers
Of the ship all to-broken?
And one who belongs not to me
Sails in the ship!
He who comes yonder, he cannot be man! . . .
I gaze thither, but I understand it not.
I gaze thither, but I grasp it not." . . .

Utnapishtim says to him, to Gilgamesh:
"What is thy name? Say forth!
I am Utnapishtim who hath found Life."
Gilgamesh says to him, to Utnapishtim:

"My name is Gilgamesh.
I have come from wide-away . . .
Now I behold thee, Utnapishtim, thou far one."
Utnapishtim says to him, to Gilgamesh:
"Why are thy cheeks so wasted,
Thy visage so sunken,
Thy heart so sad,
Thy shape so undone?
Why is woe in thy heart?
Why art thou like a wanderer of far ways?
Why is thy countenance
So destroyed with grief and pain?
Why hast thou from wide-away
Made haste over the steppes?"

Gilgamesh says to him, to Utnapishtim:
"Why should my cheeks not be so wasted,
My visage so sunken,
My heart so sad,
My shape so undone?
How should woe not be in my heart?
Why should I not be like a wanderer of far ways?
Why should not my countenance
Be destroyed with grief and pain?
Why should I not from wide-away
Make haste over the steppes?
My belovèd friend, the panther of the steppes,
Engidu, my belovèd friend,
Who could do all things,
So that we climbed the mountain,
Overthrew Khumbaba,
Who housed in the cedar-forest,
So that we seized and slew the bull-of-heaven,
So that we laid lions low
In the ravines of the mountain,
My friend,
Who with me ranged through all hardships,
Engidu, my friend, who with me laid lions low,
Who with me ranged through all hardships,

Him hath the fate of mankind overtaken.
Six days and six nights have I wept over him,
Until the seventh day
Would I not have him buried.
Then I began to be afraid . . .
And fear of death seized upon me.
Therefore I make haste over the steppes.
The fate of my friend weigheth me down.
Therefore I make haste,
On a far way over the steppes.
The fate of Engidu, my friend,
Weigheth me down.
Therefore I make haste on a long road
Over the steppes.
Why should I be silent thereon?
Why should I not cry it forth?
My friend, whom I love,
Hath turned into earth.
Must I not too, as he,
Lay me down,
And rise not up again
For ever and for ever?"

Gilgamesh says again to him, to Utnapishtim:
"Methought, I will go and see
Utnapishtim, of whom men tell.
So I betook me through all lands to and fro,
So I betook me over the mountains
That are hard to cross over,
So I fared over all seas.
With good have I not been glutted . . .
I filled my body with pain;
Ere ever I got to Siduri, the cup-bearer,
Was my clothing gone . . .
I had to hunt all the wild of the fields,
Lions and panthers,
Hyenas, and deer, and ibex.
Their flesh do I eat,
With their skins do I clothe me." . . .

Utnapishtim says to him, to Gilgamesh:

[*The greater part of Utnapishtim's reply is lost.*]

". . . infuriate is Death,
Who is the slayer of Life.
Build we a house for ever?
Seal we compacts for ever?
Divide brothers for ever their heritage?
Doth bringing forth of young
Take place on the earth for ever?
Doth the river for ever swell
And bear along the flood-waters? . . .
For all time hath there been
No everlastingness . . .
The Annunaki, the great gods,
Assemble together;
Mammetum, maker of fate,
Ordaineth with them the lots;
They store away Death and Life;
But they ordain not the days of death."

TABLET XI

Gilgamesh says to him,
To Utnapishtim, the far one:
"I look upon thee, Utnapishtim:
Thy form is not unlike;
Even as I, so too art thou;
Yes, thou art not unlike;
Even as I, so too art thou.
Yet I was born unto this:
To fight and to do battle.
But thou art idle and liest on thy back.
How camest thou, then, into the assembly
Of the gods and foundest Life?"

Utnapishtim says to him, to Gilgamesh:

"I will lay open before thee, Gilgamesh,
Knowledge deep-hidden,
And a secret of the gods will I tell thee:
Shurippak is a city (thou thyself knowest her),
Which lieth on Euphrates' banks.
She is an ancient city,
And the gods are kind to her.
Once the great gods conceived a plan
To make a stormflood.
There foregathered Anu, their father,
Their overlord, the hero Ellil,
Their herald Ninurta, their prince Ennugi.
The bright-eyed Ea had sat with them at counsel.
He told their discussion to a reed-hut:
'Reed-hut, reed-hut! Hut-wall, hut-wall!
Reed-hut, listen! Wall, take it in!
Thou man from Shurippak, son of Ubara-Tutu,
Tear down thy house, build a ship!
Let riches go, seek Life,
Despise possessions, save thy life!
Bring living things of all kinds into the ship!
The ship that thou art to build,
Be its measurements strictly laid out,
For its length and its breadth to match—
On the holy lake set it at anchor!'
I understood, and I say to Ea, my lord:
'I perceive, my lord, what thou sayest;
I hold it dear, and will carry it out.
But what shall I say to the city,
To the folk and to the elders?'
Ea opened his mouth and speaks,
Says to me, his bondman:
'Man, thus shalt thou speak unto them:
Ellil hath taken a loathing to me,
Therefore will I not any longer dwell in your city;
The land of Ellil I will not see more.
I will betake me off to the holy lake,
To dwell with Ea, my lord.
But over you will he make to rain down

Riches upon riches,
Catch of fish, catch of birds,
And with great harvests will he bless you—
When of an evening the Sender of darkness
Will let a cloudburst come down upon you.'


"When a shimmer of morning shone,
I began to do what Ea had ordered . . .
On the fifth day
I planned the form of the ship:
Its walls measured one hundred and twenty ells.
And one hundred and twenty ells
Measured the rim of its roof.
I planned the bows and made a drawing,
I gave it six storeys,
Divided it sevenfold on the outside,
Divided it ninefold on the inside,
And hammered calk-plugs amidships.
I chose me out a pole,
And laid ready what I needed.
Six measures of asphalt I cast into the furnace,
Three measures of pitch I poured therein.
Three measures of oil did the people drag thither in baskets,
Aside from one measure of oil, which the offering consumed,
And two measures of oil which the shipman hid.
I slaughtered beeves for the people,
Slew sheep every day;
I gave the folk to drink
Must and beer, oil and juice of grape,
As if the waters of the river.
I made a feast as on the day of the new year,
Opened the box of ointment and put my hands within.
Before sunset the ship was finished . . .
All that I had I laded upon it,
All that I had of silver I laded upon it,
I laded upon it all that I had of gold,
I laded upon it all that I had
Of living things of all kinds.
I made my whole family and kin

To go aboard the ship;
Cattle of the field, animals of the field,
All handworkers I made go aboard.
Shamash had given me the appointed time:
'Of an evening will the Sender of darkness
Let a cloudburst stream from on high.
Then enter the ship and close thy door.'
This appointed time came on.
The Sender of darkness
Of an evening let a cloudburst come down.
I observed the look of the tempest,
I was afraid to gaze on the tempest,
I went within the ship and shut my gate.
To the pilot of the ship,
The shipman Pusur-Amurri,
I gave over the giant ship with all it held.
When a shimmer of morning shone,
Black thunderheads rose in the deeps of heaven,
Adad thundered therein,
Shullat and Hanish, the gods, go on before,
Go as heralds over mountain and land.
Irragal tears out the dock-posts,
Ninurta goes forth and breaks down the dikes.
The Annunaki lift up their torches,
With their terrible glare
Inflaming the land.
Adad's fury mounts even to heaven,
Turning all brightness to dark.
He shattered the wide land like a pot.
All one day raged the southstorm,
Roared hastening along,
And made the waters reach the hills.
The waters fell upon men like a battle,
No one seeth the other;
From above in heaven
One could no more make out man and man.
The gods were afraid before the stormflood,
Fled, and mounted up to the heaven of Anu.
The gods cringe down like dogs,

Cowering on the ground.
Ishtar shrieks like a woman in birth-pangs,
The lovely-voiced lady of the gods yells aloud:
'The times before are indeed turned to earth,
Because I myself in the gods' assembly
Gave the ill counsel!
How could I in the gods' assembly
Give such ill counsel,
To decree the fight
For the destruction of my mankind?
I alone give birth to my mankind.
Now they fill, like the spawn of the fishes, the sea!'
The gods of the Annunaki weep with her,
The gods are bowed down, sit weeping there . . .
Their lips are shut . . .
Six days and six nights swirls the stormflood,
And the southstorm is a weight on the land.
As the seventh day came on,
The southstorm gave up the fight,
Which it had fought like an army.
The sea grew quiet, and gathered up its waters.
The stormflood ceased.
I looked for the tempest, all had become still.
The whole race of man was turned to earth.
Like a flat roof were the plains.
Then I opened a hatch,
And light streamed into my face.
I sat me down weeping,
And my tears ran over my face.
I gazed about for solid earth
In the dominions of the sea.
After twelve hours an island emerged.
The ship drove for Mount Nissir.
Mount Nissir holds the ship fast
And keeps it from rocking.
One day, a second day, Mount Nissir
Holds the ship fast and keeps it from rocking.
A third and fourth day Mount Nissir
Holds the ship fast and keeps it from rocking.

A fifth, a sixth day Mount Nissir
Holds the ship fast and keeps it from rocking.

"As the seventh day came on,
I held a dove outside and set it free;
The dove flew forth and came back.
She found no resting-place, so she turned home.
I held a swallow outside and set it free;
The swallow flew forth and came back.
She found no resting-place, so she turned home.
I held a raven outside and set it free;
The raven flew forth, saw the water run dry,
He feeds, scrapes, croaks, and turned not home.

"Then I let all out unto the four winds,
And offered a sacrifice,
Set up a burnt-offering
On the top of the mountain.
Seven and again seven vessels of consecration
Did I put in place.
I heaped under them reeds,
Cedarwood and myrtle.
The gods savoured the smell,
The gods savoured the sweet smell;
The gods foregathered, like flies,
Above the maker of the offering.
But when Ishtar, the lady of the gods, came nigh,
She lifted aloft the great jewels
Which Anu had fashioned after her wishes,
And cried out:
'Ye gods here,
As surely as I forget not
These precious-stones on my neck,
Will I be mindful of these days
And forget them not to eternity.
May the gods come to the burnt-offering,
But Ellil shall not come to the burnt-offering,
Because without taking thought
He brought on the stormflood,

[56]

And ordained ruin for my mankind!'
As Ellil came nigh, he saw the ship.
Then Ellil grew wroth and was angry at the gods:
'Someone hath escaped, a living soul!
No man was to have remained alive in this ruin.'
Ninurta opened his mouth and speaks,
He says to the hero Ellil:
'Can anyone devise plans except Ea?
Why, Ea understands every matter!'
Ea opened his mouth and speaks,
Says to the hero Ellil:
'Thou hero and wise one among the gods,
How couldst thou without heed
Rouse up a stormflood?
He who doeth sin let him bear his sin,
He who doeth sacrilege let him bear his sacrilege;
Yet see to it that he be not destroyed,
Be long-suffering that he be not rooted out.
Instead of thy rousing a stormflood,
A lion could have risen up
And diminished mankind;
Instead of thy rousing a stormflood,
A wolf could have risen up
And diminished mankind;
Instead of thy rousing a stormflood,
Famine could have come
And stricken down the land;
Instead of thy rousing a stormflood,
The god of pestilence could have risen
And stricken down the land.
I myself have not betrayed
The secret of the great gods.
I let Utnapishtim, the Very-Wise, see dream-pictures,
And so the secret of the great gods he learned.
Ye now, devise counsel for him.'
Then Ea went aboard the ship,
Took me by the hands, led me onto the land,
And had my wife kneel down at my side.
He stepped into our midst,

Touched our foreheads and blessed us:
'Until now was Utnapishtim only a man;
Henceforth are Utnapishtim and his wife
To be like unto us gods.
And Utnapishtim is to live in the far-away,
At the mouth of the rivers!'
So they took me,
And had me live at the mouth of the rivers.
But who of the gods, Gilgamesh,
Will be taking thee to himself,
That thou too mayst find Life, which thou seekest?
Go to, lie not down to sleep
For six days, seven nights!"

And whilst Gilgamesh sits there in a posture of rest,
Sleep bloweth upon him like a stormwind.
Utnapishtim says to her, to his wife:
"Look at the strong one
Who longed after Life—
Like a stormwind, sleep bloweth against him!"
His wife speaks to him, to Utnapishtim,
To the far one:
"Touch him, that the man may wake up!
Let him, on the way whence he came,
Safe and sound return home.
Through the gate, through which he went,
May he return back to his land!"
Utnapishtim says to her, to his wife:
"Oh, thou hast pity upon the man!
Go to, bake loaves for him,
And lay them at his head!
And the days which he sleeps
Do thou mark on the house-wall."
She baked loaves for him and laid them at his head.
And the days which he slept she marked on the wall.
Utnapishtim announced to him:
"One is dry, a loaf for him,
A second is kneaded, a third damp,
A fourth is become white, a roasted loaf for him,

A fifth is become old,
A sixth is baked, a seventh—"
Then of a sudden he touched him,
And the man awoke.
Gilgamesh says to him,
To Utnapishtim, the far one:
"I was benumbed by the sleep that fell on me.
Then didst thou touch me quick and awaken me."
Utnapishtim says to him, to Gilgamesh:
"Go to, Gilgamesh, thy loaves are counted . . .
One was dry, a loaf for thee,
A second was kneaded, a third damp,
A fourth was become white, a roasted loaf for thee,
A fifth was become old,
A sixth was baked, a seventh—
Then of a sudden I touched thee,
And thou awokest!"
Gilgamesh says to him,
To Utnaphishtim, the far one:
"What shall I do, Utnapishtim?
Whither shall I go,
Now that the Snatcher hath laid hold on my body?
In my sleeping-chamber dwells Death,
And whithersoever I flee, is he, is Death, there."

Utnapishtim says to him,
To Ur-Shanabi, the shipman:
"Ur-Shanabi, the landing-place
Shall no more desire thee;
The crossing-spot shall hate thee . . .
The man whom thou leddest hither,
Whose body filth covers,
From whom beast-skins have taken
The beauty of the body,
Escort him, Ur-Shanabi,
And bring him to the bathing-place;
Let him wash clean as snow
His filth in the water!
Let him cast off his skins

That the sea bear them away!
His body shall again show beautiful!
Be the band round his head made new!
Let him be clad in a robe,
In a shirt for his nakedness!
Until he comes again to his city,
Until he gets to his journey's end,
The robe shall not grow old,
Shall always be made new."

Then Ur-Shanabi took him
And led him to the bathing-place.
He washed clean as snow
His filth in the water.
He cast off his skins
That the sea bore them away.
His body showed beautiful,
The band round his head was made new.
He became clad in a robe,
In a shirt for his nakedness.
Until he returned again home to his city,
Until he got to his journey's end,
The robe should not grow old,
Should always be made new.

Gilgamesh and Ur-Shanabi boarded the ship,
They headed the ship into the flood,
And sailed away.
Then said his wife to him,
To Utnapishtim, the far one:
"Gilgamesh hath set forth;
He hath worn himself out, and suffered torments.
What wilt thou give him,
That with it he may reach his homeland?"

And Gilgamesh has already lifted the pole,
And brings the ship again near the shore:
Utnapishtim says to him, to Gilgamesh:
"Gilgamesh, thou hast set forth;

Thou hast worn thyself out, and suffered torments.
What shall I give thee
That with it thou reachest thy homeland?
I will lay open before thee
Knowledge deep-hidden;
About a plant of life will I tell thee.
The plant looks like the prick-thorn . . .
Its thorn like the thorn of the rose
Can prick the hand hard.
When thou gettest this plant in thy hands,
Eat thereof and thou wilt live."

When Gilgamesh learned of this . . .
He bound heavy stones on his feet;
These drew him down deep in the sea.
He himself took the plant,
And it pricked his hand hard.
He cut off the heavy stones . . .
And laid the plant beside him.
Gilgamesh says to him,
To Ur-Shanabi, the shipman:
"Ur-Shanabi, this plant
Is a plant-of-promise,
Whereby a man obtains his desire.
I will bring it to ramparted Uruk;
I will make the warriors eat thereof . . .
Its name is: 'The-old-man-becomes-young-again.'
I myself will eat thereof,
And return back to my youth."

After twenty miles they took a little food,
After thirty miles they rested for the night.
Then Gilgamesh saw a pit with cool water;
He stepped into it and bathed in the water.
Then a serpent savoured the smell of the plant;
She crept along and took the plant . . .
When he returned, he shrieked out a curse.
Gilgamesh sat himself down and weeps,
His tears run over his face.

He speaks and says to Ur-Shanabi, the shipman:
"For whom, Ur-Shanabi,
Have my arms worn themselves out?
For whom hath been spent the blood of my heart?
I worked good not for myself—
For the worm of the earth have I wrought good. . . ."

After twenty miles they took a little food,
After thirty miles they rested for the night.
At last they reached ramparted Uruk.
Gilgamesh says to him,
To Ur-Shanabi, the shipman:
"Mount up, Ur-Shanabi,
Go up along the walls of ramparted Uruk,
Observe the bricks, behold the ground-work,
If the bricks are not firm and lasting,
And if the foundations were not
Laid by the seven wise-men. . . ."

## TABLET XII

[*Gilgamesh finds no rest. He goes to his mother Ninsun and asks her
how he can have sight of Engidu to inquire of him the fate of the dead;
and she answers:*]

"Gilgamesh, if thou wilt decend into earth
And reach the sanctuary of Irkalla,
Thou mayst not put on a clean robe . . .
With precious oil from the ointment-box,
Mayst thou not anoint thyself;
Else at its smell will the spirits of the dead
Come crowding around thee.
The bow mayst thou not set on the earth;
Else will those who were smitten by the bow
Make a circle around thee.
The staff mayst thou not take into the hand;
Else will the spirits of the dead
Stand trembling before thee.

[ 62 ]

Shoes mayst thou not put on thy feet,
Not a sound mayst thou make toward the earth.
Thy wife whom thou lovest, thou mayst not kiss.
Thy wife whom thou likest not, thou mayst not strike.
Thy child whom thou lovest, thou mayst not kiss.
Thy child whom thou likest not, thou mayst not strike.
Else will the sorrow of earth seize upon thee.
She who rests there, who rests there,
The goddess of earth, who rests there,
Whose clean body is covered with no robe . . .
She will not else let Engidu
Rise up out of the earth.

[*There is a gap in the text and what immediately follows has been diversely interpreted. Gilgamesh has apparently broken at least some of these taboos.*]

Hath he put on a clean robe?
With precious oil from the ointment-box
Hath he anointed himself?
Hath he set the bow on the earth?
Hath he taken the staff into the hand?
Hath he put shoes on his feet?
Hath he made any sound toward the earth?
His wife whom he loved, hath he kissed?
His wife whom he liked not, hath he struck?
His child whom he loved, hath he kissed?
His child whom he liked not, hath he struck?—
The sorrow of earth seized upon him.

She who rests there, who rests there,
The goddess of earth, who rests there,
Whose clean body is covered with no robe . . .
She granted not
That Engidu rose up out of the earth!
Then Ninsun laments
And weeps over her bondman Engidu . . .
Gilgamesh went alone to Ekur,
To the temple of Ellil and spake:

"Father Ellil, on a day
A snare tripped me to the ground,
A trap tripped me to the ground.
Engidu, whom the goddess
Grants not to be led up from below,
Not the pestgod has seized him,
A mischance has not seized him,
Not the merciless steward of Nergal has seized him.
Earth has seized him!
Not on the battle-field of men is he fallen.
Earth has seized him!"
Father Ellil returned him no word.

[*Gilgamesh goes next to Sin, the moongod, and speaks:*]

"Father Sin, on a day
A snare tripped me to the ground,
A trap tripped me to the ground.
Engidu, whom the goddess
Grants not to be led up from below,
Not the pestgod has seized him,
A mischance has not seized him.
Earth has seized him!
Not the merciless steward of Nergal has seized him.
Earth has seized him!
Not on the battle-field of men is he fallen.
Earth has seized him!"
Father Sin returned him no word.

[*Gilgamesh goes finally to Ea, lord of depths of the waters, and speaks:*]

"Father Ea, on a day
A snare tripped me to the ground,
A trap tripped me to the ground.
Engidu, whom the goddess
Grants not to be led up from below,
Not the pestgod has seized him,
A mischance has not seized him.
Earth has seized him!

Not the merciless steward of Nergal has seized him.
Earth has seized him!
Not on the battle-field of men is he fallen.
Earth has seized him!"
Father Ea heard his speaking.
He said to the hero, the manful **Nergal**:
"Nergal, manful hero . . .
Open forthwith a hole in the earth,
Lead Engidu's shadow up out of the earth,
That he talk to his brother Gilgamesh."

As Nergal, the manful hero, this heard,
He opened forthwith a hole in the earth,
Led Engidu's shadow like a wind
Up out of the earth . . .
They talked with one another . . .
"Say forth, my friend!
Say forth, my friend!
The statute of the earth,
Which thou hast beheld,
Say forth!"
"I will not tell thee, my friend,
I will not tell thee.
If I told thee the statute of the earth,
Which I have beheld,
Thou wouldst needs sit thee down
And weep all the day."
"So then will I sit me down
And weep all the day."
"See, the body which thou hast clasped
So that thy heart was glad—
The worms eat it like an old garment.
My body, which thou hast clasped
So that thy heart was glad,
Is vanished away, full of dust,
In dust is it sunken away,
In dust is it sunken away." . . .
"He who died a death of iron—
Sawest thou such a one?"

"I saw him! He rests on a bed of rest
And drinketh clear water."
"He who was slain in battle—
Sawest thou such a one?"
"I saw him!
His father and mother hold his head,
And his wife bends over him."
"Him whose corpse was thrown into the field—
Sawest thou such a one?"
"I saw him!
His dead ghost has no rest in the earth."
"Him whose dead ghost has no care-taker—
Sawest thou such a one?"
"I saw him!
What was left over in the pot,
What was thrown into the street,
That is his fare."

# 2 The Father and the Teen-Ager

From a Sumerian essay pieced together from seventeen clay tablets and fragments emerges a depiction of the age-old concern of a father for his wayward son. Many of the father's complaints and much of his advice have a familiar ring, having changed little in the passage of the millennia and the rises and falls of civilizations.

※※※※※

[*The father begins by asking his son:*]

"Where did you go?"
"I did not go anywhere."
"If you did not go anywhere, why do you idle about? Go to school, stand before your 'school-father,' recite your assignment, open your schoolbag, write your tablet, let your 'big brother' write your new tablet for you. After you have finished your assignment and reported to your monitor,

SOURCE: Samuel Noah Kramer, *History Begins at Sumer* (Garden City, N.Y.: Doubleday and Co.—Doubleday Anchor Books, 1959). Reprinted by permission of the author.

come to me, and do not wander about in the street. Come now, do you know what I said?"

"I know, I'll tell it to you."

"Come, now, repeat it to me."

"I'll repeat it to you."

"Tell it to me.

"Come on, tell it to me."

"You told me to go to school, recite my assignment, open my schoolbag, write my tablet, while my 'big brother' is to write my new tablet. After finishing my assignment, I am to proceed to my work and to come to you after I have reported to my monitor. That's what you told me."

[*The father now continues with a long monologue:*]

"Come now, be a man. Don't stand about in the public square, or wander about the boulevard. When walking in the street, don't look all around. Be humble and show fear before your monitor. When you show terror, the monitor will like you."

[*About fifteen lines destroyed.*]

"You who wander about in the public square, would you achieve success? Then seek out the first generations. Go to school, it will be of benefit to you. My son, seek out the first generations, inquire of them.

"Perverse one over whom I stand watch—I would not be a man did I not stand watch over my son—I spoke to my kin, compared its men, but found none like you among them.

"What I am about to relate to you turns the fool into a wise man, holds the snake as if by charms, and will not let you accept false phrases. Because my heart had been sated with weariness of you, I kept away from you and heeded not your fears and grumblings—no, I heeded not your fears and grumblings. Because of your clamorings, yes, because of your clamorings—I was angry with you—yes, I was angry with you. Because you do not look to your humanity, my heart was carried off as if by an evil wind. Your grumblings have put an end to me, you have brought me to the point of death.

"I, never in all my life did I make you carry reeds to the canebrake. The reed rushes which the young and the little carry, you, never in your life did you carry them. I never said to you 'Follow my caravans.' I never sent you to work, to plow my field. I never sent you to work to dig up my field. I never sent you to work as a laborer. 'Go, work and support me,' I never in my life said to you.

"Others like you support their parents by working. If you spoke to your kin, and appreciated them, you would emulate them. They provide 10 *gur* barley each—even the young ones provided their fathers with 10 *gur* each. They multiplied barley for their father, maintained him in barley, oil, and wool. But you, you're a man when it comes to perverseness, but compared to them you are not a man at all. You certainly don't labor like them—they are the sons of fathers who make their sons labor, but me—I didn't make you work like them.

"Perverse one with whom I am furious—who is the man who can really be furious with his son—I spoke to my kin and found something hitherto unnoticed. The words which I shall relate to you, fear them and be on your guard because of them. Your partner, your yokemate—you failed to appreciate him; why do you not emulate him? Your friend, your companion— you failed to appreciate him; why do you not emulate him? Emulate your older brother. Emulate your younger brother. Among all mankind's craftsmen who dwell in the land, as many as Enki[1] called by name, no work as difficult as the scribal art did he call by name. For if not for song—like the banks of the sea, the banks of the distant canals, is the heart of song distant —you wouldn't be listening to my counsel, and I wouldn't be repeating to you the wisdom of my father. It is in accordance with the fate decreed by Enlil for man that a son follows the work of his father.

"I, night and day am I tortured because of you. Night and day you waste in pleasures. You have accumulated much wealth, have expanded far and wide, have become fat, big, broad, powerful, and puffed. But your kin waits expectantly for your misfortune, and will rejoice at it because you looked not to your humanity."

[*Here follows an obscure passage of 41 lines which seems to consist of proverbs and old saws; the essay then concludes with the father's poetic blessing.*]

"From him who quarrels with you may Nanna, your god, save you,
From him who attacks you may Nanna, your god, save you,
May you find favor before your god,
May your humanity exalt you, neck and breast,
May you be the head of your city's sages,
May your city utter your name in favored places,
May your god call you by a good name,
May you find favor before your god Nanna,
May you be regarded with favor by the goddess Ningal."

1. The god of arts and crafts.

# 3 Sargon of Agade

The Sumerians engaged in destructive intercity wars for hundreds of years until an invader appeared who in about 2250 B.C. put a stop to these activities by conquering all of Sumer. The conqueror was Sargon of Agade, the first major historical personage in Mesopotamian history, the first empire builder in all history.

Just north of Sumer was the land of Akkad, inhabited by a people who learned from their neighbors and adopted Sumerian achievements, including the cuneiform system of writing, and who thus themselves became civilized. The Akkadians belonged to a group of peoples whose languages, all closely related to each other, were of the Semitic language group. Included are most of the peoples who eventually rose to prominence in the ancient history of the Near East: Akkadians, Amorites, Assyrians, Canaanites (Phoenicians), Hebrews, and Aramaeans.

The Akkadians were able to unite themselves, and under Sargon they expanded their territorial control south into Sumer and north and west to the shores of the Mediterranean, perhaps even including the island of Cyprus. Sargon's dynasty lasted only about a hundred years, but his empire was the first major achievement in the organization of a large territory composed of different peoples. More important, it contributed to the development of a single Near Eastern civilization in which individual countries were to be only local variations of a cultural pattern founded upon the Sumerian model. The various peoples retained their local languages, but the Akkadian language became the normal language for the conduct of international relations, and it remained so in the entire Near East for some fifteen hundred years.

So great a figure as Sargon had an enormous impact. Our sources of knowledge are compounded of legend and romance, boastful exaggeration and hard historical fact. The tales of his remarkable birth and upbringing provided the model for many later rulers, including the Persian empire builder of the sixth century, Cyrus the Great, and the Biblical Moses.

The three passages about Sargon that follow illustrate the kind of leg-

SOURCE: L. W. King, *Chronicles Concerning Early Babylonian Kings*, Vol. II (*Studies in Eastern History*, Vol. III) (London: Luzac and Co., 1907). Reprinted by permission of the publisher.
George A. Barton, *The Royal Inscriptions of Sumer and Akkad* (*Library of Ancient Semitic Inscriptions*, Vol. I) (New Haven: Yale University Press for the American Oriental Society, 1929), pp. 101–107. Reprinted by permission of the publisher.

endary and historical source material found in the ancient Mesopotamian documents. The first two are translated by L. W. King, the third by George A. Barton.

❀❀❀❀❀❀

Sargon, the mighty king, the king of Agade, am I.
My mother was lowly, my father I knew not,
and the brother of my father dwelleth in the mountain.
My city is Azupiranu, which lieth on the bank of the Euphrates.
My lowly mother conceived me, in secret she brought me forth.
She set me in a basket of rushes, with bitumen she closed my door;
she cast me into the river, which rose not over me.
The river bore me up, unto Akki, the irrigator it carried me.
Akki, the irrigator, with . . . lifted me out,
Akki, the irrigator, as his own son . . . reared me,
Akki, the irrigator, as his gardener appointed me.
While I was a gardener the goddess Ishtar loved me,
and for . . . -four years I ruled the kingdom.
The black-headed peoples I ruled, I governed;
mighty mountains with axes of bronze did I destroy.
I bolted fast the upper mountains;
I burst through the lower mountains.
The Country of the Sea three times did I besiege;
Dilmun did. . . .
Unto the great Dur-ilu I went up, I. . . .
. . . I altered. . . .
Whatsoever king shall be exalted after me, . . .
let him rule, let him govern the black-headed peoples;
mighty mountains with axes of bronze let him destroy.
Let him bolt fast the upper mountains;
let him burst through the lower mountains.
The Country of the Sea let him three times besiege;
let Dilmun. . . .
Unto the great Dur-ilu let him go up, and let him. . . .
. . . from my city of Agade. . . .

 • • • • •

Sargon, king of Agade, through the royal gift of Ishtar was exalted, and he possessed no foe nor rival. His glory over the world he poured out. The Sea in the East he crossed, and in the eleventh year the Country of the West in its full extent his hand subdued. He united them under one control; he set up his images in the West; their booty he brought over at his word. The sons of his palace for five *kasbu* around he settled, and over the hosts of the world he reigned supreme.

Against Kasalla he marched, and he turned Kasalla into mounds and heaps of ruins; he destroyed the land and left not enough for a bird to rest thereon.

Afterwards in his old age all the lands revolted against him, and they besieged him in Agade; and Sargon went forth to battle and defeated them; he accomplished their overthrow, and their wide-spreading host he destroyed.

Afterwards he attacked the land of Subartu[1] in his might, and they submitted to his arms, and Sargon settled that revolt, and defeated them; he accomplished their overthrow, and their wide-spreading host he destroyed, and he brought their possessions into Agade. The soil from the trenches of Babylon he removed, and the boundaries of Agade he made like those of Babylon. But because of the evil which he had committed the great lord Marduk was angry, and he destroyed his people by famine. From the rising of the Sun unto the setting of the Sun they opposed him and gave him no rest.

Naram-Sin, the son of Sargon, marched against the city of Apirak, and he constructed mines against it, and Rish-Adad, the king of Apirak, and the governor of Apirak his hand subdued. He marched against Magan,[2] and Mannu-dannu, the king of Magan, his hand subdued.

Dungi, the son of Ur-Engur, cared greatly for the city of Eridu, which was on the shore of the sea. But he sought after evil, and the treasure of Esagila and of Babylon he brought out as spoil. And Bel was . . . and body and . . . he made an end of him.

Ura-imitti, the king, set Bel-ibni, the gardener, upon his throne, that the dynasty might not come to an end; and the crown of his sovereignty he placed upon his head, Ura-imitti in his palace . . . died. Bel-ibni, who sat upon the throne, did not arise therefrom, but as king he was established. Ilu-shuma, king of Assyria, against Su-abu.

. . . . .

Sargon, king of Agade, overseer of Ishtar, king of Kish, *pasisu*-priest of Anu, king of the land, the great vice-gerent of Enlil, the city of Erech he subjugated, and its wall he destroyed; the men of Erech with mighty weapons he cut off: all the fields he destroyed. Lugalzaggisi, king of Erech was overthrown, his hand overpowered, in vile fetters, by the gate of Enlil

1. Assyria.    2. Perhaps Egypt.

he placed him. Sargon, king of Agade, with the man of Ur fought, all the fields he destroyed. His city he subjugated, and its wall destroyed. The temple of Ninmar he subjugated, its wall he destroyed and all its country from Lagash unto the sea he subjugated. His weapons in the sea he washed. With the men of Umma he fought, all the fields he devastated, their city he subjugated, and its wall he destroyed.

Unto Sargon, king of the land, the god Enlil gave, no one opposing, from the upper sea to the lower sea Enlil gave unto him; and from the lower sea the citizens of Agade the viceroy of . . . Uga, the man of Mari and Elam before Sargon, king of the land, stood. Sargon, king of the lands of the earth, Kish—its place he restored; their city he made strong for them.

Whoever this inscription destroys, may Shamash his foundation tear out, and his seed remove!

Inscription on its pedestal: Lugalzaggisi, king of Erech, the man who was *patesi* of Umma. . . .

# 4  The Law Code of the City of Eshnunna

After the end of Sargon's dynasty, the Sumerian cities regained their independence. The final period of Sumerian achievement, from about 2150 to 2000 B.C., saw Ur once again prominent and is known as that of the Third Dynasty of Ur. In the eighteenth century B.C. all of Mesopotamia was subjected by the Amorites, whose rule lasted until about 1600 B.C. Thereafter the land was once again subjected to the experience of repeated invasion, conquest, and dismemberment until about 1550 B.C., when the Kassites, a people from the mountains to the east, imposed their rule. By then greater powers had arisen, and the scene of history's main events had shifted westward. Mesopotamia's civilization had placed its permanent mark upon them, but the country itself was left in semi-isolation, unimportant until the rise to power of its northern component, Assyria, in the ninth and eighth centuries B.C.

The greatest single source of our knowledge of Mesopotamian life and society comes from the law codes. The celebrated Code of Hammurabi is the longest and most complete. For a long time it was the earliest law code known and was thought to be an original achievement of the Amorites (or Babylonians), whose sixth king, Hammurabi, ruled a powerful Mesopotamian empire from 1728 to 1686 B.C. In recent years other, earlier codes have been found. So far they bring the codification of law back as far as about 2400 B.C. and indicate that local city law codes were regularly issued by the Sumerian kings. These codes are a treasure house of detailed information: class divisions, slavery, regulation of business activity, contractual obligations, family relations, rights of women, property, moral standards, and concepts of justice are among the many topics on which they give us precise information.

The code of the city of Eshnunna, dating from the early eighteenth century B.C., a hundred years before Hammurabi's, is translated by Albrecht Goetze.

⊛⊛⊛⊛⊛

*[There is a prologue or preamble, which contains the name of the king Bilalama, thereby giving the approximate date of the document. It is otherwise too fragmentary to be of use.]*

1. 1 *kor* of grain is priced at 1 shekel of silver, 3 *qa* of "best oil" are priced at 1 shekel of silver, 1 *seah* and 2 *qa* of "tree-oil" are priced at 1 shekel of silver, 1 *seah* and 5 *qa* of lard are priced at 1 shekel of silver, 4 *seah* of "river-oil" are priced at 1 shekel of silver, 6 minas of wool are priced at 1 shekel of silver, 2 *kor* of salt are priced at 1 shekel of silver, 1 *kor* of . . . is priced at 1 shekel of silver, 3 minas of copper are priced at 1 shekel of silver, 2 minas of refined copper are priced at 1 shekel of silver.

2. 1 *qa* of "tree-oil" *sa nishatim,*[1] its value in grain is 3 *seah*. 1 *qa* of lard *sa nishatim,* its value in grain is 2 *seah* and 5 *qa*. 1 *qa* of "river-oil" *sa nishatim,* its value in grain is 8 *qa*.

3. The hire for a wagon together with its oxen and its driver is 1 *massiktum* and 4 *seah* of grain. If it is paid in silver, its hire is ⅓ of a shekel. He may drive it the whole day.

4. The hire for a boat is 2 *qa* per *kor* of capacity, and 4 *massiktum* and 1 *qa* is the hire for a boat-man. He may drive it the whole day.

5. If the boat-man is negligent and causes the sinking of the boat, he shall pay in full for everything the sinking of which he caused.

6. If a man takes possession of a boat which is not his at its berth, he shall pay 10 shekels of silver.

SOURCE: Albrecht Goetze, "The Laws of Eshnunna—Discovered at Tell Harmal," *Sumer,* IV : 2 (Sept. 1948), 69–91. Reprinted with the permission of the Director-General of Antiquities, Republic of Iraq.

1. Meaning unknown.

7. The wages of a harvester are 2 *seah* of grain; if they are paid in silver, the wages are 12 "grain."

8. The wages of a winnower are 1 *seah* of grain.

9. Should a man pay 1 shekel of silver to a hired man for harvesting—if he does not fulfil his obligations and does not complete for him the harvest everywhere, he shall pay 10 shekels of silver. He shall receive 1 *seah* and 5 *qa* of grain as wages and leave the service. His rations of grain, oil and cloth shall be returned.

10. The hire for a donkey is 1 *seah* of grain and the wages for its driver are 1 *seah* of grain. He may drive it the whole day.

11. The wages for a hired man are 1 shekel of silver; his provender is 1 "grain" of silver. He shall work for one month.

12. A man who is caught in the field of a *muskenum*[2] in the crop during day-time, shall pay 10 shekels of silver. He who is caught in the crop at night, shall die, he shall not get away alive.

13. A man who is caught in the house of a *muskenum* in the house during day-time, shall pay 10 shekels of silver. He who is caught in the house at night, shall die, he shall not get away alive.

14. The fee of a . . . —should he bring 5 shekels of silver the fee is 1 shekel of silver; should he bring 10 shekels of silver the fee is 2 shekels of silver.

15. The *tamkarrum* and the *sabitum* shall not receive silver, grain, wool or "tree oil" from a slave or a slave-girl as an investment.

16. To a coparcener or a slave a mortgage cannot be furnished.

17. Should a man bring the bride-money to the house of his father-in-law —if one of the two deceases, the silver shall revert to its owner.

18. If he has taken her and she has entered his house and after a while the young woman deceases, he her father shall get refunded not merely that which she brought in, he shall obtain also its accrued increase. He shall add 1 sixth and 6 "grain" per shekel, 1 *massiktum* and 4 *seah* per *kor* as interest.

19. A man who gives in terms of his retake shall make the debtor pay on the threshing-floor.

20. If a man gives . . . to . . . and expresses the value of the silver in grain for him, he shall at harvest-time obtain the grain and its interest, 1 *massiktum* and 4 *seah* per *kor*.

21. If a man gives silver at face value, he shall obtain the silver and its interest, 1 sixth and 6 "grain" per shekel.

2. A member of a social class which at Eshnunna seems to have been connected with the palace or temple.

22. If a man has no claims against another man, but nevertheless distrains on the other man's slave-girl, the owner of the slave-girl shall declare under oath: "You have no claims against me" and he shall pay silver in full compensation for the slave-girl.

23. If a man has no claims against another man, but nevertheless distrains on the other man's slave-girl, detains her in his house and causes her death, he shall give two slave-girls to the owner of the slave-girl in compensation.

24. If he has no claims against him, but nevertheless distrains on the wife of a *muskenum* or the child of a *muskenum,* detains the distrainee in his house and causes his death, it is a capital offense. The distrainer who distrained shall die.

25. If a man calls at the house of his father-in-law and his father-in-law accepts him, but nevertheless gives his daughter to another man, the father of the girl shall refund the bride-money which he received twofold.

26. If a man gives bride-money for another man's daughter, but another man seizes her forcibly without asking the permission of her father and her mother and violates her, it is a capital offence and he shall die.

27. If a man seizes another man's daughter without asking the permission of her father and her mother and concludes no formal marriage contract with her father and her mother, even though she may live in his house for a year, she is not a housewife.

28. Otherwise, if he concludes a formal contract with her father and her mother and cohabits with her, she is a housewife. When she is caught with another man, she shall die, she shall not get away alive.

29. If a man has been lost in a raid or an invasion, or if he has been carried off as a prisoner and lived in a foreign country for long days, and if another man has taken his wife and she has borne him a son—when he returns, he shall get his wife back.

30. If a man hates his town and his lord and becomes a fugitive and another man takes his wife—when he returns, he shall have no right to claim his wife.

31. If a man violates another man's slave-girl, he shall pay ⅔ of a mina of silver; the slave-girl remains the property of her owner.

32. If a man gives his son away for nursing him and bringing him up, but does not give the grain-ration, oil-ration and wool-ration for three years, he shall pay 10 shekels of silver for bringing up his son and she the nurse shall care for his son.

33. If he wrongs a slave-girl and she gives her child to another man's daughter, if its lord sees it when it has become older, he may seize it and then shall have to care for it.

34. If a slave-girl of the palace gives her son or her daughter to a *muskenum* for bringing him/her up, the palace may take back the son or the daughter whom she gave.

35. Also he who took the child of a slave-girl of the palace shall recompense the palace with its equivalent.

36. If a man gives property of his on deposit with a view to subsequent redemption and if the deposited property which he gave has disappeared without that the house was burglarized, the *sippu* broken down or the window forced, he the depositee will replace his the depositor's property.

37. If a man's house indeed collapses and, together with the property of the depositor which he gave him, loss on the part of the owner of the house is incurred, the owner of the house shall swear him an oath in the gate of Tishpak saying: "Together with your property my property was lost; I have done nothing improper or wrong." If he swears him such oath, he shall have no claim against him.

38. If one of several brothers wants to sell his share in property which is common to them and his brother wishes to buy it, he shall pay half of what an outsider would have to pay.

39. If a man is hard up and sells his house, on the day on which the buyer pays, the owner of the house shall vacate it.

40. If a man buys a slave, a slave-girl, an ox or any other valuable object but cannot legally establish the seller, he is a thief.

41. If an *ubarum,* a *naptarum* or a *mudum* wants to sell his beer, the *sabitum* shall sell the beer for him at the current price.

42. If a man bites the nose of another man and severs it, he shall pay 1 mina of silver. For an eye he shall pay 1 mina of silver; for a tooth ½ mina; for an ear ½ mina; for a slap in the face 10 shekels of silver.

43. If a man severs another man's finger, he shall pay ⅔ of a mina of silver.

44. If a man throws another man to the floor in an altercation and breaks his hand, he shall pay ½ mina of silver.

45. If he breaks his foot, he shall pay ½ mina of silver.

46. If a man assaults another man and breaks his . . . he shall pay ⅔ of a mina of silver.

47. If a man hits another man accidentally, he shall pay 10 shekels of silver.

48. And in addition, in cases involving penalties from ⅔ of a mina to 1 mina, they shall formally try the man. A capital offence comes before the king.

49. If a man is caught with a stolen slave or a stolen slave-girl, he shall surrender slave by slave and slave-girl by slave-girl.

50. If the *sakanakku* of the River district or an official, whoever it may be, seizes a lost slave, a lost slave-girl, a lost ox, a lost donkey belonging to the palace or a *muskenum* and does not surrender it to Eshnunna but keeps it in his house, even though he may have let pass only seven days of one month, the palace will prosecute him for theft.

51. A slave or a slave-girl of Eshnunna which is marked with a *kannum*, a *maskanum* or an *abbuttum* shall not leave the gate of Eshnunna without its owner's permission.

52. A slave or a slave-girl which has entered the gate of Eshnunna in the custody of a foreign envoy shall be marked with a *kannum*, a *maskanum* and an *abbuttum* but remain in the custody of its master.

53. If an ox gores another ox and causes its death, both ox-owners shall divide among themselves the price of the live ox and the equivalent of the dead ox.

54. If an ox habitually gores other oxen and the authorities have brought the fact to the notice of its owner, if nevertheless he does not have it de-horned, it gores a man and causes his death, the owner of the ox shall pay ⅔ of a mina of silver.

55. If it gores a slave and causes its death, he shall pay 15 shekels of silver.

56. If a dog is mad and the authorities have brought the fact to the notice of its owner, if nevertheless he does not subdue it, it bites a man and causes his death, the owner of the dog shall pay ⅔ of a mina of silver.

57. If it bites a slave and causes its death, he shall pay 15 shekels of silver.

58. If a wall is threatening to fall and the authorities have brought the fact to the notice of its owner, if nevertheless he does not strengthen his wall, the wall collapses and causes a free man's death, it is a capital offence; jurisdiction of the king.

59. If a man divorces his wife after having made her bear children and takes another wife, he shall be driven from his house and whatever he owns and go after. . . .

[*60 and 61 are fragmentary*]

# 5 *The Law Code of Hammurabi*

Aside from its completeness and the resultant wealth of information it provides, the historical importance of Hammurabi's code is now seen to be its achievement in creating a law to be applied not simply to the local level of the Sumerian codes but to a large kingdom, one that contained within it a variety of local usages as well as major differences between the Sumerian juridical tradition and that of the Semitic-speaking peoples. The most striking difference between the Sumerian codes and Hammurabi's is seen in the law of *talio,* the principle of "an eye for an eye, a tooth for a tooth" in exacting punishment. This principle is absent from the Sumerian codes, while it is a conspicuous feature of the Code of Hammurabi and all later Semitic codes including, of course, the Biblical one. The Sumerian codes display a notable preference for the payment of fines rather than for the bodily punishment frequent in Hammurabi's code. The harshness of punishment in the latter, especially the frequency with which the death penalty is stipulated, has led many scholars to believe that the penalties prescribed in the code were maximal and that in actual practice a judge could at his discretion impose a lesser sentence.

It is particularly noteworthy that, while the gods are invoked and Hammurabi is depicted as issuing his laws under the guidance of the sun god Shamash, the Near Eastern law codes were not religious but were all secular in content and in tone. The translation of the Code of Hammurabi, from which part of the prologue and part of the epilogue have been omitted, is that of D. D. Luckenbill (edited by E. Chiera).

❀❀❀❀❀

PROLOGUE

When the lofty Anu, king of the Anunnaki, and Enlil, lord of heaven and earth, who determines the destinies of the land, committed the rule of all mankind to Marduk, the first-born son of Ea, and made him great among the Igigi; when they pronounced the lofty name of Babylon, made it great among the quarters of the world and in its midst established for him an everlasting kingdom whose foundations were firm as heaven and earth— at that time Anu and Enlil named me, Hammurabi, the exalted prince, the worshiper of the gods, to cause righteousness to prevail in the land, to

SOURCE: Reprinted from *The Origin and History of Hebrew Law* by J. M. P. Smith by permission of The University of Chicago Press. Copyright 1931 by The University of Chicago.

destroy the wicked and the evil, to prevent the strong from plundering the weak, to go forth like the sun over the black-headed race, to enlighten the land and to further the welfare of the people. Hammurabi, the shepherd, named by Enlil am I, who increased plenty and abundance; who made everything complete for Nippur, the bond of heaven and earth; the exalted supporter of Ekur; the wise king, who restored Eridu to its place . . . .

*[Some 210 poetic lines reciting the religious, civil, and military achievements of the king are here omitted.]*

. . . The ancient seed of royalty, the powerful king, the sun of Babylon, who caused light to go forth over the lands of Sumer and Akkad; the king who caused the four quarters of the world to render obedience; the favorite of Innanna am I. When Marduk sent me to rule the people and to bring help to the land, I established law and justice in the language of the land and promoted the welfare of the people.

### THE LAWS

1. If a man[1] accuse a man, and charge him with murder, but cannot convict him, the accuser shall be put to death.

2. If a man charge a man with sorcery, but cannot convict him, he who is charged with sorcery shall go to the sacred river, and he shall throw himself into the river; if the river overcome him, his prosecutor shall take to himself his house. If the river show that man innocent and he come forth unharmed, he that charged him with sorcery shall be put to death. He who threw himself into the river shall take to himself the house of his accuser.

3. If a man, in a case before the court, offer testimony concerning deeds of violence, and do not establish the testimony that he has given—if that case be a case involving life, that man shall be put to death.

4. If he offer testimony concerning grain or money, he shall himself bear the penalty imposed in that case.

5. If a judge pronounce a judgment, render a decision, deliver a sealed verdict, and afterward reverse his judgment, they shall prosecute the judge for reversing the judgment which he has pronounced, and he shall pay

---

1. The term *awilum* is ambiguous, sometimes meaning a noble, sometimes a free man of any class, sometimes any man from king to slave. In the Code it has in general the signification of a free man.

twelvefold the damages which were awarded in said judgment; and publicly they shall expel him from his seat of judgment, and he shall not return, and with the judges in a case he shall not take his seat.

6. If a man steal the property of god or palace, that man shall be put to death; and he who receives from his hand the stolen property shall be put to death.

7. If a man purchase silver or gold, manservant or maidservant, ox, sheep, or ass, or anything else from a man's son, or from a man's servant without witnesses or contracts, or if he receive the same for safekeeping, that man is a thief, he shall be put to death.

8. If a man steal ox or sheep, ass or pig, or boat—if it belonged to god or palace, he shall pay thirty fold; if it belonged to a common man,[2] he shall restore tenfold. If the thief have nothing wherewith to pay, he shall be put to death.

9. If a man who has lost anything find that which was lost in the hand of another man; and the man in whose hand the lost property is found say, "A man sold it to me, I purchased it in the presence of witnesses"; and the owner of the lost property say, "I will bring witnesses who know the lost property"; if the purchaser produce the seller who has sold it to him and the witnesses in whose presence he purchased it, and the owner of the lost property produce witnesses who know his lost property, the judges shall look into their matters. The witnesses in whose presence the purchase was made and the witnesses who know the lost property shall declare what they know in the presence of God. The seller shall be put to death as a thief; the owner of the lost property shall receive his lost property; the purchaser shall take from the estate of the seller the money which he paid out.

10. If the alleged purchaser do not produce the seller who sold it to him, and the witnesses in whose presence he purchased it, and if the owner of the lost property produce witnesses who know the lost property, the purchaser is a thief, he shall be put to death; the owner of the lost property shall receive his lost property.

11. If the alleged owner of the lost property do not produce witnesses who know his lost property, he is a mischief-maker, he has stirred up strife, he shall be put to death.

12. If the seller has died, the purchaser shall recover damages in said case fivefold from the estate of the seller.

13. If the witnesses of the man be not at hand, the judges shall grant him

2. The term distinguishes a private citizen from one who is a dependent of temple or palace.

a delay of six months; and if he do not produce his witnesses within the six months, that man is a mischief-maker, he shall bear the penalty imposed in that case.

14. If a man steal a man's son who is a minor, he shall be put to death.

15. If a man aid a male or a female slave of the palace, or a male or a female slave of a common man, to escape from the city, he shall be put to death.

16. If a man harbor in his house a runaway male or female slave of the palace or of a common man and do not bring him forth at the call of the commandant, the owner of the house shall be put to death.

17. If a man catch a runaway male or female slave, in the country, and bring him back to the owner, the owner of the slave shall pay him two shekels of silver.

18. If that slave will not name his owner, he shall bring him to the palace, his past shall be looked up, and they shall return him to his owner.

19. If he detain that slave in his house and later the slave be found in his possession, that man shall be put to death.

20. If the slave escape from the hand of his captor, that man shall make declaration under oath, to the owner of the slave, and shall go free.

21. If a man make a breach in a house, they shall put him to death in front of that breach, and they shall bury him there.

22. If a man practice brigandage and be captured, that man shall be put to death.

23. If the brigand be not captured, the man who has been robbed shall establish the amount of his loss before the god, and the city and the governor, in whose land or border the robbery was committed, shall compensate him for whatsoever was lost.

24. If there were loss of life, the city and governor shall pay one mina of silver to his heirs.

25. If a fire break out in a man's house and a man who goes to extinguish it cast his eye on the household property of the owner of the house, and take the household property of the owner of the house, that man shall be thrown into the fire.

26. If either an officer or a constable who is ordered to go on an errand of the king do not go, or if he hire a substitute and he carry out his task, that officer or constable shall be put to death. His hired substitute shall take to himself his house.

27. If an officer or a constable in a campaign of the king be captured, and afterward they give his field and garden to another and he perform

his feudal service, if he return and reach his city, they shall restore to him his field and garden, and he himself shall perform his service.

28. If an officer or a constable who is in a fortress of the king be captured, and his son be able to perform his service, the field and garden shall be given to him and he shall perform the service of his father.

29. If his son be a minor and be not able to perform the service of his father, one-third of the field and of the garden shall be given to his mother, and his mother shall rear him.

30. If an officer or a constable abandon his field, his garden, and his house along with his service, and leave them uncared for and another after him take his field, his garden, and his house, and perform service three years; if he return and ask for his field, his garden, and his house, they shall not be given to him; he who has taken them and performed his service shall continue to perform the service.

31. If he leave them uncared for but one year and return, his field, his garden, and his house shall be given to him, and he shall perform his service.

32. If a merchant ransom either an officer or a constable who has been captured on an errand of the king, and enable him to reach his city; if there be in his house wherewith to ransom him, he shall ransom himself; if there be not in his house, by the temple of his city he shall be ransomed; if there be not in the temple of his city wherewith to ransom him, the palace shall ransom him. His field, his garden, and his house shall not be given for his ransom.

33. If a governor or a magistrate get a dismissed soldier, or accept and send a hired substitute on an errand of the king, that governor or magistrate shall be put to death.

34. If a governor or a magistrate take the property of an officer, plunder an officer, let an officer for hire, betray an officer in a judgment to a man of influence, take the gift which the king has given to an officer, that governor or magistrate shall be put to death.

35. If a man buy from the hand of an officer the cattle or sheep which the king has given to that officer, he shall forfeit his money.

36. The field, garden, and house of an officer, constable, or taxgatherer shall not be sold for silver.

37. If a man purchase the field, garden, and house of an officer, constable, or taxgatherer, his deed-tablet shall be broken and he shall forfeit his money. The field, garden, and house shall revert to the owner.

38. An officer, constable, or taxgatherer shall not deed to his wife or daughter the field, garden, and house which are his feudal holding, nor shall he assign them for debt.

39. He may deed to his wife or daughter the field, garden, and house which he has purchased and acquired or he may assign them for debt.

40. A priestess, merchant, or other holder of fiefland may sell his field, his garden, or his house; the purchaser shall perform the feudal service of the field, garden, and house which he has purchased.

41. If a man have exchanged some property of his for the field, garden, and house of an officer, constable, or taxgatherer and have given money to boot, the officer, constable, or taxgatherer shall return to his field, garden, and house and he shall take to himself the money which was given to him to boot.

42. If a man rent a field for cultivation and do not produce any grain in the field, because he has not performed the necessary work on the field they shall convict him, and he shall give to the owner of the field grain on the basis of the adjacent fields.

43. If he do not cultivate the field but neglect it, he shall give to the owner of the field grain on the basis of the adjacent fields; and the field which he has neglected he shall break up with the spade, he shall harrow, and he shall return to the owner of the field.

44. If a man rent an uncultivated field for three years to develop it, and neglect it and do not develop the field, in the fourth year he shall break up the field with the spade, he shall spade and harrow it, and he shall return it to the owner of the field and shall measure out ten *kor* of grain for each ten *gan*.

45. If a man rent his field to a tenant for rent and receive the rent of his field and later Adad [*the storm god*] inundate the field, or carry away the produce, the loss is the tenant's.

46. If he have not received the rent of his field whether he had rented the field for one-half or one-third of the crop, the grain which is in the field the tenant and the owner of the field shall divide by shares.

47. If the tenant offer a cultivated field into the charge of another because in a former year he had not made his expenses, the owner of the field need not permit him to do so. He is his cultivator, and his field shall be cultivated and at the time of harvest he shall take grain according to his contracts.

48. If a man owe a debt and Adad inundate the field or the flood carry the produce away, or, through lack of water, grain have not grown in the field, in that year he shall not make any return of grain to the creditor, he shall alter his contract-tablet and he need not pay the interest for that year.

49. If a man obtain money from a merchant and give as security to the merchant a field prepared for grain or sesame, and say to him, "Cultivate the field, and harvest and take to thyself the grain and sesame which is

produced"; and the cultivator raise grain or sesame in the field, at the time of harvest the owner of the field shall receive the grain or sesame which is in the field and he shall give to the merchant grain for the loan which he had obtained from him and for the interest and for the expenses of the cultivation.

50. If he give as security a field planted with grain or a field planted with sesame, the owner of the field shall receive the grain or the sesame which is in the field and he shall return the loan and its interest to the merchant.

51. If he have not the money to return, he shall give to the merchant grain or sesame, as their market value according to the scale fixed by the king, for the loan and its interest which he has obtained from the merchant.

52. If the tenant do not raise a crop of grain or sesame, he shall not change his contract.

53. If a man neglect to strengthen his dike, and do not strengthen his dike, and a break be made in his dike and he let the water carry away the farmland, the man in whose dike the break has been made shall restore the grain which he has damaged.

54. If he be not able to restore the grain, they shall sell him and his goods, and the farmers whose grain the water has carried away shall divide the results of the sale.

55. If a man open his canal for irrigation and neglect it and he let the water carry away an adjacent field, he shall measure out grain on the basis of the adjacent fields.

56. If a man open up the water and he let the water carry away the preparations of an adjacent field, he shall measure out ten *kor* of grain for each *gan*.

57. If a shepherd have not come to an agreement with the owner of a field to pasture his sheep on the grass, and if he pasture his sheep on the field without the consent of the owner, the owner of the field shall harvest his field, and the shepherd who has pastured his sheep on the field without the consent of the owner of the field shall give over and above twenty *kor* of grain for each ten *gan* to the owner of the field.

58. If, after the sheep have gone up from the meadow and have crowded their way through the gate into the public common, the shepherd turn the sheep into the field, and pasture the sheep on the field, the shepherd shall oversee the field on which he pastures and at the time of harvest he shall measure out sixty *kor* of grain for each ten *gan* to the owner of the field.

59. If a man cut down a tree in a man's orchard without the consent of the owner of the orchard, he shall pay one-half mina of silver.

60. If a man give a field to a gardener to plant as an orchard and the gardener plant the orchard and care for the orchard four years, in the fifth year the owner of the orchard and the gardener shall share equally; the owner of the orchard shall choose his share and take it.

61. If the gardener do not plant the whole field, but leave a portion uncultivated, they shall assign the uncultivated portion to his share.

62. If he do not plant as an orchard the field which was given to him, if it be a cultivated field, as rent for the field for the years during which it has been neglected, the gardener shall measure out grain to the owner of the field on the basis of the adjacent fields, and he shall perform the required work on the field and he shall restore it to the owner of the field.

63. If the field be an uncultivated one, he shall perform the required work on the field and he shall restore it to the owner of the field and he shall measure out ten *kor* of grain per *gan* for each year.

64. If a man give his orchard to a gardener to manage, the gardener, as long as he is in possession of the orchard, shall give to the owner of the orchard two-thirds of the produce of the orchard; he himself shall take one-third.

65. If the gardener do not pollinate the orchard, and he diminish the yield, the gardener shall measure out the yield of the orchard on the basis of the adjacent orchards.

66. If a man borrow money from a merchant, and his merchant foreclose on him, if he have no money for repayment but give his orchard, after it has been pollinated, to the merchant, and say to him, "The dates, as many as there are produced in the orchard, take for your money," that merchant shall not agree. The dates, as many as there are in the orchard, the owner shall take and shall pay the merchant the money and its interest according to the wording of his tablet; and the remaining dates which are in the orchard the owner shall take for himself.

*[Sections 67–70 are fragmentary.]*

71. If he pay grain, silver, or personal property for a fief estate which is of the estate of his neighbor which he is purchasing, he shall lose everything which he paid; the estate shall return to its holder. If that estate have not vassalage obligation resting upon it, he may buy it; for that estate he may pay grain, silver, or personal property.

*[Sections 72–77 are fragmentary.]*

78. If a man who is a tenant have paid the full amount of money for

his rent for the year to the owner of the house, and he the owner say to him before "his days are full," "Vacate," the owner of the house, because he made the tenant move out of his house before "his days were full," shall lose the money which the tenant paid him.

[*Sections 79–85 are not preserved.*]

86. If a merchant put out money [a scribe's error; "grain" is intended] at interest, for one *kor* he shall receive one hundred *sila* of grain as interest.

87. If he put out money at interest, for one shekel of silver he shall receive one-fifth of a shekel as interest.

88. If a man who owes money at interest have no money wherewith to repay, but have grain, according to the regulation of the king he shall measure out grain for his interest, and the merchant shall receive it.

89. If a merchant increase the interest on grain beyond one hundred *sila* for one *kor,* for the interest on silver beyond one-sixth shekel plus six *she* and take this interest, he shall lose whatever he put out at interest.

90. If a merchant put out grain or silver at interest, the interest . . . of grain or silver . . . he received . . . the grain or . . . he shall not . . .

[*Section 91 is not preserved.*]

92. If a merchant put out grain or silver at interest but do not deduct the grain or silver which he received and do not write a new document, or if he add the interest to the principal, that merchant shall pay back double the grain or silver which he received.

93. If a merchant put out grain or silver at interest and when he puts it out at interest he give silver by the small stone and grain by the small measure but when he receives it back he receive silver by the large stone and grain by the large measure, that man shall lose whatever he put out.

[*Section 94 is fragmentary.*]
[*Section 95 is not preserved.*]

96. If a man receive grain or silver from a merchant and do not have grain or silver to repay, but have personal property, whatever there is in his hand, when he brings it before witnesses, he shall give to the merchant. The merchant shall not refuse it, he shall receive it.

[*Section 97 is fragmentary.*]

98. If a man give silver to a man for a partnership, they shall divide equally before God the profit and the loss, whatever there is of either.

99. If a merchant give money at interest to a peddler for trading and send him out on the road and the peddler, on the road . . . .

100. If he the peddler made money where he went, he shall write down the interest on all the money he received, and he shall count up his days, and make his return to the merchant.

101. If he made no money where he went, the agent shall double the amount of money obtained and he shall pay it to the merchant.

102. If a merchant give money to an agent as a favor, and the latter meet with a reverse where he goes, he shall return the principal of the money to the merchant.

103. If, when he goes on a journey, an enemy rob him of anything he was carrying, the agent shall take an oath in the name of God and go free.

104. If a merchant give an agent grain, wool, oil, or goods of any kind with which to trade, the agent shall write down the money received and return it to the merchant. The agent shall take a sealed receipt for the money which he gives to the merchant.

105. If the agent be careless and do not take a receipt for the money which he has given to the merchant, the money not receipted for shall not be placed to his account.

106. If an agent obtain money from a merchant and have a dispute with the merchant, that merchant shall call the agent to account in the presence of God and witnesses for the money obtained and the agent shall give to the merchant threefold the amount of the money which he obtained.

107. If a merchant lend money to an agent and the agent return to the merchant anything of what the merchant had given him; and if the merchant deny that the agent has given to him anything, that agent shall call the merchant to account in the presence of God and witnesses; and the merchant, because he has had a dispute with his agent, shall give to him sixfold the amount which he obtained.

108. If a barmaid do not take grain in payment of drink, but if she take money by the great stone, or make the measure of drink smaller than the measure of grain, they shall prosecute that barmaid, and they shall throw her into the water.

109. If outlaws hatch a conspiracy in the house of a wine-seller, and she do not arrest these outlaws and bring them to the palace, that wine-seller shall be put to death.

110. If a priestess or a nun who is not resident in a convent open a wineshop or enter a wineshop for a drink, they shall burn that woman.

111. If a barmaid give sixty *ka* of *pihu*-wine on credit, at the time of harvest she shall receive fifty *ka* of grain.

112. If a man be on a journey and he give silver, gold, precious stones, or his portable property to a man, delivering them to him for transportation, and if that man do not deliver that which was to be transported where it was to be transported, but take it to himself, the owner of the transported goods shall call that man to account for the goods to be transported which he did not deliver, and that man shall give to the owner of the transported goods fivefold the amount which was given to him.

113. If a man hold a debt of grain or money against a man, and if he help himself to grain without the consent of the owner from the heap or the granary, they shall call that man to account for taking grain without the consent of the owner from the heap or the granary, and he shall return as much grain as he took, and he shall forfeit all that he has lent, whatever it be.

114. If a man do not hold a debt of grain or money against a man, and seize him or his family as his pledge, for each pledge seized he shall pay one to three mina of silver.

115. If a man hold a debt of grain or money against a man, and seize his pledge, and the pledge die a natural death in the house of him who seized him, that case has no penalty.

116. If the pledge die of a blow or bad treatment in the house of him who seized him, the owner of the pledge shall call his merchant to account; and if it be a man's son, they shall put his son to death; if it be a man's servant, he shall pay one to three mina of silver and he shall forfeit whatever amount he had lent.

117. If an obligation of a man mature and he give his wife, his son, or his daughter, or bind them over to service, for three years they shall work in the house of their purchaser or master; in the fourth year their freedom shall be given them.

118. If he bind over to service a male or female slave, and if the merchant transfer or sell such slave, there is no ground for a suit.

119. If an obligation of a man mature and he sell for silver his maidservant who has borne him children, the owner of the maidservant shall repay the money which the merchant paid, and he shall redeem his maidservant.

120. If a man pour out his grain in the house of another for storage and a loss happen in the granary, or the owner of the house open the granary and take the grain or he raise a dispute about the grain which was stored in his house, the owner of the grain shall declare his grain in the

presence of God, and the owner of the house shall double the amount of the grain which he took and restore it to the owner of the grain.

121. If a man store grain in the house of another, he shall pay, per year, a storage charge of five *ka* of grain per *kor*.

122. If a man give to another silver, gold, or anything else for safekeeping, whatever he gives he shall show to witnesses and he shall draw up contracts and then give it for safekeeping.

123. If a man give for safekeeping without witnesses or contracts, and at the place of deposits they dispute with him, that case has no penalty.

124. If a man give to another silver, gold, or anything else for safekeeping in the presence of witnesses and the latter dispute with him or deny it, they shall call that man to account and he shall double whatever he has disputed and repay it.

125. If a man give anything of his for safekeeping and at the place of deposit either by burglary or by pillage his property along with the property of the owner of the house be carried off, the owner of the house who has been negligent and has lost whatever was given to him on deposit shall make good the loss and restore it to the owner of the goods; the owner of the house may institute a search for what has been lost and take it from the thief.

126. If a man, nothing of whose has been carried off, say, "Something of mine has been carried off," alleging he sustained loss when nothing of his had been carried off, he shall declare his alleged loss in the presence of God, and he shall double and pay the amount for which he had made claim for his alleged loss.

127. If a man point the finger at a nun or the wife of a man and cannot justify it, they shall drag that man before the judges and they shall cut the hair of his forehead.

128. If a man take a wife and do not draw up a contract with her, that woman is not a wife.

129. If the wife of a man be taken in lying with another man, they shall bind them and throw them into the water. If the husband of the woman spare the life of his wife, the king shall spare the life of his servant.

130. If a man force the betrothed wife of a man, who has not known a male and is living in her father's house, and lie in her bosom, and they take him, that man shall be put to death and that woman shall go free.

131. If a man accuse his wife and she have not been taken in lying with another man, she shall take an oath in the name of God and she shall return to her house.

132. If the finger have been pointed at the wife of a man because of another man, and she have not been taken in lying with another man, for her husband's sake she shall throw herself into the sacred river.

133. If a man be taken captive and there be something to eat in his house and his wife go out of her house and she do not protect her body and she enter into another house, because that woman did not protect her body and entered into another house they shall convict that woman and they shall throw her into the water.

134. If a man be taken captive and there be nothing to eat in his house and his wife enter into another house, that woman has no blame.

135. If a man be taken captive and there be nothing to eat in his house, and his wife enter into another house and bear children; if later her husband return and reach his city, that woman shall return to her husband; the children shall go to their father.

136. If a man desert his city and run away, and afterward his wife enter into another house, if that man return and seize his wife, because he hated his city and fled, the wife of the fugitive shall not return to her husband.

137. If a man set his face to put away a concubine who has borne him children or a wife who has presented him with children, they shall return to that woman her dowry and shall give to her part of field, garden, and goods, and she shall bring up her children; from the time that her children are grown up, from whatever is given to her children they shall give to her a portion corresponding to that of a son and the man of her choice may marry her.

138. If a man put away his wife who has not borne him children, he shall give her money to the amount of her marriage settlement and he shall make good to her the dowry which she brought from her father's house and then he may put her away.

139. If there were no marriage settlement, he shall give to her one mina of silver for a divorce.

140. If he be a common man, he shall give her one to three mina of silver.

141. If the wife of a man who is living in his house set her face to go out, playing the fool, ruining her house, and belittling her husband, they shall convict her; if her husband announce her divorce, he may put her away. For her journey home no alimony shall be given to her. If her husband do not announce her divorce, her husband may take another woman. That woman [the first wife] shall dwell in the house of her husband as a maidservant.

142. If a woman hate her husband and say, "Thou shalt not have me,"

her past shall be inquired into for any deficiency of hers; and if she have been careful and be without past sin and her husband have been going out and greatly belittling her, that woman has no blame. She shall take her dowry and go to her father's house.

143. If she have not been careful, have been going out, ruining her house and belittling her husband, they shall throw that woman into the water.

144. If a man take a wife and that wife give a maidservant to her husband and cause him to have children, if that man set his face to take a concubine, they shall not countenance him. He may not take a concubine.

145. If a man take a wife and she do not present him with children, and he set his face to take a concubine, that man may take a concubine and bring her into his house. That concubine shall not take precedence of his wife.

146. If a man take a wife and she give a maidservant to her husband, and she bear children and afterward that maidservant would take precedence of her mistress; because she has borne children, her mistress may not sell her for money, but she may reduce her to bondage and count her among the maidservants.

147. If she have not borne children, her mistress may sell her for money.

148. If a man take a wife and disease seize her, and he set his face to take a concubine, he may do so. His wife whom disease has seized he may not put away. She shall dwell in the house which he has built and he shall maintain her as long as she lives.

149. If that woman be not willing to dwell in her husband's house, he shall make good to her the dowry which she brought from her father's house and she may go her way.

150. If a man make his wife a present of field, garden, house, and goods and deliver to her a sealed deed, after the death of her husband her children may not make any claim against her. The mother after her death may give them to her child whom she loves, but to a brother she may not give them.

151. If a woman who is living in the house of a man make a contract with her husband that his creditors may not seize her for his debts and have him deliver a written agreement; if that man were in debt before he took that woman, his creditors may not seize his wife, and if that woman were in debt before she entered into the house of the man, her creditors may not seize her husband.

152. If they contract a debt after the woman has entered into the house of the man, both of them shall be answerable to the merchant.

153. If the wife of a man bring about the death of her husband because of another man, they shall impale that woman.

154. If a man have sexual intercourse with his daughter, they shall expel that man from the city.

155. If a man have betrothed a bride to his son and his son have had sexual intercourse with her, and if he the father afterward lie in her bosom and they take him, they shall bind that man and throw him into the water.

156. If a man have betrothed a bride to his son and his son have not had sexual intercourse with her, and he the father lie in her bosom, he shall pay her one to two mina of silver, and he shall make good to her whatever she brought from the house of her father and the man of her choice may take her.

157. If a man, after the death of his father, lie in the bosom of his mother, they shall burn both of them.

158. If a man, after the death of his father, be taken in the bosom of his father's chief wife who has borne children, that man shall be driven away from his father's house.

159. If a man who has brought a present to the house of his father-in-law and has given the marriage settlement look with longing upon another woman and say to his father-in-law, "I will not take thy daughter," the father of the daughter shall take to himself whatever was brought to him.

160. If a man bring a present to the house of his father-in-law and give a marriage settlement and the father of the daughter say, "I will not give thee my daughter," he the father-in-law shall double everything which was brought to him and return it.

161. If a man bring a present to the house of his father-in-law and give a marriage settlement, and his friend slander him and his father-in-law say to the "lord of the wife," "My daughter thou shalt not take," he the father-in-law shall double everything which was brought to him and return it, but his friend may not take his wife.

162. If a man take a wife and she bear him children and that woman die, her father may not lay claim to her dowry. Her dowry belongs to her children.

163. If a man take a wife and she do not present him with children and that woman die; if his father-in-law return to him the marriage settlement which that man brought to the house of his father-in-law, her husband may not lay claim to the dowry of that woman. Her dowry belongs to the house of her father.

164. If his father-in-law do not return to him the marriage settlement, he

may deduct from her dowry the full amount of the marriage settlement and return the rest of her dowry to the house of her father.

165. If a man make a present of field, garden, and house to his son who is first in his eyes and write for him a sealed deed; after the father dies, when the brothers divide, he shall take the present which the father gave him, and over and above they shall divide the goods of the father's house equally.

166. If a man take wives for his sons and do not take a wife for his youngest son; after the father dies, when the brothers divide, they shall give from the goods of the father's house to their youngest brother, who has not taken a wife, in addition to his portion, money for a marriage settlement, and they shall enable him to take a wife.

167. If a man take a wife and she bear him children and that woman die, and after her death he take another woman and she bear him children and later the father die, the children shall not divide the estate according to mothers. They shall receive the dowries of their respective mothers and they shall divide equally the goods of the house of their father.

168. If a man set his face to disinherit his son and say to the judges, "I will disinherit my son," the judges shall inquire into his past, and if the son have not committed a crime sufficiently grave to cut him off from sonship, the father may not cut off his son from sonship.

169. If he have committed a crime against his father sufficiently grave to cut him off from sonship, they shall condone his first offense. If he commit a grave crime a second time, the father may cut off his son from sonship.

170. If a man's wife bear him children and his maidservant bear him children, and the father during his lifetime say to the children which the maidservant bore him, "My children," and reckon them with the children of his wife; after the father dies the children of the wife and the children of the maidservant shall divide the goods of the father's house equally. The child of the wife shall have the right of choice at the division.

171. But if the father during his lifetime have not said to the children which the maidservant bore him, "My children," after the father dies the children of the maidservant shall not share in the goods of the father's house with the children of the wife. The maidservant and her children shall be given their freedom. The children of the wife may not lay claim to the children of the maidservant for service. The wife shall take her dowry and the gift which her husband gave and deeded to her on a tablet and she may dwell in the house of her husband and enjoy the property as long as she lives. She may not sell it. Her residue belongs to her children.

172. If her husband have not given her a gift, they shall make good her dowry and she shall receive from the goods of her husband's estate a portion corresponding to that of a son. If her children keep plaguing her, to drive her out of the house, the judges shall inquire into her past and place the blame on the children. That woman need not go out from her husband's house.

172A. If the woman set her face to go out, she shall leave to her children the gift which her husband gave her; she shall receive the dowry of her father's house, and the husband of her choice may take her.

173. If that woman bear children to her later husband into whose house she has entered, and later that woman die, the earlier and the later children shall divide her dowry.

174. If she do not bear children to her later husband, the children of her first husband shall receive her dowry.

175. If either a slave of the palace or a slave of a common man take the daughter of a gentleman and she bear children, the owner of the slave may not lay claim to the children of the daughter of the gentleman for service.

176. But if a slave of the palace or a slave of a common man take the daughter of a gentleman, and when he takes her she enter into the house of the slave of the palace or the slave of the common man with the dowry of her father's house, whereupon they join hands and acquire property, and later the slave of the palace or the slave of the common man die, the daughter of the man shall receive her dowry; and they shall divide into two parts whatever her husband and she had acquired from the time they joined hands; the owner of the slave shall receive one-half and the daughter of the man one-half for her children.

176A. If the daughter of the man have no dowry, they shall divide into two parts whatever her husband and she acquired from the time they joined hands; the owner of the slave shall receive one-half and the daughter of the man shall receive one-half for her children.

177. If a widow whose children are minors set her face to enter another house, she may not enter it without the consent of the judges. When she enters another house, the judges shall inquire into the condition of the estate of her former husband and they shall intrust the estate of her earlier husband to the later husband and that woman, and they shall require them to furnish a receipt. They shall administer the estate and rear the minors. They may not sell the household goods; the purchaser who purchases household goods belonging to the sons of a widow shall lose his money. The goods shall revert to their owner.

178. If to a nun, a priestess, or a palace woman her father have given a dowry and written a deed; if in the deed which he has written for her he have not granted her permission to give her inheritance to whomsoever she may please—have not granted her full discretion; after the father dies her brothers shall take her field and her garden and they shall give her grain, oil, and wool according to the value of her share and they shall make her content. If her brothers do not give her grain, oil, and wool according to the value of her share and they do not make her content, she may give her field and her garden to any tenant she may please and her tenant shall maintain her. She shall enjoy the field, garden, and anything else which her father gave her as long as she lives; she may not sell them or transfer them. Her heritage belongs to her brothers.

179. If to a nun, a priestess, or a palace woman her father have given a dowry and written a deed; if in the deed which he has written for her he have granted her permission to give her inheritance to whomsoever she may please—have granted her full discretion; after the father dies she may give her inheritance to whomsoever she may please. Her brothers may not bring any claim against her.

180. If a father do not give a dowry to his daughter who is a cloister nun or a palace woman, after her father dies she shall receive as her share in the goods of her father's house a portion as of a son, and she shall enjoy it as long as she lives. After her death it belongs to her brothers.

181. If a father devote his daughter as a nun, sacred prostitute, or temple woman to a god and do not give her a dowry, after her father dies she shall receive as her share in the goods of her father's house one-third of the portion of a son and she shall enjoy it as long as she lives. After her death it belongs to her brothers.

182. If a father do not give a dowry to his daughter, a priestess of Marduk of Babylon, and do not write for her a deed, after her father dies she shall receive as her share with her brothers one-third the portion of a son in the goods of her father's house, but she need not render any feudal services pertaining thereto. A priestess of Marduk after her death may give to whomsoever she may please.

183. If a father present a dowry to his daughter who is a concubine and give her to a husband and write her a deed, after the father dies she shall not share in the goods of her father's house.

184. If a man do not present a dowry to his daughter who is a concubine, and do not give her to a husband; after her father dies her brothers shall

present her a dowry proportionate to the value of her father's estate and they shall give her to a husband.

185. If a man with his father's consent take a young child for sonship and rear him, one may not bring claim for that adopted son.

186. If a man take a young child for sonship and, when he takes him, he use undue influence upon his father and mother, that adopted son shall return to the house of his father.

187. One may not bring claim for the son of a chamberlain who is a palace servant or the son of a palace woman.

188. If an artisan take a son for rearing and teach him his handicraft, one may not bring claim for him.

189. If he do not teach him his handicraft, that adopted son may return to his father's house.

190. If a man do not reckon among his sons the young child whom he has taken for sonship and reared, that adopted son may return to his father's house.

191. If a man who has taken a young child for sonship and reared him establish a house and later have children; if he set his face to cut off the adopted son, that son shall not go away empty. The father who reared him shall give to him of his goods one-third the portion of a son, and then he shall go. He need not give to him of field, garden, or house.

192. If the adopted son of a chamberlain or the son of a palace woman say to his father who has reared him or his mother who has reared him, "Thou art not my father," "Thou art not my mother," they shall cut out his tongue.

193. If the adopted son of a chamberlain or the son of a palace woman identify his father's house (discover his parentage) and hate the father who has reared him and the mother who has reared him and go back to his father's house, they shall pluck out his eye.

194. If a man give his son to a nurse and that son die in the hands of the nurse, and without the knowledge of his father and mother the nurse come to an agreement with some other family to substitute another son, they shall convict her, and because she has made an agreement to substitute another son without the consent of the father and mother, they shall cut off her breast.

195. If a man strike his father, they shall cut off his hand.

196. If a man destroy the eye of another man, they shall destroy his eye.

197. If he break a man's bone, they shall break his bone.

198. If he destroy the eye of a common man or break a bone of a common man, he shall pay one mina of silver.

199. If he destroy the eye of a man's slave or break a bone of a man's slave, he shall pay one-half his price.

200. If a man knock out a tooth of a man of his own rank, they shall knock out his tooth.

201. If he knock out a tooth of a common man, he shall pay one-third mina of silver.

202. If a man smite on the cheek a man who is his superior, he shall receive sixty strokes with an oxtail whip in public.

203. If the son of a gentleman smite the son of a gentleman of his own rank on the cheek, he shall pay one mina of silver.

204. If a common man smite a common man on the cheek, he shall pay ten shekels of silver.

205. If a man's slave smite the son of a gentleman on the cheek, they shall cut off his ear.

206. If a man strike another man in a quarrel and wound him, that man shall swear, "I did not strike him intentionally," and he shall be responsible for the physician.

207. If he die as the result of the blow, he shall swear as above, and if it were the son of a gentleman, he shall pay one-half mina of silver.

208. If it were a common man, he shall pay one-third mina of silver.

209. If a man strike the daughter of a man and bring about a miscarriage, he shall pay ten shekels of silver for her miscarriage.

210. If that woman die, they shall put his daughter to death.

211. If through a blow he bring about a miscarriage to the daughter of a common man, he shall pay five shekels of silver.

212. If that woman die, he shall pay one-half mina of silver.

213. If he strike the maidservant of a man and bring about a miscarriage, he shall pay two shekels of silver.

214. If that maidservant die, he shall pay one-third mina of silver.

215. If a physician make a deep incision upon a man with his bronze lancet and save the man's life; or if he operate on the eye socket of a man with his bronze lancet and save that man's eye, he shall receive ten shekels of silver.

216. If it were a common man, he shall receive five shekels.

217. If it were a man's slave, the owner of the slave shall give two shekels of silver to the physician.

218. If a physician make a deep incision upon a man with his bronze lancet and cause the man's death, or operate on the eye socket of a man with his bronze lancet and destroy the man's eye, they shall cut off his hand.

219. If a physician make a deep incision upon a slave of a common man

with his bronze lancet and cause his death, he shall substitute a slave of equal value.

220. If he operate on the eye socket with his bronze lancet and destroy his eye, he shall pay silver to the extent of half his price.

221. If a physician set a broken bone for a man or cure a sprained tendon, the patient shall give five shekels of silver to the physician.

222. If it were a common man, he shall give three shekels of silver.

223. If it were a man's slave, the owner of the slave shall give two shekels of silver to the physician.

224. If a veterinary surgeon make a deep incision upon an ox or an ass and save its life, the owner of the ox or ass shall give to the surgeon as his fee one-sixth of a shekel of silver.

225. If he make a deep incision upon an ox or an ass and cause its death, he shall give to the owner of the ox or ass one-fourth its value.

226. If a barber without the consent of the owner of the slave cut the hair of the forehead of a slave making him unrecognizable, they shall cut off the hand of that barber.

227. If a man deceive a barber and he cut the hair of the forehead of a slave making him unrecognizable, they shall put that man to death, and they shall cover him up by his gate. The barber shall swear, "I did not cut his hair knowingly," and he shall go free.

228. If a builder erect a house for a man and complete it, he shall give him two shekels of silver per *sar* of house as his wage.

229. If a builder erect a house for a man and do not make its construction firm, and the house which he built collapse and cause the death of the owner of the house, that builder shall be put to death.

230. If it cause the death of a son of the owner of the house, they shall put to death a son of that builder.

231. If it cause the death of a slave of the owner of the house, he shall give to the owner of the house slave for slave.

232. If it destroy property, he shall restore whatever he destroyed, and because he did not make the house which he built firm and it collapsed, he shall rebuild the house which collapsed from his own property.

233. If a builder erect a house for a man and do not surround it with walls of proper construction, and a wall fall in, that builder shall strengthen that wall at his own expense.

234. If a shipbuilder construct a boat of sixty-*gur* capacity for a man, he shall give to him two shekels of silver as his wage.

235. If a shipbuilder construct a boat for a man and he do not make its

construction trustworthy, and that boat develop structural weakness the same year and have an accident, the shipbuilder shall dismantle that boat and he shall strengthen it at his own expense and he shall give the strengthened boat to the owner of the boat.

236. If a man hire his boat to a boatman and the boatman be careless and sink or wreck the boat, the boatman shall replace the boat to the owner of the boat.

237. If a man hire a boatman and a boat and freight it with grain, wool, oil, dates, or any other kind of freight, and that boatman be careless and sink the boat or lose its cargo, the boatman shall replace the boat which he sank and whatever portion of the cargo he lost.

238. If a boatman sink a man's boat and refloat it, he shall pay the owner one-half its value.

239. If a man hire a boatman, he shall give him six *gur* of grain per year.

240. If a boat going forward strike a boat going across stream, and sink it, the owner of the boat whose boat was sunk shall establish, before God, what was lost in his boat and the owner of the boat going forward which sank the boat going across stream shall replace his boat and whatever he lost.

241. If a man carry off an ox as security for debt, he shall pay one-third mina of silver.

242, 243. If a man hire cattle for a year, he shall give to the owner four *gur* of grain as the hire of a plow ox and three *gur* of grain as the hire of a . . . cow.

244. If a man hire an ox or an ass and a lion kill it on the plain, the loss is the owner's affair.

245. If a man hire an ox and cause its death through neglect or abuse, he shall restore ox for ox to the owner of the ox.

246. If a man hire an ox and break its foot or cut its neck tendon, he shall restore ox for ox to the owner of the ox.

247. If a man hire an ox and destroy its eye, he shall pay the owner of the ox half its value.

248. If a man hire an ox and break its horn or cut off its tail, or pull out the flesh of its ring, he shall pay one-fourth of its value.

249. If a man hire an ox and a god strike it and it die, the man who hired the ox shall take an oath before God and go free.

250. If an ox when passing through the street gore a man and bring about his death, that case has no penalty.

251. If a man's ox have been wont to gore and they have made known to him his fault of goring, and he have neither cut off his horns nor tied him

up, and that ox gore the son of a man and bring about his death, he shall pay one-half mina of silver.

252. If it were the servant of a man, he shall pay one-third mina of silver.

253. If a man hire a man to oversee his farm and hand over to him implements and intrust him with oxen and contract with him for the cultivation of the field; if that man steal either the seed grain or the fodder and it be found in his hand, they shall cut off his hand.

254. If he take the implements and weaken the oxen, he shall restore the stand of grain which he sowed.

255. If he hire out the oxen of the man, or steal the seed grain and do not raise anything in the field, they shall convict that man and he shall measure out sixty *gur* of grain per ten *gan*.

256. If he be not able to meet his obligation, they shall leave him in that field with the oxen.

257. If a man hire a plowman, he shall pay him eight *gur* of grain per year.

258. If a man hire an ox herder, he shall pay him six *gur* of grain per year.

259. If a man steal a plow in a field, he shall pay five shekels of silver to the owner of the plow.

260. If a man steal a plow point or a beam of a plow, he shall pay three shekels of silver.

261. If a man hire a herdsman to pasture oxen or sheep, he shall pay him eight *gur* of grain per year.

[*Section 262 is fragmentary.*]

263. If he lose an ox or sheep which is given to him, he shall restore to their owner ox for ox, sheep for sheep.

264. If a shepherd to whom oxen or sheep have been given to pasture be in possession of his hire and his heart be satisfied, and he let the cattle or sheep decrease in number, or lessen the increase according to the word of his contract he shall hand over both increase and his share.

265. If a shepherd to whom oxen or sheep have been given to pasture become unfaithful, alter the brand, or sell them, they shall convict him and he shall restore tenfold to their owner the oxen and sheep he has stolen.

266. If a visitation of God happen to a fold, or a lion kill, the shepherd shall show himself innocent before God, and the owner of the fold shall accept the loss of the fold.

267. If a shepherd be careless and allow disease to develop in the fold,

the shepherd shall make good in cattle and sheep the loss through the disease which he allowed to develop in the fold, and give them to their owner.

268. If a man hire an ox to thresh, twenty *ka* of grain is its hire.

269. If he hire an ass to thresh, ten *ka* of grain is its hire.

270. If he hire a young animal to thresh, one *ka* of grain is its hire.

271. If a man hire oxen, a wagon, and a driver, he shall pay 180 *ka* of grain per day.

272. If a man hire a wagon only, he shall pay forty *ka* of grain per day.

273. If a man hire a day laborer, from the beginning of the year until the fifth month he shall pay six *she* of silver per day; from the sixth month till the end of the year he shall pay five *she* of silver per day.

274. If a man hire an artisan, the wage of a . . . is five *she* of silver; the wage of a baker is five *she* of silver; the wage of a tailor is five *she* of silver; the wage of a lapidary is . . . *she* of silver; the wage of a . . . is . . . *she* of silver; the wage of a smith is . . . *she* of silver; the wage of a carpenter is four *she* of silver; the wage of a leather worker is . . . *she* of silver; the wage of a basketmaker is . . . *she* of silver; the wage of a mason is . . . *she* of silver; so much per day shall he pay.

275. If a man hire a . . . its hire is three *she* of silver per day.

276. If he hire a . . . he shall pay two and one-half *she* of silver per day as its hire.

277. If a man hire a boat of sixty *gur* tonnage, he shall pay one-sixth of a shekel of silver as its hire per day.

278. If a man buy a male or female slave, and the slave have not completed his month when epilepsy attacks him, the buyer shall return him to the seller and shall receive the money which he paid.

279. If a man buy a male or female slave of a man in a foreign country, and there be a claim against him, the seller shall be responsible for the claim.

280. If a man buy a male or female slave of a man in a foreign country, and if when he comes back to his own land the former owner of the male or female slave recognize his male or female slave, if the male or female slave be natives of the land, their freedom shall be granted without money.

281. If they be natives of another land, the buyer shall declare before God the money which he paid for them, and the owner of the male or female slave shall give to the merchant the money which he paid out, and shall thus redeem his male or female slave.

282. If a male slave say to his master, "Thou art not my master," his master shall prove him to be his slave and shall cut off his ear.


## EPILOGUE

The righteous laws which Hammurabi the wise king established and by which he gave the land a firm support and a gracious rule. Hammurabi the perfect king am I. I was not careless nor was I neglectful of the black-headed people, whom Bel presented to me and whose care Marduk gave to me. Regions of peace I spied out for them, grievous difficulties I over-came—caused light to shine forth for them. With the powerful weapon which Zamama and Innanna intrusted to me, with the breadth of vision which Ea allotted to me, with the might which Marduk gave me, I expelled the enemy north and south; I made an end of their raids; I promoted the welfare of the land; I made the peoples to rest in habitations of security; I permitted no one to molest them. The great gods have named me and I am the guardian shepherd whose scepter is righteous; my beneficent shadow is spread over the city. In my bosom I have carried the peoples of the land of Sumer and Akkad, under my protection I brought their brethren into secur-ity; with my wisdom I covered them; that the strong might not oppress the weak, and that they should give justice to the orphan and the widow, in Babylon, the city whose head Anu and Enlil raised aloft, in Esagila, the temple whose foundations stand firm as heaven and earth, to pronounce judgments for the land, to render decisions for the land, to give justice to the oppressed, my weighty words I have written upon my monument, and in the presence of the image of me, king of righteousness, have I set it up.

The king who is preeminent among kings am I. My words are precious, my wisdom is unrivaled. By the command of Shamash, the great judge of heaven and earth, may I make righteousness to shine forth on the land; by the word of Marduk, my lord, may there be none to set aside my statutes; in Esagila which I love may my name be remembered with favor forever. Let any oppressed man who has a cause come before the image of me, the king of righteousness! Let him have read to him the writing on my monument! Let him give heed to my weighty words! And may my monument enlighten him as to his cause and may he understand his case! May it set his heart at ease. "Hammurabi indeed is a ruler who is like a real father to his people; he has given reverence to the word of Marduk, his lord; he has obtained Marduk's victory north and south; he has made glad the heart of Marduk, his lord; he has established prosperity for the people for all time and has led the land aright," let him proclaim aloud and let him pray with his whole heart before Marduk, my lord, and Zarpanit, my lady, and may the protecting deities, the gods who enter Esagila, the walls of Esagila, make his thoughts acceptable daily before Marduk, my lord, and Zarpanit, my lady!

In the days to come, for all time, let the king who arises in the land observe the words of righteousness which I have written upon my monument! Let him not alter the judgments of the land which I have pronounced, the decisions of the country which I have rendered! Let him not efface my statutes! If that man have wisdom and be able to guide his land aright, let him give attention to the words which I have written upon my monument! And may this monument enlighten him as to procedure and administration, the judgments of the land which I have pronounced, and the decisions of the land which I have rendered! And let him guide aright his black-headed people; let him pronounce their judgments and render their decisions! Let him root out the wicked and evildoer from his land! Let him promote the welfare of his people! Hammurabi, the king of righteousness, to whom Shamash has presented these laws am I. . . .

[*The Epilogue concludes with some three hundred lines containing curses against any future king who may in any way fail to follow or acknowledge these laws.*]

# EGYPT

WHERE the early history of Mesopotamia is filled with turmoil and uncertainty, wars and conquests, the rise and fall of empires, the history of Egypt in the same period displays a stability that is appropriately mirrored in the stately procession of the dynasties of the pharaohs. The regularity of the Nile River, unlike the fierce floods of the Tigris and Euphrates, made Egypt readily susceptible of unification, an accomplishment that was also aided by a homogeneous population. In late predynastic times Egypt was divided into Two Lands, Lower Egypt (the Nile Delta) and Upper Egypt (the rest of the country as far south as the First Cataract). The dynastic system begins with the uniting of Upper and Lower Egypt under the rule of Menes (or Narmer) about 3100 B.C. It is at this time that writing was introduced and the history of Egypt begins.

For the first two dynasties the records are sparse, and conventionally the first major division of Egyptian history, the Old Kingdom, begins with Dynasty III about 2700 B.C. and continues through Dynasty VI for about five hundred years. This is the period, contemporaneous with the Sumerian period in Mesopotamia, that saw the development of Egypt's independent civilization, of the way of life, the political organization, the cultural and intellectual achievements that set the pattern for the later epochs of Egyptian history. The Egyptian monarchy, centralized and bureaucratized under the authority of the pharaoh, a king who was a living god to his subjects, is one of the most powerful forms of political organization and control known in history. For over a thousand years, until about 1700 B.C., Egypt remained immune to foreign conquest, and the succession of the dynasties has in that period only one real break—from the fall of the Old Kingdom about 2200 B.C. until the restoration of unity in the Middle Kingdom some two hundred years later. Dynasties VII to XI were thus regional rulers in a divided country; the period of their rule is often referred to as the "Feudal Period."

With the reunification of the country about 2000 B.C., the Middle Kingdom commences. It endured just over two hundred years under the rule of Dynasty XII. It is from the Middle Kingdom that most of the literary sources date—the prophecies and prayers, the stories and poems. The great mass of these writings found in modern times owes its survival mainly to the distinctive religion and the distinctive climate of Egypt. The emphasis of Egyptian religion upon the afterlife led to the building of stone tombs for the preservation of the earthly remains of the dead. On the walls of these elaborate structures were painted scenes commemorating the life of the departed; records of their deeds were painted or carved there, too. The dry climate of Egypt makes for natural dehydration of organic matter. Preserved thereby from rotting, such matter lasts indefinitely. The process of mummification exploits this quality, and writings on papyrus were buried with the mummy. More important still, the embalming process itself required that the body be wrapped in linen or, when mummification spread to the lower classes of society during the Middle Kingdom, papyrus. For this purpose whatever paper lay conveniently to hand was used, and from mummy wrappings comes a considerable sampling of Egyptian literature, permanently preserved.

The Middle Kingdom ended in the decline of royal power and an internal split that lasted eighty years. At the end of this time, about 1700 B.C., the Nile delta was invaded by a band of adventurers from the Semitic East, the Hyksos. These, finding a divided country, were able to end Egypt's independence and to impose foreign rule for the first time in Egyptian history. Their rule lasted 120 years.

The expulsion of the Hyksos kings occurred in 1580 B.C. The national hero, Ah-mose, who performed the exploit, became the first pharaoh of a new dynasty, the Eighteenth, and ushered in a new epoch in Egyptian history, the period of the Empire (or New Kingdom). The Empire, which endured until about 1000 B.C., was the final period of an independent Egypt. Thereafter, except for very brief episodes, the country was under the rule of one foreign power after another—not only in antiquity but for nearly three thousand years. It regained its independence only in our own century, following the First World War.

In creating the first nation-state in history the Egyptians of the Old Kingdom built upon the immensely strong foundation of a centralized monarchy under a divine king. While the fortunes of individual pharaohs varied, the essential stability of the monarchy survived through the Old and Middle Kingdoms and on into the Empire. The pharaoh was in theory the owner of the entire land of Egypt, its people and its resources. A bureaucratic officialdom reached into every village and farm. A noble class of high public officials administered the economy and the affairs of state, for which they were rewarded with lavish grants of land. These rewards bound the nobles to loyal service to the throne, for although they tended to be hereditary, they could be revoked at the will of the sovereign. Various aspects of Egyptian government are illustrated in Selections 6 to 9.

The life of Egyptian society was not limited to the court. There was a variety of tastes and interests, of values and emotions, and numerous stories and poems provide us with glimpses into some of this variety and into the lives of people of different classes (Selections 10 to 13).

Egypt's major discoveries and accomplishments were made early, during the Old Kingdom. The Middle Kingdom can be considered in this respect as mainly an effort to preserve and to use this knowledge rather than to extend it, just as in the political sphere the Middle Kingdom's work was the re-establishment of the order instituted during the Old.

The intellectual achievement of ancient Egypt is seen most clearly in her great monuments, especially the Pyramids, which stand as silent symbols of an impressive engineering knowledge as well as of amazing technological skill. The buildings, the irrigation works, the development of a solar calendar and a system of mathematical calculation—these and other achievements bespeak the spirit of inquiry that we associate with scientific endeavor. Selection 14 illustrates a major aspect of Egypt's technical and intellectual achievement.

# 6 A Vizier of Egypt

The topmost civil official was the vizier, to whom most other officials were responsible and who was himself responsible directly to the pharaoh. The excerpts here are from a lengthy text found on the walls of the tomb of the vizier Rekh-mi-Re, consisting of an autobiographical account of the vizier's career and accompanied by numerous paintings illustrating the text. Included are important details about the functions and powers of the office and about the bureaucratic operation of the Egyptian government. Although the text was written in the fifteenth century B.C., during the period of the Empire, it gives a picture that for most details is equally appropriate for the Old and Middle Kingdoms.

SOURCE: Norman de Garis Davies, *The Tomb of Rekh-mi-Re at Thebes* (*Publications of the Metropolitan Museum of Art Egyptian Expedition,* Vol. XI) (New York: Metropolitan Museum of Art, 1943). Reprinted by permission of the Metropolitan Museum of Art.

It is worth noting, apropos of the vizier's function as chief judicial officer of Egypt, that no law codes like those of Mesopotamia have been found in Egypt. Most scholars are agreed that, as the text seems clearly to indicate, the reason is that a published law code would have been irrelevant in Egypt, where law was by royal decree in which administrative precedent was followed.

The translation is by N. deG. Davies and A. H. Gardiner.

❀❀❀❀❀

### THE AUTOBIOGRAPHY OF REKH-MI-RE

". . . It was the first time of my being summoned; all my brothers were in the outer thousand. I came forth . . . clad in festal attire; my household rejoiced over me. I reached the door of the palace-gate; the courtiers bent their backs. Having found the elders of the forecourt clearing the way for me, I went . . . My ability was not as it had been before; my yesterday's nature had altered itself since I had come forth in the adornments of the vizier, promoted to be the priest of Maet. . . .

"When a second day had dawned and the morrow was come, I was summoned again into the presence of the good god, King Men-kheper-Re [Thut-mose III]—may he live forever—even Horus, the victorious bull appearing gloriously in Thebes. . . .

"So then His Majesty opened his mouth and spake his words before me: 'Behold, my eyes send me to my heart, forasmuch as My Majesty knows that decisions are many and there is no end to them, and the judgment of cases never flags. Mayest thou act according as I say; then will Maet rest in her place.' He admonished me very greatly: 'Armor thyself; be strong in action; weary not; accuse evil.'

". . . I acted according as he had ordained. He gave me a court of justice under my authority, and none of them could overrule me. Then I strode forth, acting with stick on back; the dogs were not let loose; my voice went up to heaven. . . .

"I was the heart of the Lord, the ears and eyes of the Sovereign. Yea, I was his own skipper, and knew not slumber night or day. Whether I stood or sat, my heart was set upon prow rope and stern rope, and the sounding-pole never was idle in my hands. I was watchful for any chance of stranding. Every king of Upper and Lower Egypt is a god by whose guidance men live. He is the father and mother of all men, alone by himself, without an equal. I did not suffer evil to overtake me. No neglect of mine led to misfortune.

". . . I judged poor and rich alike. I rescued the weak from the strong. I opposed the rage of the ill-disposed and quelled the covetous in his hour. I checked the passionate moment of the infuriated. I restrained weeping by replacing it with an avenger. I defended the husbandless widow. I established the son and heir on the seat of his father. I gave bread to the hungry, water to the thirsty, meat and ointment and clothes to him who had nothing. I relieved the old man, giving him my staff, and causing the old women to say, 'What a good action!' I hated iniquity, and wrought it not, causing false men to be fastened head downwards. I was innocent before God. No one who knew said concerning me, 'What has he done?' I judged great matters. . . . I caused both parties to go forth at peace. I did not pervert justice for reward. I was not deaf to the empty-handed, nay more, I never accepted anyone's bribe. . . .

". . . I was clever in all undertakings, deliberate in counsel, ready to listen. I was skilled in past matters, and the condition of yesterday caused me to know tomorrow.

"I judged the suppliant. I did not incline to one side. I paid no attention to rewards. I was not angry with him who came as a suppliant. I did not rebuff him. I tolerated him in his moment of passion. I rescued the timid man from the violent. . . ."

## THE INSTALLATION OF THE VIZIER

The guiding principles enjoined on the vizier Rekh-mi-Re: the assembling of the council at the audience hall of Pharaoh—life, prosperity, and health to him!—and causing the newly appointed vizier Rekh-mi-Re to be brought in.

His Majesty said to him: "Look thou to the hall of the vizier and be vigilant over all the procedure in it. Lo, it is the consolidation of the entire land. Lo, as to the position of a vizier, lo, it is not pleasant at all; no, it is bitter as gall. Lo, it is the bronze which surrounds the gold of the house of its lord. Lo, it is to have no consideration for himself or for the officials of the magistracy, and not to make slaves of the general public. . . .

"Lo, if a petitioner of Upper or Lower Egypt, that is the entire land, come prepared for the court . . . to hear his case, thou shalt see well to it that all the procedure is in accord with what has legal sanction, that all the procedure is in accord with due regularity. . . .

"Lo, whenever an administrator hears cases let there be publicity and let water and air report about all that he may do. Lo, then, his conduct is by no means unperceived. If he does anything unseemly and he is to blame, he is not to be reinstalled on the authority of an acting official, but men shall learn of it on the authority of his proper judge by a pronouncement with regard to it, he the judge being associated with the acting official by the formula 'It is not a case for my giving my verdict, I send the litigant to be judged by the vizier or a high official.' Thus people are not ignorant of what has been done by him.

"Lo, to proceed in accordance with first principles is the safeguard of the administrator in the execution of current instructions. Then a litigant who is judged may say, 'There was no impediment to my having my right.' . . .

"Beware of what is said of the Vizier Akhtoy, namely that he damnified men who were his relatives in favor of others, from fear of the objection that he was partial. Therein he favored the unjust. . . . Now this was an exaggeration of justice. . . .

"Thou shalt give attention to one whom thou knowest as to one whom thou dost not know, to one who has recourse to thee in person as to one who is far away. . . . If an administrator act on this wise, he will be successful here in this department. Do not pass over a litigant before thou hast attended to his plea. If there be a litigant who wishes to petition thee, do not dismiss what he says with a word; if thou rejectest him let him hear the reason why thou rejectest him. Lo, it is said that a litigant would rather that his argument were attended to than that the case about which he has come should be judged.

"Do not be angry with a man unfairly, but be angry about that which justifies anger. Inspire thou fear, so that men fear thee. That official whom men fear is a real official. Lo, the luster of an official is that he does what is right. . . . Lo, thou wilt reach a point where 'Thou doest thy office' and 'Thou doest what is right' are one. Lo, the ideal is that right-dealing should constitute the success of the vizier. . . .

"Now the hall in which thou hearest cases has a broad room in it which contains records of all legal decisions. . . . Do not follow thine inclination in matters whereof thou knowest the pertinent regulations. . . . Do thou act in accordance with the directions which have been given thee. . . ."

## THE DUTIES OF THE VIZIER

Regarding the exact procedure of His Excellency the Vizier when he gives a hearing in the hall of the vizier—he is to sit on a backed chair, a reed mat being on the ground, the chain of office on him, a skin under his back, another under his feet, and a matwork cape on him, a baton near him, forty leathern rods laid out before him, the Chiefs of Ten of Upper Egypt before him on either hand, the chamberlain on his right hand, the Controller of Ingress on his left, and the scribes of the vizier near him. . . .

Report is to be made to him [the vizier] of the closing of repositories at the proper time and of their opening at the proper time. Report is to be made to him of the condition of the strongholds of the South and the North and of the outgoing of all that goes out from the Royal Demesne. Report is to be made to him of the incoming of all that comes into the Royal Demesne. Report is to be made to him too of all incomings and outgoings to and from the grounds of the Residence, they that enter and they that leave. They shall come in and go out through his apparitor. Superintendents of bailiffs, bailiffs, and superintendents of landholdings are to report their affairs to him.

But he [the vizier] is to enter to greet the monarch—life, prosperity, and health to him!—and the state of the land may be reported to him [the king] daily in his palace. He [the vizier] is to enter the Great House as soon as the High Treasurer has taken up his position by the northern column. When the vizier is in movement and is visible in the gate of the two great pylons, then the High Treasurer shall come to join him, and report is to be made to him [the vizier] saying, "All thy affairs are safe and sound. Every official on duty has reported to me saying, 'All thy affairs are safe and sound and the Royal Demesne is safe and sound.'" Then the vizier is to report to the High Treasurer saying, "All thy affairs are safe and sound and every department of the Residence is safe and sound. Report has been made to me that the repositories were closed at the proper time and opened at the proper time by every official on duty." Then, after these two officials have reported to one another, the vizier is to send to open every gate of the Royal Demesne and to allow entrance to all that enters and likewise to all that goes out. It is his apparitor who has it put in writing. . . .

As to any apparitor whom the vizier sends on a mission to any official, from one of highest rank down to one of the lowest, it is not to be permitted that he take a friendly attitude and it is not permitted that the official summon him to audience; but he is to utter the message of the vizier, standing in the presence of that official and uttering the message to him personally and then going out to his waiting room. . . . . If the apparitor who is sent with his message should make complaint, saying, "When I was sent with a message to such and such an official he had me summoned and had something of value placed on my neck,"[1] and there is a hearing of the case of the official versus the apparitor, then the official is to be punished in proportion to that which was the subject of their quarrel, by the vizier in his hall, by any penalty other than a punishment by severance of a limb. . . . .

As for any documents that the vizier sends for which belong to any court, being such as are not confidential, they are to be removed for him together with the registrar's records relating to them, under the seal of the magistrates and of the scribes in their employ who are concerned therewith. Then he is to open it, and after he has inspected it, it shall be removed to its department again, sealed with the seal of the vizier. . . . .

It is he who dispatches every apparitor of the Royal Demesne and who sends to nomarchs and heads of divisions. It is he who dispatches any courier and all commissions of the Royal Demesne. It is he who appoints anyone from the bureaucracy as superintendent of Upper or Lower Egypt, the Front of the South, or the Great Territory [the province of Abydos]. They are to report to him all that has happened in their zones at the beginning of each four-monthly season, and they are to bring to him the official scribes attached to them and their council.

It is he who sees that soldiers mobilize and move as an escort of the monarch when he sails north or south. It is he who appoints to vacancies whether in the Southern City or in the Residence, following a decision of the Royal Demesne. There shall be brought before him the guild of victuallers to the Ruler, that his hall and the military council may be supplied and that the army regulation may be issued to them. . . . .

It is he who sends out men to cut down sycamores, following a decision of the Royal Demesne. It is he who sends out the councillors of the nome to make irrigation canals throughout the entire land. It is he who dispatches mayors and heads of divisions for summer tillage. It is he who appoints superintendents of bailiffs in the hall of the Royal Demesne. It is he who appoints one who shall hear the case of mayors and heads of divisions and

---

1.   Attempted bribery is to be understood.

who shall go on circuit in his [the vizier's] name to Upper or Lower Egypt. Report is to be made to him of all legal cases.

. . . It is he who is to fix the boundaries of any nome, any additional marshland, any temple fief, and any entry on possession. . . .

. . . It is he who makes inventories of all oxen of which inventories have to be made. It is he who inspects the water supply on the first of every ten-day period. . . . Report is to be made to him of the ascent of Sirius and the slackening of the Nile. Report shall be made to him of rains. . . .

# 7 *Instruction of Ptah-hotep*

Order and stability are the words that most succinctly describe the character of ancient Egypt. In view of the almost unvarying climate and the remarkable regularity of the Nile, these qualities seem to have emanated from nature itself and were reflected throughout Egyptian life, thought, and institutions. They are seen in the political stability of the country and, more familiarly and graphically, in the austere monumentality of its sculpture and architecture.

Egyptian moral thought, too, is aimed at order and permanence. Whether in the sphere of religion, where the goal was salvation in an eternal after-life, or whether in secular morality, the emphasis is upon the sober virtues of self-control, respect for authority, and devotion to duty.

A literary form that appears to have been highly prized in Egypt was the so-called "instruction," which approximates a modern book of etiquette in laying down rules of behavior. For the Egyptian moralist the reward of virtue is success; the penalty for failure to act in accordance with his wise precepts is misery and disorder.

The Instruction of Ptah-hotep is contained in a papyrus dating from the Middle Kingdom and purporting to be from the pen of the vizier of King Izezi of Dynasty V. It is expressly intended for the education of the children of high officials, and its wisdom consists of the kind of advice that young men who hope to get on in the world have been receiving ever since. The following selection is abridged from Aylward M. Blackman's English rendering of the German translation by Adolf Erman.

SOURCE: Adolf Erman, *The Literature of the Ancient Egyptians,* translated into English by Aylward M. Blackman (London: Methuen and Co., 1927). Reprinted by permission of the publisher.

✸✸✸✸✸

## TITLE

The instruction of the superintendent of the capital, the vizier, Ptah-hotep, under the majesty of King Izezi, who liveth for ever and ever.

## INTRODUCTION

So spake he unto the majesty of King Izezi: Old age hath come and dotage hath descended. The limbs are painful and the state of being old appeareth as something new. Strength hath perished for weariness. The mouth is silent and speaketh not. The eyes are shrunken and the ears deaf. . . . The heart is forgetful and remembereth not yesterday. The bone, it suffereth in old age, and the nose is stopped up and breatheth not. To stand up and to sit down are alike ill. Good is become evil. Every taste hath perished. What old age doeth to a man is that it fareth ill with him in all things.

Let therefore the servant there be bidden to make him a staff of old age; let my son be set in my place, that I may instruct him in the discourse of them that hearken, and in the thoughts of them that have gone before, them that have served the ancestors in times past. May they do the like for thee, that strife may be banished from among the people, and the Two River-banks may serve thee.

Said his majesty: "Instruct thou him in discourse first. . . . May he set an example to the children of the great; may obedience enter into him, and every right conception of him that speaketh unto him. There is no child that of itself hath understanding."

## SECOND TITLE

The beautifully expressed utterances, spoken by the prince and count, the father of the god and beloved of the god, the bodily son of the king, the superintendent of the capital and vizier, Ptah-hotep, while instructing the ignorant in knowledge and in the rules of elegant discourse, the weal of him that will hearken thereto and the woe of him that shall transgress them.

1. *Thou canst learn something from every one.* Be not arrogant because of thy knowledge, and have no confidence in that thou art a learned man.

Take counsel with the ignorant as with the wise, for the limits of art cannot be reached, and no artist fully possesseth his skill. A good discourse is more hidden than the precious green stone, and yet is it found with slave-girls over the mill-stones.

2–4. *Concerning behaviour towards an orator.* If thou findest an orator at his time, with sound sense and better than thou, bend thine arm and bow thy back. But if he speaketh ill, then fail not to withstand him, in order that men may call out to him: "Thou ignorant one."

But if it is an equal of thine, show thyself by silence to be better than he, when he speaketh ill. Then will he be praised by the listeners, but thy name will be accounted good among the great.

If he is a humble person, who is not thine equal, be not wrathful against him, for thou knowest that he is miserable. . . . Disregard him, and so he punisheth himself. It is bad if one injureth one that is despicable. . . . Thou smitest him with the punishment of the great.

5. *Thou wilt get on best in life with the aid of right and truth.* If thou art a leader and givest command to the multitude, strive after every excellence, until there be no fault in thy nature. Truth is good and its worth is lasting, and it hath not been disturbed since the day of its creator, whereas he that transgresseth its ordinances is punished. It lieth as a right path in front of him that knoweth nothing. Wrong-doing hath never yet brought its venture to port. Evil indeed winneth wealth, but the strength of truth is that it endureth, and the upright man saith: "It is the property of my father."

6. *Thou canst obtain nothing in life by bluster;* what hath come to pass is the command of God.

7. *Concerning behaviour as a guest.* If thou art one that sitteth where standeth the table of one who is greater than thou, take, when he giveth, that which is set before thee. Look not at that which lieth before him, but look at that which lieth before thee. Shoot not many glances at him, for it is an abhorrence to the *ka*[1] if one offendeth it.

Cast down thy countenance until he greeteth thee, and speak only when he hath greeted thee. Laugh when he laugheth. That will be well pleasing in his heart, and what thou doest will be acceptable; one knoweth not what is in the heart.

A great man, when he sitteth behind the food, his resolves depend upon

1. Upon this vital force in a man also depended, according to the view here held, his disposition and therewith his whole conduct. In social intercourse, therefore, particular care must be taken to avoid what is unpleasant to another's *ka*.

the command of his *ka*. A great man giveth to the man that is within reach of him, but the *ka* stretcheth out the hands for him further. Bread is eaten by the decree of God. . . .

8. *Be faithful in the delivering of messages.* If thou art one of the trusted ones, whom one great man sendeth to another, act rightly in the matter when he sendeth thee. Thou shalt deliver the message as he saith it. Be not secretive concerning what may be said to thee, and beware of any forgetfulness. Hold fast to the truth and overstep it not, even if thou therewith recountest nothing that is gratifying. Beware also of worsening words, such as might make one great man contemptible to the other through the manner of speech of all men. "A great man, an insignificant one"—that is what the *ka* abhorreth.

9. If thou ploughest and there is growth in the field and God giveth it thee liberally, satisfy not thy mouth beside thy kindred. . . .

10. *Do not slight those who have risen in the world.* If thou art an humble person and art in the train of a man of repute, one that standeth well with the god, know thou nothing of his former insignificance. Raise not up thine heart against him on account of what thou knowest about him aforetime. Reverence him in accordance with what hath happened unto him, for wealth cometh not of itself. . . . It is God that createth repute. . . .

11. *Permit thyself time for recreation.* Follow thine heart so long as thou livest, and do not more than is said. Diminish not the time in which thou followest the heart, for it is an abhorrence to the *ka* if its time is diminished. In particular a warning is uttered against too much care for thine house.

12. *Conduct towards thy son.* If thou art held in esteem, and hast an household, and begettest a son that pleaseth God—if he doeth right, and inclineth to thy nature, and hearkeneth to thine instruction, and his designs do good in thine house, and he hath regard for thy substance as it befitteth, search out for him everything that is good.

He is thy son, whom thy *ka* hath begotten for thee; separate not thine heart from him.

But if he doeth wrong and trespasseth against thy designs, and acteth not after thine instructions, and his designs are worthless in thine house, and he defieth all that thou sayest . . . then drive him away, for he is not thy son, he is not born to thee. . . .

13. *On behaviour in the vestibule of the great.* If thou standest or sittest in the vestibule, wait quietly until thy turn cometh. Give heed to the servant that announceth; he that is called hath a broad place. The vestibule hath its rule, and every arrangement therein is in accordance with the

measuring-cord. It is God who assigneth the foremost place—but one attaineth nothing with the elbow.

14. *Be discreet in thine intercourse with people.*

15. *Proclaim thy business without concealment.* Give out thy thoughts in the council of thy lord. . . . One ought to say plainly what one knoweth and what one knoweth not. . . . he is silent and saith: "I have spoken."

16. The high official ought to have in mind the days that are yet to come.

17. *Behaviour towards petitioners.* If thou art one to whom petition is made, be kindly when thou hearkenest to the speech of a petitioner. Deal not roughly with him, until he hath swept out his body, and until he hath said that on account of which he is come. A petitioner liketh it well if one noddeth to his addresses, until he hath made an end of that about which he came. . . . A favourable audience gladdeneth the heart.

But whoso acteth the churl towards petitioners, then men say: "Why is it, pray, that he so doeth?"

18. *Warning against women.* If thou wouldst prolong friendship in an house to which thou hast admittance, as master, or as brother, or as friend, into whatsoever place thou enterest, beware of approaching the women. The place where they are is not good.

On that account a thousand go to perdition: Men are made fools by their gleaming limbs, and lo! they are already become *herset*-stones. A trifle, a little, the likeness of a dream, and death cometh as the end. . . .

19. *Warning against covetousness.* If thou desirest thy conduct to be good, to set thyself free from all that is evil, then beware of covetousness, which is a malady, diseaseful, incurable. Intimacy with it is impossible; it maketh the sweet friend bitter, it alienateth the trusted one from the master, it maketh bad both father and mother, together with the brothers of the mother, and it divorceth a man's wife. It is a bundle of every kind of evil, and a bag of everything that is blameworthy. Long lived is the man whose rule of conduct is right, and who goeth in accordance with his right course; he winneth wealth thereby, but the covetous hath no tomb.

20. *The same. (Older version.)* Be not covetous regarding division, and be not exacting, except with regard to what is due to thee. Be not covetous towards thy kindred; the request of the meek availeth more than strength. . . . Just the little of which he hath been defrauded, createth enmity even in one of a cool disposition.

21. *The advantage of marriage.* If thou art a man of note, found for thyself an household, and love thy wife at home, as it beseemeth. Fill her belly,

[ 116 ]

clothe her back; unguent is the remedy for her limbs. Gladden her heart, so long as she liveth; she is a goodly field for her lord.

22. *Be liberal towards thine intimates.* Satisfy thine intimates with that which hath accrued to thee, as one favoured of God. To do this is prudent, for there is none that knoweth his condition, if he thinketh of the morrow. If, therefore, a misfortune befalleth the favoured ones, it is the intimates that still say "Welcome!" to him. . . . Thus retain for thyself their attachment against the time of displeasure that threateneth.

23. Repeat not frivolous speeches, the utterance for instance of one that is heated.

24. *Be cautious in speech.* If thou art a man of note, that sitteth in the council of his lord, fix thine heart upon what is good. Be silent—this is better than *teftef*-flowers. Speak only if thou knowest that thou canst unravel the difficulty. It is an artist that speaketh in council, and to speak is harder than any other work. . . .

25. If thou art strong and inspirest respect, through knowledge or through pleasantness of speech. . . .

26. Approach not a great one in his hour, and anger not the heart of him that is laden. . . . this is a dangerous thing, which detacheth the *ka* from him that loveth him, him that supplieth food together with the god. . . .

27. Instruct a great one in that which is profitable to him; that will also be of advantage to thee, for thy sustenance dependeth upon his *ka,* and thy back will be clothed thereby. . . .

28. If thou art the son of a man of the bureaucracy, an envoy, that is to make the multitude content . . . be not partial. . . .

29. Do not harbour a grudge.

30. *Trust not fortune.* If thou be grown great, after that thou wast of small account, and have gotten thee substance, after that thou wast aforetime needy in the city which thou knowest, forget not how it fared with thee in time past. Trust not in thy riches, that have accrued to thee as a gift of God. Thou art not better than another that is thine equal, to whom the same hath happened.

31. *Respect for superiors.* Bend thy back to him that is over thee, thy superior of the king's administration. So will thine house endure with its substance, and thy pay be duly awarded. To resist him that is set in authority is evil. One liveth so long as he is indulgent. . . .

32. Do not have intercourse with a woman with child.

33. *Prudence in engaging in friendships.* If thou lookest for a state of friendship, ask no question, but draw near him and be with him alone. . . .

Prove his heart by a conversation. If he betrayeth aught that he hath seen, or doeth aught with which thou art vexed, then take heed, even in thine answers. . . .

34. Have a cheerful countenance when thou celebratest a feast and distributest bread thereat.

35. Riches are inconstant, but a good disposition is a lasting possession.

36. [Unintelligible.]

37. *Let not thy concubine starve.* If thou takest to wife one that is well-nurtured, one that is cheerful, one that the people of her city know . . . put her not away, but give her to eat.

### EPILOGUE

If thou hearest this that I have spoken unto thee, thy whole state will be as good as that of them who have gone before. What remaineth over of their truth is noble, and the remembrance of them perisheth not in the mouth of men, because their maxims are so goodly. Every word of theirs will be used always as a thing imperishable in this land, and will beautify the utterances with which the princes speak. . . .

# 8 A Trial for Conspiracy

Down through the dynasties the governmental form remained unchanged, kingship passing from father to son. The change from one dynasty to the next might reflect nothing more drastic than the failure of a royal line to produce a male heir. More likely, however, it occurred as the result of a successful palace plot whereby an ambitious noble managed to overthrow his king and to set himself upon the throne, thus establishing a new royal line. The stability of the governmental apparatus endured through these violent events, the only outcome of which was to put new persons in power at the top. In the "Trial for Conspiracy" an abridged account is given of one such plot involving high officials and women of the court. It contains what almost amounts to a roster of the top officialdom of the Egyptian

SOURCE: A. de Buck, "The Judicial Papyrus of Turin," *Journal of Egyptian Archaeology,* XXIII (1937), pp. 154–156. Reprinted by permission of the officers of the Egypt Exploration Society.

court, and one wonders where enough loyal officers were found to bring the conspirators to trial. Indeed, some of the "great officials of the Court of Examination" in the first list of accused turn up in later lists as members of the conspiracy. The first part of the papyrus, which presumably described the background of the conspiracy, is lost. The events described are from the reign of Ramses III of Dynasty XX and date about the middle of the twelfth century B.C. The translation is by A. de Buck.

❀❀❀❀❀

. . . I[1] commissioned the overseer of the treasury Montemtowe; the overseer of the treasury Pefrowe; the standard-bearer Kara; the butler Paibese, the butler Kedendenna; the butler Baalmahar; the butler Peirswene; the butler Dhutrekhnefer; the king's adjutant Penernute; the clerk Mai; the clerk of the archives Preemhab; the standard-bearer of the infantry Hori; saying: "As for the matters which the people—I do not know who—have plotted, go and examine them." And they went and examined them, and they caused to die by their own hands those whom they caused so to die, though I do not know who, and they also punished the others, though I do not know who. But I had charged them strictly, saying: "Take heed, have a care lest you allow that somebody be punished wrongfully by an official who is not over him." Thus I spoke to them again and again.

As for all this that has been done, it is they who have done it. May the responsibility for all that they have done fall upon their own heads, while I am consecrated and exempted forever, while I am among the just kings who are before Amen-Re, King of the Gods, and before Osiris, Ruler of Eternity.

### FIRST LIST OF ACCUSED

Persons brought in because of the great crimes which they had committed, and placed in the Court of Examination before the great officials of the Court of Examination in order to be examined by the overseer of the treasury Montemtowe, the overseer of the treasury Pefrowe, the standard-bearer Kara, the butler Paibese, the clerk of the archives Mai, the standard-

---

1. The speaker is the pharaoh himself, who in this introductory passage disclaims all personal responsibility in the conduct and results of the inquiry, as emphasized in the formula "I do not know who."

bearer Hori; they examined them; they found them guilty; they caused their punishment to overtake them; their crimes seized them.

The great criminal, Paibekkamen,[2] who was then chief of the chamber. He was brought in because he had been in collusion with Teye and the women of the harem; he had made common cause with them; he had begun to bring out their words to their mothers and their brothers who were there, saying: "Stir up the people! Incite enmity in order to make rebellion against their lord!" He was placed before the great officials of the Court of Examination; they examined his crimes; they found that he had committed them; his crimes seized him; the officials who examined him caused his punishment to overtake him. . . .

Wives of men of the gate of the harem, who had united with the men who plotted the matters, who were placed before the officials of the Court of Examination; they found them guilty; they caused their punishment to overtake them. Six women. . . .

The great criminal Beyenemwese, who was then captain of archers of Nubia. He was brought in because his sister who was in the harem in the suite had written to him, saying: "Stir up people, make enmity and come back to make rebellion against your lord." He was placed before Kedendenna, Baalmahar, Peirswene, and Dhutrekhnefer; they examined him; they found him guilty; they caused his punishment to overtake him.

## SECOND LIST OF ACCUSED

Persons brought in because of their crimes, because they had been in collusion with Paibekkamen, Paiis, and Pentawere. They were placed before the officials of the Court of Examination in order to be examined; they found them guilty; they left them on their own hands in the Court of Examination; they took their own lives, no harm having been done to them. . . .

## THIRD LIST OF ACCUSED

. . . Pentawere, to whom had been given that other name.[3] He was

2. The name means "This Blind Slave." A number of the accused bear patently fictitious names of opprobrium, presumably with the double purpose of holding them in contempt and of concealing their previously honored names.
3. He is presumably the prince who would have acquired the throne had his mother's plot been successful.

brought in because he had been in collusion with Teye, his mother, when she had plotted the matters with the women of the harem concerning the making rebellion against his lord. He was placed before the butlers in order to be examined; they found him guilty; they left him where he was; he took his own life. . . .

### FOURTH LIST OF ACCUSED

Persons punished by cutting off their noses and their ears because they had forsaken the good instructions given to them; the women had gone; they had reached them at the place where they were; they had caroused with them and with Paiis. Their crime seized them.

The great criminal Paibese, who was then butler. This punishment was executed upon him; he was left alone; he took his own life.

The great criminal Mai, who was then clerk of the archives.

The great criminal Tainakhte, who was then officer of infantry.

The great criminal Nanai, who was then captain of police.

### FIFTH LIST OF ACCUSED

Person who had been connected with them. He was scolded sternly with bad words; he was left alone, no harm having been done to him.

The great criminal, Hori, who was then standard-bearer of the infantry.

# 9 *Pepi II and the Dancing Dwarf*

In the Old and Middle Kingdoms the foreign relations of Egypt consisted largely of sending royal caravans southward into the interior of Africa to obtain exotic products such as ivory, incense, spices, and gold, which were in demand at the court. These expeditions were thus primarily for trading purposes, and the products of Egypt were bartered for those she lacked. Nevertheless, the caravans are depicted as in part military, in part diplomatic missions. Their commanders were high officials who enjoyed great prestige.

SOURCE: From *Never to Die* by Josephine Mayer and Tom Prideaux. Copyright 1938 by Josephine Mayer and Tom Prideaux. Reprinted by permission of The Viking Press, Inc.

The exchanging of gifts between the leaders of such an expedition, acting in the pharaoh's name, and a chieftain in the interior is frequently described as the offering of tribute to the Egyptian king in acknowledgement of his suzerainty. In addition to such peaceful barter, the caravans no doubt occasionally plundered. The following selection is a communication from the pharaoh to the caravan commander Hark-huf, making his way back from an expedition that took him to a little-known area deep in central Africa, the land of the pygmies. Pepi II was one of the last kings, possibly the last, of the Old Kingdom. He succeeded to the throne as a child and remained on it for ninety years, surely one of the longest reigns in history. At the time of this document the pharaoh was eight years old. The translation is that of James H. Breasted.

❈❈❈❈❈

*Royal seal, year 2, third month of the first season, day 15. Royal decree to the sole companion, the ritual priest and caravan conductor, Hark-huf.*

I have noted the matter of this thy letter, which thou hast sent to the king, to the palace, in order that one might know that thou hast descended in safety from Yam with the army which was with thee. Thou hast said in this thy letter, that thou hast brought all great and beautiful gifts, which Hathor, mistress of Imu, hath given to the *ka*[1] of the king of Upper and Lower Egypt, Neferkere,[2] who liveth for ever and ever. Thou hast said in this thy letter, that thou hast brought a dancing dwarf of the god from the land of spirits, like the dwarf which the treasurer of the god, Burded, brought from Punt in the time of Izezi. Thou hast said to my majesty: "Never before has one like him been brought by any other who has visited Yam."

Come northward to the court immediately; thou shalt bring this dwarf with thee, which thou bringest living, prosperous, and healthy from the land of spirits, for the dances of the god, to rejoice and gladden the heart of the king of Upper and Lower Egypt, Neferkere, who lives for ever. When he goes down with thee into the vessel, appoint excellent people, who shall be beside him on each side of the vessel; take care lest he fall into the water. When he sleeps at night appoint excellent people, who shall sleep beside him in his tent; inspect ten times a night. My majesty desires to see this dwarf more than the gifts of Sinai and of Punt. If thou arrivest

1. The soul or spirit.   2.   Throne-name of Pepi II.

at court this dwarf being with thee alive, prosperous, and healthy, my majesty will do for thee a greater thing than that which was done for the treasurer of the god, Burded, in the time of Izezi, according to the heart's desire of my majesty to see this dwarf.

Commands have been sent to the chief of the New Towns, the companion, and superior prophet, to command that sustenance be taken from him in every store-city and in every temple, without stinting therein.

# 10 Story of Sinuhe

Love of country is the main theme of the "Story of Sinuhe." It tells of an official during the Middle Kingdom who fled into exile from Egypt during an anxious moment between the death of the king and the accession of his successor. Sinuhe, the hero of the story, went on to live a successful and prosperous life in Palestine. The one thing lacking to him in his old age is his native land, and his longing for it is at last satisfied by a royal invitation to return, to live out his life in honor and be buried in his own land. The English rendering is by Aylward M. Blackman from the German translation of Adolf Erman.

❀❀❀❀❀

The prince and count, administrator of the domains of the sovereign in the lands of the Asiatics, the true acquaintance of the king, whom he loveth, the henchman Sinuhe. He saith: I was a henchman who followed his lord, and a servant of the king's harem waiting on the princess, the greatly praised, the Royal Consort of Sesostris, the Royal Daughter of Amenemhet in the Pyramid-town of Ka-nefru, even Nefru the revered.

In the year 30, on the ninth day of the third month of Inundation, the god entered his horizon. King Amenemhet flew away to heaven and was united with the sun, and the god's body was merged with his creator. The Residence was hushed, hearts were filled with mourning, the Two Great Portals were shut, the courtiers sat head on knees, and the people grieved.

Now his majesty had sent forth an army to the land of the Temehu, and his eldest son was captain thereof, the good god Sesostris; and even

SOURCE: Adolf Erman, *The Literature of the Ancient Egyptians,* translated into English by Aylward M. Blackman (London: Methuen and Co., 1927). Reprinted by permission of the publishers.

now he was returning, having carried away captives of the Tehenu and all manner of cattle without count.

And the Chamberlains of the Royal Palace sent to the western border of the Delta to inform the king's son of the event that had befallen at the Court. And the messengers met him on the road and reached him at eventide. Not a moment did he tarry; the hawk flew away with his henchmen, and did not make it known unto his army. Howbeit, a message had been sent unto the king's children that were with him in this army, and one of them had been summoned. And lo, I stood and heard his voice as he spake, being a little way off.

Then was mine heart distraught, mine arms sank, and trembling fell on all my limbs. I betook me thence leaping, to seek me a hiding-place; I placed me between two bushes so as to sunder the road from its traveller.

I set out southward, yet did I not purpose to reach the Residence, for I thought that strife would arise, and I was not minded to live after him. I crossed the waters of Maaty, hard by the Sycamore, and came to the island of Snefru, and tarried there in a plot of ground. I was afoot early, and when it was day I met a man who stood in my path; he shrank from me and was afraid. The time of the evening meal came, and I drew nigh to Ox-town. I crossed over in a barge without a rudder, with the aid of the breath of the west wind, and passed on east of the quarry, in the region of the Mistress of the Red Mountain. I gave a road to my feet northwards, and attained the Wall of the Prince, which was made to repel the Asiatics. I bowed me down in a thicket for fear lest the watcher for the day on the wall should espy me.

At eventide I passed on, and when day dawned I reached Peten and halted on the island of Kemwer. There it o'ertook me that I fell down for thirst, I was parched, my throat burned, and I said: "This is the taste of death." Then lifted I up mine heart and gathered up my body, for I heard the sound of the lowing of cattle and descried Bedouins. The sheikh among them, who had been in Egypt, recognized me. He gave me water and cooked milk for me, and I went with him to his tribe, and they entreated me kindly.

Land gave me to land. I set forth from Byblos and drew near to Kedemi and spent half a year there. Nenshi the son of Amu, the prince of Upper Retenu,[1] took me and said unto me: "Thou farest well with me, for thou hearest the speech of Egypt." This said he, for he had become aware of my

1. Palestine.

[ 124 ]

qualities, and had heard of my wisdom; Egyptians that dwelt with him had testified to him concerning me.

He said unto me: "Why art thou come hither? Hath aught befallen at the Residence?" And I said unto him: "King Sehetepibre hath gone to the horizon, and none knoweth what hath happened in the matter." And I said again, dissembling: "I came from the expedition to the land of the Temehu, and report was made unto me, and mine heart trembled and mine heart was no longer in my body. It carried me away upon the pathways of the wastes. Yet none had gossiped about me, none had spat in my face; I had heard no reviling word, and my name had not been heard in the mouth of the herald. I know not what brought me to this land; it was like the dispensation of God." Then said he unto me: "How will yon land fare without him, that beneficent god, the fear of whom was throughout the lands like that of Sekhmet in a year of plague?" But I said unto him answering him: "Nay, but his son hath entered into the palace and hath taken the inheritance of his father, he, the god without peer, whom none surpasseth, a lord of prudence, excellent in counsel, efficacious in giving orders. Going out and coming in are at his command. He it was that subdued the foreign lands, while his father sat within in his palace, that he might report to him that what had been commanded him had been done.

"He is the strong one that achieveth with his mighty arm, the champion without peer.

He is seen charging down on the foe, attacking the warriors.

It is he that curbeth the horn and maketh weak the hands, and his foes cannot marshal their ranks.

It is he that venteth his wrath and smasheth the foreheads, and none can stand in his neighbourhood.

It is he that is wide of stride when he shooteth the fugitive, and there is no end to flight for him that turneth on him his back.

Steadfast of heart is he at the moment of a repulse; he is the repeller and turneth not his back.

Stout of heart is he when he seeth a multitude; he alloweth his heart no rest.

Bold is he, when he falleth upon the Easterners; his delight it is to take captive the enemy.

He seizeth his buckler, he trampleth under foot; he repeateth not his blow in order to kill.

There is none that hath turned his shaft, there is none that hath bent his bow.

The People-of-the-Bow flee before him, as before the might of the Great Goddess.

He fighteth without end, he . . . eth not, and there is no remnant.

He is a master of grace, rich in sweetness, and through love hath he conquered.

His city loveth him more than itself, and they rejoice over him more than over their god.

Men and women pass by and exult over him.

He is a king, and he conquered while yet in the womb; on that was he set ever since he was born.

He it is that multiplieth them that were born with him; he is unique, god-given.

How this land which he ruleth rejoiceth! It is he that extendeth the borders.

He will conquer the southern lands, but as yet he payeth no heed to the northern lands.

Still he was created to smite the Bedouins, to crush the sand-farers.

"Send to him, let him know thy name, utter no curse against his majesty. He faileth not to do good to a land that will be loyal to him."

Then said he unto me: "Verily Egypt is happy, for it knoweth that he flourisheth. But see, thou art here and shalt abide with me, and I will entreat thee kindly."

And he placed me at the head of his children, and mated me with his eldest daughter. He caused me to choose for myself of his country, of the best of what belonged to him on his border to another country. It was a goodly land called Yaa. There were figs in it and vines, and it had more wine than water. Plentiful was its honey, abundant its oil, and all fruits were on its trees. There was barley in it and wheat, and countless cattle of all kinds. Great too was that which accrued to me by reason of the love bestowed upon me. He made me ruler of a tribe of the best of his country. Bread was made for me for my daily fare, wine for my daily drink, cooked meat and roast fowl, over and above the wild game of the desert; for that men hunted for me and laid it before me, besides the spoils of my hounds. And many . . . were made for me, and milk prepared in every way.

I spent many years, and my children grew up to be mighty men, each one having his tribe in subjection. The envoy who went north or south to the Residence tarried with me. I made all men to tarry. I gave water to the thirsty, set upon the road him that had strayed, and rescued him that had been plundered. When the Bedouins began to wax bold and to withstand the chieftains of the lands, I counselled their movements. This prince of Retenu caused me to pass many years as the captain of his host, and every country against which I marched, when I had made my attack, it was driven from its pastures and its wells. I plundered its cattle and carried off its people and took away their food. I slew people in it by my strong arm, my bow, my marchings, and my excellent counsels. That found favour with him and he loved me; he marked how brave I was, and placed me at the head of his children, for he saw how my hands prevailed.

There came a mighty man of Retenu, that he might challenge me in my camp. He was a champion without peer, and had subdued the whole of Retenu. He vowed that he would fight with me, he planned to rob me, he plotted to take my cattle as a spoil, by the counsel of his tribe. That prince communed with me and I said: "I know him not; forsooth, I am no confederate of his, that I should stride about his encampment. Or have I ever opened his door or overthrown his fence? Nay, it is envy, because he seeth me doing thy behest. Assuredly I am like a bull of the cattle in the midst of a strange herd, and the steer of the kine attacketh him, the long-horned bull chargeth him. I am even so a foreigner whom none loveth, any more than a Bedouin would be loved in the Delta. But if that man is a bull and loveth combat, I also am a fighting bull and am not afraid to try conclusions with him. If his heart be set on fighting, let him speak his will. Doth God not know what is ordained for him . . . ."

At night-time I strung my bow and shot my arrows. I drew out my dagger and burnished my weapons. At dawn when Retenu came, it had stirred up its tribes, it had assembled the countries of a half of it, and it had planned this combat. Every heart burned for me; the men's wives jabbered, and every heart was sore for me. They said: "Is there another mighty man who can fight against him?"

Then his shield, his axe, and his armful of javelins. . . . But after I had drawn out his weapons, I caused his arrows to pass by me, uselessly sped. As one approached the other, he charged me, and I shot him, mine arrow sticking in his neck. He cried out and fell on his nose. I laid him low with his own axe, and raised my shout of victory on his back. Every Asiatic bellowed. I offered praise to Month, and his following mourned for him. This prince Nenshi, the son of Amu, took me to his embrace.

Then carried I off his goods and spoiled his cattle. That which he had devised to do to me I did to him. I seized what was in his tent and plundered his encampment. I became great thereby, wide in my riches, abundant in mine herds.

And this hath God done, in order to be gracious to one that had trespassed against him, that had fled away unto another land. To-day his heart is again glad.

> Once a fugitive fled in his season—
> now the report of me is in the Residence.
> Once a laggard lagged because of hunger—
> now give I bread to my neighbour.
> Once a man left his country because of nakedness—
> now am I shining white in raiment and linen.
> Once a man sped for lack of one to send—
> now have I slaves in plenty.
> Fair is my house, wide my dwelling-place,
> and I am remembered in the palace.

O God, whosoever thou art, that didst ordain this flight, be merciful and bring me again to the Residence. Peradventure thou wilt suffer me to see the place wherein mine heart dwelleth. What is a greater matter than that my corpse should be buried in the land wherein I was born? Come to mine aid! May good befall, may God show me mercy . . . in order to make good the end of him whom he hath afflicted, his heart being compassionate on him whom he hath compelled to live abroad. Is he in truth appeased to-day? Then may he hearken to the prayer of one that is afar off . . . .

O may the king of Egypt show me mercy, that I may live by his mercy. May I ask the Lady of the Land that is in his palace what her will is. May I hear the behests of her children.

O may my body grow young again, for now hath old age befallen, and weakness hath overtaken me. Mine eyes are heavy, mine arms are weak, and my legs have ceased to follow. Mine heart is weary, and death draweth nigh unto me. May they bring me to the cities of Eternity. May I serve the Sovereign Lady; O may she speak well to me of her children; may she spend eternity over me.

Now it had been told unto the majesty of King Kheperkere concerning this state in which I was. Thereupon his majesty sent to me with presents of the royal bounty, to gladden the heart of the servant there, as it had been the prince of any foreign country. And the royal children in his palace caused me to hear their behests.

COPY OF THE DECREE WHICH WAS BROUGHT TO THE SERVANT
THERE CONCERNING HIS RETURN TO EGYPT

Horus, Life-of-Births, Two Crown-Goddesses, Life-of-Births, King of
Upper and Lower Egypt, Kheperkere, Son of Re, Sesostris, that liveth for
ever and ever.

A royal decree unto the henchman Sinuhe. Behold, this decree of the
King is brought to thee to instruct thee as here followeth: Thou hast
traversed the foreign lands and art come forth from Kedemi to Retenu, and
land gave thee to land, by the counsel of thine own heart. What hast thou
done that aught should be done against thee? Thou didst not curse, that
thy speech should be reproved, and thou didst not so speak in the council
of the magistrates, that thine utterances should be thwarted. Only this
thought, it carried away thine heart . . . . But this thine heaven, that is in
the palace, yet abideth and prospereth to-day; she hath her part in the
kingdom of the land, and her children are in the council-chamber. Thou
wilt long subsist on the good things which they give thee, thou wilt live
on their bounty. Come back to Egypt, that thou mayest see the Residence
wherein thou didst grow up, that thou mayest kiss the earth at the Two
Great Portals, and mingle with the Chamberlains.

Even to-day thou hast begun to be old, thou hast lost thy manhood, and
hast bethought thee of the day of burial, the passing to honour. An evening is devoted to thee with cedar-oil and with bandages from the hand of
Tait. A funeral procession is made for thee on the day of burial; the
mummy-shell is of gold, with head of lapis lazuli; the heaven is above
thee, and thou art placed upon a sledge. Oxen drag thee, and singers go
before thee, and the dance of the Muu is performed for thee at the door
of thy tomb. The Requirements of the Offering-Table are recited for thee,
and victims are slain at thine offering-stones. Thy pillars are wrought of
white stone in the midst of the tombs of the royal children. Thus shalt
thou not die abroad, nor shall the Asiatics bury thee. Thou shalt not be
placed in a sheep-skin, . . . . Wherefore bethink thee of thy corpse and return.

This decree reached me as I stood in the midst of my tribe. It was read to
me, and I threw myself on my belly; I touched the dust and strewed it on
my hair. I strode about my encampment rejoicing and saying: "How
should such things be done to a servant, whom his heart led astray to
barbarous lands? Yea, good indeed is the Benevolent One that delivereth
me from death. Thy *ka* will suffer me to bring my life to an end in the
Residence."

[ 129 ]

## COPY OF THE ACKNOWLEDGMENT OF THIS DECREE

The servant of the palace Sinuhe saith: In very beautiful peace! Ascertained is this flight, which the servant there made unwillingly, by thy *ka,* thou Good God, Lord of the Two Lands, beloved of Re, praised of Month, lord of Thebes. Amun, lord of Karnak, Sobk, Re, Horus, Hathor, Atum with his Ennead of gods, Sopdu-Neferbau-Semseru the Eastern Horus, the Mistress of Buto that resteth on thy head, the Conclave on the Waters, Min-Horus that is in the foreign countries, Wereret mistress of Punt, Nut, Harueris-Re, the gods of Egypt and of the islands of the sea—may they all give life and happiness to thy nose, may they endue thee with their gifts, may they give thee eternity without limit, everlastingness without end!

Men tell of the fear of thee in the plains and hill-countries; what the sun encircleth hast thou subdued. This prayer of the servant there to his lord that rescueth from the West—the lord of Perception, that perceiveth men, he perceived it in the majesty of the Palace. The servant there feared to say it, for it is a grave matter to repeat it, but the great god, who is like unto Re, giveth discretion even unto him that serveth him . . . . Thy majesty is the victorious Horus and thine arms are strong against all lands.

Now let thy majesty command that Meki be brought from Kedemi, Khentiuiaush from Khentkeshu, and Menus from the lands of the Fenekhu. They are princes and . . . witnesses, that have grown up in love of thee—without my making mention of Retenu, for that is thine, as it were thy dogs.

This flight, which the servant there made, I planned it not, it was not in mine heart, and I had not conceived it. I know not what sundered me from my place. It was after the manner of a dream, as if a man of the Delta should see himself suddenly in Elephantine,[2] or a man of the marshes in Nubia. I had nought to fear, none had persecuted me, I had heard no reviling speech, my name had not been heard in the mouth of the herald. Only this befell, that my body quivered, my feet quaked, mine heart led me on, and the god that ordained the flight drew me away. And yet I was not presumptuous aforetime, and a man that knoweth his land is afraid, for Re hath put the fear of thee throughout the land, the dread of thee in every foreign country. Whether I am in the Residence or in this place, it is ever thou that obscurest this horizon, and the sun ariseth at thy pleasure; the water in the river is drunk when thou willest, and the air in heaven is breathed when thou biddest.

2. An island in the Nile, traditionally marking the southern border of Egypt. See Selection 33.

The servant there will hand over my viziership, which the servant there hath exercised in this place.

Thereupon men came to the servant there—thy majesty wilt do as he pleaseth; men live on the breath which thou givest. May Re, Horus, and Hathor love this thine august nose which Month, lord of Thebes, willeth shall live for ever.

I was suffered to spend a day in Yaa, and handed over my substance to my children, so that my eldest son had charge of my tribe and all my substance was in his hand, my serfs, all my cattle, my fruits, and every pleasant tree of mine.

Then the servant there came southwards and I halted at Paths-of-Horus. The commander there, who was in charge of the patrol, sent a message to the Residence to bear tidings. And his majesty despatched a trusty overseer of the peasants of the royal domain, having with him ships laden with presents of the royal bounty for the Bedouins that had followed me and had conducted me to Paths-of-Horus. And I named each one of them with his name.

Every cook was at his task, and I set out and sailed; and men kneaded and brewed beside me, until I reached the town of Conqueress-of-the-Two-Lands. And at daybreak, very early, they came to summon me; ten men came and ten men went and conducted me to the palace.

I touched the ground between the sphinxes with my forehead, and the royal children stood in the gateway and received me, and the Chamberlains, that conduct to the hall, set me on the way to the Privy Chamber. I found his majesty on his great throne in the golden gateway. When I had stretched myself on my belly, my wits forsook me in his presence, albeit this god addressed me kindly. I was as a man that is carried off in the dusk, my soul fled, my body quaked, mine heart was no longer in my body, and I wist not whether I were alive or dead.

Then said his majesty to one of these Chamberlains: "Raise him up, let him speak to me." And his majesty said: "See, thou art returned, after thou hast trodden the foreign lands . . . . Eld assaileth thee and thou hast reached old age. It is no small matter that thy body be laid in the ground, and that the barbarians bury thee not. But be not silent, be not silent; speak, thy name is pronounced . . . ."

I answered thereto with the answer of one that is afraid: "What saith my lord unto me? Would that I might answer it, but I cannot. It is as it were the hand of God, it is a dread; it is in my body, as it were that which once caused that destined flight. Behold, I am in thy presence. Thine is life, and thy majesty will do as it pleaseth thee."

Then the royal children were caused to be ushered in. Said his majesty to the Queen: "See, this is Sinuhe, who hath come back as an Asiatic, a creature of the Bedouins." She uttered an exceeding loud cry, and the royal children shrieked out altogether. They said unto his majesty: "It is not he in sooth, O king, my lord." His majesty said: "It is he in sooth." Now they had brought with them their necklaces, their rattles, and their sistra. And they held them out to his majesty: "Thy hands be on the Beauteous One, O longliving King, on the ornament of the Lady of Heaven. May the Golden One give life to thy nose, and the Mistress of the Stars join herself to thee. May the Upper Egyptian crown go down stream, and the Lower Egyptian crown go up stream, and be joined both together in the mouth of thy majesty. May the serpent be set on thy brow. Thou hast delivered the poor from evil. May Re be gracious unto thee, O Lord of the Two Lands! Hail to thee as to the Mistress of All. Loose thine horn and pull out thine arrow; give breath to him that is stifled, and bestow on us as our goodly festival-gift this sheikh, the son of the Goddess of the North, the barbarian born in Egypt. He fled through fear of thee; he left the land through dread of thee. But a face that hath seen thy majesty shall no more blench, and an eye that hath regarded thee shall not fear."

Then said his majesty: "He shall not fear, he shall not dread. He shall be a Chamberlain among the magistrates, and be placed in the midst of the courtiers. Get you gone to the Chamber of Adoration in order to make . . . ."

So when I was gone forth from the Privy Chamber, the royal children giving me their hands, we then went to the Two Great Portals. And I was placed in the house of a king's son, in which there was noble equipment, and a bath was therein and . . . . Precious things of the Treasury were in it, garments of royal linen, myrrh, and fine oil of the king. Counsellors whom he loveth were in every chamber, and every serving man was at his task. Years were made to pass away from my body, I was shaved, and my hair was combed. A load of dirt was given over to the desert, and the filthy clothes to the Sand-farers. And I was arrayed in finest linen and anointed with the best oil. I slept on a bed, and gave up the sand to them that be in it, and the oil of wood to him that smeareth himself therewith.

And I was given the house of a . . ., such as appertaineth to a Chamberlain. Many artificers built it, and all its woodwork was new appointed.

And meals were brought me from the palace, three times and four times a day, over and above that which the royal children gave, without cessation at any time.

And there was constructed for me a pyramid out of stone within the precinct of the pyramids. The chief architect began the building of it, the painter designed in it, the master-sculptor carved in it, the master-builders of the necropolis busied themselves with it. All the glistening gear that is placed in a tomb-shaft, its (the tomb's) needs were supplied therefrom. And funerary priests were given me, and there was made for me a sepulchral garden, in which were fields, over against the abode, even as is done for a chief Chamberlain. And my statue was overlaid with gold and its apron was of fine gold. It was his majesty who caused it to be made. There is no humble man for whom the like had been done.

And so live I, rewarded by the king, until the day of my death cometh.

# 11 *Tale of Two Brothers*

The "Tale of Two Brothers" is a popular story of virtue falsely accused. An interesting feature is the close similarity between the central incident, in which Bata resists the advances of his brother's wife, and the familiar Biblical story of Joseph and Potiphar's wife (Genesis 39). The following selection is the first half of the story, which in its latter part, here omitted, changes its tone and character to become a tale of magical transformations. The English rendering is by Aylward M. Blackman from the German translation of Adolf Erman.

@@@@@

It is related that there were once two brothers by one mother and one father; and the name of the elder was Anubis, and the name of the younger Bata. Now Anubis, he had an house and he had a wife, while his younger brother dwelt with him as a son. It was he who made clothes for him, tended his cattle in the field, ploughed and reaped for him, and did for him all the tasks that are in the field. Yea, his younger brother was a good husbandman, who had not his equal in the whole land, and the strength of a god was in him.

Now many days after this his younger brother tended his cattle, as he did every day, and he came home to his house every evening laden with all manner of herbs of the field, and with milk, and with . . . wood of the

SOURCE: Adolf Erman, *The Literature of the Ancient Egyptians*, translated into English by Aylward M. Blackman (London: Methuen and Co., 1927). Reprinted by permission of the publishers.

field, and set it down before his elder brother, while he sat with his wife; and then he drank and ate, and laid him down to sleep in his stall, and kept watch over his kine.

Now when it was dawn and another day had come, he made ready cooked victuals and set them before his elder brother, and he gave him bread for the field, and he drave out his cattle in order to pasture them in the field. He walked behind his cattle, and they said unto him: "The herbage is good in such and such a place," and he heard all that they said and took them to the place where was the good herbage which they desired. Thus the cattle which he tended flourished exceedingly and calved very, very often.

Now at the season of ploughing his elder brother said unto him: "Make ready an yoke of oxen for ploughing, for the land hath come forth and it is now good for ploughing. Also come to the field with seed, for we will plough with a will in the early morn." So spake he unto him, and his younger brother did all the things that his elder brother said unto him, "Do them."

Now when day dawned and another day had come, they went afield with their . . . and ploughed with a will, and were exceeding glad of heart because of their work at their beginning of work.

And many days after this they were in the field and were short of seed. And he sent his younger brother, saying: "Go and fetch us seed from the village." And his younger brother found the wife of his elder brother as she sat having her hair done. And he said unto her: "Up, and give me seed, that I may go to the field, for mine elder brother waiteth for me. Tarry not."

And she said unto him: "Go, open the bin thyself, and take away for thee what thou willest; make me not to leave unfinished the dressing of my hair."

And the lad went into his stall and took a great vessel, with the intent to take away much seed. And he loaded himself with barley and wheat and went out with it. And she said unto him: "How much is it that thou hast upon thy shoulder?" And he said unto her: "Three sacks of wheat and two sacks of barley, five in all, have I upon my shoulder." So spake he unto her. And she . . . and said: "Then thou hast great strength. Yea, I see daily how strong thou art." And her desire was to know him as one knoweth a youth.

And she arose and took hold of him and said: "Come, we will take our pleasure and sleep. It will also be for thine advantage, for I will make thee goodly garments."

And the lad became enraged like a leopard . . . at this wicked thing which she said unto him, and she was sore afraid. And he spake unto her, saying: "Lo, thou art unto me as a mother, and thine husband is unto me as a father, for as the elder hath he brought me up. What is this great abomination that thou hast spoken? Say it not again unto me. But I will tell it to no man, and will not suffer it to come forth from my mouth to any man." And he took up his burden and went into the field. And he came to his elder brother, and they worked at their work with a will.

Then at eventide his elder brother went home to his house, but his younger brother tended his cattle, and loaded himself with all manner of things of the field, and he drave his cattle before him, in order to let them sleep in their stall in the village.

Now the wife of his elder brother was afraid because of that which she had said. So she took fat and . . . and made as though she had been cruelly beaten, desiring to say to her husband: "It was thy younger brother that did beat me." And her husband came home at even, as was his daily wont. He came to his house and found his wife lying down and made cruelly sick. She poured no water upon his hands according to his wont; she had kindled no light against his return, and his house was in darkness; and there she lay and vomited. And her husband said unto her: "Who hath spoken with thee?" And she said unto him: "No one hath spoken with me save thy younger brother. When he came to fetch the seed and found me sitting all alone, he said unto me: 'Come, we will take our pleasure and sleep. Put on thy ringlets.' So spake he unto me, but I heeded him not. 'Lo, am I not thy mother, and thine elder brother is unto thee as a father,' so spake I unto him. Then he was afraid, and he beat me so that I might not report it unto thee. If, therefore, thou sufferest him to live, I will take mine own life; for behold, when he cometh home at even and I tell this evil tale, he will have made it look white."

Then his elder brother became enraged as a leopard, and made his lance sharp and took it in his hand.

And his elder brother took up his stand behind the door of his stall, in order to slay his younger brother, when he came home at even to drive his cattle into the stall.

And when the sun set, he loaded himself with all herbs of the field, according to his daily wont. He came, and the first cow entered the stall. And she said unto her herdsman: "Have a care! Thine elder brother stand-eth before thee with his lance, in order to slay thee. Flee from before him." And he understood what his first cow said. The next entered, and she said likewise. And he looked under the door of his stall and saw the feet of his elder brother, as he stood behind the door with his lance in his hand. So he laid his load down on the ground and started to run away quickly, and his elder brother pursued after him with his lance.

And his younger brother called to Re-Harakhti, saying: "My good lord, thou art he that judgest between the wrong-doer and the righteous!" And Re heard all his petitions, and Re caused a great stretch of water, that was full of crocodiles, to spring up between him and his elder brother, and one of them came to be upon the one side and the other upon the other. And his elder brother smote twice upon his hand, because he had not slain him.

And his younger brother called to him from the other side, saying: "Abide here until day-break. When the sun ariseth, I will be judged with thee in his presence, and he will give the wrong-doer to the righteous. For I will never more be with thee, nor be in a place where thou art. I will go to the Valley of the Cedar." Now, when it was dawn and another day had come, Re-Harakhti arose, and the one beheld the other. And the lad communed with his elder brother, saying: "What meaneth thy pursuing after me in order to slay me by guile, without first hearing what I had to say? For I am indeed thy younger brother, and thou art unto me as a father and thy wife is unto me as a mother. Is it not so? Now when I was sent to fetch us seed, thy wife said unto me: 'Come, let us take our pleasure and sleep.' But behold, that hath been perverted for thee into some different thing." And he acquainted him with all that had befallen him with his wife.

And he swore by Re-Harakhti, saying: "Alas, that thou desiredst to slay me by guile, and didst take thy lance on the word of a dirty strumpet!" And he took a reed knife and cut off his privy member and cast it unto the water, and the shad swallowed it. And he was faint and became wretched. And his elder brother was exceeding sorrowful, and stood and wept loudly over him, yet could he not cross over to where his younger brother was because of the crocodiles.

Then his younger brother cried unto him, saying: "If thou hast thought of an evil thing, wilt thou not think of a good thing, or of something that I also might do for thee? Go now to thine house, and thyself tend thy cattle, for I will no more abide in the place where thou art. I shall go away to the Valley of the Cedar. . . ."

And he went away to the Valley of the Cedar, and his elder brother went unto his house, his land laid on his head, and he was smeared with mud. And he came unto his house, and he slew his wife, cast her to the dogs, and sat mourning for his younger brother. . . .

# 12 Is Life Worth Living?

"The Dispute over Suicide" is a dialogue between a man and his soul about the futility of life in a world of treachery and evil. Dating from the period between the Old and Middle Kingdoms, it has been called the first important philosophical poem in world literature. The prose passages, containing the arguments of the man who finds life not worth living and the counterarguments of his soul (*ka*), which advises steadfastness and patience, have been omitted. The poetic passages, descriptive of the man's despair, are given in their entirety. The English rendering is by Aylward M. Blackman from the German translation of Adolf Erman.

❀❀❀❀❀

Lo, my name is abhorred,
Lo, more than the odour of carrion
On days in summer, when the sky is hot.

Lo, my name is abhorred,
Lo, more than catching fish
On the day of the catch, when the sky is hot.

Lo, my name is abhorred,
Lo, more than the odour of birds,
More than the hill of willows with the geese.

Lo, my name is abhorred,
Lo, more than the odour of fishermen,
More than the shores of the swamps, when they have fished.

Lo, my name is abhorred,
Lo, more than the odour of crocodiles,
More than sitting on . . . where are the crocodiles.

Lo, my name is abhorred,
Lo, more than that of a wife
When lies are told against her to the husband.

source: Adolf Erman, *The Literature of the Ancient Egyptains*, translated into English by Aylward M. Blackman (London: Methuen and Co., 1927). Reprinted by permission of the publishers.

Lo, my name is abhorred,
Lo, more than that of a stalwart child
Against whom it is said, he . . . to him that hateth him.

Lo, my name is abhorred,
Lo, more than that of a . . . city,
Than that of a rebel, whose back is seen.

To whom do I speak to-day?
Brothers are evil,
Friends of to-day, they are not lovable.

To whom do I speak to-day?
Men are covetous,
Every one seizeth his neighbour's goods.

To whom do I speak to-day?
Gentleness hath perished,
Insolence hath come to all men.

To whom do I speak to-day?
He that hath a contented countenance is bad,
Good is disregarded in every place.

To whom do I speak to-day?
He that maketh wrathful a good man by his evil deeds,
The same moveth all men to laughter, when his iniquity is grievous.

To whom do I speak to-day?
Men rob,
Every man seizeth his neighbour's goods.

To whom do I speak to-day?
The sick man is the trusty friend,
The brother that is with him, hath become the enemy.

To whom do I speak to-day?
None remembereth the past,
None at this moment doeth good to him that hath done it.

To whom do I speak to-day?
Brothers are evil,
A man is treated as an enemy in spite of a right disposition.

To whom do I speak to-day?
Faces are invisible,
Every man hath his face downcast against his brethren.

To whom do I speak to-day?
Hearts are covetous,
The man on whom men rely, hath no heart.

To whom do I speak to-day?
There are none that are righteous,
The earth is given over to the workers of iniquity.

To whom do I speak to-day?
A trusty friend is lacking,
A man is treated as one that is unknown, albeit he have made himself known.

To whom do I speak to-day?
There is none that is peaceable;
That one who went with him, he is not existent.

To whom do I speak to-day?
I am laden with misery,
And lack a trusty friend.

To whom do I speak to-day?
The sin that smiteth the land,
It hath no end.

Death is before me to-day
As when a sick man becometh whole,
As when one walketh abroad after sickness.

Death is before me to-day
As the odour of myrrh,
As when one sitteth under the sail on a windy day.

Death is before me to-day
As the odour of lotus flowers,
As when one sitteth on the shore of drunkenness.

Death is before me to-day
As a well-trodden path,
As when a man returneth from the war unto his house.

Death is before me to-day
As a clearing of the sky,
As a man . . . to that which he knew not.

Death is before me to-day
As when a man longeth to see his house again,
After he hath spent many years in captivity.

Why he that is yonder will be
One that . . . as a living god,
And will inflict punishment for sin on him that doeth it.

Why he that is yonder will be
One that standeth in the sun's ship,
And will therein assign the choicest things unto the temples.

Why he that is yonder will be
A man of knowledge, and he is not hindered,
And he petitioneth Re when he speaketh.

# 13 Love Songs

No sampling of the literature of ancient Egypt would be satisfactory if it omitted the sensuous beauty of the love songs from the period of the Empire. From indications in the papyrus manuscripts on which these lyrics are found it appears that they were to be accompanied by a musical instru-

SOURCE: Adolf Erman, *The Literature of the Ancient Egyptians*, translated into English by Aylward M. Blackman (London: Methuen and Co., 1927). Reprinted by permission of the publishers.

ment. The atmosphere of the songs is strikingly similar to the Song of Solomon, that perfumed love poem that found its way into the Old Testament. The lovers in the Egyptian songs call each other "brother" and "sister." While this is probably literary convention, it should be remembered that brother-sister marriage was in fact practiced in ancient Egypt. The English rendering is by Aylward M. Blackman from the German translation of Adolf Erman.

❋❋❋❋❋

DISCOURSES OF THE LOVERS, I

*The Maiden*   . . . my god.
My brother,
it is pleasant to go to the pond
in order to bathe me in thy presence,
that I may let thee see my beauty
in my tunic of finest royal linen,
when it is wet. . . .
I go down with thee into the water,
and come forth again to thee
with a red fish,
which lieth beautiful on my fingers. . . .
Come and look at me.

*The Youth*   The love of my sister
is upon yonder side,
a stretch of water is between us both,
and a crocodile waiteth on the sandbank.
But when I go down into the water
I tread upon the flood;
mine heart is courageous upon the waters . . .
and the water is like land to my feet.
Her love it is that maketh me so strong;
yea, it maketh the water-spell for me.

I see my sister coming
and mine heart rejoiceth.
Mine arms are opened wide to embrace her,
and mine heart rejoiceth upon its place

like . . . eternally,
when the mistress cometh unto me.

If I embrace her and her arms are opened,
it is for me as if I were one
that is from Punt. . . .

If I kiss her and her lips are open,
I am happy even without beer. . . .

[*What follows is probably spoken by the youth to a maid-servant.*]

I say to thee:
Put the finest linen between her limbs,
make not her bed with royal linen
and beware of white linen.
Adorn her couch with . . .
and sprinkle it with *tishepes*-oil.

Ah, would I were her negress
that is her handmaid,
then would I behold the color
of all her limbs.

Ah, would I were the washerman
. . . in a single month,
. . . I would wash out the unguents
which are in her clothing. . . .

Ah, would I were the signet-ring
which is on her finger. . . .

DISCOURSES OF THE LOVERS, II

*The Maiden*   If thou desirest to caress my thigh,
my breast will . . . thee.
Wilt thou go away
because thou hast bethought thee of eating?
Art thou a glutton?
Wilt thou go away

and clothe thyself?
But I have a sheet.
Wilt thou go away,
because thou art thirsty?
Take to thee my breast;
what it hath overfloweth for thee.
Fair is the day whereon. . . .

The love of thee penetrateth my body
like . . . mixed with water,
like the love-apple
when . . . is mingled therewith,
and like as dough is mixed with. . . .

Hasten to see thy sister,
as an horse. . . .

*The Youth*　. . . the . . . of the sister is a field
with lotus buds,
and her breast
one with love-apples.
Her arms are. . . .
Her brow is the bird-trap of *meru*-wood,
and I am the goose
which is snared by the worm.

*The Maiden*　Hath not mine heart compassion
on thy love for me?
My young wolf is . . . thy drunkenness.
I will not let go of thy love,
even if I am beaten . . .
as far as the land of Palestine
with *shebet* and clubs,
and unto the land of Ethiopia with palm-ribs,
as far as the hill with sticks,
and unto the field with cudgels.
I will not heed their designs
so as to forsake love.

*The Youth*  I voyage downstream in the ferry-boat
. . . with my bundle of reeds on my shoulder.
I will go to Memphis
and will say unto Ptah, Lord of Truth:
"Give me my sister tonight."
The stream is wine,
Ptah is its reeds;
Sekhmet its lotus,
Earit its bud,
and Nefertem its flower; . . .


The dawn breaks through her beauty.
Memphis is a dish of love-apples
set before the Fair of Face.

I will lay me down in mine house
and be sick for the wrong done me.
My neighbors will enter to see me.
If my sister cometh with them
she will put to shame the physicians,
for she knoweth my malady.

The castle of the sister,
her doorway
is in the midst of her house,
and her doors they stand open
. . . the sister cometh forth wroth.
Ah, that I were made the porter,
so that she might chide me.
Then would I hear her voice, when she is wroth,
like a child in dread of her.

*The Maiden*  Mine arms
are full of branches of the *persea,*
and my hair
is weighed down with unguent.
I am like a princess
of the Lord of the Two Lands,
when I am in thine arms.

[ 144 ]

## THE TREES IN THE GARDEN

The . . . -tree speaketh:

My stones are like unto her teeth
and my shape unto her breasts.
I am the best of the orchard,
I abide at every season,
that the sister may recline beneath me
with her brother,
when they are drunken with wine and *shedeh,*
and besprinkled with *ķemi-*oil. . . .
All trees in the garden save me fade away;
I endure twelve months. . . .
I stand . . .
and if the blossom falleth off,
that of the year before is still upon me.

I am the first of all trees and will not
that I should be regarded as second.
If this is done again
I will no longer keep silence
and will betray them,
that the wrongdoing may be seen
and the beloved be chastized,
that she may not. . . .
. . . the feast
with its lotus flowers, blossoms and buds,
its unguent and beer of all kinds,
that she may cause thee to pass
the day in merriment.
The booth of rushes is a sheltered spot. . . .
I see him,
he is really coming.
Let us go and flatter him.
May he pass the whole day. . . .

The fig-tree moveth its mouth, and its foliage cometh
        and saith:

. . . to the mistress.
Was there ever a lady like me?
Yet if thou hast no slave
I will be thy servant.

I was brought from the land of . . .
as a spoil for the beloved.
She hath had me set in her orchard,
she putteth not for me. . . .
I busy myself with drinking,
and my belly hath not become full of well-water.

I am found for pleasure . . .
to one that drinketh not.
By my *ka*! O beloved,
. . . bringeth me into thy presence.

The little sycamore,
which she hath planted with her hand,
it moveth its mouth to speak.
The whispering of its leaves
is as sweet as refined honey.
How charming are its pretty branches,
verdant as. . . .
It is laden with *neku*-fruits
that are redder than jasper.
Its leaves are like unto malachite,
and are . . . as glass.
Its wood is in color like unto *neshmet*-stone
and is . . . as the *besbes*-tree.
It draweth them that be not already under it,
its shadow is so cool.

It slippeth a letter into the hand of a
little maid,
the daughter of its chief gardener,
and maketh her run to the beloved:
"Come, and pass the time in the midst
of thy maiden.

[ 146 ]

The garden is in its day.
There are bowers and shelters there for thee.
My gardeners are glad and rejoice
when they see thee.
Send thy slaves ahead of thee,
supplied with their utensils.
Of a truth one is already drunken
when one hasteneth to thee,
ere one hath yet drunken.
But the servants come from thee
with their vessels,
and bring beer of every sort
and all manner of mixed loaves,
and many flowers of yesterday
and today,
and all manner of refreshing fruit.

"Come, and spend the day
in merriment,
and tomorrow
and the day after,
three whole days,
and sit in my shadow."

Her lover sitteth on her right hand.
She maketh him drunken,
and heedeth all that he sayeth.
The feast is disordered with drunkenness,
and she stayeth on with her brother.

Her . . . is spread out under me,
when the sister walketh about.
But I am discreet,
and speak not
of what I see.
I will say no word.

# 14  *The Book of Surgery*

Egypt was famous throughout all of antiquity for her physicians and her medical knowledge, even long after Greek contributions to medicine had surpassed her own. From a number of papyri we can gain some appreciation of what Egypt achieved in this field, and the modern reader, while suitably impressed, is usually disappointed to observe that the quite rational prescriptions of Egyptian medicine are generously interspersed with prayers and incantations. In one document this magical element has been almost entirely eliminated: "The Book of Surgery" (or the Edwin Smith Papyrus, as it is less descriptively known, in tribute to the American who acquired it in Egypt) is a manual for the use of physicians in treating injuries and wounds. It proceeds systematically from wounds in the head downward through the body. Each case is separately described and the account is given in a regular and systematic way, including a title which defines the condition, an examination, the diagnosis, the prognosis, and the treatment. The papyrus dates from the Middle Kingdom but has been shown on the basis of the language to have been copied from an Old Kingdom original. While the document does not make pleasant reading for those squeamish about medical details, it is one of the most important evidences we have for the achievement of ancient Egyptian civilization and has been called the greatest scientific work prior to the Greeks. The manuscript was left unfinished, the forty-eight cases contained in it going from the head only as far down as the chest and the upper spinal vertebrae. In the following selection each of the separate cases that have been included is in itself complete and unabridged. The translation is by James H. Breasted.

CASE 1[1]: A WOUND IN THE HEAD PENETRATING TO THE BONE

*Title*

Instructions concerning a wound in his head, penetrating to the bone of his skull.

SOURCE: Reprinted from *The Edwin Smith Surgical Papyrus,* Vol. I, by James H. Breasted by permission of The University of Chicago Press. Copyright 1930 by The University of Chicago.

1.  It should be noted that the case numbers and the titles of the case subdivisions are insertions of the modern editor.

### Examination

If thou examinest a man having a wound in his head, penetrating to the bone of his skull, but not having a gash, thou shouldst palpate his wound (or, thou shouldst lay thy hand upon it); shouldst thou find his skull uninjured, not having a perforation, a split, or a smash in it,

### Diagnosis

Thou shouldst say regarding him: "One having a wound in his head, while his wound does not have two lips . . . nor a gash, although it penetrates to the bone of his head. An ailment which I will treat."

### Treatment

Thou shouldst bind it with fresh meat the first day and treat afterward with grease, honey and lint every day until he recovers.

### Gloss A

As for: "Thou examinest a man," it means counting any one . . . like counting things with a bushel. For examining is like one's counting a certain quantity with a bushel, or counting something with the fingers, in order to know. . . . It is measuring things with a bushel which . . . one in whom an ailment is counted, like measuring the ailment of a man; in order to know the action of the heart. There are canals (vessels) in it (the heart) to every member. Now if the priests of Sekhmet or any physician put his hands or his fingers upon the head, upon the back of the head, upon the two hands, upon the pulse, upon the two feet, he measures to the heart, because its vessels are in the back of the head and in the pulse; and because its pulsation is in every vessel of every member. He says "measure" regarding his wound because of the vessels to his head and to the back of his head and to his two feet . . . his heart in order to recognize the indications which have arisen therein; meaning to measure it in order to know what is befalling therein.

### Gloss B

As for: "While his wound does not have two lips," it means his wound is narrow, not wide; without gaping of one lip from the other.

## Gloss C

As for: "Penetrating to the bone of his skull, but not having a gash," it means that there is a gaping of the flesh, although . . . over the bone of his skull, without gaping of one lip from the other, being narrow, not wide.

### CASE 2: A GAPING WOUND IN THE HEAD PENETRATING TO THE BONE

#### Title

Instructions concerning a gaping wound in his head, penetrating to the bone.

#### Examination

If thou examinest a man having a gaping wound in his head, penetrating to the bone, thou shouldst lay thy hand upon it and thou shouldst palpate his wound. If thou findest his skull uninjured, not having a perforation in it,

#### Diagnosis

Thou shouldst say regarding him, "One having a gaping wound in his head. An ailment which I will treat."

#### Treatment

Thou shouldst bind fresh meat upon it the first day; thou shouldst apply for him two strips of linen, and treat afterward with grease, honey, and lint every day until he recovers.

### CASE 4: A GAPING WOUND IN THE HEAD PENETRATING TO THE BONE AND SPLITTING THE SKULL

#### Title

Instructions concerning a gaping wound in his head, penetrating to the bone, and splitting his skull.

## Examination

If thou examinest a man having a gaping wound in his head, penetrating to the bone, and splitting his skull, thou shouldst palpate his wound. Shouldst thou find something disturbing therein under thy fingers, and he shudders exceedingly, while the swelling which is over it protrudes, he discharges blood from both his nostrils and from both his ears, he suffers with stiffness in his neck, so that he is unable to look at his two shoulders and his breast,

## Diagnosis

Thou shouldst say regarding him: "One having a gaping wound in his head, penetrating to the bone, and splitting his skull; while he discharges blood from both his nostrils and from both his ears, and he suffers with stiffness in his neck. An ailment with which I will contend."

## Treatment

Now when thou findest that the skull of that man is split, thou shouldst not bind him, but moor him at his mooring stakes[2] until the period of his injury passes by. His treatment is sitting. Make for him two supports of brick, until thou knowest he has reached a decisive point. Thou shouldst apply grease to his head, and soften his neck therewith and both his shoulders. Thou shouldst do likewise for every man whom thou findest having a split skull.

## Gloss A

As for: "Splitting his skull," it means separating shell from shell of his skull, while fragments remain sticking in the flesh of his head, and do not come away.

## Gloss B

As for: "The swelling which is over it protrudes," it means that the swelling which is over this split is large, rising upward.

---

2.   A gloss in Case 3 explains that "moor him at his mooring stakes" means putting the patient on his customary diet, without administering to him a prescription.

## Gloss C

As for: "Until thou knowest he has reached a decisive point," it means until thou knowest whether he will die or he will live; for he is a case of "an ailment with which I will contend."

## CASE 5: A GAPING WOUND IN THE HEAD WITH COMPOUND COMMINUTED FRACTURE OF THE SKULL

### Title

Instructions concerning a gaping wound in his head, smashing his skull.

### Examination

If thou examinest a man having a gaping wound in his head, penetrating to the bone, and smashing his skull; thou shouldst palpate his wound. Shouldst thou find that smash which is in his skull deep and sunken under thy fingers, while the swelling which is over it protrudes, he discharges blood from both his nostrils and both his ears, and he suffers with stiffness in his neck, so that he is unable to look at his two shoulders and his breast,

### Diagnosis

Thou shouldst say regarding him, "One having a gaping wound in his head, penetrating to the bone, and smashing his skull, while he suffers with stiffness in his neck. An ailment not to be treated."

### Treatment

Thou shalt not bind him but moor him at his mooring stakes, until the period of his injury passes by.

### Gloss A

As for: "Smashing his skull," it means a smash of his skull such that bones, getting into that smash, sink into the interior of his skull. The "Treatise on What Pertains to His Wounds" states: "It means a smash of his skull into numerous fragments, which sink into the interior of his skull."

14

CASE 17: COMPOUND COMMINUTED FRACTURE OF THE BONE
IN THE REGION OF THE MAXILLA AND THE ZYGOMA

*Title*

Instructions concerning a smash in his cheek.

*Examination*

If thou examinest a man having a smash in his cheek, thou shouldst place thy hand on his cheek at the point of that smash. Should it crepitate under thy fingers, while he discharges blood from his nostril, and from his ear on the side of him having that injury; and at the same time he discharges blood from his mouth, while it is painful when he opens his mouth because of it,

*Diagnosis*

Thou shouldst say concerning him: "One having a smash in his cheek, while he discharges blood from his nostril, from his ear, and from his mouth, and he is speechless. An ailment not to be treated."

*Treatment*

Thou shouldst bind with fresh meat the first day. His relief is sitting until its swelling is reduced. Thou shalt treat it afterward with grease, honey, and lint every day until he recovers.

CASE 20: A WOUND IN THE TEMPLE PERFORATING THE BONE

*Title*

Instructions concerning a wound in his temple, penetrating to the bone, and perforating his temporal bone.

*Examination*

If thou examinest a man having a wound in his temple, penetrating to the bone, and perforating his temporal bone, while his two eyes are bloodshot, he discharges blood from both his nostrils, and a little drops; if thou puttest thy fingers on the mouth of that wound and he shudder exceedingly; if thou ask of him concerning his malady and he speak not to thee; while copious tears fall from both his eyes, so that he thrusts his hand often to his face that he may wipe both his eyes with the back of his hand as a child does, and knows not that he does so,

## Diagnosis

Thou shouldst say concerning him: "One having a wound in his temple, penetrating to the bone, and perforating his temporal bone; while he discharges blood from both his nostrils, he suffers with stiffness in his neck, and he is speechless. An ailment not to be treated."

## Examination

## Treatment

Now when thou findest that man speechless, his relief shall be sitting; soften his head with grease, and pour milk into both his ears.

### CASE 28: A GAPING WOUND IN THE THROAT
### PENETRATING TO THE GULLET

## Title

Instructions concerning a wound in his throat.

If thou examinest a man having a gaping wound in his throat, piercing through to his gullet; if he drinks water he chokes and it comes out of the mouth of his wound; it is greatly inflamed, so that he develops fever from it; thou shouldst draw together that wound with stitching.

## Diagnosis

Thou shouldst say concerning him: "One having a wound in his throat, piercing through to his gullet. An ailment with which I will contend."

## First Treatment

Thou shouldst bind it with fresh meat the first day. Thou shouldst treat it afterward with grease, honey, and lint every day, until he recovers.

## Second Examination

If, however, thou findest him continuing to have fever from that wound,

## Second Treatment

Thou shouldst apply for him dry lint in the mouth of his wound, and moor him at his mooring stakes until he recovers.

## CASE 29: A GAPING WOUND IN A CERVICAL VERTEBRA

### Title

Instructions concerning a gaping wound in a vertebra of his neck.

### Examination

If thou examinest a man having a gaping wound in a vertebra of his neck, penetrating to the bone, and perforating a vertebra of his neck; if thou examinest that wound, and he shudders exceedingly, and he is unable to look at his two shoulders and his breast,

### Diagnosis

Thou shouldst say concerning him: "One having a wound in his neck, penetrating to the bone, perforating a vertebra of his neck, and he suffers with stiffness in his neck. An ailment with which I will contend."

### Treatment

Thou shouldst bind it with fresh meat the first day. Now afterward moor him at his mooring stakes until the period of his injury passes by.

## CASE 32: DISPLACEMENT OF A CERVICAL VERTEBRA

### Title

Instructions concerning a displacement in a vertebra of his neck.

### Examination

If thou examinest a man having a displacement in a vertebra of his neck, whose face is fixed, whose neck cannot turn for him, and thou shouldst say to him: "Look at thy breast and thy two shoulders," and he is unable to turn his face that he may look at his breast and his two shoulders,

### Diagnosis

Thou shouldst say concerning him: "One having a displacement in a vertebra of his neck. An ailment which I will treat."

### Treatment

Thou shouldst bind it with fresh meat the first day. Thou shouldst loose his bandages and apply grease to his head as far as his neck, and thou shouldst bind it with *ymrw*. Thou shouldst treat it afterward with honey every day, and his relief is sitting until he recovers.

### Gloss A

As for: "A displacement in a vertebra of his neck," he is speaking concerning a sinking of a vertebra of his neck to the interior of his neck, as a foot settles into cultivated ground. It is a penetration downward.

## CASE 33: A CRUSHED CERVICAL VERTEBRA

### Title

Instructions concerning a crushed vertebra in his neck.

### Examination

If thou examinest a man having a crushed vertebra in his neck and thou findest that one vertebra has fallen into the next one, while he is voiceless and cannot speak; his falling head downward has caused that one vertebra crush into the next one; and shouldst thou find that he is unconscious of his two arms and his two legs because of it,

## Diagnosis

Thou shouldst say concerning him: "One having a crushed vertebra in his neck; he is unconscious of his two arms and his two legs, and he is speechless. An ailment not to be treated."

## Gloss A

As for: "A crushed vertebra in his neck," he is speaking of the fact that one vertebra of his neck has fallen into the next, one penetrating into the other, there being no movement to and fro.

## Gloss B

As for: "His falling head downward has caused that one vertebra crush into the next," it means that he has fallen head downward upon his head, driving one vertebra of his neck into the next.

## CASE 35: A FRACTURE OF THE CLAVICLE

### Title

Instructions concerning a break in his collar-bone.

### Examination

If thou examinest a man having a break in his collar-bone, and thou shouldst find his collar-bone short and separated from its fellow,

### Diagnosis

Thou shouldst say concerning him: "One having a break in his collar-bone. An ailment which I will treat."

## Treatment

Thou shouldst place him prostrate on his back, with something folded between his two shoulder-blades; thou shouldst spread out with his two shoulders in order to stretch apart his collar-bone until that break falls into its place. Thou shouldst make for him two splints of linen, and thou shouldst apply one of them both on the inside of his upper arm and the other on the under side of his upper arm. Thou shouldst bind it with *ymrw*, and treat it afterward with honey every day, until he recovers.

CASE 39: TUMORS OR ULCERS IN THE BREAST
PERHAPS RESULTING FROM INJURY

## Title

Instructions concerning tumors with prominent head in his breast.

## Examination

If thou examinest a man having tumors with prominent head in his breast, and thou findest that the swellings have spread with pus over his breast, and have produced redness, while it is very hot therein, when thy hand touches him,

## Diagnosis

Thou shouldst say concerning him: "One having tumors with prominent head in his breast, and they produce cists of pus. An ailment which I will treat with the fire-drill."

## Treatment

Thou shouldst burn for him over his breast and over those tumors which are on his breast. Thou shouldst treat him with wound treatment. Thou shouldst not prevent its opening of itself, that there may be no *mnhy-w* in his wound. Every wound that arises in his breast dries up as soon as it opens of itself.

## Gloss A

As for: "Tumors with prominent head in his breast," it means that there are swellings spreading over his breast because of his injury; they produce pus and redness on his breast; as it is said: "It is like parti-colored things," whose product is pus.

## CASE 47: A GAPING WOUND IN THE SHOULDER

### Title

Instructions concerning a gaping wound in his shoulder.

### First Examination

If thou examinest a man having a gaping wound in his shoulder, its flesh being laid back and its sides separated, while he suffers with swelling in his shoulder blade, thou shouldst palpate his wound. Shouldst thou find its gash separated from its sides in his wound, as a roll of linen is unrolled, and it is painful when he raises his arm on account of it, thou shouldst draw together for him his gash with stitching.

### First Diagnosis

Thou shouldst say concerning him: "One having a gaping wound in his shoulder, its flesh being laid back and its sides separated, while he suffers with swelling in his shoulder blade. An ailment which I will treat."

### First Treatment

Thou shouldst bind it with fresh meat the first day.

### Second Examination and Treatment

If thou findest that wound open and its stitching loose, thou shouldst draw together for him its gash with two strips of linen over that gash; thou shouldst treat it afterward with grease, honey, and lint every day until he recovers.

If thou findest a wound, its flesh laid back, its sides separated, in any member of a man, thou shouldst treat it according to these directions.

### Third Examination

If, however, thou findest that his flesh has developed inflammation from

[ 159 ]

that wound which is in his shoulder, while that wound is inflamed, open, and its stitching loose, thou shouldst lay thy hand upon it. Shouldst thou find inflammation issuing from the mouth of his wound at thy touch, and secretions discharging therefrom are cool like *wenesh*-juice,

## Diagnosis Following Third Examination

Thou shouldst say concerning him: "One having a gaping wound in his shoulder, it being inflamed, and he continues to have fever from it. An ailment with which I will contend."

## Fourth Examination

If then, thou findest that man continuing to have fever, while that wound is inflamed,

## Treatment Following Fourth Examination

Thou shalt not bind it; thou shalt moor him at his mooring stakes, until the period of his injury passes by.

## Fifth Examination

If, however, his fever abates and the inflammation in the mouth of his wound dissipates entirely,

## Treatment Following Fifth Examination

Thou shouldst treat him afterward with grease, honey, and lint every day, until he recovers.

### CASE 48: A SPRAIN IN A SPINAL VERTEBRA

## Title

Instructions concerning a sprain in a vertebra of his spinal column.

## Examination

If thou examinest a man having a sprain in a vertebra of his spinal column, thou shouldst say to him: "Extend now thy two legs and contract them both again." When he extends them both he contracts them both immediately because of the pain he causes in the vertebra of his spinal column in which he suffers.

## Diagnosis

Thou shouldst say concerning him: "One having a sprain in a vertebra of his spinal column. An ailment which I will treat."

## Treatment

Thou shouldst place him prostrate on his back; thou shouldst make for him . . . .

[*Here the papyrus ends.*]

# THE EXPANDED WORLD

MOST of the major achievements of Mesopotamia and Egypt belong to the earliest centuries of their civilizations. Their failure thereafter to introduce any remarkable discoveries or to make dramatic progress in technology, political organization, and intellectual activity, or in any other realm of human affairs has often been pointed out. In the view held by many historians, the reason for this lay in the narrow material basis of their culture. In this view the term "Bronze Age Civilization" is not merely a convenient way of referring to the period from the beginning of recorded history down to about 1200 B.C. but contains a decisive explanation for the limitations of that civilization. The limits imposed by the use of bronze as the chief material for tools and weapons prevented an intensification of the early bursts of achievement. As the archaeologist Gordon Childe has put it, "If the economy of the Early Bronze Age cities could not expand internally . . . if its ideological expressions were doomed to fossilization . . . the urban economy must—and did—expand externally."

As early as 2200 B.C. the Sumerian civilization had been adopted by the neighboring Akkadians. Other peoples continued to be drawn into what was rapidly becoming a fairly homogeneous civilization in the Near East or were being reached out to by the influence of that civilization through the agency of the two great historical catalysts of culture: trade and war. In the second millennium (2000–1000) B.C., civilization had spread from its original homes on the lower Tigris and Euphrates and on the Nile, throughout the Near East to the upper Tigris and Euphrates, to the Syrian coastlands, to Asia Minor, to the islands of the eastern Mediterranean, notably Cyprus and Crete, and into the Aegean Sea and its islands. Modern archaeology has uncovered the fragmentary records of numerous peoples who were drawn into the orbit of the civilized world. Some of them, like the Mari and Nuzi cultures, played only a minor historical role before being absorbed by their more powerful neighbors. Others maintained their identities and became the great powers of a later epoch, as the Assyrians and the Persians did. A few, such as the Hittites and the Mitanni, were to develop rapidly into important actors in the history of the second millennium. Thus the world of the second millennium was one of numerous peoples

[ 162 ]

and nations, and from about 1500 B.C. on, it was a world of national rivalries, of war and conquest, of the building and the decline of empires.

Of the "new" peoples the outstanding were the Hittites, whose culture is illustrated in Selections 15–18. The discovery of the empire of the Hittites is one of the most dramatic events of twentieth-century archaeology. A people almost completely lost to history, known only from a few passing references in the Old Testament, they have been revealed to us as one of the two greatest powers of their times, rulers of a considerable territory, rivals in imperial grandeur of mighty Egypt itself. The first important Indo-European speaking people to appear on the stage of history, the Hittites (or Hatti) entered Asia Minor shortly after 2000 B.C. They settled within the great bend of the Halys River and gradually over the centuries built up a strong monarchy and from the capital city, Hattusas, extended their rule over neighboring peoples. The Hittites had their own cultural traditions, their own language, their own gods; but they were civilized by the Mesopotamian civilization and assimilated much of its way of life. The adoption of cuneiform writing is but the most conspicuous symbol of the immense cultural debt of the Hittites to Mesopotamia.

# 15  Hittite Law Code

Like their neighbors, the Hittites followed Sumerian precedent in developing a law code. The very considerable portion of the Hittite law code that has been preserved makes for an instructive comparison with the early Sumerian codes and the Code of Hammurabi: there are similarities that reflect the influence of Mesopotamian civilization, and there are differences that bespeak an independent tradition of the Hittites themselves. The code as we have it contains evidence of at least two revisions in it during antiquity. As presented in the following selection, it has been abridged to omit repetitions and also some of the detail that the Hittite jurists—who were admirable at making minute distinctions—indulged in. The translation is by Arnold Walther.

❀❀❀❀❀

SOURCE: Reprinted from *The Origin and History of Hebrew Law* by J. M. P. Smith by permission of The University of Chicago Press. Copyright 1931 by The University of Chicago.

1. If anyone slay a man or a woman in a quarrel, he shall bring this one. He shall also give four persons, either men or women, he shall let them go to his family's home.[1]

2. If anyone slay a male or female slave in a quarrel, he shall bring this one and give two persons, either men or women, he shall let them go to his home.

3. If anyone smite a free man or woman and this one die, only his hand doing evil,[2] he shall bring this one and give two persons, he shall let them go to his home.

4. If anyone smite a male or female slave, only his hand doing evil, he shall bring this one also and give one person, he shall let him or her go to his home. [*Later version of 4:*] But if it be a woman or a female slave, he shall give two pounds[3] of silver.

5. If anyone slay a merchant of Hatti, he shall give one and a half [*the signs may read "one hundred"*] pounds of silver, he shall let it go to his family's home. If it happen in the land of Luia or in the land of Pala, he shall give one and a half [*one hundred*] pounds of silver and compensate his property. If it happen in the land of Hatti, then he shall bring that merchant. [*Later version of 5:*] If anyone slay a merchant of Hatti for property in this land, he shall give . . . pounds of silver and compensate for the property threefold. But if anyone do not retain the property and slay him in a quarrel, he shall give six pounds of silver. If only his hand do evil, he shall give two pounds of silver.

6. If one, man or woman, die in this or that village, he in whose circuit he dies shall cut off one hundred rods of field, and he the heir may take it. [*Later version of 6:*] If a man die in another field and ground, if it be a free man, he shall give field, ground, house, and one pound, twenty half-shekels[4] of silver; if it be a woman, he shall give three pounds of silver. But if there be no field and ground, in the place of the other shall be put this way three double-leagues, that way three double-leagues, and whatever village is met or determined by an oracle therein, he the heir may take these men for compensation. If there be no village, he shall go away empty.

7. If anyone blind a free man or knock out his teeth, formerly they would give one pound of silver, now he shall give twenty half-shekels of silver, he shall let it go to his home.

1. This formula appears to mean that an individual's (or family's) personal estate is to be pledged as security.
2. This formula appears to mean involuntarily or accidentally.
3. The word regularly rendered in this translation as "pound" is the "mina."
4. The "half-shekel" that is the standard monetary unit throughout is rendered by some other translators as the simple shekel.

8. If anyone blind a male or female slave or knock out his or her teeth, he shall give ten half-shekels of silver, he shall let it go to his home. [*Later version of 7 and 8:*] If anyone blind a free man in a quarrel, he shall give one pound of silver. If only the hand do evil, he shall give twenty half-shekels of silver. If anyone knock out a free man's teeth, if he knock out two teeth or three teeth, he shall give twelve half-shekels of silver. If it be a slave, he shall give six half-shekels of silver.

9. If anyone injure a man's head, formerly they would give six half-shekels of silver: the injured man was to take three half-shekels, for the palace they would take three half-shekels of silver. Now the king has remitted the palace's dues; so only the injured man may take three half-shekels of silver.

10. If anyone injure a man so that he cause him suffering, he shall take care of him. Yet he shall give him a man in his place, who shall work for him in his house until he recovers. But if he recover, he shall give him six half-shekels of silver. And to the physician this one shall also give the fee, three half-shekels of silver, but if it be a slave, two half-shekels.

11. If anyone break a free man's hand or foot, he shall give him twenty half-shekels of silver, he shall let it go to his home.

12. If anyone break the hand or the foot of a male or female slave, he shall give ten half-shekels of silver, he shall let it go to his home. [*Later version of 11 and 12:*] If anyone break a freeman's hand or foot and if he remain crippled, he shall give him twenty half-shekels of silver; but if he be not crippled, he shall give him ten half-shekels of silver.

13. If anyone cut off the nose of a free man, he shall give one pound of silver, he shall let it go to his home.

14. If anyone cut off the nose of a male or female slave, he shall give three half-shekels of silver, he shall let it go to his home.

15. If anyone tear the ear of a free man, he shall give twelve half-shekels of silver, he shall let it go to his home.

16. If anyone tear the ear of a male or a female slave, he shall give three half-shekels of silver.

17. If anyone cause a free woman to miscarry, if it be the tenth month, he shall give ten half-shekels of silver, if it be the fifth month, he shall give five half-shekels of silver, he shall let it go to her home.

18. If anyone cause a female slave to miscarry, if it be the tenth month, he shall give five half-shekels of silver.

27. If a man take a woman for his wife and lead her into his house and put down some of her patrimony there, if the woman die, and they burn the

property of this man, the man may take from her patrimony. If she die at her father's house and he the father have sons or children, for his son the man dare not take her patrimony.

28. If a daughter be betrothed to a man and another elope with her and elope with the bride price too, whatever the first man's bride price was, then he the other man shall compensate him; father and mother do not compensate. If father and mother give her to the other man, father and mother shall compensate. If father and mother refuse it, they shall separate her from him.

29. If a daughter be bound to a man and he convey the bride price to her, and afterward father and mother oppose this, they may separate her from the man, but they shall compensate double the price.

30. If the man have not yet taken the daughter and refuse her, he however forfeits the bride price that he conveyed.

31. If a free man and female slave be fond of each other and come together and he take her for his wife and they set up house and get children, and afterward they either become hostile or come to close quarters, and they divide the house between them, the man shall take the children, only one child the woman shall take.

32. If a slave take a woman as his wife, their case is the same.

33. If a slave take a female slave, their case is the same.

34. If a slave convey the bride price to a woman and take her for his wife, nobody dare surrender her to slavery.

35. If an administrator or a shepherd elope with a free woman and do not convey the bride price, she becomes a slave for three years.

36. If a slave convey the bride price to a free son and take him as husband for his daughter, nobody dare surrender him to slavery.

37. If anyone elope with a woman, but afterward a rescuer come to them, if two men or three men die, there is no compensation: "Thou hast turned into a wolf."[5]

38. If men be seized and brought into the court of justice, and any rescuer come to them, and then they rage at the wood of the lock, and someone smite the rescuer, and he die, there shall be no compensation.

39. If a man hold the vacant fields of another and perform the tenancy duties, if he abandon the fields, and another take the fields, he dare not dispose of them.

57. If anyone steal a bull—if it be an ox half a year old, it is not a bull; if it be a yearling ox, it is not a bull; if it be an ox two years old, this

5. The meaning of this formula is not known.

one is a bull—formerly they would give thirty oxen, now he shall give fifteen oxen: he shall give five two-years old, five yearling oxen, five oxen half a year old, he shall let them go to his home.

58. If anyone steal a stallion—if the horse be half a year old, it is not a stallion; if it be a yearling, it is not a stallion; if it be two years old, this one is a stallion—formerly they would give thirty horses, now he shall give fifteen horses: he shall give five horses two years old, five yearling horses, five horses half a year old, he shall let them go to his home.

59. If anyone steal a ram, formerly they would give thirty sheep, now he shall give fifteen sheep; he shall give five wool-ewes, five wethers, five lambs, he shall let them go to his home.

60. If anyone find a bull, then release it, and its owner discover it, he shall give seven oxen: he shall give two oxen two years old, three yearling oxen, two oxen half a year old, he shall let them go to his home.

61. If anyone find a stallion, then release it and its owner discover it, he shall give seven horses: he shall give two horses two years old, three yearling horses, two half a year old, he shall let them go to his home.

62. If anyone find a ram, then release it and its owner discover it, he shall give seven sheep: he shall give two wool-ewes, three wethers, two lambs, he shall let them go to his home.

72. If an ox die in the field of anyone, the owner of the field shall give two oxen, he shall let them go to his home.

73. If anyone appropriate a living ox, also this one is a thief equally.

74. If anyone break the horn of an ox or the foot of an ox, then he shall take this ox and give the owner of the ox a sound ox. If the owner of the ox say, "I will take just my ox," he shall take his ox, and he the other shall give two half-shekels of silver.

75. If anyone borrow and yoke an ox, a horse, a mule, an ass, and it die, or a wolf devour it, or it go astray, he shall give it in good condition. But if he say, "By the hand of a god it died," then he shall take an oath.

76. If anyone borrow an ox, a horse, a mule, an ass, and it die with him on the spot, he shall bring it and give its hire.

77. If anyone smite a pregnant cow and cause it to miscarry, he shall give two half-shekels of silver. If anyone smite a pregnant ass and cause it to miscarry, he shall give two half-shekels of silver. If anyone destroy the eye of an ox or a horse, he shall give six half-shekels of silver, he shall let it go to his home.

78. If anyone hire an ox for lighter work, as threshing, and impose a

yoke harness or a collar harness on it and its owner find it, he shall give one peck of barley as additional food for one pair.

79. If oxen go upon a field and the owner of the field find them, he may yoke them one day, until the stars come; then he shall return them to their owner.

80. If anyone throw a sheep before the wolf, its owner shall take its fat, and he himself the shepherd shall take the skin of the sheep.

81. If anyone steal a fattened pig, formerly they would give one pound of silver. Now he shall give twelve half-shekels of silver, he shall let it go to his home.

82. If anyone steal a pig of the portico,[6] he shall give six half-shekels of silver, he shall let it go to his home.

83. If anyone steal a pregnant pig, he shall give six half-shekels of silver. Also the little pigs they shall count; for two little pigs he shall give one peck of barley, he shall let it go to his home.

84. If anyone smite a pregnant pig so that it dies, his case is the same.

85. If anyone separate a little young pig and steal it, for a pair he shall give one peck of barley.

86. If a pig go upon a meadow or a field or a garden, and then the owner of the meadow, the field, or the garden smite it so that it dies, he shall give it back to its owner. But if he do not give it back, he becomes a thief.

87. If anyone smite the dog of a shepherd so that it dies, he shall give twenty half-shekels of silver, he shall let it go to his home.

88. If anyone smite the dog of a dogman so that it dies, he shall give twelve half-shekels of silver and shall let it go to his home.

89. If anyone smite a dog of the portico so that it dies, he shall give one half-shekel of silver.

90. If a dog devour pig's lard and the owner of the lard find the dog and kill it in order to tear the lard out of its stomach, there is no compensation.

91. If anyone steal bees in the sunshine: formerly they would give one pound of silver; now he shall give five half-shekels of silver, he shall let it go to his home.

92. If anyone steal two beehives or three beehives: formerly covering with bee-stings was inflicted; now he shall give six half-shekels of silver. If anyone steal a beehive, if no bees are therein, he shall give three half-shekels of silver.

93. If they seize a free man at a storehouse before he has gone in, he

6. The meaning is not clear.

shall give twelve half-shekels of silver. If they seize a slave at a storehouse, before he has gone in, he shall give six half-shekels of silver.

94. If a free man steal in a house, he shall give it in the same good condition. Formerly for a theft they would give one pound of silver; now he shall give twelve half-shekels of silver. If he steal much, they shall impose upon him much; if he steal little, they shall impose upon him little, he shall let it go to his home.

95. If a slave steal in a house, he shall give it in the same good condition. For the theft he shall give six half-shekels of silver. And he the victim of the theft shall cut off the nose of the slave and his ears. Then they give him back to his master. If he steal much, they shall impose upon him much; if he steal little, they shall impose upon him little. If his master say, "I will compensate for him," he shall compensate. If he refuse, then he shall give up that slave.

96. If a free man steal in a granary and he obtain the grain of the granary, he shall fill the granary with grain. And he shall give twelve half-shekels of silver and let it go to his home.

97. If a slave steal in a granary and he obtain the grain of the granary, he shall fill the granary with grain. And he shall give six half-shekels of silver, he shall let it go to his home.

98. If a free man set a house ablaze, he shall build the house, again. And whatever is inside the house, be it a man, an ox, or a sheep, that perishes, nothing of these he need compensate.

99. If a slave set a house ablaze, his master shall compensate for him. The nose of the slave and his ears they shall cut off, and give him back to his master. But if he do not compensate, then he shall give up this one.

100. If anyone set a barn ablaze, he shall feed the other's oxen and shall bring the fodder until spring. He shall give back the barn. If straw was not therein, then he shall only build the barn.

146. If anyone be going to sell house or village, or . . . or . . . and another come and prevent it by dissuading the buyer, then he make the trade himself or at a lower price, the evildoer shall give one pound of silver and he shall buy according to the first trade.

147. If anyone be going to sell an unskilled man and another prevent it, the evildoer shall give . . . half-shekels of silver.

148. If anyone be going to sell an ox, horse, mule, or ass, and another prevent it, the evildoer shall give . . . half-shekels of silver.

149. If anyone trade away a tamed . . . and say "It died," and its owner

trace it, he the owner may take it, and, in addition, he the purloiner shall give two persons.

150. If a man go for wages, for one month his wages are . . . half-shekels of silver. If a woman go for wages, for one month her wages are . . . half-shekels of silver.

151. If anyone hire a plow-ox, for one month its hire is one half-shekel of silver. If anyone hire a . . . for one month its hire is . . . half-shekel of silver.

152. If anyone hire a horse . . . for one month its hire is . . . half-shekel of silver.

158. If a man go for wages, bind sheaves, load it into carts, spread it on the straw barn and so forth till they clear the threshing-floor, for three months his wages are thirty pecks of barley. If a woman go for wages in the harvest, for two months he the proprietor shall give twelve pecks of barley.

159. If anyone harness a yoke of oxen, his wages are one-half peck of barley.

166. If anyone sow seed upon seed, his neck shall be put upon the plow, then they shall harness a yoke of oxen, directing the face of this one this way, and the face of that one that way. The man shall die, and the oxen shall die. And he who sowed the field first, this one then may take it. Formerly they did thus.

167. Now, one sheep shall be fetched as the substitute of the man, and two sheep shall be fetched as the substitutes of the oxen. And thirty loaves, three jugs of beer he shall give. Then he cleanses it again by the offering. And he who sowed the field first, this one then may reap it.

170. If a free man kill a serpent and speak the name of another, he shall give one pound of silver; if a slave, this one shall die.

172. If anyone keep a free man alive in a hungry year, then this one shall give indemnification for it; if a slave, he shall give ten half-shekels of silver.

173. If anyone oppose the judgment of the king, his house shall become a ruin. If anyone oppose the judgment of a dignitary, his head shall be cut off. If a slave rise against his master, he shall go into the pit.

174. If men fight one another, and then one dies, he who killed shall give one person.

175. If a shepherd or an administrator take a free woman, she shall be a slave for two years or for four years, and they may pelt her children and nobody shall dare seize the missiles.

[ 170 ]

176A. If anyone remove a part of the fence of a bull, it falls under the judgment of the king. They trade as follows. In the third year the bull genders. The plow-ox, the wether, the he-goat gender in the third year.

176B. If anyone buy an artisan's apprentice, buy either a potter, a smith, a carpenter, a leatherworker, a tailor, a weaver, or a lace-maker, he shall give ten half-shekels of silver.

177. If anyone buy an expert fowler, he shall give twenty-five half-shekels of silver. If anyone buy an unskilled man or woman, he shall give twenty half-shekels of silver.

178. A plow-ox costs fifteen half-shekels of silver, a bull costs ten half-shekels of silver, a great cow costs seven half-shekels of silver, a plow-ox, a cow one year old costs five half-shekels of silver, and for an ox half a year old one shall give four half-shekels of silver; if for a pregnant cow, eight half-shekels of silver; a calf costs two half-shekels of silver. One male horse, one mare for breeding, one he-ass, one she-ass for breeding, cost correspondingly.

187. If a man do evil with a cow, it is a capital crime, he shall die. They shall lead him to the king's hall. But the king may kill him, and the king may grant him his life. But he shall not approach the king.

189. If a man do evil with his own mother, it is a capital crime. If a man do evil with a daughter, it is a capital crime. If a man do evil with a son, it is a capital crime.

190. But if they come willingly, man and woman, there shall be no punishment. And if a man do evil with his stepmother, there shall be no punishment. But if his father be living, it is a capital crime.

191. If a free man picks up now this one, now that one, now in this country, then in that country, there shall be no punishment. If both live in one place and he know them, it is a capital crime.

192. If the man of a woman die, his wife may take the man's patrimony.

193. If a man have taken a woman, then the man die and his brother take her, then his father take her; if again also his father die and one brother of his take the woman whom he had taken, there is no punishment.

194. If a free man pick up female slaves, now one, now another, there is no punishment. If brothers or relations sleep with a free woman, there is no punishment. If father and son sleep with a female slave or a harlot, there is no punishment.

195. If a man sleep with the wife of his brother, but his brother is living, it is a capital crime. If a man have taken a free woman, then have intercourse also with her daughter, it is a capital crime. If he have taken her

daughter, then have intercourse with her mother or her sister, it is a capital crime.

196. If anyone's male and female slaves practice harlotry, then they shall bring them and let them dwell, this one at this village, that one at that village. For this one one sheep, for that one one sheep, shall be fetched as a substitute.

197. If a man seize a woman in the mountain, it is the man's wrong, he shall die. But if he seize her in the house, it is the woman's fault, the woman shall die. If the man find them and then kill them, there is no punishing him.

198. If he lead them to the gate of the palace and say, "My wife shall not die," then he shall grant life to his wife and likewise to the adulterer, then mark his head. If he say, "These two shall die," then they shall suffer for their crime. The king may kill them; the king may grant them their lives.

200B. If anyone give a son for instruction, be it a carpenter, or a potter, or a weaver, or a leather-worker, or a tailor, or a smith, he shall give six half-shekels of silver for the instruction. If he the artisan have taught him, he the father shall give him a person.

# 16 Instructions for Temple Officials

The "Instructions for Temple Officials" provide impressive evidence for the close tie between the state and religion in early societies as well as for the extremely rigorous and legalistic nature of religious observances, also a feature common to most ancient religions. They are regulations governing the professional duties and behavior of officials of the Hittite state religious cults rather than injunctions respecting clerical piety. The translation (abridged) is by E. H. Sturtevant and G. Bechtel.

❀❀❀❀❀

*[The first regulation is missing.]*

SOURCE: Edgar H. Sturtevant and George Bechtel, *A Hittite Chrestomathy* (William Dwight Whitney Linguistic Series) (Philadelphia: Linguistic Society of America and University of Pennsylvania, 1935). Reprinted by permission of Professor Konstantin Reichardt for the Whitney Linguistic Series.

2. Furthermore let those who prepare the daily bread be clean; let them be washed and cleansed; let their hair and finger-nails be removed, and let them have on clean clothes. If not, let them not prepare it. Let those who propitiate the heart and soul of the gods prepare them (the loaves). And let the baker's house in which they prepare them be swept and sprinkled. Furthermore let not a pig or a dog approach the door of the place of the broken bread. Is the disposition of men and of the gods at all different? No! Even in this matter somewhat different? No; but their disposition is quite the same. When a slave stands before his master, he is washed and he has on clean clothes; and either he gives him something to eat, or he gives him something to drink. And he, his master, eats and drinks something and he is relaxed in spirit and he is favorably inclined to him. If, however, he the slave is ever dilatory, and is not observant, there is a different disposition toward him. And if ever a slave vexes his master, either they kill him or they injure his nose, his eyes, or his ears; or he the master calls him to account and also his wife, his sons, his brother, his sister, his relatives by marriage, and his family, whether it be a male slave or a female slave. Then they revile him in public, and they consider him nothing at all. And if ever he dies, he does not die alone, but his family is included with him.

3. If then, on the other hand, anyone vexes the feelings of a god, does the god punish him alone for it? Does he not punish his wife, his children, his descendants, his family, his slaves male and female, his cattle, his sheep, and his harvest for it, and remove him utterly? Now, of your own accord, be very much afraid of the word of a god.

4. Within, however, there is a festival of the month, a festival of the year, a festival for *ayalas,* a festival of the autumn, a festival of the spring, a festival of the thunder, a rain festival, a festival of *pudahas,* a festival of *isuwas,* a festival of *issalas,* a festival of the drinking horn, festivals of the pure priest, festivals of the old men, festivals of the mothers of god, a festival of *dahis,* festivals of the men of the east, festivals of *pulas,* festivals of *hahratar,* or whatever festival there is in behalf of Hattusas. If you do not perform them set up with all the cattle, sheep, bread, beer, and wine, and you, temple officials, accept pay from those who give it the food and drink, you will cause the festival to fall short of the desire of the god.

5. Or if you take the food and drink for the festival, when it has been set up, and do not bring it right to the gods themselves, and you carry it away from them to your houses, and your wives, your children and your slaves eat it up, or if, on the other hand, a relative by marriage or a good

citizen comes to you, and you give it to such a person—if you take it from the god himself, and do not bring it straight to him, and share by share you give it away, then let this charge of division lie against you with a capital penalty. Do not divide it. But whoever divides it, let him die; let there be no pardon for him.

6. Of the bread, beer, and wine carry everything up into the temple. Let no one leave the god's ordinary bread or thin bread. And let no one dip up beer or wine from the libation bowl; devote every bit to the god. Furthermore, in the presence of the god speak for yourselves these words: "Whoever has taken anything from thy divine ordinary bread, or from the libation bowl, may the god, my lord, hereafter destroy him, and turn his house upside down." And if you can eat and drink everything on that day, eat and drink it. But if you cannot, keep on eating and drinking it for three days; and with you let your wives, your children, and your slaves eat and drink. But let no other person open the door of the gods. But if a citizen comes to anyone and he has the privilege of going up to the temple and he habitually opens the king's door also, let that man conduct him up to the temple, and let him eat and drink. But if he is a foreigner and he is not a Hittite man and he visits the gods, let him die; and whoever conducts him to the temple, for him there is the capital penalty.

7. If an ox or a sheep is brought for the god to eat, but you take for yourselves either a fat ox or a fat sheep, and put in its place a thin animal that you have cut up for yourselves, and if you either eat that ox up or put it into your pen, or put it under the yoke . . . or if you put the sheep into your fold, or kill it, and if your wishes are gratified; or if you give it in exchange to another man, and take a price for it; why then do you withdraw meat from the mouth of the god, and take it for yourselves or give it to another, and speak as follows? "Since he is a god he will not say anything, and he will not do anything to us." Just look at the man who takes thy choice meat from before thine eyes! Afterwards, when it operates, the will of the gods is strong. It does not make haste to seize; but when it seizes, it does not thereafter let go. Now be very much afraid of the will of the gods.

8. And in the temples what silver, gold, clothing, or bronze implements of the gods you have—and your metal-workers—belongs to the gods. There is none for you. In the courtyard of the gods there is nothing which you possess; whatever there is belongs to the god. Now be very much afraid. Let a temple official have no silver or gold. Let him not take it into his house; and let him not make it into an ornament for his wife or his

children. But if they give him as a present from the palace silver, gold, garments, or bronze implements, let them be named: "So-and-so, the king, gave it to him." And how great its weight is, let that be set down. And furthermore let it be set down as follows: "At such-and-such a festival they gave it to him." And after that let the witnesses be set down: "When they gave it to him, so-and-so and so-and-so were present." Furthermore let him not leave it in his house; let him offer it for sale. However, when he sells it, let him not sell it in a secret place; let the lords of Hatti be present, and let them observe. And let them make an inventory of what the purchaser buys, and let them seal it in his presence. Moreover, when the king comes up to Hattusas, let him take it directly to the palace, and let them seal it for him. If, however, he (the recipient of the gift) exchanges it just as he pleases (without due formality), there is the capital penalty for him. But whoever is not selling a gift of the king, for which the king's name has been stamped upon a tablet, and he nevertheless sells silver, gold, garments, or bronze utensils, and whoever receives it and hides it, and does not bring it to the royal gate, for them both there is the capital penalty; let them both die. . . . Let there not be pardon for them.

10. Now you who are temple officials in the temple, be very careful of the reputation of the precinct. At nightfall promptly go down into the town; and eat and drink, and if thoughts of a woman overcome anyone, let him sleep with a woman. And as long as the omens are favorable for them, let them stay. Afterwards let each come up to the temple to spend the night, whoever is a temple official—great priests, small priests, and all *imme*-priests—and whoever else opens the temple door. Let them severally not neglect to spend the night up in the temple. Furthermore, at night let patrolmen be chosen, and let them patrol all night. Outside in the precinct let the keepers watch; but inside in the temples let the temple officials patrol all night; and let them not sleep. Now from night to night let one important priest be in command of the patrolmen. And besides, of those who are priests, let someone be door-keeper; let him guard the temple. Let no one spend the night in his own house with his wife; and whomsoever they find down in his own house, it is a capital offense for him. Now of your own accord guard the temples diligently; and do not sleep. Furthermore, let the precinct be divided among you; then the one in whose part of the precinct sin occurs shall die; let him not be pardoned.

12. Furthermore, you priests, *imme*-priests, mothers of god, temple officials, some voluntary giver of a festival might get drunk in a temple or in another sacred building. If he gets drunk in the temple and causes a quarrel, and

then injures the festival, let them injure him; let him later perform that festival set up with cattle, sheep, bread, and beer; let him not omit even the thin bread. Whoever avoids the festival, and does not perform the festival fully set up, let that be a great sin for him; thereafter let him repeat the festival. Now be very much afraid of a drunken quarrel.

17. Now you who care for the plow oxen belonging to the granary on the lands of the temple, if you sell a plow ox, or kill it and eat it, and if you conceal it from the gods, saying: "It died from thinness, or it had been smashing things, or it ran away, or a bull gored it"; and you eat it up; and it nevertheless afterwards becomes known; you will replace that ox. But if it does not become known, and you go before the god—if you are acquitted, it is due to your protecting deity; if you are convicted, it is a capital sin for you.

19. Again, if in the temple properties you ever castrate animals, and they bring the castrated animals to the gods, your lords, let the cow-herd or shepherd go with the castrated animals; and as it has been castrated from the stable or the fold, just so let them bring it in to the gods; and let them not later, on the road, make an exchange. But if any cow-herd or shepherd does wrong on the road, and then exchanges a fat ox or a fat sheep, and makes a trade, or if he kills it and they eat it up, and put in its place a thin animal, and it becomes known, that is a capital sin for them; they have taken the best meat of the gods' desire. But if it does not become known, whenever they arrive, thereupon let them take down from the stand the cup of the god of life. Let them deliver the animals with these words: "If we have drawn forth for ourselves the best meat from the mouth of the gods, and have devoted it to ourselves, or have sold it for ourselves, or have accepted pay and made a trade for ourselves and have put in its place a thin animal, then do thou, god, pursue us, with our wives and our children, on account of the meat of thy desire."

The first tablet of the duties of all the temple officials, of the kitchen workers of the gods, of the farmers of the gods, and of the cow-herds of the god, and the shepherds of the god, is finished.

# 17 Plague Prayers

In the "Plague Prayers of Mursilis" the vigor of Hittite religious literature is illustrated, as well as that repetitiousness which is so evident a feature of ancient Near Eastern literature, both religious and secular. Mursilis reigned in the late fourteenth century B.C. The appeal by the king himself attests to the seriousness of the medical situation in which appeal is made to the gods and especially to the Storm-god, the chief of the Hittite pantheon. Only the first half of the prayer has been retained in the following selection. The translation is by Albrecht Goetze.

❀❀❀❀❀

1. Hattian Storm-god, my lord, and ye, Hattian gods, my lords! Mursilis,[1] the great king, your servant, has sent me with the order: Go! To the Hattian Storm-god, my lord, and to the gods, my lords, speak as follows: What is this that ye have done? A plague ye have let into the land. The Hatti land has been cruelly afflicted by the plague. For twenty years now men have been dying in my father's days, in my brother's days, and in mine own since I have become the priest of the gods. When men are dying in the Hatti land like this, the plague is in no wise over. As for me, the agony of my heart and the anguish of my soul I cannot endure any more.

2. When I celebrated festivals, I worshiped all the gods, I never preferred one temple to another. The matter of the plague I have laid in prayer before all the gods making vows to them and saying: "Hearken to me, ye gods, my lords! Drive ye forth the plague from the Hatti land! The reason for which people are dying in the Hatti land—either let it be established by an omen, or let me see it in a dream, or let a prophet declare it!" But the gods did not hearken to me and the plague got no better in the Hatti land. The Hatti land was cruelly afflicted.

3. The few people who were left to give sacrificial loaves and libations were dying too. Matters again got too much for me. So I made the anger of the gods the subject of an oracle. I learnt of two ancient tablets. The first tablet dealt with the offerings to the river Mala. The old kings had regularly presented offerings to the river Mala. But now a plague has been rampant

SOURCE: Reprinted from *Ancient Near Eastern Texts Relating to the Old Testament* ed. James B. Pritchard by permission of Princeton University Press. Copyright, 1950, by Princeton University Press.

1. Hittite king, son of Suppiluliumas; see Selection 22.

in the Hatti land since the days of my father, and we have never performed the offerings to the river Mala.

4. The second tablet concerned Kurustama. When the Hattian Storm-god had brought people of Kurustama to the country of Egypt and had made an agreement concerning them with the Hattians so that they were under oath to the Hattian Storm-god—although the Hattians as well as the Egyptians were under oath to the Hattian Storm-god, the Hattians ignored their obligations; the Hattians promptly broke the oath of the gods. My father sent foot soldiers and charioteers who attacked the country of Amka,[2] Egyptian territory. Again he sent troops, and again they attacked it. When the Egyptians became frightened, they asked outright for one of his sons to take over the kingship. But when my father gave them one of his sons, they killed him as they led him there. My father let his anger run away with him, he went to war against Egypt and attacked Egypt. He smote the foot soldiers and the charioteers of the country of Egypt. The Hattian Storm-god, my lord, by his decision even then let my father prevail; he vanquished and smote the foot soldiers and the charioteers of the country of Egypt. But when they brought back to the Hatti land the prisoners which they had taken a plague broke out among the prisoners and they began to die.

5. When they moved the prisoners to the Hatti land, these prisoners carried the plague into the Hatti land. From that day on people have been dying in the Hatti land. Now, when I found that tablet dealing with the country of Egypt, I made the matter the subject of an oracle of the god and asked: "Those arrangements which were made by the Hattian Storm-god—namely that the Egyptians and the Hattians as well were put under oath by the Hattian Storm-god, that the Damnassaras deities were present in the temple of the Hattian Storm-god, and that the Hattians promptly broke their word—has this perhaps become the cause of the anger of the Hattian Storm-god, my lord?" And so it was established.

6. Because of the plague, I made the offerings to the river Mala the subject of an oracle also. And in that matter too it was established that I should have to account for myself before the Hattian Storm-god. See now! I have admitted my guilt before the Storm-god and said: "It is so. We have done it." I know for certain that the offence was not committed in my days, that it was committed in the days of my father. . . . But, since the Hattian Storm-god is angry for that reason and people are dying in the Hatti land, I am nevertheless making the offerings to the Hattian Storm-god, my lord, on that account.

2.   The region between Lebanon and Antilibanus.

7. Because I humble myself and cry for mercy, hearken to me, Hattian Storm-god, my lord! Let the plague stop in the Hatti land!

8. The reasons for the plague that were established when I made the matter the subject of a series of oracles, these have I removed. I have made ample restitution. The matter of the broken oath which was established as a cause in connection with the plague, offerings for those oaths I have made to the Hattian Storm-god, my lord. I have also made offerings to the other gods. The offerings have been presented to thee, Hattian Storm-god, my lord; the offerings have been presented to them too. As for the offerings to the river Mala that were established as a cause in connection with the plague—since I am now on my way to the river Mala, acquit me of that offering to the river Mala, O Hattian Storm-god my lord, and ye gods, my lords! The offering to the river Mala I promise to make, I promise to complete it properly. The reason for which I make it—namely the plague—O gods, my lords, take pity on me and let that plague abate in the Hatti land!

# 18  *Apology of Hattusilis*

Hattusilis III ruled the Hittite empire from about 1275 to about 1250 B.C. His claim to the throne was in question, and he wrote an autobiographical narrative in an effort to justify his career against any charge of usurpation. This document, that has come to be known as the "Apology of Hattusilis," is especially remarkable as a contribution to historical writing. Although it is scarcely impartial, it comes much closer to what we would call narrative history than do the boastful annals (such as Selection 19) or the bare chronological memoranda (such as Selection 30) that are most typical of the earliest historical writing. It may be instructive to compare the work in this respect to the Biblical account of King David's reign (Selection 26). The translation (slightly abridged) is by E. H. Sturtevant and G. Bechtel.

❀❀❀❀❀

Thus speaks King Hattusilis, the great king, king of the land of Hatti, son of Mursilis, the great king, king of the land of Hatti, grandson of Suppululiumas, the great king, king of the land of Hatti, descendant of Hattusilis, king of the city of Kussaras.

SOURCE: Edgar H. Sturtevant and George Bechtel, *A Hittite Chrestomathy* (William Dwight Whitney Linguistic Series) (Philadelphia: Linguistic Society of America and University of Pennsylvania, 1935). Reprinted by permission of Professor Konstantin Reichardt for the Whitney Linguistic Series.

I tell Ishtar's divine power; let mankind hear it. And in the future among the gods of My Majesty, of his son, of his grandson, of the descendants of My Majesty, let there be reverence to Ishtar.

My father Mursilis begot us four children, Halpasulupis, Muwattallis, Hattusilis, and Dingirmesiris, a daughter. Now of them all I was the last child. And while I was still a child and was groom, My Lady Ishtar by means of a dream sent to my father Mursilis my brother Muwattallis with this message: "For Hattusilis the years are short; he is not to live. Now give him to me; and let him be my priest. Then he shall be alive." And my father took me, still a child, and gave me to the goddess for service. And, serving as priest to the goddess, I poured libations. And so at the hand of My Lady Ishtar I saw prosperity. And My Lady Ishtar took me by the hand; and she guided me.

But when my father Mursilis became a god, and my brother Muwattallis sat upon the throne of his father, I became a general in the presence of my brother, and then my brother appointed me to the office of chief of the Mesedi,[1] and gave me the Upper Country to rule. Then I governed the Upper Country. Before me, however, Armadattas, son of Zidas, had been ruling it. Now because My Lady Ishtar had favored me and my brother Muwattallis was well disposed toward me, when people saw My Lady Ishtar's favor toward me and my brother's kindness, they envied me. And Armadattas, son of Zidas, and other men too began to stir up ill will against me. They brought malice against me, and I had bad luck; and my brother Muwattallis named me for the wheel.[2] My Lady Ishtar, however, appeared to me in a dream, and by means of the dream said this to me: "Shall I abandon you to a hostile deity? Fear not." And I was cleared from the hostile deity. And since the goddess, My Lady, held me by the hand, she did not ever abandon me to the hostile deity, the hostile court; and the weapon of my enemy never overthrew me. My Lady Ishtar always rescued me. If ever ill-health befell me, even while ill I observed the goddess's divine power. The goddess, My Lady, always held me by the hand. Because I, for my part, was an obedient man, and because I walked before the gods in obedience, I never pursued the evil course of mankind. Thou, goddess, My Lady, dost always rescue me. Has it not been so? In fact, the goddess, My Lady, did not ever in time of danger pass me by; to an enemy she did not ever abandon me, and no more to my opponents in court, my enviers, did

1. The Mesedi were high officials of the royal court.
2. The metaphorical phrase is probably to be understood in a judicial context, something like "brought an indictment against me."

she abandon me. If it was a plot of an enemy, if it was a plot of an opponent at law, if it was a plot of the palace, My Lady Ishtar always held over me protection. She always rescued me. Envious enemies My Lady Ishtar put into my hand; and I destroyed them utterly.

When, however, my brother Muwattallis came to understand the matter, and there remained no ill repute against me, he took me back; and he put the infantry and charioteers of the land of Hatti into my hand, and I commanded all the infantry and charioteers of the land of Hatti. And my brother Muwattallis used to send me on expeditions. And as My Lady Ishtar had granted me her favor, wherever among the countries of the enemy I turned my eyes, not an enemy turned back his eyes upon me. And I kept conquering the countries of the enemy. The favor of My Lady Ishtar, as ever, was mine. And whatever enemy there was within the lands of Hatti, I drove clear out of the lands of Hatti. However, what countries of the enemy I conquered while I was a minor, that I shall make into a tablet separately; and I shall set it up before the goddess.

When, however, my brother Muwattallis at the command of his patron deity went down to the Lower Country and left Hattusas, my brother took the gods of Hatti and the Manes and carried them down into the Lower Country. During his absence all the land of Gasga, the land of Pishurus, the land of Ishupitta, and the land of Daistipassa revolted.[3] And they took away the land of Landas and the land of Maristas and the fortified cities. And the enemy crossed the Halys and he began to attack the land of . . . and he began to attack the land of Kanes. . . . However H . . ., Kurustamas, and Gaziuras immediately made war, and they began to attack the ruined cities of Hatti. The enemy from the land of Durmittas, however, began to attack the land of Tuhuppiya. And since the land of Ippassanama was deserted, he kept making incursions into the country of Suwatara. And only the cities of . . . and Istaharas escaped. But in the districts that had been cut off they did not plant seed for ten years. Thenceforth, moreover, during the years while my brother Muwattallis was in the land of Hatti, all the Gasga countries made war; and they devastated the land of Sadduppa and the land of Dankuwa. Now my brother Muwattallis sent me into the field, and established my headquarters in Pattiyarigas. However, he gave me troops and charioteers in small numbers. Now I took with me auxiliary troops of the country in small numbers; and I marched and cut the enemy off in Hahhas, and I gave him battle. Then My Lady Ishtar

3.  The cities and regions of the Hittite empire that are named here and in the following passages are for the most part not identifiable with certainty.

marched before me, and I defeated him. And I set up a trophy. And every Hittite he had brought with him I took away and established again in his former dwelling place. Moreover, I took his allies and delivered them to my brother. And this was my first manly deed; My Lady Ishtar in this campaign for the first time proclaimed my name. . . .

[*The following omitted passage recounts Hattusilis' military achievements.*]

And he (Muwattallis) gave me these depopulated countries to govern. I ruled over the country of Ishupitta, the country of Maristas, the country of Hissashapa, the country of Katapas, the country of Hanhana, the country of Darahna, the country of Hattena, the country of Durmittas, the country of Pala, the country of Tumanna, the country of Gassiya, the country of Sappa, the country of the Yellow River, the charioteers and all the golden grooms. The land of Hakpissas, moreover, and the land of Istaharas he gave me to be my subjects; and he made me king in the land of Hakpissas. Now in the above mentioned depopulated countries which my brother had put into my hands, since My Lady Ishtar held me by the hand, I conquered some enemies and others made peace with me. And My Lady Ishtar stood with me. And these depopulated countries I myself caused to be inhabited again. And I made them Hittite again.

When once my brother came and marched against the land of Egypt,[4] these countries which I had caused to be inhabited again—the army and charioteers of this country I led for my brother's campaign against the land of Egypt. Now because, in the presence of my brother, infantry and charioteers of the land of Hatti were in my hands, I commanded them. Now when Armadattas, son of Zidas, saw the kindness to me of My Lady Ishtar and of my brother, he nevertheless did not in any respect show them any reverence; and thereupon he with his wife and his sons tried to bewitch me. And he filled Samuhas, the city of the goddess, with witchcraft. When, however, I was on my way back from the land of Egypt, I journeyed to Lawazantiyas to pour libations to the goddess; and I worshipped the goddess. And at the command of the goddess I took in marriage Puduhepas, the daughter of Pentipsarris, the priest. And we founded a family, and the goddess gave us the love of husband and wife. And we got us sons and daughters. Furthermore the goddess, My Lady, said to me: "Do you with your house be subject to me." And with my house I was true to the god-

---

4. The campaign against Ramses II, the ultimate result of which was the treaty presented in Selection 23.

dess. And for us the goddess dwelt within the house that we were making us. . . . Hakpissas, however, revolted; and I drove out the men of the Gasga countries, and I subjected it. And I became king of the land of Hakpissas and you became queen of the land of Hakpissas.

When, however, an indictment was brought again from the palace, My Lady Ishtar at that time also showed her divine power. And she brought a new indictment out of the indictment. Now they found witchcraft in Armadattas along with his wife and his sons, and they established it against him; and he had filled even Samuhas, the city of the goddess, with witchcraft. Now the goddess, My Lady, made him lose the case to me; and my brother delivered him to me with his wife, his sons, and his house. Then my brother said to me: "Sippaluis is not in it." And because my brother made me, the innocent party, victorious in the trial, I did not thereafter repay him in malice. Now because Armadattas was a man related to me, and besides he was an aged man, and he was ill, I let him off. And I let Sippaluis off. When, however, I had let them off and had done nothing to them, I actually sent Armadattas and his son to Alasiya, and I took half of his estate and gave it back to Armadattas.

And my brother died. I, however, firm in my respect for my brother, did not act selfishly; but, as at this time my brother did not yet have a legitimate son, I took Urhitesupas, the son of a secondary wife, and set him in authority in the land of Hatti. And I put all the army in his hands. And in the lands of Hatti he was the great king. I, however, was king in Hakpissas. And with army and charioteers I took the field. And, since Nerikkas had been in ruins from the day of Hantilis,[5] I took it and rebuilt it. And the countries which were near Nerikkas and had made Neras and Hassuras their boundary, all these I subjected and made tributaries. . . .

Now when Urhitesupas thus observed the kindness of the goddess to me, he envied me, and he brought ill will upon me. He took away from me all my subjects; Samuhas also he took away from me; the depopulated lands also that I had settled again, all those too he took away from me, and he made me weak. Hakpissas, however, according to the command of a god he did not take away from me. Because I was priest of the storm god of Nerikkas, for that reason he did not take it away from me. And, firm in my respect for my brother, I did not act selfishly. And for seven years I submitted. But Urhitesupas at the command of a god and the suggestion of man tried to destroy me. And he took Hakpissas and Nerikkas away from me. And I did not submit any longer. And I made war upon him. But

5. Ruled in the first half of the sixteenth century B.C.

when I made war upon him, I did not do it as a crime. Did I rebel against him in the chariot or rebel against him within the palace? I sent him a declaration of war as an open enemy: "You started hostilities with me. Now you are a great king; but as for me, the one fortress that you have left me— of that one I am king. Come! Ishtar of Samuhas and the storm god of Nerikkas shall decide the case for us." Now whereas I wrote Urhitesupas thus, if any one speaks as follows: "Why did you formerly establish him on the throne? And why are you now declaring war upon him?" I answer, "Very well, if he had never started hostilities with me." Would the gods have subjected a great king who was upright to a small king? Now because he started hostilities with me, they subjected him to me in the trial. Now when I communicated these words to him, saying "Come on" to him, he marched out from Marassantiyas, and came to the Upper Country. And Sippaluis, the son of Armadattas, was with him. And he appointed him to gather the troops of the Upper Country. But because Sippaluis was hostile to me, he did not succeed against me.

Now, while My Lady Ishtar had even before this been promising me the kingship, at that time My Lady Ishtar appeared to my wife in a dream: "I shall march before your husband. And all Hattusas shall be led with your husband. Since I thought highly of him, I did not—no, not ever— abandon him to the hostile trial, the hostile deity. Now also I will exalt him, and make him priest of the sun goddess of Arinnas. Do you also make me, Ishtar, your patron deity." And My Lady Ishtar stood behind me; and whatever she promised me occurred. And My Lady Ishtar then also showed me her divine power abundantly. To whatever nobles Urhitesupas had ever banished My Lady Ishtar appeared in a dream: "You are summoned to your strength; but I, Ishtar, have turned all the lands of Hatti to the side of Hattusilis." And then also I saw the divine power of Ishtar abundantly. Whereas she did not ever at another time abandon Urhitesupas, she shut him up in Samuhas like a pig in a sty. As for me, however, the Gasga men who had been hostile supported me; and all Hattusas supported me. But, firm in my respect for my brother, I did not act selfishly. And I marched back to Samuhas to be with Urhitesupas and I brought him down like a captive. And I gave him fortified towns in the land of Nuhasse, and he dwelt there. He would have planned another plan, and would have proceeded into the land of Karaduniya; but when I heard of the matter, I arrested him and banished him across the sea. And they sent Sippaluis across the border; but I took his house from him, and gave it to My Lady Ishtar. Now I gave that to My Lady Ishtar, and My Lady Ishtar thereafter granted me desire after desire.

Now I was a prince, and became chief of the Mesedi. Again I, chief of the Mesedi, became king of Hakpissas. Again I, king of Hakpissas, later became a great king. Thereupon My Lady Ishtar put into my hands my enviers, enemies, and opponents at law. And some of them died by the weapon, but others died on the appointed day; and I completely got rid of them all. And My Lady Ishtar gave me the kingship of the land of Hatti also, and I became a great king. My Lady Ishtar took me as a prince and placed me on the throne. And those who had been well disposed toward the kings, my predecessors, became well disposed toward me. And they began to send me messengers, and they began to send me gifts as well. But such gifts as they kept sending me, they had not sent to any of my fathers and forefathers. On the other hand, whatever king owed me homage paid me homage. But the lands that were hostile to me I conquered; I annexed district after district to the lands of Hatti. And those who had been hostile in the time of my fathers and of my forefathers made peace with me. And since the goddess, my Lady, had thus favored me, being firm in my loyalty to my brother, I did not act selfishly. And I took my brother's son Kalas, and set him upon a throne in the very spot, namely Dattasas, which my brother Muwattallis used for his palace. Insignificant as I was when thou, My Lady Ishtar, didst take me, thou didst set me in the high place in the land of Hatti, upon the throne. For my part I gave My Lady Ishtar the house of Armadattas. I consecrated it and gave it to her. What was there previously, I gave her; and what I had, that also I gave. I consecrated it and gave it to the goddess. Furthermore, as to the house of Armadattas that I gave her, and the cities that belonged to Armadattas, behind every one they are again setting up her statue, and distributing libation cups. Ishtar is my goddess, and for themselves men pour libations to Ishtar, the Highest. Whatever mausoleum I have built, that I have given to the goddess. And my son Duthaliyas I gave for thy service; may my son Duthaliyas[6] rule the house of Ishtar. I am the servant of the goddess; let him also be the servant of the goddess. . . .

In the future whatever son, grandson, or future descendant of Hattusilis and Puduhepas ascends the throne, let him be reverent toward Ishtar of Samuhas among the gods.

6.   Ruled from c. 1250 to c. 1220 B.C.

# INTERNATIONAL RELATIONS

W ITH the spreading of civilization the world of the second millennium B.C. became one of nations and national rivalries, of conquests and empires. In the second half of that thousand-year period the most noteworthy achievements of civilization were in the broad area of international relations. This being a field in which mankind up to our own day has not been markedly successful, it may be excessive to speak of "achievements." Still, it is important to observe—if only to see how little progress has since been made—that in this remote period of history practically all the apparatus of international affairs was developed: diplomacy and formal diplomatic correspondence, propaganda and patriotic bragging, treaties and trade agreements, techniques of imperial rule, dynastic marriages, and—perhaps most important of all—the arts of warfare and conquest.

# 19 *Asiatic Campaigns of Thut-mose III*

Under the Hyksos the Egyptians had learned new techniques in the art of war, notably the use of the horse and the war chariot and of arrows tipped with metal. The belligerence that expelled the Hyksos was turned to a vigorous policy of aggression, and the boundaries of Egypt were extended eastward into Asia. The pharaoh who did most for the building of a powerful Egyptian empire was Thut-mose III, "the Napoleon of Egypt," who was on the throne for some forty-two years spanning most of the first half of the fifteenth century until his death in 1449 B.C. For the first twenty years he shared the rule with his wife Hat-shepsut. The only important female ruler of pharaonic Egypt, Hat-shepsut kept affairs of state in her own hands. After her death Thut-mose, released from his subordinate position, launched the career of conquest that saw him almost incessantly at war for the rest of his reign.

The "Asiatic Campaigns of Thut-mose III" are narratives of the military expeditions in which the pharaoh established Egyptian power in Syria-Palestine. They are abridged from a number of different inscriptions in which he officially recorded his deeds. The long first part of the selection recounts the details of the capture of the powerful Canaanite fortress city Megiddo during Thut-mose's first campaign. The translation is by James H. Breasted (*Ancient Records of Egypt,* Vol. II).

⊕⊕⊕⊕⊕

### INTRODUCTION

His Majesty commanded to cause to be recorded his victories which his father, Amon, gave to him, upon a tablet in the temple which His Majesty made for his father, Amon, setting forth each expedition by its name, together with the plunder which His Majesty carried away therein. It was done according to all the command which his father, Re, gave to him.

### FIRST CAMPAIGN

Year 23, first month of the third season, on the fifth day. Departure from this place in might . . . in power, and in triumph, to overthrow that wretched foe, to extend the boundaries of Egypt, according as his father, Amon-Re, had commanded that he seize.

Year 23, first month of the third season, on the sixteenth day. Arrival at the city of Yehem. His Majesty ordered a consultation with his valiant troops, saying as follows: "That wretched enemy, the chief of Kadesh, has come and entered into Megiddo; he is there at this moment. He has gathered to himself the chiefs of all the countries which are subject to Egypt, and as far as Naharin,[1] consisting of the countries of the Kharu, the Kode, their horses, their troops. Thus he speaks, 'I have arisen to fight against His Majesty in Megiddo.' "

. . . His Majesty halted outside and waited there, protecting the rear of his victorious army. Behold, when the front had reached the exit upon this road, the shadow had turned, and when His Majesty arrived at the south of Megiddo on the bank of the brook of Kina, the seventh hour was turning, measured by the sun.

Then was set up the camp of His Majesty, and command was given to the whole army, saying: "Equip yourselves! Prepare your weapons, for we

1. Northwestern Mesopotamia, the region around the great bend of the Euphrates River.

shall advance to fight with that wretched foe in the morning." Therefore the king rested in the royal tent, the affairs of the chiefs were arranged, and the provisions of the attendants. The watch of the army went about, saying: "Steady of heart! Steady of heart! Watchful! Watchful! Watch for life at the tent of the king." One came to say to His Majesty: "The land is well, and the infantry of the South and North likewise."

Year 23, first month of the third season, on the twentieth day, the day of the feast of the new moon, corresponding to the royal coronation. Early in the morning, behold, command was given to the entire army to move. His Majesty went forth in a chariot of electrum, arrayed in his weapons of war, like Horus, the Smiter, lord of power; like Montu of Thebes, while his father, Amon, strengthened his arms.

The southern wing of this army of His Majesty was on a hill south of the brook of Kina, the northern wing was at the northwest of Megiddo, while His Majesty was in their center, with Amon as the protection of his members, the valor of his limbs. Then His Majesty prevailed against them at the head of his army, and when they saw His Majesty prevailing against them they fled headlong to Megiddo in fear, abandoning their horses and their chariots of gold and silver. The people hauled them up, pulling them by their clothing into the city. The people of the city, having closed it against them, lowered clothing to pull them up into the city. Now, if only the army of His Majesty had not given their heart to plundering the things of the enemy, they would have captured Megiddo at this moment, when the wretched foe of Kadesh and the wretched foe of this city were hauled up in haste to bring them into the city. The fear of His Majesty had entered their hearts, their arms were powerless, his serpent diadem was victorious among them.

Then were captured their horses, their chariots of gold and silver were made spoil; their champions lay stretched out like fishes on the ground. The victorious army of His Majesty went around counting their portions. Behold, there was captured the tent of that wretched foe in which was his son. The whole army made jubilee, giving praise to Amon for the victory which he had granted to his son on this day, giving praise to His Majesty, exalting his victories. They brought up the booty which they had taken, consisting of hands, of living prisoners, of horse, chariots of gold and silver, of. . . .

Then spoke His Majesty on hearing the words of his army, saying: "Had ye captured this city, behold, I would have given very many offerings to Re this day; because every chief of every country that has revolted is in it;

and because it is the capture of a thousand cities, this capture of Megiddo. Capture ye mightily, mightily!"

His Majesty commanded the officers of the troops, assigning to each his place. They measured the city, surrounding it with an enclosure, walled about with green timber from all their pleasant trees. His Majesty himself stood upon the fortification east of the city, inspecting. It was walled about with a thick wall. The wall's name was made: "Men-kheper-Re [Thut-mose III]-Is-the-Surrounder-of-the-Asiatics." People were stationed to watch over the tent of His Majesty; to whom it was said: "Steady of heart! Watch!" His Majesty commanded, saying: "Let not one among them come forth outside, beyond this wall, except to come out in order to offer them-selves as prisoners."

Now, all that His Majesty did to this city, to that wretched foe and his wretched army, was recorded on each day by the day's name, under the title of. . . . Then it was recorded upon a roll of leather in the temple of Amon this day.

Behold, the chiefs of the country came to render their portions, to do obeisance to the fame of His Majesty, to crave breath for their nostrils, because of the greatness of his power, because of the might of the fame of His Majesty. . . . They came, bearing their gifts, consisting of silver, gold, lapis lazuli, malachite; bringing clean grain, wine, large cattle, and small cattle—for the army of His Majesty. Each of the Kode bore the tribute southward. Behold, His Majesty appointed the chiefs anew. . . .

*[The spoils from Megiddo]*

. . . 340 living prisoners; 83 hands; 2,041 mares; 191 foals; 6 stallions; . . .; a chariot, wrought with gold, its pole of gold, belonging to that foe; a beautiful chariot, wrought with gold, belonging to the chief of Megiddo; . . . ; 892 chariots of his wretched army; total, 924 chariots; a beautiful suit of bronze armor, belonging to that foe; a beautiful suit of bronze armor, belonging to the chief of Megiddo; . . . ; 200 suits of armor, belonging to his wretched army; 502 bows; 7 poles of *mry*-wood, wrought with silver, belonging to the tent of that foe. Behold, the army of His Majesty took . . . , 297 . . . , 1,929 large cattle, 2,000 small cattle, 20,500 white small cattle.

List of that which was afterwards taken by the king, of the household goods of that foe who was in the city of Yenoam, in Nuges, and in Heren-keru, together with all the goods of those cities which submitted them-selves, which were brought to His Majesty: 474 . . . ; 38 lords[2] of theirs, 87

2. Members of the warrior or officer class.

children of that foe and of the chiefs who were with him, 5 lords of theirs, 1,796 male and female slaves with their children, non-combatants who surrendered because of famine with that foe, 103 men; total, 2,503. Besides, flat dishes of costly stone and gold, various vessels, . . . , a large two-handled vase of the work of Kharu, . . . -vases, flat dishes, . . . -dishes, various drinking vessels, 3 large kettles, 87 knives, amounting to 784 *deben*. Gold in rings found in the hands of the artificers, and silver in many rings, 966 *deben* and 1 *ḳidet*. A silver statue in beaten work, . . . the head of gold, the staff with human faces; 6 chairs of that foe, of ivory, ebony, and carob wood, wrought with gold; 6 footstools belonging to them; 6 large tables of ivory and carob wood, a staff of carob wood, wrought with gold and all costly stones in the fashion of a scepter, belonging to that foe, all of it wrought with gold; a statue of that foe, of ebony wrought with gold, the head of which was inlaid with lapis lazuli . . . ; vessels of bronze, much clothing of that foe.

Behold, the cultivable land was divided into fields, which the inspectors of the royal house—life, prosperity, health!—calculated, in order to reap their harvest. Statement of the harvest which was brought to His Majesty from the fields of Megiddo: 208,200 fourfold *heḳet* of grain, besides that which was cut as forage by the army of His Majesty.

## FIFTH CAMPAIGN

Year 29. Behold, His Majesty was in Zahi[3] subduing the countries revolting against him, on the fifth victorious campaign. . . .

List of the plunder taken out of this city, from the infantry of that foe of Tunip: the chief of this city, 1; warriors, 329; silver, 100 *deben;* gold, 100 *deben;* lapis lazuli, malachite, vessels of bronze and copper.

Behold, ships were taken, laden with everything, with slaves male and female; copper, lead, emery, and everything good. Afterward His Majesty proceeded southward to Egypt, to his father, Amon-Re, with joy of heart.

Behold, His Majesty overthrew the city of Arvad, with its grain, cutting down all its pleasant trees. Behold, there were found the products of all Zahi. Their gardens were filled with their fruit, their wines were found remaining in their presses as water flows, their grain on the terraces; it was more plentiful than the sand of the shore. The army were overwhelmed with their portions. . . . Behold, the army of His Majesty was drunk and anointed with oil every day as at a feast in Egypt.

3. Syria-Palestine.

THE AUTOBIOGRAPHY OF AMEN-EM-HEB[4]

The officer, Amen-em-heb; he says:

"I was the very faithful one of the sovereign—life, prosperity, health!—the wise-hearted of the King of Upper Egypt, the excellent-hearted of the King of Lower Egypt. I followed my lord on his expeditions in the northern and the southern country. He desired that I should be the companion of his feet, while he was upon the battlefield of his victories, while his valor fortified the heart.

"I fought hand to hand in the land of Negev. I brought off three men, Asiatics, as living prisoners.

"When His Majesty came to Naharin I brought off three men from the fight there; I set them before Thy Majesty as living prisoners.

"Again I fought hand to hand in the expedition in the land of 'The-Height-of-Wan' on the west of Aleppo. I brought off 13 Asiatics as living prisoners, 13 men; 70 living asses; 13 bronze spears; the bronze was wrought with gold.

"Again I fought in the expedition in the land of Carchemish. I brought off . . . as living prisoners. I crossed over the water of Naharin, while they were in my hand, to . . . ; I set them before my lord. He rewarded me with a great reward; list thereof: . . . .

"Again I beheld his bravery, while I was among his followers. He captured the city of Kadesh; I was not absent from the place where he was; I brought off two men, lords, as living prisoners; I set them before the king, the Lord of the Two Lands, Thut-mose III, living forever. He gave to me gold because of bravery, before the whole people; list thereof: of the finest gold, a lion; 2 necklaces, 2 flies, 4 arm rings. . . .

"Again I beheld another excellent deed which the Lord of the Two Lands did in Niy. He hunted 120 elephants, for the sake of their tusks and. . . . I engaged the largest which was among them, which fought against His Majesty; I cut off his hand[5] while he was alive, before His Majesty, while I stood in the water between two rocks. Then my lord rewarded me with gold; he gave . . . and three changes of clothing.

"The prince of Kadesh sent forth a mare before the army; in order to . . .[6] she entered among the army. I pursued her on foot, with my sword, and I ripped open her belly; I cut off her tail, I set it before the king; while

4.  From the wall paintings in the tomb of an Egyptian soldier in Thebes.
5.  Presumably the elephant's trunk is meant.
6.  To arouse the stallions of the Egyptian chariots and throw the battle line into confusion.

there was thanksgiving to god for it! He gave me joy, it filled my body, with rejoicing he endued my limbs.

"His Majesty sent forth every valiant man of his army, in order to pierce the wall for the first time, which Kadesh had made. I was the one who pierced it, being the first of all the valiant; no other before me did it. I went forth, I brought off 2 men, lords, as living prisoners. Again my lord rewarded me because of it, with every good thing for satisfying the heart."

# 20 Diplomatic Correspondence

The most striking event of the Empire period is the so-called "Amarna Revolution." Amen-hotep IV came to the throne in 1380 B.C. as a young man. He promptly set about deliberately creating a break with the ancient and static traditions of his country. His revolution centers about his instituting the worship of Aton as the new chief deity of Egypt to supplant Amon, whose great temple at Thebes had been the religious center of the nation. To symbolize this revolution he changed his name to Akh-en-Aton (or Akhnaton or Ikhnaton) and moved his capital from Thebes to Aketaton (the modern village of el-Amarna), where he built a palace and a whole new city.

The actual motives of the Amarna Revolution are obscure. Most historians emphasize its purely religious aspect, observing that in a hymn to Aton, supposedly written by the pharaoh himself, the deity is presented as the god of all living things. From this, Akh-en-Aton has been called "the first monotheist in history," a clearly erroneous claim in that the king made no effort to abolish the worship of the other traditional gods. On balance, whatever its ultimate goals, Akh-en-Aton's revolution seems to have been aimed at a thoroughgoing renovation of all aspects of Egyptian life. Its character is most strikingly seen in the remains of the art of the period, in which there is a realism quite foreign to the stylized rigidity of traditional Egyptian art. The king himself is regularly depicted in contemporary portraits with a startling realism that emphasizes his deformed legs, while the portraits of his queen, Nefer-titi, have made her features one of the best-known symbols of feminine beauty that the ancient world has left to us.

In the political realm Akh-en-Aton's revolution can best be seen as an effort to restore to the monarchy the power it had been steadily losing to the major priesthoods, especially that of Amon. The priestly estates had become immensely rich by the grants of land given by each succeeding pharaoh upon his accession to the throne and accumulated through the centuries. Akh-en-Aton did not succeed in breaking the power of the priests, and immediately after his death in 1362 B.C. the revolution was overthrown. The new capital of Aket-aton was destroyed and the site was abandoned. This has turned out to be a boon to the historian, for nearly four hundred clay tablets have been unearthed there. They form a part of the diplomatic correspondence from the royal archives during the last years of Amen-hotep III and his successor Akh-en-Aton. Most of them are written in Akkadian, the international language of the Near East at the time, and are from the puppet princelings of Syria-Palestine through whom the pharaohs maintained their control—with the aid of Egyptian troops. From these documents some historians have inferred a neglect of his imperial possessions by Akh-en-Aton, preoccupied with the struggle to establish his domestic revolution. For the student of diplomatic history the "Amarna Letters" are a fascinating treasure, with their fine combination of pleas, flattery, veiled threats, whining, protestations of loyalty, slander—and, again and again, requests for more money and more troops. Of the selected letters that follow, numbers 1, 2, 4, 5, 6, and 8 are translated by the present editor from the German translation by J. A. Knudtzon (*Die El-Amarna Tafeln*, nos. 137, 244, 252, 254, 270, and 280); number 3 from the French translation by F. Thureau-Dangin (*Revue d'Assyriologie*, 1922, pp. 97–98); and number 7 from the French translation by G. Dossin (*Revue d'Assyriologie*, 1934, pp. 126–128).

@@@@@@

I

Rib-addi[1] spoke to the king, his lord, the Sun of the lands:

Beneath the foot of the king, my lord, seven and seven times I prostrate myself. I have repeatedly written for garrison troops, but they have not been given, and the king, my lord, has not listened to the words of his servant. And I sent my messenger to the palace, but he returned empty-handed: he had no garrison troops. The people of my palace became aware of the situation: since no silver was given to me they, like my brother governors, insulted and despised me.

Further: I have gone to Hamuniri[2]; and my younger brother is subvert-

1. Prince of Byblos.
2. Prince of Berytus (Beirut).

ing Byblos in order to hand the city over to the sons of Abdi-ashirtis.[3] When my brother saw that my messenger had returned with nothing, that no garrison troops were with him, then he despised me and committed the outrage of driving me out of the city. May the king, my lord, not restrain himself in dealing with the deed of this dog!

Behold, I cannot enter the lands of Egypt. I am aged and serious illness is in my body. And may the king, my lord, know that the gods of Byblos are angry and in consequence my ailment is severe, and I have confessed my sins to the gods. In these circumstances I have not entered into the presence of the king, my lord. But behold I have sent my son, the servant of the king, my lord, before the king, my lord. May the king then hear the words of his servant and give regular troops to take Byblos and prevent the disaffected and the sons of Abdi-ashirtis from taking possession of it. Regular troops of the king, my lord, are needed to take the city. Behold, in the city are numerous people who love me; those in it who are inimical are few in number. If they hear that a regular army has set out, on the very day of its arrival the city will return to the king, my lord. And may the king know that I am willing to die for him. When I was in the city I protected it for my lord and my heart was directed toward the king, my lord, that I might not yield the city to the sons of Abdi-ashirtis. But my brother has subverted the city with the aim of handing it over to the sons of Abdi-ashirtis. May the king, my lord, not hold back from the city, for in it a very great quantity of silver and gold is at hand, and in the temple of its gods everything possible is in huge amount. If they take possession of it, may the king, my lord, do what he will with his servant. But may he give me the town of Buruzilim for a dwelling place. Behold, I am with Hamuniri. When the cities became disaffected they were hostile also to Buruzilim, which is afraid of the sons of Abdi-ashirtis. When I went to Hamuniri because the sons of Abdi-ashirtis had become powerful against me and there was not a breath of the mouth of the king on my behalf, then I said to my lord: "Behold, Byblos is your city. In it, open to hand, is a great amount of the king's wealth, the possessions of our ancestors. If the king holds back from the city then all the cities of Canaan will be lost to him. May the king not stay his hand from this task!"

Behold, I have sent thy servant, my son, before the king, my lord, and may the king send him straightway back with soldiers to take the city! If the king, my lord, has mercy on my plight and brings me back to the city, then will I protect it as before for the king, my lord. If the king, my lord,

3. Nomad chieftains.

[ 194 ]

does not bring me back to it, then . . . to the city from Buruzilim. . . . May he do to his servant what he will and may he not abandon . . . Hamuniri. . . . How long shall I remain with him?

May the king, my lord, hear the words of his servant straight away and send soldiers with all speed to take the city! May the king, my lord, not withhold his hand from this serious crime, which is being perpetrated against the lands of the king, my lord! But may the king, my lord, quickly send soldiers to take the city with all speed! If respecting the city it is said to the king: "The city is strong," may he know it is not strong enough to withstand the soldiers of the king, my lord.

## 2

To the king, my lord and my Sun. Thus spoke Biridiya,[4] the true servant of the king:

Beneath the two feet of the king, my lord and my Sun, seven and seven times I prostrate myself. May the king, my lord, know that since the troops returned to Egypt, Labaya[5] has conducted warfare against me! And we cannot . . . and we cannot go out of the gate, on account of Labaya, since he came to know of it. And still have you given no soldiers.

And behold, indeed, his face is therefore directed to take Megiddo. But verily, let the king hold his city, that Labaya may not conquer it, with the city fallen through death and pestilence into dust. May the king then in very deed give one hundred garrison troops for the protection of his city, that Labaya may not conquer it! For there is no other intention in Labaya —but he seeks to destroy Megiddo.

## 3

To the king, my lord and my Sun, speak as follows: Thus says Biridiya. the faithful servant of the king:

At the feet of the king, my lord and my Sun, seven and seven times I prostrate myself. May the king, my lord, take cognizance concerning his servant and his city. Behold, I am working in the territory of the town of Shunama[6] and I bring men for the forced labor corvée. Behold, the governors who are along with me do not do as I do: they do not work in the

4.  Prince of Megiddo.
5.  Prince of Shechem.
6.  These towns were several hours march eastward of Megiddo.

territory of the town of Shunama, and they do not bring men for the corvée. I alone bring men for the corvée from the town of Yapu.[5] They likewise come from the town of Nuribda.[6] So may the king, my lord, take cognizance concerning his city!

### 4

To the king, my lord. Thus spoke Labaya, thy servant:

Beneath the feet of my lord I prostrate myself. With regard to what you wrote to me asking: "Are the people strong who have conquered the city? How then can they be put under arrest?" I reply thus: "By fighting the city was taken. Has the truth been destroyed? . . . is an important man in my sight. The city is conquered, and indeed slander has been spoken against me in the presence of the king, my lord."

Further: When . . . are struck, they do not fight back, and so become powerful the hands of the man who. . . . So am I oppressed and . . . for my two cities have been taken.

Further: If you on that account should still say: ". . . and so let them strike you," then I. . . . The people who have captured the city will be brought to book, just as my father. . . . Yes, they will be brought to book.

### 5

To the king, my lord and Sun. Thus spoke Labaya, thy servant and the dust on which thou walkest:

Beneath the feet of the king, my lord and my Sun, seven and seven times I prostrate myself. I have heard the words that the king wrote to me. And who am I that the king should lose his land on my account? Behold, I am a faithful servant of the king, and I have not committed any crime, nor have I sinned, nor do I refuse to pay tribute, nor do I refuse the demands of my superior.

Behold, they slander me and treat me badly, and the king, my lord, has not even given me notice of my imputed crime.

Further: Here is my crime: that I entered Gezer and said: "The king has appropriated absolutely everything that belongs to me, but all the property of Milkilu,[7] where is *it*? I know what Milkilu has accomplished against me."

Further: The king has written regarding Dumuya. I did not know

7. Prince of Gezer.

Dumuya trafficked with the Habiru.[8] But I have now handed him over to Addaya.

Further: Even suppose the king should write to ask for my wife, would I then refuse her? Even suppose the king should write to me: "Plunge a bronze dagger into your heart and die!" Even then would I not carry out the king's command?

## 6

To the king, my lord, my gods, my Sun. Thus spoke Milkilu, thy servant, the dust beneath thy feet:

Beneath the feet of the king, my lord, my gods, my Sun, seven and seven times I prostrate myself. May the king, my lord, know what Yanhamu[9] has done to me since my leaving of the king's presence. Behold, he demands two thousand shekels of silver from my hand and he has said to me: "Give me your wife and your children! Or else I will surely strike." Indeed, may this deed be known to the king without fail and may the king, my lord, send chariots and may he take me to himself, that I may not perish.

## 7

To Milkilu, prince of the city of Gezer. Thus speaks the king:[10]

Behold, I have had the present tablet brought to thee to inform thee: Behold, I have sent Hanya, the commandant of the troops, along with all sorts of goods to procure beautiful women:[11] silver, gold, apparel, carnelian and all sorts of precious stones, chairs of ebony, all kinds of beautiful objects of a total in all of 160 *deben*. There are, then, a total of 40 women, and 40 shekels of silver is the price of each. Send me therefore very fine women, with not one of poor quality among them, of such sort that the king, thy master, may be enabled to declare to thee: "Well done! To thee has thy life been granted."

May thou know that the king waxes strong like the Sun and that his troops, his chariots, and his horses are also in excellent condition.

Behold, the god Amon has put the upper land, the lower land, the east, and the west beneath the feet of the king.

8. See Selection 25.
9. A high Egyptian official.
10. Amen-hotep III, presumably, for Amon (not Aton) is the god named at the end of the letter.
11. Presumably for the pharaoh's harem.

To the king, my lord, my gods, my Sun. Thus spoke Shuwardata,[12] thy servant, the dust beneath thy feet:

Beneath the feet of the king, my lord, my gods, my Sun, seven and seven times I prostrate myself. The king, my lord, has sent me to make war against Kelta. I have made war; I was successful; my city has been restored to me.

Why has Abdi-hiba[13] written to the people of Kelta: "Bring silver and come follow me!"? May the king, my lord, know that Abdi-hiba had taken my city out of my hands.

Further: Let the king, my lord, inquire whether I have taken from him a man or a head of cattle or an ass. If so then let him be found in the right.

Further: Labaya, who had taken our cities, is dead. But behold, Abdi-hiba is another Labaya, and he now takes our cities. And may the king be concerned for his servant on account of this deed! And now I shall take no further action until the king sends a reply to his servant.

# 21 Tut-ankh-Amon's Restoration

Akh-en-Aton died under somewhat mysterious circumstances after eighteen years of rule, and he was succeeded in 1362 b.c. by his very young son-in-law Tut-ankh-Aton. The new king was promptly forced by the priesthoods and the high civil officials to undo the revolution of his predecessor, to move back to Thebes, and to change his name to Tut-ankh-Amon. He is the celebrated "King Tut," the discovery of whose intact tomb provided our own century with one of its most sensational archaeological finds. In life he was a pawn of the powerful elements in his realm and at his court, and he died after only ten years on the throne. For three years thereafter his widow was a center for intrigue as various groups plotted and negotiated to place their respective candidates on the throne by marrying her. Finally an army general, Hor-em-heb (Harmhab), managed a military coup and

SOURCE: John Bennett, "The Restoration Inscription of Tut-ankhamun," *Journal of Egyptian Archaeology,* XXV (1939), pp. 9–11 (revised). Reprinted by permission of the officers of the Egypt Exploration Society.

12.   Prince of the Hebron district.        13.   Prince of Jerusalem.

placed himself upon the throne, ruling from 1349 until his death in 1319 B.C. He rooted out the last vestiges of Akh-en-Aton's ill-fated revolution, completely restoring the traditional order. With him the great Dynasty XVIII comes to an end.

The following selection is an inscription from the mammoth temple of Amon at Karnak (on the east side of the Nile opposite Thebes) commemorating Tut-ankh-Amon's restoration of the traditional worship. The translation is by John Bennett, who revised his published version especially for the present edition.

✹✹✹✹✹✹

Year . . . fourth month of the inundation season, day 19, under the majesty of Horus "Strong bull, beautiful of birth," Two Ladies "Goodly of laws, he who pacifies the Two Lands," Horus of Gold "Exalted of crowns, who placates the gods," King of Upper and Lower Egypt "Neb-khepru-Re," Son of Re "Tut-ankh-Amon, ruler of Hermonthis," given life like Re for ever and ever; beloved of Amen-Re, lord of the Thrones of the Two Lands, chief of Ipt-isut; Atum, lord of the Two Lands and Heliopolis; Re-Harakhte; Ptah, South of his Wall, lord of Ankhtawe; and Thoth, lord of the god's speech; he who appears on the Horus-throne of the living, like his father Re every day; the good god, son of Amun; image of Kamephis, glorious seed, splendid offspring, scion of Amun himself; father of the Two Lands, who moulds his moulder, who fashions his fashioner; for whom the souls of Heliopolis assembled, in order that he might be fashioned to act as king of eternity, as the enduring Horus of everlastingness; the good ruler, who does things beneficial to his Father and all the gods, he has made that which was in ruins to flourish as a monument of eternal age; he has suppressed wrongdoing throughout the Two Lands; Truth is established, she causes falsehood to be the abomination of the land, as in its [the land's] first time.

Now when His Majesty arose as king, the temples of the gods and goddesses, beginning from Elephantine down to the marshes of the Delta, their . . . had fallen into neglect, their shrines had fallen into desolation and become mounds overgrown with . . . -plants, their sanctuaries were as if they had never been, their halls were a trodden path. The land was in confusion, the gods forsook this land. If an army was sent to Djahy[1] to

1.  Or Zahi: Syria-Palestine.

widen the frontiers of Egypt, it met with no success at all. If one prayed to a god to ask things of him, in no wise did he come. If one made supplication to a goddess in like manner, in no wise did she come. Their hearts were weak of themselves [with anger], and they thwarted what would be done.

After some days had passed this way, His Majesty appeared on the throne of his father; he ruled the countries of Horus, the Black Land and the Red Land were under his dominion, and every land was in obeisance to his might.

Behold His Majesty was in his palace, which is in the estate of A-kheper-ka-Re, like Re in the heavens, and His Majesty was administering this land, and making daily governance of the Two Riverbanks. Then His Majesty took counsel with his heart, searching out every excellent occasion, seeking what was beneficial to his father Amon, for fashioning his august image of real fine-gold. He has added to what was done in former time, he has fashioned an image of his father Amon upon thirteen carrying-poles, his holy image being of fine-gold, lapis-lazuli, turquoise, and every rare costly stone, whereas formerly the majesty of this august god had been upon eleven carrying-poles. He has fashioned an image of Ptah, South of his Wall, lord of Ankhtawe, his august image being of fine-gold, upon eleven carrying-poles, his holy image being of fine-gold, lapis-lazuli, turquoise, and every rare costly stone, whereas formerly the majesty of this august god had been upon six carrying-poles.

And His Majesty has made monuments for the gods, fashioning their statues of real fine-gold, the best of foreign lands, building anew their sanctuaries as monuments of eternal age, they being endowed with property for ever, establishing for them divine gifts as a lasting daily sacrifice, and supplying them with food-offerings upon earth. He has added to what was in former time, he has surpassed that done since the time of the ancestors, he has inducted priests and prophets, children of the notables of their towns, each the son of a noted man, and one whose name is known; he has multiplied their wealth with gold, silver, bronze and copper, without limit of all things, he has filled their storehouses with slaves, men and women, the fruit of His Majesty's plundering. All the possessions of the temples are doubled, trebled and quadrupled with silver, gold, lapis-lazuli, turquoise, all rare costly stones, royal linen, white cloth, fine linen, olive oil, gum, fat, . . . , incense, *ihmt* incense and myrrh, without limit of all good things.

His Majesty—may he live, prosper and be in health—has hewn their

[ 200 ]

barques which are on the river of fresh cedar, the best of the hill-slope, the pick of Negev, worked with gold, the best of foreign lands; and they illumine the river. His Majesty—may he live, prosper and be in health—has consecrated men and women slaves, singers and dancers, who are servants in the house of the King; and their wages are charged to the . . . palace of the Lord of the Two Lands.

"I cause them to be protected and preserved for my fathers, all the gods, in the desire to placate them by doing that which their *kas* love, so that they may protect Ta-mery."

The gods and goddesses who are in this land, their hearts are joyful, the possessors of shrines are glad, lands are in a state of jubilation and merry-making, exaltation is throughout the whole land; a goodly state has come to pass.

The ennead of the gods who are in the temple, their arms are raised in adoration, their hands are full of jubilees of eternity and everlastingness, all life and prosperity with them are placed to the nose of Horus who is born again, beloved son of his father Amen-Re, lord of the Thrones of the Two Lands . . . ; he [Amon] has fashioned him that he himself may be fashioned; king of Upper and Lower Egypt, Neb-khepru-Re, beloved of Amon, his beloved, real eldest son, who protects the father who fashioned him that he may exercise the kingship over kings in all lands, son of Re, Tut-ankh-Amon, ruler of Hermonthis, a son who is profitable to him who fashioned him, wealthy in monuments, rich in wonders, who makes monuments in righteousness of heart for his father Amon; beautiful of birth, sovereign who assumed the crowns in Chemmis.

On this day One was in the goodly palace, which is in the estate of A-kheper-ka-Re, justified; behold, His Majesty—may he live, prosper and be in health—was young; but neglectfulness was taken from his body. Khnumu has moulded him as a mighty one . . . he is mighty of arm, great of strength, one distinguished more than the mighty, vast of strength like the son of Nut . . . mighty of arm like Horus, there exists no equal to him among the mighty one of all lands together; he who knows like Re, who . . . like Ptah, who understands like Thoth, who ordains excellent laws, who commands . . . excellent of utterance; King of Upper and Lower Egypt, lord of the Two Lands, lord of rites, lord of the strong arm, Nebkhepru-Re, he who placates the gods, beloved son of Re of his body, lord of every foreign land, lord of crowns, Tut-ankh-Amon, ruler of Hermonthis, given life, stability and prosperity like Re for ever and ever.

# 22 Suppiluliumas and Egypt

From the fourteenth century B.C. on, Egypt and the Hittites were the two greatest powers of the world. Their imperial ambitions met head on in Syria-Palestine, where for centuries the fortunes of war favored first one then the other of the contenders. In the struggle for power all manner of devices were used in addition to outright warfare. The greatest weakness of the Hittites was the existence on the upper Euphrates of the powerful state of Mitanni, flanking the southward drive of Hittite arms and thereby posing a permanent threat. A major goal of Egyptian foreign policy was an alliance with Mitanni, and a successful moment in the implementation of this policy may be seen in the person of Akh-en-Aton's wife, Nefer-titi, who was a Mitanni princess.

In the fourteenth century the greatest of the Hittite kings, Suppiluliumas (ruled c. 1375–1335), managed to defeat Mitanni and to make it a Hittite dependency. The Syrian princes saw a winner and defected from their Egyptian alliance. In the turmoil that followed the death of Tut-ankh-Amon the opportunity presented itself which might have put the crown upon Suppiluliumas' successes. In the following passage, from the annals of Suppiluliumas' reign compiled by his son Mursilis, we learn that Tut-ankh-Amon's widow, the last surviving daughter of Akh-en-Aton, wrote to the Hittite king requesting one of his sons in marriage. After an appropriate show of reluctance, Suppiluliumas hastened to comply. Unfortunately for the king the plan fell through, for we learn from a passage in the "Plague Prayers" (Selection 17) that the Hittite prince never got to Egypt but was murdered on the way. The translation is by Albrecht Goetze.

❀❀❀❀❀

While my father was down in the country of Karkamis,[1] he dispatched Lupakkis and Tessub-zalmas to the country of Amqa.[2] They proceeded to attack the country of Amqa and brought deportees, cattle and sheep home before my father. When the people of the land of Egypt heard about the attack on Amqa, they became frightened. Because, to make matters worse,

SOURCE: Reprinted from *Ancient Near Eastern Texts Relating to the Old Testament* ed. James B. Pritchard by permission of Princeton University Press. Copyright, 1950, by Princeton University Press.
1.   Today Jerablus on the Euphrates.
2.   Between Lebanon and Antilibanus.

their lord Bibhururiyas[3] had just died, the Egyptian queen who had become a widow, sent an envoy to my father and wrote him as follows: "My husband died and I have no son. People say that you have many sons. If you were to send me one of your sons, he might become my husband. I am loath to take a servant of mine and make him my husband." When my father heard that, he called the great into council saying: "Since of old such a thing has never happened before me." He proceeded to dispatch Hattu-zitis, the chamberlain, saying: "Go! Bring you reliable information back to me. They may try to deceive me: As to whether perhaps they have a prince bring reliable information back to me!"

During Hattu-zitis' absence in the land of Egypt my father vanquished the city of Karkamis. . . .

The Egyptian envoy, the Honorable Hanis, came to him. Because my father had instructed Hattu-zitis while sending him to the land of Egypt as follows: "Perhaps they have a prince; they may try to deceive me and do not really want one of my sons to take over the kingship," the Egyptian queen answered my father in a letter as follows: "Why do you say: 'They may try to deceive me'? If I had a son, would I write to a foreign country in a manner which is humiliating to myself and to my country? You do not trust me and tell me even such a thing. He who was my husband died and I have no sons. Shall I perhaps take one of my servants and make him my husband? I have not written to any other country, I have written only to you. People say that you have many sons. Give me one of your sons and he is my husband and king in the land of Egypt." Because my father was generous, he complied with the lady's wishes and decided for sending the son.

# 23 *"Treaty of the Silver Tablet"*

The rivalry of the Egyptian and Hittite empires for control of the Syria-Palestine region gave rise to constant warfare. A high point in this struggle was a major battle fought about 1295 B.C. at the city of Kadesh on the Orontes River, the chief strong point in northern Syria. Historians are in some doubt as to which side, if either, was the winner, but the Egyptian troops were commanded on the occasion by the pharaoh himself, who claimed a victory. The pharaoh was Ramses II, who, whatever his merits, ruled for so long (1300–1233 B.C.) and left to posterity so many statues and

3. Tut-ankh-Amon.

buildings and inscriptions that he seems to loom as one of the greatest of the pharaohs.

About 1280 B.C., some fifteen years after the Battle of Kadesh, the Egyptians and the Hittites were ready to declare their mutual incapacity to inflict decisive defeat. A treaty was negotiated in which each recognized the other's territorial claims and vowed eternal alliance. The original text of this treaty, which must have been in Akkadian, the language of diplomacy of the time, is lost, but we are uniquely fortunate in having both the Egyptian and the Hittite versions. The Egyptian version, inscribed on the walls of the Great Temple at Karnak, has been known since the beginnings of Egyptology in the early nineteenth century; the Hittite version was discovered in the imperial archives during the excavation of Hattusas a hundred years later and a thousand miles distant. It is instructive to observe, in addition to the Egyptian version's greater completeness, the differences in wording and in emphasis in the two texts. The translation of the Egyptian version of the treaty is by A. H. Gardiner; that of the Hittite version is by S. Langdon.

⊛⊛⊛⊛⊛

## EGYPTIAN VERSION

Year 21, first month of winter, day 21, under the Majesty of the King of Upper and Lower Egypt Usi-ma-Re-setpen-Re, son of Re, Ramesse-mi-Amun, granted life eternally and forever, beloved of Amen-Re, Harakhte, Ptah South-of-His-Wall, lord of Onkhtowe, Mut lady of Ishru and Khons-Neferhotpe, being arisen upon the Horus-throne of the Living like his father Harakhte eternally and for evermore.

On this day, when His Majesty was at the town of Pi-Ramesse-mi-Amun doing the pleasure of his father Amen-Re, Harakhte, Atum lord-of-the-two-lands-of-Heliopolis, Amun of Ramesse-mi-Amun, Ptah of Ramesse-mi-Amun and Setekh great-of-valour, son of Nut, according as they give to him an infinity of Sed-festivals and an eternity of peaceful years, all lands and all hill-countries being prostrate under his sandals eternally; there came the king's messenger, the deputy-commander . . . the king's messenger . . . Usi-ma-Re-setpen-Re, Tartesub . . . and the messenger of Hatti . . . carrying the tablet of silver which the great chief of Hatti, Hattusilis, caused to be

SOURCE: S. Langdon and Alan H. Gardiner, "The Treaty of Alliance Between Hattusili, King of the Hittites, and the Pharaoh Ramesses II of Egypt," *Journal of Egyptian Archaeology*, VI (1920), pp. 186–192. Reprinted by permission of the officers of the Egypt Exploration Society.

brought to Pharaoh in order to beg peace from the Majesty of Usi-ma-Re-setpen-Re, son of Re, Ramesse-mi-Amun, granted life eternally and forever like his father Re every day.

Copy of the tablet of silver which the great chief of Hatti, Hattusilis, caused to be brought to Pharaoh by the hand of his messenger Tartesub and his messenger Ramose, in order to beg peace from the Majesty of Usi-ma-Re-setpen-Re, son of Re, Ramesse-mi-Amun, bull of rulers, who makes his boundary where he will in every land.

### Preamble

The treaty which the great prince of Hatti, Hattusilis, the strong, the son of Mursilis, the great chief of Hatti, the strong, the son of the son of Suppiluliumas, the great chief of Hatti, the strong, made upon a tablet of silver for Usi-ma-Re-setpen-Re, the great ruler of Egypt, the strong, the son of Men-ma-Re, the great ruler of Egypt, the strong, the son of the son of Men-pehti-Re, the great ruler of Egypt, the strong: the good treaty of peace and brotherhood, giving peace and brotherhood . . . between us by means of a treaty of Hatti with Egypt forever.

### Previous Relations

Now aforetime, since eternity, as regards the policy of the great ruler of Egypt and the great chief of Hatti—the god did not permit hostility to be made between them, by means of a treaty.

But in the time of Muwattallis, the great chief of Hatti, my brother, he fought with Ramesse-mi-Amun, the great ruler of Egypt.

But hereafter, beginning from this day, behold Hattusilis, the great chief of Hatti, is in a treaty for making permanent the policy which Re made and Setekh made for the land of Egypt with the land of Hatti, so as not to permit hostilities to be made between them forever.

### Present Treaty

Behold, Hattusilis, the great chief of Hatti, has made himself in a treaty with Usi-ma-Re-setpen-Re, the great ruler of Egypt, beginning with this day, to cause to be made good peace and good brotherhood between us forever; and he is in brotherhood with me and at peace with me, and I am in brotherhood with him and at peace with him forever.

And since Muwattallis, the great chief of Hatti, my brother, hastened after his fate, and Hattusilis took his seat as great chief of Hatti on the throne of his father; behold I have become with Ramesse-mi-Amun, the great ruler of Egypt, we being together in our peace and our brotherhood; and it is better than the peace and the brotherhood of formerly, which was in the land.

Behold, I, being the great chief of Hatti, am with Ramesse-mi-Amun, the great ruler of Egypt, in good peace and good brotherhood.

And the children of the children of the great chief of Hatti shall be in brotherhood and at peace with the children of the children of Ramesse-mi-Amun, the great ruler of Egypt; they being in our policy of brotherhood and our policy of peace.

And the land of Egypt with the land Hatti shall be at peace and in brotherhood like us forever; and hostilities shall not be made between them forever.

## Mutual Non-Aggression

And the great chief of Hatti shall not trespass into the land of Egypt forever to take aught from it; and Usi-ma-Re-setpen-Re, the great ruler of Egypt, shall not trespass into the land of Hatti to take aught from it forever.

## Validity of Earlier Treaties

As to the regular treaty which there was in the time of Suppiluliumas, the great chief of Hatti, and likewise the regular treaty which was in the time of Muwattallis,[1] the great chief of Hatti, my father, I take hold of it. Behold, Ramesse-mi-Amun, the great ruler of Egypt, takes hold of the peace which it makes together with us from this day; and we will act according to this regular policy.

## Mutual Defense of Egypt

And if another enemy come to the lands of Usi-ma-Re-setpen-Re, the great ruler of Egypt, and he send to the great chief of Hatti saying, "Come with me as help against him"; the great chief of Hatti shall come to him, the great chief of Hatti shall slay his enemy.

But if it be not the desire of the great chief of Hatti to come, he shall send his troops and his chariotry and shall slay his enemy.

1.  Apparently a scribe's error. Mursilis was Hattusilis' father, Muwattallis his brother; see Selection 18.

Or if Ramesse-mi-Amun, the great ruler of Egypt, become incensed against servants of his, and they do another offense against him, and he go to slay his enemy; the great chief of Hatti shall act with him to destroy everyone against whom they shall be incensed.

### Mutual Defense of Hatti

But if another enemy come against the great chief of Hatti; then shall Usi-ma-Re-setpen-Re, the great ruler of Egypt, come to him as help to slay his enemy.

But if it be not the desire of Ramesse-mi-Amun, the great ruler of Egypt, to come, he . . . Hatti, and he shall send his troops and his chariotry, besides returning answer to the land of Hatti.

But if servants of the great chief of Hatti trespass against him, and Ramesse-mi-Amun, the great ruler of Egypt. . . .

### Contingency of Ruler's Death[2]

. . . the land of Hatti and the land of Egypt . . . the life. Supposing I shall go after my fate, then Ramesse-mi-Amun, the great ruler of Egypt, living forever, shall act . . . coming to the land of Hatti . . . to cause to make . . . them to make him for themselves to lord, so as to cause Usi-ma-Re-setpen-Re, the great ruler of Egypt, to be silent with his mouth forever. And after . . . the land of Hatti and he return to place the great chief of Hatti and similarly the. . . .

### Extradition of Egyptian Fugitives

If any great man flee from the land of Egypt and he come to the lands of the great chief of Hatti; or a town or a district . . . belonging to the lands of Ramesse-mi-Amun, the great ruler of Egypt, and they come to the great chief of Hatti: the great chief of Hatti shall not receive them. The great chief of Hatti shall cause them to be brought to Usi-ma-Re-setpen-Re, the great ruler of Egypt, their lord, on account of it.

Or if one man or two men who are unknown flee . . . and they come to the land of Hatti to be servants of another, they shall not be left in the land of Hatti, they shall be brought to Ramesse-mi-Amun, the great ruler of Egypt.

2.   Its fragmentary condition makes clear interpretation of this clause impossible.

## Extradition of Hittite Fugitives

Or if a great man flee from the land of Hatti, and he come to the lands of Usi-ma-Re-setpen-Re, the great ruler of Egypt; or a town or a district or . . . belonging to the land of Hatti, and they come to Ramesse-mi-Amun, the great ruler of Egypt: Usi-ma-Re-setpen-Re, the great ruler of Egypt, shall not receive them. Ramesse-mi-Amun, the great ruler of Egypt, shall cause them to be brought to the chief . . . they shall not be left.

Likewise, if one man or two men who are not known flee to the land of Egypt to be subjects of others, Usi-ma-Re-setpen-Re, the great ruler of Egypt, shall not leave them; he shall cause them to be brought to the great chief of Hatti.

## Divine Witnesses

As for these words of the treaty made by the great chief of Hatti with Ramesse-mi-Amun, the great ruler of Egypt, in writing upon this tablet of silver; as for these words, a thousand gods, male gods and female gods of those of the land of Hatti, together with a thousand gods, male gods and female gods of those of the land of Egypt—they are with me as witnesses hearing these words: Re, the lord of the sky; Re of the town of Arinna; Setekh, the lord of the sky; Setekh of Hatti; Setekh of the town of Arinna; Setekh of the town of Zippalanda; Setekh of the town of Betiarik; Setekh of the town of Hissashapa; Setekh of the town of Sarissa; Setekh of the town of Halab; Setekh of the town of Lihzin; Setekh of the town of . . . ; Setekh of the town of . . . ; Setekh of the town of S-m-s; Setekh of the town of S-h-p-n; Astarte of the land of Hatti; the god of Zitharias; the god of Karzis; the god of Hapantarias; the goddess of the town Karahna; the goddess of Tyre; the goddess of -w-k; the goddess of D-n- ; the god of P-n-t; the god of . . . ; the god of H-b-t; the queen of the sky; the gods lords of swearing; this goddess, the mistress of the earth; the mistress of swearing, Ishara; the mistress of . . . ; the mountains and the rivers of the land of Hatti; the gods of the land of Kizuwadna; Amun; Re; Setekh; the male gods and the female gods; the mountains and the rivers of the land of Egypt; the sky; the earth; the great sea; the winds; the clouds.

## Curses and Blessings

As to these words which are upon this tablet of silver of the land of Hatti

[ 208 ]

and of the land of Egypt, as to him who shall not keep them, a thousand gods of the land of Hatti and a thousand gods of the land of Egypt shall destroy his house, his land and his servants. But he who shall keep these words which are on this tablet of silver, be they Hatti, or be they Egyptians, and who do not neglect them, a thousand gods of the land of Hatti and a thousand gods of the land of Egypt will cause him to be healthy and to live, together with his houses and his land and his servants.

### Immunity of Egyptian Fugitives

If one man flee from the land of Egypt, or two, or three, and they come to the great chief of Hatti, the great chief of Hatti shall seize them and shall cause them to be brought back to Usi-ma-Re-setpen-Re, the great ruler of Egypt. But as for the man who shall be brought to Ramesse-mi-Amun, the great ruler of Egypt, let not his crime be charged against him, let not his house, his wives or his children be destroyed, let him not be killed, let no injury be done to his eyes, to his ears, to his mouth or to his legs, let not any crime be charged against him.

### Immunity of Hittite Fugitives

Likewise, if a man flee from the land of Hatti, be he one, be he two, or be he three, and they come to Usi-ma-Re-setpen-Re, the great ruler of Egypt, let Ramesse-mi-Amun, the great ruler of Egypt, cause them to be brought to the great chief of Hatti, and the great chief of Hatti shall not charge their crime against them, and they shall not destroy his house, his wives or his children, and they shall not kill him, and they shall not do injury to his ears, to his eyes, to his mouth or to his legs, and they shall not charge any crime against him.

### Description of the Tablet

What is in the middle of the tablet of silver. On its front side: a relief consisting of an image of Setekh embracing an image of the great prince of Hatti, surrounded by a legend saying: the seal of Setekh, the ruler of the sky, the seal of the treaty made by Hattusilis, the great chief of Hatti, the strong, the son of Mursilis, the great chief of Hatti, the strong. What is within the surrounding frame of the relief: the seal of Setekh, the ruler of the sky. What is on its other side: a relief consisting of a female image of the goddess of Hatti embracing a female image of the chieftainess of Hatti, surrounded by a legend saying: the seal of Re of the town of Arinna, the lord of the land, the seal of Puduhepa, the chieftainess of the land of Hatti, the daughter of the land of Kizuwadna, the priestess of the town of Arinna, the lady of the land, the servant of the goddess. What is within the surrounding frame of the relief: the seal of Re of Arinna, the lord of every land.

## HITTITE VERSION

And so be it. Riamasesa-mai-Amana, the great king, king of Egypt, the strong, with Hattusilis, the great king, king of the land Hatti, his brother, in order to give good peace, good brotherhood and to obtain a mighty kingdom between them as long as we live and forever a treaty has made.

### Preamble

Riamasesa-mai-Amana, the great king, king of Egypt, the strong in all lands, son of Minmuaria, the great king, king of Egypt, the strong, son of the son of Minpahiritaria, the great king, king of Egypt, the strong, unto Hattusilis, the great king, king of the land Hatti, the strong, the son of Mursilis, the great king, king of the land Hatti, the strong, son of the son of Suppiluliumas, the great king, king of the land Hatti, the strong, behold now I give good brotherhood, good peace between us forever, in order to give good peace, good brotherhood by means of a treaty of Egypt with Hatti forever. So it is.

### Previous Relations

Behold, the policy of the great king, king of Egypt, and of the great king, king of Hatti since eternity—god did not permit the making of hostility between them, by means of a treaty forever.

Behold, Riamasesa-mai-Amana, the great king, king of Egypt, in order to make the policy which Samas and Tesub[3] made for Egypt with the land Hatti because of his policy which is from eternity, wickedly will not become hostile to make hostility between them unto everlasting and unto all time.

3. The Sun-god and the Storm-god.

[ 210 ]

## Present Treaty

Riamasesa-mai-Amana, the great king, king of Egypt, has made himself in a treaty upon a silver tablet with Hattusilis, the great king, king of the land Hatti, his brother, from this day to give good peace and good brotherhood between us forever; and he is a brother to me and at peace with me, and I am a brother to him and at peace with him forever.

And we have made brotherhood, peace and goodwill more than the brotherhood and peace of former times, which was between Egypt and Hatti.

Behold, Riamasesa-mai-Amana, the great king, king of Egypt, is in good peace and good brotherhood with Hattusilis, the great king, king of the land Hatti.

Behold, the sons of Riamasesa-mai-Amana, the king of Egypt, are at peace and are brothers with the sons of Hattusilis, the great king, king of the land Hatti, forever; and they are according to our policy of our brotherhood and our peace.

And Egypt with the land Hatti—they are at peace, they are brothers like us forever.

## Mutual Non-Aggression

And Riamasesa-mai-Amana, the great king, king of Egypt, shall not trespass into the land Hatti to take aught from therein forever; and Hattusilis, the great king, king of the land Hatti, shall not trespass into Egypt to take aught from therein forever.

## Validity of Earlier Treaty

Behold, the decree of eternity which Samas and Tesub have made for Egypt and the land Hatti to make peace and brotherhood in order not to give hostility between them.

And behold, Riamasesa-mai-Amana, the great king, king of Egypt, takes hold of it to make peace from this day.

Behold, Egypt and Hatti are at peace, and they are brothers forever.

## Mutual Defense of Hatti

And if another enemy come against the land Hatti, and Hattusilis, the great king of the land Hatti, send to me saying, "Come unto me for my help against him"; then Riamasesa-mai-Amana, the great king, king of Egypt shall send his troops and his chariots and shall slay his enemy and he shall restore confidence to the land Hatti.

And if Hattusilis, the great king, king of the land Hatti, become incensed against servants of his and they sin against him, and thou send to Riamasesa, the great king, king of Egypt concerning it; straightway Riamasesa-mai-Amana his troops and his chariots shall send, and they shall destroy all of them against whom thou art become incensed.

### Mutual Defense of Egypt

And if another enemy come against Egypt, and Riamasesa-mai-Amana, the king of Egypt, thy brother, send to Hattusilis, king of the land Hatti, his brother, saying, "Come for my help against him"; straightway then shall Hattusilis, king of the land Hatti, send his troops and his chariots; he shall slay my enemy.

And if Riamasesa, the great king, king of Egypt, become incensed against servants of his, and they commit sin against him, and I send to Hattusilis, king of the land Hatti, my brother, concerning it; then Hattusilis, the great king, shall send his troops and his chariots and they shall destroy all of them; and I will. . . .

### Contingency of Ruler's Death

And behold the son of Hattusilis, king of the land Hatti, the treaty which we have made . . . in the place of Hattusilis, his father, after years . . . of the land Hatti have committed sin . . . chariots where shall I return . . . in the land Hatti. . . .

[*The text breaks off here.*]

# 24 Journey of Unamun to Phoenicia

One of the reasons why both Egypt and the Hittites were ready to suspend their ancient hostility was that both were having troubles elsewhere. A wave

SOURCE: Adolf Erman, *The Literature of the Ancient Egyptians,* translated into English by Aylward M. Blackman (London: Methuen and Co., 1927). Reprinted by permission of the publishers.

of invasions by peoples from outside the orbit of civilization required both countries to protect their homelands. The wave grew in strength, and by the end of the thirteenth century B.C. it threatened to engulf all the civilized world. It did destroy much of it. The Hittites disappeared from history; Mesopotamia under Kassite rule was left for centuries in semi-isolation and silence; the civilization of Crete, Greece, and the Aegean islands was wiped out. Egypt succeeded in repelling invaders from Libya and others who came by sea into the Delta, but her imperial greatness was gone, and she survived only as a nation much shrunk in power. On the Syrian-Palestinian coast the small Canaanite principalities, relieved of their burden of struggle with the contending forces of the now defunct Hittite and Egyptian empires, lived on with a new independence, and by plying their old profession of trade and business enterprise, they prospered. Almost alone they kept alive the cultural contacts and other amenities of civilization.

The "Journey of Unamun" (or Wen-Amon) is a story dating from about 1100 B.C. It describes the misadventures of an Egyptian official on a mission to Syria to obtain timber, a product that Egypt had always had to import but that was one of Syria's chief resources, from the famous cedars of Lebanon. The treatment of the Egyptian at the hands of Zakar-baal, prince of Byblos, is a measure of the decline of Egypt's power at this time. The English rendering (slightly abridged) is by Aylward M. Blackman from the German translation by Adolf Erman.

⁂⁂⁂⁂⁂

Year 5, day 16 of the third month of Summer. On this day Unamun, Eldest of the Hall of the Administration of Amun of Karnak, departed in order to fetch the timber for the great august ship of Amunre, king of gods, which is on the river and is called Userhet-Amun.

On the day whereon I came to Tanis, the abode of Smendes and Tentamun, I gave unto them the writings of Amunre, king of gods. They had them read in their presence and said: "Yea, I will do even as Amunre, king of gods, our lord, saith."

I remained until the fourth month of Summer in Tanis. Smendes and Tentamun then sent me with the ship-captain, Mengebet, and on the first day of the fourth month of Summer I went down to the great Syrian sea.

And I came to Dor, a city of the Zakar and its prince Beder caused to be brought to me fifty loaves, one measure of wine, and a leg of beef.

A man of my ship ran away and stole in

| Gold: . . . vessels, | amounting to 5 *deben*. |
| Silver: 4 vessels, | amounting to 20 *deben*. |

Silver: in a bag, amounting to 11 *deben.*

[*Total of what he stole:*] Gold, 5 *deben;* silver, 31 *deben.*

On the same morning I arose and went to where the prince was, and said unto him: "I have been robbed in thine harbour. Now thou art the prince of this land, and thou art its judge, so look for my money. Of a truth the money belongeth to Amunre, king of gods, the lord of the countries; it belongeth to Smendes; it belongeth to Hrihor, my lord, and the other great men of Egypt. To thee it belongeth, and it belongeth to Weret, and belongeth to Mekemer, and belongeth to Zakarbaal, the prince of Byblos."

And he said unto me: "Art thou aggrieved, or art thou friendly? For behold, I understand nought of this matter that thou hast told me. Had it been a thief belonging to mine own country that went aboard thy ship and stole thy money, then would I have repaid it thee out of my treasury, until thy thief aforesaid had been apprehended. But the thief that hath robbed thee, he is thine, he belongeth to thy ship. So tarry a few days here with me, that I may seek for him."

So I spent nine days moored in his harbour. Then I went unto him and said: "Behold, thou hast not found my money, so I will now depart with the captain and with them that go away. . . ."

[*In the badly damaged section which follows, Unamun meets up with certain Zakar-people, takes property of theirs to compensate himself for the theft of which he had been the victim, and thus makes enemies of the Zakar-people.*]

They departed and he came to the harbour of Byblos. There he sought for himself some place of safety. I hid therein Amun of the Road and placed his possessions in it. The prince of Byblos sent unto me and said: "Get thee out of my harbour."

[*Of Unamun's answer to this demand only the last words are preserved:*]

"If men sail, let them take me away to Egypt."

I passed nineteen days in his harbour, and every day he continued sending to me, saying: "Get thee out of my harbour."

Now when he was making offering to his gods, the god seized one of his noble youths and made him frenzied, and he said: "Bring the god hither! Bring the messenger, that hath him. It is Amun that sent him, it is he that caused him to come."

[ 214 ]

Thus the frenzied one continued in frenzy throughout this night, when I had just found a ship bound for Egypt, and I was stowing all that I had aboard her, and was watching for the darkness, thinking that when it descends I will also embark the god, so that no other eye may see him.

And the harbour-master came to me, saying: "Remain until morning at the disposition of the prince." I said unto him: "Art thou not he that continued coming to me every day, saying: 'Get thee out of my harbour,' and never didst thou say: 'Remain'? And now the prince will let the ship, which I have found, depart, and thou wilt come again saying: 'Get thee gone!'"

So he went and told it to the prince, and the prince sent unto the ship's captain, saying: "Remain until morning at the disposition of the prince."

And when the morning was come he sent and had me brought up, while the god rested in the . . . in which he was, on the shore of the sea. I found him sitting in his upper chamber, with his back leaning against a window, while the waves of the great Syrian sea beat upon his neck.

I said unto him: "The kindness of Amun!" He said unto me: "How long is it until to-day since thou camest from the abode of Amun?" I said unto him: "Five full months until now." He said unto me: "Dost thou indeed speak the truth? Where then is the writing of Amun, which thou shouldest have? Where is the letter of the High Priest of Amun, which thou shouldest have?" And I said unto him: "I gave them to Smendes and Tentamun." And he was very wroth, and said unto me: "Behold, writing and letter hast thou none. Where is then at least the ship of cedar-wood that Smendes hath given thee? And where is her Syrian crew? He surely did not hand thee over to this ship's captain, to be slain and to be cast into the sea! From whom had they sought the god then? And thee, pray, from whom had they sought thee, pray?" So spake he unto me. . . .

I was silent in this great moment. And he answered and said unto me: "Upon what kind of behest art thou come hither?" I said unto him: "I am come after the timber for the great august vessel of Amunre, king of gods. Thy father used to do it, thy grandfather used to do it, and thou wilt do it also." So spake I unto him. And he said unto me: "They did it in sooth, and if thou wilt give me something for doing it, I will do it. Of a truth my people did execute this behest, but the Pharaoh had six ships sent hither, laden with the wares of Egypt, and they unloaded them into their storehouses. So do thou bring somewhat for me also." And he had fetched the daily registers of his fathers, and he had them read aloud in my presence, and it was found that it was a thousand *deben* of every kind of silver that was entered in his book.

And he said unto me: "If the ruler of Egypt were the lord of my possessions, and I were also his servant, he would not have sent silver and gold, when he said: 'Execute the behest of Amun.' Nor was it a king's gift that they assigned to my father. And I too, I am not thy servant, nor yet am I the servant of him that sent thee. If I cry out to the Lebanon, the heaven openeth, and the trees are here lying on the shore of the sea. . . ."

And I said unto him: ". . . There is not a ship upon the water that belongeth not to Amun. His is the sea and his is Lebanon, whereof thou sayest: 'It belongeth unto me.' . . . But behold, thou hast caused this great god to spend twenty-nine days, after that he had landed in thy harbour, and thou knewest well that he was here! He is still the same as ever he was, and thou standest and wouldest bargain about Lebanon with Amun its lord.

"As for thy saying: 'The former kings sent silver and gold'—if they had offered life and health, they would not have sent these things. Rather they sent thy fathers these things instead of life and health.

"Now as for Amunre, king of gods, he is the lord of life and health, and he was the lord of your fathers, who passed their term of life making offering to Amun. And thou too, thou art a servant of Amun. If now thou sayest: 'Yea, I will do it,' and fulfillest his behest, thou wilt live and prosper and be in health, and thou wilt be a benefactor to thy whole land and to thy people. But covet not for thyself anything that belongeth to Amunre, king of gods; verily a lion loveth his own!

"Let my scribe be brought unto me, that I may send him to Smendes and Tentamun, the officers of the land, whom Amun hath given to the northern portion of his land, and they will send all that is needed. I will write to them, saying: 'Send it, until I be come to the south and send thee all that I owe thee.'" So spake I unto him.

And he gave my letter into the hand of his messenger, and loaded the keel and the bow- and stern-post, together with four other hewn logs—seven in all—and had them brought to Egypt.

And his messenger went to Egypt and came back to me to Syria in the first month of Winter. And Smendes and Tentamun sent me:

Gold: 4 ewers and 1 *kakment*-vessel.

Silver: 5 ewers.

Garments of royal linen: 10 pieces.

Good Upper Egyptian linen: 10 *khered*.

Fine papyrus: 500.

Ox-hides: 500.

Ropes: 500.

Lentils: 20 sacks.

Fish: 30 baskets.

They also had brought to me:

Garments of good Upper Egyptian linen: 5 pieces.

Good Upper Egyptian linen: 5 *khered*.

Lentils: 1 sack.

Fish: 5 baskets.

And the prince rejoiced, and appointed three hundred men and three hundred oxen, and set overseers at their head, in order that they might fell the trees. And they felled them, and they remained lying over the winter. But in the third month of summer they were dragged to the shore of the sea.

And the prince came forth and took up his stand upon them, and sent for me, saying: "Come." . . . And I was brought nigh unto him, and he answered and said unto me: "Behold, the behest that my fathers fulfilled in times past, I have also fulfilled it, albeit thou on thy part hast not done for me what thy fathers did for me. Behold, the last of thy timber hath now arrived and there it is stacked. Now do according to my wish and come to stow it, for in truth it is given unto thee. . . .

And I went to the shore of the sea to where the timber was stacked, and I descried eleven ships drawing nigh on the sea. They belongeth to the Zakar and came with the order: "Take him prisoner, suffer not a ship of his to get to the land of Egypt." Thereupon I sat down and wept.

And the letter-writer of the prince came out to me and said unto me: "What aileth thee?" And I said unto him: "Surely thou seest the birds that for the second time go down into Egypt. Look at them! They go to the cool pool, but how long am I to be left here? Surely thou seest them that come back to take me prisoner."

And he went and told it to the prince, and the prince began to weep because of the tidings told him, that were so grievous. And he sent out his letter-writer unto me, and he brought me two measures of wine and a ram. Moreover, he had brought unto me Tentnut, an Egyptian singer that was with him, saying unto her: "Sing unto him; let not his heart harbour cares!" And he sent unto me, saying: "Eat and drink! Let not thine heart harbour cares! Thou wilt hear all that I shall say to-morrow." And when the morrow came he had his . . . called, and he stood in their midst and said unto the Zakar: "What meaneth this coming of yours?" And they said unto him: "We are come after the shivered ships which thou sendest unto

Egypt with our . . . comrades." And he said unto them: "I cannot take the messenger of Amun prisoner in my land. Let me send him away, and then do ye pursue him in order to take him prisoner."

He put me on board and sent me away . . . to the harbour of the sea. And the wind drave me to the land of Arsa. And they of the city came forth against me to slay me, and between them I was hustled to the place of abode of Heteb, the queen of the city. And I found her as she was coming from her one house and was entering into her other.

And I saluted her, and said unto the people that stood beside her: "Surely there is one among you that understandeth Egyptian." And one of them said: "I understand it." And I said unto him: "Say unto my mistress: 'As far as Thebes, even unto the abode of Amun, I have heard it said that wrong is done in every city, but right is done in the land of Arsa. And now here also wrong is done every day.'" And she said unto me: "But what meaneth it, that thou sayest this?" And I said unto her: "If the sea raged and the wind drave me to the land wherein thou dwellest, thou wilt not suffer them to arrest me in order to slay me, seeing that I am a messenger of Amun. Look well to it. I am one for whom search will be made unceasingly. And as for this crew of the prince of Byblos that they seek to slay, if their lord findeth ten crews of thine he too will slay them."

So she had the people summoned and they were brought forward. And she said unto me: "Lie down and sleep——"

[*Here the papyrus breaks off.*]

# II

# PEOPLES OF THE
# EARLY IRON AGE

The disaster that overtook the civilized world about 1200 B.C. and tore down its structure of nations and empires is perhaps best described as the coming of the Iron Age. It is a characteristic found often in nature—and many historians find it in human society too—that the most highly specialized, the most complexly developed organisms adapt very poorly to environmental change. A profound conservatism leads them to continue to do what they have always done, even when altered conditions render the pattern no longer efficacious.

The use of iron as a material for the manufacture of tools and weapons had potentially far-reaching consequences. Iron is more versatile, more durable, harder and stronger than bronze, but these advantages do not appear to have been so much as noticed by the great Bronze Age powers. A practical method for working iron was developed about 1500 B.C. The invention is usually credited to the Hittites, and if that is correct it is one of their very few original contributions to civilization. In any case, neither they nor their contemporaries saw the potential significance of the new material. The few iron objects that are found in the archaeological remains of the next several centuries are decorative. They are novelties, not utilitarian devices. It was the barbarians from without who, having no age-old commitment to bronze as a way of life, so to speak, first exploited the new material. They came with iron weapons, and the old nations *crumbled before their onslaught. They came from the north, and the destruction in the northern tier of civilized peoples was so great that, until the discoveries of modern archaeology, nothing remained even as a reminder that a civilization had existed in early times in Asia Minor or Greece or Crete. In these areas the light of civilization was extinguished. The cities are gone. Written records occur no more. Farther south, civilization was kept alive and, maintaining its continuity with the past, adopted the new materials, and gradually there developed a dynamism which ultimately produced a rebirth and renewed spreading of civilized life.*

# THE HEBREWS

IT IS on the Syrian-Palestinian coast that the first Iron Age awakenings can be observed. There the destruction of the Bronze Age empires was not a disaster but an opportunity for independent development. The Semitic-speaking Canaanite peoples of this region were to provide the seeds · of the spectacular future. In the northern half of the coast, in Syria, the people who were finally to be known as the Phoenicians continued to flourish in their little principalities centering on trading cities such as Tyre, Sidon, and Byblos. In the southern half, Palestine, a new people took the center of the stage, a people whose influence upon subsequent history is out of all proportion to its size or to its role as a national power.

The Hebrews were an ill-organized group of tribes closely related ethnically to the other Canaanite peoples of the region. They came late to civilization, being still desert nomads when their cousins of the Ugaritic culture (see section on *The Alphabet* in the introduction on Sources for Ancient History) were at their height in the fifteenth century B.C.

## 25 *The Primitive Habiru*

From the Amarna Letters (see Selection 20) of the fourteenth century B.C. come what are believed to be the earliest notices we have of the Hebrews. The *Habiru* (or *Hapiru* or *'Apiru*) to whom reference is made in a number of the letters are generally believed to be the Hebrews of the patriarchal age, although the identification cannot as yet be taken as certain. In the letters the *Habiru* appear as a seminomadic people hungry for land in Palestine, marauders whose depredations provide the puppet princes with an opportunity to show how loyal they are in fighting to maintain the integrity of the pharaoh's territories.

Of the selected letters that follow, numbers 1, 3, 4, and 5 are translated by the present editor from the German translation of J. A. Knudtzon (*Die El-Amarna Tafeln,* numbers 271, 286. 288, and 290); number 2 from the French translation of F. Thureau-Dangin (*Revue d'Assyriologie,* 1922, pp. 98–99).

⊛⊛⊛⊛⊛

I

To the king, my lord, my gods, my Sun. Thus spoke Milkilu,[1] thy servant, the dust beneath thy feet:

Beneath the feet of the king, my lord, my gods, my Sun, seven and seven times I prostrate myself. May the king, my lord, know that the hostilities against me and against Shuwardata have grown to serious proportions. May the king, my lord, then rescue his territory from the hand of the Habiru! If not, then may the king, my lord, send chariots to fetch us away, lest our own servants slay us.

And further: May the king, my lord, inquire of Yanhamu, his servant, concerning the things that are done in his land.

2

To the king, my lord, my Sun, my god, say as follows: Thus speaks Shuwardata, thy servant, the servant of the king and the dust beneath his two feet, the earth that thou treadest:

Beneath the feet of the king, my lord, the Sun of the Heavens, seven and seven times have I prostrated myself both on my belly and on my back. May the king, my lord, know that the Habiru are in arms in the land that the god of the king, my lord, has granted to me, and that I have defeated them.

Further: May the king, my lord, know that all my brothers have abandoned me and that Abdi-hiba and I are making war on the Habiru. Zurata, prince of Accho, and Indaruta, prince of Achshaph, are the allies who came to help me with fifty chariots. Behold, they are with me in the war.

May it please the king, my lord, to send Yanhamu so that we may bring the war to a conclusion and that thou restorest the land of the king, my lord, to. . . .

3

To the king, my lord. Thus spoke Abdi-hiba, thy servant:

Beneath the two feet of my lord, the king, seven and seven times I prostrate myself. What have I done to the king, my lord? I am being slandered before the king, my lord: "Abdi-hiba is disloyal to the king, his

1.  For the identity of the persons named in these letters, see Selection 20.

lord." Behold, neither my father nor my mother put me in this place; the mighty hand of the king established me in the house of my father. Why should I commit crime against the king, my lord? As long as the king, my lord, lives, I shall say to the commissioner of the king, my lord: "Why do you love the Habiru and hate the princes?" But it is for that that I am slandered before the king, my lord. Because I say, "The lands of the king, my lord, are being lost," that is why I am being slandered before the king, my lord.

May the king, my lord, know that when the king, my lord, installed garrison troops, Yanhamu took them all. . . . Egypt . . . of the king, my lord. And so there are no garrison troops.

May the king have a care for his land!

May the king have a care for his land!

The lands of the king, my lord, are all in rebellion. Ilimilku is destroying the entire land of the king. So may the king, my lord, have a care for his land!

I say: "I shall go before the king, my lord, and I shall see the two eyes of the king, my lord." But enemies have grown powerful against me and so I cannot appear before the king, my lord. Therefore may it seem right to the king. . . . to send a garrison and to let me enter and see the two eyes of the king, my lord! As long as the king, my lord, lives; as long as his commissioners desert, will I continue to say: "The king's lands are being lost." But you hear me not. All the princes are being lost; not a prince remains to the king, my lord.

May the king direct his face to his armed forces, that the soldiers of the king, my lord, march forth! The king's lands are no longer his. The Habiru plunder all the king's lands. But if troops are forthcoming this year, then the lands of the king, my lord, can still be retained; if not, then the lands of the king, my lord, are lost.

To the scribe of the king, my lord. Thus spoke Abdi-hiba, thy servant:

Bring words, eloquent words, to the king, my lord. Lost are all the lands of the king, my lord!

4

To the king, my lord, my Sun. Thus spoke Abdi-hiba, thy servant:

Beneath the two feet of the king, my lord, seven and seven times I prostrate myself. Behold, the king, my lord, has set his name upon the rising of the sun and upon the setting of the sun. Behold the infamy they have committed against me. Behold, I am not a prince; I am but a subordinate official of the king, my lord. Behold, I am a shepherd of the king and one who bears the burden of the king's tribute. Not my father, not my mother, but the mighty hand of the king has established me in the house of my father. . . . came to me. . . . I gave him ten servants. Shuta, the king's commissioner, came to me. Into the hand of Shuta I gave twenty-one maidens and eighty . . . -persons as a gift to the king, my lord.

May the king have a care for his land! The king's land is being lost. Everything is being taken from me; hostilities are going on against me. As far as the lands of Shiri and Gath-carmel the lands are slipping away from their princes; and I am attacked. Once I produced a . . . and now I do not see the two eyes of the king, my lord, for warfare presses upon me. On another occasion I launched a ship on the sea, and the mighty hand of the king took Naharim and Kapasi. But now the Habiru capture the king's cities. No prince is left to the king, my lord; all are being lost. Behold, Turbazu has been killed before the city gate of Zilu; yet the king holds back. Behold, Zimrida of Lachish: he was cut down by slaves who had joined with the Habiru. Yaptih-Adda was killed at the city gate of Zilu; still the king holds back and does not bring them to account.

Then let the king have a care for his land, and may he turn his face to the need for soldiers for the land that gives its tribute! For if soldiers are not supplied this year, then all the lands of the king, my lord, will be lost. May no one be able to say before the king, my lord, that the land of the king, my lord, is going to be lost and that all the princes will be lost. If soldiers are not sent this year, then may the king send a commissioner who will take me to himself together with my brothers, and we shall die in the presence of the king, our lord.

To the scribe of the king, my lord. Thus spoke Abdi-hiba, the servant: Beneath the two feet I prostrate myself. Bring words, eloquent words, to the king. Thy faithful servant and thy son am I.

5

To the king, my lord. Thus spoke Abdi-hiba, thy servant: Beneath the two feet of the king, my lord, seven and seven times I prostrate myself. Behold the criminal deed done by Milkilu and Shuwardata to the land of the king, my lord. They have hired men from Gezer, from Gath, from Kilti and taken the land belonging to the town of Rubuta. The king's land has fallen to the Habiru, and now to add to that, a town of the land of Jerusalem, by the name of Beth-Ninib, a town belonging to the king, has gone over to the people of Kilti.

May the king listen to Abdi-hiba, thy servant, and send troops to secure the king's land to the king once more! But if no troops are forthcoming, then the king's land will fall to the Habiru. This fate of the land will indeed have come about through Milkilu and through Shuwardata. . . . And may the king have a care for his land!

# 26  The Old Testament as History

By the twelfth century B.C. the Hebrews had filtered into Palestine and settled there. They assimilated—and were civilized by—the Canaanite inhabitants. Early in the tenth century their hold on the country was threatened: one of the "peoples of the sea," the Philistines, who had attempted to invade the Nile Delta, upon failing there had moved eastward and settled at the southeastern corner of the Mediterranean around Gaza. There for two centuries they prospered, and about 1000 B.C. they were attempting to expand northward into Hebrew territory.

Little is known about the Philistines, and it is variously believed that they came originally from Crete, from Albania, or from Asia Minor. It is one of the ironies of history that it is from the Philistines that has come the name of "Palestine," the land they failed to win. The sole historical importance of the Philistines is that the threat they posed caused the Hebrews to unite into a nation.

The United Kingdom of the Hebrews lasted for only about seventy years under Saul, David, and Solomon. After the death of Solomon about 930 B.C., the country divided into the northern kingdom of Israel and the southern kingdom of Judah, and its political fortunes are all downhill thereafter. At no time were the Hebrews very powerful, and their neighbors did not take them much into account. Even their height in the splendor of Solomon's reign did not cause more than a ripple in the international world of the time. Solomon's building, his trading operations, his vaunted visit by the queen of Sheba merely indicate that he had wrought well enough to find a modest place for his nation among the trading peoples of the eastern Mediterranean.

The importance of the Hebrews lies, of course, in their monotheistic religion and in the book which is the testimonial to that faith. The Old

Testament happens to be the most important single literary contribution in the whole range of what we today call "the Western tradition," but it would form one of the world's major literatures in any case. It is a strange fact that this great compilation seems to have been completely unknown until Christian times to any of the ancient peoples with whom the Hebrews were in contact through all the long centuries of their Dispersion. The writing and the compilation of the books that comprise the Old Testament were the work of a millennium, from as far back as 900 B.C. until the collection reached its canonical form in the first century A.D. The historical study of the Old Testament is a career in itself. The modern discovery of the earlier literatures of the Near East and Egypt have shed much light on the origins and significance of its legends, hymns, proverbs, songs, laws—as the most superficial reading of many of the preceding selections will immediately suggest to anyone at all familiar with the Old Testament.

For the student of history there is one aspect of the Old Testament that automatically claims attention: the question of its reliability as a historical source. In the nineteenth century A.D. the systematic study of the Bible tended to belittle it as a source for historically credible information, but twentieth-century study and archaeological finds have brought a new credit to the historical accuracy of the Old Testament. Indeed, the assertion has been made that in its historical books is to be found the earliest true narrative history ever written, an original intellectual and literary achievement far surpassing the annalistic records of the Egyptian or Hittite kings and antedating by several centuries the works of the Greek historians.

It is instructive to compare the following narrative from the account of the reign of King David as found in II Samuel 11–19 with various selections from the Greek historians (see Part III) for what can be learned of the writers' methods and purposes, their ideas about the nature and meaning of past events. The translation is that of the King James Version.

❁❁❁❁❁

And it came to pass, after the year was expired, at the time when kings go forth to battle, that David sent Joab, and his servants with him, and all Israel; and they destroyed the children of Ammon, and besieged Rabbah. But David tarried still at Jerusalem.

And it came to pass in an eveningtide, that David arose from off his bed, and walked upon the roof of the king's house: and from the roof he saw a woman washing herself; and the woman was very beautiful to look upon. And David sent and inquired after the woman. And one said, Is not this Bathsheba, the daughter of Eliam, the wife of Uriah the Hittite? And David sent messengers, and took her; and she came in unto him, and he lay with her; for she was purified from her uncleanness: and she returned unto her house. And the woman conceived, and sent and told David, and said, I am with child.

And David sent to Joab, saying, Send me Uriah the Hittite. And Joab sent Uriah to David. And when Uriah was come unto him, David demanded of him how Joab did, and how the people did, and how the war prospered. And David said to Uriah, Go down to thy house, and wash thy feet. And Uriah departed out of the king's house, and there followed him a mess of meat from the king. But Uriah slept at the door of the king's house with all the servants of his lord, and went not down to his house. And when they had told David, saying, Uriah went not down unto his house, David said unto Uriah, Camest thou not from thy journey? why then didst thou not go down unto thine house? And Uriah said unto David, The ark, and Israel, and Judah, abide in tents; and my lord Joab, and the servants of my lord, are encamped in the open fields; shall I then go into mine house, to eat and to drink, and to lie with my wife? as thou livest, and as thy soul liveth, I will not do this thing. And David said to Uriah, Tarry here today also, and to morrow I will let thee depart. So Uriah abode in Jerusalem that day, and the morrow. And when David had called him, he did eat and drink before him; and he made him drunk: and at even he went out to lie on his bed with the servants of his lord, but went not down to his house.

And it came to pass in the morning, that David wrote a letter to Joab, and sent it by the hand of Uriah. And he wrote in the letter, saying, Set ye Uriah in the forefront of the hottest battle, and retire ye from him, that he may be smitten, and die. And it came to pass, when Joab observed the city, that he assigned Uriah unto a place where he knew that valiant men were. And the men of the city went out, and fought with Joab: and there fell some of the people of the servants of David; and Uriah the Hittite died also.

Then Joab sent and told David all the things concerning the war; And charged the messenger, saying, When thou hast made an end of telling the matters of the war unto the king, And if so be that the king's wrath arise, and he say unto thee, Wherefore approached ye so nigh unto the city when ye did fight? knew ye not that they would shoot from the wall? Who smote Abimelech the son of Jerubbesheth? did not a woman cast a piece of a millstone upon him from the wall, that he died in Thebez? why went ye nigh the wall? then say thou, Thy servant Uriah the Hittite is dead also.

So the messenger went, and came and shewed David all that Joab had sent him for. And the messenger said unto David, Surely the men prevailed against us, and came out unto us into the field, and we were upon them even unto the entering of the gate. And the shooters shot from off the wall upon thy servants; and some of the king's servants be dead, and thy servant Uriah the Hittite is dead also. Then David said unto the messenger, Thus shalt thou say unto Joab, Let not this thing displease thee, for the sword devoureth one as well as another: make thy battle more strong against the city, and overthrow it: and encourage thou him.

And when the wife of Uriah heard that Uriah her husband was dead, she mourned for her husband. And when the mourning was past, David sent and fetched her to his house, and she became his wife, and bare him a son. But the thing that David had done displeased the Lord.

And the Lord sent Nathan unto David. And he came unto him, and said unto him, There were two men in one city; the one rich, and the other poor. The rich man had exceeding many flocks and herds: But the poor man had nothing, save one little ewe lamb, which he had bought and nourished up: and it grew up together with him, and with his children; it did eat of his own meat, and drank of his own cup, and lay in his bosom, and was unto him as a daughter. And there came a traveller unto the rich man, and he spared to take of his own flock and of his own herd, to dress for the way-faring man that was come unto him; but took the poor man's lamb, and dressed it for the man that was to come to him. And David's anger was greatly kindled against the man; and he said to Nathan, As the Lord liveth, the man that hath done this thing shall surely die: And he shall restore the lamb fourfold, because he did this thing, and because he had no pity.

And Nathan said to David, Thou art the man. Thus saith the Lord God of Israel, I anointed thee king over Israel, and I delivered thee out of the hand of Saul; And I gave thee thy master's house, and thy master's wives into thy bosom, and gave thee the house of Israel and of Judah; and if that had been too little, I would moreover have given unto thee such and such things. Wherefore hast thou despised the commandment of the Lord, to do evil in his sight? thou hast killed Uriah the Hittite with the sword, and hast taken his wife to be thy wife, and hast slain him with the sword of the children of Ammon. Now therefore the sword shall never depart from thine house; because thou hast despised me, and hast taken the wife of Uriah the Hittite to be thy wife. Thus saith the Lord, Behold, I will raise up evil against thee out of thine own house, and I will take thy wives before thine eyes, and give them unto thy neighbour, and he shall lie with thy wives in the sight of this sun. For thou didst it secretly, but I will do this thing before all Israel, and before the sun. And David said unto Nathan, I have sinned against the Lord. And Nathan said unto David, The Lord also hath put away thy sin; thou shalt not die. Howbeit, because by this deed thou hast given great occasion to the enemies of the Lord to blaspheme, the child also that is born unto thee shall surely die.

And Nathan departed into his house. And the Lord struck the child that Uriah's wife bare unto David, and it was very sick. David therefore besought God for the child; and David fasted, and went in, and lay all night upon the earth. And the elders of his house arose, and went to him, to raise him up from the earth: but he would not, neither did he eat bread with them. And it came to pass on the seventh day, that the child died. And the servants of David feared to tell him that the child was dead: for they said, Behold, while the child was yet alive, we spake unto him, and he would not hearken unto our voice: how will he then vex himself, if we tell him that the child is dead? But when David saw that his servants whispered, David perceived that the child was dead: therefore David said unto his servants, Is the child dead? And they said, He is dead. Then David arose from the earth, and washed, and anointed himself, and changed his apparel, and came into the house of the Lord, and worshipped: then he came to his own house; and when he required, they set bread before him, and he did eat. Then said his servants unto him, What thing is this that thou hast done? thou didst fast and weep for the child, while it was alive; but when the child was dead, thou didst rise and eat bread. And he said, While the child was yet alive, I fasted and wept: for I said, Who can tell whether God will be gracious to me, that the child may live? But now he is dead, wherefore should I fast? can I bring him back again? I shall go to him, but he shall not return to me.

And David comforted Bathsheba his wife, and went in unto her, and lay with her: and she bare a son, and he called his name Solomon: and the Lord loved him. And he sent by the hand of Nathan the prophet; and he called his name Jedidiah, because of the Lord.

And Joab fought against Rabbah of the children of Ammon, and took the royal city. And Joab sent messengers to David, and said, I have fought against Rabbah, and have taken the city of waters. Now therefore gather the rest of the people together, and encamp against the city, and take it: lest I take the city, and it be called after my name. And David gathered all the people together, and went to Rabbah, and fought against it, and took it. And he took their king's crown from off his head, the weight whereof was a talent of gold with the precious stones: and it was set on David's head.

And he brought forth the spoil of the city in great abundance. And he brought forth the people that were therein, and put them under saws, and under harrows of iron, and under axes of iron, and made them pass through the brick-kiln: and thus did he unto all the cities of the children of Ammon. So David and all the people returned unto Jerusalem.

And it came to pass after this, that Absalom the son of David had a fair sister, whose name was Tamar; and Amnon the son of David loved her. And Amnon was so vexed, that he fell sick for his sister Tamar; for she was a virgin; and Amnon thought it hard for him to do anything to her. But Amnon had a friend, whose name was Jonadab, the son of Shimeah David's brother: and Jonadab was a very subtil man. And he said unto him, Why art thou, being the king's son, lean from day to day? wilt thou not tell me? And Amnon said unto him, I love Tamar, my brother Absalom's sister. And Jonadab said unto him, Lay thee down on thy bed, and make thyself sick: and when thy father cometh to see thee, say unto him, I pray thee, let my sister Tamar come, and give me meat, and dress the meat in my sight, that I may see it, and eat it at her hand.

So Amnon lay down, and made himself sick: and when the king was come to see him, Amnon said unto the king, I pray thee, let Tamar my sister come, and make me a couple of cakes in my sight, that I may eat at her hand. Then David sent home to Tamar, saying, Go now to thy brother Amnon's house, and dress him meat. So Tamar went to her brother Amnon's house; and he was laid down. And she took flour, and kneaded it, and made cakes in his sight, and did bake the cakes. And she took a pan, and poured them out before him; but he refused to eat. And Amnon said, Have out all men from me. And they went out every man from him. And Amnon said unto Tamar, Bring the meat into the chamber, that I may eat of thine hand. And Tamar took the cakes which she had made, and brought them into the chamber to Amnon her brother. And when she had brought them unto him to eat, he took hold of her, and said unto her, Come lie with me my sister. And she answered him, Nay, my brother, do not force me; for no such thing ought to be done in Israel: do not thou this folly. And I, whither shall I cause my shame to go? and as for thee, thou shalt be as one of the fools in Israel. Now therefore, I pray thee, speak unto the king; for he will not withhold me from thee. Howbeit he would not hearken unto her voice: but, being stronger than she, forced her, and lay with her.

Then Amnon hated her exceedingly; so that the hatred wherewith he hated her was greater than the love wherewith he had loved her. And Amnon said unto her, Arise, be gone. And she said unto him, There is no cause: this evil in sending me away is greater than the other that thou didst unto me. But he would not hearken unto her. Then he called his servant that ministered unto him, and said, Put now this woman out from me, and bolt the door after her. And she had a garment of divers colours upon her: for with such robes were the king's daughters that were virgins apparelled. Then his servant brought her out, and bolted the door after her.

And Tamar put ashes on her head, and rent her garment of divers colours that was on her, and laid her hand on her head, and went on crying. And Absalom her brother said unto her, Hath Amnon thy brother been with thee? but hold now thy peace, my sister: he is thy brother; regard not this thing. So Tamar remained desolate in her brother Absalom's house.

But when King David heard of all these things, he was very wroth. And Absalom spake unto his brother Amnon neither good nor bad: for Absalom hated Amnon, because he had forced his sister Tamar.

And it came to pass after two full years, that Absalom had sheepshearers in Baal-hazor, which is beside Ephraim: and Absalom invited all the king's sons. And Absalom came to the king, and said, Behold now, thy servant hath sheepshearers; let the king, I beseech thee, and his servants go with thy servant. And the king said to Absalom, Nay, my son, let us not all now go, lest we be chargeable unto thee. And he pressed him: howbeit he would not go, but blessed him. Then said Absalom, If not, I pray thee, let my brother Amnon go with us. And the king said unto him, Why should he go with thee? But Absalom pressed him, that he let Amnon and all the king's sons go with him.

Now Absalom had commanded his servants, saying, Mark ye now when Amnon's heart is merry with wine, and when I say unto you, Smite Amnon; then kill him, fear not: have not I commanded you? be courageous, and be valiant. And the servants of Absalom did unto Amnon as Absalom had commanded. Then all the king's sons arose, and every man gat him up upon his mule, and fled.

And it came to pass, while they were in the way, that tidings came to David, saying, Absalom hath slain all the king's sons, and there is not one of them left. Then the king arose, and tare his garments, and lay on the earth; and all his servants stood by with their clothes rent. And Jonadab, the son of Shimeah David's brother, answered and said, Let not my lord suppose that they have slain all the young men the king's sons; for Amnon only is dead: for by the appointment of Absalom this hath been determined from the day that he forced his sister Tamar. Now therefore let not my lord the king take the thing to his heart, to think that all the king's sons are dead: for Amnon only is dead. But Absalom fled. And the young man that kept the watch lifted up his eyes, and looked, and, behold, there came much people by the way of the hillside behind him. And Jonadab said unto the king, Behold, the king's sons come: as thy servant said, so it is. And it came to pass, as soon as he had made an end of speaking, that, behold, the king's sons came, and lifted up their voice and wept: and the king also and all his servants wept very sore.

But Absalom fled, and went to Talmai, the son of Ammihud, king of Geshur. And David mourned for his son every day. So Absalom fled, and went to Geshur, and was there three years. And the soul of King David longed to go forth unto Absalom: for he was comforted concerning Amnon, seeing he was dead.

Now Joab the son of Zeruiah perceived that the king's heart was toward Absalom. And Joab sent to Tekoah, and fetched thence a wise woman, and said unto her, I pray thee, feign thyself to be a mourner, and put on now mourning apparel, and anoint not thyself with oil, but be as a woman that had a long time mourned for the dead: And come to the king, and speak on this manner unto him. So Joab put the words in her mouth.

And when the woman of Tekoah spake to the king, she fell on her face to the ground, and did obeisance, and said, Help, O king. And the king said unto her, What aileth thee? And she answered, I am indeed a widow woman, and mine husband is dead. And thy handmaid had two sons, and they two strove together in the field, and there was none to part them, but the one smote the other, and slew him. And, behold, the whole family is risen against thine handmaid, and they said, Deliver him that smote his brother, that we may kill him, for the life of his brother whom he slew; and we will destroy the heir also: and so they shall quench my coal which is left, and shall not leave to my husband neither name nor remainder upon the earth. And the king said unto the woman, Go to thine house, and I will give charge concerning thee. And the woman of Tekoah said unto the king, My lord, O king, the iniquity be on me, and on my father's house: and the king and his throne be guiltless. And the king said, Whosoever saith ought unto thee, bring him to me, and he shall not touch thee any more. Then said she, I pray thee, let the king remember the Lord thy God, that thou wouldest not suffer the revengers of blood to destroy any more, lest they destroy my son. And he said, As the Lord liveth, there shall not one hair of thy son fall to the earth. Then the woman said, Let thine handmaid, I pray thee, speak one word unto my lord the king. And he said, Say on. And the woman said, Wherefore then hast thou thought such a thing against the people of God? for the king doth speak this thing as one which is faulty, in that the king doth not fetch home again his banished. For we must needs die, and are as water spilt on the ground, which cannot be gathered up again; neither doth God respect any person: yet doth he devise means, that his banished be not expelled from him. Now therefore that I am come to speak of this thing unto my lord the king, it is because the people have made me afraid: and thy handmaid said, I will now speak unto the king; it may be that the king will perform the request of his handmaid. For the king will hear, to deliver his handmaid out of the hand of the man that would destroy me and my son together out of the inheritance of God. Then thine handmaid said, The word of my lord the king shall now be comfortable: for as an angel of God, so is my lord the king to discern good and bad: therefore the Lord thy God will be with thee. Then the king answered and said unto the woman, Hide not from me, I pray thee, the thing that I shall ask thee. And the woman said, Let my lord the king now speak. And the king said, Is not the hand of Joab with thee in all this? And the woman answered and said, As thy soul liveth, my lord the king, none can turn to the right hand or to the left from ought that my lord the king hath spoken: for thy servant Joab, he bade me, and he put all these words in the mouth of thine handmaid: To fetch about this form of speech hath thy servant Joab done this thing: and my lord is wise, according to the wisdom of an angel of God, to know all things that are in the earth.

And the king said unto Joab, Behold now, I have done this thing: go therefore, bring the young man Absalom again. And Joab fell to the ground on his face, and bowed himself, and thanked the king: and Joab said, To day they servant knoweth that I have found grace in thy sight, my lord, O king, in that the king hath fulfilled the request of his servant. So Joab arose and went to Geshur, and brought Absalom to Jerusalem. And the king said, Let him turn to his own house, and let him not see my face. So Absalom returned to his own house, and saw not the king's face.

But in all Israel there was none to be so much praised as Absalom for his beauty: from the sole of his foot even to the crown of his head there was no blemish in him. And when he polled his head, (for it was at every year's end that he polled it: because the hair was heavy on him, therefore he polled it:) he weighed the hair of his head at two hundred shekels after the king's weight. And unto Absalom there were born three sons, and one daughter, whose name was Tamar: she was a woman of a fair countenance.

So Absalom dwelt two full years in Jerusalem, and saw not the king's face. Therefore Absalom sent for Joab, to have sent him to the king; but he would not come to him: and when he sent again the second time, he would not come. Therefore he said unto his servants, See, Joab's field is near mine, and he hath barley there; go and set it on fire. And Absalom's servants set the field on fire. Then Joab arose, and came to Absalom unto his house, and said unto him, Wherefore have thy servants set my field on fire? And Absalom answered Joab, Behold, I sent unto thee, saying, Come hither, that I may send thee to the king, to say, Wherefore am I come from Geshur? it had been good for me to have been there still: now therefore let me see the king's face; and if there be any iniquity in me, let him kill me. So Joab came to the king, and told him: and when he had called for Absalom, he came to the king, and bowed himself on his face to the ground before the king: and the king kissed Absalom.

And it came to pass after this, that Absalom prepared him chariots and horses, and fifty men to run before him. And Absalom rose up early, and stood beside the way of the gate: and it was so, that when any man that had a controversy came to the king for judgment, then Absalom called unto him, and said, Of what city art thou? And he said, Thy servant is of one of the tribes of Israel. And Absalom said unto him, See, thy matters are good and right; but there is no man deputed of the king to hear thee. Absalom said moreover, O that I were made judge in the land, that every man which hath any suit or cause might come unto me, and I would do him justice! And it was so, that when any man came nigh to him to do him obeisance, he put forth his hand, and took him, and kissed him. And on this manner did Absalom to all Israel that came to the king for judgment: so Absalom stole the hearts of the men of Israel.

And it came to pass after forty years, that Absalom said unto the king, I pray thee, let me go and pay my vow, which I have vowed unto the Lord, in Hebron. For thy servant vowed a vow while I abode at Geshur in Syria, saying, If the Lord shall bring me again indeed to Jerusalem, then I will serve the Lord. And the king said unto him, Go in peace. So he arose, and went to Hebron.

But Absalom sent spies throughout all the tribes of Israel, saying, As soon as ye hear the sound of the trumpet, then ye shall say, Absalom reigneth in Hebron. And with Absalom went two hundred men out of Jerusalem, that were called; and they went in their simplicity, and they knew not any thing. And Absalom sent for Ahithophel the Gilonite, David's counseller, from his city, even from Giloh, while he offered sacrifices. And the conspiracy was strong; for the people increased continually with Absalom. And there came a messenger to David, saying, The hearts of the men of Israel are after Absalom. And David said unto all his servants that were with him at Jerusalem, Arise, and let us flee; for we shall not else escape from Absalom: make speed to depart, lest he overtake us suddenly, and bring evil upon us, and smite the city with the edge of the sword. And the king's servants said unto the king, Behold, thy servants are ready to do whatsoever my lord the king shall appoint. And the king went forth, and all his household after him. And the king left ten women, which were concubines, to keep the house. And the king went forth, and all the people after him, and tarried in a place that was far off. And all his servants passed on beside him; and all the Cherethites, and all the Pelethites, and all the Gittites, six hundred men which came after him from Gath, passed on before the king.

Then said the king to Ittai the Gittite, Wherefore goest thou also with us? return to thy place, and abide with the king: for thou art a stranger, and also an exile. Whereas thou camest but yesterday, should I this day make thee go up and down with us? seeing I go whither I may, return thou, and take back thy brethren: mercy and truth be with thee. And Ittai answered the king, and said, As the Lord liveth, and as the lord my king liveth, surely in what place my lord the king shall be, whether in death or life, even there also will thy servant be. And David said to Ittai, Go and pass over. And Ittai the Gittite passed over, and all his men, and all the little ones that were with him. And all the country wept with a loud voice, and all the people passed over: the king also himself passed over the brook Kidron, and all the people passed over, toward the way of the wilderness.

And lo Zadok also, and all the Levites were with him, bearing the ark of the covenant of God: and they set down the ark of God; and Abiathar went up, until all the people had done passing out of the city. And the king said unto Zadok, Carry back the ark of God into the city: if I shall find favour in the eyes of the Lord, he will bring me again, and shew me both it, and his habitation: But if he thus say, I have no delight in thee; behold, here am I, let him do to me as seemeth good unto him. The king said also unto Zadok the priest, Art not thou a seer? return into the city in peace, and your two sons with you, Ahimaaz thy son, and Jonathan the son of Abiathar. See, I will tarry in the plain of the wilderness, until there come word from you to certify me. Zadok therefore and Abiathar carried the ark of God again to Jerusalem: and they tarried there.

And David went up by the ascent of mount Olivet, and wept as he went up, and had his head covered, and he went barefoot; and all the people that was with him covered every man his head, and they went up, weeping as they went up.

And one told David, saying, Ahithophel is among the conspirators with Absalom. And David said, O Lord, I pray thee, turn the counsel of Ahithophel into foolishness.

And it came to pass, that when David was come to the top of the mount, where he worshipped God, behold, Hushai the Archite came to meet him with his coat rent, and earth upon his head: Unto whom David said, If thou passest on with me, then thou shalt be a burden unto me: But if thou return to the city, and say unto Absalom, I will be thy servant, O king; as I have been thy father's servant hitherto, so will I now also be thy servant: then mayest thou for me defeat the counsel of Ahithophel. And hast thou not there with thee Zadok and Abiathar the priests? therefore it shall be, that what thing soever thou shalt hear out of the king's house, thou shalt tell it to Zadok and Abiathar the priests. Behold, they have there with them their two sons, Ahimaaz Zadok's son, and Jonathan Abiathar's son; and by them ye shall send unto me every thing that ye can hear. So Hushai David's friend came into the city, and Absalom came into Jerusalem.

And when David was a little past the top of the hill, behold, Ziba the servant of Mephibosheth met him, with a couple of asses saddled, and upon them two hundred loaves of bread, and an hundred bunches of raisins, and an hundred of summer fruits, and a bottle of wine. And the king said unto Ziba, What meanest thou by these? And Ziba said, The asses be for the king's household to ride on; and the bread and summer fruit for the young men to eat; and the wine, that such as be faint in the wilderness may drink. And the king said, And where is thy master's son? And Ziba said unto the king, Behold, he abideth at Jerusalem: for he said, To day shall the house of Israel restore me the kingdom of my father. Then said the king to Ziba, Behold, thine are all that pertained unto Mephibosheth. And Ziba said, I humbly beseech thee that I may find grace in thy sight, my lord, O king.

And when king David came to Bahurim, behold, thence came out a man of the family of the house of Saul, whose name was Shimei, the son of Gera: he came forth, and cursed still as he came. And he cast stones at David, and at all the servants of king David: and all the people and all the mighty men were on his right hand and on his left. And thus said Shimei when he cursed, Come out, come out, thou bloody man, and thou

[ 236 ]

man of Belial: The Lord hath returned upon thee all the blood of the house of Saul, in whose stead thou hast reigned; and the Lord hath delivered the kingdom into the hand of Absalom thy son: and, behold, thou art taken in thy mischief, because thou art a bloody man.

Then said Abishai the son of Zeruiah unto the king, Why should this dead dog curse my lord the king? let me go over, I pray thee, and take off his head. And the king said, What have I to do with you, ye sons of Zeruiah? so let him curse, because the Lord hath said unto him, Curse David. Who shall then say, Wherefore hast thou done so? And David said to Abishai, and to all his servants, Behold, my son, which came forth of my bowels, seeketh my life: how much more now may this Benjamite do it? let him alone, and let him curse; for the Lord hath bidden him. It may be that the Lord will look on mine affliction, and that the Lord will requite me good for his cursing this day. And as David and his men went by the way, Shimei went along on the hill's side over against him, and cursed as he went, and threw stones at him, and cast dust. And the king, and all the people that were with him, came weary, and refreshed themselves there.

And Absalom, and all the people the men of Israel, came to Jerusalem, and Ahithophel with him. And it came to pass, when Hushai the Archite, David's friend, was come unto Absalom, that Hushai said unto Absalom, God save the king, God save the king. And Absalom said to Hushai, Is this thy kindness to thy friend? why wentest thou not with thy friend? And Hushai said unto Absalom, Nay; but whom the Lord, and this people, and all the men of Israel choose, his will I be, and with him will I abide. And again, whom should I serve? should I not serve in the presence of his son? as I have served in thy father's presence, so will I be in thy presence.

Then said Absalom to Ahithophel, Give counsel among you what we shall do. And Ahithophel said unto Absalom, Go in unto thy father's concubines, which he hath left to keep the house; and all Israel shall hear that thou art abhorred of thy father: then shall the hands of all that are with thee be strong. So they spread Absalom a tent upon the top of the house; and Absalom went in unto his father's concubines in the sight of all Israel. And the counsel of Ahithophel, which he counselled in those days, was as if a man had inquired at the oracle of God: so was all the counsel of Ahithophel both with David and with Absalom.

Moreover Ahithophel said unto Absalom, Let me now choose out twelve thousand men, and I will arise and pursue after David this night: And I will come upon him while he is weary and weak handed, and will make him afraid: and all the people that are with him shall flee; and I will smite the king only: And I will bring back all the people unto thee: the man whom thou seekest is as if all returned: so all the people shall be in peace. And the saying pleased Absalom well, and all the elders of Israel. Then said Absalom, Call now Hushai the Archite also, and let us hear likewise what he saith. And when Hushai was come to Absalom, Absalom spake unto him, saying, Ahithophel hath spoken after this manner: shall we do after his saying? if not; speak thou. And Hushai said unto Absalom, The counsel that Ahithophel hath given is not good at this time. For, said Hushai, thou knowest thy father and his men, that they be chafed in their minds, as a bear robbed of her whelps in the field: and thy father is a man of war, and will not lodge with the people. Behold, he is hid now in some pit, or in some other place: and it will come to pass, when some of them be overthrown at the first, that whosoever heareth it will say, There is a slaughter among the people that follow Absalom. And he also that is valiant, whose heart is as the heart of a lion, shall utterly melt: for all Israel knoweth that thy father is a mighty man, and they which be with him are valiant men. Therefore I counsel that all Israel be generally gathered unto thee, from Dan even to Beersheba, as the sand that is by the sea for multitude; and that thou go to battle in thine own person. So shall we come upon him in some place where he shall be found, and we will light upon him as the dew falleth on the ground: and of him and of all the men that are with him there shall not be left so much as one. Moreover, if he be gotten into a city, then shall all Israel bring ropes to that city, and we will draw it into the river, until there be not one small stone found there. And Absalom and all the men of Israel said, The counsel of Hushai the Archite is better than the counsel of Ahithophel. For the Lord had appointed to defeat the good counsel of Ahithophel, to the intent that the Lord might bring evil upon Absalom.

Then said Hushai unto Zadok and to Abiathar the priests, Thus and thus did Ahithophel counsel Absalom and the elders of Israel; and thus and thus have I counselled. Now therefore send quickly, and tell David, saying, Lodge not this night in the plains of the wilderness, but speedily pass over; lest the king be swallowed up, and all the people that are with him. Now Jonathan and Ahimaaz stayed by En-rogel; for they might not be seen to come into the city: and a wench went and told them; and they went and told king David. Nevertheless a lad saw them, and told Absalom: but they went both of them away quickly, and came to a man's house in Bahurim, which had a well in his court; whither they went down. And the woman took and spread a covering over the well's mouth, and spread ground corn thereon; and the thing was not known. And when Absalom's servants came to the woman to the house, they said, Where is Ahimaaz and Jonathan? And the woman said unto them, They be gone over the brook of water. And when they had sought and could not find them, they returned to Jerusalem. And it came to pass, after they were departed, that they came up out of the well, and went and told king David, and said unto David, Arise, and pass quickly over the water: for thus hath Ahithophel counselled against you. Then David arose, and all the people that were with him, and they passed over Jordan: by the morning light there lacked not one of them that was not gone over Jordan.

And when Ahithophel saw that his counsel was not followed, he saddled his ass, and arose, and gat him home to his house, to his city, and put his household in order, and hanged himself, and died, and was buried in the sepulchre of his father. Then David came to Mahanaim. And Absalom passed over Jordan, he and all the men of Israel with him.

And Absalom made Amasa captain of the host instead of Joab: which Amasa was a man's son, whose name was Ithra an Israelite, that went in to Abigail the daughter of Nahash, sister to Zeruiah Joab's mother. So Israel and Absalom pitched in the land of Gilead.

And it came to pass, when David was come to Mahanaim, that Shobi the son of Nahash of Rabbah, of the children of Ammon, and Machir the son of Ammiel of Lo-debar, and Barzillai the Gileadite of Rogelim, brought beds, and basons, and earthen vessels, and wheat, and barley, and flour, and parched corn, and beans, and lentiles, and parched pulse, and honey, and butter, and sheep, and cheese of kine, for David and for the people that were with him, to eat: for they said, The people is hungry, and weary, and thirsty, in the wilderness.

And David numbered the people that were with him, and set captains of thousands and captains of hundreds over them. And David sent forth a third part of the people under the hand of Joab, and a third part under the hand of Abishai the son of Zeruiah, Joab's brother, and a third part under the hand of Ittai the Gittite. And the king said unto the people, I will surely go forth with you myself also. But the people answered, Thou shalt not go forth: for if we flee away, they will not care for us; neither if half of us die, will they care for us: but now thou art worth ten thousand of us: therefore now it is better that thou succour us out of the city. And the king said unto them, What seemeth you best I will do. And the king stood by the gate side, and all the people came out by hundreds and by thousands. And the king commanded Joab and Abishai and Ittai, saying, Deal gently for my sake with the young man, even Absalom. And all the people heard when the king gave all the captains charge concerning Absalom.

So the people went out into the field against Israel: and the battle was in the wood of Ephraim; where the people of Israel were slain before the servants of David, and there was there a great slaughter that day of twenty thousand men. For the battle was there scattered over the face of all the country: and the wood devoured more people that day than the sword devoured.

And Absalom met the servants of David. And Absalom rode upon a mule, and the mule went under the thick boughs of a great oak, and his head caught hold of the oak, and he was taken up between the heaven and the earth; and the mule that was under him went away. And a certain man saw it, and told Joab, and said, Behold, I saw Absalom hanged in an oak. And Joab said unto the man that told him, And, behold, thou sawest him, and why didst thou not smite him there to the ground? and I would have given thee ten shekels of silver, and a girdle. And the man said unto Joab, Though I should receive a thousand shekels of silver in mine hand, yet would I not put forth mine hand against the king's son: for in our hearing the king charged thee and Abishai and Ittai, saying, Beware that none touch the young man Absalom. Otherwise I should have wrought falsehood against mine own life: for there is no matter hid from the king, and thou thyself wouldest have set thyself against me. Then said Joab, I may not tarry thus with thee. And he took three darts in his hand, and thrust them through the heart of Absalom, while he was yet alive in the midst of the oak. And ten young men that bare Joab's armour compassed about and smote Absalom, and slew him. And Joab blew the trumpet, and the people returned from pursuing after Israel: for Joab held back the people. And they took Absalom, and cast him into a great pit in the wood, and laid a very great heap of stones upon him: and all Israel fled every one to his tent.

Now Absalom in his lifetime had taken and reared up for himself a pillar, which is in the king's dale: for he said, I have no son to keep my name in remembrance: and he called the pillar after his own name: and it is called unto this day, Absalom's place.

Then said Ahimaaz the son of Zadok, Let me now run, and bear the king tidings, how that the Lord hath avenged him of his enemies. And

Joab said unto him, Thou shalt not bear tidings this day, but thou shalt bear tidings another day: but this day thou shalt bear no tidings, because the king's son is dead. Then said Joab to Cushi, Go tell the king what thou hast seen. And Cushi bowed himself unto Joab, and ran. Then said Ahimaaz the son of Zadok yet again to Joab, But howsoever, let me, I pray thee, also run after Cushi. And Joab said, Wherefore wilt thou run, my son, seeing that thou hast no tidings ready? But howsoever, said he, let me run. And he said unto him, Run. Then Ahimaaz ran by the way of the plain, and overran Cushi. And David sat between the two gates: and the watchman went up to the roof over the gate unto the wall, and lifted up his eyes, and looked, and behold a man running alone. And the watchman cried, and told the king. And the king said, If he be alone, there is tidings in his mouth. And he came apace, and drew near. And the watchman saw another man running: and the watchman called unto the porter, and said, Behold, another man running alone. And the king said, He also bringeth tidings. And the watchman said, Me thinketh the running of the foremost is like the running of Ahimaaz the son of Zadok. And the king said, He is a good man, and cometh with good tidings. And Ahimaaz called, and said unto the king, All is well. And he fell down to the earth upon his face before the king, and said, Blessed be the Lord thy God, which hath delivered up the men that lifted up their hand against my lord the king. And the king said, Is the young man Absalom safe? And Ahimaaz answered, When Joab sent the king's servant, and me thy servant, I saw a great tumult, but I knew not what it was. And the king said unto him, Turn aside, and stand here. And he turned aside, and stood still. And, behold, Cushi came; and Cushi said, Tidings, my lord the king: for the Lord hath avenged thee this day of all them that rose up against thee. And the king said unto Cushi, Is the young man Absalom safe? And Cushi answered, The enemies of my lord the king, and all that rise against thee to do thee hurt, be as that young man is.

And the king was much moved, and went up to the chamber over the gate, and wept: and as he went, thus he said, O my son Absalom, my son, my son Absalom! would God I had died for thee, O Absalom, my son, my son!

And it was told Joab, Behold, the king weepeth and mourneth for Absalom. And the victory that day was turned into mourning unto all the people: for the people heard say that day how the king was grieved for his son. And the people gat them by stealth that day into the city, as people being ashamed steal away when they flee in battle. But the king covered his face, and the king cried with a loud voice, O my son Absalom, O Absalom, my son, my son! And Joab came into the house to the king, and said, Thou hast shamed this day the faces of all thy servants, which this day have saved thy life, and the lives of thy sons and of thy daughters, and the lives of thy wives, and the lives of thy concubines; in that thou lovest thine enemies, and hatest thy friends. For thou hast declared this day, that thou regardest neither princes nor servants: for this day I perceive, that if Absalom had lived, and all we had died this day, then it had pleased thee well. Now therefore arise, go forth, and speak comfortably unto thy servants: for I swear by the Lord, if thou go not forth, there will not tarry one with thee this night: and that will be worse unto thee than all the evil that befell thee from thy youth until now. Then the king arose, and sat in the gate. And they told unto all the people, saying, Behold, the king doth sit in the gate. And all the people came before the king: for Israel had fled every man to his tent.

And all the people were at strife throughout all the tribes of Israel, saying, The king saved us out of the hand of our enemies, and he delivered us out of the hand of the Philistines; and now he is fled out of the land for Absalom. And Absalom, whom we anointed over us, is dead in battle. Now therefore why speak ye not a word of bringing the king back?

And king David sent to Zadok and to Abiathar the priests, saying, Speak unto the elders of Judah, saying, Why are ye the last to bring the king back to his house? seeing the speech of all Israel is come to the king, even to his house. Ye are my brethren, ye are my bones and my flesh: wherefore then are ye the last to bring back the king? And say ye to Amasa, Art thou not of my bone, and of my flesh? God do so to me, and more also, if thou be not captain of the host before me continually in the room of Joab. And he bowed the heart of all the men of Judah, even as the heart of one man; so that they sent this word unto the king, Return thou, and all thy servants. So the king returned, and came to Jordan. And Judah came to Gilgal, to go to meet the king, to conduct the king over Jordan.

And Shimei the son of Gera, a Benjamite, which was of Bahurim, hasted and came down with the men of Judah to meet king David. And there were a thousand men of Benjamin with him, and Ziba the servant of the house of Saul, and his fifteen sons and his twenty servants with him; and they went over Jordan before the king. And there went over a ferry boat to carry over the king's household, and to do what he thought good. And Shimei the son of Gera fell down before the king, as he was come over Jordan; And said unto the king, Let not my lord impute iniquity unto me, neither do thou remember that which thy servant did perversely the day that my lord the king went out of Jerusalem, that the king should take it to his heart. For thy servant doth know that I have sinned: therefore, behold, I am come the first this day of all the house of Joseph to go down to meet my lord the king. But Abishai the son of Zeruiah answered and said, Shall not Shimei be put to death for this, because he cursed the Lord's anointed? And David said, What have I to do with you, ye sons of Zeruiah, that ye should this day be adversaries unto me? shall there any man be put to death this day in Israel? for do not I know that I am this day king over Israel? Therefore the king said unto Shimei, Thou shalt not die. And the king sware unto him.

And Mephibosheth the son of Saul came down to meet the king, and had neither dressed his feet, nor trimmed his beard, nor washed his clothes, from the day the king departed until the day he came again in peace. And it came to pass, when he was come to Jerusalem to meet the king, that the king said unto him, Wherefore wentest thou not with me, Mephibosheth? And he answered, My lord, O king, my servant deceived me: for thy servant said, I will saddle me an ass, that I may ride thereon, and go to the king; because thy servant is lame. And he hath slandered thy servant unto my lord the king; but my lord the king is as an angel of God: do therefore what is good in thine eyes. For all of my father's house were but dead men before my lord the king: yet didst thou set thy servant among them that did eat at thine own table. What right therefore have I yet to cry any more unto the king? And the king said unto him, Why speakest thou any more of thy matters? I have said, Thou and Ziba divide the land. And Mephibosheth said unto the king, Yea, let him take all, forasmuch as my lord the king is come again in peace unto his own house.

And Barzillai the Gileadite came down from Rogelim, and went over Jordan with the king, to conduct him over Jordan. Now Barzillai was a very aged man, even fourscore years old: and he had provided the king of sustenance while he lay at Mahanaim; for he was a very great man. And the king said unto Barzillai, Come thou over with me, and I will feed thee with me in Jerusalem. And Barzillai said unto the king, How long have I to live, that I should go up with the king unto Jerusalem? I am this day fourscore years old: and can I discern between good and evil? can thy servant taste what I eat or what I drink? can I hear any more the voice of singing men and singing women? wherefore then should thy servant be yet a burden unto my lord the king? Thy servant will go a little way over Jordan with the king: and why should the king recompense it me with such a reward? Let thy servant, I pray thee, turn back again, that I may die in mine own city, and be buried by the grave of my father and of my mother. But behold thy servant Chimham; let him go over with my lord the king; and do to him what shall seem good unto thee. And the king answered, Chimham shall go over with me, and I will do to him that which shall seem good unto thee: and whatsoever thou shalt require of me, that will I do for thee. And all the people went over Jordan. And when the king was come over, the king kissed Barzillai, and blessed him; and he returned unto his own place. Then the king went on to Gilgal, and Chimham went on with him: and all the people of Judah conducted the king, and also half the people of Israel.

# THE ASSYRIANS

THE early centuries of the Iron Age witnessed the building of empires that dwarfed those of the Egyptians and Hittites in the Bronze Age. The use of iron offered new opportunities for military power. Not only is iron from many points of view a better material than bronze but it also has the advantage of being found in more places and in greater quantity than copper, the main ingredient of bronze. The use of iron weapons meant the possibility of bigger and better armies and consequently greater concentrations of power and larger empires than the world had known before. These were not the only potential fruits nor the necessary results of the use of iron, but they were the possibilities most readily grasped by rulers.

The first to exploit the new opportunities were the Assyrians. Their achievement was the conquest and rule of an empire which at its height in the eight and seventh centuries B.C. extended throughout Mesopotamia from the Persian Gulf to the borders of Armenia, took in the eastern corner of Asia Minor, the Syria-Palestine coastal lands, and included Egypt.

## 27 The Middle Assyrian Laws

Although the people who created such an empire were best known to their contemporaries for their military talents, warfare was not traditionally the first interest of the Assyrians. Just another of the Semitic-speaking peoples of the ancient Near East, occupying a territory on the upper Tigris, the Assyrians are known from documents dating back at least as far as the time of Sargon, the Akkadian conqueror, about 2250 B.C. They appear as a trading people who quietly prospered through the centuries from the advantages of their geographic position along the ancient route of east-

SOURCE: Reprinted from *The Origin and History of Hebrew Law* by J. M. P. Smith by permission of The University of Chicago Press. Copyright 1931 by The University of Chicago.

west trade. It has been said that the chief Assyrian contribution to this trade was the selling of "protection" to the caravans that passed through or near their territory.

The Assyrians appear in Bronze Age history as an off-shoot of the Mesopotamian civilization, partaking of the achievements of their neighbors, contributing little if anything original themselves. The derivative quality of the Assyrian culture can be seen in the Middle Assyrian Laws, which date from between 1450 and 1250 B.C. (although the actual copy was made later), and display many similarities to earlier codes (see Selections 4 and 5). A distinctly Assyrian aspect may be the noteworthy stress on marriage and family law and on the area of the criminal law dealing with sexual transgressions. On the other hand, the laws do not form a code and are not complete, so that it may be that they are simply a special collection dealing solely with those subjects. The translation (here abridged) is that of D. D. Luckenbill as edited by F. W. Geers.

⚜⚜⚜⚜⚜

## PART I

1. If a woman, whether the wife of a man, or the daughter of a man, enter a temple, in the temple steal anything from a bin, and it be found in her hand, whether they prosecute her, or convict her, the one prosecuting, before the god they shall inquire. According as he orders to be done, they shall do unto her.

2. If a woman, whether the wife of a man or the daughter of a man, utter vulgarity or indulge in low talk, that woman bears her own sin; against her husband, her sons, or her daughters they shall have no claim.

3. If a man be sick or dead, and his wife steal anything from his house, to a man or to a woman or to anybody else give it, the wife of that man and those who received the stolen goods they shall put to death. And if the wife of a man whose husband is in good health steal from the house of her husband, to a man or to a woman or to anybody else give the stolen goods, the man shall prosecute his wife and shall impose a penalty. And the recipient of the stolen goods who received them from the hand of the wife of the man shall give up the stolen goods and a penalty like that which the man imposes upon his wife they shall impose upon the recipient of the stolen goods.

4. If a male or a female slave from the hand of the wife of a man re-

ceive anything, the nose of the male or the female slave and their ears they shall cut off. The stolen goods they shall restore in full. The man shall cut off the ears of his wife. But if he pardon his wife, do not cut off her ears, they shall not cut off the ears of the male or female servant; the stolen goods they need not restore in full.

5. If the wife of a man from the house of another man steal anything, and the value of the goods exceed five minas of lead, the owner of the stolen goods shall take oath, "Verily, I did not cause her to take anything, saying, 'Steal from my house.'" If her husband be willing, he may return the stolen goods and ransom her. He may cut off her ears. If her husband be not willing to ransom her, the owner of the stolen goods may seize her and cut off her nose.

7. If a woman bring her hand against a man, they shall prosecute her; thirty minas of lead she shall pay; twenty blows they shall inflict on her.

8. If a woman in a quarrel injure the testicle of a man, one of her fingers they shall cut off. And if a physician bind it up and the other testicle which is beside it be infected thereby, or take harm; or if in a quarrel she injure the other testicle, they shall destroy both of her eyes.

9. If a man bring his hand against the wife of a man, treating her like a little child, and they prove it against him, and convict him, one of his fingers they shall cut off. If he kiss her, his lower lip with the blade of an ax they shall "draw down," they shall cut off.

12. If the wife of a man be walking on the highway and a man seize her, say to her, "I will surely have intercourse with thee"; if she be not willing and defend herself, and he seize her by force and have intercourse with her, whether they catch him with the wife of a man, or whether at the word of the woman whom he has raped, the elders prosecute, they shall put that man to death. There is no punishment for the woman.

13. If the wife of a man go out from her house and visit a man where he lives, and he have intercourse with her, knowing that she is a man's wife, the man and also the woman they shall put to death.

15. If a man catch a man with his wife, they shall prosecute him, they shall convict him; both of them they shall put to death. He the husband is not to be blamed. If the two be caught and brought before the king or before the judges, they shall prosecute him, they shall convict him. If the husband of the woman put his wife to death, he shall also put the man to death. If he cut off the nose of his wife, he shall turn the man into a eunuch; and they shall disfigure the whole of his face. But if he spare his wife, he shall also acquit the man.

18. If a man say to his companion, either in secret or in a quarrel, "They have had intercourse with thy wife; I will prove it," and be not able to prove it, and do not prove it, on that man they shall inflict forty blows, a month of days he shall perform the king's work, they shall mutilate him, and one talent of lead he shall pay.

20. If a man have intercourse with his companion, they shall prosecute him, they shall convict him, because he had intercourse with him they shall turn him into a eunuch.

21. If a man strike the daughter of a man and cause her to drop what is in her, they shall prosecute him, they shall convict him, two talents and thirty minas of lead he shall pay, fifty blows they shall inflict on him, one month of days he shall do the king's work.

24. If the wife of a man withdraw from the presence of her husband of her own accord, and in the midst of the city or in a suburban garrison, where they point out a house to her, she enter an Assyrian's house, dwelling with the mistress of the house, spending the night there three or four times; the master of the house not knowing that the wife of a man was dwelling in his house, and finally that woman be caught; the master of the house whose wife of her own accord withdrew from his presence shall take his wife home. Of the wife of the man with whom his wife was dwelling they shall cut off her ears. Her husband, if willing, may pay three talents of lead as her price, or if he wish it to be so, they shall seize his wife. But if the master of the house knew that a man's wife was dwelling in his house with his wife, he shall pay threefold. But if he deny it saying, "I did not know," they shall go to the river. And if the man in whose house a man's wife was dwelling return from the river, threefold he shall pay. If the man whose wife of her own accord withdrew herself from his presence return from the river, he is free. The river has settled everything in connection with her case. And if the man whose wife withdrew of her own accord from his presence do not cut off his wife's ears, he shall take his wife back. There is no other penalty.

26. If a woman be dwelling in the house of her father, and her husband have died, any gift which her husband settled upon her—if there be any sons of her husband's, they shall receive it. If there be no sons of her husband's she receives it.

28. If a woman, who is a widow enter into the house of a man, bringing her minor son with her, and he grow up in the house of the one who has taken her in marriage but a document of his sonship is not written, he has no share in the house of him who brought him up; he is not responsible

for a debt; from the house of his parents he receives a portion according to his share.

29. If a woman enter into the house of her husband, her dowry and anything which she brought from the house of her father, as well as that which her father-in-law gave her on her entering her husband's house, is free to her sons. The sons of her father-in-law shall make no claim, and if her husband survive her, he may give to his sons as he wishes.

31. If a man to the house of his father-in-law have presented a present, and his wife die, his father-in-law having other daughters, if the father-in-law be willing, another daughter of his father-in-law in place of his dead wife he may take. Or if he wish, the silver which he gave he may take back. But again, grain or sheep or anything else which is food, they need not give back to him. The silver only he may receive.

32. If a woman be dwelling in the house of her father, but has been given to her husband, whether she has been taken to the house of her father-in-law or whether she has not been taken, debts, misdemeanors, and crimes of her husband she bears.

33. If a woman be dwelling in the house of her father, and her husband die, and she have a son . . . then her father to her father-in-law shall give her in marriage. If her husband and her father-in-law be both dead, and she have no sons, she is a widow; where she wishes she may go.

36. If a woman be dwelling in the house of her father, although her husband had caused her to spend the night in his house, and her husband have since gone to the "field," and have left her neither oil, nor wool, nor clothes, nor food, nor anything else, and have not sent her any goods out of "the field"—this woman shall wait for her husband five years, she shall not live with another husband. If she have sons, they shall be hired out and eat. The woman shall wait for her husband, shall not dwell with another husband. If she have no sons, she shall wait for her husband five years; on the arrival of the sixth year she may dwell with the husband of her choice. Her husband on coming back shall have no claim on her; she is free to her later husband. If he prove on his coming back that for a period of five years he delayed, not having drawn near of his own accord, because an overseer had seized him and he had run away, or as a rebel he had been seized and so had delayed, a woman he shall give in place of his wife, and his wife he may take back. Or if the king send him to another country, and he delay for a period of five years, his wife shall wait for him, shall not dwell with another husband. And if before the five years are up she dwell with another husband, and bear children, her husband, on coming back,

because she had not waited the full time, but had been given in marriage to that one, her children he may take.

40. If the wives of a man, or the daughters of a man, or his women go out into the street, their heads are to be veiled. The daughters of a man . . . with a . . . garment, or with . . . garments, are to be veiled. As for widows their heads . . . with . . . garments or with . . . garments . . . they are to be veiled. When they go out into the streets, and go about, they shall veil themselves. The concubine, who apart from her mistress goes into the streets, is to be veiled. The sacred prostitute, whom a husband has married, is to be veiled in the streets. But one whom a husband has not married is to have her head uncovered in the streets; she is not to veil herself. The harlot is not to veil herself, her head is to be uncovered. The one who sees a veiled harlot is to seize her, secure witnesses, and bring her for the judgment of the palace. Her ornaments they shall not seize. The one who seized her shall take her garment. Fifty blows they shall inflict on her. Bitumen they shall pour on her head. But if a man see a veiled harlot and let her go, and do not bring her for the judgment of the palace, on that man they shall inflict fifty blows; the one who caused his apprehension shall take his garment. His ears they shall pierce, string them with a string, and bind them on his back. A month of days he shall do the king's work. Maidservants are not to veil themselves. The one who sees a veiled maidservant shall seize her, for the judgment of the palace he shall bring her; they shall cut off her ears. The one who seized her shall take her garments. If a man see a veiled maidservant and let her go, and do not seize her, do not bring her for the judgment of the palace, they shall prosecute him; they shall convict him; fifty blows they shall inflict upon him; his ears they shall pierce; they shall string them with a string; they shall bind them to his back. The one who caused his apprehension shall take his garments. A month of days he shall do the king's work.

41. If a man veil his concubine, five or six of his companions he shall cause to sit down; before them he shall veil her. He shall say, "She is my wife." She is his wife. But the captive woman who was not veiled in front of the men, whose husband did not say, "She is my wife," she is not a wife. She is a captive woman. If the man die, not having sons by his veiled wife, the sons of captive women shall be their sons, they shall receive a portion of the paternal estate.

46. If a woman whose husband is dead on the death of her husband do not go out from her house, if her husband did not leave her anything, she shall dwell in the house of one of her sons. The sons of her husband shall

support her; her food and her drink, as for a fiancée whom they are courting, they shall agree to provide for her. If she be a second wife, and have no sons of her own, with one of her husband's sons she shall live and the group shall support her. If she have sons of her own, and the sons of the former marriage be not willing to support her, in the house of one of her own sons, where she chooses, she may dwell. Her own sons shall support her, and she shall do their work. But if there be one among the sons of her husband who marries her, and is willing to support her, the other sons need not support her.

47. If a man or a woman practice sorcery, and they be caught with it in their hands, they shall prosecute them, they shall convict them. The practicer of magic they shall put to death. The man who saw the practice of magic or hears of it from the mouth of one who saw the magic practiced and who said to him, "I saw it"—the one who heard of it shall go and report to the king. If the one who saw it, who reported to the king, deny it, he shall declare before the Gudbanda, the son of Shamash, "Verily, he has told me," and he goes free. The one who saw it, who reported it, and then denied it, the king, if he wish, shall question him, and he shall examine his past career. The sorcerer, on the day they bring him to trial, shall make the man speak out, and that one shall say: "The oath which before the king and his son thou didst take will not free you from it; according to the word of the document to which before the king and his son thou didst swear, thou hast sworn."

50. If a man strike the wife of a man, in her first stage of pregnancy, and cause her to drop that which is in her, it is a crime; two talents of lead he shall pay.

51. If a man strike a harlot and cause her to drop that which is in her, blows for blows they shall lay upon him; he shall make restitution for a life.

52. If a woman of her own accord drop that which is in her, they shall prosecute her, they shall convict her; they shall crucify her; they shall not bury her. If she die from dropping that which was in her, they shall crucify her. They shall not bury her. If because she dropped what was in her they hide that woman. . . .

54. If a man seize a virgin who is dwelling in the house of her father, whose husband have not yet been chosen, whose . . . have not been opened, who have not been taken in marriage, against the house of whose father they have no claims, if the man, either in the city, or in the country, or at night in the street, or in a "warehouse," or at a city festival—the man by means of force seize the virgin, and make her pregnant, the father of the

virgin shall seize the wife of the adulterer and give her to be raped, he shall not return her to her husband, he shall take her. The father shall give his ravished daughter to the one who raped her as a wife. If he have no wife, the ravisher shall pay to her father threefold the price of a virgin in silver. Her ravisher shall marry her, he shall not abuse her. If the father be not willing, he shall take threefold the price of a virgin in silver, and give his daughter to whom he pleases.

55. If a virgin of her own accord give herself to a man, the man shall take oath, against his wife they shall not draw nigh. Threefold the price of a virgin the ravisher shall pay. The father shall do with his daughter what he pleases.

57. In the case of every crime for which there is the penalty of the cutting-off of ear or nose, or ruining of reputation or condition, as it is written it shall be carried out.

58. Except in case of the crime concerning the wife of a man: what is in the tablet need not be carried out. The man may strike his wife, pull her hair, her ear he may bruise or pierce. He commits no misdeed thereby.


PART II


2. If a man among brothers who have not yet divided the paternal estate commit murder, to the avenger of blood[1] they shall give him. If he choose, the avenger of blood may kill him, or if he choose, he may be spared. His portion in the paternal estate he may seize.

6. . . . for silver shall not take. Before he takes field or house for silver, three times in a month of days the buyer shall make proclamation in the city of Ashur, and three times he shall have proclamation made in the city in which he would buy the field and house. Thus: "Field and house of so-and-so, son of so-and-so, situated in the cultivable area of this city, I am buying. Such as are in possession, or have objection, or who have any claims against the property, let them bring their tablets, let them lay them before the magistrates, let them present their claims, let them prove their title, and let them take what is theirs. Those who during this month of days cannot bring even one of their tablets to me, lay them before the magistrates, then the buyer shall receive in full whatever belongs to him up to the fence of his field." On the day that the buyer makes proclamation in the midst of the city of Ashur, one of the officials who stand before the king, the scribe

1. Probably the next of kin to the victim.

of the city of the buyer, and the magistrates of the king shall confer and of the city in which he is buying field and house the governor and the three nobles of the city shall meet; if the buyer shall have made proclamation, they shall write their tablets, they shall give them to him, saying: "In this month of days, the buyer made proclamation three times, 'He who in this month of days brought not his tablets to me, did not lay them before the magistrates, shall forfeit his claim to share in field and house.' To the one making the proclamation, who is a buyer, it shall be free." Three tablets of the judges, containing the proclamation of the buyer they shall write. . . .

8. If a man meddle with the "large boundary" of his neighbor, they shall prosecute him, they shall convict him. Whatever the amount of field which he seized upon, threefold he shall restore. One of his fingers they shall cut off, a hundred blows they shall inflict upon him, one month of days he shall do the king's work.

9. If a man change the "small boundary" which is of reed palings, they shall prosecute him, they shall convict him. One talent of lead he shall pay; whatever the amount of field which he seized threefold he shall restore; fifty blows they shall inflict upon him; one month of days he shall do the king's work.

10. If a man, in a field not his, dig a well, build a strengthening wall, he forfeits his claim to his well and his strengthening wall; twenty blows they shall inflict upon him; twenty days he shall do the king's work. . . .

12. If a man in the field of a man plant a garden, dig a well, raise trees, the owner of the field looking on, not objecting, then the garden is "free" to the one who set it out. Field for field to the owner of the garden he shall give.

13. If a man on ground not his plant a garden or dig a well, raise vegetables or trees, they shall prosecute him; they shall convict him; on the day the owner of the field comes he shall take the garden together with its improvements.

21. If a man in a field not his, or its . . . surround it with a boundary, and set up a boundary stone, and say, "This is my field," they shall prosecute him, they shall convict him. . . .

## PART III

2. If a man sell the son of a man or the daughter of a man, who on account of money matters or as a pledge was dwelling in his house, for silver

to another man, or if he sell any animal which was dwelling in his house, they shall convict him, he shall lose his money; and he shall give his minor to the owner of the property; . . . lashes they shall inflict upon him, twenty days he shall do the king's work.

9. If a man when . . . or a jewel of any kind and weight . . . as a pledge in a transaction outside was deposited, and the man in whose house the pledge was deposited do not close the doors which guard his house, and anything be taken from his house, that man is a thief, he shall bear the theft.

10. If a man make too large the debt of his partner, they shall prosecute him, they shall convict him; a thief he is; a penalty the king shall impose upon him according to his heart.

# 28  *The Hebrew View*

The Assyrians survived the debacle in which the Bronze Age came to an end, and gradually they built a powerful state and an efficient army under a succession of able rulers. They expanded slowly and then in the eighth and seventh centuries B.C. won their vast empire.

This nation contributed almost nothing to civilization. It was as preservers and transmitters of the culture of the ancient Near East that their rulers saw themselves. They were remarkably conscious of this heritage. One of the great eighth-century monarchs is known to history as Sargon II, having taken as his name that of the Akkadian builder of the Near East's earliest empire, who lived some fifteen hundred years earlier. The last of the great Assyrian kings, Ashurbanipal, devoted his later years to antiquarian studies and built a library in his palace at Nineveh where he housed the literary treasures of the past. It is from the ruins of Ashurbanipal's library that much of our knowledge of early Mesopotamian literature comes, including the chief texts of the Gilgamesh epic (Selection 1). Indeed, it is to Ashurbanipal's scholarly pursuits and neglect of the duties of empire that some historians attribute the fall of Assyria.

The Assyrian kings produced numerous inscriptions recording their deeds. Moved by both pride and piety, they endeavored to insure permanence to their achievements. These chronicles of so many battles won, of so many enemies slaughtered and prisoners mutilated, of so many vassal kings acknowledging the Assyrian monarch's overlordship, of so many temples built or rebuilt, do not contain enough of interest to warrant reprinting them. Like so much that the Assyrians did, it has all been seen before.

It is thus easy enough to belittle the Assyrians for their lack of originality. Yet they did contribute significantly in one important area of human activity—the techniques of imperial conquest and rule. It is upon Assyrian precedents that later empires built, even when they rejected Assyrian devices. It was the Assyrians who put the art of military conquest on a systematic footing and who systematized the moving of populations, the keeping of hostages, the maintaining of garrisons as adjuncts of imperial rule. There is one trait that runs throughout Assyrian royal inscriptions and is often visible in the impressive objects of Assyrian art: cruelty. To the Assyrians probably goes the melancholy credit of having been the first rulers to elevate cruelty and the promulgation of fear into instruments of policy.

This "tough" policy is best seen from the point of view of their subjects, among whom were the Hebrews. In the following Old Testament selection, Nahum 3, the anguished victim of Assyrian rule prophesies the destruction of the hated capital at Nineveh. The English is that of the King James version.

❋❋❋❋❋

Woe to the bloody city! it is all full of lies and robbery; the prey departeth not; the noise of a whip, and the noise of the rattling of the wheels, and of the pransing horses, and of the jumping chariots. The horseman lifteth up both the bright sword and the glittering spear: and there is a multitude of slain, and a great number of carcasses; and there is none end of their corpses; they stumble upon their corpses: Because of the multitude of the whoredoms of the well favoured harlot, the mistress of witchcrafts, that selleth nations through her whoredoms, and families through her witchcrafts.

Behold, I am against thee, saith the Lord of hosts; and I will discover thy skirts upon thy face, and I will shew the nations thy nakedness, and the kingdoms thy shame. And I will cast abominable filth upon thee, and make thee vile, and will set thee as a gazing-stock. And it shall come to pass, that all they that look upon thee shall flee from thee, and say, Nineveh is laid waste: who will bemoan her? whence shall I seek comforters for thee? Art thou better than populous No, that was situate among the rivers, that had the waters round about it, whose rampart was the sea, and her wall was from the sea? Ethiopia and Egypt were her strength, and it was infinite; Put and Lubim were thy helpers. Yet was she carried away, she went into captivity: her young children also were dashed in pieces at the top of all the streets: and they cast lots for her honourable men, and all her great men were bound in chains.

Thou also shalt be drunken: thou shalt be hid, thou also shalt seek strength because of the enemy. All thy strongholds shall be like fig trees with the first-ripe figs: if they be shaken, they shall even fall into the mouth of the eater. Behold, thy people in the midst of thee are women: the gates of thy land shall be set wide open unto thine enemies: the fire shall devour thy bars. Draw thee waters for the siege, fortify thy strongholds: go into clay, and tread the mortar, make strong the brickkiln. There shall the fire devour thee; the sword shall cut thee off, it shall eat thee up like the cankerworm: make thyself many as the cankerworm, make thyself many as the locusts. Thou hast multiplied thy merchants above the stars of heaven: the cankerworm spoileth, and flieth away. Thy crowned are as the locusts, and thy captains as the great grasshoppers, which camp in the hedges in the cold day, but when the sun ariseth they flee away, and their place is not known where they are.

Thy shepherds slumber, O king of Assyria: thy nobles shall dwell in the dust: thy people is scattered upon the mountains, and no man gathereth them. There is no healing of thy bruise; thy wound is grievous: all that hear the bruit of thee shall clap the hands over thee: for upon whom hath not thy wickedness passed continually?

# 29 *The Greek View*

In a later period, when the writing of history was becoming a literary form among the Greeks, increasing contacts with their exotic eastern neighbors aroused an interest in that region. In the early fourth century B.C. a Greek physician serving at the Persian court undertook to write a history of Persia that included as much of ancient Near Eastern history as his researches could encompass. The surviving fragments of Ctesias' history contain a lengthy section on the Assyrian monarchy and empire, which, in contrast to the Old Testament's contemporary picture, emphasizes the triumphant, glamorous, and legendary qualities that the Greeks associated with the Assyrians.

The following selection[1] consists of passages from this work: Ctesias,

1.  Reprinted by permission of the translator.

*Persika* Fragment I, 1.1–2.1; 3.1–7.2; 16.1–21.8; 23. The translation is by Truesdell S. Brown.

❀❀❀❀❀❀

The preceding book . . . includes the deeds in Egypt . . . . In this book we shall describe what happened in Asia in ancient times, beginning with the rule of Assyria. In antiquity there were native rulers in Asia to whom no famous deeds are attributed and whose names are not remembered. The first name handed down to us as a historical figure is Ninus, the Assyrian king, who accomplished great deeds. We will accordingly attempt a partial account. Being of a warlike nature and desirous of distinction he armed the sturdiest of the young men, and trained them over a long period of time to endure every kind of hardship and the perils of war. Assembling a worthy army he made an alliance with Ariaeus the King of Arabia, for at that time Arabia seems to have abounded in men of might. This people generally is liberty-loving and in no wise amenable to foreign domination. . . .

Now Ninus, King of the Assyrians, winning over the Arabian ruler, marched against the Babylonians, who lived in a neighboring country. In those days the present Babylon had not been built, though there were many other memorable cities in Babylonia. After an easy conquest of the inhabitants, who had had no experience in war, he enjoined them to pay a fixed tribute every year. But the king of this conquered people, whom he had taken prisoner along with his children, he put to death. After that he invaded Armenia with a great host, where he terrified the natives and expelled the inhabitants from some of the cities. Accordingly, when their king, Barzanes, saw he was no match for him, he met him with many gifts and promised to do whatever he might command. Ninus treated him with magnanimity and permitted him to rule Armenia and to be his friend. Also he was to send him an army and to pay their expenses. As his strength continued to grow he marched against Media. Their king, Pharnus, offered battle with a sizeable army, but was worsted. He lost most of his men, while he himself was crucified after being captured together with his wife and seven children.

Since Ninus was so successful in his undertakings he conceived a great desire to conquer all Asia between the Tanaïs[2] and the Nile. As is usual with fortunate people the steady flow of successes led to the desire for still more. Consequently he appointed one of his friends as satrap of Media,

2. The Don.

while he himself turned to the conquest of the Asiatic peoples. In a space of seventeen years he made himself master of all of them except for India and Bactria. . . .

Now that he had accomplished more illustrious deeds than anyone who preceded him he was anxious to build a city so great that not only would it be the largest city in the world at that time, but so that it would not be easy for any later ruler to surpass it. Now after rewarding the Arabian king with splendid gifts and booty he sent him home with his army. But he himself gathered forces from all directions, and stores of all sorts of supplies and built a well-constructed city beside the Euphrates river,[3] in the shape of a rectangle. The two long sides of the city were each 150 *stades,* and the short ones 90 *stades.* Thus the whole circuit, consisting of 480 *stades* did not fall short of his hopes. For no one afterwards founded a city with such an extensive perimeter or such splendid walls. For the height of the wall was 100 feet, and it was wide enough to drive three chariots abreast. There were 1,500 towers all told, and they were over 200 feet high. He settled the majority of the ablest Assyrians there along with those who so desired from other nations. He named the city Ninus after himself, and he assigned much of the adjoining land to the inhabitants.

Since Ninus campaigned against Bactria after founding this city, and since it was there that he married Semiramis, the most famous of all the women we know of, it will be necessary to speak about her and of how she attained such great glory from a humble beginning. In Syria there is a city, Ascalon, with a lake not far away, a large deep lake well stocked with fish. Beside the lake is a precinct sacred to an illustrious goddess whom the Syrians call Derceto. She has a woman's face, but the rest of her body is that of a fish, and for these reasons: The most informed natives say that Aphrodite took offense at the aforementioned goddess and inspired her with love for a youth, one of the mortals who offered sacrifice. Derceto, mingling with the Syrian, gave birth to a daughter. Shamed by her mistake she caused the young man to disappear, and exposed the child in a rocky deserted region. . . . She herself plunged into the lake, overwhelmed with shame and anguish, and her body was transformed into that of a fish. As a result the Syrians refrain from this creature and to the present day they regard fish as divine.

Near the place where the child was exposed flocks of doves made their nests, and in wonderful fashion the child was cared for by them. For some wrapped their plumage all around the girl's body to warm it, while others

3.  Ancient Nineveh was actually on the Tigris.

kept an eye on the cattle pens nearby. When the cowherds and the other herdsmen were away they carried off milk in their beaks, dropping it between the child's lips. When the child was a year old and in need of more solid food, the doves would snip off bits of cheese and provide sufficient nourishment. When the herdsmen went back and saw the cheeses nibbled away they marvelled at the phenomenon. Then, keeping watch, and finding out the reason they discovered a child of surpassing beauty. They promptly brought it to their shelter and presented it to Simmas, supervisor of the royal herds. He was childless, so he brought up the infant as his own daughter, treating her with every consideration and naming her Semiramis —which is derived from the word for doves in Syrian. And from that time on all Syrians have honored them as goddesses.

Now that is how the myth goes about the birth of Semiramis. When she was already of marriageable age and far surpassed other maidens in beauty, an official was sent out by the king to inspect the royal herds. This man was called Onnes, and he was chief of the royal council and designated as hyparch of all Syria. When he lodged with Simmas and beheld Semiramis he was enchanted with her loveliness. He begged Simmas to give him the maiden for his lawful wife, and then took her away to Nineveh where he married her and begat two children, Hypates and Hydaspes. Semiramis, who excelled all women in every other way just as much as she excelled them in beauty, gained a complete ascendancy over her husband, who never did anything without consulting her, and who prospered in all his undertakings.

Meanwhile, having completed the construction of his eponymous city, the king turned his attention to the campaign against Bactria. Realizing that the inhabitants were many and warlike, and also that many parts of the country were strong and hard to reach, he enlisted a host of men from all the subject peoples. Having failed in his earlier expedition he exerted himself to march against Bactria with an army many times larger than before. . . . This army was recruited from every direction, and comprised 1,700,000 infantry, 210,000 cavalry and almost 16,000 scythebearing chariots. At first report the size of this army is incredible, but it will not seem beyond range of possibility to those who take into account the extent of Asia and the numerous nations that live there. . . .

Campaigning in Bactria with such a large army, Ninus was obliged to divide his forces because the country was difficult of access through narrow passes. While Bactria contained many large cities there was one which is specially famous, the city called Bactra, where the palace was. It far surpassed all the rest in size and in the strength of its fortifications. Oxyartes, the king, enlisted everyone of military age, and 400,000 men were brought together. Taking over this army he went to meet the enemy at the pass, where he permitted a part of Ninus' army to get through. When he decided that enough enemy troops had reached the plain he brought out his own army. A great battle took place in which, after routing the Assyrians, the Bactrians chased them back up into the mountains, slaughtering as many as 100,000 of them. But later, when the whole army got through the pass the Bactrians were outmatched by their numbers, so they dispersed to the various cities, each contingent going to the aid of its own city. Ninus easily subdued the others, but he was unable to take Bactra by force because of its natural strength and advance preparations.

The siege had already lasted a long time when Semiramis' husband, who was campaigning with the king, and who doted on his wife, sent for her. She, who was gifted with intelligence, daring and every other asset for winning favor, seized on the opportunity to display her talents. First, meaning to travel many days by road, she devised a costume which, once it was put on, made it impossible to tell whether the wearer was a man or a woman. It was also serviceable in protecting the surface of the body from the intense heat of the journey, and in adapting itself to the needs of the wearer; for it permitted a fine freedom of movement. In general the garment was so pleasing that later when the Medes ruled Asia they adopted Semiramis' costume, as did the Persians after them. When she had arrived in Bactria and looked over the siege she noticed that the assaults were all being made in the plains and in accessible areas, while no attacks were directed against the acropolis because of its strength, with the result that those inside neglected to guard it; instead they moved down to the assistance of those defending the fortifications lower down. Accordingly, she commandeered some soldiers experienced in rock climbing, and with them she scaled a rugged ravine and seized one section of the acropolis, signalling to the men besieging the fortifications down below in the plain. Those inside, dismayed by the capture of this high place, abandoned the walls and gave up all hope of safety.

When the city had been taken in this manner the king was astounded by the woman's valor. At first he rewarded her with magnificent presents, but later on, when he was overcome by love for her beauty, he tried to induce her husband to resign her voluntarily, promising that in return for this favor he would give him his daughter Sosane in marriage. But when he took this badly, he threatened to deprive him of his sight if he did not obey his injunctions. And Onnes, partly because he was terrified by the king's threats and partly because his love drove him into a mad frenzy, slipped a noose around his neck and hanged himself. By reason of these things Semiramis attained royal dignity.

Now Ninus appropriated the Bactrian treasures which included quantities of gold and silver, and after arranging matters in Bactria he dismissed his army. Afterwards, when he had a son, Ninyas, by Semiramis, he died, leaving his widow as Queen. Semiramis buried Ninus in the capital and built an enormous mound for him, nine *stades* high and ten *stades* across. . . . Since the city lay in a plain beside the Euphrates the mound was visible for many *stades,* like an acropolis. It has remained down to my day, though Nineveh was destroyed by the Medes when they overthrew the Assyrian empire.[4]

Since her nature inclined her to great undertakings Semiramis was eager to surpass the previous ruler. . . .

. . . Since her army was large and since she had remained at peace for a long time she was desirous of accomplishing something notable in war. When she learned that the Indians were the most populous nation in the world, and that they occupied the largest and finest territory she decided to march into India, which was ruled then by Stabrobates with innumerable soldiers. He also possessed a very large number of elephants superlatively well trained for the terrors of war.

India is an extraordinarily beautiful land traversed by many rivers, and well watered throughout. It yields two crops every year, and supplies such an abundance of provisions that the inhabitants always enjoy inexhaustible supplies of food. It is said the climate is so propitious that there has never been a crop failure, let alone a famine. It produces an unheard of number of elephants which are far superior to the Libyan variety in courage and bodily strength. Likewise there are gold, silver, iron and copper. In addition there are quantities of all sorts of precious stones in India, and just about anything else contributing to luxury and wealth.

Although Semiramis had heard only a part of this, still she was persuaded to make war on the Indians, who had not previously committed any offense. Perceiving that she would need overwhelming forces she sent out messengers to all the satrapies[5] ordering the eparchs to enlist the pick of the young men in numbers proportionate to the size of the district. She also ordered them all to furnish new armor and to appear with all the rest in military array

4.   See Selection 30.
5.   Major regional divisions of the empire.

at Bactra after the third year. She also sent for ship builders from Phoenicia, Syria, Cyprus and other countries on the sea, ordering them to bring down an unlimited supply of timber, and to manufacture river boats capable of being broken up into sections. Since the Indus river, which marked the boundary of the empire, was the largest in the region, many boats were required for transport and also to guard against the Indians. As there was no timber near the river the vessels had to be transported overland from Bactria.

Further, seeing that the lack of elephants was a great handicap she devised a most unusual scheme concerning these beasts, hoping by this means to startle the Indians, who were under the impression that no elephants existed anywhere except for the ones in India. She collected 300,000 head of black cattle, then distributed their carcasses among the craftsmen and others who knew how to make things. She had them stitch hides together and stuff them with fodder, moulding them into exact replicas of elephants. Inside each dummy elephant was a man, to manipulate it, and a camel. When carried by a camel the dummy looked just like a real elephant to anyone who saw it from a distance. The workmen who made these contrivances for her were kept under constant guard inside a walled enclosure with gates, to prevent any of the workmen from getting outside or anyone from the outside from getting in where the workmen were. She did this to stop anyone else from finding out what she was doing, lest a report about it might reach the Indians.

The ships and the beasts were finished within two years, so in the third year she summoned her forces to Bactria from all directions. . . . The assembled armies amounted to 3,000,000 infantry, 200,000 cavalry and 100,000 chariots. In addition the number of men riding camels equalled the number of chariots, and they carried swords four cubits long. She constructed 2,000 river boats in sections, the hulls being transported overland by camel. Likewise, as has been pointed out, camels bore the counterfeit elephants. The soldiers led their horses alongside to overcome their fear of these terrifying beasts. . . .

When the Indian king, Stabrobates, heard of the size of the aforementioned forces and of their excellent military preparations he was eager to surpass Semiramis in everything. First he constructed 4,000 river boats out of reeds. India produces vast numbers of reeds along the river and in marshy places, reeds so thick a man can hardly grasp them. It is also said that reed vessels are remarkably durable because their wood will not rot. Devoting great attention to the manufacture of arms and traversing the whole of India, he gathered together an army many times as large as the army of Semiramis. In an elephant hunt he captured wild elephants in numbers many times the elephants he had before, and then equipped them magnificently with trappings calculated to terrify in warfare. The result was that the towers they carried and their great numbers gave them the appearance of being beyond the powers of human beings to resist.

When his warlike preparations were complete he sent messengers to Semiramis, who was already on the move, upbraiding her for starting war without any provocation. He also reviled her in unmentionable language as a whore, calling on the gods as his witnesses that after victory he would nail her to a cross. But Semiramis laughed when she read his letter, saying the Indian would find out about her courage by her deeds.

When she reached the Indus with her forces she found the enemy fleet prepared for battle. Thereupon she immediately put together her own ships, embarked the picked crews and began a naval action on the Indus, while the land forces, drawn up on the bank, lent them encouragement. In the end Semiramis was victorious but only after a prolonged battle in which each side made a strong fight of it. She destroyed about 1,000 ships and took no small number of prisoners. Puffed up with success she made slaves of the inhabitants of the island cities and took more than 100,000 prisoners.

The Indian king, meanwhile, withdrew his army from the river, pretending to fly in panic, but actually hoping to induce the enemy to cross the river.

And in point of fact, when Semiramis saw things going according to plan she constructed a long and elaborate pontoon bridge across the river. Leaving a guard of 60,000 men behind, she moved the rest of the army across the bridge and led them on against the Indians. In front were the dummy elephants, so that enemy scouts would tell the king she had a multitude of elephants. And in this she was not deceived, for the Indian scouts reported the great numbers of elephants, and everyone was puzzled to explain where this vast assemblage of beasts had come from. But the ruse did not remain undetected for long. Some of Semiramis' soldiers who had been remiss in night guard duty at camp, were so afraid of their impending punishment that they deserted to the enemy, and told them about the elephant hoax. Heartened by this news the Indian monarch told his soldiers about the dummy elephants, then turned back and drew his army up in line of battle against the Assyrians.

Semiramis followed suit, and when the armies approached one another Stabrobates the King of the Indians, sent his cavalry and chariotry out ahead of the phalanx. As the queen was bravely awaiting the cavalry attack with her dummy elephants posted at equal intervals in front of the phalanx, the Indian horses turned in panic. From the distance the dummies resembled real elephants, so the Indian horses which were used to elephants came on with a will. But when they got close, the unaccustomed smell and other differences completely terrified the horses. As a consequence some of the Indians were thrown to the ground, while others were carried over intact inside the enemy lines when the horses refused to be guided by the reins.

Meanwhile, leading a picked body of soldiers, Semiramis took full advantage of this success and drove the Indians back. But when they reached the phalanx in their flight, King Stabrobates was undismayed. He brought up regiments of infantry preceded by elephants. Riding the largest elephant into battle on the right wing he advanced menacingly against the queen, who happened to be posted opposite him. The rest of the elephants followed, and for a short time Semiramis' army resisted the onslaught of these beasts. But the elephants were very powerful. Confident in their own strength they easily overpowered anyone who tried to resist them. Therefore, the slaughter was great and varied, some being trampled underfoot, others ripped up by the elephants' tusks, still others tossed on their trunks. The growing heap of the slain and the impending danger struck terror into those who beheld it.

No one dared maintain his place in the ranks. As the entire host turned in flight the Indian monarch pressed on after Semiramis. First drawing his bow, he hit her in the arm; then he hurled his javelin, striking the queen on the back with a glancing blow. But Semiramis was not seriously hurt and she soon got away on horseback, the pursuing elephant being much slower. When the mass of fugitives reached the float there was such a crowding of people in a narrow space, that the queen's men caused one another's death, being trampled underfoot. The footsoldiers and the cavalry were unnaturally crowded together, while the Indians kept pressing them. There was a mighty rush for the bridge, inspired by terror, which resulted in many men being pushed off both sides into the river.

As soon as Semiramis had crossed the river safely with the majority of the survivors of the battle, she cut the cables. Thereupon the floating bridge was broken up into many separate sections, and the crowd of pursuing Indians on the bridge were caught, just as they were, by the swift current, and many of them destroyed. This was Semiramis' salvation, for it prevented the enemy from crossing over to attack her. After this there were divine omens which the soothsayers interpreted as a sign not to cross the river, so the Indian ruler called a halt. After exchanging prisoners Semiramis returned to Bactra, having lost two-thirds of her army.

Some time later, when she was informed by a eunuch that her son Ninyas was conspiring against her she remembered the oracle of Ammon. Instead of harming the conspirator in any way she turned the kingdom over to him and ordered her governors to accept his orders. She herself soon disappeared, as though translated to the gods in fulfillment of the oracle. Some mythologers maintain she was turned into a dove, and that when a flock of birds flew down into her house, she flew away with them. For this reason the Assyrians honor the dove as sacred, and pay divine honors to Semiramis. Thus after ruling over all of Asia except India she died in the manner indicated above after living for sixty-two years and ruling for forty-two. . . .

After her death Ninyas, the son of Ninus and Semiramis, succeeded to the throne. He ruled peacefully, not emulating the dangerous military policies of his mother to the slightest degree. He spent all his time primarily in the palace, seen only by the concubines and eunuchs who surrounded him. He cared for nothing but luxury and amusement without unpleasantness or even serious thoughts, for he thought the object in ruling a prosperous kingdom was to indulge oneself in every kind of pleasure without interruption. To safeguard his rule and keep his subjects in awe, he sent for a stipulated number of soldiers and a general from each nation. He kept this army, recruited from every region, outside the city, appointing leaders for each national contingent from the men in his entourage who were most well disposed towards him. When the year elapsed he would send again to the nations for the same number of soldiers, discharging the soldiers he had, to return to their native land.

This arrangement terrified all the king's subjects, for they saw that there were always strong forces camping out in the open country, ready to punish rebellion or disobedience. He devised the annual succession of soldiers so that they would all return to their native lands before becoming well acquainted with their generals or with one another. For long periods of service make the generals expert in war, and also contribute to their arrogance; such periods usually offer many opportunities for conspiracy and rebellion of their followers. To prevent any outsider from seeing the luxurious way he lived, he kept them all in ignorance. No one dared even say a word against him for fear of him, as though he were an invisible god. Accordingly, after appointing generals and satraps, administrators and judges for each nation, men suited to his interests, Ninyas lived out his time.

Like him the other kings inherited the kingdom from father to son, and continued to rule for thirty generations down to the time of Sardanapallus.[6] But in his time the Assyrians lost their empire to the Medes, after it had lasted for more than 1,300 years. . . .

Sardanapallus, the thirtieth king after Ninus established the Assyrian rule, was also the last. He outdid all his predecessors in luxury and frivolity, for not only were no outsiders allowed to see him, but he even lived like a woman. He spent his time with his concubines, spinning the finest purple-dyed wool, while clad in a woman's robes. He painted his face, his entire body in fact, with white lead and other preparations courtesans employ, to make his skin softer than that of the most delicate women. He also affected a woman's voice. At banquets not only did he partake of food and drink especially designed to prolong the pleasure, but he surrendered himself to the delights of both male and female love. He used both forms of intercourse without restraint, not troubling himself in the least over the shamefulness of his actions.

He reached such a pitch of luxury and shameless unbridled pleasure that he composed an elegy for himself which he ordered his successor to inscribe on his tomb after he died. While he wrote this in barbarian speech, some Greek later on translated it thus:

"Know well thou art mortal, gratify thy desires,
Rejoice in merry-making. There is no profit after thou art dead.
For I am but dust, though king of mighty Nineveh.
All I keep are food, indolence and love,
From which I received pleasure. The multitude of other possessions are meaningless."

Such behavior not only brought about his own shameful death, but also finally ended the Assyrian rule, which had endured longer than any other recorded empire.

6. Ashurbanipal.

# THE CHALDEANS
# (NEO-BABYLONIANS)

IN THE late seventh century B.C. a coalition brought about the Assyrian empire's downfall. Its chief parties were the Medes, an Indo-European-speaking people inhabiting territory east of Mesopotamia, and a revived Babylonian kingdom aiming at independence from the Assyrian yoke. When the capital, Nineveh, fell and was destroyed in 612 B.C., the Assyrian empire was finished. Of the victors the Babylonians received the chief spoils, and set up an empire of their own which included most of the Assyrian territory. This so-called Chaldean, or Neo-Babylonian (the reference is to the past glories of the Babylonian empire of Hammurabi, over a thousand years earlier), empire lasted only a little more than half a century, but its magnificence, symbolized by the famous Hanging Gardens of Babylon, was legendary throughout the rest of antiquity. It succeeded, in a way that the Assyrians had not, in recalling the splendors of an ancient past.

## 30 *The Fall of Nineveh*

This selection recounts in summary fashion the military events which brought about the end of the Assyrian empire. It is taken from one of a number of Babylonian chronicles narrating the military history of the period. The section here deals with the tenth to the sixteenth year of the reign of Nabopolassar, the first king of the Neo-Babylonian monarchy, referred to here as "king of Akkad." Nabopolassar had been an official of the Assyrian empire in Babylon. He revolted successfully and was crowned king in Babylon in 626 B.C., then he went on to attack his former masters. The account of his fourteenth year covers with its laconic words the major historical catastrophe of the Assyrian capital's fall in 612. The translation is by C. J. Gadd.

SOURCE: C. J. Gadd, *The Fall of Nineveh* (London: Trustees of the British Museum, 1923). Reprinted by permission of the Trustees of the British Museum.

[ 267 ]

✿✿✿✿✿

In the tenth year Nabopolassar, in the month of Iyyar, mustered the army of Akkad, and marched up the Euphrates. The men of Suhu and Hindanu did not fight against him; their tribute they laid before him.

In the month of Ab they reported that the army of Assyria was in the city of Qablinu. Nabopolassar went up against them, in the month of Ab, the 12th day, he did battle against the army of Assyria, and the army of Assyria was routed before him, and a great havoc was made of Assyria; prisoners in great number they took. The Mannaeans who had come to their aid and the chief men of Assyria were captured. On that day the city of Qablinu was captured. Also in the month of Ab the king of Akkad his army sent against the cities of Mane, Sahiru, and Balihu; prisoners from them they took, and carried off a great booty from them, and brought out their gods.

In the month of Elul the king of Akkad and his army turned back. On his march the city of Hindanu and its gods he took to Babylon.

In the month of Tisri the army of Egypt and the army of Assyria marched after the king of Akkad as far as the city of Qablinu, but did not overtake the king of Akkad. He hastened after them.

In the month of Adar the army of Assyria and the army of Akkad in the city of Madanu which is in the territory of the city of Araphu did battle against each other. The army of Assyria before the army of Akkad was routed; they made great havoc of them and threw them back to the river Zab; their asses and horses were captured, and prisoners they took in great number. His many . . . they brought with them across the Tigris and made them to enter Babylon.

In the eleventh year, the king of Akkad mustered his army, and marched up the bank of the Tigris, and in the month of Iyyar encamped against Ashur.

On the . . . day of the month of Sivan he made an assault upon the city, but did not capture the city. The king of Assyria mustered his army, and the king of Akkad was driven from Ashur, and as far as the city of Takritain the Assyrian marched after him along the bank of the Tigris. The king of Akkad made his army to go up into the citadel of Takritain. The king of Assyria and his army against the army of the king of Akkad, which was shut up in Takritain, encamped. For ten days he made assault on them, but did not capture the city. The army of the king of Akkad, which was shut up in the citadel, made great havoc of the Assyrians; wherefor the king of Assyria and his army ceased, and returned to his land.

In the month of Marcheswan the Mede came down upon the land of Arrapha, and made an assault upon the city of . . . .

In the twelfth year in the month of Ab the Mede against Nineveh . . . and hastened, and the city of Tarbis, a city in the district of Nineveh, they captured. . . . Down the bank of the Tigris he pursued, and encamped against Ashur. An assault he made upon the city. . . . The city he destroyed, and cruel havoc he made of the chief men; he took prisoners from it and plundered its spoils. The king of Akkad and his army, who had come to the help of the Mede, were not in time for the assault; the city. . . . The king of Akkad and Kyaxares[1] at the city met one with the other. Friendship and alliance they established together. Kyaxares and his army returned to his land; the king of Akkad and his army returned to his land.

In the thirteenth year in the month of Iyyar the men of Suhu against the king of Akkad revolted and committed hostilities. The king of Akkad mustered his army and marched to Suhu.

In the month of Sivan, the fourth day, he made an assault upon Rahilu, a city which is in the middle of the Euphrates. On that day the city was captured. . . . Its . . . he built; stone from the bank of the Euphrates they laid down against it. . . . Against the city of Anatu he encamped, and siege-engines from the westerly direction. . . . The siege-engines he brought near to the city wall and made an assault upon the city, but did not capture it. . . . The king of Assyria and his army came down, and the king of Akkad and his army turned and went back to his land.

In the fourteenth year the king of Akkad mustered his army. . . . The men of the king of the Umman-Manda[2] to meet the king of Akkad. . . . They met one with the other, the king of Akkad . . . and Kyaxares. . . . He made to cross; by the bank of the Tigris they marched . . . against Nineveh. . . .

From the month of Sivan to the month of Ab three battles. . . . A mighty assault they made upon the city, and in the month of Ab, the . . . day, the city was captured. . . . A great havoc of the chief men was made. At that time Sin-shar-ishkun, king of Assyria. . . . The spoil of the city, a quantity beyond counting, they plundered, and turned the city into a

---

1. King of the Medes.     2. The Scythians.

mound and a ruin. . . . The king escaped and the forces of the king of Akkad. . . .

In the month of Elul, the 20th day, Kyaxares and his army returned to his land, and the king of Akkad turned back. . . . They went as far as the city of Nisibis, and the prisoners and the slaves . . . of the land of Rusapu they brought to Nineveh before the face of the king of Akkad.

In the month of . . . Ashur-uballit in the city of Harran sat upon the throne as king of Assyria. . . .

In the fifteenth year in the month of Tammuz . . . the king of Akkad . . . marched to Assyria . . . victoriously. . . . The army of the land of Hazzu . . . and of the land of Shu . . . he conquered; prisoners they took from them, their spoil and. . . .

In the month of Marcheswan the king of Akkad turned the front of his army and against the city of Rugguliti. . . . He made an assault upon the city, and on the 28th of the month of Marcheswan he captured the city. . . . No man he. . . . To his land he returned.

In the sixteenth year in the month of Iyyar the king of Akkad mustered his army and marched to Assyria. From the month of Iyyar to the month of Marcheswan they marched victoriously in Assyria.

In the month of Marcheswan the Umman-Manda . . . came to the help of the king of Akkad; their armies they united and to the city of Harran after Ashur-uballit, who had sat upon the throne in Assyria, they marched. Ashur-uballit and the army of the land of . . . which to his help had come. . . . Fear of the enemy fell upon them; they abandoned the city. . . . The king of Akkad reached Harran. . . . The city was captured. The spoil of the city, a quantity beyond counting, he plundered.

In the month of Adar the king of Akkad . . . he left behind. He himself returned to his land, and the Umman-Manda, who had come to the help of the king of Akkad. . . .

# 31 The Jewish View

It is from the Old Testament that we derive our most familiar image of the splendor and wickedness of Babylon in the sixth century B.C. under the Chaldean empire. This is the time of the "Babylonian exile" and the subsequent Diaspora ("dispersion") of the Hebrew nation, who from this time on are known as the Jews. Although the Old Testament writers were scarcely impartial, they were eyewitnesses, and the picture they draw gives something of the flavor of the brief flowering of Neo-Babylonian power under Nebuchadnezzar (or Nebuchadrezzar) and his ill-fated successors, Nabonidus and Belshazzar (whose "reign" lasted only a matter of weeks).

The following passages, Jeremiah 39 and Daniel 3 and 5, are in the King James Version.

⊛⊛⊛⊛⊛⊛

In the ninth year of Zedekiah king of Judah,[1] in the tenth month, came Nebuchadnezzar king of Babylon and all his army against Jerusalem, and they besieged it. And in the eleventh year of Zedekiah, in the fourth month, the ninth day of the month, the city was broken up. And all the princes of the king of Babylon came in, and sat in the middle gate, even Nergal-sharezer, Samgar-nebo, Sarsechim, Rab-saris, Nergal-sharezer, Rab-mag, with all the residue of the princes of the king of Babylon.

And it came to pass, that when Zedekiah the king of Judah saw them, and all the men of war, then they fled, and went forth out of the city by night, by the way of the king's garden, by the gate betwixt the two walls: and he went out the way of the plain. But the Chaldeans' army pursued after them, and overtook Zedekiah in the plains of Jericho: and when they had taken him, they brought him up to Nebuchadnezzar king of Babylon to Riblah in the land of Hamath, where he gave judgment upon him. Then the king of Babylon slew the sons of Zedekiah in Riblah before his eyes: also the king of Babylon slew all the nobles of Judah. Moreover he put out Zedekiah's eyes, and bound him with chains, to carry him to Babylon.

And the Chaldeans burned the king's house, and the houses of the people, with fire, and brake down the walls of Jerusalem. Then Nebuzar-adan the captain of the guard carried away captive into Babylon the remnant of the people that remained in the city, and those that fell away, that fell to him, with the rest of the people that remained. But Nebuzar-adan the captain of the guard left of the poor of the people, which had nothing, in the land of Judah, and gave them vineyards and fields at the same time.

Now Nebuchadnezzar king of Babylon gave charge concerning Jeremiah to Nebuzar-adan the captain of the guard, saying, Take him, and look well to him, and do him no harm; but do unto him even as he shall say unto thee. So Nebuzar-adan the captain of the guard sent, and Nebushasban, Rab-saris, and Nergal-sharezer, Rab-mag, and all the king of Babylon's

1.  587 B.C.

princes; even they sent, and took Jeremiah out of the court of the prison, and committed him unto Gedaliah the son of Ahikam the son of Shapan, that he should carry him home: so he dwelt among the people.

Now the word of the Lord came unto Jeremiah, while he was shut up in the court of the prison, saying, Go and speak to Ebed-melech the Ethiopian, saying, Thus saith the Lord of hosts, the God of Israel; Behold, I will bring my words upon this city for evil, and not for good; and they shall be accomplished in that day before thee. But I will deliver thee in that day, saith the Lord: and thou shalt not be given into the hand of the men of whom thou art afraid. For I will surely deliver thee, and thou shalt not fall by the sword, but thy life shall be for a prey unto thee: because thou hast put thy trust in me, saith the Lord.

. . . . .

Nebuchadnezzar the king made an image of gold, whose height was threescore cubits, and the breadth thereof six cubits: he set it up in the plain of Dura, in the province of Babylon. Then Nebuchadnezzar the king sent to gather together the princes, the governors, and the captains, the judges, the treasurers, the counsellers, the sheriffs, and all the rulers of the provinces, to come to the dedication of the image which Nebuchadnezzar the king had set up. Then the princes, the governors, and captains, the judges, the treasurers, the counsellers, the sheriffs, and all the rulers of the provinces, were gathered together unto the dedication of the image that Nebuchadnezzar the king had set up; and they stood before the image that Nebuchadnezzar had set up. Then an herald cried aloud, To you it is commanded, O people, nations, and languages, that at what time ye hear the sound of the cornet, flute, harp, sackbut, psaltery, dulcimer, and all kinds of musick, ye fall down and worship the golden image that Nebuchadnezzar the king hath set up: And whoso falleth not down and worshippeth shall the same hour be cast into the midst of a burning fiery furnace. Therefore at that time, when all the people heard the sound of the cornet, flute, harp, sackbut, psaltery, and all kinds of musick, all the people, the nations, and the languages, fell down and worshipped the golden image that Nebuchadnezzar the king had set up.

Wherefore at that time certain Chaldeans came near, and accused the Jews. They spake and said to the king Nebuchadnezzar, O king, live for ever. Thou, O king, hast made a decree, that every man that shall hear the sound of the cornet, flute, harp, sackbut, psaltery, and dulcimer, and all kinds of musick, shall fall down and worship the golden image: And whoso falleth not down and worshippeth, that he should be cast into the midst of a burning fiery furnace. There are certain Jews whom thou hast set over the affairs of the province of Babylon, Shadrach, Meshach, and Abed-nego; these men, O king, have not regarded thee: they serve not thy gods, nor worship the golden image which thou hast set up.

Then Nebuchadnezzar in his rage and fury commanded to bring Shadrach, Meshach, and Abed-nego. Then they brought these men before the king. Nebuchadnezzar spake and said unto them, Is it true, O Shadrach, Meshach, and Abed-nego, do not ye serve my gods, nor worship the golden image which I have set up? Now if ye be ready that at what time ye hear the sound of the cornet, flute, harp, sackbut, psaltery, and dulcimer, and all kinds of musick, ye fall down and worship the image which I have made; well: but if ye worship not, ye shall be cast the same hour into the midst of a burning fiery furnace; and who is that God that shall deliver you out of my hands? Shadrach, Meshach, and Abed-nego, answered and said to the king, O Nebuchadnezzar, we are not careful to answer thee in this matter. If it be so, our God whom we serve is able to deliver us from the burning fiery furnace, and he will deliver us out of thine hand, O king. But if not, be it known unto thee, O king, that we will not serve thy gods, nor worship the golden image which thou hast set up.

Then was Nebuchadnezzar full of fury, and the form of his visage was changed against Shadrach, Meshach, and Abed-nego: therefore he spake, and commanded that they should heat the furnace one seven times more than it was wont to be heated. And he commanded the most mighty men that were in his army to bind Shadrach, Meshach, and Abed-nego, and to cast them into the burning fiery furnace. Then these men were bound in their coats, their hosen, and their hats, and their other garments, and were cast into the midst of the burning fiery furnace. Therefore because the king's commandment was urgent, and the furnace exceeding hot, the flame of the fire slew those men that took up Shadrach, Meshach, and Abed-nego. And these three men, Shadrach, Meshach, and Abed-nego, fell down bound into the midst of the burning fiery furnace. Then Nebuchadnezzar the king was astonished, and rose up in haste, and spake, and said unto his counsellers, Did not we cast three men bound into the midst of the fire? They answered and said unto the king, True, O king. He answered and said, Lo, I see four men loose, walking in the midst of the fire, and they have no hurt; and the form of the fourth is like the Son of God.

Then Nebuchadnezzar came near to the mouth of the burning fiery furnace, and spake, and said, Shadrach, Meshach, and Abed-nego, ye servants of the most high God, come forth, and come hither. Then Shadrach, Meshach, and Abed-nego, came forth of the midst of the fire. And the princes, governors, and captains, and the king's counsellers, being gathered together, saw these men, upon whose bodies the fire had no power, nor was an hair of their head singed, neither were their coats changed, nor the smell of fire had passed on them. Then Nebuchadnezzar spake, and said, Blessed be the God of Shadrach, Meshach, and Abed-nego, who hath sent his angel, and delivered his servants that trusted in him, and have changed the king's word, and yielded their bodies, that they might not serve nor worship any god, except their own God. Therefore I make a decree, That every people, nation, and language, which speak any thing amiss against the God of Shadrach, Meshach, and Abed-nego, shall be cut in pieces, and their houses shall be made a dunghill: because there is no other God that can deliver after this sort. Then the king promoted Shadrach, Meshach, and Abed-nego, in the province of Babylon.

. . . . .

Belshazzar the king made a great feast to a thousand of his lords, and drank wine before the thousand. Belshazzar, whiles he tasted the wine, commanded to bring the golden and silver vessels which his father Nebuchadnezzar had taken out of the temple which was in Jerusalem; that the king, and his princes, his wives, and his concubines, might drink therein. Then they brought the golden vessels that were taken out of the temple of the house of God which was at Jerusalem; and the king, and his princes, his wives, and his concubines, drank in them. They drank wine, and praised the gods of gold, and of silver, of brass, of iron, of wood, and of stone.

In the same hour came forth fingers of a man's hand, and wrote over against the candlestick upon the plaister of the wall of the king's palace: and the king saw the part of the hand that wrote. Then the king's countenance was changed, and his thoughts troubled him, so that the joints of his loins were loosed, and his knees smote one against another. The king cried aloud to bring in the astrologers, the Chaldeans, and the soothsayers. And the king spake, and said to the wise men of Babylon, Whosoever shall read this writing, and shew me the interpretation thereof, shall be clothed with scarlet, and have a chain of gold about his neck, and shall be the third ruler in the kingdom. Then came in all the king's wise men: but they could not read the writing, nor make known to the king the interpretation thereof. Then was king Belshazzar greatly troubled, and his countenance was changed in him, and his lords were astonished.

[ 274 ]

Now the queen, by reason of the words of the king and his lords, came into the banquet house: and the queen spake and said, O king, live for ever: let not thy thoughts trouble thee, nor let thy countenance be changed: There is a man in thy kingdom, in whom is the spirit of the holy gods; and in the days of thy father light and understanding and wisdom, like the wisdom of the gods, was found in him; whom the king Nebuchadnezzar thy father, the king, I say, thy father, made master of the magicians, astrologers, Chaldeans, and soothsayers; forasmuch as an excellent spirit, and knowledge, and understanding, interpreting of dreams, and shewing of hard sentences, and dissolving of doubts, were found in the same Daniel, whom the king named Belteshazzar: now let Daniel be called, and he will shew the interpretation. Then was Daniel brought in before the king, and the king spake and said unto Daniel, Art thou that Daniel, which art of the children of the captivity of Judah, whom the king my father brought out of Jewry? I have even heard of thee, that the spirit of the gods is in thee, and that light and understanding and excellent wisdom is found in thee. And now the wise men, the astrologers, have been brought in before me, that they should read this writing, and make known unto me the interpretation thereof: but they could not shew the interpretation of the thing: And I have heard of thee, that thou canst make interpretations, and dissolve doubts: Now if thou canst read the writing, and make known to me the interpretation thereof, thou shalt be clothed with scarlet, and have a chain of gold about thy neck, and shalt be the third ruler in the kingdom.

Then Daniel answered and said before the king, Let thy gifts be to thyself, and give thy rewards to another; yet I will read the writing unto the king, and make known to him the interpretation. O thou king, the most high God gave Nebuchadnezzar thy father a kingdom, and majesty, and glory, and honour: And for the majesty that he gave him, all people, nations, and languages, trembled and feared before him: whom he would he slew; and whom he would he kept alive; and whom he would he set up; and whom he would he put down. But when his heart was lifted up, and his mind hardened in pride, he was deposed from his kingly throne, and they took his glory from him: And he was driven from the sons of men; and his heart was made like the beasts, and his dwelling was with the wild asses: they fed him with grass like oxen, and his body was wet with the dew of heaven; till he knew that the most high God ruled in the kingdom of men, and that he appointeth over it whomsoever he will. And thou his son, O Belshazzar, hast not humbled thine heart, though thou knewest all this; but hast lifted up thyself against the Lord of heaven; and they have brought the vessels of his house before thee, and thou, and thy lords, thy wives, and thy concubines, have drunk wine in them; and thou hast praised the gods of silver, and gold, of brass, iron, wood, and stone, which see not, nor hear, nor know: and the God in whose hand thy breath is, and whose are all thy ways, hast thou not glorified: Then was the part of the hand sent from him; and this writing was written.

And this is the writing that was written, MENE, MENE, TEKEL, UPHARSIN. This is the interpretation of the thing: MENE; God hath numbered thy kingdom, and finished it. TEKEL; Thou art weighed in the balances and art found wanting. PERES; Thy kingdom is divided, and given to the Medes and Persians. Then commanded Belshazzar, and they clothed Daniel with scarlet, and put a chain of gold about his neck, and made a proclamation concerning him, that he should be the third ruler in the kingdom.

In that night was Belshazzar the king of the Chaldeans slain. And Darius the Median took the kingdom, being about threescore and two years old.

# THE PERSIANS

T HE power of the Medes too, like that of the Neo-Babylonians, was short-lived. Both fell to the Persians. This was a people closely related to the Medes, and these two branches of the same ethnic stock with similar traditions and language became so thoroughly assimilated to each other as to be for practical purposes indistinguishable. The Greeks indeed never succeeded in making the distinction accurately, finally following the practice of referring to either Persians or Medes according to whim.

The Persians, after conquering the Medes, went on to subdue the rest of the ancient Near East, putting under their sway all of the former possessions of the Assyrian empire and extending eastward to western India. This immense territory, comparable in size to the continental United States, was far greater than that ruled by any of their predecessors. Its efficient organization and administration, without the benefit of machines for communication and transportation, was one of history's greatest feats of statecraft.

The Persian empire was divided into major provinces, called satrapies, reflecting the chief national divisions of the conquered peoples. Each of these was governed by a satrap chosen from the Persian nobility, who had great powers and was responsible to the central administration in the royal city of Persepolis. The outstanding characteristic of the Persian empire was the mildness of its rule. It gave internal peace and orderly government to most of the civilized world of its time, and it is not too great an oversimplification to say that in return for these blessings it demanded only two things: payment of taxes, that were on the whole reasonably based upon ability to pay, and provision of soldiers to serve in the imperial armies that maintained internal peace and protected and extended the empire.

# 32 The Babylonian View

The architect of the Persian empire was Cyrus the Great, who ascended the throne as a tribal prince in 559 B.C., and by the time of his death thirty years later had conquered almost the whole of the empire (Egypt was added by his son Cambyses in 525 B.C.) and had set down the main lines of policy and administration. Cyrus could not be everywhere at once and it was not until 539 B.C. that, having already extended his empire north and west to the Aegean coast of Asia Minor and east to India, he conquered Babylonia and put an end to the Neo-Babylonian empire under its last monarch, Nabonidus. This event is recorded in a contemporary inscription which, while reflecting Cyrus' imperial propaganda about himself, also gives a clear insight into the role that he played and the policy that he instituted to make his rule welcome to a conquered people. In the troubled Near East of his time Cyrus was indeed looked upon as a savior rather than as a foreign invader. The translation of the inscription is by A. Leo Oppenheim.

❀❀❀❀❀

[*one line destroyed*]

. . . rims of the world . . . a weakling has been installed as the *enu* of his country; the correct images of the gods he removed from their thrones, imitations he ordered to place upon them. A replica of the temple Esagila he has . . . for Ur and the other sacred cities inappropriate rituals . . . daily he did blabber incorrect prayers. He furthermore interrupted in a fiendish way the regular offerings, he did . . . he established within the sacred cities. The worship of Marduk, the king of the gods, he changed into abomination, daily he used to do evil against his [i.e. Marduk's] city. . . . He tormented its inhabitants with corvée-work without relief, he ruined them all.

Upon their complaints the lord of the gods became terribly angry and he departed from their region, also the other gods living among them left their mansions, wroth that he had brought them into Babylon. But Marduk who does care for . . . on account of the fact that the sanctuaries of all their settlements were in ruins and the inhabitants of Sumer and Akkad had become like living dead, turned back his countenance his anger abated

SOURCE: Reprinted from *Ancient Near Eastern Texts Relating to the Old Testament* ed. James B. Pritchard by permission of Princeton University Press. Copyright, 1950, by Princeton University Press.

and he had mercy upon them. He scanned and looked through all the countries, searching for a righteous ruler willing to lead him [Marduk] in the annual procession. Then he pronounced the name of Cyrus, king of Anshan, declared him to become the ruler of all the world. He made the Guti country and all the Manda-hordes bow in submission to his [Cyrus'] feet. And he [Cyrus] did always endeavour to treat according to justice the black-headed whom he [Marduk] has made him conquer. Marduk, the great lord, a protector of his worshipers, beheld with pleasure his [Cyrus'] good deeds and his upright mind and therefore ordered him to march against his city Babylon. He made him set out on the road to Babylon, going at his side like a real friend. His widespread troops—their number, like that of the water of a river, could not be established—strolled along, their weapons packed away. Without any battle, he made him enter his town Babylon, sparing Babylon any calamity. He delivered into his hands Nabonidus, the king who did not worship him. All the inhabitants of Babylon as well as of the entire country of Sumer and Akkad, princes and governors included, bowed to him and kissed his feet, jubilant that he had received the kingship, and with shining faces. Happily they greeted him as a master through whose help they had come again to life from death and had all been spared damage and disaster, and they worshiped his very name.

I am Cyrus, king of the world, great king, legitimate king, king of Babylon, king of Sumer and Akkad, king of the four rims of the earth, son of Cambyses, great king, king of Anshan, grandson of Cyrus, great king, king of Anshan, descendant of Teispes, great king, king of Anshan, of a family which always exercised kingship; whose rule Bel and Nebo love, whom they want as king to please their hearts.

When I entered Babylon as a friend and when I established the seat of the government in the palace of the ruler under jubilation and rejoicing, Marduk, the great lord, induced the magnanimous inhabitants of Babylon to love me, and I was daily endeavouring to worship him. My numerous troops walked around in Babylon in peace, I did not allow anybody to terrorize any place of the country of Sumer and Akkad. I strove for peace in Babylon and in all his other sacred cities. As to the inhabitants of Babylon, who against the will of gods were . . . I abolished the corvée which was against their social standing. I brought relief to their dilapidated housing, putting thus an end to their main complaints. Marduk, the great lord, was well pleased with my deeds and sent friendly blessings to myself, Cyrus, the king who worships him, to Cambyses, my son, the offspring of my loins, as well as to all my troops, and we all praised his great godhead joyously, standing before him in peace.

All the kings of the entire world from the Upper to the Lower Sea, those who are seated in throne rooms, those who live in other types of buildings as well as all the kings of the West land living in tents, brought their heavy tributes and kissed my feet in Babylon. As to the region from . . . as far as Ashur and Susa, Agade, Eshnunna, the towns Zamban, Me-Turnu, Der as well as the region of the Gutians, I returned to these sacred cities on the other side of the Tigris, the sanctuaries of which have been ruins for a long time, the images which used to live therein and established for them permanent sanctuaries. I also gathered all their former inhabitants and returned to them their habitations. Furthermore, I resettled upon the command of Marduk, the great lord, all the gods of Sumer and Akkad whom Nabonidus has brought into Babylon to the anger of the lord of the gods, unharmed, in their former chapels, the places which make them happy.

May all the gods whom I have resettled in their sacred cities ask daily Bel and Nebo for a long life for me and may they recommend me to him; to Marduk, my lord, they may say this: "Cyrus, the king who worships you, and Cambyses, his son . . ." . . . all of them I settled in a peaceful place . . . ducks and doves . . . I endeavoured to repair their dwelling places. . . .

# 33 A Jewish View

In depicting himself as the supporter of a conquered people's national religious tradition (as in the preceding selection), Cyrus had discovered a major secret of rule. Thereafter it was a consistently followed policy of the Persian kings (with the exception of Cambyses, who was considered mad by his contemporaries) to show the utmost care for the local religious cults within their empire. Imperial funds were generously used for the rebuilding of ancient temples and for re-instituting ancestral cults and worship that had been destroyed by the predecessors of the Persians or had fallen into disuse. The fruits of this policy are seen in the respectful treatment accorded the Persian monarchy in the Old Testament, for the Jews were among the beneficiaries.

The documents that follow illustrate the pains that the Persian government was willing to take to satisfy the religions of its peoples. A Persian

SOURCE: Reprinted from *Aramaic Papyri of the Fifth Century B.C.* by A. Cowley by permission of the Clarendon Press, Oxford (Eng.).

garrison at Elephantine (Yeb), an island in the Nile that marks the southern border of Egypt, was manned by a regiment of Jewish soldiers who had been conscripted for service in the imperial army. In the first document, dated 419 B.C., official instructions are given to these men for the proper observation of the festival of the Passover, a ritual celebration recalling the Hebrews' liberation from their enslavement in Egypt nearly a thousand years before. The second document is a petition of 407 B.C. in which the Jewish community requests permission to rebuild the island's temple. The translations are by A. Cowley.

✸✸✸✸✸

To my brethren, Yedoniah and his colleagues the Jewish garrison, your brother Hananiah. The welfare of my brethren may the gods seek. Now this year, the 5th year of King Darius, word was sent from the king to Arsames, saying: In the month of Tybi let there be a Passover for the Jewish garrison. Now you accordingly count fourteen days of the month Nisan and keep the Passover, and from the 15th day to the 21st day of Nisan are seven days of Unleavened bread. Be clean and take heed. Do no work on the 15th day and on the 21st day. Also drink no beer, and anything at all in which there is leaven do not eat, from the 15th day from sunset till the 21st day of Nisan, seven days, let it not be seen among you; do not bring it into your dwellings, but seal it up during those days. Let this be done as Darius the king commanded. [*Address:*] To my brethren Yedoniah and his colleagues the Jewish garrison, your brother Hananiah.

. . . . .

To our lord Bigvai, governor of Judea, your servants Yedoniah and his colleagues, the priests who are in Yeb the fortress. The health of your lordship may the God of Heaven seek after exceedingly at all times, and give you favor before Darius the king and the princes of the palace more than now a thousand times, and may he grant you long life, and may you be happy and prosperous at all times. Now your servant Yedoniah and his colleagues depose as follows: In the month of Tammuz in the 14th year of Darius the king, when Arsames departed and went to the king, the priests of the god Khnub, who is in the fortress of Yeb, were in league with Waidrang who was governor here, saying: The temple of Ya'u the God, which is in the fortress of Yeb let them remove from there. Then that Waidrang, the reprobate, sent a letter to his son Nephayan who was commander of the garrison in the fortress of Syene saying: The temple which is in Yeb the fortress let them destroy. Then Nephayan led out the Egyptians with the other forces. They came to the fortress of Yeb with their weapons, they entered that temple, they destroyed it to the ground, and the pillars of stone which were there they broke. Also it happened, 5 gateways of stone, built with hewn blocks of stone, which were in that temple they destroyed, and their doors they lifted off, and the hinges of those doors were bronze, and the roof of cedar wood, all of it with the rest of the furniture and other things which were there, all of it they burnt with fire, and the basins of gold and silver and everything that was in that temple, all of it, they took and made their own. Already in the days of the kings of Egypt our fathers had built that temple in the fortress of Yeb, and when Cambyses came into Egypt[1] he found that temple built, and the temples of the gods of Egypt all of them they overthrew, but no one did any harm to that temple. When this was done, we with our wives and our children put on sack-cloth and fasted and prayed to Ya'u the Lord of Heaven, who let us see our desire upon that Waidrang. The dogs tore off the anklet from his legs, and all the riches he had gained were destroyed, and all the men who had sought to do evil to that temple, all of them, were killed and we saw our desire upon them. Also before this, at the time when this evil was done to us, we sent a letter to your lordship and to Johanan the high priest and his colleagues the priests who are in Jerusalem, and to Ostanes the brother of Anani, and the nobles of the Jews. They have not sent any letter to us. Also since the month of Tammuz in the 14th year of Darius the king till this day we wear sack-cloth and fast. Our wives are made widow-like, we do not anoint ourselves with oil and we drink no wine. Also from that time till the present day in the 17th year of Darius the king, neither meal-offering, incense, nor sacrifice do they offer in that temple. Now your servants Yedoniah and his colleagues and the Jews, all of them inhabitants of Yeb, say as follows: If it seem good to your lordship, take thought for that temple to build it, since they do not allow us to build it. Look upon your well-wishers and friends who are here in Egypt, and let a letter be sent from you to them concerning the temple of the God Ya'u to build it in the fortress of Yeb as it was built before, and they shall offer the meal-offering and incense and sacrifice on the altar of the God Ya'u on your behalf, and we will pray for you at all times, we, our wives, our children, and the Jews, all who are here, if they do so that that temple be re-built, and it shall be a merit to you before Ya'u the God of Heaven more than a man who offers to him sacrifice and burnt-offerings worth as much as the sum of a thousand talents. As to gold, about this we have sent and given instruc-

1. 525 B.C.

tions. Also the whole matter we have set forth in a letter in our name to Delaiah and Shelemiah the sons of Sanballat governor of Samaria. Also of all this which was done to us Arsames knew nothing. On the 20th of Marcheswan the 17th year of Darius the king.

# *34 A Greek View*

The struggle of the Greeks with the Persian Empire (see Selections 48–50) did not blind them to the greatness and the many virtues of their adversary. The calm view taken of the Persians by one enlightened Greek observer is expressed in this selection—a compound of legend, hearsay, and sharp observation—describing Persian customs. The passages are from Herodotus' *History of the Persian Wars,* 1.131–140, written about 425 B.C. The translation is by George Rawlinson.

❁❁❁❁❁

The customs which I know the Persians to observe are the following. They have no images of the gods, no temples nor altars, and consider the use of them a sign of folly. This comes, I think, from their not believing the gods to have the same nature with men, as the Greeks imagine. Their wont, however, is to ascend the summits of the loftiest mountains, and there to offer sacrifice to Zeus, which is the name they give to the whole circuit of the firmament. They likewise offer to the sun and moon, to the earth, to fire, to water, and to the winds. These are the only gods whose worship has come down to them from ancient times. At a later period they began the worship of Aphrodite, which they borrowed from the Arabians and Assyrians. Mylitta is the name by which the Assyrians know this goddess, whom the Arabians call Alitta, and the Persians Mitra.

To these gods the Persians offer sacrifice in the following manner: they raise no altar, light no fire, pour no libations, there is no sound of the flute, no putting on of chaplets, no consecrated barley-cake; but the man who wishes to sacrifice brings his victim to a spot of ground which is pure from pollution, and there calls upon the name of the god to whom he intends to offer. It is usual to have the turban encircled with a wreath, most commonly of myrtle. The sacrificer is not allowed to pray for blessings on himself alone, but he prays for the welfare of the king, and of the whole Persian people, among whom he is of necessity included. He cuts the victim in pieces, and having boiled the flesh, he lays it out upon the softest grass that he can find, trefoil especially. When all is ready, one of the Magi comes forward and chants a hymn, which they say recounts the origin of the gods. It is not lawful to offer sacrifice unless there is a Magus present. After waiting a short time the sacrificer carries the flesh of the victim away with him, and makes whatever use of it he pleases.

Of all the days in the year, the one which they celebrate most is their birthday. It is customary to have the board furnished on that day with an ampler supply than common. The richer Persians cause an ox, a horse, a camel, and an ass to be baked whole and so served up to them: the poorer classes use instead the smaller kinds of cattle. They eat little solid food but abundance of dessert, which is set on table a few dishes at a time; this it is which makes them say that "the Greeks, when they eat, leave off hungry, having nothing worth mention served up to them after the meats; whereas, if they had more put before them, they would not stop eating." They are very fond of wine, and drink it in large quantities. To vomit or obey natural calls in the presence of another, is forbidden among them. Such are their customs in these matters.

It is also their general practice to deliberate upon affairs of weight when they are drunk; and then on the morrow, when they are sober, the decision to which they came the night before is put before them by the master of the house in which it was made; and if it is then approved of, they act on it; if not, they set it aside. Sometimes, however, they are sober at their first deliberation, but in this case they always reconsider the matter under the influence of wine.

When they meet each other in the streets, you may know if the persons meeting are of equal rank by the following token; if they are, instead of speaking, they kiss each other on the lips. In the case where one is a little inferior to the other, the kiss is given on the cheek; where the difference of rank is great, the inferior prostrates himself upon the ground. Of nations, they honour most their nearest neighbours whom they esteem next to themselves; those who live beyond these they honour in the second degree; and so with the remainder, the further they are removed, the less the esteem in which they hold them. The reason is, that they look upon themselves as very greatly superior in all respects to the rest of mankind, regarding others as approaching to excellence in proportion as they dwell nearer to them; whence it comes to pass that those who are the farthest off must be the most degraded of mankind. Under the dominion of the Medes, the several nations of the empire exercised authority over each other in this order. The Medes were lords over all, and governed the nations upon their borders, who in their turn governed the States beyond, who likewise bore rule over the nations which adjoined on them. And this is the order which the Persians also follow in their distribution of honour; for that people, like the Medes, has a progressive scale of administration and government.

There is no nation which so readily adopts foreign customs as the Persians. Thus, they have taken the dress of the Medes, considering it superior to their own; and in war they wear the Egyptian breastplate. As soon as they hear of any luxury, they instantly make it their own: and hence, among other novelties, they have learned pederasty from the Greeks. Each of them has several wives, and a still larger number of concubines.

Next to prowess in arms, it is regarded as the greatest proof of manly excellence, to be the father of many sons. Every year the king sends rich gifts to the man who can show the largest number: for they hold that number is strength. Their sons are carefully instructed from their fifth to their twentieth year, in three things alone,—to ride, to draw the bow, and to speak the truth. Until their fifth year they are not allowed to come into the sight of their father, but pass their lives with the women. This is done that, if the child die young, the father may not be afflicted by its loss.

To my mind it is a wise rule, as also is the following—that the king shall not put any one to death for a single fault, and that none of the Persians shall visit a single fault in a slave with any extreme penalty; but in every case the services of the offender shall be set against his misdoings; and, if the latter be found to outweigh the former, the aggrieved party shall then proceed to punishment.

The Persians maintain that never yet did any one kill his own father or mother; but in all such cases they are quite sure that, if matters were sifted to the bottom, it would be found that the child was either a changeling or else the fruit of adultery; for it is not likely they say that the real father should perish by the hands of his child.

They hold it unlawful to talk of any thing which it is unlawful to do. The most disgraceful thing in the world, they think, is to tell a lie; the next worse, to owe a debt: because, among other reasons, the debtor is obliged to tell lies. If a Persian has the leprosy he is not allowed to enter into a city, or to have any dealings with the other Persians; he must, they say, have sinned against the sun. Foreigners attacked by this disorder, are forced to leave the country: even white pigeons are often driven away, as guilty of the same offense. They never defile a river with the secretions of their bodies, nor even wash their hands in one; nor will they allow others to do so, as they have a great reverence for rivers. There is another peculiarity, which the Persians themselves have never noticed, but which has not escaped my observation. Their names, which are expressive of some bodily or mental excellence, all end with the same letter—the letter which is called San by the Dorians, and Sigma by the Ionians. Any one who examines will find that the Persian names, one and all without exception, end with this letter.

Thus much I can declare of the Persians with entire certainty, from my own actual knowledge. There is another custom which is spoken of with reserve, and not openly, concerning their dead. It is said that the body of a male Persian is never buried, until it has been torn either by a dog or a bird of prey.[1] That the Magi have this custom is beyond a doubt, for they practise it without any concealment. The dead bodies are covered with wax, and then buried in the ground.

The Magi are a very peculiar race, differing entirely from the Egyptian priests, and indeed from all other men whatsoever. The Egyptian priests make it a point of religion not to kill any live animals except those which they offer in sacrifice. The Magi, on the contrary, kill animals of all kinds with their own hands, excepting dogs and men. They even seem to take a delight in the employment, and kill, as readily as they do other animals, ants and snakes, and such like flying or creeping things. However, since this has always been their custom, let them keep to it. I return to my former narrative.

# 35 *Persian Religious Literature*

In addition to their mighty achievement in imperial rule (in which the place of religion has been noted), a second important historical contribution of the Persians was in their own religion. This contribution is associated with the name of a great religious innovator, the prophet Zarathustra (or Zoroaster in the Greek rendering of his name). His dates are not certain, but he appears to have flourished in the sixth century B.C. His teachings are found in the Zend-Avesta, one of the great works among the sacred literatures of the world. They had a profound influence upon later religious developments, most importantly in the theology of early Christianity.

The teaching of the Zarathustrian religion is thought to be the crowning point of a long religious development. In this religion all functions of deity

1. This strange custom still prevails among the Parsees, wherever they are found, whether in Persia or in India.

[ 286 ]

are contained in one great Spirit of Light and Goodness, Ahura Mazda, a god who has lost all anthropomorphic character, a purely spiritual conception. He is seen as being opposed by Angra Mainyu, the Spirit of Darkness and Evil. In the sacred book of the Zarathustrian faith, the Avesta, are contained elements from various historical stages of the religion's development. The whole work itself is fragmentary and the immense task of organizing, translating, and interpreting it may never be completed entirely satisfactorily.

The portion of the Avesta known as the Vendidad has been described as a book of laws, and most of it does contain prescriptions dealing with ritual purification and similar subjects. Another section of the Avesta, the Yasts, consists of a monthly cycle of daily prayers to various ancient deities now representing facets of the all-embracing Ahura Mazda. The Gathas, yet another section, are believed to be the remnants of writings by Zarathustra himself. In these hymns allusion is frequently made to a struggle with the adherents of a hostile religion. These are understood as referring to the actual historical difficulties encountered by the Zarathustrian cult. The selection that follows is from the second of these principal parts of the Avesta. It is Yast XXII, which describes the fate after death of the souls of the righteous and of the wicked. The translation is by James Darmesteter (in F. Max Müller, *The Sacred Books of the East,* Vol. XXIII: *The Zend-Avesta,* Part II, The Sirozahs, Yasts, and Nyahis, pp. 314–322).

@@@@@

Zarathustra asked Ahura Mazda: "O Ahura Mazda, most beneficent Spirit, Maker of the material world, thou Holy One!

"When one of the faithful departs this life, where does his soul abide on that night?"

Ahura Mazda answered:

"It takes its seat near the head, singing the Ustavaiti Gatha and proclaiming happiness: 'Happy is he, happy the man, whoever he be, to whom Ahura Mazda gives the full accomplishment of his wishes!' On that night his soul tastes as much of pleasure as the whole of the living world can taste."

—"On the second night where does his soul abide?"

Ahura Mazda answered: "It takes its seat near the head, singing the Ustavaiti Gatha and proclaiming happiness: 'Happy is he, happy the man, whoever he be, to whom Ahura Mazda gives the full accomplishment of his wishes!' On that night his soul tastes as much of pleasure as the whole of the living world can taste."

—"On the third night where does his soul abide?"

Ahura Mazda answered: "It takes its seat near the head, singing the Ustavaiti Gatha and proclaiming happiness: 'Happy is he, happy the man, whoever he be, to whom Ahura Mazda gives the full accomplishment of his wishes!' On that night his soul tastes as much of pleasure as the whole of the living world can taste."

At the end of the third night, when the dawn appears, it seems to the soul of the faithful one as if it were brought amidst plants and scents: it seems as if a wind were blowing from the region of the south, from the regions of the south, a sweet-scented wind, sweeter-scented than any other wind in the world.

And it seems to the soul of the faithful one as if he were inhaling that wind with the nostrils, and he thinks: "Whence does that wind blow, the sweetest-scented wind I ever inhaled with my nostrils?"

And it seems to him as if his own conscience were advancing to him in that wind, in the shape of a maiden fair, bright, white-armed, strong, tall-formed, high-standing, thick-breasted, beautiful of body, noble, of a glorious seed, of the size of a maid in her fifteenth year, as fair as the fairest things in the world.

And the soul of the faithful one addressed her, asking: "What maid art thou, who art the fairest maid I have ever seen?"

And she, being his own conscience, answers him: "O thou youth of good thoughts, good words, and good deeds, of good religion, I am thy own conscience!

"Everybody did love thee for that greatness, goodness, fairness, sweet-scentedness, victorious strength and freedom from sorrow, in which thou dost appear to me;

"And so thou, O youth of good thoughts, good words, and good deeds, of good religion! didst love me for that greatness, goodness, fairness, sweet-scentedness, victorious strength, and freedom from sorrow, in which I appear to thee.

"When thou wouldst see a man making derision and deeds of idolatry, or rejecting the poor and shutting his door, then thou wouldst sit singing the Gathas and worshipping the good waters and Atar, the son of Ahura Mazda, and rejoicing the faithful that would come from near or from afar.

"I was lovely and thou madest me still lovelier; I was fair and thou madest me still fairer; I was desirable and thou madest me still more desirable; I was sitting in a forward place and thou madest me sit in the foremost place, through this good thought, through this good speech, through this good deed of thine; and so henceforth men worship me for my having long sacrificed unto and conversed with Ahura Mazda.

"The first step that the soul of the faithful man made, placed him in the Good-Thought Paradise;

"The second step that the soul of the faithful man made, placed him in the Good-Word Paradise;

"The third step that the soul of the faithful man made, placed him in the Good-Deed Paradise;

"The fourth step that the soul of the faithful man made, placed him in the Endless Lights."

Then one of the faithful, who had departed before him, asked him, saying: "How didst thou depart this life, thou holy man? How didst thou come, thou holy man! from the abodes full of cattle and full of the wishes and enjoyments of love? From the material world into the world of the spirit? From the decaying world into the undecaying one? How long did thy felicity last?"

And Ahura Mazda answered: "Ask him not what thou askest him, who has just gone the dreary way, full of fear and distress, where the body and the soul part from one another.

"Let him eat of the food brought to him, of the oil of Zaremaya: this is the food for the youth of good thoughts, of good words, of good deeds, of good religion, after he has departed this life; this is the food for the holy woman, rich in good thoughts, good words, and good deeds, well-principled and obedient to her husband, after she has departed this life."

Zarathustra asked Ahura Mazda: "O Ahura Mazda, most beneficent Spirit, Maker of the material world, thou Holy One!

"When one of the wicked perishes, where does his soul abide on that night?"

Ahura Mazda answered: "It rushes and sits near the skull, singing the Kima Gatha, O holy Zarathustra!

" 'To what land shall I turn, O Ahura Mazda? To whom shall I go with praying?'

"On that night his soul tastes as much of suffering as the whole of the living world can taste."

—"On the second night, where does his soul abide?"

Ahura Mazda answered: "It rushes and sits near the skull, singing the

Kima Gatha, O holy Zarathustra! 'To what land shall I turn, O Ahura Mazda? To whom shall I go with praying?'

"On that night his soul tastes as much of suffering as the whole of the living world can taste."

—"On the third night, where does his soul abide?"

Ahura Mazda answered: "It rushes and sits near the skull, singing the Kima Gatha, O holy Zarathustra! 'To what land shall I turn, O Ahura Mazda? To whom shall I go with praying?'

"On that night his soul tastes as much of suffering as the whole of the living world can taste."

At the end of the third night, O holy Zarathustra! when the dawn appears, it seems to the soul of the faithful one as if it were brought amidst snow and stench, and as if a wind were blowing from the region of the north, from the regions of the north, a foul-scented wind, the foulest-scented of all the winds in the world.

And it seems to the soul of the wicked man as if he were inhaling that wind with the nostrils, and he thinks: "Whence does that wind blow, the foulest-scented wind that I ever inhaled with my nostrils?"

The first step that the soul of the wicked man made laid him in the Evil-Thought Hell;

The second step that the soul of the wicked man made laid him in the Evil-Word Hell;

The third step that the soul of the wicked man made laid him in the Evil-Deed Hell;

The fourth step that the soul of the wicked man made laid him in the Endless Darkness.

Then one of the wicked who departed before him addressed him, saying: "How didst thou perish, O wicked man? How didst thou come, O fiend! from the abodes full of cattle and full of the wishes and enjoyments of love? From the material world into the world of the Spirit? From the decaying world into the undecaying one? How long did thy suffering last?"

Angra Mainyu, the lying one, said: "Ask him not what thou askest him, who has just gone the dreary way, full of fear and distress, where the body and the soul part from one another.

"Let him eat of the food brought unto him, of poison and poisonous stench: this is the food, after he has perished, for the youth of evil thoughts, evil words, evil deeds, evil religion after he has perished; this is the food for the fiendish woman, rich in evil thoughts, evil words, and evil deeds, evil religion, ill-principled, and disobedient to her husband.

[ 290 ]

"We worship the Fravashi of the holy man, whose name is Asmo-hvanvant; then I will worship the Fravashis of the other holy Ones who were strong of faith.

"We worship the memory of Ahura Mazda, to keep the Holy Word.

"We worship the understanding of Ahura Mazda, to study the Holy Word.

"We worship the tongue of Ahura Mazda, to speak forth the Holy Word.

"We worship the mountain that gives understanding, that preserves understanding; we worship it by day and by night, with offerings of libations well-accepted.

"O Maker! how do the souls of the dead, the Fravashis of the holy Ones, manifest themselves?"

Ahura Mazda answered: "They manifest themselves from goodness of spirit and excellence of mind."

# THE GREEKS:
# THE MYCENAEAN AGE

A FTER 500 B.C. the people who came to dominate the civilization of the Mediterranean world, who deeply impressed their stamp upon the subsequent course of what is now called Western civilization, were the Greeks. The radical departure of the Greek achievement from that of all previously studied peoples, the departure which formed the foundation of Western civilization, should not, however, blind us to the fact that the Greeks were a part of their contemporary world, a world in which other powers and other traditions also flourished. In the early stages of Greek history these other traditions played an important part in the formation of Greek civilization, and in later periods there continued a fruitful interaction between Greeks and the peoples of what we have called the Ancient Near East.

The earliest stage of Greek history, in the Bronze Age, is known to us through the obscurity of the myths and the legends handed on through centuries in the oral tradition of folklore and written down by the poets and genealogists of later epochs. This tradition—corrected, confirmed, or extended by the findings of modern archaeology—informs us in sketchy outline of the entrance into the Balkan peninsula of a primitive, tribally organized people speaking various dialects of an Indo-European language. Their entry into the peninsula began shortly after 2000 B.C. and was a part of that same movement of peoples on the fringe of the civilized world that contemporaneously brought the Hittites into Asia Minor. Throughout the second millennium B.C. the Greek tribes continued to press down into the peninsula, where they fell under the domination of an expanding Bronze Age civilization based on the island of Crete.

The civilization of Crete had developed its own characteristics, in particular a unique and splendid art, but in general the archaeological evidence depicts a Bronze Age civilization much like those of the Near Eastern peoples. No "history" of Bronze Age Crete is possible, for alone among the civilized peoples in the second millennium B.C. the Cretans left no literary remains. All that we have to show that they knew how to write at all are a few score of clay tablets inscribed in a script known as Linear A, which has not yet been fully deciphered.

In the first half of the second millennium the power and influence of Crete extended into the mainland of Greece and over the islands of the Aegean Sea. Then, in the fifteenth century B.C.—at the time when the Egyptians were forming their empire and the Hittites were reaching the height of their imperial power—the mainland asserted its independence of Crete and subsequently gained control of that island itself. The fortress cities on both the mainland and Crete were ruled by the descendants of the Greek tribesmen who for hundreds of years had been filtering into the peninsula. The period that follows contains the earliest history of the Greeks. This Bronze Age history of Greece from about 1400 to 1100 B.C. is known as the Mycenaean Age, from the name of Mycenae, the leading city during that epoch. This is the period recalled in the earliest monuments of Greek literature, the epic poems of Homer.

# *36   The Decipherment of Linear B*

From the archaeological investigations of Mycenaean Greece came a gradually increasing quantity of inscribed clay tablets which by 1950 numbered some three thousand. Similar in form to the Linear A tablets of Crete, these tablets were written in a script sufficiently different to be dubbed Linear B. For decades linguistic scholars in many countries applied themselves to the decipherment of Linear B, and though several hopeful solutions turned out to be premature and were promptly disproved, slow progress was made. It became clear that the tablets contained only lists and inventories, that they were palace records, not literature, and could reveal only modest aspects of the society and the people that produced them. One question was of particular significance: what would the language of the tablets turn out to be? Upon the answer to this question hinged the major historical problem of whether in fact the dominant people of the Mycenaean period were indeed Greeks or of some other linguistic stock. In 1952 came the announcement of a decipherment of Linear B so conclusive that it

SOURCE: John Chadwick, *The Decipherment of Linear B* (Cambridge: Cambridge University Press, 1958; New York: Random House, Modern Library Paperbooks, 1959). Reprinted by permission of the publishers.

quickly gained complete acceptance by a skeptical scholarly world. And the language was Greek, an odd, archaic, primitive sort of Greek, but indisputably Greek.

No less dramatically appealing than the discovery was the discoverer. Michael Ventris, a thirty-year-old Englishman, was not a professional scholar but an architect, who had passionately pursued the problem of the tablets ever since they first captured his interest when he was a schoolboy of fourteen. In the later stages of his work he had allied himself with an expert in linguistics, the Cambridge University scholar John Chadwick, and they jointly published the articles and the book in which the successful decipherment was proved. In 1956 Michael Ventris was killed in an automobile accident.

The following passages are by John Chadwick.

❋❋❋❋❋

In 1940 a new name appears for the first time in the literature of the subject: Michael Ventris, then only eighteen years old. His article called "Introducing the Minoan Language" was published in the *American Journal of Archaeology;* in writing to the editor he had been careful to conceal his age, but although in later years he dismissed the article as "puerile," it was none the less soundly written. The basic idea was to find a language which might be related to Minoan. Ventris' candidate was Etruscan; not a bad guess, because the Etruscans, according to an ancient tradition, came from the Aegean to Italy. Ventris attempted to see how the Etruscan language would fit with Linear B. The results, as he admitted, were negative; but the Etruscan idea remained a fixation, which possessed him until in 1952 the Greek solution finally imposed itself on him. So firmly was Evans' Minoan theory based that at this date Greek seemed out of the question. "The theory that Minoan could be Greek," Ventris wrote, "is based of course upon a deliberate disregard for historical plausibility." Hardly anyone would have ventured to disagree. . . .

There is an obvious resemblance between an unreadable script and a secret code; similar methods can be employed to break both. But the differences must not be overlooked. The code is deliberately designed to baffle the investigator; the script is only puzzling by accident. The language underlying the coded text is ordinarily known; in the case of a script there are three separate possibilities. The language may be known or partially known, but written in an unknown script; this, for instance, was the case with the decipherment of the Old Persian inscriptions by the German scholar

Grotefend in 1802; the cuneiform signs were then quite unknown, but the language, as revealed by recognition of proper names, turned out to be largely intelligible through the medium of the Avestan texts.[1] Secondly, the script may be known, the language unknown. This is the case of Etruscan, which is written in a modified form of the Greek alphabet that presents little difficulty to the understanding of its sounds; but no language has yet been found sufficiently closely related to throw any light on the meaning of the words. Thus in spite of a large collection of inscriptions our knowledge of Etruscan is still very elementary and uncertain. Lastly, we have the situation which confronted the decipherers of the Minoan script, an unknown script *and* an unknown language. The fact that the language *subsequently* proved to be known is irrelevant; that fact could not be used in the first stages of the decipherment.

In the last case decipherments have usually been judged to be possible only when they could start from a bilingual text. The Egyptian hieroglyphs began to yield their secret only when the discovery of the Rosetta stone, with the Egyptian text repeated in Greek, made it possible to equate the royal names in the two versions. No such document exists for Minoan; but it was useless to sit back and wait for one to appear.

Cryptography has contributed a new weapon to the student of unknown scripts. It is now generally known that any code can in theory be broken, provided sufficient examples of coded texts are available; the only method by which to achieve complete security is to ensure continuous change in the coding system, or to make the code so complicated that the amount of material necessary to break it can never be obtained. The detailed procedures are irrelevant, but the basic principle is the analysis and indexing of coded texts, so that underlying patterns and regularities can be discovered. If a number of instances can be collected, it may appear that a certain group of signs in the coded text has a particular function; it may, for example, serve as a conjunction. A knowledge of the circumstances in which a message was sent may lead to other identifications, and from these tenuous gains further progress becomes possible, until the meaning of most of the coded words is known. The application of this method to unknown languages is obvious; such methods enable the decipherer to determine the *meaning* of sign-groups without knowing how to pronounce the signs. Indeed it is possible to imagine a case where texts in an unknown language might be understood without finding the phonetic value of a single sign.

The first step is of course to determine the type of system employed and,

1.   The holy book of the Persians; see Selection 35.

in the case of Linear B, this is not so difficult as it seems at first sight. There are only three basic ways of committing language to writing, and all known graphic systems use one or a combination of these. The simplest method is to draw a picture to represent a word; these pictograms are then often simplified until they become unrecognizable, but the principle remains that one sign represents one word. This is called 'ideographic' writing, and it has been carried to the highest stage of development by the Chinese, who still write in this way, although the Communist government is now trying to introduce reforms. . . .

Ideograms of course give no direct clue to the pronunciation of the word, and in fact the different Chinese dialects pronounce the characters very differently. It is as if everyone in Europe wrote CANIS, but read this as *cane, chien, perro, dog, Hund, sobaka, skili* and so forth; just as 5 is read *cinque, cinq, cinco, five, fünf, piat', pende,* etc. The other two systems are both made up of elements which, taken together, represent the sound of the word. Thus a number of signs are needed to write all but the shortest words. The difference between them is that the units of sound represented by the signs may be either whole syllables (pronounceable) or single letters (partly unpronounceable abstractions). A syllabic system splits words up like a child's first reading book: thus *in-di-vi-du-al* would require five signs. The total number of signs needed is obviously much less than in the ideographic system; but it may still be high if a language, like English, uses many complicated groups of consonants. A word like *strength,* for instance, is from the syllabic point of view a single unit. . . .

Alphabetic writing is generally held to be a Semitic invention, though the Egyptian script pointed the way to it, and it was only fully developed by the Greeks. Its characteristic feature is the small number of signs needed. Thus we use twenty-six letters in English (some of them redundant, like *c, k,* and *q* all for the same sound in some words), and the more complicated alphabets rarely exceed the thirty-two of modern Russian.

Equipped with this knowledge we can turn to our Linear B texts. These consist of groups of signs separated by small vertical bars; the length of the groups varies from two to eight signs. Accompanying these in many cases are other signs which stand alone followed by a numeral; many of these are recognizable pictograms. It is easy to guess that single signs standing alone are probably ideographic, that is, representing a whole word; those used in groups are likely to be either syllabic or alphabetic. A count of these signs shows that they number about eighty-nine—the exact total is still disputed, because some are very rare, and it is not yet clear whether certain forms are separate signs or variants of others. But the number is significant; it is far too small for a wholly ideographic system, and it is much too large for an alphabet. It must therefore be syllabic, and a fairly simple form of syllabary like the Cypriot or Japanese, not the more complicated systems of the cuneiform script. This elementary deduction was neglected by many of the would-be decipherers.

The first step towards the solution was the explanation of the numerical and metrical systems. The numerals were straightforward, and were tabulated by Evans at an early stage. They are based on the decimal system, but are not positional; there is no notation for zero, and figures up to 9 are represented by repeating the sign the appropriate number of times, much as in Roman numerals. . . .

The basis of the metrical system was worked out by Bennett in 1950. . . .

The signs on the tablets then could be divided into two classes: ideograms (together with metric signs and numerals) and syllabic signs. . . .

. . . the meaning of some of these ideographic signs was obvious. But there was still a large number of signs too stylized to allow guesswork; though now that we have worked out the meaning by reference to the context, we can sometimes see their derivation. It was, however, possible to classify many more of the ideograms with the help of those which could be recognized. Thus along with HORSE and PIG were regularly found three other ideograms which were therefore likely to belong to the same category of livestock. It was not easy to tell which was which, and here some understandable mistakes were made. It was also noticed that variants of the livestock ideograms occurred, the commonest being to modify the main vertical stroke or axis of the sign by adding two short cross bars, or dividing it into a fork. . . . Evans correctly guessed that these signified male and female animals, but Sundwall reversed the sexes. Miss Kober finally settled the question by showing that the ideograms for men and male animals share one form of the word for "total," while women and female animals have another form; the distinction of men and women was of course clear.

Thus in many cases it was possible to deduce the general subject-matter of the tablets before a single syllable could be read; almost without exception it was clear that they were lists, inventories or catalogues. For instance, a list of single sign-groups ("words"), each followed by the ideogram MAN and the numeral 1, was clearly a list of men's names, a muster roll or the like. . . .

In order to work successfully on texts of this kind, it is essential to become completely familiar with their appearance. The signs must be thoroughly learnt, so that there is no risk of confusing one with another, and sign-groups and even portions of text must be committed to memory, so that similar groups elsewhere can be identified. Careful indexing will reveal the repetitions of identical sign-groups; but the most significant discoveries are often not the exact repetitions, but groups which are very much alike but show slight variations. Ventris laid great stress on the need for a good visual memory; in this, as in so much else, he was richly endowed.

Ventris' first contribution to the study of Linear B has been described. . . . After the war, when he had completed his training as an architect, he returned to it with renewed vigour. At the beginning of 1950 he took the unusual step of circulating a questionnaire to a group of a dozen scholars of international reputation, whom he knew to be actively working on the Minoan scripts. The questions were drawn up to elicit opinions on the type of language or languages concealed by the scripts, any possible evidence of inflexion, the relationship of Linear A, Linear B and Cypriot, and so forth. It says a great deal, not only for international co-operation but also for the acuity of his questionnaire, that ten scholars supplied answers. These Ventris translated into English if necessary, and circulated at his own expense to all the rest, together with an analysis and his own views. The official title was: "The Languages of the Minoan and Mycenaean Civilizations"; but since it was deliberately designed to review the position fifty years after Evans' discovery of the first tablets, it came to be known as the "Mid-Century Report."

The ten scholars who sent answers were Bennett (U.S.A.), Bossert and Grumach (Germany), Schachermeyr (Austria), Pugliese Carratelli and Peruzzi (Italy), Georgiev (Bulgaria), Ktistopoulos (Greece), Sundwall (Finland), and Myres (Great Britain). There was the widest diversity in their views; Georgiev and Ktistopoulos both believed they had already achieved at least a partial solution. The others were reserved, but this exchange of opinions served to clear the air, and to show at least how little agreement there was on the basic issues.

The two who failed to reply were Hrozny (Czechoslovakia), who was by this time an old man, and had in any case recently published his own attempt at decipherment; and Miss Kober (U.S.A.), whose work was to prove so fruitful. She replied briefly that she thought the questionnaire was a waste of time; but this rebuff did not prevent Ventris from establishing friendly relations with her.

In one sense Miss Kober was right; the discussion of unproven theories

[ 298 ]

is often barren, and much that was written at this time now seems unreal and blind. It is astonishing to think that no one then seriously contemplated Greek as a possible language for Linear B. Ventris suggested that even if there were some Greeks living on the mainland, the principal language was something else. The majority opinion was that it would prove to be a language of the Indo-European family, to which Greek belongs, but perhaps more closely related to Hittite. The minority view, to which Ventris himself adhered, was that it was an "Aegean" language of a poorly known type, but probably represented by Etruscan.

The most interesting part of this document is the section by Ventris himself. In this he makes it plain that the first step must be to establish the relationships between alternating signs, independently of the phonetic values; all the rest, apart from Miss Kober, had concentrated attention on finding phonetic values, and the possibility of grouping the undeciphered signs had escaped them. The search for a pattern was the essential cryptographic procedure that made possible his success. . . .

Ventris intended his summing up to be the end of his own work on the problem for the time being. He had now a full-time job as an architect on the staff of the Ministry of Education, and he did not expect to be able to spare time and energy for the Minoan scripts. He ended the Report with these words: "I have good hopes that a sufficient number of people working on these lines will before long enable a satisfactory solution to be found. To them I offer my best wishes, being forced by pressure of other work to make this my last small contribution to the problem."

But it is not so easy to let a fascinating problem rest unsolved; it continues to fret one's mind at odd moments, and sooner or later one comes back to it, even at the expense of more urgent tasks. During the following two years Ventris, so far from letting it rest, followed up the Report with an intensive period of work on his own. It was typical of him that the series of twenty long Work Notes—in all 176 foolscap pages—that he prepared during this period were all duplicated and circulated (to a limited number of scholars) at his own expense. By means of these we are able to follow the complete history of the decipherment and the stages by which he reached it. . . .

Little real progress could be made until the publication in 1951 of Bennett's *The Pylos Tablets,* a transcript of the tablets found in 1939. This for the first time contained reliable lists of the signs; hitherto there had been much confusion of similar signs. The first task was the compilation of statistical tables showing the over-all frequency of each sign, and its frequency in initial, final and other positions in the sign groups. Simultaneously with Ventris similar tables were prepared by Bennett and Ktistopoulos. This in itself made certain conclusions possible. . . .

Another useful line of approach was offered by certain words which appeared in two different spellings. In some cases it was not easy to be sure that these were not two different words; but if they were long enough, but differed in only one syllable, then it was a reasonable assumption that they had something in common, especially if they were in like contexts. . . .

The greatest number of variations in words, however, was to be found in their endings. Miss Kober had already found some examples and suggested that they represented inflexions, that is, modifications of the ending of the word to denote grammatical relationship; as, for instance, in English *boxes* and *boxing* might be recognized as inflected forms of the simple word *box*. Fortunately lists such as the tablets contain consist almost entirely of nouns, so that the problems of inflexions in the verb could at this stage be left aside, and almost all variations explained as inflexions in the declension of nouns. With the new material Ventris was able to go far beyond her observations and distinguish various types of inflexion. . . .

Now these variations might be due to adding unrelated suffixes, like the Japanese "postpositions" which behave much as inflected endings: "nominative" *hito-ha,* "genitive" *hito-no,* "accusative" *hito-wo.* But if it is a true inflexion, it is more likely to follow the pattern of Latin: *domin-us, domin-i, domin-o.* The Japanese *hito* is an independent word which can stand alone; but in Latin there is no independent *domin*—it must be completed by the grammatical ending. If the Latin forms are written in a syllabic script, the termination will in fact represent *-nus, -ni, -no,* that is to say the consonant of the alternating suffixes, being part of the stem, remains unchanged. The existence of a number of different types of inflexion pointed to the second possibility; in Japanese all nouns show the same limited set of suffixes, and there is no true inflexion.

By this means it was possible to establish a fresh series of links, between signs which could be suspected of containing the same consonant but different vowels. . . . Ventris in August 1951 prepared a list of 159 words from the Pylos tablets which showed what he took to be inflexional variation; and from this and other lists of Knossos words he derived a large number of possible links between signs sharing the same consonant. Not all of these could be right, he pointed out, but those which occurred several times in different words were at least likely. . . .

In some cases the inflexional variation seemed to be due to a change of gender rather than case; this could be seen from the use of these words

[ 300 ]

with the ideograms for men and women. . . .This gender table suggested a further series of links, which Ventris worked on in September 1951. . . .

At this stage it was difficult to judge which of the links so found were correct, but Ventris built up a table showing which were the most probable and consistent. The signs were allotted to columns according to the function of the suffix. Not only masculine and feminine, but the other recognizable cases and derivatives each had a column, thus allowing the principle of links between signs having the same vowel to be extended.

"We may in this way," wrote Ventris in Work Note 15 of 3 September 1951, "be able to construct a second dimension to our 'GRID' which will make it the skeleton of a true table of phonetic values. It will then only need the identification of a small number of syllabic values for the more or less complete system of consonants and vowels to fit into place. Though it would evidently be better to wait until the 'GRID' can be further corrected by the full Knossos evidence, it is conceivable that some happy accident or intuition might lead to such a solution at any time now." Clearly Ventris felt that the solution was not far off; but he was still convinced that the language would prove to be of the little known pre-Greek type, to which Etruscan afforded the only clue, and that a poor one.

The next stage was to construct from this table a rough syllabic grid, using as many of the equations as seemed to be consistent and valid. The result was to bring together the different types of linkage found, so that the vowel columns could be reduced to five, and the consonant lines to fifteen. . . .

Work Note 20 (1 June 1952) was introduced by its author as "a frivolous digression" and was headed: "Are the Knossos and Pylos tablets written in Greek?" *Scripta Minoa II* was now available, but no one, not even Ventris, had yet made a full analysis. Ventris was well aware that he was flying in the face of expert opinion in daring to consider the possibility of Greeks at Knossos in the fifteenth century B.C. Hence the rather casual way in which he treated this theory, which he expected shortly to disprove.

However, he did not start with the Greek hypothesis and see if it would fit. The title was a description added after the work had been done, for the starting-point was deliberately chosen to be independent of the Greek language. This was the group of words which Ventris had classified as 'Category 3', and they included Miss Kober's "triplets". . . . The key supposition was that these were place-names, a step Miss Kober had not taken. Ventris analysed them as follows:

They are sign-groups which are not personal names, and yet figure as the subjects of very varied lists of commodities, often recurring in a fixed order. . . . Their commonest members are formed, in each case [i.e., at both Knossos and Pylos], by a group of about a dozen . . . which are found in a disproportionately large number of entries.

From the analogy of the contemporary accounts from Ras Shamra/Ugarit . . . which should be one of our most valuable aids, I think it is likely that the Category 3 sign-groups correspond to the 'towns and corporations' of Ugarit. . . . Those which occur *both* at Pylos and at Knossos are probably "corporations"; those which are peculiar to each are the "towns" and villages of the region. . . .

That is to say, the longer forms would be the adjectives (masculine and feminine) derived from the names of the towns, like *Athens/Athenian.* The Knossos names offered some hope of identification with names surviving into the classical period. . . .

A name which is likely to occur at Knossos is that of the nearby harbour town, Amnisos, mentioned by Homer. The consonant group *–mn–* will have to be spelled out by inserting an extra vowel, since every consonant must be followed by a vowel. It should therefore have the form approximately *a-mi-ni-so.* . . . We find in the tablets one suitable word, and only one, containing these signs. . . .

Ventris then reverted to the adjectival forms of the place-names, which now appear as, for example, *a-mi-ni-si-jo* (masculine) and *a-mi-ni-si-ja* (feminine). He acutely observed that if we suppose the final *-s, -n* and *-i* after another vowel are omitted, these forms are precisely the Greek derivative forms: masculine *Amnisios* (or plural *Amnisioi*), feminine *Amnisia* (or plural *Amnisiai*). The puzzling genitive ending . . . will be *-jo-jo* agreeing with the archaic Greek genitives in *-(i)-oio.* . . .

Ventris ended this Note with a warning: "If pursued, I suspect that this line of decipherment would sooner or later come to an impasse, or dissipate itself in absurdities." He called attention to features which appeared not to fit Greek. . . .

But even while this Note was in the post, on its way to scholars all over the world, Ventris did pursue this lead, and found to his astonishment that the Greek solution was inescapable. Slowly and painfully the mute signs were being forced to speak, and what they spoke was Greek—mangled and truncated it is true, but recognizable none the less as the Greek language.

Cryptography is a science of deduction and controlled experiment; hypotheses are formed, tested and often discarded. But the residue which passes the test grows and grows until finally there comes a point when the experimenter feels solid ground beneath his feet: his hypotheses cohere, and fragments of sense emerge from their camouflage. The code "breaks." Perhaps this is best defined as the point when the likely leads appear faster than they can be followed up. It is like the initiation of a chain-reaction in atomic physics; once the critical threshold is passed, the re-action propagates itself. Only in the simplest experiments or codes does it complete itself with explosive violence. In the more difficult cases there is much work still to be done, and the small areas of sense, though sure proof of the break, remain for a while isolated; only gradually does the picture become filled out.

In June 1952 Ventris felt that the Linear B script had broken. Admittedly the tentative Greek words suggested in Work Note 20 were too few to carry conviction; in particular they implied an unlikely set of spelling conventions. But as he transcribed more and more texts, so the Greek words began to emerge in greater numbers; new signs could now be identified by recognizing a word in which one sign only was a blank, and this value could then be tested elsewhere. The spelling rules received confirmation, and the pattern of the decipherment became clear.

It so happened that at this moment Ventris was asked by the B.B.C. to give a talk on the Third Programme in connexion with the publication of *Scripta Minoa II*. He determined to take this opportunity of bringing his discovery before the public. He gave first a brief historical account of the script and its discovery, and then proceeded to outline his method. Finally came the astonishing announcement:

During the last few weeks, I have come to the conclusion that the Knossos and Pylos tablets must, after all, be written in Greek—a difficult and archaic Greek, seeing that it is 500 years older than Homer and written in a rather abbreviated form, but Greek nevertheless.

Once I made this assumption, most of the peculiarities of the language and spelling which had puzzled me seemed to find a logical explanation; and although many of the tablets remain as incomprehensible as before, many others are suddenly beginning to make sense.

He went on to quote four well known Greek words which he claimed to have found (*poimēn*, "shepherd," *kerameus*, "potter," *khalkeus*, "bronze-smith," *khrusoworgos*, "gold-smith"), and to translate eight phrases. He ended on a suitably cautious note: "I have suggested that there is now a better chance of reading these earliest European inscriptions than ever before, but there is evidently a great deal more work to do before we are all agreed on the solution of the problem."

I do not think it can be said that this broadcast made a great impression; but I for one was an eager listener. In view of the recurrent claims that had been made, I did not regard Ventris' system as standing much chance; in particular I already had a pretty clear notion what Mycenaean Greek should look like, and I doubted whether Ventris had. . . .

The claim of Ventris, however, was too important and too relevant to my subject, the Greek dialects, to be overlooked. The first thing was to see Sir John Myres and ask his opinion, for I knew he was in touch with Ventris. He sat as usual in his canvas chair at a great desk, his legs wrapped in a rug. He was too infirm to move much, and he motioned me to a chair. "Mm, Ventris," he said in answer to my question, "he's a young architect." As Myres at that time was himself eighty-two, I wondered if "young" meant less than sixty. "Here's his stuff," he went on, "I don't know what to make of it. I'm not a philologist." On the whole he appeared sceptical, though admitting that he had not sufficient specialized knowledge to judge if the proposed Greek was sound. But he had some of Ventris' notes, including the latest version of the grid, which he let me copy, promising at the same time to put me in direct contact with Ventris.

I went home eager to try out the new theory. I approached the matter very cautiously, for impressed as I had been by the broadcast, I had a horrid feeling the Greek would turn out to be only vague resemblances to Greek words. . . . I set to work transcribing words from the two sets of texts, and in four days I had convinced myself that the identifications were in the main sound. I collected a list of twenty-three plausible Greek words I had found in the tablets, some of which had not then been noted by Ventris, and on 9 July I wrote to Myres stating my conclusion. I wrote, too, to Ventris, congratulating him on having found the solution, and putting forward a number of new suggestions.

His reply (13 July) was typically frank and modest. "At the moment," he wrote, "I feel rather in need of moral support. . . . I'm conscious that there's a *lot* which so far can't be very satisfactorily explained." I had tentatively asked if I could be any help to him; he replied: "I've been feeling the need of a 'mere philologist' to keep me on the right lines. . . . It would be extremely useful to me if I could count on your help, not only in trying to make sense out of the material, but also in drawing the correct conclusions about the formations in terms of dialect and stage of development." Thus was formed a partnership which was to last more than four years. . . .

My correspondence with Ventris developed into a rapid exchange of views, and although we met from time to time to discuss problems and plan our work, most of it was done alone and then submitted to the other for criticism. We followed this method in our joint publications; each drafted sections, which the other then criticized, and the whole was often rewritten to take account of objections raised. This method could never have worked, had we not been so much in harmony in our general attitude to the problem. We had many differences, but they were never serious, and most were resolved before we put anything into print; and the advantage of having everything checked by a second person in no small measure contributed to our confidence in our joint work.

The first project was a full length technical article on the decipherment, and I was flattered when Ventris asked me to contribute to it. I had no wish to take more than the small share of credit due to me, but he was anxious that it should be published jointly; my suggestions could in this way be incorporated without detailed acknowledgement, and, more important, joint authorship was some guarantee that it was at the least a shared delusion.

The title was carefully chosen to avoid extravagant claims: "Evidence for Greek Dialect in the Mycenaean Archives." . . .

The first section of the article advanced the proposition that Linear B contained Greek as a reasonable historical hypothesis. Next came an analysis of the texts entirely on internal evidence, explaining very briefly the principles of the syllabic grid. . . .

"Evidence" gave a full list of the words which had provided the equations of vowels and consonants for the grid. . . .

This part of the article ended with four explanations intended to disarm any critics who might protest at the incompleteness of the decipherment: (1) the dialect is 1000 years older than classical Attic, as great a gap as between *Beowulf* and Shakespeare; (2) the archives are not literary essays but highly abbreviated accounts; (3) the article represented only the first three months' work on an entirely new subject; (4) no attempt could be made to deal with all the material; attention was concentrated on the most significant tablets.

Then came a section demonstrating the variations due to gender. . . . An analysis of the personal names showed the different types of declension, which were further confirmed by a study of occupational terms, a hundred of which were listed. Verbs are relatively rare, but four forms of the verb *ekhō* "have" were demonstrated, and some other verbs were identified and discussed. . . .

"Evidence" ended with a short section on the position of the Mycenaean dialect. We outlined the principal features of the dialect and commented on their relation to the dialects of the classical period, and to other related languages. . . .

Between the writing of "Evidence" and its appearance in the autumn of 1953 we had to possess ourselves in as much patience as we could. In conversation with colleagues we had already succeeded in gaining some converts, and as a result both of us were asked to lecture on the decipherment to learned, and less learned, societies in various parts of England. In this way the ground was prepared for the article.

We had been fortunate in gaining quickly the adherence of L. R. Palmer, recently appointed to the chair of Classical Philology at Oxford, and two leading Swedish scholars, Professors A. Furumark and G. Björck of Uppsala. Their further help and support at this critical period did much to overcome the hesitations which we naturally encountered among our colleagues.

It was Furumark who gave us our first publicity, as early as November 1952, when he was interviewed by the Swedish press. He had been receiving the Work Notes, and when the Experimental Vocabulary reached him, he described it as a "bombshell dropped through his letter-box." The praise he lavished on Ventris caught the eye of journalists elsewhere; but too few people had then seen the decipherment, and Bennett in Yale, when asked his opinion, was studiously non-committal.

In private correspondence with Ventris, Bennett had expressed himself more freely. On 6 July he wrote: "I don't know whether to congratulate you or offer condolences on your recent decipherment, because it came at a deucedly inconvenient time, just when I was checking entries in the index. . . . On the face of it I don't like your freedom to supply l r m n t q w e r t, etc., but there were some other things that seemed quite reasonable." Later that year he was still too busy to devote the time necessary to check the decipherment, and on receiving an advance draft of "Evidence" in October wrote: "I shall probably return now to wavering back and forth, thinking one day that you have it, and the next that you haven't."

The lecture given by Ventris in London on 24 June 1953 was reported by *The Times;* a leading article discussed the claim and its possible consequences. The coincidence that it stood next to a comment on the conquest of Everest was not missed; and it was not long before the decipherment was being described as "the Everest of Greek Archaeology." But of course the one feat was certain and provable; the other was still a doubtful claim to be authenticated, and *The Times* was right to head its comment "On the Threshold?"

We had expected that our article would touch off a long and bitter controversy before the theory was finally accepted. Scholars do not accept revolutionary changes without the deepest probing; and even then some are always reluctant. But in this we were wrong. Even before the theory could be published, Professor Blegen had put into our hands a decisive confirmation, a weapon so powerful that the failure of the opposition was certain before it had begun.

One afternoon in May 1953 the telephone rang in my flat in Cambridge. Michael Ventris had called me from London in a great state of excitement—he rarely showed signs of emotion, but for him this was a dramatic moment. The cause was a letter he had received from Professor Blegen, the excavator of Pylos. We knew that Blegen had found more tablets in 1952, but no one had yet examined them carefully; they had been cleaned during the winter and only the next spring were they ready for study. Blegen's letter ran:

Since my return to Greece I have spent much of my time working on the tablets from Pylos, getting them properly ready to be photographed. I have tried your experimental syllabary on some of them.

Enclosed for your information is a copy of P641, which you may find interesting. It evidently deals with pots, some on three legs, some with four handles, some with three, and others without handles. The first word by your system seems to be *ti-ri-po-de* and it recurs twice as *ti-ri-po* (singular?). The four-handled pot is preceded by *qe-to-ro-we,* the three-handled by *ti-ri-o-we* or *ti-ri-jo-we,* the handleless pot by *a-no-we.* All this seems too good to be true. Is coincidence excluded?

The odds against getting this astonishing agreement purely by accident are astronomical, and this was a proof of the decipherment which was undeniable. A few people have of course remained unconvinced. . . . But all who were unprejudiced could now be convinced that the system worked; further refinements would no doubt be possible, but the basis was obviously sound. . . .

To Ventris and myself this tablet was a godsend: not that either of us wanted convincing further, but we knew that here was a proof to carry conviction with any impartial judge. Blegen did his best to hasten its publication, and Ventris was able to publish his own version in the spring of 1954 in the American journal *Archaeology.* But before that it had been mentioned in lectures, and the news had leaked out to the wide circle of scholars whose interest had been aroused by "Evidence."

[ 307 ]

The Hellenic Society reprinted "Evidence" as a separate pamphlet and more than a thousand copies were sold, an event without parallel in the annals of the society. Reviews of it soon began to appear in learned journals all over the world, and not a few articles were published by newspapers and more popular magazines. How far the news of the confirmation influenced reviewers it is hard to tell; and but for that its reception might not have been so enthusiastic. A typical comment was that of Professor M. S. Ruipérez, writing in the Spanish periodical *Zephyrus* early in 1954:

Although it may be susceptible of further refinements and corrections the interpretation . . . (which comes to crown many years of tenacious effort by the young English architect Mr Michael Ventris) unites—let us say it at once—all the guarantees which can be demanded (reading of whole phrases with meaning suited to that expected from the ideograms, reading of known place and personal names, perfect coherence in orthography and grammar) and must in consequence be regarded as definitive.

This view was echoed by other scholars, but not entirely without criticism; indeed right from the first the decipherment was subjected to the most careful testing and probing. . . .

During this period Ventris received many letters from experts abroad whom he had kept informed of his work. Their tone was extraordinarily favourable. Professor Sittig, for instance, who was committed to his own line of decipherment, was generous enough to abandon his theory and support Ventris. On 22 May 1953 he wrote: "I repeat: your demonstrations are cryptographically the most interesting I have yet heard of, and are really fascinating. If you are right, the methods of the archaeology, ethnology, history and philology of the last fifty years are reduced *ad absurdum*." . . .

Ventris and I were not of course standing still. We had already in December 1953 written a more popular account of the results and decipherment methods in the journal *Antiquity*. In August 1954 Ventris' lecture to the International Classical Congress at Copenhagen was a triumph; when he showed the slide of the tripod tablet deciphered the whole of the large audience burst into applause, before he had said a word. . . .

The present state of research on the Mycenaean texts and related problems is best illustrated by some figures from the bibliographies which have been published by the London University Institute of Classical Studies. The four issues which have appeared cover articles and books from the publication of "Evidence" down to the end of 1958. In this period alone we have recorded 432 articles, pamphlets or books by 152 authors from 23 different countries. This rate of work still continues, and if anything is increasing. It would be invidious to single out any particular authors, but a few comments are necessary. These figures exclude the work on the publication of the texts, which has fallen chiefly to Bennett. Two useful glossaries have been compiled in transliteration, one by Meriggi, one by Georgiev. The London Institute of Classical Studies has not only held a series of Linear B Seminars, which have provided a forum for discussion among British scholars, but has also undertaken the publication of texts and bibliographies.

The respectability of this new branch of classical studies is evident from the fact that it has been accepted as a proper subject for research degrees, and that it now appears in the examination syllabus at the Universities of Cambridge and Oxford. Needless to say, it is not yet suited for the ordinary level of undergraduate instruction, but its importance is recognized, and it will remain a growing field for specialists.

In April 1956 the French Centre National de la Recherche Scientifique, under the direction of Professors Chantraine and Lejeune, organized the first International Colloquium on the Mycenaean texts. Nine French and eleven foreign scholars from seven countries met for a week at Gif near Paris to discuss the work done and to plan for the future. Their contributions were printed in a volume entitled *Études Mycéniennes;* but the happiest result of the meeting was the friendly spirit in which we resolved our differences. Now at the first sign of a quarrel, we have only to appeal to the "esprit de Gif," and I hope that this beginning will be followed by all who now seek to enter the circle of specialists in Mycenaean. At this meeting Ventris was of course the leading figure; his fluency in French made a great impression, but he was equally at home chatting to the Swiss in Schwyzerdeutsch, or to the Greek delegate in Greek.

Five months later he was dead; but the work he did lives, and his name will be remembered so long as the ancient Greek language and civilization are studied.

# 37 Mycenaean Kings

The Mycenaean Age was the period which the Greeks looked back upon as their dimly remembered "heroic age." It is the epoch from which their

SOURCE: Reprinted from *The Iliad of Homer* tr. Richmond Lattimore by permission of The University of Chicago Press. Copyright 1951 by The University of Chicago.

legends and folk tales derive and is recalled in the epic poems of Homer, the *Iliad* and the *Odyssey*. These two great poems, the earliest monuments of European literature, were put into writing in their final form in the eighth century B.C. During the preceding three to four hundred years the stories they tell were part of an oral literature in which the deeds of a glorious past were recounted in song by bards who gave their own versions, embroidered upon the basic material of historical fact. Until the findings of modern archaeology it was not known whether the tradition preserved in the Homeric poems had any historical value at all. Now, used with caution and checked wherever possible with the archaeological data, the poems can be made to reveal illuminating details about Bronze Age, Mycenaean Greece. The following passages from the *Iliad* show something of the flavor of Mycenaean monarchy. The translation is by Richmond Lattimore of *Iliad* 1.101–192, 245–305.

❀❀❀❀❀

He spoke thus and sat down again, and among them stood up
Atreus' son the hero wide-ruling Agamemnon
raging, the heart within filled black to the brim with anger
from beneath, but his two eyes showed like fire in their blazing.
First of all he eyed Kalchas bitterly and spoke to him:
"Seer of evil: never yet have you told me a good thing.
Always the evil things are dear to your heart to prophesy,
but nothing excellent have you said nor ever accomplished.
Now once more you make divination to the Danaans, argue
forth your reason why he who strikes from afar afflicts them,
because I for the sake of the girl Chryseis would not take
the shining ransom; and indeed I wish greatly to have her
in my own house; since I like her better than Klytaimestra
my own wife, for in truth she is no way inferior,
neither in build nor stature nor wit, not in accomplishment.
Still I am willing to give her back, if such is the best way.
I myself desire that my people be safe, not perish.
Find me then some prize that shall be my own, lest I only
among the Argives go without, since that were unfitting;
you are all witnesses to this thing, that my prize goes elsewhere."
Then in answer again spoke brilliant swift-footed Achilleus:
"Son of Atreus, most lordly, greediest for gain of all men,

how shall the great-hearted Achaians give you a prize now?
There is no great store of things lying about I know of.
But what we took from the cities by storm has been distributed;
it is unbecoming for the people to call back things once given.
No, for the present give the girl back to the god; we Achaians
thrice and four times over will repay you, if ever Zeus gives
into our hands the strong-walled citadel of Troy to be plundered."
    Then in answer again spoke powerful Agamemnon:
"Not that way, good fighter though you be, godlike Achilleus,
strive to cheat, for you will not deceive, you will not persuade me.
What do you want? To keep your own prize and have me sit here
lacking one? Are you ordering me to give this girl back?
Either the great-hearted Achaians shall give me a new prize
chosen according to my desire to atone for the girl lost,
or else if they will not give me one I myself shall take her,
your own prize, or that of Aias, or that of Odysseus,
going myself in person; and he whom I visit will be bitter.
Still, these are things we shall deliberate again hereafter.
Come, now, we must haul a black ship down to the bright sea,
and assemble rowers enough for it, and put on board it
the hecatomb, and the girl herself, Chryseis of the fair cheeks,
and let there be one responsible man in charge of her,
either Aias or Idomeneus or brilliant Odysseus,
or you yourself, son of Peleus, most terrifying of all men,
to reconcile by accomplishing sacrifice the archer."
    Then looking darkly at him Achilleus of the swift feet spoke:
"O wrapped in shamelessness, with your mind forever on profit,
how shall any one of the Achaians readily obey you
either to go on a journey or to fight men strongly in battle?
I for my part did not come here for the sake of the Trojan
spearmen to fight against them, since to me they have done nothing.
Never yet have they driven away my cattle or my horses,
never in Phthia where the soil is rich and men grow great did they
spoil my harvest, since indeed there is much that lies between us,
the shadowy mountains and the echoing sea; but for your sake,
o great shamelessness, we followed, to do you favour,
you with the dog's eyes, to win your honour and Menelaos'
from the Trojans. You forget all this or else you care nothing.
And now my prize you threaten in person to strip from me,

for whom I laboured much, the gift of the sons of the Achaians.
Never, when the Achaians sack some well-founded citadel
of the Trojans, do I have a prize that is equal to your prize.
Always the greater part of the painful fighting is the work of
my hands; but when the time comes to distribute the booty
yours is far the greater reward, and I with some small thing
yet dear to me go back to my ships when I am weary with fighting.
Now I am returning to Phthia, since it is much better
to go home again with my curved ships, and I am minded no longer
to stay here dishonoured and pile up your wealth and your luxury."

Then answered him in turn the lord of men Agamemnon:
"Run away by all means if your heart drives you. I will not
entreat you to stay here for my sake. There are others with me
who will do me honour, and above all Zeus of the counsels.
To me you are the most hateful of all the kings whom the gods love.
Forever quarrelling is dear to your heart, and wars and battles;
and if you are very strong indeed, that is a god's gift.
Go home then with your own ships and your own companions,
be king over the Myrmidons. I care nothing about you.
I take no account of your anger. But here is my threat to you.
Even as Phoibos Apollo is taking away my Chryseis.
I shall convey her back in my own ship, with my own
followers; but I shall take the fair-cheeked Briseis,
your prize, I myself going to your shelter, that you may learn well
how much greater I am than you, and another man may shrink back
from likening himself to me and contending against me."

So he spoke. And the anger came on Peleus' son, and within
his shaggy breast the heart was divided two ways, pondering
whether to draw from beside his thigh the sharp sword, driving
away all those who stood between and kill the son of Atreus,
or else to check the spleen within and keep down his anger. . . .

Thus spoke Peleus' son and dashed to the ground the sceptre
studded with golden nails, and sat down again. But Atreides
raged still on the other side, and between them Nestor
the fair-spoken rose up, the lucid speaker of Pylos,
from whose lips the streams of words ran sweeter than honey.
In his time two generations of mortal men had perished,
those who had grown up with him and they who had been born to
these in sacred Pylos, and he was king in the third age.

He in kind intention toward both stood forth and addressed them:
"Oh, for shame. Great sorrow comes on the land of Achaia.
Now might Priam and the sons of Priam in truth be happy,
and all the rest of the Trojans be visited in their hearts with gladness,
were they to hear all this wherein you two are quarrelling,
you, who surpass all Danaans in council, in fighting.
Yet be persuaded. Both of you are younger than I am.
Yes, and in my time I have dealt with better men than
you are, and never once did they disregard me. Never
yet have I seen nor shall see again such men as these were,
men like Peirithoös, and Dryas, shepherd of the people,
Kaineus and Exadios, godlike Polyphemos,
or Theseus, Aigeus' son, in the likeness of the immortals.
These were the strongest generation of earth-born mortals,
the strongest, and they fought against the strongest, the beast men
living within the mountains, and terribly they destroyed them.
I was of the company of these men, coming from Pylos,
a long way from a distant land, since they had summoned me.
And I fought single-handed, yet against such men no one
of the mortals now alive upon earth could do battle. And also
these listened to the counsels I gave and heeded my bidding.
Do you also obey, since to be persuaded is better.
You, great man that you are, yet do not take the girl away
but let her be, a prize as the sons of the Achaians gave her
first. Nor, son of Peleus, think to match your strength with
the king, since never equal with the rest is the portion of honour
of the sceptred king to whom Zeus gives magnificence. Even
though you are the stronger man, and the mother who bore you was immortal,
yet is this man greater who is lord over more than you rule.
Son of Atreus, give up your anger; even I entreat you
to give over your bitterness against Achilleus, he who
stands as a great bulwark of battle over all the Achaians."
   Then in answer again spoke powerful Agamemnon:
"Yes, old sir, all this you have said is fair and orderly.
Yet here is a man who wishes to be above all others,
who wishes to hold power over all, and to be lord of
all, and give them their orders, yet I think one will not obey him.
And if the everlasting gods have made him a spearman,

yet they have not given him the right to speak abusively."

Then looking at him darkly brilliant Achilleus answered him:
"So must I be called of no account and a coward
if I must carry out every order you may happen to give me.
Tell other men to do these things, but give me no more
commands, since I for my part have no intention to obey you.
And put away in your thoughts this other thing I tell you.
With my hands I will not fight for the girl's sake, neither
with you nor any other man, since you take her away who gave her.
But of all the other things that are mine beside my fast black
ship, you shall take nothing away against my pleasure.
Come, then, only try it, that these others may see also;
instantly your own black blood will stain my spearpoint."

So these two after battling in words of contention
stood up, and broke the assembly beside the ships of the Achaians.

# 38 The Dark Ages

The civilization of Mycenaean Greece was extinguished in the waves of
barbarian invasion that destroyed the empire of the Hittites and eclipsed
that of Egypt, bringing centuries of chaos to the Near East. The invaders
of Greece were the Dorians, who were themselves Greek-speaking and who
destroyed as they came, sending the settled inhabitants fleeing before them.
In wave after wave they poured over Greece, and by 1100 B.C. the Bronze
Age splendors of Mycenae were no more. Throughout the lands bordering
the Aegean Sea the dreary curtain of the Dark Ages descended. Until the
eighth century B.C. the expression "Dark Ages" reflects both the wretched-
ness of the poverty-stricken, primitive conditions and the paucity of our
knowledge of this period.

For a glimpse into that world we must turn again to the Homeric poems.
The bards who sang of the heroic past could remember the stirring tales of
warrior kings and they could see the ruins of the great palaces in which
those monarchs had lived. When, however, it came to describing a way of
life splendid beyond anything in their experience, their imaginations could
not always serve. The failure to imagine what Bronze Age life was like
often resulted in pictures more applicable to the conditions of the Dark Ages
than to those of Mycenaean royalty. Thus a royal household was depicted

with a middle-class flavor and a rather rustic and naïve quality of speech and activity; a king was conceived of as a rough and unregal person, capable of doing his own farm labor or making his own household furniture.

The following passages are in the prose translation of the late-nineteenth-century English novelist, satirist, and critic Samuel Butler, who in his translation followed the practice of giving the Latin equivalents of Greek proper names: Odysseus thereby becomes Ulysses, Zeus is Jove or Jupiter, Athena is Minerva, and so forth. The selections are *Odyssey* 6.48–315 and 23.152–230.

@@@@@

By and by morning came and woke Nausicaa, who began wondering about her dream; she therefore went to the other end of the house to tell her father and mother all about it, and found them in their own room. Her mother was sitting by the fireside spinning her purple yarn with her maids around her, and she happened to catch her father just as he was going out to attend a meeting of the town council, which the Phaeacian aldermen had convened. She stopped him and said:

"Papa dear, could you manage to let me have a good big waggon? I want to take all our dirty clothes to the river and wash them. You are the chief man here, so it is only right that you should have a clean shirt when you attend meetings of the council. Moreover, you have five sons at home, two of them married, while the other three are good-looking bachelors; you know they always like to have clean linen when they go to a dance, and I have been thinking about all this."

She did not say a word about her own wedding, for she did not like to, but her father knew and said, "You shall have the mules, my love, and whatever else you have a mind for. Be off with you, and the men shall get you a good strong waggon with a body to it that will hold all your clothes."

On this he gave his orders to the servants, who got the waggon out, harnessed the mules, and put them to, while the girl brought the clothes down from the linen room and placed them on the waggon. Her mother prepared her a basket of provisions with all sorts of good things, and a goat skin full of wine; the girl now got into the waggon, and her mother gave her also a golden cruse of oil, that she and her women might anoint themselves. Then she took the whip and reins and lashed the mules on, whereon they set off, and their hoofs clattered on the road. They pulled without flagging, and carried not only Nausicaa and her wash of clothes, but the maids also who were with her.

When they reached the water side they went to the washing-cisterns, through which there ran at all times enough pure water to wash any quantity of linen, no matter how dirty. Here they unharnessed the mules and turned them out to feed on the sweet juicy herbage that grew by the water side. They took the clothes out of the waggon, put them in the water, and vied with one another in treading them in the pits to get the dirt out. After they had washed them and got them quite clean, they laid them out by the sea side, where the waves had raised a high beach of shingle, and set about washing themselves and anointing themselves with olive oil. Then they got their dinner by the side of the stream, and waited for the sun to finish drying the clothes. When they had done dinner they threw off the veils that covered their heads and began to play at ball, while Nausicaa sang for them. As the huntress Diana goes forth upon the mountains of Taygetus or Erymanthus to hunt wild boars or deer, and the wood-nymphs, daughters of Aegis-bearing Jove, take their sport along with her (then is Leto proud at seeing her daughter stand a full head taller than the others, and eclipse the loveliest amid a whole bevy of beauties), even so did the girl outshine her handmaids.

When it was time for them to start home, and they were folding the clothes and putting them into the waggon, Minerva began to consider how Ulysses should wake up and see the handsome girl who was to conduct him to the city of the Phaeacians. The girl, therefore, threw a ball at one of the maids, which missed her and fell into deep water. On this they all shouted, and the noise they made woke Ulysses, who sat up in his bed of leaves and began to wonder what it might all be.

"Alas," said he to himself, "what kind of people have I come amongst? Are they cruel, savage, and uncivilized, or hospitable and humane? I seem to hear the voices of young women, and they sound like those of the nymphs that haunt mountain tops, or springs of rivers and meadows of green grass. At any rate I am among a race of men and women. Let me try if I cannot manage to get a look at them."

As he said this he crept from under his bush, and broke off a bough covered with thick leaves to hide his nakedness. He looked like some lion of the wilderness that stalks about exulting in his strength and defying both wind and rain; his eyes glare as he prowls in quest of oxen, sheep, or deer, for he is famished, and will dare break even into a well-fenced homestead, trying to get at the sheep—even such did Ulysses seem to the young women, as he drew near to them all naked as he was, for he was in great want. On seeing one so unkempt and so begrimed with salt water, the others scampered off along the spits that jutted out into the sea, but the daughter of Alcinous stood firm, for Minerva put courage into her heart and took away all fear from her. She stood right in front of Ulysses, and he doubted whether he should go up to her, throw himself at her feet, and embrace her knees as a suppliant, or stay where he was and entreat her to give him some clothes and show him the way to the town. In the end he deemed it best to entreat her from a distance in case the girl should take offence at his coming near enough to clasp her knees, so he addressed her in honeyed and persuasive language.

"O queen," he said, "I implore your aid—but tell me, are you a goddess or are you a mortal woman? If you are a goddess and dwell in heaven, I can only conjecture that you are Jove's daughter Diana, for your face and figure resemble none but hers; if on the other hand you are a mortal and live on earth, thrice happy are your father and mother—thrice happy, too, are your brothers and sisters; how proud and delighted they must feel when they see so fair a scion as yourself going out to a dance; most happy, however, of all will he be whose wedding gifts have been the richest, and who takes you to his own home. I never yet saw any one so beautiful, neither man nor woman, and am lost in admiration as I behold you. I can only compare you to a young palm tree which I saw when I was at Delos growing near the altar of Apollo—for I was there, too, with much people after me, when I was on that journey which has been the source of all my troubles. Never yet did such a young plant shoot out of the ground as that was, and I admired and wondered at it exactly as I now admire and wonder at yourself. I dare not clasp your knees, but I am in great distress; yesterday made the twentieth day that I had been tossing about upon the sea. The winds and waves have taken me all the way from the Ogygian island, and now fate has flung me upon this coast that I may endure still further suffering; for I do not think that I have yet come to the end of it, but rather that heaven has still much evil in store for me.

"And now, O queen, have pity upon me, for you are the first person I have met, and I know no one else in this country. Show me the way to your town, and let me have anything that you may have brought hither to wrap your clothes in. May heaven grant you in all things your heart's desire—husband, house, and a happy, peaceful home; for there is nothing better in this world than that man and wife should be of one mind in a house. It discomfits their enemies, makes the hearts of their friends glad, and they themselves know more about it than any one."

To this Nausicaa answered, "Stranger, you appear to be a sensible, well-disposed person. There is no accounting for luck; Jove gives prosperity to rich and poor just as he chooses, so you must take what he has seen fit to send you, and make the best of it. Now, however, that you have come to this our country, you shall not want for clothes nor for anything else that a foreigner in distress may reasonably look for. I will show you the way to the town, and will tell you the name of our people; we are called Phaeacians, and I am daughter to Alcinous, in whom the whole power of the state is vested."

Then she called her maids and said, "Stay where you are, you girls. Can you not see a man without running away from him? Do you take him for a robber or a murderer? Neither he nor any one else can come here to do us Phaeacians any harm, for we are dear to the gods, and live apart on a land's end that juts into the sounding sea, and have nothing to do with any other people. This is only some poor man who has lost his way, and we must be kind to him, for strangers and foreigners in distress are under Jove's protection, and will take what they can get and be thankful; so, girls, give the poor fellow something to eat and drink, and wash him in the stream at some place that is sheltered from the wind."

On this the maids left off running away and began calling one another back. They made Ulysses sit down in the shelter as Nausicaa had told them, and brought him a shirt and cloak. They also brought him the little golden cruse of oil, and told him to go and wash in the stream. But Ulysses said, "Young women, please to stand a little on one side that I may wash the brine from my shoulders and anoint myself with oil, for it is long enough since my skin has had a drop of oil upon it. I cannot wash as long as you all keep standing there. I am ashamed to strip before a number of good-looking young women."

Then they stood on one side and went to tell the girl, while Ulysses washed himself in the stream and scrubbed the brine from his back and from his broad shoulders. When he had throughly washed himself, and had got the brine out of his hair, he anointed himself with oil, and put on the clothes which the girl had given him; Minerva then made him look taller and stronger than before, she also made the hair grow thick on the top of his head, and flow down in curls like hyacinth blossoms; she glorified him about the head and shoulders as a skilful workman who has studied art of all kinds under Vulcan and Minerva enriches a piece of silver plate by gilding it—and his work is full of beauty. Then he went and sat down a little way off upon the beach, looking quite young and handsome, and the girl gazed on him with admiration; then she said to her maids:

"Hush, my dears, for I want to say something. I believe the gods who live in heaven have sent this man to the Phaeacians. When I first saw him I thought him plain, but now his appearance is like that of the gods who dwell in heaven. I should like my future husband to be just such another as he is, if he would only stay here and not want to go away. However, give him something to eat and drink."

They did as they were told, and set food before Ulysses, who ate and drank ravenously, for it was long since he had had food of any kind. Meanwhile, Nausicaa bethought her of another matter. She got the linen folded and placed in the waggon, she then yoked the mules, and, as she took her seat, she called Ulysses:

"Stranger," said she, "rise and let us be going back to the town; I will introduce you at the house of my excellent father, where I can tell you that you will meet all the best people among the Phaeacians. But be sure and do as I bid you, for you seem to be a sensible person. As long as we are going past the fields and farm lands, follow briskly behind the waggon along with the maids and I will lead the way myself. Presently, however, we shall come to the town, where you will find a high wall running all round it, and a good harbour on either side with a narrow entrance into the city, and the ships will be drawn up by the road side, for every one has a place where his own ship can lie. You will see the market place with a temple of Neptune in the middle of it, and paved with large stones bedded in the earth. Here people deal in ship's gear of all kinds, such as cables and sails, and here, too, are the places where oars are made, for the Phaeacians are not a nation of archers; they know nothing about bows and arrows, but are a seafaring folk, and pride themselves on their masts, oars, and ships, with which they travel far over the sea.

"I am afraid of the gossip and scandal that may be set on foot against me later on; for the people here are very ill-natured, and some low fellow, if he met us, might say, 'Who is this fine-looking stranger that is going about with Nausicaa? Where did she find him? I suppose she is going to marry him. Perhaps he is a vagabond sailor whom she has taken from some foreign vessel, for we have no neighbours; or some god has at last come down from heaven in answer to her prayers, and she is going to live with him all the rest of her life. It would be a good thing if she would take herself off and find a husband somewhere else, for she will not look at one of the many excellent young Phaeacians who are in love with her.' This is the kind of disparaging remark that would be made about me, and I could not complain, for I should myself be scandalized at seeing any other girl do the like, and go about with men in spite of everybody, while her father and mother were still alive, and without having been married in the face of all the world.

"If, therefore, you want my father to give you an escort and to help you home, do as I bid you; you will see a beautiful grove of poplars by the road side dedicated to Minerva; it has a well in it and a meadow all round it. Here my father has a field of rich garden ground, about as far from the town as a man's voice will carry. Sit down there and wait for a while till the rest of us can get into the town and reach my father's house. Then, when you think we must have done this, come into the town and ask the way to the house of my father Alcinous. You will have no difficulty in finding it; any child will point it out to you, for no one else in the whole town has anything like such a fine house as he has. When you have got past the gates and through the outer court, go right across the inner court till you come to my mother. You will find her sitting by the fire and spinning her purple wool by firelight. It is a fine sight to see her as she leans back against one of the bearing-posts with her maids all ranged behind her. Close to her seat stands that of my father, on which he sits and topes like an immortal god. Never mind him, but go up to my mother, and lay your hands upon her knees if you would get home quickly. If you can gain her over, you may hope to see your own country again, no matter how distant it may be."

. . . . .

[*Odysseus has returned home, but his wife Penelope does not recognize him after his twenty-year absence.*]

This was what they said, but they did not know what it was that had been happening. The upper servant Eurynome washed and anointed Ulysses in his own house and gave him a shirt and cloak, while Minerva made him look taller and stronger than before; she also made the hair grow thick on the top of his head, and flow down in curls like hyacinth blossoms; she glorified him about the head and shoulders just as a skilful workman who has studied art of all kinds under Vulcan or Minerva—and his work is full of beauty—enriches a piece of silver plate by gilding it. He came from the bath looking like one of the immortals, and sat down opposite his wife on the seat he had left. "My dear," said he, "heaven has endowed you with a heart more unyielding than woman ever yet had. No other woman could bear to keep away from her husband when he had come back to her after twenty years of absence, and after having gone through so much. But come, nurse, get a bed ready for me; I will sleep alone, for this woman has a heart as hard as iron."

"My dear," answered Penelope, "I have no wish to set myself up, nor to depreciate you; but I am not struck by your appearance, for I very well remember what kind of a man you were when you set sail from Ithaca.

[ 320 ]

Nevertheless, Euryclea, take his bed outside the bed chamber that he himself built. Bring the bed outside this room, and put bedding upon it with fleeces, good coverlets, and blankets."

She said this to try him, but Ulysses was very angry and said, "Wife, I am much displeased at what you have just been saying. Who has been taking my bed from the place in which I left it? He must have found it a hard task, no matter how skilled a workman he was, unless some god came and helped him to shift it. There is no man living, however strong and in his prime, who could move it from its place, for it is a marvellous curiosity which I made with my very own hands. There was a young olive growing within the precincts of the house, in full vigour, and about as thick as a bearing-post. I built my room round this with strong walls of stone and a roof to cover them, and I made the doors strong and well-fitting. Then I cut off the top boughs of the olive tree and left the stump standing. This I dressed roughly from the root upwards and then worked with carpenter's tools well and skilfully, straightening my work by drawing a line on the wood, and making it into a bed-prop. I then bored a hole down the middle, and made it the centre-post of my bed, at which I worked till I had finished it, inlaying it with gold and silver; after this I stretched a hide of crimson leather from one side of it to the other. So you see I know all about it, and I desire to learn whether it is still there, or whether any one has been removing it by cutting down the olive tree at its roots."

When she heard the sure proofs Ulysses now gave her, she fairly broke down. She flew weeping to his side, flung her arms about his neck, and kissed him. "Do not be angry with me Ulysses," she cried, "you, who are the wisest of mankind. We have suffered, both of us. Heaven has denied us the happiness of spending our youth, and of growing old, together; do not then be aggrieved or take it amiss that I did not embrace you thus as soon as I saw you. I have been shuddering all the time through fear that someone might come here and deceive me with a lying story; for there are many very wicked people going about. Jove's daughter Helen would never have yielded herself to a man from a foreign country, if she had known that the sons of Achaeans would come after her and bring her back. Heaven put it in her heart to do wrong, and she gave no thought to that sin, which has been the source of all our sorrows. Now, however, that you have convinced me by showing that you know all about our bed (which no human being has ever seen but you and I and a single maid servant, the daughter of Actor, who was given me by my father on my marriage, and who keeps the doors of our room) hard of belief though I have been I can mistrust no longer."

# THE GREEKS:
# THE ARCHAIC PERIOD

T HE world that emerged from the Dark Ages was a very different one from the Bronze Age civilization of Mycenae. Poor and primitive at first, it developed rapidly to the point at which the Greeks were prepared for the brilliant achievement of the Classical Age. The three centuries from about 800 to 500 B.C. may be conveniently referred to as the Archaic Period. In these centuries the Greeks, under the stimulating influence of Phoenician traders, came out of their Dark Age isolation and began to find their destiny as a versatile, ingenious, seafaring people. During the Archaic Period emerged the characteristic institutions, ideas, and attitudes that are the hallmark of ancient Greece. It was also during this epoch that those economic and political developments occurred which were to set the stage for Classical Greece.

## 39 *The World of Hesiod*

In the Near East the empires that arose from 800 to 500 B.C. were realizing one side of the potential development inherent in the use of iron: greater concentrations of power. There was, however, a diametrically opposite potential, and it was in Greece that the first steps were taken toward its realization. If the larger and more readily acquired supply of iron, as contrasted with copper, meant that more powerful empires could be built, it meant equally as well that the wide distribution of iron tools and iron weapons could lead to a new independence for individuals. Instead of bronze implements monopolized by royal power and distributed for the use of peasantry and craftsmen, who remained thereby the dependents of the palace economy, iron tools could become the private possession of independent farmers and artisans. Instead of bronze weapons issued to the soldiers of a royal army, it would be possible for iron weapons to be owned

SOURCE: Reprinted from *Hesiod* tr. Richmond Lattimore by permission of The University of Michigan Press. Copyright © by the University of Michigan 1959.

by the individual soldiers in a citizen army. This is in fact what happened in Greece, where for hundreds of years the citizen-soldier when called to the ranks provided his own arms and when mustered out returned to his own farm or workbench.

The appearance of the independent individual is one of the fateful moments in human history. We are inclined to think of it as glorious, but it did not look entirely that way to those who first witnessed it. To them it appeared not as the fruition of an ideal but as an incomprehensible historical accident. In place of the humble peasant who shared in the protective tradition of collective welfare guaranteed by the clan or tribe or royal power, they saw the independent farmer as a man left alone to pursue his fate in a world indifferent to his welfare, the world of private enterprise, of "every man for himself," of "dog eat dog." That is the hard world depicted in the *Works and Days,* a kind of farmer's almanac in poetry, written by the eighth-century farmer-poet Hesiod. It is a world both exhilarating and frightening.

The translation of the following passages, *Works and Days* lines 1–49, 106–382, is by Richmond Lattimore.

❋❋❋❋❋

Muses, who from Pieria give glory through singing,
come to me, tell of Zeus, your own father, sing his praises, through whose
will
mortal men are named in speech or remain unspoken.
Men are renowned or remain unsung as great Zeus wills it.
For lightly he makes strong, and lightly brings strength to confusion,
lightly diminishes the great man, uplifts the obscure one,
lightly the crooked man he straightens, withers the proud man,
he, Zeus, of the towering thunders, whose house is highest.

Hear me, see me, Zeus: hearken: direct your decrees in righteousness.
To you, Perses, I would describe the true way of existence.

It was never true that there was only one kind of strife. There have always
been two on earth. There is one you could like when you understand her.
The other is hateful. The two Strifes have separate natures.
There is one Strife who builds up evil war, and slaughter.
She is harsh; no man loves her, but under compulsion

and by will of the immortals men promote this rough Strife.
But the other one was born the elder daughter of black Night.
The son of Kronos, who sits on high and dwells in the bright air,
set her in the roots of the earth and among men; she is far kinder.
She pushes the shiftless man to work, for all his laziness.
A man looks at his neighbor, who is rich: then he too
wants work; for the rich man presses on with his plowing and planting
and the ordering of his state. So the neighbor envies the neighbor
who presses on toward wealth. Such Strife is a good friend to mortals.
Then potter is potter's enemy, and craftsman is craftman's
rival; tramp is jealous of tramp, and singer of singer.

So you, Perses,[1] put all this firmly away in your heart,
nor let that Strife who loves mischief keep you from working
as you listen at the meeting place to see what you can make of
the quarrels. The time comes short for litigations and lawsuits,
too short, unless there is a year's living laid away inside
for you, the stuff that the earth yields, the pride of Demeter.
When you have got a full burden of that, you can push your lawsuits,
scheming for other men's goods, yet you shall not be given another chance
to do so. No, come, let us finally settle our quarrel
with straight decisions, which are from Zeus, and are the fairest.
Now once before we divided our inheritance, but you seized
the greater part and made off with it, gratifying those barons
who eat bribes, who are willing to give out such a decision.
Fools all! who never learned how much better than the whole the half is,
nor how much good there is in living on mallow and asphodel.

For the gods have hidden and keep hidden what could be men's
livelihood.
It could have been that easily in one day you could work out
enough to keep you for a year, with no more working.
Soon you could have hung up your steering oar in the smoke of the fireplace,
and the work the oxen and patient mules do would be abolished,
but Zeus in the anger of his heart hid it away
because the devious-minded Prometheus had cheated him;
and therefore Zeus thought up dismal sorrows for mankind.

. . . . .

---

1. The poet's brother, who was bringing suit against him in a dispute over their
joint inheritance.

Or if you will, I will outline it for you in a different story,
well and knowledgeably—store it up in your understanding—
the beginnings of things, which were the same for gods as for mortals.

In the beginning, the immortals who have their homes on Olympos
created the golden generation of mortal people.
These lived in Kronos' time, when he was the king in heaven.
They lived as if they were gods, their hearts free from all sorrow,
by themselves, and without hard work or pain; no miserable
old age came their way; their hands, their feet, did not alter.
They took their pleasure in festivals, and lived without troubles.
When they died, it was as if they fell asleep. All goods
were theirs. The fruitful grainland yielded its harvest to them
of its own accord; this was great and abundant, while they at their pleasure
quietly looked after their works, in the midst of good things
prosperous in flocks, on friendly terms with the blessed immortals.

Now that the earth has gathered over this generation,
these are called pure and blessed spirits; they live upon earth,
and are good, they watch over mortal men and defend them from evil;
they keep watch over lawsuits and hard dealings; they mantle
themselves in dark mist and wander all over the country;
they bestow wealth; for this right as of kings was given them.
Next after these the dwellers upon Olympos created
a second generation, of silver, far worse than the other.
They were not like the golden ones either in shape or spirit.
A child was a child for a hundred years, looked after and playing
by his gracious mother, kept at home, a complete booby.
But when it came time for them to grow up and gain full measure,
they lived for only a poor short time; by their own foolishness
they had troubles, for they were not able to keep away from
reckless crime against each other, nor would they worship
the gods, nor do sacrifice on the sacred altars of the blessed ones,
which is the right thing among the customs of men, and therefore
Zeus, son of Kronos, in anger engulfed them, for they paid no due
honors to the blessed gods who live on Olympos.

But when the earth had gathered over this generation
also—and they too are called blessed spirits by men, though under

the ground, and secondary, but still they have their due worship—
then Zeus the father created the third generation of mortals,
the age of bronze. They were not like the generation of silver.
They came from ash spears. They were terrible and strong, and the ghastly
action of Ares was theirs, and violence. They ate no bread,
but maintained an indomitable and adamantine spirit.
None could come near them; their strength was big, and from their
    shoulders
the arms grew irresistible on their ponderous bodies.
The weapons of these men were bronze, of bronze their houses,
and they worked as bronzesmiths. There was not yet any black iron.
Yet even these, destroyed beneath the hands of each other,
went down into the moldering domain of cold Hades;
nameless; for all they were formidable black death
seized them, and they had to forsake the shining sunlight.

Now when the earth had gathered over this generation
also, Zeus, son of Kronos, created yet another
fourth generation on the fertile earth, and these were better and nobler,
the wonderful generation of hero-men, who are also
called half-gods, the generation before our own on this vast earth.
But of these too, evil war and the terrible carnage
took some; some by seven-gated Thebes in the land of Kadmos
as they fought together over the flocks of Oidipous; others
war had taken in ships over the great gulf of the sea,
where they also fought for the sake of lovely-haired Helen.
There, for these, the end of death was misted about them.
But on others Zeus, son of Kronos, settled a living and a country
of their own, apart from human kind, at the end of the world.
And there they have their dwelling place, and hearts free of sorrow
in the islands of the blessed by the deep-swirling stream of the ocean,
prospering heroes, on whom in every year three times over
the fruitful grainland bestows its sweet yield. These live
far from the immortals, and Kronos is king among them.
For Zeus, father of gods and mortals, set him free from his bondage,
although the position and the glory still belong to the young gods.

After this, Zeus of the wide brows established yet one more
generation of men, the fifth, to be on the fertile earth.

[ 326 ]

And I wish that I were not any part of the fifth generation
of men, but had died before it came, or been born afterward.
For here now is the age of iron. Never by daytime
will there be an end to hard work and pain, nor in the night
to weariness, when the gods will send anxieties to trouble us.
Yet here also there shall be some good things mixed with the evils.
But Zeus will destroy this generation of mortals also,
in the time when children, as they are born, grow gray on the temples,
when the father no longer agrees with the children, nor children with their
     father,
when guest is no longer at one with host, nor companion to companion,
when your brother is no longer your friend, as he was in the old days.
Men will deprive their parents of all rights, as they grow old,
and people will mock them too, babbling bitter words against them,
harshly, and without shame in the sight of the gods; not even
to their aging parents will they give back what once was given.
Strong of hand, one man shall seek the city of another.
There will be no favor for the man who keeps his oath, for the righteous
and the good man, rather men shall give their praise to violence
and the doer of evil. Right will be in the arm. Shame will
not be. The vile man will crowd his better out, and attack him
with twisted accusations and swear an oath to his story.
The spirit of Envy, with grim face and screaming voice, who delights
in evil, will be the constant companion of wretched humanity,
and at last Nemesis and Aidos, Decency and Respect, shrouding
their bright forms in pale mantles, shall go from the wide-wayed
earth back on their way to Olympos, forsaking the whole race
of mortal men, and all that will be left by them to mankind
will be wretched pain. And there shall be no defense against evil.

Now I will tell you a fable for the barons; they understand it.
This is what the hawk said when he had caught a nightingale
with spangled neck in his claws and carried her high among the clouds.
She, spitted on the clawhooks, was wailing pitifully,
but the hawk, in his masterful manner, gave her an answer:
"What is the matter with you? Why scream? Your master has you.
You shall go wherever I take you, for all your singing.
If I like, I can let you go. If I like, I can eat you for dinner.
He is a fool who tries to match his strength with the stronger.

He will lose his battle, and with the shame will be hurt also."
So spoke the hawk, the bird who flies so fast on his long wings.

But as for you, Perses, listen to justice; do not try to practice
violence; violence is bad for a weak man; even a noble
cannot lightly carry the burden of her, but she weighs him down
when he loses his way in delusions; that other road is the better
which leads toward just dealings. For Justice wins over violence
as they come out in the end. The fool knows after he's suffered.
The spirit of Oath is one who runs beside crooked judgments.
There is an outcry when Justice is dragged perforce, when bribe-eating
men pull her about, and judge their cases with crooked decisions.
She follows perforce, weeping, to the city and gatherings of people.
She puts a dark mist upon her and brings a curse upon all those
who drive her out, who deal in her and twist her in dealing.
　But when men issue straight decisions to their own people
and to strangers, and do not step at all off the road of rightness,
their city flourishes, and the people blossom inside it.
Peace, who brings boys to manhood, is in their land, nor does Zeus
of the wide brows ever ordain that hard war shall be with them.
Neither famine nor inward disaster comes the way of those people
who are straight and just; they do their work as if work were a holi-
　day;
the earth gives them great livelihood, on their mountains the oaks
bear acorns for them in their crowns, and bees in their middles.
Their wool-bearing sheep are weighted down with fleecy burdens.
Their women bear them children who resemble their parents.
They prosper in good things throughout. They need have no traffic
with ships, for their own grain-giving land yields them its harvest.
　But when men like harsh violence and cruel acts, Zeus
of the wide brows, the son of Kronos, ordains their punishment.
Often a whole city is paid punishment for one bad man
who commits crimes and plans reckless action. On this man's people
the son of Kronos out of the sky inflicts great suffering,
famine and plague together, and the people die and diminish.
The women bear children no longer, the houses dwindle
by design of Olympian Zeus; or again at other times,
he destroys the wide camped army of a people, or wrecks
their city with its walls, or their ships on the open water.

You barons also, cannot even you understand for yourselves
how justice works? For the immortals are close to us, they mingle
with men, and are aware of those who by crooked decisions
break other men, and care nothing for what the gods think of it.
Upon the prospering earth there are thirty thousand immortal
spirits, who keep watch for Zeus and all that men do.
They have an eye on decrees given and on harsh dealings,
and invisible in their dark mist they hover on the whole earth.
Justice herself is a young maiden. She is Zeus's daughter,
and seemly, and respected by all the gods of Olympos.
When any man uses force on her by false impeachment
she goes and sits at the feet of Zeus Kronion, her father,
and cries out on the wicked purpose of men, so that their people
must pay for the profligacy of their rulers, who for their own greedy purposes
twist the courses of justice aslant by false proclamations.
Beware, you barons, of such spirits. Straighten your decisions
you eaters of bribes. Banish from your minds the twisting of justice.

The man who does evil to another does evil to himself,
and the evil counsel is most evil for him who counsels it.
The eye of Zeus sees everything. His mind understands all.
He is watching us right now, if he wishes to, nor does he fail
to see what kind of justice this community keeps inside it.
Now, otherwise I would not myself be righteous among men
nor have my son be so; for it is a hard thing for a man
to be righteous, if the unrighteous man is to have the greater right.
But I believe that Zeus of the counsels will not let it end thus.

You, Perses, should store away in your mind all that I tell you,
and listen to justice, and put away all notions of violence.
Here is the law, as Zeus established it for human beings;
as for fish, and wild animals, and the flying birds,
they feed on each other, since there is no idea of justice among them;
but to men he gave justice, and she in the end is proved the best thing
they have. If a man sees what is right and is willing to argue it,
Zeus of the wide brows grants him prosperity.
But when one, knowingly, tells lies and swears an oath on it,
when he is so wild as to do incurable damage against justice,
this man is left a diminished generation hereafter,

but the generation of the true-sworn man grows stronger.

I mean you well, Perses, you great idiot, and I will tell you.
Look, badness is easy to have, you can take it by handfuls
without effort. The road that way is smooth and starts here beside you.
But between us and virtue the immortals have put what will make us
sweat. The road to virtue is long and goes steep up hill,
hard climbing at first, but the last of it, when you get to the summit
(if you get there) is easy going after the hard part.

That man is all-best who himself works out every problem
and solves it, seeing what will be best late and in the end.
That man, too, is admirable who follows one who speaks well.
He who cannot see the truth for himself, nor, hearing it from others,
store it away in his mind, that man is utterly useless.
As for you, remember what I keep telling you over and over:
work, O Perses, illustrious-born, work on, so that Famine
will avoid you, and august and garlanded Demeter
will be your friend, and fill your barn with substance of living;
Famine is the unworking man's most constant companion.
Gods and men alike resent that man who, without work
himself, lives the life of the stingless drones,
who without working eat away the substance of the honeybees'
hard work; your desire, then, should be to put your works in order
so that your barns may be stocked with all livelihood in its season.
It is from work that men grow rich and own flocks and herds;
by work, too, they become much better friends of the immortals.
And to men too, for they hate the people who do not labor.
Work is no disgrace; the disgrace is in not working;
and if you do work, the lazy man will soon begin to be envious
as you grow rich, for with riches go nobility and honor.
It is best to work, at whatever you have a talent for doing,
without turning your greedy thought toward what some other man
possesses, but take care of your own livelihood, as I advise you.
Shame, the wrong kind of shame, has the needy man in convoy,
shame, who does much damage to men, but prospers them also,
shame goes with poverty, but confidence goes with prosperity.

Goods are not to be grabbed; much better if God lets you have them.

If any man by force of hands wins him a great fortune,
or steals it by the cleverness of his tongue, as so often
happens among people when the intelligence is blinded
by greed, a man's shameless spirit tramples his sense of honor;
lightly the gods wipe out that man, and diminish the household
of such a one, and his wealth stays with him for only a short time.
It is the same when one does evil to guest or suppliant,
or goes up into the bed of his brother, to lie in secret
love with his brother's wife, doing acts that are against nature;
or who unfeelingly abuses fatherless children,
or speaks roughly with intemperate words to his failing
father who stands upon the hateful doorstep of old age;
with all these Zeus in person is angry, and in the end
he makes them pay a bitter price for their unrighteous dealings.
Keep your frivolous spirit clear of all such actions.
As far as you have the power, do sacrifice to the immortals,
innocently and cleanly; burn them the shining thighbones;
at other times, propitiate them with libations and burnings,
when you go to bed, and when the holy light goes up the sky;
so They may have a complacent feeling and thought about you;
so you may buy someone else's land, not have someone buy yours.

Invite your friend to dinner; have nothing to do with your enemy.
Invite that man particularly who lives close to you.
If anything, which ought not to happen, happens in your neighborhood,
neighbors come as they are to help; relatives dress first.
A bad neighbor's as great a pain as a good one's a blessing.
One lucky enough to draw a good neighbor draws a great prize.
Not even an ox would be lost, if it were not for the bad neighbor.
Take good measure from your neighbor, then pay him back fairly
with the same measure, or better yet, if you can manage it;
so, when you need him some other time, you will find him steadfast.
No greedy profits; greedy profit is a kind of madness.
Be a friend to your friend, and come to him who comes to you.
Give to him who gives; do not give to him who does not give.
We give to the generous man; none gives to him who is stingy.
Give is a good girl, but Grab is a bad one; what she gives is death.
For when a man gives willingly, though he gives a great thing,
yet he has joy of his gift and satisfaction in his heart,

while he who gives way to shameless greed and takes from another,
even though the thing he takes is small, yet it stiffens his heart.
For even if you add only a little to a little, yet if
you do it often enough, this little may yet become big.
When one adds to what he has, he fends off staring hunger.
What is stored away in a man's house brings him no trouble.
Better for it to be at home, since what is abroad does damage.
It is fine to draw on what is on hand, and painful to have need
and not have anything there; I warn you to be careful in this.
When the bottle has just been opened, and when it's giving out, drink deep;
be sparing when it's half-full; but it's useless to spare the fag end.

Let the hire that has been promised to a friend be made good.
When you deal with your brother, be pleasant, but get a witness; for too
  much
trustfulness, and too much suspicion, have proved men's undoing.
 Do not let any sweet-talking woman beguile your good sense
with the fascinations of her shape. It's your barn she's after.
Anyone who will trust a woman is trusting flatterers.
 One single-born son would be right to support his father's
house, for that is the way substance piles up in the household;
if you have more than one, you had better live to an old age;
yet Zeus can easily provide abundance for a greater number,
and the more there are, the more work is done, and increase increases.
 If the desire within your heart is for greater abundance,
do as I tell you: keep on working with work and more work.


# 40 Colonization and Tyranny

As the new way of life gathered momentum, one consequence was a notable
growth of population that the rocky soil of Greece could not support. The
solution to this problem, consistent with the increasing venturesomeness
with which the Greeks were taking to the sea, was to seek an outlet through
settlements in unoccupied territory. In the eighth and seventh centuries
B.C. scores of expeditions were sent out to found new settlements. In the
Dark Ages, Greece had consisted of the mainland (especially its southern
part), the islands of the Aegean Sea, and the western coast of Asia Minor.

By the end of the Archaic Period, as a result of the colonization movement Greeks were permanently settled in many coastal areas from the
Crimea and the shores of the Black Sea in the northeast to the Mediterranean coasts of France and Spain in the west. The heaviest concentrations
were in the Black Sea region and in southern Italy and Sicily, but there
were also Greek cities founded in a few places on the North African
coast—including one, Naucratis, in the Nile Delta—as well as farther west
than Sicily, the most noteworthy being Massilia (modern Marseilles) at the
mouth of the Rhone River.

The rapid economic advances that led to this colonization movement were
not without the accompaniment of political unrest and change. The Greece
that emerged from the Dark Ages was one of numerous independent
city-states, not unlike the earliest political divisions of Sumer. The small,
mountain-locked fertile valley typical of the Aegean region contributed to
this division of the Greeks into city-states. In each of them the political
structure was much the same: kings had largely disappeared during the
Dark Ages, and power was held by a cohesive noble class who ruled by
virtue of a traditional monopoly of state offices and judicial functions which
they wielded in the name of an ancestral law known only to themselves.
This hereditary aristocracy had large land-holdings as the original source
of its power, and it maintained its wealth and status through the income
derived from the land.

As trade and industry developed, new social classes arose. The traders,
the businessmen, and the artisans found the administration conducted by
the agrarian aristocracy unsuited to their interests. Yet the traditional
constitution of the state gave these new classes no voice in introducing
change, and the nobility would not yield its privileges. In this situation
revolution was almost inevitable. The form that it took in the seventh and
sixth centuries B.C., as the social and economic evolution in city-state after
city-state reached this impasse, was "tyranny." An individual—sometimes
from among the wealthy businessmen, quite often from the ranks of the
nobility itself—with the backing of the discontented groups seized the
governmental power by force and set himself up as a "tyrant." The tyrant
effected a one-man rule whose outstanding characteristic was the introduction of economic reforms, such as the institution of coinage and standard
weights and measures, the building of ports and dockyards, the improvement of civic facilities in the way of water supply, streets, and public
buildings. Politically the tyrant was usually content to admit to the aristocratic class the wealthiest of the new business groups. Otherwise he did
nothing to alter the sacred tradition of the ancestral constitution of the

state. During his rule the traditional forms of government were maintained but were manipulated at his whim.

The tyrant was thus an extraconstitutional ruler whose function was the modernizing of the state to take into account the new facts of economic and social advance, while leaving the constitutional structure unaltered. When his work was done there was no longer need for him, and although most tyrants tried to perpetuate their rule and handed power on to their sons, it was a rare tyranny that lasted beyond the second generation. The tyrant's successor was usually murdered, and power in the modernized state went back into the hands of an aristocracy expanded to include the leading men of the business classes. "Tyranny" then, was originally a phase in economic and social progress; it was in the regimes of the second-generation tyrants that the word took on the connotation of arbitrary and oppressive government it has had ever since.

The early tyrants provided an endless source of anecdote illustrating the ingenious ways in which they had seized power, maintained it, and effected their reforms. The following passage, taken from Herodotus, concerns the tyranny founded at Corinth in the seventh century by Cypselus and carried on by his son Periander. The translation by George Rawlinson is of Herodotus 5.92.

❀❀❀❀❀

Such was the address of the Spartans. The greater number of the allies listened without being persuaded. None however broke silence, but Sosicles the Corinthian, who exclaimed:

"Surely the heaven will soon be below, and the earth above, and men will henceforth live in the sea, and fish take their place upon the dry land, since you, Lacedaemonians, propose to put down free governments in the cities of Greece, and to set up tyrannies in their stead. There is nothing in the whole world so unjust, nothing so bloody, as a tyranny. If, however, it seems to you a desirable thing to have the cities under despotic rule, begin by putting a tyrant over yourselves, and then establish despots in the other states. While you continue yourselves, as you have always been, unacquainted with tyranny, and take such excellent care that Sparta may not suffer from it, to act as you are now doing is to treat your allies unworthily. If you knew what tyranny was as well as ourselves, you would be better advised than you now are in regard to it. The government at Corinth was once an oligarchy—a single race, called Bacchiadae, who intermarried only among themselves, held the management of affairs. Now it happened that Amphion, one of these, had a daughter, named Labda, who was lame, and whom

therefore none of the Bacchiadae would consent to marry; so she was taken
to wife by Aetion, son of Echecrates, a man of the township of Petra, who
was, however, by descent of the race of the Lapithae, and of the house of
Caeneus. Aetion, as he had no child either by this wife, or by any other,
went to Delphi to consult the oracle concerning the matter. Scarcely had
he entered the temple when the priestess saluted him in these words:

> No one honours thee now, Aetion, worthy of honour;
> Labda shall soon be a mother—her offspring a rock,
>     that will one day
> Fall on the kingly race, and right the city of Corinth.

By some chance this address of the oracle to Aetion came to the ears of the
Bacchiadae, who till then had been unable to perceive the meaning of
another earlier prophecy which likewise bore upon Corinth, and pointed
to the same event as Aetion's prediction. It was the following:

> When mid the rocks an eagle shall bear a carnivorous lion,
> Mighty and fierce, he shall loosen the limbs of many
>     beneath them—
> Brood ye well upon this, all ye Corinthian people,
> Ye who dwell by fair Peirene, and beetling Corinth.

"The Bacchiadae had possessed this oracle for some time, but they were
quite at a loss to know what it meant until they heard the response given to
Aetion; then however they at once perceived its meaning, since the two
agreed so well together. Nevertheless, though the bearing of the first
prophecy was now clear to them, they remained quiet, intending to put to
death the child which Aetion was expecting. As soon, therefore, as his wife
was delivered, they sent ten of their number to the township where Aetion
lived, with orders to make away with the baby.

"So the men came to Petra, and went into Aetion's house, and there asked
if they might see the child; and Labda, who knew nothing of their purpose,
but thought their inquiries arose from a kindly feeling towards her husband,
brought the child, and laid him in the arms of one of them. Now they had
agreed by the way that whoever first got hold of the child should dash it
against the ground. It happened, however, by a providential chance, that
the babe, just as Labda put him into the man's arms, smiled in his face.
The man saw the smile, and was touched with pity, so that he could not
kill it; he therefore passed it on to his next neighbour, who gave it to a
third; and so it went through all the ten without any one choosing to be

the murderer. The mother received her child back, and the men went out of the house, and stood near the door, and there blamed and reproached one another; chiefly however accusing the man who had first had the child in his arms, because he had not done as had been agreed upon. At last, after much time had been thus spent, they resolved to go into the house again and all take part in the murder. But it was fated that evil should come upon Corinth from the progeny of Aetion, and so it chanced that Labda, as she stood near the door, heard all that the men said to one another, and fearful of their changing their mind, and returning to destroy her baby, she carried him off and hid him in what seemed to her the most unlikely place to be suspected, a cypsel or corn-bin. She knew that if they came back to look for the child, they would search all her house; and so indeed they did, but not finding the child after looking everywhere, they thought it best to go away, and declare to those by whom they had been sent that they had done their bidding. And thus they reported on their return home.

"Aetion's son grew up, and, in remembrance of the danger from which he had escaped, was named Cypselus, after the corn-bin. When he reached to man's estate, he went to Delphi, and on consulting the oracle, received a response which was two-sided. It was the following:

See there comes to my dwelling a man much favour'd of fortune,
Cypselus, son of Aetion, and king of the glorious Corinth,—
He and his children too, but not his children's children.

Such was the oracle; and Cypselus put so much faith in it that he forthwith made his attempt, and thereby became master of Corinth. Having thus got the tyranny, he showed himself a harsh ruler—many of the Corinthians he drove into banishment, many he deprived of their fortunes, and a still greater number of their lives. His reign lasted thirty years, and was prosperous to its close; insomuch that he left the government to Periander, his son. This prince at the beginning of his reign was of a milder temper than his father; but after he corresponded by means of messengers with Thrasybulus, tyrant of Miletus, he became even more sanguinary.

"On one occasion he sent a herald to ask Thrasybulus what mode of government it was safest to set up in order to rule with honour. Thrasybulus led the messenger without the city, and took him into a field of corn, through which he began to walk, while he asked him again and again concerning his coming from Corinth, ever as he went breaking off and throwing away all such ears of corn as overtopped the rest. In this way he went through the whole field, and destroyed all the best and richest part of the crop; then, without a word, he sent the messenger back. On the return of the man to Corinth, Periander was eager to know what Thrasybulus had counselled, but the messenger reported that he had said nothing; and he wondered that Periander had sent him to so strange a man, who seemed to have lost his senses, since he did nothing but destroy his own property. And upon this he told how Thrasybulus had behaved at the interview. Periander, perceiving what the action meant, and knowing that Thrasybulus advised the destruction of all the leading citizens, treated his subjects from this time forward with the very greatest cruelty. Where Cypselus had spared any, and had neither put them to death nor banished them, Periander completed what his father had left unfinished.

"One day he stripped all the women of Corinth stark naked, for the sake of his own wife Melissa. He had sent messengers into Thesprotia to consult the oracle of the dead upon the Acheron concerning a pledge which had been given into his charge by a stranger, and Melissa appeared, but refused to speak or tell where the pledge was. 'She was chill,' she said, 'having no clothes; the garments buried with her were of no manner of use, since they had not been burnt. And this should be her token to Periander, that what she said was true—the oven was cold when he baked his loaves in it.' When this message was brought him, Periander knew the token for he had had intercourse with the dead body of Melissa; wherefore he straightway made proclamation, that all the wives of the Corinthians should go forth to the temple of Hera. So the women apparelled themselves in their bravest, and went forth, as if to a festival. Then, with the help of his guards, whom he had placed for the purpose, he stripped them one and all, making no difference between the free women and the slaves; and, taking their clothes to a pit, he called on the name of Melissa, and burnt the whole heap. This done, he sent a second time to the oracle, and Melissa's ghost told him where he would find the stranger's pledge. Such, Lacedaemonians, is tyranny, and such are the deeds which spring from it. . . ."

# 41 *"The Greek Renaissance"*

Liberation of the individual, colonization, tyranny—these were the main economic and political developments in the Archaic Period. They were accompanied by a cultural flowering often referred to as the "Greek Renaissance." It was indeed a "rebirth" in the sense that Greek culture had slumbered since the fall of the brilliant Bronze Age civilization of Mycenae. But in their specific characteristics the art, the literature, and the intellectual productivity of the seventh and sixth centuries B.C. were not a rebirth but an original achievement. At first—and this is especially notable in art— they owed much to the influence of the contemporary cultures of the East, chiefly in Asia Minor, Phoenicia, and Egypt. For example, it is from the Phoenicians that the Greeks borrowed the alphabet which allowed them to be literate. What they produced, however, in art, literature, and philosophy became stamped with their own unique quality. It was different from anything to be found in previous epochs or among other peoples. The tone, the range, the variety, and the quality are Greek and nothing else. This remarkable outpouring of artistic and intellectual expression in the seventh and sixth centuries forms the foundation upon which the subsequent cultural achievement of Western civilization has been built.

Works of art must, of course, be seen rather than merely talked about; and the work of the early philosophers is too fragmentary, in the form in which it has come down to us, to be conveniently readable. This selection and the two that follow it are, therefore, all purely "literary" works— poetry, for prose literature did not appear in Greece until well into the 5th century B.C.

Among the early poems of the Greeks it is not surprising to find hymns to their gods. In their devotional quality the hymns do not differ much from the religious poetry of the Near East. In the use of language, however, in the imagery, and especially in the human quality that pervades them, these so-called "Homeric Hymns"—of unknown authorship—are distinctly Greek and are characteristic of Greek ideas and attitudes. The *Hymn to Hermes* is strikingly illustrative of the remarkable combination of reverence and impudent intimacy that typifies the relation of the Greek to his gods. This translation of stanzas 1–3, 17–25, and 42–47 is by Percy Bysshe Shelley, who followed the fashion of his day in calling the Greek gods by their Latin names. Thus Hermes is (usually) called Mercury, Zeus is called Jove, and so forth.

❀❀❀❀❀

Sing, Muse, the son of Maia and of Jove,
　　The Herald-child, king of Arcadia
And all its pastoral hills, whom, in sweet love
　　Having been interwoven, modest May

Bore Heaven's dread Supreme. An antique grove
Shadowed the cavern where the lovers lay
In the deep night, unseen by Gods or Men,
And white-armed Juno slumbered sweetly then.

Now, when the joy of Jove had its fulfilling,
 And Heaven's tenth moon chronicled her relief,
She gave to light a babe all babes excelling,
 A schemer subtle beyond all belief,
A shepherd of thin dreams, a cow-stealing,
 A night-watching, and door-waylaying thief,
Who 'mongst the Gods was soon about to thieve,
And other glorious actions to achieve.

The babe was born at the first peep of day;
 He began playing on the lyre at noon,
And the same evening did he steal away
 Apollo's herds. The fourth day of the moon,
On which him bore the venerable May,
 From her immortal limbs he leaped full soon,
Nor long could in the sacred cradle keep,
But out to seek Apollo's herds would creep. . . .

Now to Alpheus he had driven all
 The broad-foreheaded oxen of the Sun;
They came unwearied to the lofty stall
 And to the water troughs which ever run
Through the fresh fields; and when with rushgrass tall,
 Lotus and all sweet herbage, every one
Had pastured been, the great God made them move
Towards the stall in a collected drove.

A mighty pile of wood the God then heaped,
 And, having soon conceived the mystery
Of fire, from two smooth laurel branches stripped
 The bark, and rubbed them in his palms; on high
Suddenly forth the burning vapor leaped,
 And the divine child saw delightedly.

Mercury first found out for human weal
Tinder-box, matches, fire-irons, flint and steel.

And fine dry logs and roots innumerous
   He gathered in a delve upon the ground—
And kindled them—and instantaneous
   The strength of the fierce flame was breathed around;
And, whilst the might of glorious Vulcan thus
   Wrapped the great pile with glare and roaring sound,
Hermes dragged forth two heifers, lowing loud,
Close to the fire—such might was in the God.

And on the earth upon their backs he threw
   The panting beasts, and rolled them o'er and o'er,
And bored their lives out. Without more ado
   He cut up fat and flesh, and down before
The fire on spits of wood he placed the two,
   Toasting their flesh and ribs, and all the gore
Pursed in the bowels; and while this was done
He stretched their hides over a craggy stone.

We mortals let an ox grow old, and then
   Cut it up after long consideration,—
But joyous-minded Hermes from the glen
   Drew the fat spoils to the more open station
Of a flat smooth space, and portioned them; and when
   He had by lot assigned to each a ration
Of the twelve Gods, his mind became aware
Of all the joys which in religion are.

For the sweet savor of the roasted meat
   Tempted him though immortal. Natheless
He checked his haughty will and did not eat,
   Though what it cost him words can scarce express,
And every wish to put such morsels sweet
   Down his most sacred throat he did repress;
But soon within the lofty portaled stall
He placed the fat and flesh and bones and all.

[ 340 ]

And every trace of the fresh butchery
And cooking the God soon made disappear,
As if it all had vanished through the sky;
    He burned the hoofs and horns and head and hair,—
The insatiate fire devoured them hungrily;
    And, when he saw that everything was clear,
He quenched the coals, and trampled the black dust,
And in the stream his bloody sandals tossed.

All night he worked in the serene moonshine.
    But when the light of day was spread abroad
He sought his natal mountain-peaks divine.
    On his long wandering neither man nor god
Had met him, since he killed Apollo's kine,
    Nor house-dog had barked at him on his road;
Now he obliquely through the key-hole passed,
Like a thin mist or an autumnal blast.

Right through the temple of the spacious cave
    He went with soft light feet, as if his tread
Fell not on earth; no sound their falling gave;
    Then to his cradle he crept quick, and spread
The swaddling-clothes about him; and the knave
    Lay playing with the covering of the bed
With his left hand about his knees—the right
Held his belovèd tortoise-lyre tight. . . .

Latona's offspring, after having sought
    His herds in every corner, thus did greet
Great Hermes:—"Little cradled rogue, declare
Of my illustrious heifers, where they are!

"Speak quickly! or a quarrel between us
    Must rise, and the event will be that I
Shall hurl you into dismal Tartarus,
    In fiery gloom to dwell eternally;
Nor shall your father nor your mother loose
    The bars of that black dungeon; utterly

[ 341 ]

You shall be cast out from the light of day,
To rule the ghosts of men, unblessed as they."

To whom thus Hermes slyly answered:—"Son
Of great Latona, what a speech is this!
Why come you here to ask me what is done
  With the wild oxen which it seems you miss?
I have not seen them, nor from any one
  Have heard a word of the whole business;
If you should promise an immense reward,
I could not tell more than you now have heard.

"An ox-stealer should be both tall and strong,
  And I am but a little new-born thing,
Who, yet at least, can think of nothing wrong.
  My business is to suck, and sleep, and fling
The cradle-clothes about me all day long,—
  Or half asleep, hear my sweet mother sing,
And to be washed in water clean and warm,
And hushed and kissed and kept secure from harm.

"Oh, let not e'er this quarrel be averred!
  The astounded Gods would laugh at you, if e'er
You should allege a story so absurd
  As that a new-born infant forth could fare
Out of his home after a savage herd.
  I was born yesterday—my small feet are
Too tender for the roads so hard and rough.
And if you think that this is not enough,

"I swear a great oath, by my father's head,
  That I stole not your cows, and that I know
Of no one else, who might, or could, or did.
  Whatever things cows are I do not know,
For I have only heard the name." This said,
  He winked as fast as could be, and his brow
Was wrinkled, and a whistle loud gave he,
Like one who hears some strange absurdity.

[*Hermes refuses to confess his crime and the dispute between the two gods is brought before Zeus for judgment. No satisfactory solution is found, but finally Hermes teaches Apollo to play the lyre and to sing, and in return he receives the right to share Apollo's herd equally with him. The two end by becoming fast friends.*]

# 42 Battle Between the Frogs and the Mice

If one had to single out one thing that separates the Greeks from their predecessors and contemporaries, that symbolizes the novelty of their achievement and of the approach to life out of which it sprang, perhaps nothing better could be picked than their ability to laugh at themselves. If, as has often been noted, the Greeks are the discoverers of the importance and value of man (see Selections 79–82), it is even more noteworthy to observe that they discovered in man both the sublime and the ridiculous. The sense of tragedy goes hand in hand with the sense of comedy. Just as the Greek could be impudent with his gods, so could he also mock at his most prized human possessions. The epic poems of Homer were nearly a Bible for the Greeks, but that did not prevent their poking fun at them.

The *Batrachomyomachia*—"Battle Between the Frogs and the Mice"— is a parody (by an unknown author) of the epic grandeur of the *Iliad*. The names of the characters are all plays on words that introduce appropriately mouselike and froglike characteristics. For example, Psycarpax (the mouse whose death causes the war) means "he who plunders granaries"; Physignathus (the king of the frogs) is "he who swells his cheeks." The following selection, consisting of the first two-thirds of the mock-epic poem, is the translation by the early-eighteenth-century English clergyman and poet Thomas Parnell.

@@@@@

## BOOK I

To fill my rising song with sacred fire,
Ye tuneful Nine, ye sweet celestial quire!
From helicon's embowering height repair,
Attend my labours, and reward my prayer.
The dreadful toils of raging Mars I write,

The springs of contest, and the fields of fight;
How threatening mice advanc'd with warlike grace,
And wag'd dire combats with the croaking race.
Not louder tumults shook Olympus' towers,
When earth-born giants dar'd immortal powers.
These equal acts an equal glory claim,
And thus the Muse records the tale of fame.

Once on a time, fatigu'd and out of breath,
And just escap'd the stretching claws of death,
A gentle mouse, whom cats pursu'd in vain,
Fled swift of foot across the neighb'ring plain,
Hung o'er a brink, his eager thirst to cool,
And dipt his whiskers in the standing pool;
When near a courteous frog advanc'd his head
And from the water's, hoarse-resounding, said,
What art thou, stranger? What the line you boast?
What chance has cast thee panting on our coast?
With strictest truth let all thy words agree,
Nor let me find a faithless mouse in thee.
If worthy friendship, proffer'd friendship take,
And entering view the pleasurable lake:
Range o'er my palace, in my bounty share,
And glad return from hospitable fare.
This silver realm extends beneath my sway,
And me, their monarch, all its frogs obey.
Great Physignathus I, from Peleus' race,
Begot in fair Hydromeduse' embrace,
Where by the nuptial bank that paints his side,
The swift Eridanus delights to glide.
Thee too, thy form, thy strength, and port proclaim
A sceptred king; a son of martial fame;
Then trace thy line, and aid my guessing eyes.
Thus ceas'd the frog, and thus the mouse replies.

Known to the gods, the men, the birds that fly
Through wild expanses of the midway sky,
My name resounds; and if unknown to thee,

The soul of great Psycarpax lives in me,
Of brave Troxartes' line, whose sleeky down
In love compress'd Lychomile the brown.
My mother she, and princess of the plains
Where'er her father Pternotroctes reigns:
Born where a cabin lifts its airy shed,
With figs, with nuts, with varied dainties fed.
But since our natures nought in common know,
From what foundation can a friendship grow?
These curling waters o'er thy palace roll;
But man's high food supports my princely soul.
In vain the circled loaves attempt to lie
Conceal'd in flaskets from my curious eye;
In vain the tripe that boasts the whitest hue,
In vain the gilded bacon shuns my view;
In vain the cheeses, offspring of the pail,
Or honey'd cakes, which gods themselves regale.
And as in arts I shine, in arms I fight,
Mix'd with the bravest, and unknown to flight,
Though large to mine the human form appear,
Not man himself can smite my soul with fear:
Sly to the bed with silent steps I go,
Attempt his finger, or attack his toe,
And fix indented wounds with dext'rous skill;
Sleeping he feels and only seems to feel.
Yet have we foes which direful dangers cause,
Grim owls with talons arm'd, and cats with claws,
And that false trap, the den of silent fate,
Where death his ambush plants around the bait:
All dreaded these, and dreadful o'er the rest
The potent warriors of the tabby vest:
If to the dark we fly, the dark they trace,
And rend our heroes of the nibbling race.
But me, nor stalks, nor watrish herbs delight,
Nor can the crimson radish charm my sight,
The lake-resounding frog's selected fare,
Which not a mouse of any taste can bear.
As thus the downy prince his mind express'd,

His answer thus the croaking king address'd.
Thy words luxuriant on thy dainties rove,
And, stranger, we can boast of bounteous Jove:
We sport in water, or we dance on land,
And born amphibious, food from both command.
But trust thyself where wonders ask thy view,
And safely tempt those seas, I'll bear thee through:
Ascend my shoulders, firmly keep thy seat,
And reach my marshy court, and feast in state.

He said, and bent his back; with nimble bound
Leaps the light mouse, and clasps his arms around;
Then wondering floats, and sees with glad survey
The winding banks resembling ports at sea.
But when aloft the curling water rides,
And wets with azure wave his downy sides,
His thoughts grow conscious of approaching woe,
His idle tears with vain repentance flow;
His locks he rends, his trembling feet he rears,
Thick beats his heart with unaccustom'd fears;
He sighs, and chill'd with danger, longs for shore:
His tail extended forms a fruitless oar,
Half drench'd in liquid death his prayers he spake,
And thus bemoan'd him from the dreadful lake.

So pass'd Europa through the rapid sea,
Trembling and fainting all the venturous way;
With oary feet the bull triumphant row'd,
And safe in Crete depos'd his lovely load.
Ah safe at last! may thus the frog support
My trembling limbs to reach his ample court.

As thus he sorrows, death ambiguous grows,
Lo! from the deep a water-hydra rose;
He rolls his sanguin'd eyes, his bosom heaves,
And darts with active rage along the waves.
Confus'd the monarch sees his hissing foe,
And dives, to shun the sable fates, below.
Forgetful frog! The friend thy shoulders bore,

Unskill'd in swimming, floats remote from shore.
He grasps with fruitless hands to find relief,
Supinely falls, and grinds his teeth with grief;
Plunging he sinks, and struggling mounts again,
And sinks, and strives, but strives with fate in vain.
The weighty moisture clogs his hairy vest,
And thus the prince his dying rage express'd.

Nor thou, that fling'st me floundering from thy back,
As from hard rocks rebounds the shattering wrack,
Nor thou shalt 'scape thy due, perfidious king!
Pursu'd by vengeance on the swiftest wing:
At land thy strength could never equal mine,
At sea to conquer, and by craft, was thine.
But heaven has gods, and gods have searching eyes:
Ye mice, ye mice, my great avengers, rise!
This said, he sighing gasp'd, and gasping died.
His death the young Lychopinax espied,
As on the flowery brink he pass'd the day,
Bask'd in the beams, and loiter'd life away.
Loud shrieks the mouse, his shrieks the shores repeat;
The nibbling nation learn their hero's fate;
Grief, dismal grief ensues; deep murmurs sound,
And shriller fury fills the deafen'd ground.
From lodge to lodge the sacred heralds run,
To fix their council with the rising sun;
Where great Troxartes crown'd in glory reigns,
And winds his lengthening court beneath the plains:
Psycarpax' father, father now no more!
For poor Psycarpax lies remote from shore;
Supine he lies! the silent waters stand,
And no kind billow wafts the dead to land!

## BOOK II

When rosy-finger'd morn had ting'd the clouds
Around their monarch-mouse the nation crowds;
Slow rose the sovereign, heav'd his anxious breast,
And thus, the council fill'd with rage, address'd.

For lost Psycarpax much my soul endures,
'Tis mine the private grief, the public, yours.
Three warlike sons adorn'd my nuptial bed,
Three sons, alas! before their father dead!
Our eldest perish'd by the ravening cat,
As near my court the prince unheedful sat.
Our next, an engine fraught with danger drew,
The portal gap'd, the bait was hung in view,
Dire arts assist the trap, the fates decoy,
And men unpitying kill'd my gallant boy.
The last, his country's hope, his parents' pride,
Plung'd in the lake by Physignathus, died.
Rouse all the war, my friends! avenge the deed,
And bleed that monarch, and his nation bleed.

His words in every breast inspir'd alarms,
And careful Mars supplied their host with arms.
In verdant hulls despoil'd of all their beans,
The buskin'd warriors stalk'd along the plains:
Quills aptly bound, their bracing corselet made,
Fac'd with the plunder of a cat they flay'd;
The lamp's round boss affords their ample shield;
Large shells of nuts their covering helmet yield;
And o'er the region with reflected rays,
Tall groves of needles for their lances blaze.
Dreadful in arms the marching mice appear;
The wondering frogs perceive the tumult near,
Forsake the waters, thickening form a ring,
And ask and hearken, whence the noises spring.
When near the crowd, disclos'd to public view,
The valiant chief Embasichytros drew:
The sacred herald's sceptre grac'd his hand,
And thus his words express'd his king's command.

Ye frogs! the mice, with vengeance fir'd, advance,
And deck'd in armour shake the shining lance:
Their hapless prince by Physignathus slain,
Extends incumbent on the watery plain.
Then arm your host, the doubtful battle try;
Lead forth those frogs that have the soul to die.

[ 348 ]

The chief retires, the crowd the challenge hear,
And proudly-swelling yet perplex'd appear:
Much they resent, yet much their monarch blame,
Who rising, spoke to clear his tainted fame.

O friends, I never forc'd the mouse to death,
Nor saw the gasping of his latest breath.
He, vain of youth, our art of swimming tried,
And venturous, in the lake the wanton died.
To vengeance now by false appearance led,
They point their anger at my guiltless head.
But wage the rising war by deep device,
And turn its fury on the crafty mice.
Your king directs the way; my thoughts elate
With hopes of conquest, form designs of fate.
Where high the banks their verdant surface heave,
And the steep sides confine the sleeping wave,
There, near the margin, clad in armour bright,
Sustain the first impetuous shocks of fight:
Then, where the dancing feather joins the crest,
Let each brave frog his obvious mouse arrest;
Each strongly grasping, headlong plunge a foe,
Till countless circles whirl the lake below;
Down sink the mice in yielding waters drown'd;
Loud flash the waters; and the shores resound:
The frogs triumphant tread the conquer'd plain,
And raise their glorious trophies of the slain.

He spake no more: his prudent scheme imparts
Redoubling ardour to the boldest hearts.
Green was the suit his arming heroes chose,
Around their legs the greaves of mallows close;
Green were the beets about their shoulders laid,
And green the colewort, which the target made;
Form'd of the varied shells the waters yield,
Their glossy helmets glisten'd o'er the field;
And tapering sea-reeds for the polish'd spear,
With upright order pierc'd the ambient air.
Thus dress'd for war, they take th' appointed height,
Poise the long arms, and urge the promis'd fight.

But now, where Jove's irradiate spires arise,
With stars surrounded in ethereal skies,
(A Solemn council call'd) the brazen gates
Unbar; the gods assume their golden seats;
The sire superior leans, and points to show
What wond'rous combats mortals wage below:
How strong, how large, the numerous heroes stride;
What length of lance they shake with warlike pride;
What eager fire, their rapid march reveals;
So the fierce Centaurs ravag'd o'er the dales;
And so confirm'd, the daring Titans rose,
Heap'd hills on hills, and bid the gods be foes.

This seen, the power his sacred visage rears,
He casts a pitying smile on worldly cares,
And asks what heavenly guardians take the list,
Or who the mice, or who the frogs assist?

Then thus to Pallas. If my daughter's mind
Have join'd the mice, why stays she still behind?
Drawn forth by savoury steams they wind their way,
And sure attendance round thine altar pay,
Where while the victims gratify their taste,
They sport to please the goddess of the feast.
Thus spake the ruler of the spacious skies;
But thus, resolv'd, the blue-ey'd maid replies.
In vain, my father! all their dangers plead;
To such, thy Pallas never grants her aid.
My flowery wreaths they petulantly spoil,
And rob my crystal lamps of feeding oil,
Ills following ills: but what afflicts me more,
My veil, that idle race profanely tore.
The web was curious, wrought with art divine;
Relentless wretches! all the work was mine;
Along the loom the purple warp I spread,
Cast the light shoot, and cross'd the silver thread.
In this their teeth a thousand breaches tear;
The thousand breaches skilful hands repair;
For which vile earthly duns thy daughter grieve:

The gods, that use no coin, have none to give;
And learning's goddess never less can owe:
Neglected learning gains no wealth below
Nor let the frogs to win my succour sue,
Those clamorous fools have lost my favour too.
For late, when all the conflict ceas'd at night,
When my stretch'd sinews work'd with eager fight;
When spent with glorious toil, I left the field,
And sunk for slumber on my swelling shield;
Lo from the deep, repelling sweet repose,
With noisy croakings half the nation rose:
Devoid of rest, with aching brows I lay,
Till cocks proclaim'd the crimson dawn of day.
Let all, like me, from either host forbear,
Nor tempt the flying furies of the spear;
Let heavenly blood, or what for blood may flow,
Adorn the conquest of a meaner foe.
Some daring mouse may meet the wondrous odds,
Though gods oppose, and brave the wounded gods.
O'er gilded clouds reclin'd, the danger view,
And be the wars of mortals scenes for you.

So mov'd the blue-ey'd queen; her words persuade,
Great Jove assented, and the rest obey'd.


## BOOK III

Now front to front the marching armies shine,
Halt ere they meet, and form the lengthening line:
The chiefs conspicuous seen and heard afar,
Give the loud signal to the rushing war;
Their dreadful trumpets deep-mouth'd hornets sound,
The sounded charge remurmurs o'er the ground;
E'en Jove proclaims a field of horror nigh,
And rolls low thunder through the troubled sky.

First to the fight the large Hypsiboas flew,
And brave Lychenor with a javelin slew.

[ 351 ]

The luckless warrior fill'd with generous flame,
Stood foremost glittering in the post of fame;
When in his liver struck, the javelin hung;
The mouse fell thundering, and the target rung;
Prone to the ground he sinks his closing eye,
And soil'd in dust his lovely tresses lie.

A spear at Pelion Troglodytes cast,
The missive spear within the bosom past;
Death's sable shades the fainting frog surround,
And life's red tide runs ebbing from the wound.
Embasichytros felt Seutlaeus' dart
Transfix and quiver in his panting heart;
But great Artophagus aveng'd the slain,
And big Seutlaeus tumbling loads the plain,
And Polyphonus dies, a frog renown'd
For boastful speech and turbulence of sound;
Deep through the belly pierc'd, supine he lay,
And breath'd his soul against the face of day. . . .

[*The poem goes on with a recital of the deeds of valor in individual
combat. At length the mice prevail and commence a slaughter of the
frogs. The gods have pity and try to intervene, but the mice storm
on in the fury of victory. Finally from the lake the gods send an army
of crabs against the mice, who are forced to flee. The surviving frogs
are saved and thus ends the one-day war.*]

# 43 Lyric Poetry

If Greek lyric poetry does not seem fresh and new to the modern reader,
it is because the imagery, the subject matter, the verse forms, and the metre
have all formed the substance of the English (and the whole European)

SOURCE: F. L. Lucas, *Greek Poetry for Everyman* (Boston: Beacon Press—Beacon
Paperbacks, 1956; New York: The Macmillan Co., 1951). Reprinted by permission of
the copyright holders, J. M. Dent & Sons, Ltd. (London), and The Macmillan Company. First printed in the United States in 1951.

poetic tradition. The outpouring of verse in the seventh and sixth centuries
B.C. is one of the most impressive evidences of the novelty and originality of
the Greeks. The variety of mood, style, and form is immense. The poems
here are a sample of that output. They are translated by F. L. Lucas, with
the exception of the final four-line verse by Theognis, which is translated
by John Hookham Frere, an early-nineteenth-century English literary man.

⊛⊛⊛⊛⊛

### ARCHILOCHUS OF PAROS
[EARLY SEVENTH CENTURY]

Some Thracian now goes strutting with the shield I left behind me,
Under a bush—a peerless shield—regretfully.
However—I came home living. Plague take it! I will find me
Another one hereafter—and just as good to me!

.  .  .  .  .

Heart, my heart, with cares past curing thou that liest sore opprest,
Lift thee up now and defend thee. Grapple closely, breast to breast,
Foes that lie in ambush for thee—undismayed and undistrest!
When thou winnest, let not all men see thee too triumphant stand,
When thou losest, hie not homeward there to lie and mourn unmanned.
Grieve in sadness, joy in gladness, not past measure—thine to know
How the tides of human fortunes must for ever ebb and flow.

### TYRTAEUS OF SPARTA
[LATE SEVENTH CENTURY]

It is a fair death, fighting in the front of battle
For the cause of country like the brave to fall;
But to flee his city, his fields of corn and cattle,
And beg!—among man's sorrows *this* is worst of all.
A banished wretch, with aged sire and her that bore him,
With his little children and the wife he wed,
To all men he is hateful, wherever he comes, and o'er him
Beggary is master, and the cry for bread.
A brand he brings upon his fathers; ay, disgraces

His body's grace; and with him all blame and shame must live.
Therefore, since dishonour and scorn in all men's faces,
Both for him and his children, wait on the fugitive,
For our sons, for Lacedaemon, for this land that gave us birth,
Fight and die, accounting mere life of little worth.

## MIMNERMUS OF COLOPHON
### [LATE SEVENTH CENTURY]

Ah, what is life?—what is joy?—but Aphrodite the golden?
Let me die, when I am gladdened no more by things like these—
Her gifts honey-sweet, and the bed of love, by none beholden,
And all the flowers of youth, that are so sweet to seize,
For the hands of man and woman. But he who is once o'ertaken
By grim old age, that makes him ugly at once and base,
With misery and anguish his heart without cease is shaken,
No more to the sun rejoicing, thenceforth, he turns his face.
Hateful he grows to boyhood, a scorn to women's gaze—
Such is the bitter burden God made life's latter days.

## SEMONIDES OF AMORGOS
### [ABOUT 600 B.C.]

God from the first created diversely
The minds of women. One from a bristly sow
He made, within whose house the goods and chattels
Lie filthy, tumbling higgledy-piggledy,
While she, the slattern, dressed in dirty clothes
Sits in her muck and fattens.
    Another kind, God made from a vicious vixen—
Omniscient. There's nothing, good or bad,
Escapes her comprehension.
    Evil she'll twist to good, and good to evil,
Just as, from day to day, the whimsy takes her.
    Another has a dog's soul—nimble mongrel,
That needs must know all, hear all, everywhere
Nosing, and scurrying, and giving tongue,

Though none be there to bark at. Nothing stops her,
Not threats, not gentleness—not though in rage
One lifted up a stone and dashed her teeth out.
Even as guest, sitting at others' tables,
Still, unabashed, she plies her futile yapping.
    Then there's another sort the Olympians made
From simple clay—a half-wit, knowing nothing—
Nor good, nor bad—all that *she* understands
Is eating—*that* apart, she has not sense,
In the depth of the worst winter God can send,
Although she's shivering, to pull near the fire.
    Another was created from the sea,
Two persons in one body—one day laughing,
So gay that any stranger seeing her
At home, will sing her praises—'Never woman
So sweet in all the world, so lovable!'
Let a day pass—and she's insufferable,
To come near or to look at; in a frenzy,
Like a bitch with puppies, snapping at everyone,
To friend and foe a universal shrew.
Just as the sea will often lie so calm
And gentle—sheer delight to all that sail it—
Through summer days; and no less often rages
In a convulsion of deep-thundering breakers.
Nothing in all the world's so like such women.
    Another's made from a dusty, stubborn ass
That only blows and endless objurgation
Can make consent to labour.
And all the while, day-long, night-long, she eats—
Eats at the table, eats in a private corner.
In love, no less, she is omnivorous,
Greedy to grasp whatever lover comes. . . .
    Another's born of a dainty, long-maned filly,
Shying away from trouble and drudgery—
Never ask *her* to grind flour, or to finger
Dishes, or empty slops.
As for an oven—lest a smut fall on her,
She'll not go near it. *Her* love's tyranny.
Never a day but twice or thrice she washes,

And daubs herself with perfume; and her hair,
Flows deep, smooth-combed, all shaded o'er with flowers.
A lovely thing to look at, such a woman,
For other men; but a curse to him that has her—
Unless he be a king or a dictator,
To glorify his fancy with such toys.
  Then there's the ape. *She* is, beyond compare,
The deadliest pest of all that Zeus has sent us—
A sort of woman that's so foul to look at,
She's the laughter of the town, as she goes by—
Short-necked, and wooden-jointed; limbs like sticks,
And skimpy-hipped—poor miserable man,
That has this monster for a bed-fellow!
But every trick she knows, and every cunning,
Just like an ape—she cares not who may laugh.
She does no kindnesses, her only thought,
Her study, all day long, is simply this—
To vent her utmost malice.
  Last there's the bee—and lucky he that finds her!
For she alone is a woman without reproach
And in her hands life blossoms and bears fruit.
Beloved and loving, she grows old beside
Her husband, mother of children fair and honoured;
Her name shines out among all womankind,
And on her ways a grace lies, like the Gods'. . . .

A man can gain no prize on earth that's better
Than a good woman, nor grislier than a bad.


### ALCAEUS OF MYTILENE
[BORN ABOUT 620 B.C.]


Homeward from earth's far ends thou art returned
With gold-and-ivory swordhilt—ay, and well
By service to thy comrades *that* was earned,
The men of Babylon; who saw thee quell
So stout a champion, in single fight.
Of five royal cubits, in his giant height,

But one span short he fell.

. . . . .

It is not streets where proud-roofed mansions stand,
Nor masonry of ramparts deftly planned,
  It is not dockyard, quay, or jetty,
    That, in themselves, can make a city—
But *men,* with hearts to use what comes to hand.

## SAPPHO OF MYTILENE
### [BORN ABOUT 610 B.C.]

Aphrodite, daughter of Zeus, undying
Goddess, throned in glory, of love's beguilements,
Do not now with frenzy and desperation
    Utterly crush me.

Hear and come!—if ever before Thou heardest
Cry of mine, that called from afar Thy succour;
*Then,* in haste, with chariot swiftly harnessed,
    Forth from the golden

Hall of Zeus Thy father, to me Thou camest—
*Then* Thy lovely sparrows from Heaven swept Thee
O'er the dark-loamed earth, through the ether beating
    Swift wings together.

Fast they brought Thee hither; and Thou, most blessed,
With a smile of heavenly lips didst ask me,
What it was I suffered; and why I called Thee
    Hither to aid me.

'Tell me what it is, then, that most thou cravest,
Heart so full of madness?—who *is* it, Sappho,
Passion must awake to desire and love thee?
    Who is it wrongs thee?

'For, although she shun thee, she soon shall seek thee;
Though she scorn thy presents, herself shall bring them;

Though she love thee not, yet she soon shall love thee!—
Yea, though she would not.'

Come again to-day, then, as once Thou camest.
Save my soul from sorrow, that grows too bitter—
Grant my heart's desiring—be Thou my helper,
    Thou, Aphrodite!

. . . . .

Him I hold as happy as God in Heaven,
Who can sit and gaze on your face before him,
Who can sit and hear from your lips that sweetest
    Music they utter—

Hear your lovely laughter, that sets a-tremble
All my heart with flutterings wild as terror.
For, when I behold you an instant, straightway
    All my words fail me;

Helpless halts my tongue; a devouring fever
Runs in flame through every vein within me;
Darkness veils my vision; my ears are deafened,
    Beating like hammers;

Cold the sweat runs down me; a sudden trembling
Sets my limbs a-quiver; my face grows paler
Than the grass in summer; I see before me
    Death stand, and madness.

. . . . .

Moon's set, and Pleiads;
Midnight goes by;
The hours pass onward;
Lonely I lie.

. . . . .

As the sweet apple reddens, high up against the sky,
High on the highest branch, where the pickers passed it by,
Forgetting—ah, no, not forgetting—they never could reach so high.

[ 358 ]

THEOGNIS OF MEGARA

[ABOUT 540 B.C.]

I heard, O Polypaïdes, I heard the bird's shrill crying,
That comes to tell the tiller that time has come to plough,
And it stabbed the dark heart in me, to think my lands are lying,
My flowered fields, in keeping of other masters now;
That no team of mine goes straining against the yoke this day,
Since by its cursed pilots our city's cast away.

. . . . .

Speak fair to him that hates thee, till he falls in thy hand at last,
Then linger not for reasons, but pay him for the past.

. . . . .

Whatever the worth of a man, yet poverty can bring him
Lower than burning ague, or grey senility.
Sooner than bear it, Cyrnus, better a man should fling him
From crags that no foot can clamber, or down the gulfs of sea.
He dare not do a deed, he cannot utter sound,
Once penury has chained him. His very tongue lies bound.

. . . . .

Now is the time to surrender our hearts to merry-making,
While life's fair things can give us a joy that is not vain.
For the glory of youth goes by us, swift as a thought, o'ertaking
Even the speed of steeds whose charging hoofs amain
Whirl some king in his car to the press of the spear-fought fray,
Over the young green furrows, exulting on their way.

. . . . .

Not to be born—never to see the sun!
No worldly blessing is a greater one!
And the next best is speedily to die—
And lapt beneath a load of earth to lie!

## ANACREON OF TEOS

[ABOUT 570–485 B.C.]

Thracian filly, why so heartless? Why, so shyly sidelong glancing,
Hold me ever at a distance, like a fool with wit untried?
I could clap a bridle on ye, very well, for all your prancing;
Down the course I well could rein ye, make ye wheel the way I guide.
Yet a while, across the pastures, go your ways with light feet dancing—
You have still to find the master that shall curb ye and shall ride.

. . . . .

Timocritus fought well. This is his grave.
For Ares spares the coward; and not the brave.

# THE GREEKS:
# SPARTA AND ATHENS

THE fundamental institution of Greek life was the polis, or city-state. The small, poor territory of Greece was fragmented into nearly a thousand of these states. Each of them was sovereign and had its own laws, its official religious cults, its armed forces. Most of them were small, and in the large movements of history they play an inconspicuous role, but a few, the largest and most powerful, dominate the scene of Greek history. Two of these, Sparta and Athens, are outstanding, and Classical Greek history is focused upon them. In them are displayed the extremes in the vast range of the Greek way of life, and it has become customary to see in the ultimate conflict between them the resemblance of Greek history to a tragic drama. Politically, culturally—in every way—Sparta and Athens are opposed; yet paradoxically both are exemplars of ancient Greece. So sharp is the contrast between them that their differences are readily reduced to formulas: Sparta the rigid, militarized, profoundly conservative, authoritarian state, shunning the arts, suspicious of outsiders, taking no part in trade, preferring isolation; Athens the volatile, restless nation of free men, the inventor of democracy, achieving magnificence in the arts and the life of the mind, inquisitive and acquisitive, prying everywhere and open to all.

## 44 *The Spartan Constitution*

To her contemporaries Sparta (or Lacedaemon) was a monument of stability. Her customs, her institutions, her political organization, her laws had all been fixed long ago by the great lawgiver Lycurgus, and they remained immutable; therein lay Sparta's greatness. This view was encouraged by the Spartans, and they were so admired by other Greeks for this quality of being unchanging that everything connected with Sparta became surrounded by a glow of exaggeration and legend. Since very few people got to see Sparta from the inside, there was not much chance of debunking what one modern scholar has called "the Spartiate mirage."

Xenophon of Athens (c. 430–c. 354 B.C.), journalist, historian, soldier of fortune, and country squire, spent the last years of his life in exile from Athens. He lived in the western Peloponnesus on an estate given to him by the Spartans, whom he greatly admired. Among his numerous writings is the following essay describing the Spartan constitution. Although Xenophon had good opportunity to observe for himself, he appears to have been content to accept the whole current mythology about Sparta. The upshot is a work which presents Spartan customs and the organization of the Lacedaemonian state and society with all the quaint and exotic character-istics taken at face value. To what degree reality is mirrored in Xenophon's essay is anyone's guess. Reams have been written by modern scholars on the one point alone of when the lawgiver Lycurgus lived and made the reforms that created the Spartan way of life; it is still uncertain whether there ever was such a person as Lycurgus. There is almost no detail re-garding the structure and functioning of Sparta that is above suspicion as at least an exaggeration and possibly a complete fabrication. The selection that follows is Xenophon, *The Spartan Constitution* 1–9; the translation is by H. G. Dakyns.

❁❁❁❁❁

I recall the astonishment with which I first noted the unique position of Sparta amongst the states of Hellas, the relatively sparse population, and at the same time the extraordinary power and prestige of the community. I was puzzled to account for the fact. It was only when I came to consider the peculiar institutions of the Spartans that my wonderment ceased. Or rather, it is transferred to the legislator who gave them those laws, obedience to which has been the secret of their prosperity. This legislator, Lycurgus, I must needs admire, and hold him to have been one of the wisest of mankind. Certainly he was no servile imitator of other states. It was by a stroke of invention rather, and on a pattern much in opposition to the commonly-accepted one, that he brought his fatherland to this pinnacle of prosperity.

Take for example—and it is well to begin at the beginning—the whole topic of the begetting and rearing of children. Throughout the rest of the world the young girl, who will one day become a mother (and I speak of those who may be held to be well brought up), is nurtured on the plainest food attainable, with the scantiest addition of meat or other condiments; whilst as to wine they train them either to total abstinence or to take it highly diluted with water. And in imitation, as it were, of the handicraft type, since the majority of artificers are sedentary, we, the rest of the Hellenes, are content that our girls should sit quietly and work wools. That is all we demand of them. But how are we to expect that women nurtured in this fashion should produce a splendid offspring?

Lycurgus pursued a different path. Clothes were things, he held, the furnishing of which might well enough be left to female slaves. And, believing that the highest function of a free woman was the bearing of children, in the first place he insisted on the training of the body as incumbent no less on the female than the male; and in pursuit of the same idea instituted rival contests in running and feats of strength for women as for men. His belief was that where both parents were strong their progeny would be found to be more vigorous.

And so again after marriage. In view of the fact that immoderate intercourse is elsewhere permitted during the earlier period of matrimony, he adopted a principle directly opposite. He laid it down as an ordinance that a man should be ashamed to be seen visiting the chamber of his wife, whether going in or coming out. When they did meet under such restraint the mutual longing of these lovers could not but be increased, and the fruit which might spring from such intercourse would tend to be more robust than theirs whose affections are cloyed by satiety. By a farther step in the same direction he refused to allow marriages to be contracted at any period of life according to the fancy of the parties concerned. Marriage, as he ordained it, must only take place in the prime of bodily vigour, this too being, as he believed, a condition conducive to the production of healthy offspring. Or again, to meet the case which might occur of an old man wedded to a young wife. Considering the jealous watch which such husbands are apt to keep over their wives, he introduced a directly opposite custom; that is to say, he made it incumbent on the aged husband to introduce some one whose qualities, physical and moral, he admired, to play the husband's part and to beget him children. Or again, in the case of a man who might not desire to live with a wife permanently, but yet might still be anxious to have children of his own worthy the name, the lawgiver laid down a law in his behalf. Such an one might select some woman, the wife of some man, well born herself and blest with fair offspring, and, the sanction and consent of her husband first obtained, raise up children for himself through her.

These and many other adaptations of a like sort the lawgiver sanctioned. As, for instance, at Sparta a wife will not object to bear the burden of a double establishment, or a husband to adopt sons as foster-brothers of his own children, with a full share in his family and position, but possessing no claim to his wealth and property.

So opposed to those of the rest of the world are the principles which Lycurgus devised in reference to the production of children. Whether they enabled him to provide Sparta with a race of men superior to all in size and strength I leave to the judgment of whomsoever it may concern.

With this exposition of the customs in connection with the birth of children, I wish now to explain the systems of education in fashion here and elsewhere. Throughout the rest of Hellas the custom on the part of those who claim to educate their sons in the best way is as follows. As soon as the children are of an age to understand what is said to them they are immediately placed under the charge of Paidagogoi (or tutors), who are also attendants, and sent off to the school of some teacher to be taught "grammar," "music," and the concerns of the palestra. Besides this they are given shoes to wear which tend to make their feet tender, and their bodies are enervated by various changes of clothing. And as for food, the only measure recognised is that which is fixed by appetite.

But when we turn to Lycurgus, instead of leaving it to each member of the state privately to appoint a slave to be his son's tutor, he set over the young Spartans a public guardian, the Paidonomos or "pastor," to give him his proper title, with complete authority over them. This guardian was selected from those who filled the highest magistracies. He had authority to hold musters of the boys, and as their overseer, in case of any misbehaviour, to chastise severely. The legislator further provided the pastor with a body of youths in the prime of life, and bearing whips, to inflict punishment when necessary, with this happy result that in Sparta modesty and obedience ever go hand in hand, nor is there lack of either.

Instead of softening their feet with shoe or sandal, his rule was to make them hardy through going barefoot. This habit, if practised, would, as he believed, enable them to scale heights more easily and clamber down precipices with less danger. In fact, with his feet so trained the young Spartan would leap and spring and run faster unshod than another shod in the ordinary way.

Instead of making them effeminate with a variety of clothes, his rule was to habituate them to a single garment the whole year through, thinking that so they would be better prepared to withstand the variations of heat and cold.

Again, as regards food, according to his regulation the Eiren or head of the flock, must see that his messmates gathered to the club meal, with such moderate food as to avoid that heaviness which is engendered by repletion, and yet not to remain altogether unacquainted with the pains of penurious living. His belief was that by such training in boyhood they would be better able when occasion demanded to continue toiling on an empty stomach. They would be all the fitter, if the word of command were given, to remain on the stretch for a long time without extra dieting. The craving for luxuries would be less, the readiness to take any victual set before them greater, and, in general, the regime would be found more healthy. Under it he thought the lads would increase in stature and shape into finer men, since, as he maintained, a dietary which gave suppleness to the limbs must be more conducive to both ends than one which added thickness to the bodily parts by feeding.

On the other hand, in order to guard against a too great pinch of starvation, though he did not actually allow the boys to help themselves without further trouble to what they needed more, he did give them permission to steal this thing or that in the effort to alleviate their hunger. It was not of course from any real difficulty how else to supply them with nutriment that he left it to them to provide themselves by this crafty method. Nor can I conceive that any one will so misinterpret the custom. Clearly its explanation lies in the fact that he who would live the life of a robber must forgo sleep by night, and in the daytime he must employ shifts and lie in ambuscade; he must prepare and make ready his scouts, and so forth, if he is to succeed in capturing the quarry.

It is obvious, I say, that the whole of this education tended, and was intended, to make the boys craftier and more inventive in getting in supplies, whilst at the same time it cultivated their warlike instincts. An objector may retort: "But if he thought it so fine a feat to steal, why did he inflict all those blows on the unfortunate who was caught?" My answer is: for the self-same reason which induces people, in other matters which are taught, to punish the mal-performance of a service. So they, the Lacedaemonians, visit penalties on the boy who is detected thieving as being but a sorry bungler in the art. So to steal as many cheeses as possible off the shrine of Orthia was a feat to be encouraged; but, at the same moment, others were enjoined to scourge the thief, which would point a moral not obscurely, that by pain endured for a brief season a man may earn the joyous reward of lasting glory. Herein, too, it is plainly shown that where speed is requisite the sluggard will win for himself much trouble and scant good.

Furthermore, and in order that the boys should not want a ruler, even in case the pastor himself were absent, he gave to any citizen who chanced to be present authority to lay upon them injunctions for their good, and to chastise them for any trespass committed. By so doing he created in the boys of Sparta a most rare modesty and reverence. And indeed there is nothing which, whether as boys or men, they respect more highly than the ruler. Lastly, and with the same intention, that the boys must never be reft of a ruler, even if by chance there were no grown man present, he laid down the rule that in such a case the most active of the Leaders or Prefects was to become ruler for the nonce, each of his own division. The conclusion being that under no circumstances whatever are the boys of Sparta destitute of one to rule them.

I ought, as it seems to me, not to omit some remark on the subject of boy attachments, it being a topic in close connection with that of boyhood and the training of boys.

We know that the rest of the Hellenes deal with this relationship in different ways, either after the manner of the Boeotians, where man and boy are intimately united by a bond like that of wedlock, or after the manner of the Eleians, where the fruition of beauty is an act of grace; whilst there are others who would absolutely debar the lover from all conversation and discourse with the beloved.

Lycurgus adopted a system opposed to all of these alike. Given that some one, himself being all that a man ought to be, should in admiration of a boy's soul endeavour to discover in him a true friend without reproach, and to consort with him—this was a relationship which Lycurgus commended, and indeed regarded as the noblest type of bringing up. But if, as was evident, it was not an attachment to the soul, but a yearning merely towards the body, he stamped this thing as foul and horrible; and with this result, to the credit of Lycurgus be it said, that in Lacedaemon the relationship of lover and beloved is like that of parent and child or brother and brother where carnal appetite is in abeyance.

That this, however, which is the fact, should be scarcely credited in some quarters does not surprise me, seeing that in many states the laws do not oppose the desires in question.

I have now described the two chief methods of education in vogue; that is to say, the Lacedaemonian as contrasted with that of the rest of Hellas, and I leave it to the judgment of him whom it may concern, which of the two has produced the finer type of men. And by finer I mean the better disciplined, the more modest and reverential, and, in matters where self-restraint is a virtue, the more continent.

Coming to the critical period at which a boy ceases to be a boy and becomes a youth, we find that it is just then that the rest of the world proceed to emancipate their children from the private tutor and the schoolmaster, and, without substituting any further ruler, are content to launch them into absolute independence.

Here, again, Lycurgus took an entirely opposite view of the matter. This, if observation might be trusted, was the season when the tide of animal spirits flows fast, and the froth of insolence rises to the surface; when, too, the most violent appetites for divers pleasures, in serried ranks, invade the mind. This, then, was the right moment at which to impose tenfold labours upon the growing youth, and to devise for him a subtle system of absorbing occupation. And by a crowning enactment, which said that "he who shrank from the duties imposed on him would forfeit henceforth all claim to the glorious honours of the state," he caused, not only the public authorities, but those personally interested in the several companies of youths to take serious pains so that no single individual of them should by an act of craven cowardice find himself utterly rejected and reprobate within the body politic.

Furthermore, in his desire firmly to implant in their youthful souls a root of modesty he imposed upon these bigger boys a special rule. In the very streets they were to keep their two hands within the folds of the cloak; they were to walk in silence and without turning their heads to gaze, now here, now there, but rather to keep their eyes fixed upon the ground before them. And hereby it would seem to be proved conclusively that, even in the matter of quiet bearing and sobriety, the masculine type may claim greater strength than that which we attribute to the nature of women. At any rate, you might sooner expect a stone image to find voice than one of those Spartan youths; to divert the eyes of some bronze statue were less difficult. And as to quiet bearing, no bride ever stepped in bridal bower with more natural modesty. Note them when they have reached the public table. The plainest answer to the question asked,—that is all you need expect to hear from their lips.

But if he was thus careful in the education of the stripling, the Spartan lawgiver showed a still greater anxiety in dealing with those who had reached the prime of opening manhood; considering their immense importance to the city in the scale of good, if only they proved themselves the men they should be. He had only to look around to see that wherever the spirit of emulation is most deeply seated, there, too, their choruses and gymnastic contests will present alike a far higher charm to eye and ear. And on the same principle he persuaded himself that he needed only to confront his youthful warriors in the strife of valour, and with like result. They also, in their degree, might be expected to attain to some unknown height of manly virtue.

What method he adopted to engage these combatants I will now explain. It is on this wise. Their ephors select three men out of the whole body of the citizens in the prime of life. These three are named Hippagretai, or masters of the horse. Each of these selects one hundred others, being bound to explain for what reason he prefers in honour these and disapproves of those. The result is that those who fail to obtain the distinction are now at open war, not only with those who rejected them, but with those who were chosen in their stead; and they keep ever a jealous eye on one another to detect some slip of conduct contrary to the high code of honour there held customary. And so is set on foot that strife, in truest sense acceptable to heaven, and for the purposes of state most politic. It is a strife in which not only is the pattern of a brave man's conduct fully set forth, but where, too, each against other and in separate camps, the rival parties train for victory. One day the superiority shall be theirs; or, in the day of need, one and all to the last man, they will be ready to aid the fatherland with all their strength.

Necessity, moreover, is laid upon them to study a good habit of the body, coming as they do to blows with their fists for very strife's sake wherever they meet. Albeit, any one present has a right to separate the combatants, and, if obedience is not shown to the peacemaker, the Pastor of youth hales the delinquent before the ephors, and the ephors inflict heavy damages, since they will have it plainly understood that rage must never override obedience to law.

With regard to those who have already passed the vigour of early manhood, and on whom the highest magistracies henceforth devolve, there is a like contrast. In Hellas generally we find that at this age the need of further attention to physical strength is removed, although the imposition of military service continues. But Lycurgus made it customary for that section of his citizens to regard hunting as the highest honour suited to their age; albeit, not to the exclusion of any public duty. And his aim was

[ 368 ]

that they might be equally able to undergo the fatigues of war with those in the prime of early manhood.

The above is a fairly exhaustive statement of the institutions traceable to the legislation of Lycurgus in connection with the successive stages of a citizen's life. It remains that I should endeavour to describe the style of living which he established for the whole body, irrespective of age. It will be understood that, when Lycurgus first came to deal with the question, the Spartans, like the rest of the Hellenes, used to eat privately at home. Tracing more than half the current misdemeanours to this custom, he was determined to drag his people out of holes and corners into the broad daylight, and so he invented the public mess-rooms. Whereby he expected at any rate to minimise the transgression of orders.

As to food, his ordinance allowed them so much as, while not inducing repletion, should guard them from actual want. And, in fact, there are many exceptional dishes in the shape of game supplied from the hunting field. Or, as a substitute for these, rich men will occasionally garnish the feast with wheaten loaves. So that from beginning to end, till the mess breaks up, the common board is never stinted for viands, nor yet extravagantly furnished.

So also in the matter of drink. Whilst putting a stop to all unnecessary potations, detrimental alike to a firm brain and a steady gait, he left them free to quench thirst when nature dictated; a method which would at once add to the pleasure whilst it diminished the danger of drinking. And indeed one may fairly ask how, on such a system of common meals, it would be possible for any one to ruin either himself or his family through either gluttony or wine-bibbing.

This too must be borne in mind, that in other states equals in age, for the most part, associate together, and such an atmosphere is little conducive to modesty. Whereas in Sparta Lycurgus was careful so to blend the ages that the younger men must benefit largely by the experience of the elder—an education in itself, and the more so since by custom of the country conversation at the common meal has reference to the honourable acts which this man or that man may have performed in relation to the state. The scene, in fact, but little lends itself to the intrusion of violence or drunken riot; ugly speech and ugly deeds alike are out of place. Amongst other good results obtained through this out-door system of meals may be mentioned these: There is the necessity of walking home when the meal is over, and a consequent anxiety not to be caught tripping under the influence of wine,

since they all know of course that the supper-table must be presently abandoned, and that they must move as freely in the dark as in the day, even
the help of a torch to guide the steps being forbidden to all on active service.

In connection with this matter, Lycurgus had not failed to observe the
effect of equal amounts of food on different persons. The hardworking
man has a good complexion, his muscles are well fed, he is robust and
strong. The man who abstains from work, on the other hand, may be
detected by his miserable appearance; he is blotched and puffy, and devoid
of strength. This observation, I say, was not wasted on him. On the contrary,
turning it over in his mind that any one who chooses, as a matter of
private judgment, to devote himself to toil may hope to present a very
creditable appearance physically, he enjoined upon the eldest for the time
being in every gymnasium to see to it that the labours of the class were
proportional to the meats. And to my mind he was not out of his reckoning
in this matter more than elsewhere. At any rate, it would be hard to
discover a healthier or more completely developed human being, physically
speaking, than the Spartan. Their gymnastic training, in fact, makes demands alike on the legs and arms and neck, etc., simultaneously.

There are other points in which this legislator's views run counter to
those commonly accepted. Thus: in other states the individual citizen is
master over his own children, domestics, goods and chattels, and belongings
generally; but Lycurgus, whose aim was to secure to all the citizens a considerable share in one another's goods without mutual injury, enacted that
each one should have an equal power over his neighbour's children as over
his own. The principle is this. When a man knows that this, that, and the
other person are fathers of children subject to his own authority, he must
perforce deal by them even as he desires his own children to be dealt by.
And, if a boy chance to have received a whipping, not from his own father
but some other, and goes and complains to his own father, it would be
thought wrong on the part of that father if he did not inflict a second
whipping on his son. A striking proof, in its way, how completely they trust
each other not to impose dishonourable commands upon their children.

In the same way he empowered them to use their neighbour's domestics
in case of need. This communism he applied also to dogs used for the chase;
in so far that a party in need of dogs will invite the owner to the chase,
and if he is not at leisure to attend himself, at any rate he is happy to let
his dogs go. The same applies to the use of horses. Some one has fallen
sick perhaps, or is in want of a carriage, or is anxious to reach some point

or other quickly—in any case he has a right, if he sees a horse anywhere, to take and use it, and restores it safe and sound when he has done with it.

And here is another institution attributed to Lycurgus which scarcely coincides with the customs elsewhere in vogue. A hunting party returns from the chase, belated. They want provisions—they have nothing prepared themselves. To meet this contingency he made it a rule that owners are to leave behind the food that has been dressed; and the party in need will open the seals, take out what they want, seal up the remainder, and leave it. Accordingly, by his system of give-and-take even those with next to nothing have a share in all that the country can supply, if ever they stand in need of anything.

There are yet other customs in Sparta which Lycurgus instituted in opposition to those of the rest of Hellas, and the following among them. We all know that in the generality of states every one devotes his full energy to the business of making money: one man as a tiller of the soil, another as a mariner, a third as a merchant, whilst others depend on various arts to earn a living. But at Sparta Lycurgus forbade his freeborn citizens to have anything whatsoever to do with the concerns of money-making. As freemen, he enjoined upon them to regard as their concern exclusively those activities upon which the foundations of civic liberty are based.

And indeed, one may well ask, for what reason should wealth be regarded as a matter for serious pursuit in a community where, partly by a system of equal contributions to the necessaries of life, and partly by the maintenance of a common standard of living, the lawgiver placed so effectual a check upon the desire for riches for the sake of luxury? What inducement, for instance, would there be to make money, even for the sake of wearing apparel, in a state where personal adornment is held to lie not in the costliness of the clothes they wear, but in the healthy condition of the body to be clothed? Nor again could there be much inducement to amass wealth, in order to be able to expend it on the members of a common mess, where the legislator had made it seem far more glorious that a man should help his fellows by the labour of his body than by costly outlay. The latter being, as he finely phrased it, the function of wealth, the former an activity of the soul.

He went a step farther, and set up a strong barrier (even in a society such as I have described) against the pursuance of money-making by wrongful means. In the first place, he established a coinage of so extraordinary a sort,[1] that even a single sum of ten minas could not come into a house without attracting the notice, either of the master himself, or of some member of his household. In fact, it would occupy a considerable space, and need a waggon to carry it. Gold and silver themselves, moreover, are liable to search, and in case of detection, the possessor subjected to a penalty. In fact, to repeat the question asked above, for what reason should money-making become an earnest pursuit in a community where the possession of wealth entails more pain than its employment brings satisfaction?

But to proceed. We are all aware that there is no state in the world in which greater obedience is shown to magistrates, and to the laws themselves, than Sparta. But, for my part, I am disposed to think that Lycurgus could never have attempted to establish this healthy condition, until he had first secured the unanimity of the most powerful members of the state. I infer this for the following reasons. In other states the leaders in rank and influence do not even desire to be thought to fear the magistrates. Such a thing they would regard as in itself a symbol of servility. In Sparta, on the contrary, the stronger a man is the more readily does he bow before constituted authority. And indeed, they magnify themselves on their humility, and on a prompt obedience, running, or at any rate not crawling with laggard step, at the word of command. Such an example of eager discipline, they are persuaded, set by themselves, will not fail to be followed by the rest. And this is precisely what has taken place. It is reasonable to suppose that it was these same noblest members of the state who combined to lay the foundation of the ephorate, after they had come to the conclusion themselves, that of all the blessings which a state, or an army, or a household can enjoy, obedience is the greatest. Since, as they could not but reason, the greater the power with which men fence about authority, the greater the fascination it will exercise upon the mind of the citizen, to the enforcement of obedience.

Accordingly the ephors are competent to punish whomsoever they choose; they have power to exact fines on the spur of the moment; they have power to depose magistrates in mid career,—nay, actually to imprison and bring them to trial on the capital charge. Entrusted with these vast powers, they do not, as do the rest of states, allow the magistrates elected to exercise authority as they like, right through the year of office; but, in the style rather of despotic monarchs, or presidents of the games, at the first symptom of an offence against the law they inflict chastisement without warning and without hesitation.

1. Made of iron.

But of all the many beautiful contrivances invented by Lycurgus to kindle a willing obedience to the laws in the hearts of the citizens, none, to my mind, was happier or more excellent than his unwillingness to deliver his code to the people at large, until, attended by the most powerful members of the state, he had betaken himself to Delphi, and there made inquiry of the god whether it were better for Sparta, and conducive to her interests, to obey the laws which he had framed. And not until the divine answer came: "Better will it be in every way," did he deliver them, laying it down as a last ordinance that to refuse obedience to a code which had the sanction of the Pythian god himself was a thing not illegal only, but profane.

The following too may well excite our admiration for Lycurgus. I speak of the consummate skill with which he induced the whole state of Sparta to regard an honourable death as preferable to an ignoble life. And indeed if any one will investigate the matter, he will find that by comparison with those who make it a principle to retreat in face of danger, actually fewer of these Spartans die in battle, since, to speak truth, salvation, it would seem, attends on virtue far more frequently than on cowardice—virtue, which is at once easier and sweeter, richer in resource and stronger of arm, than her opposite. And that virtue has another familiar attendant—to wit, glory— needs no showing, since the whole world would fain ally themselves after some sort in battle with the good.

Yet the actual means by which he gave currency to these principles is a point which it were well not to overlook. It is clear that the lawgiver set himself deliberately to provide all the blessings of heaven for the good man, and a sorry and ill-starred existence for the coward.

In other states the man who shows himself base and cowardly wins to himself an evil reputation and the nickname of a coward, but that is all. For the rest he buys and sells in the same market-place with the good man; he sits beside him at the play; he exercises with him in the same gymnasium, and all as suits his humour. But at Lacedaemon there is not one man who would not feel ashamed to welcome the coward at the common mess-table, or to try conclusions with such an antagonist in a wrestling bout. Consider the day's round of his existence. The sides are being picked up in a football match, but he is left out as the odd man: there is no place for him. During the choric dance he is driven away into ignominious quarters. Nay, in the very streets it is he who must step aside for others to pass, or, being seated, he must rise and make room, even for a younger man. At home he will have his maiden relatives to support in their isolation (and they will hold him to blame for their unwedded lives). A hearth with no wife to bless it—that is a condition he must face, and yet he will have to pay damages to the last farthing for incurring it. Let him not roam abroad with a smooth and smiling countenance; let him not imitate men whose fame is irreproachable, or he shall feel on his back the blows of his superiors. Such being the weight of infamy which is laid upon all cowards, I, for my part, am not surprised if in Sparta they deem death preferable to a life so steeped in dishonour and reproach.

# 45 Solon of Athens

Athens had her legends too, but after about 600 B.C. the information we have, while occasionally spotty and frequently hazy, is based upon dependable historical data. The Athenian state was an amalgamation of the independent villages of the whole region called Attica. We have no means of dating this historical event, which is credited in the ancient tradition to the deeds of the mythical hero Theseus. Probably the unification of Attica into the polis of Athens was a process that went on over an extended period of time. At any rate it was complete by the seventh century B.C., and the Athens that we glimpse in the earliest truly historical indications, from the last third of that century, is a state run by a hereditary landed aristocracy. In short, Athens was constitutionally not significantly different from other Greek city-states that had not yet been modernized by "tyranny."

The class tensions that elsewhere regularly exploded in tyranny were resolved differently in Athens. The Eupatrids ("Well-Fathered"), as the ruling aristocrats called themselves, came to terms with the new class of commercially wealthy men in an agreement to appoint for the year 594 B.C. a single man with plenary powers to revise the constitution to satisfy present-day conditions. This may seem mild enough, but it was and is a major historical event, perhaps the unique occasion in all of recorded history when a ruling class voluntarily and without violence agreed to permit restrictions upon its power.

The man who was found acceptable by the conflicting parties was Solon,

SOURCES: Kathleen Freeman, *The Work and Life of Solon* (Cardiff: University of Wales Press Board; London: Humphrey Milford, 1926). Reprinted by permission of the publisher, The University of Wales Press Board.
Kurt von Fritz and Ernst Kapp, *Aristotle's Constitution of Athens* (New York: Hafner Publishing Co., 1950). Reprinted by permission of the publisher.

himself a Eupatrid but one who had traveled widely and had engaged personally in business activity. A "solon," in the language of headline-writers for our modern tabloid newspapers, is a legislator and no man has ever better earned the right to have his name become a common noun. The constitution that Solon produced was a masterpiece. It relieved the most onerous of the injustices existing under the traditional rule of the Eupatrids, and it pointed Athens modestly but clearly in the direction of greater participation by all classes of citizens in the holding of public office and in the decision-making process; but at the same time it avoided any radical changes. It was a triumph of the spirit of moderation, of compromise—and it pleased no one.

Solon himself was as remarkable as his constitution. He was that rare being, the nonviolent, civilian statesman who manages to be influential in a revolutionary time. He was entirely unglamorous and his name is not generally associated with the trumpet blasts and the deeds of military glory that customarily hallow the memories of history's "great men." To present his ideas to his fellow citizens he wrote poems—about statecraft, economic problems, current events. Nothing is more characteristic of the man than the remark attributed to him when a friend proposed that he take advantage of the powers granted him and take over the state, making himself tyrant. Solon is said to have replied that indeed it was a sweet thing to be a tyrant, but that there was one fatal flaw in that lofty perch: it was so high that there was no place to go from it but down.

Of the two selections that follow, the first, from the poems of Solon, is the prose translation by Kathleen Freeman. The second selection is Aristotle's *Constitution of Athens* 5-11, a work composed some 250 years after the events described in this passage. It is translated by Kurt von Fritz and Ernst Kapp.

If on our city ruin comes, it will never be by the dispensation of Zeus and the purpose of the blessed immortal gods, so powerful is our great-hearted guardian, born of mighty sire, Pallas Athene, who holds over it her hands. It is the people themselves who in their folly seek to destroy our great city, prompted by desire for wealth; and their leaders, unjust of heart, for whom awaits the suffering of many woes, the fruit of their great arrogance, since they know not how to check their greed, and to enjoy with order and sobriety the pleasures set before them at the feast. . . . They have wealth through their following of unjust works and ways. . . . Neither the sacred treasure nor that of the state do they spare in any wise, but they steal, each in his own corner, like men pillaging. They take no heed of the holy foundations of Justice, who in silence marks what happens and what has been, and who in course of time comes without fail to exact the penalty. Behold, there is coming now upon the whole state an injury that cannot be avoided; she has fallen swiftly into the evil of servitude, which awakens civil strife and war from their sleep—war that destroys many men in the bloom of their youth. By the work of the disaffected, swiftly our lovely city is being worn away, in those gatherings which are dear to unjust men.

Such are the ills that are rife within our state; while of the poor great numbers are journeying to foreign lands, sold into slavery, and bound with shameful fetters. They bear perforce the accursed yoke of slavery. Thus the public ill comes home to every single man, and no longer do his court-yard gates avail to hold it back; high though the wall be, it leaps over, and finds him out unfailingly, even though in his flight he be hid in the farthest corner of his chamber.

These are the lessons which my heart bids me teach the Athenians, how that lawlessness brings innumerable ills to the state, but obedience to the law shows forth all things in order and harmony and at the same time sets shackles on the unjust. It smooths what is rough, checks greed, dims arrogance, withers the opening blooms of ruinous folly, makes straight the crooked judgement, tames the deeds of insolence, puts a stop to the works of civil dissension, and ends the wrath of bitter strife. Under its rule all things among mankind are sane and wise.

To the people I have given just as much power as suffices, neither taking away from their due nor offering more; while for those who had power and were honoured for wealth I have taken thought likewise, that they should suffer nothing unseemly. I stand with strong shield flung around both parties, and have allowed neither to win an unjust victory.

. The people will best follow its leaders if it be neither given undue liberty nor unduly oppressed; for excess bears arrogance, whenever great prosperity attends on men whose minds are not well balanced.

In great undertakings it is hard to please all.

From the cloud comes the violent snow- and hail-storm, and the thunder springs from the lightning-flash; so from the men of rank comes ruin to the state, and the people through their ignorance fall into the servitude of rule by one man. When a man has risen too high, it is not easy to check him after; now is the time to take heed of everything.

If you have grievous sufferings through your own wrong-headedness, charge not the gods with having assigned you this lot. You yourselves have raised up these men by giving means of protection, and it is through this that you have gained the evil of servitude. Each separate man of you walks with the tread of a fox, but in the mass you have the brain of an idiot; for you look to the tongue and the words of a wheedler, and never turn your eyes to the deed as it is being done.

Through the winds is the sea stirred to wrath; but if none disturb it, it is of all things the mildest.

It is very difficult to discern that hidden measure of wisdom which alone contains the ends of all things.

On every side the mind of the immortals is hidden from mankind.

Ever as I grow old I learn many things.

Happy is he who has dear children, horses with their uncloven hooves, hunting-dogs, and a friend of another land.

No greater wealth has the man who possesses much silver and gold, expanses of wheat-bearing land, and horses and mules, than he who has these things only—stomach, lungs, and feet that afford him pleasant sensations, and the youthful beauty of a boy or a wife, when these joys also come; with every season of life come its appropriate gifts. These things are true wealth for mortals; for no man shall go to Hades carrying with him all his enormous wealth, nor by offer of a ransom shall he escape death and fell disease and the evil of approaching old age.

A boy, before he has reached adolescence, while still a child, grows and casts out his 'fence of teeth' within the first seven years. When the god brings to an end the next seven years, he puts forth the signs of adolescence. In the third period, while his limbs are still growing, the down of the beard appears, and his complexion loses its bloom. In the fourth hebdomad, every man is in the prime of his strength; this men have as a sign of their worth. In the fifth, it is seasonable for a man to take thought on marriage, and to seek after a breed of sons to succeed him. In the sixth, the mind of a man is in all things fully trained, and he no longer feels the same impulse towards wild behaviour. In the seventh seven he is at his prime in mind and tongue, and in the eighth, the sum of the two being fourteen years. In the ninth, though he still has some strength, his tongue and his wisdom are too feeble for works of mighty worth. If he complete the tenth and reach its full measure, not untimely is it if he meet the fate of death. . . .

If I spared my native land, and did not defile and dishonour my good repute by laying hands on a tyranny of cruel violence, I feel no shame at all; for in this way I believe that I shall win a greater triumph—over all mankind.

Those who came as pillagers had lavish hopes; every man of them believed he would light on a great fortune, and that I, though I coaxed so smoothly, would soon reveal a harsh purpose. Vain were their imaginings then, and now in their anger against me they all eye me askance as if I were an enemy. It is undeserved; for that which I promised I have fulfilled, by heaven's aid; and other things I undertook, not without success. To achieve aught by violence of tyranny is not to my mind; nor that the unworthy should have an equal share with the good in the rich soil of my native land.

. . . Whereas I, before the people had attained to any of the things for the sake of which they had drawn my chariot, brought it to a standstill. A witness I have who will support this claim full well in the tribunal of Time —the mighty mother of the Olympian deities, black Earth, from whose bosom once I drew out the pillars everywhere implanted; and she who was formerly enslaved is now free. Many men I restored to Athens, their native city divinely-founded, men who justly or unjustly had been sold abroad, and others who through pressure of need had gone into exile, and who through wanderings far and wide no longer spoke the Attic tongue. Those here at home who were reduced to shameful slavery, and trembled at the caprices of their masters, I made free. These things I wrought by main strength, fashioning that blend of force and justice that is law, and I went through to the close as I had promised. And ordinances for noble and base alike I wrote, fitting a rule of jurisdiction straight and true to every man. Had another, a villainous and covetous man, grasped the goad as I did, he would not have held the people back. Had I complied with the wishes of my opponents then, or at a later time with the designs of the other party against them, this city would have been bereaved of many sons. Wherefore

I stood at bay, defending myself on every side, like a wolf among a pack of hounds.

. . . . .

This being the political order and the many being serfs of the few, the common people rose against the upper class. When the civil discord had become violent and the two opposing parties had been set against each other for a long time, they chose, by mutual agreement, Solon as their mediator and Archon and entrusted the state to him. This happened after he had composed the elegy that begins:

I observe, and my heart is filled with grief when I look upon the oldest land
    of the Ionian world as it totters.

In this poem he fights for both parties against both parties. He tries to distinguish the merits and demerits of the one and of the other, and, after having done so, he exhorts both of them together to end their present dispute.

Solon was by birth and renown one of the most distinguished men of the country, but by wealth and occupation he belonged to the middle class. This can be inferred from many facts and is also confirmed by Solon's own testimony in the following passage of a poem in which he exhorts the wealthy not to set their aims too high:

You who are plunged into a surfeit of many goods restrain the strong desires
    in your breast, let your proud mind be set on moderate aims.
For we shall not submit to you, and not everything will turn out according to
    your wishes.

And, in general, he attaches the blame for the conflict to the rich; and, accordingly, he says, in the beginning of the poem, that he was always afraid of "love for money and an overbearing mind," implying that these had been the cause of the conflict.

As soon as Solon had been entrusted with full powers to act, he liberated the people by prohibiting loans on the person of the debtor, both for the present and for the future. He made laws and enacted a cancellation of debts both private and public, a measure which is commonly called *seisachtheia* (the shaking-off of burdens), since in this way they shook off their burdens. In regard to this measure, some people try to discredit him. For it happened that when Solon was about to enact the *seisachtheia*, he informed some of his acquaintances of his plans, and when he did so, according to the version of the adherents of the popular party, he was outmaneuvered by his friends; but, according to those who wish to slander him, he himself shared in the gain. For these people borrowed money and bought a great extent of land; and a short time afterwards, when the cancellation of debts was put through, they became very rich. It is said that this was the origin of those who later were considered to be of ancient wealth. However, the version of the friends of the people appears much more trustworthy. For it is not likely that in all other respects Solon should have been so moderate and public-spirited that, when it would have been in his power to subdue all others and to set himself up as a tyrant, he preferred to incur the hostility of both parties and valued his honor and the common good of the state higher than his personal aggrandizement, and that yet he should have defiled himself by such a petty and unworthy trick. Now, that he did have that opportunity (that is, of setting himself up as a tyrant) is proved by the desperate situation of the state at that time; he himself mentions the fact frequently in his poems, and it is universally admitted. Hence, one must regard the accusation as completely unfounded.

Solon set up a constitution and also made other laws. After that, the Athenians ceased to make use of the laws of Draco with the exception of those relating to murder. The laws were inscribed on the Kyrbeis[1] and placed in the portico of the King, and all swore to observe them. The nine Archons, however, regularly affirmed by an oath at the Stone that they would dedicate a golden statue if they ever should be found to have transgressed one of the laws; and they still swear in the same fashion down to the present day. He made the laws unalterable for one hundred years and set up the political order in the following way:

He divided the population, according to property qualifications, into four classes as they had been divided before—namely, Pentacosiomedimni, Knights, Zeugitae, and Thetes. He distributed the higher offices, namely, those of the nine Archons, the Treasurers, the Poletae,[2] the Eleven,[3] and the Colacretae[4] so that they were to be held by men taken from the Pentacosiomedimni, the Knights, and the Zeugitae, and assigned the offices to them in proportion to their property qualifications. To those who belonged to the census of the Thetes, he gave only a share in the Assembly of the People and in the law courts. A person belonged to the census of the Pentacosiomedimni if he obtained from his own property a return of five hundred measures of dry and liquid produce, both of them reckoned to-

1. Wooden tablets set up on pillars revolving around an axis.
2. Officials who farmed out public revenues, sold confiscated property, and drew up all public contracts.
3. The superintendents of the State Prison.
4. A very ancient office connected with the administration of finances.

gether. If he had an income of three hundred measures, or, as others say, if he was able to keep horses, he was rated a Knight; and as confirmation of the latter explanation they adduce the name of the class as being derived from the fact mentioned, and some ancient votive offerings. For on the Acropolis there is a statue of Diphilus with the following inscription:

Anthemion, the son of Diphilus, has dedicated this statue to the Gods, when from the status of a Thes he had been raised to the status of a Knight.

And a horse stands beside him in testimony of the fact that the status of a Knight means this.

In spite of this, it is more probable that this class also, like that of the Pentacosiomedimni, was distinguished by measures. To the census of the Zeugitae[5] belonged those who had an income of two hundred measures liquid and dry. The rest belonged to the census of the Thetes and had no share in the magistracies. Consequently, even today when the superintending officer asks a man who is about to draw the lot for an office to what census class he belongs, nobody would ever say that he is a Thes.

Solon established the rule that the magistrates were to be appointed by lot out of candidates previously selected by each of the four Tribes. In regard to the nine Archons, each Tribe made a preliminary choice of ten, and among these they cast the lot. Hence the custom still survives with the Tribes that each of them first selects ten by lot and then they choose, again by lot, from these men. A confirmation of the fact that the magistrates were to be selected by lot from the respective property classes mentioned is the law concerning the Treasurers, which is still in use down to the present day. This law orders that the Treasurers are to be chosen by lot from among the Pentacosiomedimni.

Such, then, was Solon's legislation in regard to the nine Archons. For, in the ancient times, the Council of the Areopagus called upon suitable persons and appointed, according to its own independent judgment, for one year to the various offices whomever it found fit for the respective tasks. There were four Tribes, as before, and four Tribe-kings. Each Tribe consisted of three *trittyes,* and there were twelve *naucrariai* to each Tribe. The Naucraries were presided over by the Naucrari who were appointed to supervise the receipts and expenditures. Hence the expressions, "the Naucrari shall levy . . ." and "the Naucrari shall spend from the Naucraric fund," are frequently found in those Solonian laws which are no longer in force. Solon also established a Council of Four Hundred, one hundred from

5. The word "Zeugites" is derived from *zeugos,* which means a yoke, in this case
   probably a team of oxen.

each Tribe. Yet he still made it the task of the Areopagus to watch over the laws, just as in the preceding period it had been the guardian of the political order; and this Council (that is, the Areopagus) still supervised the greater and more important part of public life and, in particular, chastised offenders, with full power to impose punishment and fines. It deposited the money exacted through fines in the Acropolis without having to indicate the reasons for the imposition of the fine. It also tried those who had conspired to deprive the people of their political rights, Solon having enacted a law of impeachment for such cases. Finally, seeing that violent political dissensions frequently arose in the city but that some citizens, out of a tendency to take things easy, were content to accept whatever the outcome of the political struggle might appear to be, Solon made a special law for persons of this kind, enacting that whoever, in a time of political strife, did not take an active part on either side should be deprived of his civic rights and have no share in the state.

This, then, was the order established by Solon in regard to the public offices. The three most democratic features of his constitution appear to be the following: first, and most important, the law that nobody could contract a loan secured on his person; secondly, the rule that anyone who wished to do so could claim redress on behalf of a person who had been wronged; thirdly—and, according to the prevailing opinion, this more than anything else has increased the political power of the common people—the right of appeal to a jury court. For when the people have a right to vote in the courts, they become the masters of the state. Moreover, since the laws are not written down in clear and simple terms, but are like the one about inheritances and heiresses, disputes over interpretation will inevitably arise, and the court has the decision in all affairs, both public and private. Some people believe that Solon deliberately made the laws obscure so that the people would be masters of the decision. But this is not likely. The reason is rather that he was not able to formulate the best principle in general terms. It is not fair to interpret his intentions on the basis of what is happening in the present; it should be done on the basis of the general character of his constitution.

As far as his legislation is concerned, these appear to be its democratic features; but, even before his legislation, he had effected the abolition of debts and afterwards the augmentation of the measures, the weights, and the coin. For it was under his administration that the measures became larger than those of Pheidon, and the mina, which formerly had had a weight of seventy drachmae, was increased to a full hundred. The original type of coin was that of the double drachma. He also introduced trade weights corresponding to the coinage at the rate of sixty-three minae to the weight of a talent, and proportional parts of the three additional minae were apportioned to the stater and the other units of weight.

After Solon had established the political order described above, many people came to him and plagued him with all sorts of criticisms and questions in regard to his laws. So, since he did not wish to change them nor to become an object of invidious attacks if he stayed, he went on a journey to Egypt with the object of doing some business and of seeing the country at the same time; and, at his departure, he announced that he would not be back for ten years. For, he said, he did not consider it right for him to interpret the laws, as he would inevitably be called upon to do if he stayed, but that, in his opinion, every citizen should rather be careful to obey them to the letter. Moreover, it happened that many of the nobles had become his enemies because of the cancellation of debts, and that both parties were alienated from him because the settlement had turned out contrary to their expectations. For the common people had believed that he would bring about a complete redistribution of property, while the nobles had hoped he would restore the old order or at least make only insignificant changes. Solon, however, set himself against both parties, and while he would have been able to rule as a tyrant if he had been willing to conspire with whichever party he wished, he preferred to antagonize both factions while saving the country and giving it the laws that were best for it, under the circumstances.

# 46 The Tyranny of Pisistratus

In the decades following the adoption of Solon's constitution, class tensions continued. The constitution was ignored as often as it was honored, but the worst consequences of unresolved conflict—lawless violence and civil war—were avoided. Finally Athens was modernized by the means normal to Greek states: she got her tyrant, Pisistratus. After two earlier short-lived attempts, Pisistratus seized and secured power in 546 B.C. He conducted all the enterprises tyrants customarily did: reforming the currency, building dockyards and public buildings, improving the water supply, developing an army and navy, surrounding himself with the amenities of a court, acting as a patron of artists and writers. He laid the foundations for the later economic, military, and cultural eminence of Athens, and Athenians in the next century were accustomed to look back upon the time of Pisistratus as a "golden age."

Like other tyrants, Pisistratus introduced no constitutional changes but carried on his personal rule in the shadow of the existing constitutional arrangements. When he died in 529 B.C., his sons, Hippias and Hipparchus, succeeded to his power. As usual with tyranny, the work had already been done, and the personal rule of the second-generation tyrants met with increasing hostility from all classes. Hipparchus was assassinated in 514, and Hippias was forced to flee in a general uprising in 510. The old constitution was invoked, but it was the Solonian constitution, now no longer a novelty since it had been "on the books," so to speak, for nearly a century. It was the same Solonian constitution that had satisfied no one. Now that it was to become operative, it still satisfied no one. For almost two years there was disorder in Athens. An attempt to restore the ancient Eupatrid rule with the aid of a Spartan military force resulted in a violent ousting of the Eupatrid officials and the withdrawal of the Spartan troops. The following passages are the translation by George Rawlinson of Herodotus 1.59–64; 5.63–65.

❦❦❦❦❦

This Pisistratus, at a time when there was civil contention in Attica between the party of the Seacoast headed by Megacles the son of Alcmaeon, and that of the Plain headed by Lycurgus, one of the Aristolaids, formed the project of making himself tyrant, and with this view created a third faction. Gathering together a band of partisans, and giving himself out for the protector of the Highlanders, he contrived the following stratagem. He wounded himself and his mules, and then drove his chariot into the marketplace, professing to have just escaped an attack of his enemies, who had attempted his life as he was on his way into the country. He besought the people to assign him a guard to protect his person, reminding them of the glory which he had gained when he led the attack upon the Megarians, and took the town of Nisaea, at the same time performing many other exploits. The Athenians, deceived by his story, appointed him a band of citizens to serve as a guard, who were to carry clubs instead of spears, and to accompany him wherever he went. Thus strengthened, Pisistratus broke into revolt and seized the citadel. In this way he acquired the sovereignty of Athens, which he continued to hold without disturbing the previously existing offices or altering any of the laws. He administered the state according to the established usages, and his arrangements were wise and salutary.

[ 384 ]

However, after a little time, the partisans of Megacles and those of Lycurgus agreed to forget their differences, and united to drive him out. So Pisistratus, having by the means described first made himself master of Athens, lost his power again before it had time to take root. No sooner, however, was he departed than the factions which had driven him out quarrelled anew, and at last Megacles, wearied with the struggle, sent a herald to Pisistratus, with an offer to re-establish him on the throne if he would marry his daughter. Pisistratus consented, and on these terms an agreement was concluded between the two, after which they proceeded to devise the mode of his restoration. And here the device on which they hit was the silliest to be found in all history, more especially considering that the Greeks have been from very ancient times distinguished from the barbarians by superior sagacity and freedom from foolish simpleness, and remembering that the persons on whom this trick was played were not only Greeks but Athenians, who have the credit of surpassing all other Greeks in cleverness. There was in the Paeanian district a woman named Phya, whose height was almost six feet, and who was altogether comely to look upon. This woman they clothed in complete armour, and, instructing her as to the carriage which she was to maintain in order to beseem her part, they placed her in a chariot and drove to the city. Heralds had been sent forward to precede her, and to make proclamation to this effect, "Citizens of Athens, receive again Pisistratus with friendly minds. Athena, who of all men honours him the most, herself conducts him back to her own citadel." This they proclaimed in all directions, and immediately the rumour spread throughout the country districts that Athena was bringing back her favourite. They of the city also, fully persuaded that the woman was the veritable goddess, worshipped her, and received Pisistratus back.

Pisistratus, having thus recovered the sovereignty, married, according to agreement, the daughter of Megacles. As, however, he had already a family of grown-up sons, and the Alcmaeonidae were supposed to be under a curse, he determined that there should be no issue of the marriage, and he consequently had intercourse with her in an abnormal fashion. His wife at first kept this matter to herself, but after a time, either her mother questioned her, or it may be that she told it of her own accord. At any rate, she informed her mother, and so it reached her father's ears. Megacles, indignant at receiving an affront from such a quarter, in his anger instantly made up his differences with the opposite faction, on which Pisistratus, aware of what was planning against him, took himself out of the country. Arrived at Eretria, he held a council with his children to decide what was to be done. The opinion of Hippias prevailed, and it was agreed to aim at regaining the sovereignty. The first step was to obtain advances of money from such states as were under obligations to them. By these means they collected large sums from several countries, especially from the Thebans, who gave them far more than any of the rest. To be brief, time passed, and all was at length got ready for their return. A band of Argive mercenaries arrived from the Peloponnese, and a certain Naxian named Lygdamis, who volunteered his services, was particularly zealous in the cause, supplying both men and money.

In the eleventh year of their exile the family of Pisistratus set sail from Eretria on their return home. They made the coast of Attica, near Marathon, where they encamped, and were joined by their partisans from the capital and by numbers from the country districts, who loved tyranny better than freedom. At Athens, while Pisistratus was obtaining funds, and even after he landed at Marathon, no one paid any attention to his proceedings. When, however, it became known that he had left Marathon, and was marching upon the city, preparations were made for resistance, the whole force of the state was levied, and led against the returning exiles. Meantime the army of Pisistratus, which had broken up from Marathon, meeting their adversaries near the temple of the Pallenian Athena, pitched their camp opposite them. Here a certain soothsayer, Amphilytus by name, an Acarnanian, moved by a divine impulse, came into the presence of Pisistratus, and approaching him uttered this prophecy in the hexameter measure:

> Now has the cast been made, the net is out-spread in the water,
> Through the moonshiny night the tunnies will enter the meshes.

Such was the prophecy uttered under a divine inspiration. Pisistratus, apprehending its meaning, declared that he accepted the oracle, and instantly led on his army. The Athenians from the city had just finished their midday meal, after which they had betaken themselves, some to dice, others to sleep, when Pisistratus with his troops fell upon them and put them to the rout. As soon as the flight began, Pisistratus bethought himself of a most wise contrivance, whereby the Athenians might be induced to disperse and not unite in a body any more. He mounted his sons on horseback and sent them on in front to overtake the fugitives, and exhort them to be of good cheer, and return each man to his home. The Athenians took the advice, and Pisistratus became for the third time master of Athens.[1]

Upon this he set himself to root his power more firmly, by the aid of a

1.  The probable dates of Pisistratus' rule are as follows: First tyranny, 561–560; first exile, 559; second tyranny, 559; second exile, 556; third tyranny, 546; death, 529.

numerous body of mercenaries, and by keeping up a full exchequer, partly supplied from native sources, partly from the countries about the river Strymon. He also demanded hostages from many of the Athenians who had remained at home, and not left Athens at his approach; and these he sent to Naxos, which he had conquered by force of arms, and given over into the charge of Lygdamis. He also purified the island of Delos, according to the injunctions of an oracle, after the following fashion. All the dead bodies which had been interred within sight of the temple he dug up, and removed to another part of the isle. Thus was the tyranny of Pisistratus established at Athens, many of the Athenians having fallen in the battle, and many others having fled the country together with the sons of Alcmaeon.

. . . . .

These same men,[2] if we may believe the Athenians, during their stay at Delphi persuaded the priestess by a bribe to tell the Spartans, whenever any of them came to consult the oracle, either on their own private affairs or on the business of the state, that they must free Athens. So the Lacedaemonians, when they found no answer ever returned to them but this, sent at last Anchimolius, the son of Aster—a man of note among their citizens —at the head of an army against Athens, with orders to drive out the Pisistratidae, albeit they were bound to them by the closest ties of friendship. For they esteemed the things of heaven more highly than the things of men. The troops went by sea and were conveyed in transports. Anchimolius brought them to an anchorage at Phalerum, and there the men disembarked. But the Pisistratidae, who had previous knowledge of their intentions, had sent to Thessaly, between which country and Athens there was an alliance, with a request for aid. The Thessalians, in reply to their entreaties, sent them by a public vote 1,000 horsemen, under the command of their king, Cineas, who was a Coniaean. When this help came, the Pisistratidae laid their plan accordingly: they cleared the whole plain about Phalerum so as to make it fit for the movements of cavalry, and then charged the enemy's camp with their horse, which fell with such fury upon the Lacedaemonians as to kill numbers, among the rest Anchimolius, the general, and to drive the remainder to their ships. Such was the fate of the first army sent from Lacedaemon, and the tomb of Anchimolius may be seen to this day in Attica; it is at Alopecae, near the temple of Heracles in Cynosargos.

Afterwards, the Lacedaemonians despatched a larger force against Athens, which they put under the command of Cleomenes, son of Anaxandridas,

2. Of the family of the Alcmaeonidae. These implacable opponents of Pisistratus were now conspiring against Hippias, the surviving son of the old tyrant.

one of their kings. These troops were not sent by sea, but marched by the mainland. When they were come into Attica, their first encounter was with the Thessalian horse, which they shortly put to flight, killing above forty men; the remainder made good their escape, and fled straight to Thessaly. Cleomenes proceeded to the city, and, with the aid of such of the Athenians as wished for freedom, besieged the tyrants who had shut themselves up in the Pelasgic fortress.

And now there had been small chance of the Pisistratidae falling into the hands of the Spartans, who did not even design to besiege the place, which had moreover been well provisioned beforehand with stores both of meat and drink,—nay, it is likely that after a few days' blockade the Lacedaemonians would have quitted Attica altogether, and gone back to Sparta—had not an event occurred most unlucky for the besieged, and most advantageous for the besiegers. The children of the Pisistratidae were made prisoners, as they were being removed out of the country. By this calamity all their plans were deranged, and as the ransom of their children they consented to the demands of the Athenians, and agreed within five days' time to quit Attica. Accordingly they soon afterwards left the country, and withdrew to Sigeum on the Scamander, after reigning thirty-six years over the Athenians.[3]

# 47 The Creation of Democracy

The man who led the uprising against the oligarchy was Cleisthenes, himself a member of a distinguished aristocratic family. As archon (chief executive official) for the year 508 B.C. he radically changed the political structure of Athens, introducing new official bodies and making old ones serve new functions. By the devices he introduced he created at one stroke the form of government the Greeks called democracy. In essence the constitution of Cleisthenes gave power to "the people," that is, the citizenry as a whole, by drastically reducing the powers of all officials and official bodies in the state and concentrating power in the Assembly (ekklēsia), which all adult male citizens were eligible to attend. With some justice the Athenian

---

3. The date is 510 B.C., and the reckoning is from the establishment of Pisistratus' third tyranny in 546.

SOURCE: Kurt von Fritz and Ernst Kapp, *Aristotle's Constitution of Athens* (New York: Hafner Publishing Co., 1950). Reprinted by permission of the publisher.

Assembly has been compared to a New England town meeting. In it all matters of public concern—from a decision to erect a monument to some public benefactor all the way to such grave matters as the building of warships and the declaring of war—were determined by a simple majority vote.

This selection is Aristotle's laconic description of the Cleisthenian reforms. It is from the *Constitution of Athens* 20–22; the translation is by Kurt von Fritz and Ernst Kapp.

❀❀❀❀❀

After the overthrow of the tyranny, Isagoras the son of Tisander, a former supporter of the tyrants, and Cleisthenes from the family of the Alcmeonidae pitted their respective political strengths and influences against each other. When Cleisthenes was defeated in the political clubs, he won the support of the common people by promising to give the state into their hands. So Isagoras, seeing his power waning, called upon Cleomenes, with whom he was connected by ties of hospitality, to come up again and persuaded him "to drive out the curse," for the Alcmeonidae were believed to be among those who were under a curse. When, as a result of this, Cleisthenes secretly fled the country, Cleomenes arrived with a small force and expelled as accursed seven hundred Athenian families. This done, he tried to dissolve the Council and to make Isagoras, with three hundred of his supporters, master of the city. But when the Council put up a resistance and the crowd began to gather, Cleomenes and Isagoras with their troups and adherents fled to the Acropolis. There the common people of Athens besieged them for two days. On the third day, however, they permitted Cleomenes and his men to withdraw under a truce, and called back Cleisthenes and the other exiles. After the political power had come into the hands of the people in this way, Cleisthenes became their chief and "the leader of the people." For it could hardly be denied that it was the Alcmeonidae who played the most important part in the overthrow of the tyrants, since they almost incessantly made political trouble for them. Even before the Alcmeonidae, however, Cedon had made an attack on the tyrants, on account of which he, too, was celebrated in a drinking song:

> Pour wine also in honor of Cedon, boy, and let him not be forgotten
> If to drink a toast to the good and the brave is the right thing to do.

For these reasons the common people trusted Cleisthenes. So then, being the leader of the people, in the fourth year after the overthrow of the tyranny, in the year of the archonship of Isagoras, he distributed the whole population into ten tribes instead of the previous four, with the aim of mixing up the population so that a greater number would share in the administration of the state (that is, would be admitted to citizenship). This is the origin of the proverbial saying: No tribe-investigation! It was directed against those who wanted to check on family backgrounds. Then he established a Council of Five Hundred instead of the existing one of Four Hundred, taking fifty from each tribe, whereas previously there had been one hundred (from each of the previous four tribes). The reason he did not distribute them into twelve tribes was that he wished to avoid a division according to the already existing Trittyes. For the four tribes consisted of twelve Trittyes; hence, a completely new mixture of the population could not have been obtained from such a division. At the same time, he divided the whole country into thirty parts composed of demes, ten from the city quarters, ten from the shore district, and ten from the interior. These parts he called Trittyes and assigned three of them by lot to each tribe, in such a way that each tribe would have one portion from all the main regions of the country. He made those who lived in each of the demes fellow-demesmen, so that they would not, by addressing one another by their fathers' names, expose the newly enrolled citizens, but would call them by the names of their demes.[1] This is the reason the Athenians speak of one another by the names of their demes.

He also established Demarchs with the same functions as those of the former Naucrari, replacing the naucraries by the demes. He named some of the demes after the localities, others after their founders. For not all of them were still connected with their localities. But he let everybody retain his family connections, his membership in a brotherhood, and his family rites according to ancestral custom. He assigned to the tribes as eponymous heroes ten "Archegetae," who had been selected by the Delphic Oracle from a previously chosen group of one hundred.

After these reforms the political structure became much more democratic

---

1. The normal Greek way of identifying a man was by his name and his father's name: for example, Pericles son of Xanthippus. Cleisthenes changed this so that thereafter in Athens a man was known legally and officially by his name and that of his deme: for example, Leon of Cholargos. The deme, approximately equivalent to our voting district, became the foundation of the new democratic state. The change in method of identification is not mere whim, but a decisive symbol of Cleisthenes' effort to break down the ancient power of the noble families and transfer individual loyalties from the family to the state.

than it had been under Solon. This development was in part also due to the facts that the Solonian laws had fallen into disuse under the tyranny until they were eventually obliterated and that Cleisthenes enacted new ones with the aim of winning the people's favor. Among these was the law about ostracism.

In the fifth year after the introduction of this order, under the archonship of Hermocreon, they imposed for the first time on the Council of Five Hundred the oath which they still swear at the present time. Furthermore, they began to elect the generals by tribes, one from each tribe. The Polemarch, however, was the supreme commander of the whole army.

# III

# THE CLASSICAL AGE

# OF GREECE

*The Classical Age of Greek history spans a little less than two cen-turies, the fifth century and the fourth century* B.C. *to the death of Alexander the Great in 323. It is within this brief period that the greatest flowering of Greek civilization occurred; within it are con-centrated the awesome cultural achievements upon which the claim for "the glory that was Greece" rests. It is a period studded with the names of great men and famous places and events: Themistocles, Pericles, Aeschylus, Sophocles, Euripides, Aristophanes, Hippocrates, Alcibiades, Socrates, Herodotus, Thucydides, Plato, Aristotle, Demos-thenes, Philip, and Alexander; Marathon, Thermopylae, Salamis, Sparta, Athens, Thebes, and Chaeronea.*

# THE PERSIAN WARS

THE Greeks, divided politically into hundreds of independent states but aware of their common cultural heritage, became fully conscious of themselves as a people under the impact of the invasion of their country by the armed might of the Persian empire.

The fifth century, and with it the history of Classical Greece, opens with the revolt of the Ionian cities. These Greek *poleis* on the western coast of Asia Minor across the island stepping-stones of the Aegean Sea from mainland Greece had been subject to Persian rule for nearly a half century, since the building of the empire by Cyrus the Great (see Selection 32). In their revolt they received modest aid from two Greek cities, Athens and Eretria (on the island of Euboea off the eastern coast of Greece). When the revolt was crushed in 494 B.C., after nearly six years of fighting, the Persian king, Darius, determined to punish the offending cities of Athens and Eretria. The series of invasions that ensued are known collectively as the Persian Wars. There are three distinct phases. The first was a punitive naval expedition in 492 B.C. It never reached its objective but was wrecked against the rocks in a storm as the fleet rounded the headland of Mt. Athos in the peninsula of Chalcidice. The second was the invasion by sea in 490 that was aimed directly at Athens. The third, ten years later and commanded in person by King Xerxes, son and successor of Darius, was a huge assault by land and sea with the intention of permanent conquest of Greece.

# 48 The Battle of Marathon

When the Persian troops disembarked at Marathon on the east coast of Attica in the summer of 490 B.C., there were not many Athenians who considered themselves to have a chance of victory. Indeed it was a serious matter of debate whether Athens should resist or capitulate in the hope of favorable treatment. It is usually taken as a tribute to the persuasive powers of the general Miltiades that the Athenians finally did decide to defend their homeland and sent their entire army to Marathon under Miltiades' command. The description of the Battle of Marathon is from Herodotus' *History of the Persian Wars* 6.102–117. It is translated by George Rawlinson.

⊛⊛⊛⊛⊛

The Persians, having thus brought Eretria into subjection, after waiting a few days, sailed for Attica, greatly straitening the Athenians as they approached, and thinking to deal with them as they had dealt with the people of Eretria. And because there was no place in all Attica so convenient for their horse as Marathon, and it lay moreover quite close to Eretria, therefore Hippias, the son of Pisistratus, conducted them thither.[1]

When intelligence of this reached the Athenians, they likewise marched their troops to Marathon, and there stood on the defensive, having at their head ten generals, of whom one was Miltiades.

Now this man's father, Cimon, the son of Stesagoras, was banished from Athens by Pisistratus, the son of Hippocrates. In his banishment it was his fortune to win the four-horse chariot-race at Olympia, whereby he gained the very same honour which had before been carried off by Miltiades, his half-brother on the mother's side. At the next Olympiad he won the prize again with the same mares, upon which he caused Pisistratus to be proclaimed the winner, having made an agreement with him that on yielding him this honour he should be allowed to come back to his country. Afterwards, still with the same mares, he won the prize a third time, whereupon he was put to death by the sons of Pisistratus, whose father was no longer living. They set men to lie in wait for him secretly, and these men slew him near the town-hall in the night-time. He was buried outside the city, beyond what is called the Valley Road, and right opposite his tomb were buried the mares which had won the three prizes. The same success had likewise been achieved once previously, to wit, by the mares of Evagoras the Lacedaemonian, but never except by them. At the time of Cimon's death, Stesagoras, the elder of his two sons, was in the Chersonese, where he lived with Miltiades his uncle; the younger, who was called Miltiades after the founder of the Chersonesite colony, was with his father in Athens.

It was this Miltiades who now commanded the Athenians, after escaping from the Chersonese, and twice nearly losing his life. First he was chased as far as Imbrus by the Phoenicians, who had a great desire to take him and carry him up to the king; and when he had avoided this danger, and,

---

1. The exiled tyrant was in the service of the Persians in the expectation that their victory would see him installed as the Persian governor of Greek territories.

having reached his own country, thought himself to be altogether in safety, he found his enemies waiting for him, and was cited by them before a court and impeached for his tyranny in the Chersonese. But he came off victorious here likewise, and was thereupon made general of the Athenians by the free choice of the people.

And first, before they left the city, the generals sent off to Sparta a herald, one Philippides, who was by birth an Athenian, and by profession and practice a trained runner. This man, according to the account which he gave to the Athenians on his return, when he was near Mount Parthenium, above Tegea, fell in with the god Pan, who called him by his name, and bade him ask the Athenians, "Why they neglected him so entirely, when he was kindly disposed towards them, and had often helped them in times past, and would do so again in time to come?" The Athenians, entirely believing in the truth of this report, as soon as their affairs were once more in good order, set up a temple to Pan under the Acropolis, and, in return for the message which I have recorded, established in his honour yearly sacrifices and a torch-race.

On the occasion of which we speak, when Philippides was sent by the Athenian generals, and, according to his own account, saw Pan on his journey, he reached Sparta on the very next day after quitting the city of Athens. Upon his arrival he went before the rulers, and said:

"Men of Lacedaemon, the Athenians beseech you to hasten to their aid, and not allow that state, which is the most ancient in all Greece, to be enslaved by the barbarians. Eretria is already carried away captive, and Greece weakened by the loss of no mean city."

Thus did Philippides deliver the message committed to him. And the Spartans wished to help the Athenians, but were unable to give them any present aid, as they did not like to break their established law. It was the ninth day of the month, and they could not march out of Sparta on the ninth, when the moon had not reached the full. So they waited for the full of the moon.

The barbarians were conducted to Marathon by Hippias, the son of Pisistratus, who the night before had seen a strange vision in his sleep. He seemed to have intercourse with his mother, and conjectured the dream to mean that he would be restored to Athens, recover the power which he had lost, and afterwards live to a good old age in his native country. Such was the sense in which he interpreted the vision. He now proceeded to act as guide to the Persians, and in the first place he landed the prisoners taken from Eretria upon the island that is called Aegileia, belonging to the

Styreans, after which he brought the fleet to anchor off Marathon, and marshalled the bands of the barbarians as they disembarked. As he was thus employed it chanced that he sneezed and at the same time coughed with more violence than was his wont. Now as he was a man advanced in years, and the greater number of his teeth were loose, it so happened that one of them was driven out with the force of the cough, and fell down into the sand. Hippias took all the pains he could to find it, but the tooth was nowhere to be seen; whereupon he fetched a deep sigh, and said to the bystanders, "After all the land is not ours, and we shall never be able to bring it under. All my share in it is the portion of which my tooth has possession."

So Hippias believed that this fulfilled his dream.

The Athenians were drawn up in order of battle in a precinct belonging to Heracles, when they were joined by the Plataeans, who came in full force to their aid. Some time before,[2] the Plataeans had put themselves under the rule of the Athenians, and these last had already undertaken many labours on their behalf. The occasion of the surrender was the following. The Plataeans suffered grievous things at the hands of the men of Thebes; so, as it chanced that Cleomenes, the son of Anaxandridas, and the Lacedaemonians were in their neighbourhood, they first of all offered to surrender themselves to them. But the Lacedaemonians refused to receive them, and said, "We dwell too far off from you, and ours would be but cold comfort. You might oftentimes be carried into slavery before one of us heard of it. We counsel you rather to give yourselves up to the Athenians, who are your next neighbours, and well able to shelter you."

This they said, not so much out of good will towards the Plataeans as because they wished to involve the Athenians in trouble by engaging them in wars with the Boeotians. The Plataeans, however, when the Lacedaemonians gave them this counsel, complied at once; and when the sacrifice to the Twelve Gods was being offered at Athens, they came and sat as suppliants about the altar, and gave themselves up to the Athenians. The Thebans no sooner learned what the Plataeans had done than instantly they marched out against them, while the Athenians sent troops to their aid. As the two armies were about to join battle, the Corinthians, who chanced to be at hand, would not allow them to engage; both sides consented to take them for arbitrators, whereupon they made up the quarrel, and fixed the boundary-line between the two states upon this condition: that if any of the Boeotians wished no longer to belong to Boeotia, the Thebans

2.　509 B.C. is the probable date; perhaps 519.

should allow them to follow their own inclinations. The Corinthians, when they had thus decreed, departed to their homes; the Athenians likewise set off on their return, but the Boeotians fell upon them during the march, and a battle was fought wherein they were worsted by the Athenians. Hereupon these last would not be bound by the line which the Corinthians had fixed, but advanced beyond those limits, and made the Asopus the boundary-line between the country of the Thebans and that of the Plataeans and Hysians. Under such circumstances did the Plataeans give themselves up to Athens; and now they were come to Marathon to aid the Athenians.

The Athenian generals were divided in their opinions; and some advised not to risk a battle, because they were too few to engage such a host as that of the Medes; while others were for fighting at once, and among these last was Miltiades. He therefore, seeing that opinions were thus divided, and that the less worthy counsel appeared likely to prevail, resolved to go to the Polemarch, and have a conference with him. For the man on whom the lot fell to be polemarch, at Athens was entitled to give his vote with the ten generals, since anciently the Athenians allowed him an equal right of voting with them. The Polemarch at this juncture was Callimachus of Aphidnae; to him therefore Miltiades went, and said:

"With you it rests, Callimachus, either to bring Athens to slavery, or, by securing her freedom, to leave behind to all future generations a memory beyond even Harmodius and Aristogeiton.[3] For never since the time that the Athenians became a people were they in so great a danger as now. If they bow their necks beneath the yoke of the Medes, the woes which they will have to suffer when given into the power of Hippias are already determined on; if, on the other hand, they fight and overcome, Athens may rise to be the very first city in Greece. How it comes to pass that these things are likely to happen, and how the determining of them in some sort rests with you, I will now proceed to make clear. We generals are ten in number, and our votes are divided; half of us wish to engage, half to avoid a combat. Now, if we do not fight, I look to see a great disturbance at Athens which will shake men's resolutions, and then I fear they will submit themselves; but if we fight the battle before any unsoundness show itself among our citizens, let the gods but give us fair play, and we are well able to overcome the enemy. On you therefore we depend in this matter, which lies wholly

3. The men who had assassinated Hipparchus (Pisistratus' son, and partner with his brother Hippias in the tyranny). Although the murder had resulted from a personal quarrel, the two men were traditionally remembered in Athens as patriotic heroes, the "tyrant-killers."

in your own power. You have only to add your vote to my side and your country will be free, and not free only, but the first state in Greece. Or, if you prefer to give your vote to them who would decline the combat, then the reverse will follow."

Miltiades by these words gained Callimachus; and the addition of the polemarch's vote caused the decision to be in favor of fighting. Hereupon all those generals who had been desirous of hazarding a battle, when their turn came to command the army, gave up their right to Miltiades. He however, though he accepted their offers, nevertheless waited, and would not fight, until his own day of command arrived in due course.

Then at length, when his own turn was come, the Athenian battle was set in array, and this was the order of it. Callimachus the polemarch led the right wing, for it was at that time a rule with the Athenians to give the right wing to the polemarch. After this followed the tribes, according as they were numbered, in an unbroken line; while last of all came the Plataeans, forming the left wing. And ever since that day it has been a custom with the Athenians, in the sacrifices and assemblies held each fifth year at Athens, for the Athenian herald to implore the blessing of the gods on the Plataeans conjointly with the Athenians. Now as they marshalled the host upon the field of Marathon, in order that the Athenian front might be of equal length with the Median, the ranks of the centre were diminished, and it became the weakest part of the line, while the wings were both made strong with a depth of many ranks.

So when the battle was set in array, and the victims showed themselves favourable, instantly the Athenians, so soon as they were let go, charged the barbarians at a run. Now the distance between the two armies was little short of a mile. The Persians, therefore, when they saw the Greeks coming on at speed, made ready to receive them, although it seemed to them that the Athenians were bereft of their senses, and bent upon their own destruction; for they saw a mere handful of men coming on at a run without either horsemen or archers. Such was the opinion of the barbarians; but the Athenians in close array fell upon them, and fought in a manner worthy of being recorded. They were the first of the Greeks, so far as I know, who introduced the custom of charging the enemy at a run, and they were likewise the first who dared to look upon the Median garb, and to face men clad in that fashion. Until this time the very name of the Medes had been a terror to the Greeks to hear.

The two armies fought together on the plain of Marathon for a length of time; and in the mid battle, where the Persians themselves and the Sacae had their place, the barbarians were victorious, and broke and pursued the Greeks into the inner country; but on the two wings the Athenians and the Plataeans defeated the enemy. Having so done, they suffered the routed barbarians to fly at their ease, and joining the two wings in one, fell upon those who had broken their own centre, and fought and conquered them. These likewise fled, and now the Athenians hung upon the runaways and cut them down, chasing them all the way to the shore, on reaching which they laid hold of the ships and called aloud for fire.

It was in the struggle here that Callimachus the polemarch, after greatly distinguishing himself, lost his life; Stesilaus too, the son of Thrasilaus, one of the generals, was slain; and Cynaegirus, the son of Euphorion, having seized on a vessel of the enemy's by the ornament at the stern, had his hand cut off by the blow of an axe, and so perished; as likewise did many other Athenians of note and name.

Nevertheless the Athenians secured in this way seven of the vessels, while with the remainder the barbarians pushed off, and taking aboard their Eretrian prisoners from the island where they had left them, doubled Cape Sunium, hoping to reach Athens before the return of the Athenians. The Alcmaeonidae were accused by their countrymen of suggesting this course to them; they had, it was said, an understanding with the Persians, and made a signal to them, by raising a shield, after they were embarked in their ships.

The Persians accordingly sailed round Sunium. But the Athenians with all possible speed marched away to the defence of their city, and succeeded in reaching Athens before the appearance of the barbarians; and as their camp at Marathon had been pitched in a precinct of Heracles, so now they encamped in another precinct of the same god at Cynosarges. The barbarian fleet arrived, and lay to off Phalerum, which was at that time the haven of Athens; but after resting awhile upon their oars, they departed and sailed away to Asia.

There fell in this battle of Marathon, on the side of the barbarians, about 6,400 men, on that of the Athenians, 192. Such was the number of the slain on the one side and the other. A strange prodigy likewise happened at this fight. Epizelus, the son of Cuphagoras, an Athenian, was in the thick of the fray, and behaving himself as a brave man should, when suddenly he was stricken with blindness, without blow of sword or dart, and this blindness continued thenceforth during the whole of his after life. The following is the account which he himself, as I have heard, gave of the matter: he said that a gigantic warrior, with a huge beard, which shaded all his shield, stood over against him, but the ghostly semblance passed him by, and slew the man at his side. Such, as I understand, was the tale which Epizelus told.

# 49  *The Battle of Thermopylae*

Marathon has enjoyed a great reputation as one of the decisive battles of history, but it did not seem so to contemporary Athenians. They felt it to be something of a miracle that almost alone (four hundred soldiers had been sent by the city of Plataea to join with them) they had defeated the Persian force, but they had no illusions as to their power in comparison to that of the Persian empire. In the following decade Athenians were gloomy about their chances of surviving the next Persian invasion, which they knew must surely come.

When the huge expeditionary force of the Persians crossed the Hellespont in 480 B.C. and began its march into Greece, for the first time in their history the Greeks undertook something like a united effort in the defense of their country. It was not very united at that, but at least most of the major cities joined forces, and Sparta, the acknowledged military leader of Greece, was committed to fight. All of Greece north of the pass at Thermopylae had to be written off, and the inhabitants capitulated to the invaders without any struggle. The great question among the Greek commanders was where the defense could take place with any chance of success. Clearly it had to be at some point where topography would minimize the overwhelming numerical advantage of the Persians. Most modern scholars are convinced that the Spartans intended from the outset to defend at the Isthmus of Corinth, the thin neck of land connecting the Peloponnesus with central Greece. In this view the Battle of Thermopylae becomes at most a gesture, a calculated loss intended to give the Persians a taste of Greek, and especially Spartan, fighting qualities, and to encourage the Greeks north of the Isthmus not to give in. Nevertheless, the hopeless stand of the men who died in the pass at Thermopylae has rightfully gone down through the centuries as one of the epics of military valor. This account of the Battle of Thermopylae is that of Herodotus 7.200–228. The translation is by George Rawlinson.

❁❁❁❁❁

Further to the south, another river, called the Phoenix, which has no great body of water, flows from the same hills, and falls into the Asopus. Here is the narrowest place of all, for in this part there is only a causeway wide enough for a single carriage. From the river Phoenix to Thermopylae is a distance of two miles; and in this space is situated the village called Anthela, which the river Asopus passes before it reaches the sea. The space about Anthela is of some width, and contains a temple of Amphictyonian Demeter, as well as the seats of the Amphictyonic deputies, and a temple of Amphictyon himself.

King Xerxes pitched his camp in the region of Malis called Trachinia, while on their side the Greeks occupied the straits. These straits the Greeks in general call Thermopylae (the Hot Gates); but the natives and those who dwell in the neighbourhood, call them Pylae (the Gates). Here then the two armies took their stand; the one master of all the region lying north of Trachis, the other of the country extending southward of that place to the verge of the continent.

The Greeks who at this spot awaited the coming of Xerxes were the following: From Sparta, 300 men-at-arms; from Arcadia, 1,000 Tegeans and Mantineans, 500 of each people; 120 Orchomenians, from the Arcadian Orchomenus; and 1,000 from other cities: from Corinth, 400 men: from Phlius, 200: and from Mycenae eighty. Such was the number from the Peloponnese. There were also present, from Boeotia, 700 Thespians and 400 Thebans.

Besides these troops, the Locrians of Opus and the Phocians had obeyed the call of their countrymen, and sent, the former all the force they had, the latter 1,000 men. For envoys had gone from the Greeks at Thermopylae among the Locrians and Phocians, to call on them for assistance, and to say, "They were themselves but the vanguard of the host, sent to precede the main body, which might every day be expected to follow them. The sea was in good keeping, watched by the Athenians, the Aeginetans, and the rest of the fleet. There was no cause why they should fear; for after all the invader was not a god but a man; and there never had been, and never would be, a man who was not liable to misfortunes from the very day of his birth, and those greater in proportion to his own greatness. The assailant therefore, being only a mortal, must needs fall from his glory." Thus urged, the Locrians and the Phocians had come with their troops to Trachis.

The various nations had each captains of their own under whom they served; but the one to whom all especially looked up, and who had the command of the entire force, was the Lacedaemonian, Leonidas. Now

Leonidas was the son of Anaxandridas, who was the son of Leo, who was the son of Eurycratidas, who was the son of Anaxander, who was the son of Eurycrates, who was the son of Polydorus, who was the son of Alcamenes, who was the son of Telecles, who was the son of Archelaus, who was the son of Agesilaus, who was the son of Doryssus, who was the son of Labotas, who was the son of Echestratus, who was the son of Agis, who was the son of Eurysthenes, who was the son of Aristodemus, who was the son of Aristomachus, who was the son of Cleodaeus, who was the son of Hyllus, who was the son of Heracles.

Leonidas had come to be king of Sparta quite unexpectedly.

Having two elder brothers, Cleomenes and Dorieus, he had no thought of ever mounting the throne. However when Cleomenes died without male offspring, as Dorieus was likewise deceased, having perished in Sicily, the crown fell to Leonidas, who was older than Cleombrotus, the youngest of the sons of Anaxandridas, and, moreover, was married to the daughter of Cleomenes. He had now come to Thermopylae, accompanied by the 300 men which the law assigned him, whom he had himself chosen from among the citizens, and who were all of them fathers with sons living. On his way he had taken the troops from Thebes, whose number I have already mentioned, and who were under the command of Leontiades the son of Eurymachus. The reason why he made a point of taking troops from Thebes and Thebes only was, that the Thebans were strongly suspected of being well inclined to the Medes. Leonidas therefore called on them to come with him to the war, wishing to see whether they would comply with his demand, or openly refuse, and disclaim the Greek alliance. They, however, though their wishes leant the other way, nevertheless sent the men.

The force with Leonidas was sent forward by the Spartans in advance of their main body, that the sight of them might encourage the allies to fight, and hinder them from going over to the Medes, as it was likely they might have done had they seen Sparta backward. They intended presently, when they had celebrated the Carneian festival, which was what now kept them at home, to leave a garrison in Sparta, and hasten in full force to join the army. The rest of the allies also intended to act similarly; for it happened that the Olympic festival fell exactly at this same period. None of them looked to see the contest at Thermopylae decided so speedily; wherefore they were content to send forward a mere advanced guard. Such accordingly were the intentions of the allies.

The Greek forces at Thermopylae, when the Persian army drew near to the entrance of the pass, were seized with fear, and a council was held to consider about a retreat. It was the wish of the Peloponnesians generally that the army should fall back upon the Peloponnese, and there guard the Isthmus. But Leonidas, who saw with what indignation the Phocians and Locrians heard of this plan, gave his voice for remaining where they were, while they sent envoys to the several cities to ask for help, since they were too few to make a stand against an army like that of the Medes.

While this debate was going on, Xerxes sent a mounted spy to observe the Greeks, and note how many they were, and what they were doing. He had heard, before he came out of Thessaly, that a few men were assembled at this place, and that at their head were certain Lacedaemonians, under Leonidas, a decendant of Heracles. The horseman rode up to the camp, and looked about him, but did not see the whole army; for such as were on the further side of the wall (which had been rebuilt and was now carefully guarded) it was not possible for him to behold; but he observed those on the outside, who were encamped in front of the rampart. It chanced that at this time the Lacedaemonians held the outer guard, and were seen by the spy, some of them engaged in gymnastic exercises, others combing their long hair. At this the spy greatly marvelled, but he counted their number, and when he had taken accurate note of everything, he rode back quietly; for no one pursued after him, or paid any heed to his visit. So he returned, and told Xerxes all that he had seen.

Upon this, Xerxes, who had no means of surmising the truth—namely, that the Spartans were preparing to do or die manfully—but thought it laughable that they should be engaged in such employments, sent and called to his presence Demaratus the son of Ariston, who still remained with the army. When he appeared, Xerxes told him all that he had heard, and questioned him concerning the news, since he was anxious to understand the meaning of such behaviour on the part of the Spartans. Then Demaratus said, "I spoke to you, O King, concerning these men long since, when we had but just begun our march upon Greece; you, however, only laughed at my words, when I told you of all this, which I saw would come to pass. Earnestly do I struggle at all times to speak truth to you, sire; and now listen to it once more. These men have come to dispute the pass with us, and it is for this that they are now making ready. It is their custom, when they are about to hazard their lives, to adorn their heads with care. Be assured, however, that if you can subdue the men who are here and the Lacedaemonians who remain in Sparta, there is no other nation in all the world which will venture to lift a hand in their defence. You have now to deal with the first kingdom and town in Greece, and with the bravest men."

Then Xerxes, to whom what Demaratus said seemed altogether to surpass belief, asked further, "How it was possible for so small an army to contend with his?"

"O King," Demaratus answered, "let me be treated as a liar, if matters fall not out as I say."

But Xerxes was not persuaded any the more. Four whole days he suffered to go by, expecting that the Greeks would run away. When, however, he found on the fifth that they were not gone, thinking that their firm stand was mere impudence and recklessness, he grew wroth, and sent against them the Medes and Cissians, with orders to take them alive and bring them into his presence. Then the Medes rushed forward and charged the Greeks, but fell in vast numbers: others however took the places of the slain, and would not be beaten off, though they suffered terrible losses. In this way it became clear to all, and especially to the king, that though he had plenty of combatants, he had but very few warriors. The struggle, however, continued during the whole day.

Then the Medes, having met so rough a reception, withdrew from the fight; and their place was taken by the band of Persians under Hydarnes, whom the king called his Immortals: they, it was thought, would soon finish the business. But when they joined battle with the Greeks, it was with no better success than the Median detachment—things went much as before—the two armies fighting in a narrow space, and the barbarians using shorter spears than the Greeks, and having no advantage from their numbers. The Lacedaemonians fought in a way worthy of note, and showed themselves far more skilful in fight than their adversaries, often turning their backs, and making as though they were all flying away, on which the barbarians would rush after them with much noise and shouting, when the Spartans at their approach would wheel round and face their pursuers, in this way destroying vast numbers of the enemy. Some Spartans likewise fell in these encounters, but only a very few. At last the Persians, finding that all their efforts to gain the pass availed nothing, and that whether they attacked by divisions or in any other way, it was to no purpose, withdrew to their own quarters.

During these assaults, it is said that Xerxes, who was watching the battle, thrice leaped from the throne on which he sat, in terror for his army.

Next day the combat was renewed, but with no better success on the part of the barbarians. The Greeks were so few that the barbarians hoped to find them disabled, by reason of their wounds, from offering any further resistance; and so they once more attacked them. But the Greeks were drawn up in detachments according to their cities, and bore the brunt of the battle in turns, all except the Phocians, who had been stationed on the mountain to guard the pathway. So when the Persians found no difference between that day and the preceding, they again retired to their quarters.

Now, as the king was at a loss, and knew not how he should deal with the emergency, Ephialtes, the son of Eurydemus, a man of Malis, came to him and was admitted to a conference. Stirred by the hope of receiving a rich reward at the king's hands, he had come to tell him of the pathway which led across the mountain to Thermopylae; by which disclosure he brought destruction on the band of Greeks who had there withstood the barbarians. This Ephialtes afterwards, from fear of the Lacedaemonians, fled into Thessaly; and during his exile, in an assembly of the Amphictyons held at Pylae, a price was set upon his head by the Pylagorae. When some time had gone by, he returned from exile, and went to Anticyra, where he was slain by Athenades, a native of Trachis. Athenades did not slay him for his treachery, but for another reason, which I shall mention in a later part of my history: yet still the Lacedaemonians honoured him none the less. Thus then did Ephialtes perish a long time afterwards.

Besides this there is another story told, which I do not at all believe, that Onetas the son of Phanagoras, a native of Carystus, and Corydallus, a man of Anticyra, were the persons who spoke on this matter to the king, and took the Persians across the mountain. One may guess which story is true, from the fact that the deputies of the Greeks, the Pylagorae, who must have had the best means of ascertaining the truth, did not offer the reward for the heads of Onetas and Corydallus, but for that of Ephialtes of Trachis; and again from the flight of Ephialtes, which we know to have been on this account. Onetas, I allow, although he was not a Malian, might have been acquainted with the path, if he had lived much in that part of the country; but as Ephialtes was the person who actually led the Persians round the mountain by the pathway, I leave his name on record as that of the man who did the deed.

Great was the joy of Xerxes on this occasion; and as he approved highly of the enterprise which Ephialtes undertook to accomplish, he forthwith sent upon the errand Hydarnes, and the Persians under him. The troops left the camp about the time of the lighting of the lamps. The pathway along which they went was first discovered by the Malians of these parts, who soon afterwards led the Thessalians by it to attack the Phocians, at the time when the Phocians fortified the pass with a wall, and so put themselves under covert from danger. And ever since, the path has always been put to an ill use by the Malians.

The course which it takes is the following: Beginning at the Asopus, where that stream flows through the cleft in the hills, it runs along the ridge of the mountain (which is called, like the pathway over it, Anopaea), and ends at the city of Alpenus—the first Locrian town as you come from Malis—by the stone called Black-buttock and the seats of the Cercopians. Here it is as narrow as at any other point.

The Persians took this path, and crossing the Asopus, continued their march through the whole of the night, having the mountains of Oeta on their right hand, and on their left those of Trachis. At dawn of day they found themselves close to the summit. Now the hill was guarded, as I have already said, by 1,000 Phocian men-at-arms, who were placed there to defend the pathway, and at the same time to secure their own country. They had been given the guard of the mountain path, while the other Greeks defended the pass below, because they had volunteered for the service, and had pledged themselves to Leonidas to maintain the post.

The ascent of the Persians became known to the Phocians in the following manner: During all the time that they were making their way up, the Greeks remained unconscious of it, inasmuch as the whole mountain was covered with groves of oak; but it happened that the air was very still, and the leaves which the Persians stirred with their feet made, as it was likely they would, a loud rustling, whereupon the Phocians jumped up and flew to seize their arms. In a moment the barbarians came in sight, and perceiving men arming themselves, were greatly amazed; for they had fallen in with an enemy when they expected no opposition. Hydarnes, alarmed at the sight, and fearing lest the Phocians might be Lacedaemonians, inquired of Ephialtes to what nation these troops belonged. Ephialtes told him the exact truth, whereupon he arrayed his Persians for battle. The Phocians, galled by the showers of arrows to which they were exposed, and imagining themselves the special object of the Persian attack, fled hastily to the crest of the mountain, and there made ready to meet death; but while their mistake continued, the Persians, with Ephialtes and Hydarnes, not thinking it worth their while to delay on account of Phocians, passed on and descended the mountain with all possible speed.

The Greeks at Thermopylae received the first warning of the destruction which the dawn would bring on them from the seer Megistias, who read their fate in the victims as he was sacrificing. After this deserters came in, and brought the news that the Persians were marching round by the hills: it was still night when these men arrived. Last of all, the scouts came running down from the heights, and brought in the same accounts, when the day was just beginning to break. Then the Greeks held a council to consider what they should do, and here opinions were divided: some were strong against quitting their posts, while others contended to the contrary. So when the council had broken up, part of the troops departed and went their ways homeward to their several states; part however resolved to remain, and to stand by Leonidas to the last.

It is said that Leonidas himself sent away the troops who departed, because he tendered their safety, but thought it unseemly that either he or his Spartans should quit the post which they had been especially sent to guard. For my own part, I incline to think that Leonidas gave the order, because he perceived the allies to be out of heart and unwilling to encounter the danger to which his own mind was made up. He therefore commanded them to retreat, but said that he himself could not draw back with honour; knowing that, if he stayed, glory awaited him, and that Sparta in that case would not lose her prosperity. For when the Spartans, at the very beginning of the war, sent to consult the oracle concerning it, the answer which they received from the priestess was that either Sparta must be overthrown by the barbarians, or one of her kings must perish. The prophecy was delivered in hexameter verse, and ran thus:

Oh! ye men who dwell in the streets of broad Lacedaemon,
Either your glorious town shall be sacked by the children of Perseus,
Or, in exchange, must all through the whole Laconian country
Mourn for the loss of a king, descendant of great Heracles.
He cannot be withstood by the courage of bulls or of lions,
Strive as they may; he is mighty as Zeus; there is nought that shall stay him,
Till he have got for his prey your king, or your glorious city.

The remembrance of this answer, I think, and the wish to secure the whole glory for the Spartans, caused Leonidas to send the allies away. This is more likely than that they quarrelled with him, and took their departure in such unruly fashion.

To me it seems no small argument in favour of this view, that the seer also who accompanied the army, Megistias, the Acarnanian, said to have been of the blood of Melampus, and the same who was led by the appearance of the victims to warn the Greeks of the danger which threatened them, received orders to retire (as it is certain he did) from Leonidas, that he might escape the coming destruction. Megistias, however, though bidden to depart, refused, and stayed with the army; but he had an only son present with the expedition, whom he now sent away.

So the allies, when Leonidas ordered them to retire, obeyed him and forthwith departed. Only the Thespians and the Thebans remained with the Spartans; and of these the Thebans were kept back by Leonidas as hostages, very much against their will. The Thespians, on the contrary, stayed entirely of their own accord, refusing to retreat, and declaring that they would not forsake Leonidas and his followers. So they abode with the Spartans, and died with them. Their leader was Demophilus, the son of Diadromes.

At sunrise Xerxes made libations, after which he waited until the time when the market-place is wont to fill, and then began his advance. Ephialtes had instructed him thus, as the descent of the mountain is much quicker, and the distance much shorter, than the way round the hills, and the ascent. So the barbarians under Xerxes began to draw nigh; and the Greeks under Leonidas, as they now went forth determined to die, advanced much further than on previous days, until they reached the more open portion of the pass. Hitherto they had held their station within the wall, and from this had gone forth to fight at the point where the pass was the narrowest. Now they joined battle beyond the defile, and carried slaughter among the barbarians, who fell in heaps. Behind them the captains of the squadrons, armed with whips, urged their men forward with continual blows. Many were thrust into the sea, and there perished; a still greater number were trampled to death by their own soldiers; no one heeded the dying. For the Greeks, reckless of their own safety and desperate, since they knew that, as the mountain had been crossed, their destruction was nigh at hand, exerted themselves with the most furious valour against the barbarians.

By this time the spears of the greater number were all shivered, and with their swords they hewed down the ranks of the Persians; and here, as they strove, Leonidas fell fighting bravely, together with many other famous Spartans, whose names I have taken care to learn on account of their great worthiness, as indeed I have those of all the 300. There fell too at the same time very many famous Persians: among them, two sons of Darius, Abrocomes and Hyperanthes, his children by Phratagune, the daughter of Artanes. Artanes was brother of King Darius, being a son of Hystaspes, the son of Arsames; and when he gave his daughter to the king, he made him heir likewise of all his substance; for she was his only child.

Thus two brothers of Xerxes here fought and fell. And now there arose a fierce struggle between the Persians and the Lacedaemonians over the body of Leonidas, in which the Greeks four times drove back the enemy, and at last by their great bravery succeeded in bearing off the body. This combat was scarcely ended when the Persians with Ephialtes approached; and the Greeks, informed that they drew nigh, made a change in the manner of their fighting. Drawing back into the narrowest part of the pass, and retreating even behind the cross wall, they posted themselves upon a hillock, where they stood all drawn up together in one close body, except only the Thebans. The hillock whereof I speak is at the entrance of the straits, where the stone lion stands which was set up in honour of Leonidas. Here they defended themselves to the last, such as still had swords using them, and the others resisting with their hands and teeth; till the barbarians, who in part had pulled down the wall and attacked them in front, in part had gone round and now encircled them upon every side, overwhelmed and buried the remnant left beneath showers of missile weapons.

Thus nobly did the whole body of Lacedaemonians and Thespians behave, but nevertheless one man is said to have distinguished himself above all the rest, to wit, Dieneces the Spartan. A speech which he made before the Greeks engaged the Medes, remains on record. One of the Trachinians told him, "Such was the number of the barbarians, that when they shot forth their arrows the sun would be darkened by their multitude." Dieneces, not at all frightened at these words, but making light of the Median numbers, answered, "Our Trachinian friend brings us excellent tidings. If the Medes darken the sun, we shall have our fight in the shade." Other sayings too of a like nature are said to have been left on record by this same person.

Next to him two brothers, Lacedaemonians, are reputed to have made themselves conspicuous: they were named Alpheus and Maro, and were the sons of Orsiphantus. There was also a Thespian who gained greater glory than any of his countrymen: he was a man called Dithyrambus, the son of Harmatidas.

The slain were buried where they fell; and in their honour, nor less in honour of those who died before Leonidas sent the allies away, an inscription was set up, which said:

> Here did four thousand men from Pelops' land
> Against three hundred myriads[1] bravely stand.

This was in honour of all. Another was for the Spartans alone:

> Go, stranger, and to Lacedaemon tell
> That here, obeying her behests, we fell.

1. A myriad is 10,000. Thus, according to Greek tradition, the Persian army numbered 3,000,000 men.

# 50   The Battle of Salamis

The decisive event of the years between Marathon and the Persian invasion in 480 B.C. turned out to be the finding of a rich new vein of silver at the state-owned mines at Laurium in Attica. The outstanding Athenian statesman of the period, Themistocles, persuaded the people to use the income from this bonanza to build a fleet of warships. The two hundred ships thereby launched by Athens formed the heart of the Greek naval force that on September 23, 480 B.C. won the crucial battle off the island of Salamis. Before that battle was fought, however, the Athenians had had to abandon their city before the unopposed march of the Persians relentlessly continuing southward after Thermopylae. The population was evacuated to the city of Troizen in the Peloponnesus and to the island of Salamis, from which they watched Athens burn. According to Herodotus' account the evacuation was decided upon at the last moment, but the "most sensational inscription ever discovered," found at Troizen in 1959 (A.D.) by the American archaeologist Michael H. Jameson and purportedly a copy of an edict of the Athenian Assembly, indicates that on the motion of Themistocles the orderly evacuation of the city was voted. What is remarkable about the document is its date, which places the decision to abandon Athens not immediately prior to the Battle of Salamis but several months earlier at about the time of Thermopylae. This is in direct contradiction to Herodotus' account and places in question the credit of the historian on a point about which he can be presumed to have had every opportunity to be correctly informed.

The first of the following selections is the text of the "Themistocles Inscription" in the translation of M. H. Jameson. The second is the account in Herodotus 8.40–42, 49–53 of the events leading up to the Battle of Salamis. It is translated by George Rawlinson.

❁❁❁❁❁

The Gods.

Resolved by the council and the People on the motion of Themistokles, son

SOURCE: Michael H. Jameson, "A Decree of Themistokles from Troizen," *Hesperia* (Journal of the American School of Classical Studies at Athens), Vol. XXIX (1960), pp. 200–201. Reprinted by permission of the publishers.

of Neokles, of the deme Phrearrhoi: to entrust the city to Athena the Mistress of Athens and to all the other gods to guard and defend from the Barbarian for the sake of the land. The Athenians themselves and the foreigners who live in Athens are to remove their women and children to Troizen . . . the *archegetes* of the land. . . . . The old men and the movable possessions are to be removed to Salamis. The treasurers and the priestesses are to remain on the acropolis protecting the possessions of the gods.

All the other Athenians and foreigners of military age are to embark on the 200 ships that lie ready and defend against the Barbarian for the sake of their own freedom and that of the rest of the Greeks, along with the Lakedaimonians, the Corinthians, the Aiginetans, and all others who wish to share the danger.

The generals are to appoint, starting tomorrow, 200 trierarchs, one to a ship, from among those who have ancestral land in Athens and legitimate children and who are not older than fifty; to these men the ships are to be assigned by lot. They are also to enlist marines, 20 to a ship, from men between the ages of twenty and thirty, and four archers to a ship. They are also to assign the petty officers to the ships at the same time that they allot the trierarchs. The generals are also to write up the names of the crews of the ships on white boards, taking the names of the Athenians from the lexiarchic registers, the foreigners from those registered with the polemarch. They are to write up the names assigning the whole number of 200 equal divisions and to write above each division the name of the trireme and trierarch and the names of the petty officers so that each division may know on which trireme it is to embark. When all the divisions have been composed and allotted to the triremes, the Council and the generals are to complete the manning of the 200 ships, after sacrificing a placatory offering to Zeus the Almighty, Athena, Victory, and Poseidon the Securer.

When the manning of the ships has been completed, with one hundred of them they are to meet the enemy at Artemision in Euboia,[1] and with the other hundred of them they are to lie off Salamis and the rest of Attika and keep guard over the land.

In order that all Athenians may be united in their defense against the Barbarian, those who have been sent into exile for ten years are to go to Salamis and to stay there until the People come to some decision about them, while those who have been deprived of citizen rights. . . .

· · · · ·

1.  This event dates the decree securely.

[ 412 ]

Meanwhile, the Grecian fleet, which had left Artemisium, proceeded to Salamis, at the request of the Athenians, and there cast anchor. The Athenians had begged them to take up this position, in order that they might convey their women and children out of Attica, and further might deliberate upon the course which it now behoved them to follow. Disappointed in the hopes which they had previously entertained, they were about to hold a council concerning the present posture of their affairs. For they had looked to see the Peloponnesians drawn up in full force to resist the enemy in Boeotia, but found nothing of what they had expected; nay, they learnt that the Greeks of those parts, only concerning themselves about their own safety, were building a wall across the Isthmus, and intended to guard the Peloponnese, and let the rest of Greece take its chance. These tidings caused them to make the request whereof I spoke, that the combined fleet should anchor at Salamis.

So while the rest of the fleet lay to off this island, the Athenians cast anchor along their own coast. Immediately upon their arrival, proclamation was made, that every Athenian should save his children and household as he best could; whereupon some sent their families to Aegina, some to Salamis, but the greater number to Troezen. This removal was made with all possible haste, partly from a desire to obey the advice of the oracle, but still more for another reason. The Athenians say that they have in their acropolis a huge serpent, which lives in the temple, and is the guardian of the whole place. Nor do they only say this, but, as if the serpent really dwelt there, every month they lay out its food, which consists of a honey-cake. Up to this time the honey-cake had always been consumed; but now it remained untouched. So the priestess told the people what had happened; whereupon they left Athens the more readily, since they believed that the goddess had already abandoned the citadel. As soon as all was removed, the Athenians sailed back to their station.

And now, the remainder of the Grecian sea-force, hearing that the fleet which had been at Artemisium, was come to Salamis, joined it at that island from Troezen—orders having been issued previously that the ships should muster at Pogon, the port of the Troezenians. The vessels collected were many more in number than those which had fought at Artemisium, and were furnished by more cities. The admiral was the same who had commanded before, Eurybiades, the son of Eurycleides, who was a Spartan, but not of the family of the kings: the city, however, which sent by far the greatest number of ships, and the best, was Athens. . . .

When the captains from these various nations were come together at Salamis, a council of war was summoned; and Eurybiades proposed that any one who liked to advise, should say which place seemed to him the fittest, amongst those still in the possession of the Greeks, to be the scene of a naval combat. Attica, he said, was not to be thought of now; but he desired their counsel as to the remainder. The speakers mostly advised, that the fleet should sail away to the Isthmus, and there give battle in defence of the Peloponnese; and they urged as a reason for this, that if they were worsted in a sea-fight at Salamis, they would be shut up in an island, where they could get no help; but if they were beaten near the Isthmus, they could escape to their homes.

As the captains from the Peloponnese were thus advising, there came an Athenian to the camp, who brought word that the barbarians had entered Attica, and were ravaging and burning everything. For the division of the army under Xerxes was just arrived at Athens from its march through Boeotia, where it had burnt Thespiae and Plataea—both which cities were forsaken by their inhabitants, who had fled to the Peloponnese—and now it was laying waste all the possessions of the Athenians. Thespiae and Plataea had been burnt by the Persians, because they knew from the Thebans that neither of those cities had espoused their side.

Since the passage of the Hellespont and the commencement of the march upon Greece, a space of four months had gone by; one while the army made the crossing, and delayed about the region of the Hellespont; and three while they proceeded thence to Attica, which they entered in the archonship of Calliades. They found the city forsaken; a few people only remained in the temple, either keepers of the treasures, or men of the poorer sort. These persons having fortified the acropolis with planks and boards, held out against the enemy. It was in some measure their poverty which had prevented them from seeking shelter in Salamis; but there was likewise another reason which in part induced them to remain. They imagined themselves to have discovered the true meaning of the oracle uttered by the priestess, which promised "The wooden wall should never be taken." The wooden wall, they thought, did not mean the ships, but the place where they had taken refuge.

The Persians encamped upon the hill over against the citadel, which is called Ares' hill[2] by the Athenians, and began the siege of the place, attacking the Greeks with arrows whereto pieces of lighted tow were attached, which they shot at the barricade. And now those who were within the

2. The Areopagus.

citadel found themselves in a most woeful case, for their wooden rampart betrayed them; still, however, they continued to resist. It was in vain that the Pisistratidae came to them and offered terms of surrender—they stoutly refused all parley, and among their other modes of defence, rolled down huge masses of stone upon the barbarians as they were mounting up to the gates: so that Xerxes was for a long time very greatly perplexed, and could not contrive any way to take them.

At last, however, in the midst of these many difficulties, the barbarians made discovery of an access. For verily the oracle had spoken truth; and it was fated that the whole mainland of Attica should fall beneath the sway of the Persians. Right in front of the Acropolis, but behind the gates and the common ascent—where no watch was kept, and no one would have thought is possible that any foot of man could climb—a few soldiers mounted from the sanctuary of Aglaurus, Cecrops' daughter, notwithstanding the steepness of the precipice. As soon as the Athenians saw them upon the summit, some threw themselves headlong from the wall, and so perished; while others fled for refuge to the inner part of the temple. The Persians rushed to the gates and opened them, after which they massacred the suppliants. When all were slain, they plundered the temple, and fired every part of the Acropolis.

# EMPIRE AND DEMOCRACY

THE Persian Wars ended in a complete Greek triumph. In 479 B.C. the Persian army was destroyed in a land battle at Plataea in which the Greek forces were under Spartan leadership. At about the same time a combined sea and land operation under Athenian command at Mycale, a promontory on the Ionian coast, freed the Ionian cities from Persian rule and cleared the Aegean Sea of Persian ships. Out of this series of events Athens emerged with enormous prestige and a sense of her own greatness. The Spartans retreated to their traditional isolation in the Peloponnesus, and the way was left open for Athenian leadership of Greece.

The period from the Persian Wars to the outbreak of the Peloponnesian War in 431 B.C. was known to the Greeks of later times as the *Pentekontaëtia,* the "Fifty Years." It is a period completely dominated by the dazzling achievement of Athens. Her dynamism found expression externally in the building of an Athenian empire over the Greek cities of the Aegean coasts and islands and internally in the growth of democracy and in the cultural flowering that ever since has been the basis for Athens' claim to historical greatness. The two facets of Athenian development—imperialism abroad and democracy at home—are likely to appear incompatible to the modern student, but in fact they were interdependent and mutually supporting, twin expressions of the dynamism that was Athens in the fifth century B.C.

# 51 *Growth of the Athenian Empire*

The instrument that Athens used to build her empire was the Delian League. (The League took its name from the location of its meeting-place and treasury on the tiny island of Delos, sacred to Apollo from time immemorial.) Following the Persian defeat, the cities of the Aegean were invited to join a voluntary league of cities intended to provide a permanent union against Persia and any future threat that might come from Persia. Most of the major maritime states joined.

The Delian League was under Athenian leadership from the beginning, but as the years passed, and especially after it became clear that an immediate threat was no longer to be expected from Persia, Athenian leadership became increasingly Athenian rule. The League was converted step by step into an Athenian empire in which the members were no longer independent states attached voluntarily to an international treaty organization but were subjects of Athens. The techniques whereby this was accomplished were many, but essentially it was Athenian naval power that served as the means of subjection. There is no specific point at which one can say the Delian League was no longer, for the fiction was retained, but the symbol that has customarily served to mark the reality of Athenian rule is the moving of the League's treasury in 454 B.C. from Delos to Athens in order —as the Athenians explained—to insure its safety.

The following passages illustrate and describe Athenian imperial subjection of the Greek states of the Aegean. The two fragmentary inscriptions record decrees of the Athenian Assembly. The first of them dates from about 455 B.C., and in it the arrangements for a democratic constitution in the Ionian city of Erythrae are stipulated. (One of the ways in which the Athenians tried to secure the loyalty of their subject states was by making them adopt the institutions of democracy, in the age-old illusion that ideological identity will make for community of interests.) The second inscription, the date of which is problematical but is probably about 423 B.C., provides for the enforcement of an earlier decree prescribing uniform use of Athenian standards of coinage, weights, and measures by all members of the empire. The third selection is introductory to the highly compressed narrative of the military events of the *Pentekontaëtia* in Thucydides' *History of the Peloponnesian War*. The two inscriptions are translated by the editor of this volume from the texts in M. N. Tod, *Greek Historical Inscriptions,* Vol. I (2nd edition), Oxford, 1946, Nos. 29 and 67. The translation of Thucydides 1.89–97 is by R. Crawley.

❋❋❋❋❋

. . . was presiding officer, L . . . made the motion:

The people of Erythrae are to bring all the necessary sacrificial animals to the Greater Pan-Athenian festival, to a value of no less than three minas; and the priests are to distribute to those Erythraeans present a drachma's worth of the meat to each. If they bring sacrifices which are found not to be worth three minas, the priests will purchase sacrificial animals and charge the cost to the people of Erythrae; and the meat shall be distributed to anyone who wants it.

The Council of the Erythraeans is to consist of 120 men, elected by lot, those elected to undergo examination as to their fitness by the Council itself. No one is to be a Councillor who is under thirty years of age, under penalty of prosecution. Re-election may not occur for a four-year period. The present (first) Council is to be elected by lot and organized by the (Athenian) Overseers and the (Athenian) Commander of the Garrison; thereafter by the outgoing Council and the Commander of the Garrison. Before taking office each member of the Council of Erythrae is to swear by Zeus and by Apollo and by Demeter, calling down death upon himself and the same for his children if he swear falsely; the oath to be taken over burning sacrifices. The Councillor is to serve in accordance with the present law. If he does not comply, he is to be fined 1000 drachmas, and the people of Erythrae are to pay an equal amount.

The Council is to swear as follows:

"I shall serve as Councillor to the best of my ability and judgment in the interests of the people of Erythrae and the Athenians and their allies; and I will not revolt against the Athenians nor their allies, neither on my own initiative nor persuaded by another to do so. Neither will I desert of my own will, nor be subverted by anyone else to do so. Neither will I give refuge to any of the exiles, those who deserted to the Medes, nor be persuaded to do so by anyone else, without the express approval of the Athenians and the people of Erythrae; nor will I exile those who remained without the approval of the Athenians and the people of Erythrae."

If any Erythraean kill another Erythraean wilfully, let the penalty be death. If exile be decided upon, let him also be exiled from the entire alliance of the Athenians and let his goods become the public property of the Erythraeans.

If anyone is caught betraying the city of Erythrae to tyrants, let the penalty be death for himself, and for his children unless the children demonstrate themselves as having loyalty and good will toward the Erythraeans and the Athenians; all the property of one so apprehended is to be turned in by his heirs and is to become public property, the children to receive half the value of the property. Furthermore, if anyone is caught who betrayed the Athenian people or their garrison in Erythrae. . . .

[*The remainder is fragmentary.*]

. . . . .

[ 418 ]

. . . The people will choose heralds to send to the cities to proclaim the provisions hereby decreed by the people; one to be sent to Ionia, one to the Islands, one to the Hellespont, one to the region of Thrace. The heralds are to be chosen as soon as possible and the Generals are to send them out immediately, failure to do so making them subject to a fine of 10,000 drachmas.

The officials in the cities are to publish the text of the present decree inscribed on a stone stela in the market-place of each city, and the officials of the mint (in Athens) are to do the same in front of the mint. The Athenians are to carry out this stipulation if the local officials themselves are unwilling. The herald upon arrival is to demand whatever sum the Athenians order.

The Secretary of the Council is to record an addition to the Oath of the Council as follows:

"If anyone mints silver coinage in the cities and does not use the coins, weights, and measures of Athens but adopts foreign coinage, weights, and measures, the penalty is to be as ordained in the earlier decree, the decree passed on the motion of Clearchus."

It is the individual responsibility of private persons to surrender all their foreign money; and the city is to exchange it. Each person is to record in writing whatever he has, and turn the list in to the (Athenian) mint; the receiving officials of the mint are to publish the figures in front of the mint on whitened tablets available for inspection by anyone who wishes, listing both the foreign and local coinage. . . .

[*Here the text breaks off.*]

. . . . .

The way in which Athens came to be placed in the circumstances under which her power grew was this. After the Medes had returned from Europe, defeated by sea and land by the Hellenes, and after those of them who had fled with their ships to Mycale had been destroyed, Leotychides, King of the Lacedaemonians, the commander of the Hellenes at Mycale, departed home with the allies from Peloponnese. But the Athenians and the allies from Ionia and Hellespont, who had now revolted from the king, remained and laid siege to Sestos, which was still held by the Medes. After wintering before it, they became masters of the place on its evacuation by the barbarians; and after this they sailed away from Hellespont to their respective cities. Meanwhile the Athenian people, after the departure of the barbarian from their country, at once proceeded to carry over their children and wives, and such property as they had left, from the places where they had deposited them, and prepared to rebuild their city and their walls. For only isolated portions of the circumference had been left standing, and most of the houses were in ruins; though a few remained, in which the Persian grandees had taken up their quarters.

Perceiving what they were going to do, the Lacedaemonians sent an embassy to Athens. They would have themselves preferred to see neither her nor any other city in possession of a wall; though here they acted principally at the instigation of their allies, who were alarmed at the strength of her newly acquired navy, and the valour which she had displayed in the war with the Medes. They begged her not only to abstain from building walls for herself, but also to join them in throwing down the walls that still held together of the ultra-Peloponnesian cities. The real meaning of their advice, the suspicion that it contained against the Athenians, was not proclaimed; it was urged that so the barbarian, in the event of a third invasion, would not have any strong place, such as he now had in Thebes, for his base of operations; and that Peloponnese would suffice for all as a base both for retreat and offence. After the Lacedaemonians had thus spoken, they were, on the advice of Themistocles, immediately dismissed by the Athenians, with the answer that ambassadors should be sent to Sparta to discuss the question. Themistocles told the Athenians to send him off with all speed to Lacedaemon, but not to despatch his colleagues as soon as they had selected them, but to wait until they had raised their wall to the height from which defence was possible. Meanwhile the whole population in the city was to labour at the wall, the Athenians, their wives and their children, sparing no edifice, private or public, which might be of any use to the work, but throwing all down. After giving these instructions, and adding that he would be responsible for all other matters there, he departed. Arrived at Lacedaemon he did not seek an audience with the authorities, but tried to gain time and made excuses. When any of the government asked him why he did not appear in the assembly, he would say that he was waiting for his colleagues, who had been detained in Athens by some engagement; however, that he expected their speedy arrival, and wondered that they were not yet there.

At first the Lacedaemonians trusted the words of Themistocles, through their friendship for him; but when others arrived, all distinctly declaring that the work was going on and already attaining some elevation, they did not know how to disbelieve it. Aware of this, he told them that rumours are deceptive, and should not be trusted; they should send some reputable persons from Sparta to inspect, whose report might be trusted. They despatched them accordingly. Concerning these Themistocles secretly sent word to the Athenians to detain them as far as possible without putting them under open constraint, and not to let them go until they had themselves returned. For his colleagues had now joined him, Abronichus, son of Lysicles, and Aristides, son of Lysimachus, with the news that the wall was sufficiently advanced; and he feared that when the Lacedaemonians heard the facts, they might refuse to let them go. So the Athenians detained the envoys according to his message, and Themistocles had an audience with the Lacedaemonians, and at last openly told them that Athens was now fortified sufficiently to protect its inhabitants; that any embassy which the Lacedaemonians or their allies might wish to send to them, should in future proceed on the assumption that the people to whom they were going was able to distinguish both its own and the general interests. That when the Athenians thought fit to abandon their city and to embark in their ships, they ventured on that perilous step without consulting them; and that on the other hand, wherever they had deliberated with the Lacedaemonians, they had proved themselves to be in judgment second to none. That they now thought it fit that their city should have a wall, and that this would be more for the advantage of both the citizens of Athens and the Hellenic confederacy; for without equal military strength it was impossible to contribute equal or fair counsel to the common interest. It followed, he observed, either that all the members of the confederacy should be without walls, or that the present step should be considered a right one.

The Lacedaemonians did not betray any open signs of anger against the Athenians at what they heard. The embassy, it seems, was prompted not by a desire to obstruct, but to guide the counsels of their government: besides, Spartan feeling was at that time very friendly towards Athens on account of the patriotism which she had displayed in the struggle with the Mede. Still the defeat of their wishes could not but cause them secret annoyance. The envoys of each state departed home without complaint.

In this way the Athenians walled their city in a little while. To this day the building shows signs of the haste of its execution; the foundations are laid of stones of all kinds, and in some places not wrought or fitted, but placed just in the order in which they were brought by the different hands; and many columns, too, from tombs and sculptured stones were put in with the rest. For the bounds of the city were extended at every point of the circumference; and so they laid hands on everything without exception in their haste. Themistocles also persuaded them to finish the walls of Piraeus, which had been begun before, in his year of office as archon; being influenced alike by the fineness of a locality that has three natural harbours, and by the great start which the Athenians would gain in the acquisition of power by becoming a naval people. For he first ventured to tell them to stick to the sea and forthwith began to lay the foundations of the empire. It was by his advice, too, that they built the walls of that thickness which can still be discerned round Piraeus, the stones being brought up by two waggons meeting each other. Between the walls thus formed there was neither rubble nor mortar, but great stones hewn square and fitted together, cramped to each other on the outside with iron and lead. About half the height that he intended was finished. His idea was by their size and thickness to keep off the attacks of an enemy; he thought that they might be adequately defended by a small garrison of invalids, and the rest be freed for service in the fleet. For the fleet claimed most of his attention. He saw, as I think, that the approach by sea was easier for the king's army than that by land: he also thought Piraeus more valuable than the upper city; indeed, he was always advising the Athenians, if a day should come when they were hard pressed by land, to go down into Piraeus, and defy the world with their fleet.[1] Thus, therefore, the Athenians completed their wall, and commenced their other buildings immediately after the retreat of the Mede.

Meanwhile Pausanias, son of Cleombrotus, was sent out from Lacedaemon as commander-in-chief of the Hellenes, with twenty ships from Peloponnese. With him sailed the Athenians with thirty ships, and a number of the other allies. They made an expedition against Cyprus and subdued most of the island, and afterwards against Byzantium, which was in the hands of the Medes, and compelled it to surrender. This event took place while the Spartans were still supreme. But the violence of Pausanias had already begun to be disagreeable to the Hellenes, particularly to the Ionians and the newly liberated populations. These resorted to the Athenians and requested them as their kinsmen to become their leaders, and to stop any attempt at violence on the part of Pausanias. The Athenians accepted their overtures, and determined to put down any attempt of the kind and to settle everything else as their interests might seem to demand. In the meantime the

1. This advice was later improved upon by the building of the long walls connecting the city of Athens to the port of Piraeus. Athens thereby became in effect an island, impregnable as long as she could command the sea.

Lacedaemonians recalled Pausanias for an investigation of the reports which had reached them. Manifold and grave accusations had been brought against him by Hellenes arriving in Sparta; and, to all appearance, there had been in him more of the mimicry of a despot than of the attitude of a general. As it happened, his recall came just at the time when the hatred which he had inspired had induced the allies to desert him, the soldiers from Peloponnese excepted, and to range themselves by the side of the Athenians. On his arrival at Lacedaemon, he was censured for his private acts of oppression, but was acquitted on the heaviest counts and pronounced not guilty; it must be known that the charge of Medism formed one of the principal, and to all appearance one of the best-founded articles against him. The Lacedaemonians did not, however, restore him to his command, but sent out Dorkis and certain others with a small force; who found the allies no longer inclined to concede to them the supremacy. Perceiving this they departed, and the Lacedaemonians did not send out any to succeed them. They feared for those who went out a deterioration similar to that observable in Pausanias; besides, they desired to be rid of the Median war, and were satisfied of the competency of the Athenians for the position, and of their friendship at the time towards themselves.

The Athenians having thus succeeded to the supremacy by the voluntary act of the allies through their hatred of Pausanias, fixed which cities were to contribute money against the barbarian, which ships; their professed object being to retaliate for their sufferings by ravishing the king's country. Now was the time that the office of 'Treasurers for Hellas' was first instituted by the Athenians. These officers received the tribute, as the money contributed was called. The tribute was first fixed at four hundred and sixty talents. The common treasury was at Delos, and the congresses were held in the temple. Their supremacy commenced with independent allies who acted on the resolutions of a common congress. It was marked by the following undertakings in war and in administration during the interval between the Median and the present war, against the barbarian, against their own rebel allies, and against the Peloponnesian powers which would come in contact with them on various occasions. My excuse for relating these events, and for venturing on this digression, is that this passage of history has been omitted by all my predecessors, who have confined themselves either to Hellenic history before the Median war, or to the Median war itself. Hellanicus, it is true, did touch on these events in his Athenian history; but he is somewhat concise and not accurate in his dates. Besides, the history of these events contains an explanation of the growth of the Athenian empire.[2]

# 52 The Ideal of Athenian Democracy

Democracy was more than a form of government; to its admirers it was a way of life. The individual with whose name the Athenian democracy is forever linked in all its achievements and its failings was the statesman Pericles. For over thirty years, from 461 until his death in 429 B.C., he enjoyed the confidence of the people, who accepted his leadership and expressed their willingness to follow by electing him year after year to the board of ten generals, one of the few offices to which election was by vote, not by lot, and to which a man could be re-elected an indefinite number of times.

In his personality and in his policies Pericles epitomized the greatness of Athens, and it is from his lips that we have the ideal that Athenian democracy sought to be. The "Funeral Oration" that Pericles delivered in 430 B.C. in honor of the Athenians who had died in the first year of the Peloponnesian War is known to us from the version of the actual address included by Thucydides in his *History of the Peloponnesian War* 2.34–46. If it is read aloud, some idea may be gained of the effectiveness of this famous speech, which has often been compared to the Gettysburg Address. The translation is that of R. Crawley.

◈◈◈◈◈

In the same winter the Athenians gave a funeral at the public cost to those who had first fallen in this war. It was a custom of their ancestors, and the manner of it is as follows. Three days before the ceremony, the bones of the dead are laid out in a tent which has been erected; and their friends

---

2.  Hellanicus' work has not come down to us, and Thucydides' "digression" is the only connected account we have of the growth of the Athenian empire. It is compact and indeed elliptical enough to be extremely difficult to follow. Three distinct aspects of Athenian imperialism can be discerned in Thucydides' narrative: (1) efforts to enlarge the maritime empire; (2) extension of Athenian control over the subject-allies of the Delian League; (3) attempts to acquire territory in mainland Greece, bringing Athens into direct conflict with Sparta. Modern scholars have labored to expand the bare details of Thucydides, but the important "Fifty Years," the "golden age of Athens," remains one of the least satisfactorily known of the crucial periods of ancient history.

bring to their relatives such offerings as they please. In the funeral procession cypress coffins are borne in cars, one for each tribe; the bones of the deceased being placed in the coffin of their tribe. Among these is carried one empty bier decked for the missing, that is, for those whose bodies could not be recovered. Any citizen or stranger who pleases, joins in the procession: and the female relatives are there to wail at the burial. The dead are laid in the public sepulchre in the most beautiful suburb of the city, in which those who fall in war are always buried; with the exception of those slain at Marathon, who for their singular and extraordinary valour were interred on the spot where they fell. After the bodies have been laid in the earth, a man chosen by the state, of approved wisdom and eminent reputation, pronounces over them an appropriate panegyric; after which all retire. Such is the manner of the burying; and throughout the whole of the war, whenever the occasion arose, the established custom was observed. Meanwhile these were the first that had fallen, and Pericles, son of Xanthippus, was chosen to pronounce their eulogium. When the proper time arrived, he advanced from the sepulchre to an elevated platform in order to be heard by as many of the crowd as possible, and spoke as follows:

"Most of my predecessors in this place have commended him who made this speech part of the law, telling us that it is well that it should be delivered at the burial of those who fall in battle. For myself, I should have thought that the worth which had displayed itself in deeds, would be sufficiently rewarded by honours also shown by deeds; such as you now see in this funeral prepared at the people's cost. And I could have wished that the reputations of many brave men were not to be imperilled in the mouth of a single individual, to stand or fall according as he spoke well or ill. For it is hard to speak properly upon a subject where it is even difficult to convince your hearers that you are speaking the truth. On the one hand, the friend who is familiar with every fact of the story, may think that some point has not been set forth with that fulness which he wishes and knows it to deserve; on the other, he who is a stranger to the matter may be led by envy to suspect exaggeration if he hears anything above his own nature. For men can endure to hear others praised only so long as they can severally persuade themselves of their own ability to equal the actions recounted: when this point is passed, envy comes in and with it incredulity. However, since our ancestors have stamped this custom with their approval, it becomes my duty to obey the law and to try to satisfy your several wishes and opinions as best I may.

"I shall begin with our ancestors: it is both just and proper that they should have the honour of the first mention on an occasion like the present. They dwelt in the country without break in the succession from generation to generation, and handed it down free to the present time by their valour. And if our more remote ancestors deserve praise, much more do our own fathers, who added to their inheritance the empire which we now possess, and spared no pains to be able to leave their acquisitions to us of the present generation. Lastly, there are few parts of our dominions that have not been augmented by those of us here, who are still more or less in the vigour of life; while the mother country has been furnished by us with everything that can enable her to depend on her own resources whether for war or for peace. That part of our history which tells of the military achievements which gave us our several possessions, or of the ready valour with which either we or our fathers stemmed the tide of Hellenic or foreign aggression, is a theme too familiar to my hearers for me to dilate on, and I shall therefore pass it by. But what was the road by which we reached our position, what the form of government under which our greatness grew, what the national habits out of which it sprang; these are questions which I may try to solve before I proceed to my panegyric upon these men; since I think this to be a subject upon which on the present occasion a speaker may properly dwell, and to which the whole assemblage, whether citizens or foreigners, may listen with advantage.

"Our constitution does not copy the laws of neighbouring states; we are rather a pattern to others than imitators ourselves. Its administration favours the many instead of the few; this is why it is called a democracy. If we look to the laws, they afford equal justice to all in their private differences; if to social standing, advancement in public life falls to reputation for capacity, class considerations not being allowed to interfere with merit; nor again does poverty bar the way, if a man is able to serve the state, he is not hindered by the obscurity of his condition. The freedom which we enjoy in our government extends also to our ordinary life. There, far from exercising a jealous surveillance over each other, we do not feel called upon to be angry with our neighbour for doing what he likes, or even to indulge in those injurious looks which cannot fail to be offensive, although they inflict no positive penalty. But all this ease in our private relations does not make us lawless as citizens. Against this fear is our chief safeguard, teaching us to obey the magistrates and the laws, particularly such as regard the protection of the injured, whether they are actually on the statute book, or belong to that code which, although unwritten, yet cannot be broken without acknowledged disgrace.

[ 426 ]

"Further, we provide plenty of means for the mind to refresh itself from business. We celebrate games and sacrifices all the year round, and the elegance of our private establishments forms a daily source of pleasure and helps to banish the spleen; while the magnitude of our city draws the produce of the world into our harbour, so that to the Athenian the fruits of other countries are as familiar a luxury as those of his own.

"If we turn to our military policy, there also we differ from our antagonists. We throw open our city to the world, and never by alien acts exclude foreigners from any opportunity of learning or observing, although the eyes of an enemy may occasionally profit by our liberality; trusting less in system and policy than to the native spirit of our citizens; while in education, where our rivals from their very cradles by a painful discipline seek after manliness, at Athens we live exactly as we please, and yet are just as ready to encounter every legitimate danger. In proof of this it may be noticed that the Lacedaemonians do not invade our country alone, but bring with them all their confederates; while we Athenians advance unsupported into the territory of a neighbour, and fighting upon a foreign soil usually vanquish with ease men who are defending their homes. Our united force was never yet encountered by any enemy, because we have at once to attend to our marine and to despatch our citizens by land upon a hundred different services; so that, wherever they engage with some such fraction of our strength, a success against a detachment is magnified into a victory over the nation, and a defeat into a reverse suffered at the hands of our entire people. And yet if with habits not of labour but of ease, and courage not of art but of nature, we are still willing to encounter danger, we have the double advantage of escaping the experience of hardships in anticipation and of facing them in the hour of need as fearlessly as those who are never free from them.

"Nor are these the only points in which our city is worthy of admiration. We cultivate refinement without extravagance and knowledge without effeminacy; wealth we employ more for use than for show, and place the real disgrace of poverty not in owning to the fact but in declining the struggle against it. Our public men have, besides politics, their private affairs to attend to, and our ordinary citizens, though occupied with the pursuits of industry, are still fair judges of public matters; for, unlike any other nation, regarding him who takes no part in these duties not as unambitious but as useless, we Athenians are able to judge at all events if we cannot originate, and instead of looking on discussion as a stumbling-block in the way of action, we think it an indispensable preliminary to any wise

[ 427 ]

action at all. Again, in our enterprises we present the singular spectacle of daring and deliberation, each carried to its highest point, and both united in the same persons; although usually decision is the fruit of ignorance, hesitation of reflexion. But the palm of courage will surely be adjudged most justly to those, who best know the difference between hardship and pleasure and yet are never tempted to shrink from danger. In generosity we are equally singular, acquiring our friends by conferring not by receiving favours. Yet, of course, the doer of the favour is the firmer friend of the two, in order by continued kindness to keep the recipient in his debt; while the debtor feels less keenly from the very consciousness that the return he makes will be a payment, not a free gift. And it is only the Athenians who, fearless of consequences, confer their benefits not from calculations of expediency, but in the confidence of liberality.

"In short, I say that as a city we are the school of Hellas; while I doubt if the world can produce a man, who where he has only himself to depend upon, is equal to so many emergencies, and graced by so happy a versatility as the Athenian. And that this is no mere boast thrown out for the occasion, but plain matter of fact, the power of the state acquired by these habits proves. For Athens alone of her contemporaries is found when tested to be greater than her reputation, and alone gives no occasion to her assailants to blush at the antagonist by whom they have been worsted, or to her subjects to question her title by merit to rule. Rather, the admiration of the present and succeeding ages will be ours, since we have not left our power without witness, but have shown it by mighty proofs; and far from needing a Homer for our panegyrist, or other of his craft whose verses might charm for the moment only for the impression which they gave to melt at the touch of fact, we have forced every sea and land to be the highway of our daring, and everywhere, whether for evil or for good, have left imperishable monuments behind us. Such is the Athens for which these men, in the assertion of their resolve not to lose her, nobly fought and died; and well may every one of their survivors be ready to suffer in her cause.

"Indeed if I have dwelt at some length upon the character of our country, it has been to show that our stake in the struggle is not the same as theirs who have no such blessings to lose, and also that the panegyric of the men over whom I am now speaking might be by definite proofs established. That panegyric is now in a great measure complete; for the Athens that I have celebrated is only what the heroism of these and their like have made her, men whose fame, unlike that of most Hellenes, will be found to be only commensurate with their deserts. And if a test of worth be wanted, it is to be found in their closing scene, and this not only in the cases in which it set the final seal upon their merit, but also in those in which it gave the first intimation of their having any. For there is justice in the claim that steadfastness in his country's battles should be as a cloak to cover a man's other imperfections; since the good action has blotted out the bad, and his merit as a citizen more than outweighed his demerits as an individual. But none of these allowed either wealth with its prospect of future enjoyment to unnerve his spirit, or poverty with its hope of a day of freedom and riches to tempt him to shrink from danger. No, holding that vengeance upon their enemies was more to be desired than any personal blessings, and reckoning this to be the most glorious of hazards, they joyfully determined to accept the risk, to make sure of their vengeance and to let their wishes wait; and while committing to hope the uncertainty of final success, in the business before them they thought fit to act boldly and trust in themselves. Thus choosing to die resisting, rather than to live submitting, they fled only from dishonour, but met danger face to face, and after one brief moment, while at the summit of their fortune, escaped, not from their fear, but from their glory.

"So died these men as became Athenians. You, their survivors, must determine to have as unaltering a resolution in the field, though you may pray that it may have a happier issue. And not contented with ideas derived only from words of the advantages which are bound up with the defence of your country, though these would furnish a valuable text to a speaker even before an audience so alive to them as the present, you must yourselves realise the power of Athens, and feed your eyes upon her from day to day, till love of her fills your hearts; and then when all her greatness shall break upon you, you must reflect that it was by courage, sense of duty, and a keen feeling of honour in action that men were enabled to win all this, and that no personal failure in an enterprise could make them consent to deprive their country of their valour, but they laid it at her feet as the most glorious contribution that they could offer. For this offering of their lives made in common by them all they each of them individually received that renown which never grows old, and for a sepulchre, not so much that in which their bones have been deposited, but that noblest of shrines wherein their glory is laid up to be eternally remembered upon every occasion on which deed or story shall fall for its commemoration. For heroes have the whole earth for their tomb; and in lands far from their own, where the column with its epitaph declares it, there is enshrined in every breast a record unwritten with no tablet to preserve it, except that of the heart. These take as your model, and judging happiness to be the fruit of freedom and freedom of valour, never decline the dangers of war. For it is not the miserable that would most justly be unsparing of their lives; these have nothing to hope for: it is rather they to whom continued life may bring reverses as yet unknown, and to whom a fall, if it came, would be most tremendous in its consequences. And surely, to a man of spirit, the degradation of cowardice must be immeasurably more grievous than the unfelt death which strikes him in the midst of his strength and patriotism!

"Comfort, therefore, not condolence, is what I have to offer to the parents of the dead who may be here. Numberless are the chances to which, as they know, the life of man is subject; but fortunate indeed are they who draw for their lot a death so glorious as that which has caused your mourning, and to whom life has been so exactly measured as to terminate in the happiness in which it has been passed. Still I know that this is a hard saying, especially when those are in question of whom you will constantly be reminded by seeing in the homes of others blessings of which once you also boasted: for grief is felt not so much for the want of what we have never known, as for the loss of that to which we have been long accustomed. Yet you who are still of an age to beget children must bear up in the hope of having others in their stead; not only will they help you to forget those whom you have lost, but will be to the state at once a reinforcement and a security; for never can a fair or just policy be expected of the citizen who does not, like his fellows, bring to the decision the interests and apprehensions of a father. While those of you who have passed your prime must congratulate yourselves with the thought that the best part of your life was fortunate, and that the brief span that remains will be cheered by the fame of the departed. For it is only the love of honour that never grows old; and honour it is, not gain, as some would have it, that rejoices the heart of age and helplessness.

"Turning to the sons or brothers of the dead, I see an arduous struggle before you. When a man is gone, all are wont to praise him, and should your merit be ever so transcendent, you will still find it difficult not merely to overtake, but even to approach their renown. The living have envy to contend with, while those who are no longer in our path are honoured with a goodwill into which rivalry does not enter. On the other hand, if I must say anything on the subject of female excellence to those of you who will now be in widowhood, it will be all comprised in this brief exhortation. Great will be your glory in not falling short of your natural character; and greatest will be hers who is least talked of among the men whether for good or for bad.

[ 430 ]

"My task is now finished. I have performed it to the best of my ability, and in words, at least, the requirements of the law are now satisfied. If deeds be in question, those who are here interred have received part of their honours already, and for the rest, their children will be brought up till manhood at the public expense:[1] the state thus offers a valuable prize, as the garland of victory in this race of valour, for the reward both of those who have fallen and their survivors. And where the rewards for merit are greatest, there are found the best citizens.

"And now that you have brought to a close your lamentations for your relatives, you may depart."

# 53 *An Anti-Democratic View*

Modern scholars have disputed whether Athens was in reality a democracy or, as Thucydides put it, ostensibly a democracy but in fact a state ruled by its "first citizen," Pericles. It seemed clear to contemporary opponents of the Athenian democracy that it was indeed a democracy that they opposed. Their criticisms are based on that. A political pamphlet vigorously expressing its author's disapproval of the democracy has come down to us among the writings of Xenophon. Scholars are generally agreed that it is not a work by Xenophon, but comes from the pen of an opponent of democracy writing some decades before Xenophon at the time when the Periclean democracy was at its height.

The English scholar Alfred E. Zimmern nicknamed this unknown pamphleteer "The Old Oligarch." His work, sometimes referred to as Pseudo-Xenophon's "Athenian Constitution," follows in the translation of H. G. Dakyns as revised by E. G. Sihler.

⊛⊛⊛⊛⊛

Now, as concerning the Polity of the Athenians, and the type or manner of constitution which they have chosen, I praise it not, in so far as the very choice involves the welfare of the baser folk as opposed to that of the better class. I repeat, I withhold my praise so far; but, given the fact that this is the type agreed upon, I propose to show that they set about its preservation

SOURCE: G. W. Botsford and E. G. Sihler, eds., *Hellenic Civilization* (Columbia University Records of Civilization, Vol. 1) (New York: Columbia University Press, 1929). Reprinted by permission of the publishers.
1.  On the subject of social welfare in Athens, see Selection 68.

in the right way; and that those other transactions in connection with it, which are looked upon as blunders by the rest of the Hellenic world, are the reverse.

In the first place, I maintain, it is only just that the poorer classes and the People of Athens should have the advantage over the men of birth and wealth, seeing that it is the people who row the vessels, and put round the city her girdle of power. For the steersman, the boatswain, the commanders of fifty, the lookout-man at the prow, the shipwright—these are the people who engird the city with power far rather than her heavy infantry and men of birth and quality. This being the case, it seems only just that offices of state should be thrown open to every one both by the lot and by the show of hands, and that the right of speech should belong to any citizen who likes, without restriction. Further, there are many of these offices which, according as they are in good or in bad hands, are a source of safety or of danger to the People and in these the People prudently abstain from sharing; as, for instance, they do not think it incumbent on themselves to share in the drawing of lots for general or commander of cavalry. The sovereign People recognize the fact that in foregoing the personal exercise of these offices and leaving them to the control of the more competent citizens, they secure the balance of advantage to themselves. It is only those departments of government which bring emolument and assist the private households that the People care to keep in their own hands.

In the next place, in regard to what some people are puzzled to explain— the fact that everywhere greater consideration is shown to the base, to poor people and to common folk, than to persons of good quality—so far from being a matter of surprise, this, as can be shown, is the keystone of the preservation of the democracy. It is these poor people, this common folk, this riff-raff, whose prosperity, combined with the growth of their numbers, enhance the democracy. Whereas a shifting of fortune to the ad- vantage of the wealthy and the better classes implies the establishment on the part of the commonalty of a strong power in opposition to itself. In fact, all the world over the cream of society is in opposition to the democracy. Naturally, since the smallest amount of intemperance and in- justice, together with the highest scrupulousness in the pursuit of excellence, is to be found in the ranks of the better class, while within the ranks of the People will be found the greatest amount of ignorance, disorderliness and rascality—poverty acting as a strong incentive to base conduct, not to speak of lack of education and ignorance, traceable to the want of means which afflicts some portions of mankind.

[ 432 ]

The objection may be raised that it was a mistake to allow the universal right of speech and a seat in council. These privileges should have been reserved for the cleverest, the flower of the community. But here again it will be found that they are acting with wise deliberation in granting to even the baser sort the right of speech, for supposing only the better people might speak, or sit in council, blessings would fall to the lot of those like themselves, but to the commonalty the reverse of blessings. Whereas now, any one who likes, any base fellow, may get up and discover something to the advantage of himself and his equals. It may be retorted: "And what sort of advantage either for himself or for the People can such a fellow be expected to discern?" The answer is, that in their judgment the ignorance and the baseness of this fellow, together with his good will, are worth a great deal more to them than your superior person's virtue and wisdom, coupled with aversion. What it comes to, therefore, is that a state founded upon such institutions will not be the best state; but, given a democracy, these are the right means to secure its preservation. The People, it must be borne in mind, do not demand that the city should be well governed and themselves slaves. They desire to be free and to be masters. As to bad legislation, they do not concern themselves about that. In fact, what you believe to be poor legislation is the very source of the People's strength and freedom.

But if you seek for good laws, in the first place you will see the cleverest members of the community laying down the laws for the rest. And in the next place, the better class will curb and chastise the lower orders; the better class will deliberate in behalf of the state, and not suffer men in fits of madness to sit in council, or to speak or vote in the assembly. No doubt; but under the weight of such blessings the People would in a very short time be reduced to slavery.

Another point is the extraordinary amount of license granted to slaves and resident aliens at Athens, where a blow is illegal, and a slave will not step aside to let you pass him in the street. I will explain the reason of this peculiar custom. Supposing it were legal for a slave to be beaten by a free citizen, or for a resident alien or freedman to be beaten by a citizen, it would frequently happen that an Athenian might be mistaken for a slave or an alien and receive a beating; since the Athenian People are not better clothed than the slave or alien, nor in personal appearance is there any superiority.

Or if the fact itself that slaves in Athens are allowed to indulge in luxury, and indeed in some cases to live magnificently, be found astonishing, this too, it can be shown, is done of set purpose. Where we have a naval power dependent upon wealth, we must perforce be slaves to our slaves, in order that we may get in our slave-rents, and let the real slave go free. Where you have wealthy slaves it ceases to be advantageous that my slave should stand in awe of you. In Lacedaemon my slave does stand in awe of you. But if your slave is in awe of me, the chances are he will give away his own money to avoid running a risk in his own person. It is for this reason then that we have established an equality of speech between our slaves and free men; and again between our resident aliens and full citizens, because the city stands in need of her resident aliens to meet the requirements of such a multiplicity of arts and for the purposes of her navy. That is, I repeat, the justification of the equality conferred upon our resident aliens.

Citizens devoting their time to gymnastics and to the cultivation of music are not to be found in Athens; the sovereign People have dissolved their power, not from any disbelief in the beauty and honor of such training, but recognising the fact that these are things the cultivation of which is beyond their power. On the same principle, in the case of the choregia, the gymnasiarchy, and the trierarchy,[1] the fact is recognised that it is the rich man who trains the chorus, and the People, for whom the chorus is trained; it is the rich man who is trierarch or gymnasiarch, and the People that profit by their labors. In fact, what the People deem proper is to make wages by singing and running and dancing and manning the vessels but only in order that they may be the gainer, while the rich are made poorer. Thus too in the courts of justice, justice is not more an object of concern to the jurymen than what touches personal advantage.[2]

To speak next of the allies, and in reference to the point that emissaries from Athens come out and, according to common opinion, calumniate and vent their hatred upon the better sort of people, this is done on the principle that the ruler cannot help being hated by those whom he rules; but that if wealth and respectability are to wield power in the subject cities, the empire of the Athenian People has but a short lease of existence. This explains why the better people are punished with infamy, robbed of their money, driven from their homes, and put to death, while the baser sort are promoted to honor. On the other hand, the better Athenians throw their aegis over the better class in the allied cities. And why? Because they recog-

1.   The choregia, gymnasiarchy, and trierarchy were *leiturgies*, that is, public services performed by wealthy citizens at their own expense. Modern historians tend to see in the leiturgical system a substitute for a tax on property. Direct taxation imposed upon citizens was always offensive to Greek polis tradition.
2.   For another antagonistic evaluation of the democratic jury system, see Selection 63.

nise that it is to the interest of their own class at all times to protect the best element in the cities. It may be urged that if it comes to strength and power, the real strength of Athens lies in the capacity of her allies to contribute their money quota. But to the democratic mind it appears a higher advantage still for the individual Athenian to get hold of the wealth of the allies, leaving them only enough to live upon and to cultivate their estates, but powerless to harbor treacherous designs.

Again, it is looked upon as a mistaken policy on the part of the Athenian democracy to compel her allies to voyage to Athens in order to have their cases tried. On the other hand, it is easy to reckon up what a number of advantages the Athenian People derive from the practice impugned. In the first place, there is the steady receipt of salaries throughout the year derived from the court fees. Next, it enables them to manage the affairs of the allied states while seated at home without the expense of naval expeditions. Thirdly, they thus preserve the partisans of the democracy, and ruin her opponents in the law courts. Whereas, supposing the several allied states tried their cases at home, being inspired by hostility to Athens, they would destroy those of their own citizens whose friendship to the Athenian People was most marked. But besides all this the democracy derives the following advantages from hearing the cases of her allies in Athens. In the first place, the one per cent levied in Peiraeus is an advantage to the state;[3] again, the owner of a house for a number of families does better, and so, too, the owner of a pair of beasts, or of slaves to be let out for hire. Again, heralds and criers are a class of people who fare better owing to the sojourn of the allies at Athens. Further still, supposing the allies had not to resort to Athens for the hearing of cases, only those of the Athenians who sail out to them would be held in honor, such as the general, or trierarch, or ambassador; whereas now every single individual among the allies is forced to pay flattery to the People of Athens because he knows that he must betake himself to Athens and lose or win his case at the bar, not of any stray set of judges, but of the sovereign People themselves, such being the law and custom at Athens. He is compelled to behave as a suppliant in the courts of justice, and when some juryman comes into court, to grasp his hand. For this reason, therefore, the allies find themselves more and more in the position of slaves to the democracy of Athens.

Furthermore, owing to the possession of property beyond the limits of Attica, and the exercise of magistracies which take them into regions beyond the frontier, they and their attendants have insensibly acquired the

3.  This was the amount of duty levied on imports and exports.

art of navigation. A man who is perpetually voyaging is forced to handle the oar, he and his slave alike, and to learn the terms familiar in seamanship. Hence a stock of skilful navigators is produced, bred upon a wide experience of voyaging and practice. They have learnt their business, some in piloting a small craft, others a merchant vessel, whilst others have been drafted off from these activities for service on a ship-of-war. So that the majority of them are able to row the moment they set foot on board a vessel, having been in a state of preliminary practice all their lives.

As to the heavy infantry, an arm the deficiency of which at Athens is well recognized, this is how the matter stands. They recognize the fact that, in reference to the hostile power, they are themselves inferior, and must be, even if their heavy infantry were more numerous. But relatively to the allies, who pay the tribute and are quite strong on land, they are even satisfied to have the hoplite[4] element carry on the government, if they (the Athenians) are stronger than the allies. Apart from all else, to a certain extent fortune must be held responsible for the actual condition. The subjects of a power which is dominant by land have it open to them to form *one* commonwealth from several small states and fight with all their forces gathered into a compact union. But with the subjects of a naval power it is different. As far as they are groups of islanders, it is impossible for their states to meet together for united action; for the sea lies between them, and the dominant power is master of the sea. And even if it were possible for them to assemble in some single island unobserved, they will only do so to perish by famine. And as to the states subject to Athens which are not islanders, but situated on the continent, the larger are held in check by apprehension, and the small ones absolutely by want, since there is no state in existence which does not depend upon imports and exports, and these she will forfeit if she does not lend a willing ear to those who are masters by sea.

In the next place, a power dominant by sea can do certain things which a land power is debarred from doing; as, for instance, ravage the territory of a superior, since it is always possible to coast along to some point, where either there is no hostile force to deal with or merely a small body; and in case of an advance in force on the part of the enemy they can take to their ships and sail away. Such a performance is attended with less difficulty than that experienced by the relieving force on land. Again, it is open to a power so dominating by sea to leave its own territory and sail off on as long a

4. The hoplite, or heavily armed foot-soldier, was the traditional backbone of a Greek fighting force. Since he provided his own equipment, he was normally from the wealthier classes of citizens.

voyage as you please, whereas the land power cannot place more than a few days' journey between itself and its own territory, for marches are slow affairs; and it is not possible for an army on the march to have food supplies to last for any great length of time. Such an army must either march through friendly territory or it must force a way by victory in battle. The voyager meanwhile has it in his power to disembark at any point where he finds himself in superior force, or, at the worst, to coast by until he reaches either a friendly district or an enemy too weak to resist. Again, those diseases to which the fruits of the earth are liable as visitations from Zeus fall severely on a land power, but are scarcely felt by the naval power, for such sicknesses do not visit the whole earth everywhere at once. Thus the ruler of the sea can get in supplies from a thriving district.

If one may descend to more trifling particulars, it is to this same lordship of the sea that the Athenians owe the discovery, in the first place, of many of the luxuries of life through intercourse with other countries. Thus it is that the choice things of Sicily and Italy, of Cyprus and Egypt and Lydia, of Pontus, of Peloponnese, or wheresoever else it be, are all swept, as it were, into one center, and all owing, as I say, to their maritime empire. Again, in process of listening to every form of speech, they have selected for themselves this from one place and that from another. Hence while the rest of the Hellenes employ each pretty much their own peculiar mode of speech, habit of life, and style of dress, the Athenians have adopted a composite type, to which all sections of Hellas and the foreigner alike, have contributed.

As regards sacrifices and temples and festivals and sacred enclosures, the Attic Democracy sees that it is not possible for every poor citizen to do sacrifice and hold festival, or to set up temples and to inhabit a large and beautiful city. But it has hit upon a means of meeting the difficulty. They sacrifice—that is, the whole state sacrifices—at the public cost a large number of victims; but it is the Attic Democracy that keeps holiday and distributes the victims by lot amongst its members. Rich men have in some cases private gymnasia and baths with dressing-rooms, but the People take care to have built at the public cost a number of palaestras, dressing-rooms, and bathing establishments for their own special use, and the mob gets the benefit of the majority of these luxuries rather than the select few or the well-to-do.

As to wealth, the Athenians are exceptionally placed with regard to Hellenic and foreign communities alike, in their ability to hold it. For given that some state or other is rich in timber for shipbuilding, where is it to find a market for the product except by persuading the ruler of the sea? Or suppose the wealth of some state or other to consist of iron, or may be of bronze, or of hemp, where will it find a market except by permission of the supreme maritime power? Yet these are the very things, you see, which I need for my ships. Timber I must have from one, and from another iron, from a third bronze, from a fourth hemp, from a fifth wax, etc. Besides they will not suffer our antagonists in these parts to carry these products elsewhither, or they will cease to use the sea. Accordingly I, without one stroke of labor, from land possess all these good things, thanks to my supremacy on the sea; whilst not a single other state possesses as much as two of them; not timber, for instance, and hemp together, has the same city, but where hemp is abundant, the soil will be light and devoid of timber. And in the same way bronze and iron will not be products of the same city. The same rule holds for the rest, never two, or at best three, in one state, but one thing here and another thing there.

Moreover, above and beyond what has been said, the coastline of all the mainland presents either some jutting promontory, or adjacent island, or narrow strait of some sort, so that those who are masters of the sea can come to moorings at one of these points and inflict injury on the inhabitants of the mainland.

There is just one thing which the Athenians lack. Supposing they were the inhabitants of an island, and were still as now rulers of the sea, they would have had it in their power to inflict whatever mischief they liked, and to suffer no evil in return (as long as they kept command of the sea), neither the ravaging of their territory nor the expectation of an enemy's approach. At present the farming portion of the community and the wealthy landowners are ready to cringe before the enemy overmuch, whilst the People, knowing full well that, come what may, not one stock or stone of their property will suffer, nothing will be cut down, nothing burnt, live in freedom from alarm, without fawning at the enemy's approach. Besides this, there is another fear from which they would have been exempt in an island home—the apprehension of the city's being at any time betrayed by a handful of men and the gates thrown open, and an enemy bursting suddenly in. How could such incidents have taken place if an island had been their home? Again, had they inhabited an island there would have been no stirring of sedition against the people; whereas at present, in the event of a rising, those who set it on foot would base their hopes of success on the introduction of an enemy by land. But a people inhabiting an island would be free from all anxiety on that score.

[ 438 ]

Since, however, they did not chance to inhabit an island from the first, what they actually do is this—they deposit their property in the islands, trusting to their command of the sea, and they suffer the soil of Attica to be ravaged without a sigh. To expend pity on that, they know, would be to deprive themselves of other blessings still more precious.

Further, states oligarchically governed are forced to ratify their alliances and solemn oaths in a substantial fashion, and if they fail to abide by their treaties, the offence, by whomsoever committed, lies nominally at the door of the oligarchs who entered upon the contract. But in the case of engagements entered into by a democracy it is open to the People to throw the blame on the single individual who spoke in favor of some measure, or who put it to the vote, and to enter a denial for the rest of the citizens, averring that one was not present, or did not approve of the terms of the agreement. Inquiries are made in a full meeting of the People, and should any of these things be disapproved of, the Demos has devised already innumerable excuses to avoid doing whatever they do not wish. If too any mischief should spring out of any deliberations of the assembly, the People charge that a handful of men acting against the interests of the citizens have ruined the state. But if any good result ensue, they, the People, at once take the credit of that to themselves.

In the same spirit it is not allowed to caricature on the comic stage or otherwise libel the People, because they do not care to hear themselves ill spoken of. But if any one has a desire to satirize his neighbor, he has full leave to do so. And this because they are well aware that, as a general rule, the person caricatured does not belong to the People, or the masses. He is more likely to be some wealthy or well-born person, or man of means and influence. In fact, but few poor people and of the popular stamp incur the comic lash, or if they do, they have brought it on themselves by excessive love of meddling or some covetous self-seeking at the expense of the People, so that no particular annoyance is felt at seeing such folk satirized.

What I venture to assert is therefore that the People of Athens have no difficulty in recognizing which of their citizens are of the better sort and which the opposite. Recognizing, accordingly, those who are serviceable and advantageous to themselves, even though they be base, the People love them; but the good folk they are disposed the rather to hate. This excellence of theirs, the People hold, is not ingrained in their nature for any good to itself, but rather for its injury. In direct opposition to this, there are some persons who, being born of the People, are yet by natural instinct not commoners. For my part I pardon the People their democracy, as indeed it is pardonable in any one to do good to himself. But the man who, not being himself one of the People, prefers to live in a state democratically governed rather than in an oligarchical state takes steps to commit wrong. He knows that a bad man has a better chance of slipping through the fingers of justice in a democratic than in an oligarchical state.

I repeat that my position concerning the polity of the Athenians is this: the type of polity is not to my taste, but given that a democratic form of government has been agreed upon, they do seem to me to go the right way to preserve the democracy by the adoption of the particular type which I have set forth.

But there are other objections brought, as I am aware, against the Athenians by certain people, and to this effect: It not seldom happens, they tell us, that a man is unable to transact a piece of business with the council or the People, even if he sit waiting a whole year. Now this does happen at Athens, and for no other reason save that, owing to the immense mass of affairs, they are unable to work off all the business on hand and dismiss the applicants. How in the world should they be able, considering in the first place, that they, the Athenians, have more festivals to celebrate than any other state throughout the length and breadth of Hellas? During these festivals necessarily the transaction of any sort of affairs of state is still more out of the question. In the next place, only consider the number of cases they have to decide,—private suits and public causes and scrutinies of accounts, etc.—more than the whole of the rest of mankind put together; while the council has multifarious points to advise upon concerning peace and war, concerning ways and means, concerning the framing and passing of laws, and concerning the thousand and one matters affecting the state perpetually occurring, and endless questions touching the allies, besides the receipt of the tribute, the superintendence of dockyards and temples, etc. I ask again, can any one find it at all surprising that, with all these affairs on their hands, they are unequal to attending to the business of all the world?

But some people tell us that if the applicant will only address himself to the council or the People with a fee in his hand, he will have his business done. For my part I would agree with these persons that a good many things are accomplished at Athens by dint of money; and I will add that a good many more still might be done, if the money flowed still more freely and from more pockets. One thing, however, I know full well, that as to transacting with every one of these applicants all he wants, the state could not do it, not even if all the gold and silver in the world were the inducement offered.

[ 440 ]

Here are some of the cases which have to be decided on. Some one fails to fit out his ship: judgment must be given. Another puts up a building on a piece of public land: again judgment must be given. Or to take another class of cases: adjudication has to be made between the choregi for the Dionysia, the Thargelia, the Panathenaea[5] year after year. And again in behalf of the gymnasiarchs a similar adjudication for the Panathenaea, the Prometheia, and the Hephaestia,[5] also year after year. Also as between the trierarchs, four hundred of whom are appointed each year; of these, too, any who choose must have their cases adjudicated on, year after year. But that is not all. There are various magistrates to examine and approve and decide between; there are orphans whose status must be examined; and guardians of prisoners to appoint. These, be it borne in mind, are all matters of yearly occurrence; while at intervals there are exemptions and abstentions from military service which call for adjudication, or in connection with some extraordinary misdemeanor, some case of outrage and violence of an exceptional character, or some charge of impiety. A whole list of others I simply omit; I am content to have named the most important part with the exception of the assessments of tribute which occur, as a rule, at intervals of five years.

I put it to you, then: can any one suppose that all or any of these disputes may dispense with adjudication? If so, will any one say which ought, and which ought not to be adjudicated on, there and then? If, on the other hand, we are forced to admit that these are all fair cases for adjudication, it follows of necessity that they should be decided during the twelve-month; since even now the boards of judges sitting right through the year are powerless to stay the tide of evildoing by reason of the multitude of the people.

So far so good. "But," some one will say, "try the cases you certainly must, but lessen the number of the jurors." Yet if so, it follows of necessity that unless the number of courts themselves are diminished, there will be only a few jurors sitting in each court, with the further consequence that in dealing with so small a body of jurors it will be easier for a litigant to present an invulnerable front to the court, and to bribe the whole body, to the great detriment of justice.

But besides this we cannot escape the conclusion that the Athenians have their festivals to keep, during which the courts cannot sit. As a matter of fact these festivals are twice as numerous as those of any other people.

5.   These were among the numerous public religious festivals celebrated at Athens, each of them requiring appointments to the *leiturgies* involved. The Dionysia are of particular interest in that it was in their celebration that there occurred the development of the classic drama.

However I will reckon them as merely equal to those of the state which has the fewest.

This being so, I maintain that it is not possible for business affairs at Athens to stand on any very different footing from the present, except to some slight extent, by adding here and deducting there. Any large modification is out of the question, short of curtailing the democracy itself. No doubt many expedients might be discovered for improving the constitution, but if the problems be to discover some adequate means of making it better while at the same time the democracy is to remain intact, I say it is not easy to do this, except, as I have just stated, to the extent of some trifling addition here or deduction there.

There is another point in which it is sometimes felt that the Athenians are ill advised, in their adoption, namely, of the less respectable party, in those states divided by faction. But they do this advisedly. If they chose the more respectable, they would not be choosing those who held convictions identical with their own; for there is no state in which the best element is friendly to the people. It is the worst element which in every state favors the democracy—on the principle that like favors like. The case is simple enough. The Athenians choose what is most akin to themselves. Also on every occasion on which they have attempted to side with the better classes, it has not fared well with them, but within a short interval the democratic party has been enslaved, as for instance in Boeotia; or, as when they chose the aristocrats of the Milesians, and within a short time these nobles revolted and cut the people to pieces; or, as when they chose the Lacedaemonians as against the Messenians, and within a short time the Lacedaemonians subjugated the Messenians and went to war against Athens.

I seem to overhear a retort, "No one, of course, has been deprived of his civil rights at Athens unjustly." My answer is, that there are some who are unjustly deprived of their civil rights, though the cases are certainly rare. But it will take more than a few to attack the democracy at Athens. You may consider it an established fact that it is not the man who has lost his civil rights justly who takes the matter to heart, but the victims, if any, of injustice. Yet how in the world can any one imagine that many are in a state of civil disability at Athens, where the People and the holders of office are one and the same? It is from iniquitous exercise of office, from iniquity exhibited either in speech or action, and the like circumstances, that citizens are punished with deprivation of civil rights in Athens. Due reflection on these matters will serve to dispel the notion that there is any danger at Athens from persons visited with disfranchisement.

# THE PELOPONNESIAN WAR
# (431-404 B.C.)

THE climax of fifth-century B.C. history came with the outbreak of the Peloponnesian War. The war's historian, Thucydides of Athens, himself a contemporary and indeed a participant, after recounting the reasons why the combatants said they were fighting, notes that the real cause was the one least talked of: the growth of Athenian power and the fear this roused in the Spartans. The war lasted twenty-seven years, including intervals of unstable peace; it engaged almost the entire Greek world, ranging either with Sparta and her allies or Athens and her empire; it was fought with ferocity on numerous fronts from Ionia to Sicily. When it was over, the Athenian empire was destroyed and Athenian power with it. Sparta found herself the great power in a world of destruction and hatred, faced with the opportunity to put the pieces together and the necessity of shedding her centuries-old defensive policy of isolation.

Militarily the war can be seen very simply as a struggle between land power and sea power. Neither side could decisively defeat the other, and it was not until Persian aid gave Sparta a fleet that Athens was brought to her knees. In a sense the only winner to emerge from the Peloponnesian War was the Persian empire, which, without committing any of its troops, became the arbiter of Greek affairs by the expedient of financial assistance.

The war was a major event in ancient history. Perhaps even more important than the event itself is the account of it written by Thucydides. His *History* remains to this day the most celebrated work of historical literature ever written, "a possession," as its author says he intended it to be, "for all time."

## 54 *The First Phase*

The first phase of the Peloponnesian War, the Archidamian War—so called after the name of the Spartan king who commanded the Peloponnesian

[ 443 ]

armies—was fought by the Athenians in accordance with the plans of Pericles. The great statesman died, however, in 429 B.C., and thereafter policy shifted according to which of the leading politicians in Athens was able to persuade the Assembly at a given moment. The fortunes of war shifted, too, favoring first Sparta then Athens, with neither side able to strike a decisive blow. The high point of Athenian success came during the early years of the war. It was a battle that started as a relatively insignificant action in the southwestern Peloponnesus but finally became a major engagement that led to a Spartan effort to negotiate peace with Athens. Ultimately its importance lay in the fact that a detachment of Spartan soldiers had actually surrendered, ending the myth that Spartans fought either to victory or to death.

The following selection is Thucydides' account of the final events in the Battle of Sphacteria (in the harbor of Pylos) in 428 B.C. The translation is by R. Crawley of Thucydides 4.26–41.

❁❁❁❁❁

Meanwhile the Athenians at Pylos were still besieging the Lacedaemonians in the island, the Peloponnesian forces on the continent remaining where they were. The blockade was very laborious for the Athenians from want of food and water; there was no spring except one in the citadel of Pylos itself, and that not a large one, and most of them were obliged to grub up the shingle on the sea beach and drink such water as they could find. They also suffered from want of room, being encamped in a narrow space; and as there was no anchorage for the ships, some took their meals on shore in their turn, while the others were anchored out at sea. But their greatest discouragement arose from the unexpectedly long time which it took to reduce a body of men shut up in a desert island, with only brackish water to drink, a matter which they had imagined would take them only a few days. The fact was, that the Lacedaemonians had made advertisement for volunteers to carry into the island ground corn, wine, cheese, and any other food useful in a siege; high prices being offered, and freedom promised to any of the Helots who should succeed in doing so. The Helots accordingly were most forward to engage in this risky traffic, putting off from this or that part of Peloponnese, and running in by night on the seaward side of the island. They were best pleased, however, when they could catch a wind to carry them in. It was more easy to elude the look-out of the galleys, when it blew from the seaward, as it became impossible for them to anchor round the island; while the Helots had their boats rated at their value in

[ 444 ]

money, and ran them ashore, without caring how they landed, being sure to find the soldiers waiting for them at the landing-places. But all who risked it in fair weather were taken. Divers also swam in under water from the harbour, dragging by a cord in skins poppy-seed mixed with honey, and bruised linseed; these at first escaped notice, but afterwards a look-out was kept for them. In short, both sides tried every possible contrivance, the one to throw in provisions, and the other to prevent their introduction.

At Athens, meanwhile, the news that the army was in great distress, and that corn found its way in to the men in the island caused no small perplexity; and the Athenians began to fear that winter might come on and find them still engaged in the blockade. They saw that the convoying of provisions round Peloponnese would be then impossible. The country offered no resources in itself, and even in summer they could not send round enough. The blockade of a place without harbours could no longer be kept up; and the men would either escape by the siege being abandoned, or would watch for bad weather and sail out in the boats that brought in their corn. What caused still more alarm was the attitude of the Lacedaemonians, who must, it was thought by the Athenians, feel themselves on strong ground not to send them any more envoys; and they began to repent having rejected the treaty. Cleon, perceiving the disfavour with which he was regarded for having stood in the way of the convention, now said that their informants did not speak the truth; and upon the messengers recommending them, if they did not believe them, to send some commissioners to see, Cleon himself and Theagenes were chosen by the Athenians as commissioners. Aware that he would now be obliged either to say what had been already said by the men whom he was slandering, or be proved a liar if he said the contrary, he told the Athenians, whom he saw to be not altogether disinclined for a fresh expedition, that instead of sending commissioners and wasting their time and opportunities, if they believed what was told them, they ought to sail against the men. And pointing at Nicias, son of Niceratus, then general, whom he hated, he tauntingly said that it would be easy, if they had men for generals, to sail with a force and take those in the island, and that if he had himself been in command, he would have done it.

Nicias, seeing the Athenians murmuring against Cleon for not sailing now if it seemed to him so easy, and further seeing himself the object of attack, told him that for all that the generals cared, he might take what force he chose and make the attempt. At first Cleon fancied that this resignation was merely a figure of speech, and was ready to go, but finding that it was seriously meant, he drew back, and said that Nicias, not he, was general, being now frightened, and having never supposed that Nicias would go so far as to retire in his favour. Nicias, however, repeated his offer, and resigned the command against Pylos, and called the Athenians to witness that he did so. And as the multitude is wont to do, the more Cleon shrank from the expedition and tried to back out of what he had said, the more they encouraged Nicias to hand over his command, and clamoured at Cleon to go. At last, not knowing how to get out of his words, he undertook the expedition, and came forward and said that he was not afraid of the Lacedaemonians, but would sail without taking any one from the city with him, except the Lemnians and Imbrians that were at Athens, with some targeteers that had come up from Aenus, and four hundred archers from other quarters. With these and the soldiers at Pylos, he would within twenty days either bring the Lacedaemonians alive, or kill them on the spot. The Athenians could not help laughing at his fatuity, while sensible men comforted themselves with the reflexion that they must gain in either circumstance; either they would be rid of Cleon, which they rather hoped, or if disappointed in this expectation, would reduce the Lacedaemonians.

After he had settled everything in the assembly, and the Athenians had voted him the command of the expedition, he chose as his colleague Demosthenes,[1] one of the generals at Pylos, and pushed forward the preparations for his voyage. His choice fell upon Demosthenes because he heard that he was contemplating a descent on the island; the soldiers distressed by the difficulties of the position, and rather besieged than besiegers, being eager to fight it out, while the firing of the island had increased the confidence of the general. He had been at first afraid, because the island having never been inhabited was almost entirely covered with wood and without paths, thinking this to be in the enemy's favour, as he might land with a large force, and yet might suffer loss by an attack from an unseen position. The mistakes and forces of the enemy the wood would in a great measure conceal from him, while every blunder of his own troops would be at once detected, and they would be thus able to fall upon him unexpectedly just where they pleased, the attack being always in their power. If, on the other hand, he should force them to engage in the thicket, the smaller number who knew the country would, he thought, have the advantage over the larger who were ignorant of it, while his own army might be cut off imperceptibly, in spite of its numbers, as the men would not be able to see where to succour each other.

1.   Not, of course, the famous statesman and orator of a century later.

The Aetolian disaster, which had been mainly caused by the wood, had not a little to do with these reflexions. Meanwhile, one of the soldiers who were compelled by want of room to land on the extremities of the island and take their dinners, with outposts fixed to prevent a surprise, set fire to a little of the wood without meaning to do so; and as it came on to blow soon afterwards, almost the whole was consumed before they were aware of it. Demosthenes was now able for the first time to see how numerous the Lacedaemonians really were, having up to this moment been under the impression that they took in provisions for a smaller number; he also saw that the Athenians thought success important and were anxious about it, and that it was now easier to land on the island, and accordingly got ready for the attempt, sent for troops from the allies in the neighbourhood, and pushed forward his other preparations. At this moment Cleon arrived at Pylos with the troops which he had asked for, having sent on word to say that he was coming. The first step taken by the two generals after their meeting was to send a herald to the camp on the mainland, to ask if they were disposed to avoid all risk and to order the men on the island to surrender themselves and their arms, to be kept in gentle custody until some general convention should be concluded.

On the rejection of this proposition the generals let one day pass, and the next embarking all their heavy infantry on board a few ships, put out by night, and a little before dawn landed on both sides of the island from the open sea and from the harbour, being about eight hundred strong, and advanced with a run against the first post in the island. The enemy had distributed his force as follows: In this first post there were about thirty heavy infantry; the centre and most level part, where the water was, was held by the main body, and by Epitadas their commander; while a small party guarded the very end of the island, towards Pylos, which was precipitous on the sea-side and very difficult to attack from the land, and where there was also a sort of old fort of stones rudely put together, which they thought might be useful to them, in case they should be forced to retreat. Such was their disposition.

The advanced post thus attacked by the Athenians was at once put to the sword, the men being scarcely out of bed and still arming, the landing having taken them by surprise, as they fancied the ships were only sailing as usual to their stations for the night. As soon as day broke, the rest of the army landed, that is to say, all the crews of rather more than seventy ships, except the lowest rank of oars, with the arms they carried, eight hundred archers, and as many targeteers, the Messenian reinforcements, and all the other troops on duty round Pylos, except the garrison on the fort. The tactics of Demosthenes had divided them into companies of two hundred, more or less, and made them occupy the highest points in order to paralyse the enemy by surrounding him on every side and thus leaving him without any tangible adversary, exposed to the cross-fire of their host; plied by those in his rear if he attacked in front, and by those on one flank if he moved against those on the other. In short, wherever he went he would have the assailants behind him, and these light-armed assailants, the most awkward of all; arrows, darts, stones, and slings making them formidable at a distance, and there being no means of getting at them at close quarters, as they could conquer flying, and the moment their pursuer turned they were upon him. Such was the idea that inspired Demosthenes in his conception of the descent, and presided over its execution.

Meanwhile the main body of the troops in the island (that under Epitadas), seeing their outpost cut off and an army advancing against them, serried their ranks and pressed forward to close with the Athenian heavy infantry in front of them, the light troops being upon their flanks and rear. However, they were not able to engage or to profit by their superior skill, the light troops keeping them in check on either side with their missiles, and the heavy infantry remaining stationary instead of advancing to meet them; and although they routed the light troops wherever they ran up and approached too closely, yet they retreated fighting, being lightly equipped, and easily getting the start in their flight, from the difficult and rugged nature of the ground, in an island hitherto desert, over which the Lacedaemonians could not pursue them with their heavy armour.

After this skirmishing had lasted some little while, the Lacedaemonians became unable to dash out with the same rapidity as before upon the points attacked, and the light troops, finding that they now fought with less vigour, became more confident. They could see with their own eyes that they were many times more numerous than the enemy; they were now more familiar with his aspect and found him less terrible, the result not having justified the apprehensions which they had suffered, when they first landed in slavish dismay at the idea of attacking Lacedaemonians; and accordingly their fear changing to disdain, they now rushed all together with loud shouts upon them, and pelted them with stones, darts, and arrows, whichever came first to hand. The shouting accompanying their onset confounded the Lacedaemonians, unaccustomed to this mode of fighting; dust rose from the newly-burnt wood, and it was impossible to see in front of one with the arrows and stones flying through clouds of dust from the hands of numerous assailants. The Lacedaemonians had now to sustain a rude conflict; their caps would not keep out the arrows, darts had broken off in the armour of the wounded, while they themselves were helpless for offence, being prevented from using their eyes to see what was before them, and unable to hear the words of command for the hubbub raised by the enemy; danger encompassed them on every side, and there was no hope of any means of defence or safety.

At last, after many had been already wounded in the confined space in which they were fighting, they formed in close order and retired on the fort at the end of the island, which was not far off, and to their friends who held it. The moment they gave way, the light troops became bolder and pressed upon them, shouting louder than ever, and killed as many as they came up with in their retreat, but most of the Lacedaemonians made good their escape to the fort, and with the garrison in it ranged themselves all along its whole extent to repulse the enemy wherever it was assailable. The Athenians pursuing, unable to surround and hem them in, owing to the strength of the ground, attacked them in front and tried to storm the position. For a long time, indeed for most of the day, both sides held out against all the torments of the battle, thirst, and sun, the one endeavouring to drive the enemy from the high ground, the other to maintain himself upon it, it being now more easy for the Lacedaemonians to defend themselves than before, as they could not be surrounded upon the flanks.

The struggle began to seem endless, when the commander of the Messenians came to Cleon and Demosthenes, and told them that they were losing their labour: but that if they would give him some archers and light troops to go round on the enemy's rear by a way he would undertake to find, he thought he could force the approach. Upon receiving what he asked for, he started from a point out of sight in order not to be seen by the enemy, and creeping on wherever the precipices of the island permitted, and where the Lacedaemonians, trusting to the strength of the ground, kept no guard, succeeded after the greatest difficulty in getting round without their seeing him, and suddenly appeared on the high ground in their rear, to the dismay of the surprised enemy and the still greater joy of his expectant friends. The Lacedaemonians thus placed between two fires, and in the same dilemma, to compare small things with great, as at Thermopylae, where the defenders were cut off through the Persians getting round by the path, being now attacked in front and behind, began to give way, and overcome by the odds against them and exhausted from want of food, retreated.

The Athenians were already masters of the approaches when Cleon and

Demosthenes perceiving that, if the enemy gave way a single step further, they would be destroyed by their soldiery, put a stop to the battle and held their men back; wishing to take the Lacedaemonians alive to Athens, and hoping that their stubbornness might relax on hearing the offer of terms, and that they might surrender and yield to the present overwhelming danger. Proclamation was accordingly made, to know if they would surrender themselves and their arms to the Athenians to be dealt with at their discretion.

The Lacedaemonians hearing this offer, most of them lowered their shields and waved their hands to show that they accepted it. Hostilities now ceased, and a parley was held between Cleon and Demosthenes and Styphon, son of Pharax, on the other side; since Epitadas, the first of the previous commanders, had been killed, and Hippagretas, the next in command, left for dead among the slain, though still alive, and thus the command had devolved upon Styphon according to the law, in case of anything happening to his superiors. Styphon and his companions said they wished to send a herald to the Lacedaemonians on the mainland, to know what they were to do. The Athenians would not let any of them go, but themselves called for heralds from the mainland, and after questions had been carried backwards and forwards two or three times, the last man that passed over from the Lacedaemonians on the continent brought this message: 'The Lacedaemonians bid you to decide for yourselves so long as you do nothing dishonourable;' upon which after consulting together they surrendered themselves and their arms. The Athenians, after guarding them that day and night, the next morning set up a trophy in the island, and got ready to sail, giving their prisoners in batches to be guarded by the captains of the galleys; and the Lacedaemonians sent a herald and took up their dead. The number of the killed and prisoners taken in the island was as follows: four hundred and twenty heavy infantry had passed over; three hundred all but eight were taken alive to Athens; the rest were killed. About a hundred and twenty of the prisoners were Spartans. The Athenian loss was small, the battle not having been fought at close quarters.

The blockade in all, counting from the fight at sea to the battle in the island, had lasted seventy-two days. For twenty of these, during the absence of the envoys sent to treat for peace, the men had provisions given them, for the rest they were fed by the smugglers. Corn and other victual was found in the island; the commander Epitadas having kept the men upon half rations. The Athenians and Peloponnesians now each withdrew their forces from Pylos, and went home, and crazy as Cleon's promise was, he fulfilled it, by bringing the men to Athens within the twenty days as he had pledged himself to do.

Nothing that happened in the war surprised the Hellenes so much as this. It was the opinion that no force or famine could make the Lacedaemonians give up their arms, but that they would fight on as they could, and die with them in their hands: indeed people could scarcely believe that those who had surrendered were of the same stuff as the fallen; and an Athenian ally, who some time after insultingly asked one of the prisoners from the island if those that had fallen were men of honour, received for answer that the *atraktos*—that is, the arrow—would be worth a great deal if it could tell men of honour from the rest; in allusion to the fact that the killed were those whom the stones and the arrows happened to hit.

Upon the arrival of the men the Athenians determined to keep them in prison until the peace, and if the Peloponnesians invaded their country in the interval, to bring them out and put them to death. Meanwhile the defence of Pylos was not forgotten; the Messenians from Naupactus sent to their old country, to which Pylos formerly belonged, some of the likeliest of their number, and began a series of incursions into Laconia, which their common dialect rendered most destructive. The Lacedaemonians, hitherto without experience of incursions or a warfare of the kind, finding the Helots deserting, and fearing the march of revolution in their country, began to be seriously uneasy, and in spite of their unwillingness to betray this to the Athenians began to send envoys to Athens, and tried to recover Pylos and the prisoners. The Athenians, however, kept grasping at more, and dismissed envoy after envoy without their having effected anything. Such was the history of the affair of Pylos.

# 55 *The Melian Debate*

After ten years of fighting, peace was made in 421 B.C. The Peace of Nicias, named for the Athenian who negotiated it, was actually no better than a temporary truce. It left both sides about where they had been at the outset of the war and resolved none of the sources of conflict. On the part of the Spartans, the Peace reflected only their persistent reluctance to fight, especially as the theatre of war was increasingly outside the Peloponnesus. On the part of the Athenians, the Peace represented the temporary ascendancy of the "moderates," whose spokesman was Nicias. The "radicals," whose goal was an ever-expanding Athenian power, found a leader in the years following the signing of the peace. He was Alcibiades, at whose prodding the Athenians spent the years following 421 B.C. in a "tough" diplomacy aimed at bringing the neutrals over to Athens and undermining the stability of the Peloponnesian alliance wherever possible. One incident in the pursuit of this "cold war" policy has been made forever memorable by the form in which Thucydides saw fit to present it. The "Melian Debate" of 416 B.C. is the epitome of the politics of power. The translation is by R. Crawley of Thucydides 5.84–116.

❁❁❁❁❁

The next summer Alcibiades sailed with twenty ships to Argos and seized the suspected persons still left of the Lacedaemonian faction to the number of three hundred, whom the Athenians forthwith lodged in the neighbouring islands of their empire. The Athenians also made an expedition against the isle of Melos with thirty ships of their own, six Chian, and two Lesbian vessels, sixteen hundred heavy infantry, three hundred archers, and twenty mounted archers from Athens, and about fifteen hundred heavy infantry from the allies and the islanders. The Melians are a colony of Lacedaemon that would not submit to the Athenians like the other islanders, and at first remained neutral and took no part in the struggle, but afterwards upon the Athenians using violence and plundering their territory, assumed an attitude of open hostility. Cleomedes, son of Lycomedes, and Tisias, son of Tisimachus, the generals, encamping in their territory with the above armament, before doing any harm to their land, sent envoys to negotiate. These the Melians did not bring before the people, but bade them state the object of their mission to the magistrates and the few; upon which the Athenian envoys spoke as follows:

*Athenians:* "Since the negotiations are not to go on before the people, in order that we may not be able to speak straight on without interruption, and deceive the ears of the multitude by seductive arguments which would pass without refutation (for we know that this is the meaning of our being brought before the few), what if you who sit there were to pursue a method more cautious still! Make no set speech yourselves, but take us up at whatever you do not like, and settle that before going any farther. And first tell us if this proposition of ours suits you."

The Melian commissioners answered:

*Melians:* "To the fairness of quietly instructing each other as you propose there is nothing to object; but your military preparations are too far ad-

[ 452 ]

vanced to agree with what you say, as we see you are come to be judges in your own cause, and that all we can reasonably expect from this negotiation is war, if we prove to have right on our side and refuse to submit, and in the contrary case, slavery."

*Athenians:* "If you have met to reason about presentiments of the future, or for anything else than to consult for the safety of your state upon the facts that you see before you, we will give over; otherwise we will go on."

*Melians:* "It is natural and excusable for men in our position to turn more ways than one both in thought and utterance. However, the question in this conference is, as you say, the safety of our country; and the discussion, if you please, can proceed in the way which you propose."

*Athenians:* "For ourselves, we shall not trouble you with specious pretences—either of how we have a right to our empire because we overthrew the Mede, or are now attacking you because of wrong that you have done us—and make a long speech which would not be believed; and in return we hope that you, instead of thinking to influence us by saying that you did not join the Lacedaemonians, although their colonists, or that you have done us no wrong, will aim at what is feasible, holding in view the real sentiments of us both; since you know as well as we do that right, as the world goes, is only in question between equals in power, while the strong do what they can and the weak suffer what they must."

*Melians:* "As we think, at any rate, it is expedient—we speak as we are obliged, since you enjoin us to let right alone and talk only of interest—that you should not destroy what is our common protection, the privilege of being allowed in danger to invoke what is fair and right, and even to profit by arguments not strictly valid if they can be got to pass current. And you are as much interested in this as any, as your fall would be a signal for the heaviest vengeance and an example for the world to meditate upon."

*Athenians:* "The end of our empire, if end it should, does not frighten us: a rival empire like Lacedaemon, even if Lacedaemon was our real antagonist, is not so terrible to the vanquished as subjects who by themselves attack and overpower their rulers. This, however, is a risk that we are content to take. We will now proceed to show you that we are come here in the interest of our empire, and that we shall say what we are now going to say, for the preservation of your country; as we would fain exercise that empire over you without trouble, and see you preserved for the good of us both."

*Melians:* "And how, pray, could it turn out as good for us to serve as for you to rule?"

*Athenians:* "Because you would have the advantage of submitting before suffering the worst, and we should gain by not destroying you."

*Melians:* "So that you would not consent to our being neutral, friends instead of enemies, but allies of neither side."

*Athenians:* "No; for your hostility cannot so much hurt us as your friendship will be an argument to our subjects of our weakness, and your enmity of our power."

*Melians:* "Is that your subjects' idea of equity, to put those who have nothing to do with you in the same category with peoples that are most of them your own colonists, and some conquered rebels?"

*Athenians:* "As far as right goes they think one has as much of it as the other, and that if any maintain their independence it is because they are strong, and that if we do not molest them it is because we are afraid; so that besides extending our empire we should gain in security by your subjection; the fact that you are islanders and weaker than others rendering it all the more important that you should not succeed in baffling the masters of the sea."

*Melians:* "But do you consider that there is no security in the policy which we indicate? For here again if you debar us from talking about justice and invite us to obey your interest, we also must explain ours, and try to persuade you, if the two happen to coincide. How can you avoid making enemies of all existing neutrals who shall look at our case and conclude from it that one day or another you will attack them? And what is this but to make greater the enemies that you have already, and to force others to become so who would otherwise have never thought of it?"

*Athenians:* "Why, the fact is that continentals generally give us but little alarm; the liberty which they enjoy will long prevent their taking precautions against us; it is rather islanders like yourselves, outside our empire, and subjects smarting under the yoke, who would be the most likely to take a rash step and lead themselves and us into obvious danger."

*Melians:* "Well then, if you risk so much to retain your empire, and your subjects to get rid of it, it were surely great baseness and cowardice in us who are still free not to try everything that can be tried, before submitting to your yoke."

*Athenians:* "Not if you are well advised, the contest not being an equal one, with honour as the prize and shame as the penalty, but a question of self-preservation and of not resisting those who are far stronger than you are."

*Melians:* "But we know that the fortune of war is sometimes more impartial than the disproportion of numbers might lead one to suppose; to submit is to give ourselves over to despair, while action still preserves for us a hope that we may stand erect."

*Athenians:* "Hope, danger's comforter, may be indulged in by those who have abundant resources, if not without loss at all events without ruin; but its nature is to be extravagant, and those who go so far as to put their all upon the venture see it in its true colours only when they are ruined; but so long as the discovery would enable them to guard against it, it is never found wanting. Let not this be the case with you, who are weak and hang on a single turn of the scale; nor be like the vulgar, who, abandoning such security as human means may still afford, when visible hopes fail them in extremity, turn to invisible, to prophecies and oracles, and other such inventions that delude men with hopes to their destruction."

*Melians:* "You may be sure that we are as well aware as you of the difficulty of contending against your power and fortune, unless the terms be equal. But we trust that the gods may grant us fortune as good as yours, since we are just men fighting against unjust, and that what we want in power will be made up by the alliance of the Lacedaemonians, who are bound, if only for very shame, to come to the aid of their kindred. Our confidence, therefore, after all is not so utterly irrational."

*Athenians:* "When you speak of the favour of the gods, we may as fairly hope for that as yourselves; neither our pretensions nor our conduct being in any way contrary to what men believe of the gods, or practise among themselves. Of the gods we believe, and of men we know, that by a necessary law of their nature they rule wherever they can. And it is not as if we were the first to make this law, or to act upon it when made: we found it existing before us, and shall leave it to exist for ever after us; all we do is to make use of it, knowing that you and everybody else, having the same power as we have, would do the same as we do. Thus, as far as the gods are concerned, we have no fear and no reason to fear that we shall be at a disadvantage. But when we come to your notion about the Lacedaemonians, which leads you to believe that shame will make them help you, here we bless your simplicity but do not envy your folly. The Lacedaemonians, when their own interests or their country's laws are in question, are the worthiest men alive; of their conduct towards others much might be said, but no clearer idea of it could be given than by shortly saying that of all the men we know they are most conspicuous in considering what is agreeable honourable, and what is expedient just. Such a way of thinking does not promise much for the safety which you now unreasonably count upon."

[ 455 ]

*Melians:* "But it is for this very reason that we now trust to their respect for expediency to prevent them from betraying the Melians, their colonists, and thereby losing the confidence of their friends in Hellas and helping their enemies."

*Athenians:* "Then you do not adopt the view that expediency goes with security, while justice and honour cannot be followed without danger; and danger the Lacedaemonians generally court as little as possible."

*Melians:* "But we believe that they would be more likely to face even danger for our sake, and with more confidence than for others, as our nearness to Peloponnese makes it easier for them to act, and our common blood insures our fidelity."

*Athenians:* "Yes, but what an intending ally trusts to, is not the goodwill of those who ask his aid, but a decided superiority of power for action; and the Lacedaemonians look to this even more than others. At least, such is their distrust of their home resources that it is only with numerous allies that they attack a neighbour; now is it likely that while we are masters of the sea they will cross over to an island?"

*Melians:* "But they would have others to send. The Cretan sea is a wide one, and it is more difficult for those who command it to intercept others, than for those who wish to elude them to do so safely. And should the Lacedaemonians miscarry in this, they would fall upon your land, and upon those left of your allies whom Brasidas did not reach; and instead of places which are not yours, you will have to fight for your own country and your own confederacy."

*Athenians:* "Some diversion of the kind you speak of you may one day experience, only to learn, as others have done, that the Athenians never once yet withdrew from a siege for fear of any. But we are struck by the fact, that after saying you would consult for the safety of your country, in all this discussion you have mentioned nothing which men might trust in and think to be saved by. Your strongest arguments depend upon hope and the future, and your actual resources are too scanty, as compared with those arrayed against you, for you to come out victorious. You will therefore show great blindness of judgment, unless, after allowing us to retire, you can find some counsel more prudent than this. You will surely not be caught by that idea of disgrace, which in dangers that are disgraceful, and at the same time too plain to be mistaken, proves so fatal to mankind; since in too many cases the very men that have their eyes perfectly open to what they are rushing into, let the thing called disgrace, by the mere influence of a seductive name, lead them on to a point at which they become so enslaved by the phrase as in fact to fall wilfully into hopeless disaster, and incur disgrace more disgraceful as the companion of error, than when it comes as the result of misfortune. This, if you are well advised, you will guard against; and you will not think it dishonourable to submit to the greatest city in Hellas, when it makes you the moderate offer of becoming its tributary ally, without ceasing to enjoy the country that belongs to you; nor when you have the choice given you between war and security, will you be so blinded as to choose the worse. And it is certain that those who do not yield to their equals, who keep terms with their superiors, and are moderate towards their inferiors, on the whole succeed best. Think over the matter, therefore, after our withdrawal, and reflect once and again that it is for your country that you are consulting, that you have not more than one, and that upon this one deliberation depends its prosperity or ruin.''

The Athenians now withdrew from the conference; and the Melians, left to themselves, came to a decision corresponding with what they had maintained in the discussion, and answered, 'Our resolution, Athenians, is the same as it was at first. We will not in a moment deprive of freedom a city that has been inhabited these seven hundred years; but we put our trust in the fortune by which the gods have preserved it until now, and in the help of men, that is, of the Lacedaemonians; and so we will try and save ourselves. Meanwhile we invite you to allow us to be friends to you and foes to neither party, and to retire from our country after making such a treaty as shall seem fit to us both.'

Such was the answer of the Melians. The Athenians now departing from the conference said, 'Well, you alone, as it seems to us, judging from these resolutions, regard what is future as more certain than what is before your eyes, and what is out of sight, in your eagerness, as already coming to pass; and as you have staked most on, and trusted most in, the Lacedaemonians, your fortune, and your hopes, so will you be most completely deceived.'

The Athenian envoys now returned to the army; and the Melians showing no signs of yielding, the generals at once betook themselves to hostilities, and drew a line of circumvallation round the Melians, dividing the work among the different states. Subsequently the Athenians returned with most of their army, leaving behind them a certain number of their own citizens and of the allies to keep guard by land and sea. The force thus left stayed on and besieged the place.

About the same time the Argives invaded the territory of Phlius and lost eighty men cut off in an ambush by the Phliasians and Argive exiles. Meanwhile the Athenians at Pylos took so much plunder from the Lacedaemonians that the latter, although they still refrained from breaking off the treaty and going to war with Athens, yet proclaimed that any of their people that chose might plunder the Athenians. The Corinthians also commenced hostilities with the Athenians for private quarrels of their own; but the rest of the Peloponnesians stayed quiet. Meanwhile the Melians attacked by night and took the part of the Athenian lines over against the market, and killed some of the men, and brought in corn and all else that they could find useful to them, and so returned and kept quiet, while the Athenians took measures to keep better guard in future.

Summer was now over. The next winter the Lacedaemonians intended to invade the Argive territory, but arriving at the frontier found the sacrifices for crossing unfavourable, and went back again. This intention of theirs gave the Argives suspicions of certain of their fellow-citizens, some of whom they arrested; others, however, escaped them. About the same time the Melians again took another part of the Athenian lines which were but feebly garrisoned. Reinforcements afterwards arriving from Athens in consequence, under the command of Philocrates, son of Demeas, the siege was now pressed vigorously; and some treachery taking place inside, the Melians surrendered at discretion to the Athenians, who put to death all the grown men whom they took, and sold the women and children for slaves, and subsequently sent out five hundred colonists and inhabited the place themselves.

# 56 The Sicilian Expedition

The climax of the war and the climax of Thucydides' narrative follow immediately after the destruction of Melos. In 415 B.C. Alcibiades persuaded the Athenians to embark upon a new imperial expansion—the conquest of Sicily—that would by-pass Sparta and the Peloponnesus. Since the Sicilian expedition ended in catastrophe, modern historians have found it easy to interpret as a reckless adventure. It might, however, have turned out to be the bold stroke intended by Alcibiades that could have altered drastically the deadlock between Athens and Sparta and tipped the scales decisively in Athens' favor.

Things went wrong from the outset. No sooner was the expedition launched than Alcibiades' return to Athens was demanded by his political opponents. He was to face charges for sacrilege growing out of a mysterious desecration of certain religious statues. Alcibiades jumped ship and for the next several years applied his fertile brain to devising plans for Athens' defeat. The Spartans did not trust or like him, but they made good use of his advice. Meanwhile, the Sicilian adventure continued. After some tentative successes the Athenian forces prepared to assault Syracuse, the major power in Sicily, where victory would give them the island. By this time (413 B.C.) the Athenian troops were under the command of Nicias, who had been opposed to the expedition from the beginning, was ill and discouraged, and had asked to be relieved of his command. He did his disheartened best; the Athenian soldiers fought with their accustomed valor; the result for Athens was total disaster. The following passages, narrating the high points of the Sicilian campaign, are abridged from Thucydides 6.1–32 and 7.4–87. The translation is by R. Crawley.

❀❀❀❀❀

The same winter the Athenians resolved to sail again to Sicily, with a greater armament than that under Laches and Eurymedon, and, if possible, to conquer the island; most of them being ignorant of its size and of the number of its inhabitants, Hellenic and barbarian, and of the fact that they were undertaking a war not much inferior to that against the Peloponnesians. For the voyage round Sicily in a merchantman is not far short of eight days; and yet, large as the island is, there are only two miles of sea to prevent its being mainland. . . .

Such is the list of the peoples, Hellenic and barbarian, inhabiting Sicily, and such the magnitude of the island which the Athenians were now bent upon invading; being ambitious in real truth of conquering the whole, although they had also the specious design of succouring their kindred and other allies in the island. But they were especially incited by envoys from Egesta, who had come to Athens and invoked their aid more urgently than ever. The Egestaeans had gone to war with their neighbours the Selinuntines upon questions of marriage and disputed territory, and the Selinuntines had procured the alliance of the Syracusans, and pressed Egesta hard by land and sea. The Egestaeans now reminded the Athenians of the alliance made in the time of Laches, during the former Leontine war, and begged them to send a fleet to their aid, and among a number of other considerations urged as a capital argument, that if the Syracusans were allowed to go unpunished for their depopulation of Leontini, to ruin the allies still left to Athens in Sicily, and to get the whole power of the island into their hands, there would be a danger of their one day coming with a large force, as Dorians, to the aid of their Dorian brethren, and as colonists, to the aid of the Peloponnesians who had sent them out, and joining these in pulling down the Athenian empire. The Athenians would, therefore, do well to unite with the allies still left to them, and to make a stand against the Syracusans; especially as they, the Egestaeans, were prepared to furnish money sufficient for the war. The Athenians, hearing these arguments constantly repeated in their assemblies by the Egestaeans and their supporters, voted first to send envoys to Egesta, to see if there was really the money that they talked of in the treasury and temples, and at the same time to ascertain in what posture was the war with the Selinuntines.

The envoys of the Athenians were accordingly despatched to Sicily. . . .

Early in the spring of the following summer the Athenian envoys arrived from Sicily, and the Egestaeans with them, bringing sixty talents of uncoined silver, as a month's pay for sixty ships, which they were to ask to have sent them. The Athenians held an assembly, and after hearing from the Egestaeans and their own envoys a report, as attractive as it was untrue, upon the state of affairs generally, and in particular as to the money, of which, it was said, there was abundance in the temples and the treasury, voted to send sixty ships to Sicily, under the command of Alcibiades, son of Clinias, Nicias, son of Niceratus, and Lamachus, son of Xenophanes, who were appointed with full powers; they were to help the Egestaeans against the Selinuntines, to restore Leontini upon gaining any advantage in the war, and to order all other matters in Sicily as they should deem best for the interests of Athens. Five days after this a second assembly was held, to consider the speediest means of equipping the ships, and to vote whatever else might be required by the generals for the expedition; and Nicias, who had been chosen to the command against his will, and who thought that the state was not well advised, but upon a slight and specious pretext was aspiring to the conquest of the whole of Sicily, a great matter to achieve, came forward in the hope of diverting the Athenians from the enterprise....

. . . Most of the Athenians that came forward spoke in favour of the expedition, and of not annulling what had been voted, although some spoke on the other side. By far the warmest advocate of the expedition was, however, Alcibiades, son of Clinias, who wished to thwart Nicias both as his political opponent and also because of the attack he had made upon him in his speech, and who was, besides, exceedingly ambitious of a command by which he hoped to reduce Sicily and Carthage, and personally to gain in wealth and reputation by means of his successes. For the position he held among the citizens led him to indulge his tastes beyond what his real means would bear, both in keeping horses and in the rest of his expenditure; and this later on had not a little to do with the ruin of the Athenian state. Alarmed at the greatness of his license in his own life and habits, and of the ambition which he showed in all things soever that he undertook, the mass of the people set him down as a pretender to the tyranny, and became his enemies; and although publicly his conduct of the war was as good as could be desired, individually, his habits gave offence to every one, and caused them to commit affairs to other hands, and thus before long to ruin the city. Meanwhile he now came forward. . . .

. . . After hearing him [Alcibiades] and the Egestaeans and some Leontine exiles, who came forward reminding them of their oaths and imploring their assistance, the Athenians became more eager for the expedition than before. Nicias, perceiving that it would be now useless to try to deter them by the old line of argument, but thinking that he might perhaps alter their resolution by the extravagance of his estimates, came forward a second time and spoke. . . .

With this Nicias concluded, thinking that he should either disgust the Athenians by the magnitude of the undertaking, or, if obliged to sail on the expedition, would thus do so in the safest way possible. The Athenians, however, far from having their taste for the voyage taken away by the burdensomeness of the preparations, became more eager for it than ever; and just the contrary took place of what Nicias had thought, as it was held that he had given good advice, and that the expedition would be the safest in the world. All alike fell in love with the enterprise. The older men thought that they would either subdue the places against which they were to sail, or at all events, with so large a force, meet with no disaster; those in the prime of life felt a longing for foreign sights and spectacles, and had no doubt that they should come safe home again; while the idea of the common people and the soldiery was to earn wages at the moment, and make conquests that would supply a never-ending fund of pay for the future. With this enthusiasm of the majority, the few that liked it not, feared to appear unpatriotic by holding up their hands against it, and so kept quiet.

At last one of the Athenians came forward and called upon Nicias and told him that he ought not to make excuses or put them off, but say at once before them all what forces the Athenians should vote him. Upon this he said, not without reluctance, that he would advise upon that matter more at leisure with his colleagues; as far however as he could see at present, they must sail with at least one hundred galleys—the Athenians providing as many transports as they might determine, and sending for others from the allies—not less than five thousand heavy infantry in all, Athenian and allied, and if possible more; and the rest of the armament in proportion; archers from home and from Crete, and slingers, and whatever else might seem desirable, being got ready by the generals and taken with them.

Upon hearing this the Athenians at once voted that the generals should have full powers in the matter of the numbers of the army and of the expedition generally, to do as they judged best for the interests of Athens. After this the preparations began; messages being sent to the allies and the rolls drawn up at home. And as the city had just recovered from the plague and the long war, and a number of young men had grown up and capital had accumulated by reason of the truce, everything was the more easily provided.

In the midst of these preparations all the stone Hermae in the city of Athens, that is to say the customary square figures, so common in the doorways of private houses and temples, had in one night most of them their faces mutilated. No one knew who had done it, but large public rewards were offered to find the authors; and it was further voted that any one who knew of any other act of impiety having been committed should come and give information without fear of consequences, whether he were citizen, alien, or slave. The matter was taken up the more seriously, as it was thought to be ominous for the expedition, and part of a conspiracy to bring about a revolution and to upset the democracy.

Information was given accordingly by some resident aliens and body servants, not about the Hermae but about some previous mutilations of other images perpetrated by young men in a drunken frolic, and of mock celebrations of the mysteries, averred to take place in private houses.[1] Alcibiades being implicated in this charge, it was taken hold of by those who could least endure him, because he stood in the way of their obtaining the undisturbed direction of the people, and who thought that if he were once removed the first place would be theirs. These accordingly magnified the matter and loudly proclaimed that the affair of the mysteries and the mutilation of the Hermae were part and parcel of a scheme to overthrow the democracy, and that nothing of all this had been done without Alcibiades; the proofs alleged being the general and undemocratic license of his life and habits.

Alcibiades repelled on the spot the charges in question, and also before going on the expedition, the preparations for which were now complete,

1. See Selection 74.

offered to stand his trial, that it might be seen whether he was guilty of the acts imputed to him; desiring to be punished if found guilty, but, if acquitted, to take the command. Meanwhile he protested against their receiving slanders against him in his absence, and begged them rather to put him to death at once if he were guilty, and pointed out the imprudence of sending him out at the head of so large an army, with so serious a charge still undecided. But his enemies feared that he would have the army for him if he were tried immediately, and that the people might relent in favour of the man whom they already caressed as the cause of the Argives and some of the Mantineans joining in the expedition, and did their utmost to get this proposition rejected, putting forward other orators who said that he ought at present to sail and not delay the departure of the army, and be tried on his return within a fixed number of days; their plan being to have him sent for and brought home for trial upon some graver charge, which they would the more easily get up in his absence. Accordingly it was decreed that he should sail.

After this the departure for Sicily took place, it being now about midsummer. Most of the allies, with the corn transports and the smaller craft and the rest of the expedition, had already received orders to muster at Corcyra, to cross the Ionian sea from thence in a body to the Iapygian promontory. But the Athenians themselves, and such of their allies as happened to be with them, went down to Piraeus upon a day appointed at daybreak, and began to man the ships for putting out to sea. With them also went down the whole population, one may say, of the city, both citizens and foreigners; the inhabitants of the country each escorting those that belonged to them, their friends, their relatives, or their sons, with hope and lamentation upon their way, as they thought of the conquests which they hoped to make, or of the friends whom they might never see again, considering the long yoyage which they were going to make from their country. Indeed, at this moment, when they were now upon the point of parting from one another, the danger came more home to them than when they voted for the expedition; although the strength of the armament, and the profuse provision which they remarked in every department, was a sight that could not but comfort them. As for the foreigners and the rest of the crowd, they simply went to see a sight worth looking at and passing all belief.

Indeed this armament that first sailed out was by far the most costly and splendid Hellenic force that had ever been sent out by a single city up to that time. In mere number of ships and heavy infantry that against

Epidaurus under Pericles, and the same when going against Potidaea under Hagnon, was not inferior; containing as it did four thousand Athenian heavy infantry, three hundred horse, and one hundred galleys accompanied by fifty Lesbian and Chian vessels and many allies besides. But these were sent upon a short voyage and with a scanty equipment. The present expedition was formed in contemplation of a long term of service by land and sea alike, and was furnished with ships and troops so as to be ready for either as required. The fleet had been elaborately equipped at great cost to the captains and the state; the treasury giving a drachma a day to each seaman, and providing empty ships, sixty men of war and forty transports, and manning these with the best crews obtainable; while the captains gave a bounty in addition to the pay from the treasury to the *thranitae* and crews generally, besides spending lavishly upon figure-heads and equipments, and one and all making the utmost exertions to enable their own ships to excel in beauty and fast sailing. Meanwhile the land forces had been picked from the best muster-rolls, and vied with each other in paying great attention to their arms and personal accoutrements. From this resulted not only a rivalry among themselves in their different departments, but an idea among the rest of the Hellenes that it was more a display of power and resources than an armament against an enemy. For if any one had counted up the public expenditure of the state, and the private outlay of individuals—that is to say, the sums which the state had already spent upon the expedition and was sending out in the hands of the generals, and those which individuals had expended upon their personal outfit, or as captains of galleys had laid out and were still to lay out upon their vessels; and if he had added to this the journey money which each was likely to have provided himself with, independently of the pay from the treasury, for a voyage of such length, and what the soldiers or traders took with them for the purpose of exchange—it would have been found that many talents in all were being taken out of the city. Indeed the expedition became not less famous for its wonderful boldness and for the splendour of its appearance, than for its overwhelming strength as compared with the peoples against whom it was directed, and for the fact that this was the longest passage from home hitherto attempted, and the most ambitious in its objects considering the resources of those who undertook it.

The ships being now manned, and everything put on board with which they meant to sail, the trumpet commanded silence, and the prayers customary before putting out to sea were offered, not in each ship by itself, but by all together to the voice of a herald; and bowls of wine were mixed through all the armament, and libations made by the soldiers and their officers in gold and silver goblets. In their prayers joined also the crowds on shore, the citizens and all others that wished them well. The hymn sung and the libations finished, they put out to sea, and first sailing out in column then raced each other as far as Aegina, and so hastened to reach Corcyra, where the rest of the allied forces were also assembling.

. . . . .

[*In two years of desultory campaigning nothing decisive was accomplished. Now, at Syracuse, the final scenes of the drama of the Sicilian expedition are about to be enacted.*]

In the meantime, while the Syracusans were preparing for a second attack upon both elements [land and sea], Demosthenes and Eurymedon arrived with the succours from Athens, consisting of about seventy-three ships, including the foreigners; nearly five thousand heavy infantry, Athenian and allied; a large number of darters, Hellenic and barbarian, and slingers and archers and everything else upon a corresponding scale. The Syracusans and their allies were for the moment not a little dismayed at the idea that there was to be no term or ending to their dangers, seeing, in spite of the fortification of Decelea, a new army arrive nearly equal to the former, and the power of Athens proving so great in every quarter. On the other hand, the first Athenian armament regained a certain confidence in the midst of its misfortunes. Demosthenes, seeing how matters stood, felt that he could not drag on and fare as Nicias had done, who by wintering in Catana instead of at once attacking Syracuse had allowed the terror of his first arrival to evaporate in contempt, and had given time to Gylippus to arrive with a force from Peloponnese, which the Syracusans would never have sent for if he had attacked immediately; for they fancied that they were a match for him by themselves, and would not have discovered their inferiority until they were already invested, and even if they then sent for succours, they would no longer have been equally able to profit by their arrival. Recollecting this, and well aware that it was now on the first day after his arrival that he like Nicias was most formidable to the enemy, Demosthenes determined to lose no time in drawing the utmost profit from the consternation at the moment inspired by his army; and seeing that the counterwall of the Syracusans, which hindered the Athenians from investing them, was a single one, and that he who should become master of the way up to Epipolae,[2] and afterwards of the camp there, would find no difficulty in

2.  Epipolae was the name of the high point dominating Syracuse.

taking it, as no one would even wait for his attack, made all haste to attempt the enterprise. This he took to be the shortest way of ending the war, as he would either succeed and take Syracuse, or would lead back the armament instead of frittering away the lives of the Athenians engaged in the expedition and the resources of the country at large.

First therefore the Athenians went out and laid waste the lands of the Syracusans about the Anapus and carried all before them as at first by land and by sea, the Syracusans not offering to oppose them upon either element, unless it were with their cavalry and darters from the Olympieum. Next Demosthenes resolved to attempt the counterwall first by means of engines. As however the engines that he brought up were burnt by the enemy fighting from the wall, and the rest of the forces repulsed after attacking at many different points, he determined to delay no longer, and having obtained the consent of Nicias and his fellow-commanders, proceeded to put in execution his plan of attacking Epipolae. As by day it seemed impossible to approach and get up without being observed, he ordered provisions for five days, took all the masons and carpenters, and other things, such as arrows, and everything else that they could want for the work of fortification if successful; and after the first watch set out with Eurymedon and Menander and the whole army for Epipolae, Nicias being left behind in the lines. Having come up by the hill of Euryalus (where the former army had ascended at first), unobserved by the enemy's guards, they went up to the fort which the Syracusans had there, and took it, and put to the sword part of the garrison. The greater number, however, escaped at once and gave the alarm to the camps, of which there were three upon Epipolae, defended by outworks, one of the Syracusans, one of the other Siceliots, and one of the allies; and also to the six hundred Syracusans forming the original garrison for this part of Epipolae. These at once advanced against the assailants, and falling in with Demosthenes and the Athenians, were routed by them after a sharp resistance, the victors immediately pushing on, eager to achieve the objects of the attack without giving time for their ardour to cool; meanwhile others from the very beginning were taking the counterwall of the Syracusans, which was abandoned by its garrison, and pulling down the battlements. The Syracusans and the allies, and Gylippus with the troops under his command, advanced to the rescue from the outworks, but engaged in some consternation (a night attack being a piece of audacity which they had never expected), and were at first compelled to retreat. But while the Athenians, flushed with their victory, now advanced with less order, wishing to make their way as quickly as possible through the whole force of the enemy not yet engaged, without relaxing their attack or giving them time to rally, the Boeotians made the first stand against them, attacked them, routed them, and put them to flight.

The Athenians now fell into great disorder and perplexity, so that it was not easy to get from one side or the other any detailed account of the affair. By day certainly the combatants have a clearer notion, though even then by no means of all that takes place, no one knowing much of anything that does not go on in his own immediate neighbourhood; but in a night engagement (and this was the only one that occurred between great armies during the war) how could any one know anything for certain? Although there was a bright moon they saw each other only as men do by moonlight, that is to say, they could distinguish the form of the body, but could not tell for certain whether it was a friend or an enemy. Both had great numbers of heavy infantry moving about in a small space. Some of the Athenians were already defeated, while others were coming up yet unconquered for their first attack. A large part also of the rest of their forces either had only just got up, or were still ascending, so that they did not know which way to march. Owing to the rout that had taken place all in front was now in confusion, and the noise made it difficult to distinguish anything. The victorious Syracusans and allies were cheering each other on with loud cries, by night the only possible means of communication, and meanwhile receiving all who came against them; while the Athenians were seeking for one another, taking all in front of them for enemies, even although they might be some of their now flying friends; and by constantly asking for the watchword, which was their only means of recognition, not only caused great confusion among themselves by asking all at once, but also made it known to the enemy, whose own they did not so readily discover, as the Syracusans were victorious and not scattered, and thus less easily mistaken. The result was that if the Athenians fell in with a party of the enemy that was weaker than they, it escaped them through knowing their watchword; while if they themselves failed to answer they were put to the sword. But what hurt them as much, or indeed more than anything else, was the singing of the Paean, from the perplexity which it caused by being nearly the same on either side: the Argives and Corcyraeans and any other Dorian peoples in the army, struck terror into the Athenians whenever they raised their Paean, no less than did the enemy. Thus, after being once thrown into disorder, they ended by coming into collision with each other in many parts of the field, friends with friends, and citizens with citizens, and not only terrified one another, but even came to blows and could only be parted with difficulty. In the pursuit many perished by throwing themselves down the cliffs, the way down from Epipolae being narrow; and of those who got down safely into the plain, although many, especially those who belonged to the first armament, escaped through their better acquaintance with the locality, some of the newcomers lost their way and wandered over the country, and were cut off in the morning by the Syracusan cavalry and killed.

The next day the Syracusans set up two trophies, one upon Epipolae where the ascent had been made, and the other on the spot where the first check was given by the Boeotians; and the Athenians took back their dead under truce. A great many of the Athenians and allies were killed, although still more arms were taken than could be accounted for by the number of the dead, as some of those who were obliged to leap down from the cliffs without their shields escaped with their lives and did not perish like the rest.

After this the Syracusans, recovering their old confidence at such an unexpected stroke of good fortune, despatched Sicanus with fifteen ships to Agrigentum where there was a revolution, to induce if possible the city to join them; while Gylippus again went by land into the rest of Sicily to bring up reinforcements, being now in hope of taking the Athenian lines by storm, after the result of the affair on Epipolae.

In the meantime the Athenian generals consulted upon the disaster which had happened, and upon the general weakness of the army. They saw themselves unsuccessful in their enterprises, and the soldiers disgusted with their stay; disease being rife among them owing to its being the sickly season of the year, and to the marshy and unhealthy nature of the spot in which they were encamped; and the state of their affairs generally being thought desperate. Accordingly, Demosthenes was of opinion that they ought not to stay any longer; but agreeably to his original idea in risking the attempt upon Epipolae, now that this had failed, he gave his vote for going away without further loss of time, while the sea might yet be crossed, and their late reinforcement might give them the superiority at all events on that element. He also said that it would be more profitable for the state to carry on the war against those who were building fortifications in Attica, than against the Syracusans whom it was no longer easy to subdue; besides which it was not right to squander large sums of money to no purpose by going on with the siege.

This was the opinion of Demosthenes. Nicias, without denying the bad state of their affairs, was unwilling to avow their weakness, or to have it reported to the enemy that the Athenians in full council were openly voting for retreat; for in that case they would be much less likely to effect it when they wanted without discovery. Moreover, his own particular information still gave him reason to hope that the affairs of the enemy would soon be in a worse state than their own, if the Athenians persevered in the siege; as they would wear out the Syracusans by want of money, especially with the more extensive command of the sea now given them by their present navy. Besides this, there was a party in Syracuse who wished to betray the city to the Athenians, and kept sending him messages and telling him not to raise the siege. Accordingly, knowing this and really waiting because he hesitated between the two courses and wished to see his way more clearly, in his public speech on this occasion he refused to lead off the army, saying he was sure the Athenians would never approve of their returning without a vote of theirs. Those who would vote upon their conduct, instead of judging the facts as eye-witnesses like themselves and not from what they might hear from hostile critics, would simply be guided by the calumnies of the first clever speaker; while many, indeed most, of the soldiers on the spot, who now so loudly proclaimed the danger of their position, when they reached Athens would proclaim just as loudly the opposite, and would say that their generals had been bribed to betray them and return. For himself, therefore, who knew the Athenian temper, sooner than perish under a dishonourable charge and by an unjust sentence at the hands of the Athenians, he would rather take his chance and die, if die he must, a soldier's death at the hand of the enemy. Besides, after all, the Syracusans were in a worse case than themselves. What with paying mercenaries, spending upon fortified posts, and now for a full year maintaining a large navy, they were already at a loss and would soon be at a standstill: they had already spent two thousand talents and incurred heavy debts besides, and could not lose even ever so small a fraction of their present force through not paying it, without ruin to their cause; depending as they did more upon mercenaries than upon soldiers obliged to serve, like their own. He therefore said that they ought to stay and carry on the siege, and not depart defeated in point of money, in which they were much superior.

Nicias spoke positively because he had exact information of the financial distress at Syracuse, and also because of the strength of the Athenian party there which kept sending him messages not to raise the siege; besides which he had more confidence than before in his fleet, and felt sure at least of its success. Demosthenes, however, would not hear for a moment of continuing the siege, but said that if they could not lead off the army without a decree from Athens, and if they were obliged to stay on, they ought to remove to Thapsus or Catana; where their land forces would have a wide extent of country to overrun, and could live by plundering the enemy, and would thus do them damage; while the fleet would have the open sea to fight in, that is to say, instead of a narrow space which was all in the enemy's favour, a wide sea-room where their science would be of use, and where they could retreat or advance without being confined or circumscribed either when they put out or put in. In any case he was altogether opposed to their staying on where they were, and insisted on removing at once, as quickly and with as little delay as possible; and in this judgment Eurymedon agreed. Nicias however still objecting, a certain diffidence and hesitation came over them, with a suspicion that Nicias might have some further information to make him so positive. . . .

The Syracusans had now gained a decisive victory at sea, where until now they had feared the reinforcement brought by Demosthenes, and deep, in consequence, was the despondency of the Athenians, and great their disappointment, and greater still their regret for having come on the expedition. These were the only cities that they had yet encountered, similar to their own in character, under democracies like themselves, which had ships and horses, and were of considerable magnitude. They had been unable to divide and bring them over by holding out the prospect of changes in their governments, or to crush them by their great superiority in force, but had failed in most of their attempts, and being already in perplexity, had now been defeated at sea, where defeat could never have been expected, and were thus plunged deeper in embarrassment than ever.

Meanwhile the Syracusans immediately began to sail freely along the harbour, and determined to close up its mouth, so that the Athenians might not be able to steal out in future, even if they wished. Indeed, the Syracusans no longer thought only of saving themselves, but also how to hinder the escape of the enemy; thinking, and thinking rightly, that they were now much the strongest, and that to conquer the Athenians and their allies by land and sea would win them great glory in Hellas. The rest of the Hellenes would thus immediately be either freed or released from apprehension, as the remaining forces of Athens would be henceforth unable to sustain the war that would be waged against her; while they, the Syracusans, would be regarded as the authors of this deliverance, and would be held in high admiration, not only with all men now living but also with posterity. Nor were these the only considerations that gave dignity to the struggle. They would thus conquer not only the Athenians but also their numerous allies, and conquer not alone, but with their companions-in-arms, commanding side by side with the Corinthians and Lacedaemonians, having offered their city to stand in the van of danger, and having been in a great measure the pioneers of naval success.

Indeed, there were never so many peoples assembled before a single city, if we except the grand total gathered together in this war under Athens and Lacedaemon. . . .

Such were the auxiliaries brought together on either side, all of which had by this time joined, neither party experiencing any subsequent accession. It was no wonder, therefore, if the Syracusans and their allies thought that it would win them great glory if they could follow up their recent victory in the sea-fight by the capture of the whole Athenian armada, without letting it escape either by sea or by land. They began at once to close up the Great Harbour by means of boats, merchant vessels, and galleys moored broadside across its mouth, which is nearly a mile wide, and made all their other arrangements for the event of the Athenians again venturing to fight at sea. There was, in fact, nothing little either in their plans or their ideas.

The Athenians, seeing them closing up the harbour and informed of their further designs, called a council of war. The generals and colonels assembled and discussed the difficulties of the situation; the point which pressed most being that they no longer had provisions for immediate use (having sent on to Catana to tell them not to send any, in the belief that they were going away), and that they would not have any in future unless they could command the sea. They therefore determined to evacuate their upper lines, to enclose with a cross-wall and garrison a small space close to the ships, only just sufficient to hold their stores and sick, and manning all the ships, seaworthy or not, with every man that could be spared from the rest of their land forces, to fight it out at sea, and if victorious, to go to Catana, if not, to burn their vessels, form in close order, and retreat by land for the nearest friendly place they could reach, Hellenic or barbarian. This was no sooner settled than carried into effect: they descended gradually from the upper lines and manned all their vessels, compelling all to go on board who were of age to be in any way of use. They thus succeeded in manning about one hundred and ten ships in all, on board of which they embarked a number of archers and darters taken from the Acarnanians and from the other foreigners, making all other provisions allowed by the nature of their plan and by the necessities which imposed it. All was now nearly ready, and Nicias, seeing the soldiery disheartened by their unprecedented and decided defeat at sea, and by reason of the scarcity of provisions eager to fight it out as soon as possible, called them all together, and first addressed them, speaking as follows:

"Soldiers of the Athenians and of the allies, we have all an equal interest in the coming struggle, in which life and country are at stake for us quite as much as they can be for the enemy; since if our fleet wins the day, each can see his native city again, wherever that city may be. You must not lose heart, or be like men without any experience, who fail in a first essay, and ever afterwards fearfully forebode a future as disastrous. But let the Athenians among you who have already had experience of many wars, and the allies who have joined us in so many expeditions, remember the surprises of war, and with the hope that fortune will not be always against us, prepare to fight again in a manner worthy of the number which you see yourselves to be.

"Now, whatever we thought would be of service against the crush of vessels in such a narrow harbour, and against the force upon the decks of the enemy, from which we suffered before, has all been considered with the helmsmen, and, as far as our means allowed, provided. A number of archers and darters will go on board, and a multitude that we should not have employed in an action in the open sea, where our science would be crippled by the weight of the vessels; but in the present land-fight that we are forced to make from shipboard all this will be useful. We have also discovered the changes in construction that we must make to meet theirs; and against the thickness of their cheeks, which did us the greatest mischief, we have provided grappling-irons, which will prevent an assailant backing water after charging, if the soldiers on deck here do their duty; since we are absolutely compelled to fight a land battle from the fleet, and it seems to be our interest neither to back water ourselves, nor to let the enemy do so, especially as the shore, except so much of it as may be held by our troops, is hostile ground.

"You must remember this and fight on as long as you can, and must not let yourselves be driven ashore, but once alongside must make up your minds not to part company until you have swept the heavy infantry from the enemy's deck. I say this more for the heavy infantry than for the seamen, as it is more the business of the men on deck; and our land forces are even now on the whole the strongest. The sailors I advise, and at the same time implore, not to be too much daunted by their misfortunes, now that we have our decks better armed and a greater number of vessels. Bear in mind how well worth preserving is the pleasure felt by those of you who through your knowledge of our language and imitation of our manners were always considered Athenians, even though not so in reality, and as such were honoured throughout Hellas, and had your full share of the advantages of our empire, and more than your share in the respect of our subjects and in protection from ill treatment. You, therefore, with whom alone we freely share our empire, we now justly require not to betray that empire in its extremity, and in scorn of Corinthians, whom you have often conquered, and of Siceliots, none of whom so much as presumed to stand against us when our navy was in its prime, we ask you to repel them, and to show that even in sickness and disaster your skill is more than a match for the fortune and vigour of any other.

"For the Athenians among you I add once more this reflexion: you left behind you no more such ships in your docks as these, no more heavy infantry in their flower; if you do aught but conquer, our enemies here will immediately sail thither, and those that are left of us at Athens will become unable to repel their home assailants, reinforced by these new allies. Here you will fall at once into the hands of the Syracusans—I need not remind you of the intentions with which you attacked them—and your countrymen at home will fall into those of the Lacedaemonians. Since the fate of both thus hangs upon this single battle—now, if ever, stand firm, and remember, each and all, that you who are now going on board are the army and navy of the Athenians, and all that is left of the state and the great name of Athens, in whose defence if any man has any advantage in skill or courage, now is the time for him to show it, and thus serve himself and save all."

After this address Nicias at once gave orders to man the ships. . . .

. . . The Syracusan generals and Gylippus now perceived that the Athenians were manning their ships, and immediately proceeded to man their own also. Meanwhile Nicias, appalled by the position of affairs, realising the greatness and the nearness of the danger now that they were on the point of putting out from shore, and thinking, as men are apt to think in great crises, that when all has been done they have still something left to do, and when all has been said that they have not yet said enough, again called on the captains one by one, addressing each by his father's name and by his own, and by that of his tribe, and adjured them not to belie their own personal renown, or to obscure the hereditary virtues for which their ancestors were illustrious; he reminded them of their country, the freest of the free, and of the unfettered discretion allowed in it to all to live as they pleased; and added other arguments such as men would use at such a crisis, and which, with little alteration, are made to serve on all occasions alike—appeals to wives, children, and national gods—without caring whether they are thought commonplace, but loudly invoking them in the belief that they will be of use in the consternation of the moment. Having thus admonished them, not, he felt, as he would, but as he could, Nicias withdrew and led the troops to the sea, and ranged them in as long a line as he was able, in order to aid as far as possible in sustaining the courage of the men afloat; while Demosthenes, Menander, and Euthydemus, who took the command on board, put out from their own camp and sailed straight to the barrier across the mouth of the harbour and to the passage left open, to try to force their way out.

The Syracusans and their allies had already put out with about the same number of ships as before, a part of which kept guard at the outlet, and the remainder all round the rest of the harbour, in order to attack the Athenians on all sides at once; while the land forces held themselves in readiness at the points at which the vessels might put into the shore. The Syracusan fleet was commanded by Sicanus and Agatharchus, who had each a wing of the whole force, with Pythen and the Corinthians in the centre. When the rest of the Athenians came up to the barrier, with the first shock of their charge they overpowered the ships stationed there, and tried to undo the fastenings; after this, as the Syracusans and allies bore down upon them from all quarters, the action spread from the barrier over the whole harbour, and was more obstinately disputed than any of the preceding ones. On either side the rowers showed great zeal in bringing up their vessels at the boatswains' orders, and the helmsmen great skill in manœuvring, and great emulation one with another; while the ships once alongside, the soldiers on board did their best not to let the service on deck be outdone by the others; in short, every man strove to prove himself the first in his particular department. And as many ships were engaged in a small compass (for these were the largest fleets fighting in the narrowest space ever known, being together little short of two hundred), the regular attacks with the beak were few, there being no opportunity of backing water or of breaking the line; while the collisions caused by one ship chancing to run foul of another, either in flying from or attacking a third, were more frequent. So long as a vessel was coming up to the charge the men on the decks rained darts and arrows and stones upon her; but once alongside, the heavy infantry tried to board each other's vessel, fighting hand to hand. In many quarters also it happened, by reason of the narrow room, that a vessel was charging an enemy on one side and being charged herself on another, and that two, or sometimes more ships had perforce got entangled round one, obliging the helmsmen to attend to defence here, offence there, not to one thing at once, but to many on all sides; while the huge din caused by the number of ships crashing together not only spread terror, but made the orders of the boatswains inaudible. The boatswains on either side in the discharge of their duty and in the heat of the conflict shouted incessantly orders and appeals to their men; the Athenians they urged to force the passage out, and now if ever to show their mettle and lay hold of a safe return to their country; to the Syracusans and their allies they cried that it would be glorious to prevent the escape of the enemy, and conquering, to exalt the countries that were theirs. The generals, moreover, on either side, if they saw any in any part of the battle backing ashore without being forced to do so, called out to the captain by name and asked him—the Athenians, whether they were retreating because they thought the thrice hostile shore more their own than that sea which had cost them so much labour to win; the Syracusans, whether they were flying from the flying Athenians, whom they well knew to be eager to escape in whatever way they could.

Meanwhile the two armies on shore, while victory hung in the balance, were a prey to the most agonising and conflicting emotions; the natives thirsting for more glory than they had already won, while the invaders feared to find themselves in even worse plight than before. The all of the Athenians being set upon their fleet, their fear for the event was like nothing they had ever felt; while their view of the struggle was necessarily as chequered as the battle itself. Close to the scene of action and not all looking at the same point at once, some saw their friends victorious and took courage, and fell to calling upon heaven not to deprive them of salvation, while others who had their eyes turned upon the losers, wailed and cried aloud, and, although spectators, were more overcome than the actual combatants. Others, again, were gazing at some spot where the battle was evenly disputed; as the strife was protracted without decision, their swaying bodies reflected the agitation of their minds, and they suffered the worst agony of all, ever just within reach of safety or just on the point of destruction. In short, in that one Athenian army as long as the sea-fight remained doubtful there was every sound to be heard at once, shrieks, cheers, "We win," "We lose," and all the other manifold exclamations that a great host would necessarily utter in great peril; and with the men in the fleet it was nearly the same; until at last the Syracusans and their allies, after the battle had lasted a long while, put the Athenians to flight, and with much shouting and cheering chased them in open rout to the shore. The naval force, one

one way, one another, as many as were not taken afloat, now ran ashore and rushed from on board their ships to their camp; while the army, no more divided, but carried away by one impulse, all with shrieks and groans deplored the event, and ran down, some to help the ships, others to guard what was left of their wall, while the remaining and most numerous part already began to consider how they should save themselves. Indeed, the panic of the present moment had never been surpassed. They now suffered very nearly what they had inflicted at Pylos;[3] as then the Lacedaemonians with the loss of their fleet lost also the men who had crossed over to the island, so now the Athenians had no hope of escaping by land, without the help of some extraordinary accident.

The sea-fight having been a severe one, and many ships and lives having been lost on both sides, the victorious Syracusans and their allies now picked up their wrecks and dead, and sailed off to the city and set up a trophy. The Athenians, overwhelmed by their misfortune, never even thought of asking leave to take up their dead or wrecks, but wished to retreat that very night. Demosthenes, however, went to Nicias and gave it as his opinion that they should man the ships they had left and make another effort to force their passage out next morning; saying that they had still left more ships fit for service than the enemy, the Athenians having about sixty remaining as against less than fifty of their opponents. Nicias was quite of his mind; but when they wished to man the vessels, the sailors refused to go on board, being so utterly overcome by their defeat as no longer to believe in the possibility of success.

Accordingly they all now made up their minds to retreat by land. Meanwhile the Syracusan Hermocrates suspecting their intention, and impressed by the danger of allowing a force of that magnitude to retire by land, establish itself in some other part of Sicily, and from thence renew the war, went and stated his views to the authorities, and pointed out to them that they ought not to let the enemy get away by night, but that all the Syracusans and their allies should at once march out and block up the roads and seize and guard the passes. The authorities were entirely of his opinion, and thought that it ought to be done, but on the other hand felt sure that the people, who had given themselves over to rejoicing and were taking their ease after a great battle at sea, would not be easily brought to obey; besides, they were celebrating a festival, having on that day a sacrifice to Heracles, and most of them in their rapture at the victory had fallen to drinking at the festival, and would probably consent to anything sooner

3.  See Selection 54.

than to take up their arms and march out at that moment. For these reasons the thing appeared impracticable to the magistrates; and Hermocrates, finding himself unable to do anything further with them, had now recourse to the following stratagem of his own. What he feared was that the Athenians might quietly get the start of them by passing the most difficult places during the night; and he therefore sent, as soon as it was dusk, some friends of his own to the camp with some horsemen who rode up within earshot and called out to some of the men, as though they were well-wishers of the Athenians, and told them to tell Nicias (who had in fact some correspondents who informed him of what went on inside the town), not to lead off the army by night as the Syracusans were guarding the roads, but to make his preparations at his leisure and to retreat by day. After saying this they departed; and their hearers informed the Athenian generals, who put off going for that night on the strength of this message, not doubting its sincerity.

Since after all they had not set out at once, they now determined to stay also the following day to give time to the soldiers to pack up as well as they could the most useful articles, and, leaving everything else behind, to start only with what was strictly necessary for their personal subsistence. Meanwhile the Syracusans and Gylippus marched out and blocked up the roads through the country by which the Athenians were likely to pass, and kept guard at the fords of the stream and rivers, posting themselves so as to receive them and stop the army where they thought best; while their fleet sailed up to the beach and towed off the ships of the Athenians. Some few were burned by the Athenians themselves as they had intended; the rest the Syracusans lashed on to their own at their leisure as they had been thrown up on shore, without any one trying to stop them, and conveyed to the town.

After this, Nicias and Demosthenes now thinking that enough had been done in the way of preparation, the removal of the army took place upon the second day after the sea-fight. It was a lamentable scene, not merely from the single circumstance that they were retreating after having lost all their ships, their great hopes gone, and themselves and the state in peril; but also in leaving the camp there were things most grievous for every eye and heart to contemplate. The dead lay unburied, and each man as he recognised a friend among them shuddered with grief and horror; while the living whom they were leaving behind, wounded or sick, were to the living far more shocking than the dead, and more to be pitied than those who had perished. These fell to entreating and bewailing until their friends knew not what to do, begging them to take them and loudly calling to each individual comrade or relative whom they could see, hanging upon the necks of their tent-fellows in the act of departure, and following as far as they could, and when their bodily strength failed them, calling again and again upon heaven and shrieking aloud as they were left behind. So that the whole army being filled with tears and distracted after this fashion found it not easy to go, even from an enemy's land, where they had already suffered evils too great for tears and in the unknown future before them feared to suffer more. Dejection and self-condemnation were also rife among them. Indeed they could only be compared to a starved-out town, and that no small one, escaping; the whole multitude upon the march being not less than forty thousand men. All carried anything they could which might be of use, and the heavy infantry and troopers, contrary to their wont, while under arms carried their own victuals, in some cases for want of servants, in others through not trusting them; as they had long been deserting and now did so in greater numbers than ever. Yet even thus they did not carry enough, as there was no longer food in the camp. Moreover their disgrace generally, and the universality of their sufferings, however to a certain extent alleviated by being borne in company, were still felt at the moment a heavy burden, especially when they contrasted the splendour and glory of their setting out with the humiliation in which it had ended. For this was by far the greatest reverse that ever befell an Hellenic army. They had come to enslave others, and were departing in fear of being enslaved themselves: they had sailed out with prayer and paeans, and now started to go back with omens directly contrary; travelling by land instead of by sea, and trusting not in their fleet but in their heavy infantry. Nevertheless the greatness of the danger still impending made all this appear tolerable.

Nicias seeing the army dejected and greatly altered, passed along the ranks and encouraged and comforted them as far as was possible under the circumstances, raising his voice still higher and higher as he went from one company to another in his earnestness, and in his anxiety that the benefit of his words might reach as many as possible:

"Athenians and allies, even in our present position we must still hope on, since men have ere now been saved from worse straits than this; and you must not condemn yourselves too severely either because of your disasters or because of your present unmerited sufferings. I myself who am not superior to any of you in strength—indeed you see how I am in my sickness—and who in the gifts of fortune am, I think, whether in private life or otherwise, the equal of any, am now exposed to the same danger as the meanest among you; and yet my life has been one of much devotion towards the gods, and of much justice and without offence towards men. I have, therefore, still a strong hope for the future, and our misfortunes do not terrify me as much as they might. Indeed we may hope that they will be lightened: our enemies have had good fortune enough; and if any of the gods was offended at our expedition, we have been already amply punished. Others before us have attacked their neighbours and have done what men will do without suffering more than they could bear; and we may now justly expect to find the gods more kind, for we have become fitter objects for their pity than their jealousy. And then look at yourselves, mark the numbers and efficiency of the heavy infantry marching in your ranks, and do not give way too much to despondency, but reflect that you are yourselves at once a city wherever you sit down, and that there is no other in Sicily that could easily resist your attack, or expel you when once established. The safety and order of the march is for yourselves to look to; the one thought of each man being that the spot on which he may be forced to fight must be conquered and held as his country and stronghold. Meanwhile we shall hasten on our way night and day alike, as our provisions are scanty; and if we can reach some friendly place of the Sicels, whom fear of the Syracusans still keeps true to us, you may forthwith consider yourselves safe. A message has been sent on to them with directions to meet us with supplies of food. To sum up, be convinced, soldiers, that you must be brave, as there is no place near for your cowardice to take refuge in, and that if you now escape from the enemy, you may all see again what your hearts desire, while those of you who are Athenians will raise up again the great power of the state, fallen though it be. Men make the city and not walls or ships without men in them."

As he made this address, Nicias went along the ranks, and brought back to their place any of the troops that he saw straggling out of the line; while Demosthenes did as much for his part of the army, addressing them in words very similar. The army marched in a hollow square, the division under Nicias leading, and that of Demosthenes following, the heavy infantry being outside and the baggage-carriers and the bulk of the army in the middle. When they arrived at the ford of the river Anapus they there found drawn up a body of the Syracusans and allies, and routing these, made good their passage and pushed on, harassed by the charges of the Syracusan horse and by the missiles of their light troops. On that day they advanced about four miles and a half, halting for the night upon a certain hill. On the next they started early and got on about two miles further, and descended into a place in the plain and there encamped, in order to procure some eatables from the houses, as the place was inhabited, and to carry on with them water from thence, as for many furlongs in front, in the direction in which they were going, it was not plentiful. The Syracusans meanwhile went on and fortified the pass in front, where there was a steep hill with a rocky ravine on each side of it, called the Acraean cliff. The next day the Athenians advancing found themselves impeded by the missiles and charges of the horse and darters, both very numerous, of the Syracusans and allies; and after fighting for a long while, at length retired to the same camp, where they had no longer provisions as before, it being impossible to leave their position by reason of the cavalry.

Early next morning they started afresh and forced their way to the hill, which had been fortified, where they found before them the enemy's infantry drawn up many shields deep to defend the fortification, the pass being narrow. The Athenians assaulted the work, but were greeted by a storm of missiles from the hill, which told with the greater effect through its being a steep one, and unable to force the passage, retreated again and rested. Meanwhile occurred some claps of thunder and rain, as often happens towards autumn, which still further disheartened the Athenians, who thought all these things to be omens of their approaching ruin. While they were resting Gylippus and the Syracusans sent a part of their army to throw up works in their rear on the way by which they had advanced; however, the Athenians immediately sent some of their men and prevented them; after which they retreated more towards the plain and halted for the night. When they advanced the next day the Syracusans surrounded and attacked them on every side, and disabled many of them, falling back if the Athenians advanced and coming on if they retired, and in particular assaulting their rear, in the hope of routing them in detail, and thus striking a panic into the whole army. For a long while the Athenians persevered in this fashion, but after advancing for four or five furlongs halted to rest in the plain, the Syracusans also withdrawing to their own camp.

During the night Nicias and Demosthenes, seeing the wretched condition of their troops, now in want of every kind of necessary, and numbers of them disabled in the numerous attacks of the enemy, determined to light as many fires as possible, and to lead off the army, no longer by the same route as they had intended, but towards the sea in the opposite direction to that guarded by the Syracusans. The whole of this route was leading the army not to Catana but to the other side of Sicily, towards Camarina, Gela, and the other Hellenic and barbarian towns in that quarter. They accordingly lit a number of fires and set out by night. Now all armies, and the greatest most of all, are liable to fears and alarms, especially when they are marching by night through an enemy's country and with the enemy near; and the Athenians falling into one of these panics, the leading division, that of Nicias, kept together and got on a good way in front, while that of Demosthenes, comprising rather more than half the army, got separated and marched on in some disorder. By morning, however, they reached the sea, and getting into the Helorine Road, pushed on in order to reach the river Cacyparis, and to follow the stream up through the interior, where they hoped to be met by the Sicels whom they had sent for. Arrived at the river, they found there also a Syracusan party engaged in barring the passage of the ford with a wall and a palisade, and forcing this guard, crossed the river and went on to another called the Erineus, according to the advice of their guides.

Meanwhile, when day came and the Syracusans and allies found that the Athenians were gone, most of them accused Gylippus of having let them escape on purpose, and hastily pursuing by the road which they had no difficulty in finding that they had taken, overtook them about dinner-time. They first came up with the troops under Demosthenes, who were behind and marching somewhat slowly and in disorder, owing to the night-panic above referred to, and at once attacked and engaged them, the Syracusan horse surrounding them with more ease now that they were separated from the rest, and hemming them in on one spot. The division of Nicias was five or six miles on in front, as he led them more rapidly, thinking that under the circumstances their safety lay not in staying and fighting, unless obliged, but in retreating as fast as possible, and only fighting when forced to do so. On the other hand, Demosthenes was, generally speaking, harassed more incessantly, as his post in the rear left him the first exposed to the attacks of the enemy; and now, finding that the Syracusans were in pursuit, he omitted to push on, in order to form his men for battle, and so lingered until he was surrounded by his pursuers and himself and the Athenians with him placed in the most distressing position, being huddled into an enclosure with a wall all round it, a road on this side and on that, and olive-trees in great number, where missiles were showered in upon them from every quarter. This mode of attack the Syracusans had with good reason adopted in preference to fighting at close quarters, as to risk a struggle with desperate men was now more for the advantage of the Athenians than for their own; besides, their success had now become so certain that they began to spare themselves a little in order not to be cut off in the moment of victory, thinking too that, as it was, they would be able in this way to subdue and capture the enemy.

In fact, after plying the Athenians and allies all day long from every side with missiles, they at length saw that they were worn out with their wounds and other sufferings; and Gylippus and the Syracusans and their allies made a proclamation, offering their liberty to any of the islanders who chose to come over to them; and some few cities went over. Afterwards a capitulation was agreed upon for all the rest with Demosthenes, to lay down their arms on condition that no one was to be put to death either by violence or imprisonment or want of the necessaries of life. Upon this they surrendered to the number of six thousand in all, laying down all the money in their possession, which filled the hollows of four shields, and were immediately conveyed by the Syracusans to the town.

Meanwhile Nicias with his division arrived that day at the river Erineus, crossed over and posted his army upon some high ground upon the other side. The next day the Syracusans overtook him and told him that the troops under Demosthenes had surrendered, and invited him to follow their example. Incredulous of the fact, Nicias asked for a truce to send a horseman to see, and upon the return of the messenger with the tidings that they had surrendered, sent a herald to Gylippus and the Syracusans, saying that he was ready to agree with them on behalf of the Athenians to repay whatever money the Syracusans had spent upon the war if they would let his army go; and offered until the money was paid to give Athenians as hostages, one for every talent. The Syracusans and Gylippus rejected this proposition, and attacked this division as they had the other, standing all round and plying them with missiles until the evening. Food and necessaries were as miserably wanting to the troops of Nicias as they had been to their comrades; nevertheless they watched for the quiet of the night to resume their march. But as they were taking up their arms the Syracusans perceived it and raised their paean, upon which the Athenians, finding that they were discovered, laid them down again, except about three hundred men who forced their way through the guards and went on during the night as they were able.

As soon as it was day Nicias put his army in motion, pressed, as before, by the Syracusans and their allies, pelted from every side by their missiles, and struck down by their javelins. The Athenians pushed on for the Assinarus, impelled by the attacks made upon them from every side by a numerous cavalry and the swarm of other arms, fancying that they should breathe more freely if once across the river, and driven on also by their exhaustion and craving for water. Once there they rushed in, and all order was at an end, each man wanting to cross first, and the attacks of the enemy making it difficult to cross at all; forced to huddle together, they fell against and trod down one another, some dying immediately upon the javelins, others getting entangled together and stumbling over the articles of baggage, without being able to rise again. Meanwhile the opposite bank, which was steep, was lined by the Syracusans, who showered missiles down upon the Athenians, most of them drinking greedily and heaped together in disorder in the hollow bed of the river. The Peloponnesians also came down and butchered them, especially those in the water, which was thus immediately spoiled, but which they went on drinking just the same, mud and all, bloody as it was, most even fighting to have it.

At last, when many dead now lay piled one upon another in the stream, and part of the army had been destroyed at the river, and the few that escaped from thence cut off by the cavalry, Nicias surrendered himself to Gylippus, whom he trusted more than he did the Syracusans, and told him and the Lacedaemonians to do what they liked with him, but to stop the slaughter of the soldiers. Gylippus, after this, immediately gave orders to make prisoners; upon which the rest were brought together alive, except a large number secreted by the soldiery, and a party was sent in pursuit of the three hundred who had got through the guard during the night, and who were now taken with the rest. The number of the enemy collected as public property was not considerable; but that secreted was very large, and all Sicily was filled with them, no convention having been made in their case as for those taken with Demosthenes. Besides this, a large portion were killed outright, the carnage being very great, and not exceeded by any in this Sicilian war. In the numerous other encounters upon the march, not a few also had fallen. Nevertheless many escaped, some at the moment, others served as slaves, and then ran away subsequently. These found refuge at Catana.

The Syracusans and their allies now mustered and took up the spoils and as many prisoners as they could, and went back to the city. The rest of their Athenian and allied captives were deposited in the quarries, this seeming the safest way of keeping them; but Nicias and Demosthenes were butchered, against the will of Gylippus, who thought that it would be the crown of his triumph if he could take the enemy's generals to Lacedaemon. One of them, as it happened, Demosthenes, was one of her greatest enemies, on account of the affair of the island and of Pylos; while the other, Nicias, was for the same reasons one of her greatest friends, owing to his exertions to procure the release of the prisoners by persuading the Athenians to make peace. For these reasons the Lacedaemonians felt kindly towards him; and it was in this that Nicias himself mainly confided when he surrendered to Gylippus. But some of the Syracusans who had been in correspondence with him were afraid, it was said, of his being put to the torture and troubling their success by his revelations; others, especially the Corinthians, of his escaping, as he was wealthy, by means of bribes, and living to do them further mischief; and these persuaded the allies and put him to death. This or the like was the cause of the death of a man who, of all the Hellenes in my time, least deserved such a fate, seeing that the whole course of his life had been regulated with strict attention to virtue.

The prisoners in the quarries were at first hardly treated by the Syracusans. Crowded in a narrow hole, without any roof to cover them, the heat of the sun and the stifling closeness of the air tormented them during the day, and then the nights, which came on autumnal and chilly, made them ill by the violence of the change; besides, as they had to do everything in the same place for want of room, and the bodies of those who died of their wounds or from the variation in the temperature, or from similar causes, were left heaped together one upon another, intolerable stenches arose; while hunger and thirst never ceased to afflict them, each man during eight months having only half a pint of water and a pint of corn given him daily. In short, no single suffering to be apprehended by men thrust into such a place was spared them. For some seventy days they thus lived all together, after which all, except the Athenians and any Siceliots or Italiots who had joined in the expedition, were sold. The total number of prisoners taken it would be difficult to state exactly, but it could not have been less than seven thousand.

This was the greatest Hellenic achievement of any in this war, or, in my opinion, in Hellenic history; at once most glorious to the victors, and most calamitous to the conquered. They were beaten at all points and altogether; all that they suffered was great; they were destroyed, as the saying is, with a total destruction, their fleet, their army—everything was destroyed, and few out of many returned home.

# 57 The Last Phase

The war continued for another nine years. The Athenians fielded new armies and built new navies and even won victories, but the handwriting on the wall was clear. The pressure exerted by the Spartans increased. From 413 B.C. the Spartans maintained a fortified post in Attica itself, at Decelea, less than fifteen miles from the city of Athens. In 412 a Spartan-Persian alliance was signed. As the years went by, the Spartans acquired more powerful fleets and became more proficient in their employment; by the end of the war they had in Lysander a naval commander as capable as any Athenian.

Within Athens the situation was chaotic. Politicians rose and fell in popularity according to the temporary success or failure of their policies. For a brief period in 411 B.C. the democracy was overthrown by an oligarchic *coup d'état*. For a time (410–407) Alcibiades returned in glory to lead Athens once again, only to fall from favor and to flee again, this time to Persia. In the final years of the war there were wholesale revolts within the Athenian empire, and at the end Athens fought practically alone. As late as 406 B.C. the Athenians were able to win a major naval victory at the Arginusae Islands off Ionia, but they could not exploit the advantage. In 405 B.C. the last Athenian fleet was destroyed at Aegospotami in the Hellespont, and the following year Athens surrendered.

Thucydides' history was left unfinished. The narrative was resumed by Xenophon at the point where Thucydides' work was broken off when the author died. It is from Xenophon that we know the events of the last seven years of war. The following selection describing the conclusion of the war is Xenophon's *Hellenic History* 2.1.10–2.23. It is translated by H. G. Dakyns.

⊛⊛⊛⊛⊛

In the following year Lysander arrived at Ephesus, and sent for Eteonicus with his ships from Chios, and collected all other vessels elsewhere to be found. His time was now devoted to refitting the old ships and having new ones built in Antandrus. He also made a journey to the court of Cyrus with a request for money. All Cyrus could say was, that not only the money sent by the king was spent, but much more besides; and he pointed out the various sums which each of the admirals had received, but at the same time he gave him what he asked for. Furnished with this money, Lysander appointed captains to the different men-of-war, and remitted to the sailors their arrears of pay. Meanwhile the Athenian generals, on their side, were devoting their energies to the improvement of their navy at Samos.

It was now Cyrus's turn to send for Lysander. It was the moment at which the envoy from his father had arrived with the message: "Your father is on his sick-bed and desires your presence." The king lay at Thamneria, in Media, near the territory of the Cadusians, against whom he had marched to put down a revolt. When Lysander presented himself, Cyrus was urgent with him not to engage the Athenians at sea unless he had many more ships than they. "The king," he added, "and I have plenty of wealth, so that, as far as money goes, you can man plenty of vessels." He then consigned to him all the tributes from the several cities which belonged to him personally, and gave him the ready money which he had as a gift; and finally, reminding him of the sincere friendship he entertained towards the state of Lacedaemon, as well as to himself personally, he set out up country to visit his father. Lysander, finding himself thus left with the complete control of the property of Cyrus (during the absence of that prince, so summoned to the bedside of his father), was able to distribute pay to his troops, after which he set sail for the Ceramic Gulf of Caria. Here he stormed a city in alliance with the Athenians named Cedreae, and on the following day's assault took it, and reduced the inhabitants to slavery. These were of a mixed Hellene and barbarian stock. From Cedreae he continued his voyage to Rhodes. The Athenians meanwhile, using Samos as their base of operations, were employed in devastating the king's territory, or in swooping down upon Chios and Ephesus, and in general were preparing for a naval battle, having but lately chosen three new generals in addition to those already in office, whose names were Menander, Tydeus and Cephisodotus. Now Lysander, leaving Rhodes, and coasting along Ionia, made his way to the Hellespont, having an eye to the passage of vessels through the Straits, and, in a more hostile sense, on the cities which had revolted from Sparta. The Athenians also set sail from Chios, but stood out to the open sea, since the seaboard of Asia was hostile to them.

Lysander was again on the move; leaving Abydos, he passed up channel to Lampsacus, which town was allied with Athens; the men of Abydos and the rest of the troops advancing by land, under the command of the Lacedaemonian Thorax. They then attacked and took by storm the town, which was wealthy, and with its stores of wine and wheat and other commodities was pillaged by the soldiery. All free-born persons, however, were without exception released by Lysander. And now the Athenian fleet, following close on his heels, came to moorings at Elaeus, in the Chersonesus, one hundred and eighty sail in all. It was not until they had reached this place, and were getting their early meal, that the news of what had happened at Lampsacus reached them. Then they instantly set sail again to

Sestos, and having halted long enough merely to take in stores, sailed on further to Aegospotami, a point facing Lampsacus, where the Hellespont is not quite two miles broad. Here they took their evening meal.

The night following, or rather early next morning, with the first streak of dawn, Lysander gave the signal for the men to take their breakfasts and get on board their vessels; and so, having got all ready for a naval engagement, with his ports closed and movable bulwarks attached, he issued the order that no one was to stir from his post or put out to sea. As the sun rose the Athenians drew up their vessels facing the harbour, in line of battle ready for action; but Lysander declining to come out to meet them, as the day advanced they retired again to Aegospotami. Then Lysander ordered the swiftest of his ships to follow the Athenians, and as soon as the crews had disembarked, to watch what they did, sail back, and report to him. Until these look-outs returned he would permit no disembarkation from his ships. This performance he repeated for four successive days, and each day the Athenians put out to sea and challenged an engagement.

But now Alcibiades,[1] from one of his fortresses, could espy the position of his fellow-country-men, moored on an open beach beyond reach of any city, and forced to send for supplies to Sestos, which was nearly two miles distant, while their enemies were safely lodged in a harbour, with a city adjoining, and everything within reach. The situation did not please him, and he advised them to shift their anchorage to Sestos, where they would have the advantage of a harbour and a city. "Once there," he concluded, "you can engage the enemy whenever it suits you." But the generals, and more particularly Tydeus and Menander, bade him go about his business. "We are generals now—not you," they said; and so he went away. And now for five days in succession the Athenians had sailed out to offer battle, and for the fifth time retired, followed by the same swift sailers of the enemy. But this time Lysander's orders to the vessels so sent in pursuit were, that as soon as they saw the enemy's crew fairly disembarked and dispersed along the shores of the Chersonesus (a practice, it should be mentioned, which had grown upon them from day to day owing to the distance at which eatables had to be purchased, and out of sheer contempt, no doubt, of Lysander, who refused to accept battle), they were to begin their return voyage, and when in mid-channel to hoist a shield. The orders were punctually carried out, and Lysander at once signalled to his whole squadron to put across with all speed, while Thorax, with the land forces

---

1.  Now in exile, Alcibiades was living just across the Hellespont in Asia—well paid and comfortable in the service of the Persian king.

was to march parallel with the fleet along the coast. Aware of the enemy's fleet, which he could see bearing down upon him, Conon had only time to signal to the crews to join their ships and rally to the rescue with all their might. But the men were scattered far and wide, and some of the vessels had only two out of their three banks of rowers, some only a single one, while others again were completely empty. Conon's own ship, with seven others in attendance on him and the Paralus,[2] put out to sea, a little cluster of nine vessels, with their full complement of men; but every one of the remaining one hundred and seventy-one vessels were captured by Lysander on the beach. As to the men themselves, the large majority of them were easily made prisoners on shore, a few only escaping to the small fortresses of the neighbourhood. Meanwhile Conon and his nine vessels made good their escape. For himself, knowing that the fortune of Athens was ruined, he put into Abarnis, the promontory of Lampsacus, and there picked up the great sails of Lysander's ships, and then with eight ships set sail himself to seek refuge with Evagoras in Cyprus, while the Paralus started for Athens with tidings of what had taken place.

Lysander, on his side, conveyed the ships and prisoners and all other spoil back to Lampsacus, having on board some of the Athenian generals, notably Philocles and Adeimantus. On the very day of these achievements he despatched Theopompus, a Milesian privateersman, to Lacedaemon to report what had taken place. This envoy arrived within three days and delivered his message. Lysander's next step was to convene the allies and bid them deliberate as to the treatment of the prisoners. Many were the accusations here levied against the Athenians. There was talk of crimes committed against the laws of Hellas, and of cruelties sanctioned by popular decrees; which, had they conquered in the late sea-fight, would have been carried out; such as the proposal to cut off the right hand of every prisoner taken alive, and lastly the ill-treatment of two captured men-of-war, a Corinthian and an Andrian vessel, when every man on board had been hurled headlong down the cliff. Philocles was the very general of the Athenians who had so ruthlessly destroyed those men. Many other tales were told; and at length a resolution was passed to put all the Athenian prisoners, with the exception of Adeimantus, to death. He alone, it was pleaded, had taken exception to the proposal to cut off the prisoners' hands. On the other hand, he was himself accused by some people of having betrayed the fleet. As to Philocles, Lysander put to him one question, as the officer who had thrown the Corinthians and Andrians down the cliff:

2.  The sacred ship-of-state of Athens.

What fate did the man deserve to suffer who had embarked on so cruel a course of illegality against Hellenes? and so delivered him to the executioner.

When he had set the affairs of Lampsacus in order, Lysander sailed to Byzantium and Chalcedon, where the inhabitants, having first dismissed the Athenian garrison under a flag of truce, admitted him within their walls. Those citizens of Byzantium, who had betrayed Byzantium into the hands of Alcibiades, fled as exiles into Pontus, but subsequently betaking themselves to Athens, became Athenian citizens. In dealing with the Athenian garrisons, and indeed with all Athenians wheresoever found, Lysander made it a rule to give them safe conduct to Athens, and to Athens only, in the certainty that the larger the number collected within the city and Piraeus, the more quickly the want of necessaries of life would make itself felt. And now, leaving Sthenelaus, a Laconian, as governor-general of Byzantium and Chalcedon, he sailed back himself to Lampsacus and devoted himself to refitting his ships.

It was night when the Paralus reached Athens with her evil tidings, on receipt of which a bitter wail of woe broke forth. From Piraeus, following the line of the long walls up to the heart of the city, it swept and swelled, as each man to his neighbour passed on the news. On that night no man slept. There was mourning and sorrow for those that were lost, but the lamentation for the dead was merged in even deeper sorrow for themselves, as they pictured the evils they were about to suffer, the like of which they had themselves inflicted upon the men of Melos,[3] who were colonists of the Lacedaemonians, when they mastered them by siege. Or on the men of Histiaea; on Scione and Torone; on the Aeginetans, and many another Hellene city. On the following day the public assembly met, and, after debate, it was resolved to block up all the harbours save one, to put the walls in a state of defence, to post guards at various points, and to make all other necessary preparation for a siege. Such were the concerns of the men of Athens.

Lysander presently left the Hellespont with two hundred sail and arrived at Lesbos, where he established a new order of things in Mitylene and the other cities of the island. Meanwhile he despatched Eteonicus with a squadron of ten ships to the northern coasts, where that officer brought about a revolution of affairs which placed the whole region in the hands of Lacedaemon. Indeed, in a moment of time, after the sea-fight, the whole of Hellas had revolted from Athens, with the solitary exception of the men

3.   See Selection 55.

of Samos. These, having massacred the notables, held the state under their control. After a while Lysander sent messages to Agis at Decelea, and to Lacedaemon, announcing his approach with a squadron of two hundred sail.

In obedience to a general order of Pausanias, the other king of Lacedaemon, a levy in force of the Lacedaemonians and all the rest of Peloponnesus, except the Argives, was set in motion for a campaign. As soon as the several contingents had arrived, the king put himself at their head and marched against Athens, encamping in the gymnasium of the Academy, as it is called. Lysander had now reached Aegina, where, having got together as many of the former inhabitants as possible, he formally reinstated them in their city; and what he did in behalf of the Aeginetans, he did also in behalf of the Melians, and of the rest who had been deprived of their countries. He then pillaged the island of Salamis, and finally came to moorings off Piraeus with one hundred and fifty ships of the line, and established a strict blockade against all merchant ships entering that harbour.

The Athenians, finding themselves besieged by land and sea, were in sore perplexity what to do. Without ships, without allies, without provisions, the belief gained hold upon them that there was no way of escape. They must now, in their turn, suffer what they had themselves inflicted upon others; not in retaliation, indeed, for ills received, but out of sheer insolence, overriding the citizens of petty states, and for no better reason than that these were allies of the very men now at their gates. In this frame of mind they enfranchised those who at any time had lost their civil rights, and schooled themselves to endurance; and, albeit many succumbed to starvation, no thought of truce or reconciliation with their foes was breathed. But when the stock of corn was absolutely insufficient, they sent an embassage to Agis, proposing to become allies of the Lacedaemonians on the sole condition of keeping their fortification walls and Piraeus; and to draw up articles of treaty on these terms. Agis bade them betake themselves to Lacedaemon, seeing that he had no authority to act himself. With this answer the ambassadors returned to Athens, and were forthwith sent on to Lacedaemon. On reaching Sellasia, a town in Laconian territory, they waited till they got their answer from the ephors, who, having learnt their terms (which were identical with those already proposed to Agis), bade them instantly to be gone, and, if they really desired peace, to come with other proposals, the fruit of happier reflection. Thus the ambassadors returned home, and reported the result of their embassage, whereupon despondency fell upon all. It was a painful reflection that in the end they would be sold into slavery; and meanwhile, pending the return of a second embassy, many must needs fall victims of starvation. The razing of their fortifications was not a solution which any one cared to recommend. A senator,[4] Archestratus, had indeed put the question in the senate, whether it were not best to make peace with the Lacedaemonians on such terms as they were willing to propose; but he was thrown into prison. The Laconian proposals referred to involved the destruction of both long walls for a space of more than a mile. And a decree had been passed, making it illegal to submit any such proposition about the walls. Things having reached this pass, Theramenes made a proposal in the public assembly as follows: If they chose to send him as an ambassador to Lysander, he would go and find out why the Lacedaemonians were so unyielding about the walls; whether it was they really intended to enslave the city, or merely that they wanted a guarantee of good faith. Despatched accordingly, he lingered on with Lysander for three whole months and more, watching for the time when the Athenians, at the last pinch of starvation, would be willing to accede to any terms that might be offered. At last, in the fourth month, he returned and reported to the public assembly that Lysander had detained him all this while, and had ended by bidding him betake himself to Lacedaemon, since he had no authority himself to answer his questions, which must be addressed directly to the ephors. After this Theramenes was chosen with nine others to go to Lacedaemon as ambassadors with full powers. Meanwhile Lysander had sent an Athenian exile, named Aristoteles, in company of certain Lacedaemonians, to Sparta to report to the board of ephors how he had answered Theramenes, that they, and they alone, had supreme authority in matters of peace and war.

Theramenes and his companions presently reached Sellasia, and being here questioned as to the reason of their visit, replied that they had full powers to treat of peace. After which the ephors ordered them to be summoned to their presence. On their arrival a general assembly was convened, in which the Corinthians and Thebans more particularly, though their views were shared by many other Hellenes also, urged the meeting not to come to terms with the Athenians, but to destroy them. The Lacedaemonians replied that they would never reduce to slavery a city which was itself an integral portion of Hellas, and had performed a great and noble service to Hellas in the most perilous of emergencies. On the contrary, they were willing to offer peace on the terms now specified—namely, "That

4.   That is, a member of the Council (boulē).

the long walls and the fortifications of Piraeus should be destroyed; that the Athenian fleet, with the exception of twelve vessels, should be surrendered; that the exiles should be restored; and lastly, that the Athenians should acknowledge the headship of Sparta in peace and war, leaving to her the choice of friends and foes, and following her lead by land and sea." Such were the terms which Theramenes and the rest who acted with him were able to report on their return to Athens. As they entered the city, a vast crowd met them, trembling lest their mission should have proved fruitless. For indeed delay was no longer possible, so long already was the list of victims daily perishing from starvation. On the day following, the ambassadors delivered their report, stating the terms upon which the Lacedaemonians were willing to make peace. Theramenes acted as spokesman, insisting that they ought to obey the Lacedaemonians and pull down the walls. A small minority raised their voice in opposition, but the majority were strongly in favour of the proposition, and the resolution was passed to accept the peace. After that, Lysander sailed into the Piraeus, and the exiles were readmitted. And so they fell to levelling the fortifications and walls with much enthusiasm, to the accompaniment of female flute-players, deeming that day the beginning of liberty to Greece.

# THE FOURTH-CENTURY
# STRUGGLE FOR POWER

A THENS' dynamic growth in the fifth century B.C. had almost succeeded in unifying by force the Greek world of independent city-
states. In a sense the Peloponnesian War was only a drawn-out, agonizing
demonstration that no single polis had the resources to accomplish that
unity. Neither could a unity of Greeks be achieved voluntarily so long as
the independence of the polis was cherished. In the cramped world of a
poverty-ridden land the bleak future of Greece was an endless vista of wars
among the city-states. This in brief is what actually occurred in the fourth
century.

# 58 Restoration of Athenian Democracy

After Athens surrendered and ended the Peloponnesian War, an oligarchic
regime supported by a Spartan garrison stationed on the Acropolis was
established. The ruling committee of thirty men set about demolishing the
century-old institutions of democracy. The most active of their opponents
were summarily executed. In a brief reign of terror extending over a period
of a few months, the oligarchs put some three thousand of their fellow
citizens to death and earned the nickname of the Thirty Tyrants. In the
Peiraeus (or Piraeus), the Athenian port city that had always been the
stronghold of the adherents of democracy, a revolutionary movement was
begun. It gathered strength rapidly, and by the spring of 403 B.C. the oligarchy, following the withdrawal of the Spartan troops, was overthrown.

To the bitterness of defeat in war and the ferocious rule of the Thirty
Tyrants had been added the horrors of civil war. Nevertheless, under the

SOURCE: Reprinted by permission of the publishers and The Loeb Classical Library
from: *Lysias* tr. W. R. M. Lamb, Cambridge, Mass.: Harvard University Press.

leadership of Thrasybulus the democracy was restored, and its first act was one of extraordinary statesmanship and forbearance. An amnesty was declared under which all citizens were restored to their rights and reprisals against those who had supported the oligarchs were forbidden.

Revenge was ruled out, but memory could not be effaced. In the famous case of the trial and death of Socrates in 399 B.C. (Selection 81) many historians have seen the bitter fruit of those terrible days: Socrates was tried on charges of impiety and "corrupting the youth"; but was not the hidden charge, the one of which he could not be accused, his association with men known to be of the oligarchic faction, indeed with leaders of the Thirty Tyrants themselves?

A staunch adherent of the democracy was Lysias, himself a metic, that is, a resident alien. In the decades following the restoration he made a living as a professional writer of speeches for delivery in court cases. Again and again in the speeches that Lysias wrote for the litigants who hired him are heard the echoes of the terrible time of the Thirty Tyrants and the struggle to overthrow them. The following selection is abridged from Lysias' oration *Against Agoratus,* dated about 399 B.C. The accused is charged with crimes committed as an informer at the time of the oligarchy and with having a lifelong addiction to crime. Something of the atmosphere of bitterness that was a legacy of the period can be felt in the efforts of the speaker to obtain a conviction while at the same time remaining within the legal boundaries set by the amnesty of 403 B.C. The translation is that of W. R. M. Lamb.

❀❀❀❀❀

It is the duty of you all, gentlemen of the jury, to avenge the men who were put to death as supporters of your democracy, and it is also my duty in particular; for Dionysodorus was my brother-in-law and cousin. It happens, therefore, that I share with your democracy the same settled animosity against the defendant, Agoratus; the acts that he has committed are of a kind to give me good reason to hate him to-day, and justification to you for the penalty which, by Heaven's will, you are to impose on him. For Dionysodorus, my brother-in-law, and many others whose names you shall be duly told—all loyal friends of your democracy—were done to death by him in the time of the Thirty, through his act in informing against them. By this conduct he inflicted not only grievous losses on me and each of their relatives as individuals, but serious injuries—so I consider—on the whole city at large, by depriving it of men of that character. I therefore, gentlemen, consider it an act of justice and piety in all of you as well as myself

[ 494 ]

to take vengeance as far as each of us is able; and I think we should stand better both with the gods and with mankind if we did so. You must hear the whole of the circumstances, gentlemen, from the beginning, in order that you may know, first, in what manner your democracy was dissolved, and by whom; second, in what manner those men were done to death by Agoratus; and further, what injunction they gave when they were about to die. For when you have been accurately informed of all these things you will with the more pleasure and piety condemn this man Agoratus. I shall therefore start my relation at a point from which it will be easiest both for me to explain and for you to understand.

When your ships had been destroyed[1] and the resources of the city had been enfeebled, the ships of the Lacedaemonians arrived soon after at the Peiraeus, and negotiations for peace were made at once with the Lacedaemonians. At this moment those who desired to have a revolution in the State were busy with their plots, conceiving that they had found an excellent opportunity, and that this was the very moment for them to arrange the government according to their own desire. The only obstacles that they saw in their path were the leaders of the popular party and the generals and commanders. These they consequently sought to clear out of their way by fair means or foul, in order that they might achieve their ends with ease. So they began with an attack on Cleophon[2] in the following manner. When the first Assembly was held on the question of peace, and the emissaries of the Lacedaemonians stated the terms on which the Lacedaemonians were prepared to make peace—on condition that the Long Walls were demolished, each to the extent of ten stades—you then refused, men of Athens, to stomach what you had heard as to the demolition of the walls, and Cleophon arose and protested on behalf of you all that by no means could the thing be done. After that Theramenes, who was plotting against your democracy, arose and said that, if you would appoint him an ambassador to treat for peace with a free hand, he would arrange that there should be neither a breach made in the walls nor any other abasement of the city; and that he thought he would contrive even to get from the Lacedaemonians some additional boon for the city. You were persuaded, and appointed as an ambassador with a free hand the man whom in the previous year, after his election to the generalship, you had rejected on his scrutiny, because you judged him disloyal to your democracy. Well, he went to Lacedaemon and stayed there a long time, though he had left you here in a state of siege, and

1. At Aegospotami, 405 B.C. See Selection 57.
2. A democratic and anti-Spartan orator.

knew that your population was in desperate straits, as owing to the war and its distresses the majority must be in want of the necessaries of life. But he thought that, if he should reduce you to the condition to which he in fact reduced you, you would be only too glad to make peace on any sort of terms. The others remained here, with the design of subverting the democracy: they brought Cleophon to trial, on the pretext that he did not go to the camp for his night's rest, but really because he had spoken on your behalf against the destruction of the walls. So they packed a jury for his trial, and these promoters of oligarchy appeared before the court and had him put to death on that pretext.

Theramenes arrived later from Lacedaemon. Then some of the generals and commanders—among them Strombichides and Dionysodorus, and some other citizens, who were loyal to you, as indeed they showed later—went to him and protested strongly. For he came bringing a peace whose nature we learnt through the lessons of experience, since we lost a great number of worthy citizens, and ourselves were banished by the Thirty. Instead its terms required the razing of the Long Walls in their entirety; and instead of his contriving to get some additional boon for the city, we were to surrender our ships and dismantle the wall around the Peiraeus. These men perceived that, although nominally we had the promise of peace, in actual fact it was the dissolution of the democracy, and they refused to authorize such a proceeding: their motive was not pity, men of Athens, for the walls that were to come down, or regret for the fleet that was to be surrendered to the Lacedaemonians—for they had no closer concern in these than each one of you—but they could see that this would be the means of subverting your democracy; nor were they lacking, as some declare, in eagerness for the conclusion of peace, but they desired to arrange a better peace than this for the Athenian people. They believed that they would be able to do it, and they would have succeeded, had they not been destroyed by this man Agoratus. Theramenes and the others who were intriguing against you took note of the fact that there were some men proposing to prevent the subversion of the democracy and to make a stand for the defence of freedom; so they resolved, before the Assembly met to consider the peace, to involve these men first in calumnious prosecutions, in order that there should be none to take up the defence of your people at the meeting. Now, let me tell you the scheme that they laid. They persuaded Agoratus here to act as informer against the generals and commanders; not that he was their accomplice, men of Athens, in any way—for I presume they were not so foolish and friendless that for such important business they would have

[ 496 ]

called in Agoratus, born and bred a slave, as their trusty ally; they rather regarded him as a serviceable informer. Their desire was that he should seem to inform unwillingly, instead of willingly, so that the information should appear more trustworthy. But he gave it willingly, as I think you will perceive for yourselves from what has since occurred. For they sent into the Council Theocritus, the man called "the son of Elaphostictus": this Theocritus was a comrade and intimate of Agoratus. The Council which held session before the time of the Thirty had been corrupted, and its appetite for oligarchy, as you know, was very keen. For proof of it you have the fact that the majority of that Council had seats in the subsequent Council under the Thirty. And what is my reason for making these remarks to you? That you may know that the decrees issued by that Council were all designed, not in loyalty to you, but for the subversion of your democracy, and that you may study them as thus exposed. Theocritus entered this Council, and behind closed doors he informed them that certain persons were combining to oppose the system then being instituted. He declined, however, to give their several names, as he was bound by the same oaths as they were, and there were others who would give the names: he would never do it himself. Yet, if his information was not laid by arrangement, surely the Council could have compelled Theocritus to give the names, instead of laying the information with no names given. But in fact, here is the decree that they voted:

*[Decree ordering the arrest of Agoratus]*

. . . Now, they wanted him, gentlemen of the jury, to depose the names of yet more people; so firmly determined were the Council to work some mischief that they would not believe that he had yet given them the whole truth in his accusation. Well, he willingly deposed against all those men, with no compulsion upon him. When the Assembly met in the theatre at Munichia, some were so extremely anxious to have information laid before the people also in regard to the generals and commanders—as to the others, it was enough to have had it laid before the Council only—that they brought him up there also, before the people. Now answer me, Agoratus: you will not, I suppose, deny what you did in the presence of all the Athenians.

*[Interrogation]*

He admits it himself; but however, the secretary shall read the decrees of the people to you.

*[Decrees]*

That this man Agoratus deposed the names of those men, both before the Council and before the people, and that he is their murderer, I believe you understand well enough. My further point, that he was the author of all the city's troubles, and does not deserve to be pitied by anybody, I think I can make plain to you in summary fashion. For it was just when those persons had been arrested and imprisoned that Lysander sailed into your harbours, that your ships were surrendered to the Lacedaemonians, that the walls were demolished, that the Thirty were established, and that every conceivable misery befell the city. And then, as soon as the Thirty were established, they promptly brought these men to trial before the Council; whereas the people had decreed that it should be "before the court of two thousand."[3] Please read the decree.

[Decree]

Now if they had been tried before the proper court, they would have easily escaped harm; for by that time you were all apprised of the evil plight of the city, though you were unable at that stage to be of further service to her. But as it was, they were brought before the Council which sat under the Thirty. And the trial was conducted in a manner that you yourselves well know: the Thirty were seated on the benches which are now the seats of the presiding magistrates; two tables were set before the Thirty, and the vote had to be deposited, not in urns, but openly on these tables—the condemning vote on the further one . . .—so what possible chance of escape had any of them? In a word, all those who had entered that Council chamber for their trial were condemned to death: not one was acquitted, except this man Agoratus; him they let off, as being a "benefactor." And in order that you may know of the large number done to death by this man, I propose to read you their names.

[Names]

Now, when sentence of death, gentlemen, had been passed on them, and they had to die, each of them sent for his sister, or his mother, or his wife, or any female relative that he had, to see them in the prison, in order that they might take the last farewell of their people before they should end their days. In particular, Dionysodorus sent for my sister—she was his wife—to see him in the prison. On receiving the message she came, dressed in a black cloak . . . as was natural in view of the sad fate that had befallen her husband. In the presence of my sister, Dionysodorus, after dis-

3. A court of so large a size was only formed for cases of special importance.

posing of his personal property as he thought fit, referred to this man Agoratus as responsible for his death, and charged me and Dionysius his brother here, and all his friends to execute his vengeance upon Agoratus; and he charged his wife, believing her to be with child by him, that if she should bear a son she should tell the child that Agoratus had taken his father's life, and should bid him execute his father's vengeance on the man for his murder. To show the truth of what I state, I will produce witnesses to these facts.

[*Witnesses*]

So then these persons, men of Athens, lost their lives through the depositions of Agoratus. But after the Thirty had cleared them out of their way, you know well enough, I imagine, what a multitude of miseries next befell the city; and for all of them this man, by taking those people's lives, was responsible. It gives me pain, indeed, to recall the calamities that have befallen the city, but it is a necessity, gentlemen of the jury, at the present moment, so that you may know how richly Agoratus deserves your pity! For you know the character and number of the citizens who were brought away from Salamis, and the way in which they were destroyed by the Thirty. You know what a great number of the people of Eleusis shared that calamity. You remember also our people here who were haled to prison on account of private enmities; and who, having done no harm to the city, were compelled to perish by the most shameful, the most infamous, of deaths. Some left elderly parents behind them, who were expecting to be supported in their old age by their own children and, when they should end their days, to be laid by them in the grave; others left sisters unwedded, and others little children who still required much tendance. What sort of feelings, gentlemen, do you think are theirs towards this man, or what kind of vote would they give, if it rested with them, when by his act they have been deprived of their best comforts? You recollect, again, how the walls were demolished, the ships surrendered to the enemy, the arsenals destroyed, our Acropolis occupied by the Lacedaemonians, and the whole strength of the city crippled, so that our city was sunk to a level with the smallest in the world! And besides all this, you lost your private possessions and finally, at one swoop, you were all expelled by the Thirty from your native land. Impressed with these perils, those loyal citizens, gentlemen, refused their assent to the conditions of peace, and you, Agoratus, because they sought to do the State some service, brought about their death by laying information that they were intriguing against our democracy; and you are responsible for all the troubles that have befallen the city. So now let each of you remember the misfortunes caused both to individuals and to the common weal of the city, and take vengeance on their author. . . .

But I wish now, gentlemen of the jury, to represent to you the character of the men of whom Agoratus has bereft you. Had they been merely a few, one might mention them to you separately; but, as it is, I must cover them all in one brief account. Some had served you several times as generals, and then had handed on the city with added greatness to their successors in authority; some had held other high offices, and had borne the expense of many naval equipments: never before had they met with any disgraceful censure from you. Some of them survived, by having got away in safety; though this man sent them to their death none the less, and they were condemned to die: but fortune and providence delivered them. They fled the city, instead of being arrested and awaiting their trial; they have returned from the exile of Phyle, and are honoured by you as worthy men.

Such, you see, was the character of these men whom Agoratus either did to death or sent into exile from the city. And who, then, is he? You must know that he is a slave born and bred, so that you may know what manner of man it was that grossly maltreated you. For the defendant's father was Eumares, and this Eumares was the property of Nicocles and Anticles. Come forward, please, witnesses.

[*Witnesses*]

Now Agoratus, gentlemen, had three brothers. One of them, the eldest, was caught in Sicily making traitorous signals to the enemy, and by Lamachus's order he was executed on the plank.[4] The second abducted a slave from our city to Corinth, and again was taken abducting a girl from a household there: he was cast into prison and put to death. The third was arrested here by Phaenippides as a footpad, and you tried him in your court: you condemned him to death, and consigned him to execution on the plank. The truth of my statements will, I think, be admitted even by this man himself, and we shall produce witnesses to support them.

[*Witnesses*]

Now, to tell of all the other injuries and infamies, gentlemen, which have been the practice of this man and his brothers would be a lengthy task. As to his trade of slander in all the private suits that he brought, or in the various impeachments and depositions that he made, there is no

4. During the course of the ill-fated Sicilian expedition. See Selection 56.

need for me to speak in detail. To sum the whole, you all in the Assembly, and likewise in the law-court, convicted him of venal slander and made him pay a fine of ten thousand drachmae; so that this point has been sufficiently attested by your whole body. Then again, he attempted, with a character like that, to debauch and defile free-born wives of our citizens, and was taken in adultery; and for that the penalty is death. Call witnesses to the truth of my words.

[*Witnesses*]

Then is it not clearly a duty upon you all to convict this man? For if each of the brothers was thought deserving of death for a single offence, surely the man who, both publicly against the city and privately against each of you, has committed many offences, for each of which the penalty under our laws is death, must by all means be condemned to death by you.

He will say, gentlemen, attempting to deceive you, that in the time of the Four Hundred[5] he killed Phrynichus, and in reward for this, he asserts, the people made him an Athenian citizen. But he lies, gentlemen. For neither did he kill Phrynichus, nor did the people make him an Athenian citizen. It was Thrasybulus of Calydon and Apollodorus of Megara, gentlemen, who combined in a plot against Phrynichus: they lighted on him as he was out walking, and Thrasybulus struck Phrynichus, knocking him down with the blow; but Apollodorus did not touch him. Meanwhile an outcry arose, and they ran off and disappeared. But Agoratus here was neither invited to join them nor was present at the deed, nor does he know anything of the matter. The truth of my statement will be shown you by the decree itself.

[*Decree*]

That he did not kill Phrynichus is clear from the decree itself: for nowhere do we find "that Agoratus be an Athenian," as in the case of Thrasybulus. If, however, he had killed Phrynichus, he ought to appear as having been made an Athenian in the inscription on the same slab as Thrasybulus does; though some do contrive, by bribing the proposer, to have their own names added to the tablet as "benefactors." The truth of my words will be proved by this decree.

[*Decree*]

5.   The "Four Hundred" represent the brief oligarchic regime of 411 B.C. in Athens.

But yet, this man had so much contempt for you that although he was not an Athenian he took his seat in the law-court, and in the Assembly, and made impeachments of every conceivable kind, giving in his name with the addition—"of Anagyra." And besides, I have further good evidence against his having killed Phrynichus—an act for which he claims to have been made an Athenian: this Phrynichus established the Four Hundred; after his death, most of the Four Hundred fled. Do you then believe that the Thirty and the Council in session at that time, who were themselves all members of the Four Hundred who had fled, would have let off the slayer of Phrynichus when they had hold of him, instead of taking vengeance on him for Phrynichus and the exile they had suffered? In my opinion, they would have taken vengeance on him. Now, if he is pretending, as I assert, to be the slayer of Phrynichus when he is not, he is guilty there; while if you, sir, dispute this, and declare that you did kill Phrynichus, it is evident that you must have done yet greater injuries to the Athenian people so as to redeem, in the eyes of the Thirty, the blame for Phrynichus's death. For you will never persuade anyone at all that after killing Phrynichus you would have been let off by the Thirty, unless you had inflicted great and irremediable injuries upon the Athenian people. Hence, if he asserts that he killed Phrynichus, remember my words and take vengeance on this man for what he has done: if he disclaims it, ask him on what grounds he alleges that he was made an Athenian. If he fails to prove it, punish him for making use of his assumed title of Athenian to sit in both law-court and Assembly, and to bring slanderous charges against so many persons.

I am told that he is concocting for his defence the plea that he went off to Phyle, and was in the party that returned from Phyle, and that this is the mainstay of his case. But the facts were as I shall relate. This man did go to Phyle; yet, could there be an example of more abject vileness? For he knew that at Phyle there were some of those who had been banished by him, and he had the face to approach them! As soon as they saw him they laid hold of him and dragged him straight away to be killed in the place where they executed ordinary pirates or robbers that fell into their hands. Anytus, who was the general, said that they ought not to do that, on the ground that they were not yet in a position to punish certain of their enemies: at that moment they should rather keep quiet. If ever they returned home, they would then proceed to punish the guilty. By that speech he was the cause of this man's escape at Phyle: it was necessary to obey a man in the position of general, if they were to preserve themselves. Nay, further, you will find no one who has shared either this man's table or his tent, nor did the commander assign him a place in his tribe; to all he was a polluted person with whom they would not talk. Please call the commander.

*[Evidence]*

When they had reached their mutual agreement, and the Peiraeus party made their procession to the citadel, they were led by Aesimus; but there too this man showed similar audacity. For he followed along under arms, joining in the procession with the heavy-armed men to the city. But when they were close to the gates, and grounded arms before entering the city, Aesimus perceived him and went up to him, seized his shield, and flung it away, with the order—"Now, *you* go to hell! A murderer like you must not join in the procession to Athene." This was the way in which he was driven off by Aesimus; and I will produce witnesses to the truth of my statement.

*[Witnesses]*

These were the real relations, gentlemen, that he had with the heavy-armed troops, both at Phyle and in the Peiraeus. Nobody would speak to him, as a known murderer, and Anytus was the cause of his escape from death. If, therefore, he makes use of his journey to Phyle as a plea in his defence, you must retort with the question whether Anytus was the cause of his escape from death when they were ready to do justice upon him, and whether Aesimus flung away his shield and forbade him to join in the procession.

You must not accept that plea from him, nor this one either, if he should urge it,—that we are exacting the penalty a long time after the offence. For I do not think there is any statute of limitations for such crimes as his: my opinion rather is that, whether brought to his account immediately or after some time, this man must prove that he has not done the things that form the subject of the charge. Let him therefore satisfy us, either that he did not cause the death of those men, or that he did so with justice because they were doing a mischief to the Athenian people. But if we are late in punishing where we ought to have punished long ago, he is a gainer by the time in which he lived illicitly, while those men have none the less suffered death by his act.

I am told that he also takes his stand on the plea that the words "in the act" appear in the warrant for arrest; but this, I consider, is utter imbecility. So, without the addition of the words "in the act," he would be liable to the arrest; but just because the words have been added, he thinks he can extricate himself! This simply amounts, it would seem, to an admission that he has killed, but has not been taken in the act; and to insist on that is to imply that, if he was not taken in the act, but did the killing, he ought therefore to escape. But, in my view, the Eleven who authorized this arrest, without a thought of supporting Agoratus's plea—on which he was even then insisting—were quite correct in compelling Dionysius, who carried out the summary arrest, to add the words "in the act": surely that must be so, in dealing with a man who, first before five hundred, and then again before the whole body of the Athenians, made depositions whereby he took the lives of some of them, and thus was responsible for their death. For you cannot of course suppose that "in the act" only applies to a man felled with the stroke of a club or a dagger; since, by your argument, nobody will be found to have actually killed the men against whom you deposed. For no one either struck them or assassinated them, but your deposition had the effect of compelling them to die.[6] Then is not the author of their death a person caught "in the act"? Now, who can be that author but you, who made the depositions? So clearly you, who killed them, have been caught in the act.

I understand that he intends to refer to the oaths and agreements,[7] and will tell us that his prosecution is a violation of the oaths and agreements that we of the Peiraeus contracted with the party of the town. Well, if he takes his stand on these, he practically admits that he is a murderer: at least, he makes an objection of oaths, or agreements, or lapse of time, or the words "in the act"; but in itself the case affords him no confidence of success in his trial. Your duty, gentlemen of the jury, is to reject these arguments: you must bid him direct his defence to these questions—Did he make no depositions? Are those men not dead? Besides, I consider that the oaths and agreements in no way affect our position regarding this man. For the oaths have been taken between the parties of the town and of the Peiraeus. If, indeed, he was in the town while we were in the Peiraeus, the agreements would have been something for him to count upon; but the truth is that he was in the Peiraeus, like me and Dionysius and all these persons who are for punishing the man, so that we are faced with no objection there. For there was no oath taken between the men of the Peiraeus and the men of the Peiraeus.

6. By a draught of hemlock; see Selection 81.
7. Providing an amnesty for all except the Thirty, the Eleven who executed their orders, and their ten commissioners in the Peiraeus.

In every view, I consider, he deserves more deaths than one; for the same man who says that the people have made him one of them is found to have injured the people whom he himself calls his father, by treacherously sapping the resources that they had for advancing their greatness and strength. Therefore, the man who struck his own natural father and denied him all necessaries of life, he who robbed his adoptive father of the means that he possessed is certainly, on this one score, as provided by the law of such maltreatment, deserving of the penalty of death.

It is the duty of you all, gentlemen, as it is of each one of us, to avenge those men. For it was their dying injunction both to us and to all their friends, that we should avenge them on this man Agoratus as their murderer, and do him, in a word, all the injury of which each of us is capable. Now, if they have manifestly done some good service to the city or your democracy, as you yourselves acknowledge, it must follow that you all are friends and intimates of theirs, so that they enjoined this on each of you no less than on us. Hence it would be impious as well as illegal for you to absolve this man Agoratus. And now it is for you, men of Athens, to-day—since at that moment when they were to die you were unable to come to their aid because of the embarrassments of your situation—to-day, when you are able, to punish their murderer. And take heed, men of Athens, lest you commit the most abominable act of all. For if you acquit this man Agoratus, your action does not stop there, but by that same vote you condemn to death those men whom you acknowledge as your supporters. By releasing the author of their death you simply decide that they have been justly put to death by him. And thus the most awful of all fates would be theirs, if those whom they charged to avenge them as their friends should support with their votes the motion of the Thirty against those men. In the name of the Olympian gods, gentlemen of the jury, let neither art nor craft induce you to condemn those men to death who precisely for their many good services to you were put to death by the Thirty and by Agoratus here. Remember all the horrors, both those that smote the State as a whole and those that each of us felt in private, when those men lost their lives, and punish the author of them all. It has been made plain to you, alike from the decrees, the depositions and all the rest, that Agoratus is the author of their death.

Furthermore, it behoves you to vote in opposition to the Thirty: you must therefore acquit the men whom they condemned to death; and you must convict those whom they did not so condemn. Now, the Thirty condemned to death these men, who were your friends, and these you ought to acquit. Agoratus they acquitted, because he was found zealous for their destruction: him you ought to convict. If, therefore, you vote in opposition to the Thirty, first of all, you are not supporting your enemies with your votes; next, you will have avenged your own friends; and last, you will be held by all the world to have given a just and a pious vote.

# 59 The Dilemma—and a Solution: "The Ten Thousand"

The Spartans followed their victory in the Peloponnesian War by sub-jecting the Greek cities they had "liberated" from Athenian rule to an even worse tyranny. The result was no surprise: widespread rebellion and the turning against Sparta of her own allies. The Corinthian War saw ranged against Sparta an alliance of Corinth, Thebes, and Argos, joined by a revived Athens with a new fleet and new ambitions. This war lasted from 395 to 387 B.C., and was ended through the intervention of the Persian king, who acted as arbitrator. In the following years a new Athenian mari-time confederacy sought to re-establish Athens' power, and it failed. The Greek states eyed each other with suspicion; as soon as one of the larger states began to grow in power and to extend its suzerainty, the others would unite to bring it down.

An episode of the period was the brief glory of Thebes, which from 371 to 362 B.C. sat atop the heap and attempted to subject the rest of Greece. The episode illustrates at once the power struggle of the times and its futility. Theban power was begun with a stunning defeat of Sparta at Leuctra in central Greece in 371, and it ended, ironically, with another victory over Sparta at Mantinea in the Peloponnesus nine years later. The substance of Theban strength was a superb army that had been built up and maintained by Pelopidas and Epaminondas, two Theban patriots who were among the few original military minds the period produced. Pelopidas had already died, and when Epaminondas was killed at Mantinea, the bubble burst. Without the inspired leadership of these men Theban power was nothing.

SOURCE: Xenophon, The Persian Expedition, translated by Rex Warner (Harmonds-worth, England: Penguin Books, 1949). Reprinted by permission of the copyright holders, The Bodley Head Ltd., London.

A possible way out of the impasse of interpolis warfare was suggested by the rise of new-syle tyrants on the geographical fringes of the Greek world. In the course of the fourth century B.C. a number of such men acquired control over territorial states which provided a potentially greater basis for power than the severely limited resources of a single polis. Outstanding among these military despots was Dionysius of Syracuse in Sicily. In 405 B.C. he succeeded in installing himself as tyrant of the city of Syracuse, and he ruled with an iron hand from that time until his death in 368. He aimed at the conquest of all of Sicily and rule over the whole of Western Greece, and he systematically destroyed the polis basis of Greek life wherever he was successful. Ultimately he failed, and his successors could not hold what he had won. The whole episode ended in 339 B.C. with the liberation of the Greek cities of Sicily and the restoration of polis autonomy.

There was yet another possible way out of the Greek dilemma. The Greeks' habit of fighting among themselves offered the Persian king the opportunity to serve as arbiter of Greek affairs, primarily by means of judicious application of financial aid from the unlimited wealth of his empire. Persian soldiers, however, had never been a match for Greeks. If only the Greek cities could cease fighting among themselves and unite militarily for an attack on Persia, vast territories and immeasurable wealth were there for the taking; and the taking would solve Greece's problems, which were fundamentally insufficient land and insufficient resources. That this was no pipe-dream had been startlingly demonstrated at the very beginning of the fourth century. An army of ten thousand Greek soldiers had been hired by Cyrus, younger brother of the reigning Persian monarch Artaxerxes, for the purpose, so he told them, of putting down some rebellious tribes in Asia Minor. In fact his purpose was to overthrow his brother and to seat himself upon the throne. He marched his Greek soldiers almost to the gates of Babylon, and finally they were met by a Persian army at Cunaxa. The Greeks won an overwhelming victory, but Cyrus was killed. With no paymaster, no commanders, and no purpose, the Greek mercenaries wanted only to get back to their homes, and the story of their march to safety is one of the most remarkable adventure tales in all history. As some Greeks understood, however, the important part of the story was what a Greek army could do in Persia if it had a leader and a goal of conquest.

One of the soldiers hired by Cyrus was the young man who was to become the historian Xenophon. He was also one of the commanders elected by the troops to lead them out of Persian territory. The following passages are from Xenophon's first hand account (in which he austerely refers to himself in the third person) of *The Persian Expedition* 3.1; 4.4–5, 7–8. They are translated by Rex Warner.

@@@@@

With their generals arrested and the captains and soldiers who had gone with them put to death, the Greeks were in an extremely awkward position.[1] It occurred to them that they were near the King's capital and that around them on all sides were numbers of peoples and cities who were their enemies; no one was likely in the future to provide them with a chance of buying food. They were at least a thousand miles away from Greece; they had no guide to show them the way; they were shut in by impassable rivers which traversed their homeward journey; even the natives who had marched on the capital with Cyrus had turned against them, and they were left by themselves without a single cavalryman in their army, so that it was evident that, if they won a victory, they could not kill any of their enemies, and if they were defeated themselves, none of them would be left alive. With all this to reflect upon they were in a state of deep despondency. Only a few tasted food that evening, and a few lit fires. Many of them did not parade by the arms that night, but took their rest just where each man happened to be, and could not sleep because of their misery and their longing for their home lands and parents and wives and children, which they thought that they would never see again. In this state of mind they all took their rest.

There was an Athenian in the army called Xenophon, who accompanied the expedition neither as a general nor a captain nor an ordinary soldier. Proxenus, who was an old friend of his, had sent for him from his home and promised to make him the friend of Cyrus whom, he said, he valued above his own country. When Xenophon had read Proxenus's letter he consulted Socrates the Athenian[2] about the proposed expedition, and Socrates, suspecting that friendship with Cyrus might involve complaints at Athens (since Cyrus was thought to have been very active in helping the Spartans in their war with Athens), recommended Xenophon to go to Delphi and consult the god on the question of the expedition. Xenophon went there and

1. The officers had been summarily put to death when, under a truce, they had appeared before the Persian military officials to negotiate for a safe-conduct out of Persian territory.
2. The famous philosopher. See introduction to Selection 81.

asked Apollo the following question: "To what God shall I pray and sacrifice in order that I may best and most honourably go on the journey I have in mind, and return home safe and successful?" Apollo's reply was that he should sacrifice to the appropriate gods, and when Xenophon got back to Athens he told Socrates the oracle's answer. When Socrates heard it he blamed him for not first asking whether it was better for him to go on the expedition or to stay at home; instead of that he had made his own decision that he ought to go, and then enquired how he might best make the journey. "However," he said, "since this was the way you put your question, you must do what the god has told you."

Xenophon then made the sacrifices which the god had ordered and set sail. He found Proxenus and Cyrus at Sardis just on the point of starting on the march into the interior and he was introduced to Cyrus. Proxenus was eager for him to stay with them and Cyrus too joined him in this, saying that as soon as the campaign was over he would send him back home immediately. The expedition was supposed to be against the Pisidians. Xenophon thus joined the army under a false impression, though this was not the fault of Proxenus, since neither he nor anyone else among the Greeks, except for Clearchus, knew that the expedition was marching against the King. However, when they got to Cilicia, it already seemed obvious to everyone that it was against the King that they were marching. All the same, though unwillingly and with apprehensions about the journey, most people continued on the march, not wanting to lose face in each other's eyes, and in the eyes of Cyrus. Xenophon was no different from the rest, and now in their difficult position he was as miserable as anyone else and could not get to sleep. However, he got a little sleep in the end and had a dream. He dreamed that there was a thunderstorm and that a thunderbolt fell on his father's house and then the whole house was on fire. He woke up immediately, feeling very frightened, and considered that in some respects the dream was a good one, because in the midst of his difficulties and dangers he had dreamed of a great light from Zeus; but in other respects he was alarmed by it, because the dream seemed to him to have come from Zeus in his character of the King and the fire had seemed to blaze all round him and this might mean that he would not be able to leave the King's country but would be shut in on all sides by one difficulty or another. But what is really meant by having a dream like this can be seen from what happened after the dream.

This is what did happen. As soon as he woke up the first thing that came into his head was this: "What am I lying here for? The night is passing and at dawn the enemy will probably be here. If we fall into the King's hands, there is nothing to prevent us from seeing the most terrible things happening, from suffering all kinds of tortures and from being put to death in ignominy. Yet so far from anybody bothering to take any steps for our defence, we are lying here as though we had a chance of enjoying a quiet time. What city, then, do I expect will produce the general to take the right steps? Am I waiting until I become a little older? I shall never be any older at all if I hand myself over to the enemy to-day."

Then he stood up and first of all called together Proxenus's captains. When they had come together, he said: "I personally, captains, cannot sleep any more than, I expect, you can, and I can no longer lie still when I think of the position we are in. For there is no doubt that the enemy only made open war on us when they thought that their plans were complete, but on our side there is now nobody who is thinking out counter measures whereby we can put up as good a fight as possible. Yet if we relax and fall into the King's power, what sort of treatment can we expect from him? He is the man who cut off and fixed to a stake the head and hand of his own brother, his own mother's son, even when he was dead. So what sort of treatment can we expect, we who have no blood relation to take our side, and who marched against him with the intention of deposing him and making him a subject, and killing him if we could? Will he not go to all possible lengths in trying to inflict on us every conceivable misery and so make all men afraid of ever marching against him again? No, it is surely clear that we must do everything in our power to avoid falling into his hands.

"Now, personally, while the truce was in force, I could never stop feeling sorry for us and looking with envy on the King and those on his side. I considered what a large and splendid country they had, what inexhaustible supplies, what quantities of servants, of cattle and gold and clothing material; and then I thought on the other hand of our men's prospects—that we could only get a share of all these good things by paying for it (and I knew that there were not many left who had the money to do so), and that the oaths we had sworn prevented us from acquiring supplies in any other way except by paying for them. When I reckoned all this up, I sometimes used to feel more misgivings about the truce than I now do about the war. Now, however, they have put an end to the truce, and I think that the period of their arrogance and of our uneasy feelings is also ended. For now these good things lie in front of us as prizes for whichever side shows itself to be the better men; the gods are judges of the contest, and they will naturally be on our side, since it was our enemies who took their names in vain, while we, with many good things before our eyes, resolutely kept our hands off them because of the oaths we had sworn to the gods. So it seems to me that we can enter the contest with much more confidence than they can. Then we are physically better able than they are to endure cold and heat and hardship; our morale is, with the gods on our side, better than theirs; and if the gods grant us victory, as they did before, our enemies are easier to wound and kill than we are.

"Quite likely there are others who feel the same as I do. Well then, in heaven's name, let us not wait for other people to come to us and call upon us to do great deeds. Let us instead be the first to summon the rest to the path of honour. Show yourselves to be the bravest of all the captains, with more of a right to leadership than those who are our leaders at present. As for me, if you are willing to take the initiative like this, I am prepared to follow you, and if you appoint me to be your leader I am making no excuses about my age. Indeed I think I am already sufficiently grown up to act in my own defence."

This was what Xenophon said, and, after listening to him, all the captains urged him to be their leader—all except for a man there called Apollonides, who had a Boeotian accent. This Apollonides declared that it was nonsense to say that there was any chance of safety except by getting, if it was possible, the King's goodwill, and at the same time he started talking about all their difficulties. Xenophon, however, cut him short and spoke as follows: "My dear good man, you are the sort of person who neither understands what he sees nor remembers what he hears. Yet you were there with all the rest when the King, after Cyrus's death and in his pride because of it, sent and demanded that we should surrender our arms; and then, when we, so far from surrendering them, made ready for battle and went and encamped by his army, he left no stone unturned—sending people to negotiate, begging for a truce, providing us with supplies—until he got his truce. But when our generals and captains went into a conference, just as you are recommending, and left their arms behind, relying on the truce, what happened? Are they not at this moment being beaten and tortured and insulted, and are not even able, poor devils, to die, though death, I imagine, is what they are longing for? With all this knowledge in your possession, do you actually maintain that those who recommend self-defence are talking nonsense, and tell us to go and make another attempt at getting the King's goodwill? Soldiers, my view is that we should not suffer this fellow in our society; we should take away his captaincy, put the baggage on his back and use him as an animal. Being a Greek, and being what he is, he brings shame not only on his own native place but on the whole of Greece."

Then Agasias the Stymphalian broke in and said: "This fellow has got nothing to do either with Boeotia or with Greece. I have observed that he has holes in both his ears, just like a Lydian." This was actually the case, and so they drove him out.

The others went round the various detachments and where there was a general still alive they called for him, or, in cases where he was missing, for his deputy commander; where there was a captain still alive, they called for the captain. When they had all assembled they sat down in front of the place where the arms were kept. The generals and captains assembled there were about a hundred all together, and the meeting took place at about midnight. Hieronymus of Elis, the oldest of Proxenus's captains, then began the proceedings and spoke as follows: "Generals and captains, in view of our present position we decided to meet together ourselves and to invite you to join us, so that, if possible, we might come to some useful decision. I now call upon Xenophon to speak as he has already spoken to us."

Xenophon accordingly spoke as follows: "Here is one thing which we all know, namely, that the King and Tissaphernes have made prisoners of all those of us whom they could and are obviously planning, if they can manage it, to destroy the rest of us. Our part, as I see it, is to do everything possible to prevent our ever coming into the power of the natives—indeed to see rather that they are in our power. I should like to assure you of this point—that you who have assembled here in your present numbers are placed in an extraordinarily responsible position. All these soldiers of ours have their eyes on you, and if they see that you are downhearted they will all become cowards, while if you are yourselves clearly prepared to meet the enemy and if you call on the rest to do their part, you can be sure that they will follow you and try to be like you. It is right, too, I think, that you should show some superiority over them. After all you are generals, you are officers and captains. In peace time you got more pay and more respect than they did. Now, in war time, you ought to hold yourselves to be braver than the general mass of men, and to take decisions for the rest, and, if necessary, to be the first to do the hard work. I think that first of all you could do a great service to the army by appointing generals and captains as quickly as possible to take the places of those whom we have lost. For where there is no one in control nothing useful or distinguished can ever get done. This is roughly true of all departments of life, and entirely true where soldiering is concerned. Here it is discipline that makes one feel safe, while lack of discipline has destroyed many people before now.

"Then I think that, after you have appointed the required number of officers, if you were to call a meeting of the rest of the soldiers and put some heart into them, that would be just what the occasion demands. At the moment I expect you realise, just as I do, how dispirited they were in handing in their arms for the night and in going on guard. In that condition I cannot see how any use can be made of them, whether by night or by day. But there will be a great rise in their spirits if one can change the way they think, so that instead of having in their heads the one idea of 'what is going to happen to me?' they may think 'what action am I going to take?'

"You are well aware that it is not numbers or strength that bring the victories in war. No, it is when one side goes against the enemy with the gods' gift of a stronger morale that their adversaries, as a rule, cannot withstand them. I have noticed this point too, my friends, that in soldiering the people whose one aim is to keep alive usually find a wretched and dishonourable death, while the people who, realising that death is the common lot of all men, make it their endeavour to die with honour, somehow seem more often to reach old age and to have a happier life when they are alive. These are facts which you too should realise (our situation demands it) and should show that you yourselves are brave men and should call on the rest to do likewise."

So he ended his speech. Chirisophus spoke after him and said: "Up to now, Xenophon, the only thing I knew about you was that I had heard you were an Athenian. Now I congratulate you on your speech and your actions, and I should like to see here as many people of your sort as possible. Then we should have the right spirit all through the army. And now," he went on, "let us not waste time, my friends. Let us go away, and let those who are short of officers choose new ones. When you have chosen them, come to the centre of the camp and bring along those whom you have elected. Then we will muster the rest of the soldiers there. Tolmides the herald had better come with us."

With these words he got to his feet so as to show that there should be no delay, that what was necessary should be done at once. Afterwards the following were chosen as officers: Timasion, a Dardanian, to take the place of Clearchus, Xanthicles, an Achaean, to take Socrates' place, Cleanor, an Arcadian, to take Agias's place, Philesius, an Arcadian, to take that of Menon, and Xenophon, an Athenian,[3] in the place of Proxenus.

3.   The author himself. (The Socrates mentioned just above was not, of course, the philosopher.)

. . . . .

After crossing the river[4] they formed up in order about midday and marched at least fifteen miles through Armenia, over country that was entirely flat, with gently sloping hills. Because of the wars between the Armenians and the Carduchi there were no villages near the river; but the one which they reached at the end of their march was a big one, containing a palace belonging to the satrap; most of the houses were built like fortresses and there were plenty of provisions. Then a two days' march of thirty miles took them past the sources of the river Tigris, and from here a three days' march of forty-five miles brought them to the Teleboas, a beautiful river, but not a large one. There were a number of villages near the river, and all this part is called Western Armenia. Its governor was Tiribazus who was a personal friend of the King, and when he was present no one else had the right to assist the King in mounting his horse. He now rode up to the Greeks with a cavalry escort and sent forward an interpreter to say that he would like to speak with their commanders. The generals thought it best to hear what he had to say and, going forward till they were within hearing distance, asked him what he wanted. He replied that he would like to come to terms by which he would undertake to do the Greeks no harm and they would undertake not to burn the houses, though they could take any supplies which they needed. The generals agreed to this and made a treaty on these terms.

After this came a three days' march of forty-five miles over level ground. Tiribazus with his force kept pace with them, with about a mile between the armies. In the course of the march they came to a palace with a number of villages, full of all kinds of supplies, in the vicinity. There was a heavy fall of snow in the night, while they were in camp here, and at dawn it was decided that troops with their officers should take up quarters separately in the villages. There were no enemies in sight, and it seemed a safe thing to do because of the quantity of snow that had fallen. In these quarters they had all kinds of good food,—meat, corn, old wines with a delicious bouquet, raisins, and all sorts of vegetables. However, some of the soldiers who had wandered off some way from the camp reported that at night they had clearly seen a number of camp fires. The generals then decided that it was not safe for the troops to be in separate quarters, and that the whole army should be brought together again. Consequently they camped all together; and it looked also as though the weather was clearing up. However, while

4. The army had struggled northward with the ultimate goal of reaching Greek settlements on the southern shore of the Black Sea. Now, about to enter the mountain wilderness of Armenia, they face the most difficult part of their adventure.

they were spending the night here, there was a tremendous fall of snow, so much of it that it covered over both the arms and the men lying on the ground. The baggage animals too were embedded in the snow. The soldiers felt very reluctant to get to their feet, as, when they were lying down, the snow which fell on them and did not slip off kept them warm. But when Xenophon was tough enough to get up and, without putting his clothes on, to start splitting logs, someone else soon got up too and took over the job of splitting the wood from him. Then others also got up and lit fires and rubbed themselves down with ointment. A lot of ointment was found in this place and they used it instead of olive oil. It was made of hog's lard, sesame, bitter almonds and turpentine. A perfumed oil, too, made from the same ingredients, was found here.

After the snowstorm it was decided to take up separate quarters again under cover, and the soldiers went back with a lot of shouting and jubilation to the houses and the stores of food. The ones who, when they had left the houses, had acted like hooligans and burned them down, now had to pay for it by having uncomfortable quarters. The generals gave a detachment of men to Democrates of Temenus, and sent him out from here by night to the mountains where those who had been out of camp had said they had seen the fires. They chose him because he had already on previous occasions won the reputation for bringing in accurate information on subjects like this. When he said something was there, it was there; and when he said it wasn't, it wasn't. He now went out to the mountains and said that he had not seen any fires, but he returned with a prisoner who was armed with a Persian bow and quiver and a battle-axe like those which the Amazons carry. This prisoner was questioned as to where he came from, and said that he was a Persian and was going from Tiribazus's army to get provisions. They then asked him what was the size of the army and what was the purpose for which it had been mobilised. He replied that Tiribazus had under him his own force together with mercenary troops from the Chalybes and Taochi: his plan was to attack the Greeks, as they crossed the mountain, in a narrow pass through which went their only possible road.

When they heard this the generals decided to bring the army together again. They left a guard, with Sophaenetus the Stymphalian in command of those who stayed behind, and immediately set out, with the man who had been captured to show them the way. After they had crossed the mountains, the peltasts went forward, and, coming in sight of the enemy's camp, raised a shout and charged down on it without waiting for the hoplites.

When the natives heard the noise, they did not stand their ground, but took to flight. In spite of this, some of them were killed and about twenty horses were captured, as was Tiribazus's own tent which contained some couches with silver legs and some drinking vessels; also some men who said that they were his bakers and cup-bearers.

As soon as the generals of the hoplites found out what had occurred, they decided to return to their camp as quickly as possible, in case an attack might be made on those who had been left behind. So they sounded the trumpet to call the men back, set off and got back to their camp on the same day.

Next day they decided that they ought to get away as fast as they could, before the native army could reassemble and occupy the pass. They packed their belongings at once and, taking a number of guides with them, set off through deep snow. On the same day they passed the height where Tiribazus had intended to attack them, and then pitched camp. From here a three days' march of forty-five miles through desert country brought them to the river Euphrates, which they crossed without getting wet beyond the navel. The source of the river was said to be not far from here.

Next came a three days' march of forty-five miles over level ground and through deep snow. The third day's march was a hard one, with a north wind blowing into their faces, cutting into absolutely everything like a knife and freezing people stiff. One of the soothsayers then proposed making a sacrifice to the wind and his suggestion was carried out. It was agreed by all that there was then a distinct falling off in the violence of the wind. The snow was six feet deep and many of the animals and the slaves perished in it, as did about thirty of the soldiers. They kept their fires going all night, as there was plenty of wood in the place where they camped, though those who came up late got no wood. The ones who had arrived before and had lit the fires would not let the late-comers approach their fire unless they gave them a share of their corn or any other foodstuff they had. So each shared with the other party what he had. When the fires were made, great pits were formed reaching down to the ground as the snow melted. This gave one a chance of measuring the depth of the snow.

The whole of the next day's march from here was through the snow, and a number of the soldiers suffered from bulimia. Xenophon, who, as he commanded the rearguard, came upon men who had collapsed, did not know what the disease was. However, someone who had had experience of it told him that it was a clear case of bulimia, and that if they had something to eat they would be able to stand up. So he went through the baggage train and distributed to the sufferers any edibles that he could find there, and also sent round those who were able to run with more supplies to them. As soon as they had had something to eat they stood up and went on marching.

On this march Chirisophus came to a village about nightfall, and found by the well some women and girls, who had come out of the village in front of the fortification to get water. They asked the Greeks who they were, and the interpreter replied in Persian and said they were on their way from the King to the satrap. The women answered that he was not there, and said that he was about three miles away. Since it was late, they went inside the fortification with the water-carriers to see the head-man of the village. So Chirisophus and as many of the troops as could camped there, but as for the rest of the soldiers, those who were unable to finish the march spent the night without food and without fires, and some died in the course of it. Some of the enemy too had formed themselves into bands and seized upon any baggage animals that could not make the journey, fighting among themselves for the animals. Soldiers who had lost the use of their eyes through snow-blindness or whose toes had dropped off from frostbite were left behind.

It was a relief to the eyes against snow-blindness if one held something black in front of the eyes while marching; and it was a help to the feet if one kept on the move and never stopped still, and took off one's shoes at night. If one slept with one's shoes on, the straps sank into the flesh and the soles of the shoes froze to the feet. This was the more likely to happen since, when their old shoes were worn out, they had made themselves shoes of undressed leather from the skins of oxen that had just been flayed. Some soldiers who were suffering from these kinds of complaints were left behind. They had seen a piece of ground that looked black because the snow had gone from it, and they imagined that the snow there had melted—as it actually had done—this being the effect of a fountain which was sending up vapour in a wooded hollow near by. The soldiers turned aside here, sat down, and refused to go any further.

As soon as Xenophon, who was with the rearguard, heard of this, he begged them, using every argument he could think of, not to get left behind. He told them that there were large numbers of the enemy, formed into bands, who were coming up in the rear, and in the end he got angry. They told him to kill them on the spot, for they could not possibly go on. Under the circumstances the best thing to do seemed to be to scare, if possible, the enemy who were coming up and so prevent them from falling upon

[517]

the soldiers in their exhausted condition. By this time it was already dark, and the enemy were making a lot of noise as they advanced, quarrelling over the plunder which they had. Then the rearguard, since they had the use of their limbs, jumped up and charged the enemy at the double, while the sick men shouted as hard as they could and clashed their shields against their spears. The enemy were panic-stricken and threw themselves down through the snow into the wooded hollows, and not a sound was heard from them afterwards. Xenophon and his troops told the sick men that a detachment would come to help them on the next day, and he then proceeded with the march. However, before they had gone half a mile they came across some more soldiers resting by the road in the snow, all covered up, with no guard posted. Xenophon's men roused them up, but they said that the troops in front were not going forward. Xenophon then went past them and sent on the most able-bodied of the peltasts to find out what was holding them up. They reported back that the whole army was resting in this way; so Xenophon's men posted what guards they could, and also spent the night there, without a fire and without supper. When it was near daybreak Xenophon sent the youngest of his men back to the sick with instructions to make them get up and force them to march on. At this point Chirisophus sent a detachment from his troops in the village to see what was happening to the troops in the rear. Xenophon's men were glad to see them and handed over the sick to them to escort to the camp. They then went on themselves and, before they had marched two miles got to the village where Chirisophus was camping. Now that they had joined forces again, it seemed safe for the troops to take up their quarters in the villages. Chirisophus stayed where he was, and the other officers drew lots for the villages which were in sight, and each went with his men to the one he got.

On this occasion Polycrates, an Athenian captain, asked leave to go on independently and, taking with him the men who were quickest on their feet, ran to the village which had been allotted to Xenophon and surprised all the villagers, with their head-man, inside the walls, together with seventeen colts which were kept there for tribute to the King, and the head-man's daughter, who had only been married nine days ago. Her husband had gone out to hunt hares and was not captured in the village.

The houses here were built underground; the entrances were like wells, but they broadened out lower down. There were tunnels dug in the ground for the animals, while the men went down by ladder. Inside the houses there were goats, sheep, cows and poultry with their young. All these animals were fed on food that was kept inside the houses. There was also wheat, barley, beans and barley-wine in great bowls. The actual grains of barley floated on top of the bowls, level with the brim, and in the bowls there were reeds of various sizes and without joints in them. When one was thirsty, one was meant to take a reed and suck the wine into one's mouth. It was a very strong wine, unless one mixed it with water, and, when one got used to it, it was a very pleasant drink.

Xenophon invited the chief of the village to have supper with him, and told him to be of good heart, as he was not going to be deprived of his children, and that, if he showed himself capable of doing the army a good turn until they reached another tribe, they would restock his house with provisions when they went away. He promised to co-operate and, to show his good intentions, told them of where some wine was buried. So for that night all the soldiers were quartered in the villages and slept there with all sorts of food around them, setting a guard over the head-man of the village and keeping a watchful eye on his children too.

On the next day Xenophon visited Chirisophus and took the head-man with him. Whenever he went past a village he turned into it to see those who were quartered there. Everywhere he found them feasting and merry-making, and they would invariably refuse to let him go before they had given him something for breakfast. In every single case they would have on the same table lamb, kid, pork, veal and chicken, and a number of loaves, both wheat and barley. When anyone wanted, as a gesture of friendship, to drink to a friend's health, he would drag him to a huge bowl, over which he would have to lean, sucking up the drink like an ox. They invited the head-man too to take what he liked, but he refused their invitations, only, if he caught sight of any of his relatives, he would take them along with him.

When they came to Chirisophus, they found his men also feasting, with wreaths of hay round their heads, and with Armenian boys in native dress waiting on them. They showed the boys what to do by signs, as though they were deaf mutes. After greeting each other, Chirisophus and Xenophon together interrogated the head-man through the interpreter who spoke Persian, and asked him what country this was. He replied that it was Armenia. Then they asked him for whom the horses were being kept, and he said that they were a tribute paid to the King. The next country, he said, was the land of the Chalybes, and he told them the way there.

Xenophon then went away and took the head-man back to his own people. He gave him back the horse (rather an old one) which he had taken, and told him to fatten it up and sacrifice it. This was because he had heard that it was sacred to the Sun and he was afraid that it might die, as the journey had done it no good. He took some of the colts himself, and gave one colt to each of the generals and captains. The horses in this part of the world were smaller than the Persian horses, but much more finely bred. The head-man told the Greeks to tie small bags round the feet of the horses and baggage animals whenever they made them go through snow, as, without these bags, they sank in up to their bellies.

. . . . .

The Greeks arrived next at the river Harpasus which was four hundred feet across.[5] Then they marched through the territory of the Scytheni, a four days' march of sixty miles over level ground until they came to some villages, where they stayed for three days and renewed their stocks of provisions. Then a four days' march of sixty miles brought them to a large, prosperous and inhabited city, which was called Gymnias. The governor of the country sent the Greeks a guide from this city, with the idea that he should lead them through country which was at war with his own people. When the guide arrived, he said that in five days he would lead them to a place from which they could see the sea; and he said he was ready to be put to death if he failed to do so. So he led the way, and, when they had crossed the border into his enemies' country, he urged them to burn and lay waste the land, thus making it clear that it was for this purpose that he had come to them, and not because of any goodwill to the Greeks.

They came to the mountain on the fifth day, the name of the mountain being Thekes. When the men in front reached the summit and caught sight of the sea there was great shouting. Xenophon and the rearguard heard it and thought that there were some more enemies attacking in the front, since there were natives of the country they had ravaged following them up behind, and the rearguard had killed some of them and made prisoners of others in an ambush, and captured about twenty raw ox-hide shields, with the hair on. However, when the shouting got louder and drew nearer, and those who were constantly going forward started running towards the men in front who kept on shouting, and the more there were of them the more shouting there was, it looked then as though this was something of con-siderable importance. So Xenophon mounted his horse and, taking Lycus and the cavalry with him, rode forward to give support, and, quite soon,

5. The army has passed through Armenia and is now in the final stages of its journey to reach the Black Sea.

they heard the soldiers shouting out 'The sea! the sea!' and passing the word down the column. Then certainly they all began to run, the rearguard and all, and drove on the baggage animals and the horses at full speed; and when they had all got to the top, the soldiers, with tears in their eyes, embraced each other and their generals and captains. In a moment, at somebody or other's suggestion, they collected stones and made a great pile of them. On top they put a lot of raw ox-hides and staves and the shields which they had captured. The guide himself cut the shields into pieces and urged the others to do so too. Afterwards the Greeks sent the guide back and gave him as presents from the common store a horse, and a silver cup and a Persian robe and ten darics. What he particularly wanted was the rings which the soldiers had and he got a number of these from them. He pointed out to them a village where they could camp, and showed them the road by which they had to go to the country of the Macrones. It was then evening and he went away, travelling by night.

Then the Greeks did a three days' march of thirty miles through the country of the Macrones. On the first day they came to the river which forms the boundary between the territories of the Macrones and the Scytheni. On their right there was a defensive position which looked a very awkward one, and on the left there was another river, into which flowed the river that formed the boundary and which they had to cross. The banks of this river were covered with trees which, though not large, were growing thickly together. The Greeks cut the trees down when they came up to them, being anxious to get away from the place as quickly as they could. The Macrones, armed with shields and spears, and wearing hair tunics, were drawn up in battle order facing the crossing-place. They kept shouting to each other and hurling stones which fell harmlessly into the river as they failed to reach the other side.

At this point one of the peltasts came up to Xenophon. He said that he had been a slave in Athens and that he knew the language of these people. "Indeed," he went on, "I think that this is my own country. If there is no objection, I should like to speak to them."

"There is no objection at all," Xenophon said. "Speak to them and find out first of all who they are."

He asked them this, and they replied that they were Macrones.

"Now ask them," said Xenophon, "why they are drawn up to oppose us and why they want to be our enemies."

Their reply to this was: "Because it is you who are invading our country."

The generals then told the man to say, "We are not coming with any hostile intentions. We have been making war on the King, and now we are going back to Greece and want to get to the sea."

The Macrones asked whether the Greeks would give pledges that they meant what they said, and they replied that they would like both to give and to receive pledges. The Macrones then gave the Greeks a native spear, and the Greeks gave them a Greek one, as they said that these were the usual pledges. Both sides called on the gods to witness the agreement.

After exchanging pledges, the Macrones immediately helped the Greeks to cut down the trees and made a path for them in order to help them across. They mixed freely with the Greeks and provided them, as well as they could, with opportunities for buying food, and led them through their country for three days, until they brought them to the Colchian frontier. There were mountains here, which, though high, were not steep, and the Colchians were drawn up in battle order on the mountains. At first the Greeks formed up opposite them in line, with the intention of advancing on the mountain in that formation; but in the end the generals decided to meet and discuss what would be the best method of making the attack. Xenophon then expressed the opinion that it would be better to break up their present formation and to advance in columns. "The line," he said, "will lose its cohesion directly, since we shall find some parts of the mountain easy going and other parts difficult. It will immediately make the men lose heart, if after being drawn up in line they see the line broken. Then, if we advance in a line many ranks deep, the enemy will have men on both our flanks, and can use them however they like. On the other hand, if we go forward in a line which is only a few ranks deep, there would be nothing surprising in our line being broken through, with masses of missiles and men all falling on us together. And if this takes place at any single point, the whole line will suffer for it. No, I propose that we should form up with the companies in column, spaced out so as to cover the ground in such a way that the companies on our extreme flanks are beyond the two wings of the enemy. By adopting this plan we shall outflank the enemy's line, and, as we are advancing in columns, our bravest men will be the first to engage the enemy, and each officer will lead his company by the easiest route. As for the gaps between the columns, it will not be easy for the enemy to infiltrate, when there are companies both on his right and left; and it will not be easy to break through a company that is advancing in column. If any company is in difficulties, the nearest one will give support; and if at any point any one company can reach the summit, you can be sure that not a man among the enemy will stand his ground any longer."

This plan was agreed upon, and they formed the companies into columns. Xenophon rode along from the right wing to the left and said to the soldiers: "My friends, these people whom you see are the last obstacle which stops us from being where we have so long struggled to be. We ought, if we could, to eat them up alive."

When everyone was in position and they had formed the companies, there were about eighty companies of hoplites, each company with roughly the strength of a hundred. They formed up the peltasts and the archers in three divisions, one beyond the left flank, one beyond the right, and one in the centre, each division being about six hundred strong. The order was then passed along for the soldiers to make their vows and to sing the paean. When this was done, they moved forward. Chirisophus and Xenophon, with the peltasts attached to them, were advancing outside the flanks of the enemy's line, and, when the enemy observed this, they ran to meet them, some to the right, some to the left, and lost cohesion, leaving a great gap in the centre of their line. The peltasts in the Arcadian division, commanded by Aeschines the Acarnanian, thinking that the enemy were running away, raised their battle-cry and advanced at the double. They were the first to get to the top of the mountain, and the Arcadian hoplites, commanded by Cleanor of Orchomenus, came after them. As soon as they charged, the enemy failed to stand their ground and ran away in a disorganised flight.

The Greeks ascended the mountain and camped in a number of villages which were well stocked with food. There was nothing remarkable about them, except that there were great numbers of bee hives in these parts, and all the soldiers who ate the honey went off their heads and suffered from vomiting and diarrhoea and were unable to stand upright. Those who had only eaten a little behaved as though they were drunk, and those who had eaten a lot were like mad people. Some actually died. So there were numbers of them lying on the ground, as though after a defeat, and there was a general state of despondency. However, they were all alive on the next day, and came to themselves at about the same hour as they had eaten the honey the day before. On the third and fourth days they were able to get up, and felt just as if they had been taking medicine.

A two days' march of twenty-one miles from here brought them to the sea at Trapezus, an inhabited Greek city on the Euxine,[6] a colony of Sinope in Colchian territory. They stayed here, camping in the Colchian villages, for about thirty days, and, using these villages as their base, they ravaged

6.   The Greek name for the Black Sea.

the Colchian country. The people of Trapezus provided the Greeks with facilities for buying food, and gave them presents of oxen and barley and wine. They also negotiated with them on behalf of the Colchians in the neighbourhood, particularly those who lived in the plain, and from them too there arrived presents of oxen.

Then the Greeks prepared to offer the sacrifice which they had vowed. Enough cattle had come in for them to be able to sacrifice to Zeus the Saviour and to Heracles, for safe guidance, and to make the offerings which they had vowed to the other gods. They also held athletic sports on the mountain where they were camping. They elected as organiser and president of the sports the Spartan Dracontius, who had been an exile from his home since boyhood because he had accidentally killed another boy with a dagger.

When the sacrifice was finished, they gave the hides to Dracontius and told him to lead the way to the place where he had set out the course. He then pointed to the ground where they were actually standing, and said: "This hill is an excellent place for running, wherever one likes."

"But how," they asked, "will people be able to wrestle on ground that is so hard and rough?" To which he replied: "All the worse for the man who gets thrown." Boys, mostly from among the prisoners, competed in the short-distance race, and more than sixty Cretans ran in the race over a long distance. There were also wrestling and boxing events, and all-in wrestling. It was a very fine performance, as there were many entrants for the events, and, with their comrades as spectators, the rivalry was keen. There was also a horse race in which they had to gallop down a steep bit of ground, turn round in the sea, and ride back to the altar. On the way down most of them had a thorough shaking, and on the way up, when the ground got very steep, the horses could scarcely get along at walking pace. So there was a lot of noise and laughter and people shouting out encouragements.

# THE CONQUEST OF GREECE

THE possibility that Greece might be saved from tearing itself to pieces in incessant warfare depended upon the achievement of unity. As the fourth century B.C. wore on, it became increasingly clear that this unity would have to be imposed, that of themselves the independent city-states would never arrive at it. For sixty years Isocrates of Athens performed the self-appointed task of acting as a one-man lobby in propagandizing for unity and a national mission, the conquest of Persia. From among successive promising candidates, including Dionysius of Syracuse and Jason of Pherae (a Thessalian military commander), he sought the military leader who could force unity upon the warring poleis. At last, in Isocrates' old age there appeared the man who could do the job if it was to be done: King Philip of Macedon.

The kingdom of Macedon in the north of Greece was not thought of by the classical world as being Greek at all. Linguistically, Macedonian was a Greek dialect, and the Macedonians are therefore considered to be ethnically Greek by modern historians. They had, however, never developed the polis, which to Greeks was the symbol par excellence of the Greek way of life. Neither had Macedon developed into a centralized state. A series of monarchs in the fifth century had strengthened the ruling house and had made of the capital, Pella, a city of some splendor with the trappings of Greek culture. Still, Macedon was little more than a loose collection of rustic tribes owing nominal allegiance to their king when Philip II ascended the throne in 359 B.C. at the age of twenty-three.

# 60 *Philip of Macedon*

Philip had spent three years of his youth as a hostage in Thebes during the great days of Pelopidas and Epaminondas. The time proved not to have

SOURCE: Isocrates, *Orations,* translated by J. H. Freese (London: George Bell and Sons, 1894). Reprinted by permission of the publisher.

been wasted, for the first thing the young ruler did was build a national army using the innovations of the Thebans in weapons, training, and techniques. He then centralized his government and secured his borders against the northern and western barbarians. He next proceeded to extend his territory eastward along the Thracian coast and southward into Thessaly and toward Greece proper. The dazzling rise of Philip was clearly important to Greece: to traditional adherents of polis autonomy he posed a threat, to those of Isocrates' persuasion a promise. By 351 B.C., when Philip was on the point of taking the city of Olynthus, an ally of Athens, the anti-Macedonian view had found its spokesman and the spokesman had found his career. The Athenian Demosthenes spent the remaining years of his life as the champion of a reawakened Athens that would lead Greece in repelling Macedon as she had led Greece more than a century before in fighting off the Persians. He tried to persuade his fellow citizens of the danger, while on the other hand Isocrates was trying to persuade them to accept Philip as the leader who would unite them with all other Greeks for the national mission to conquer Persia.

In the writings of Isocrates and Demosthenes the opposing arguments stand in sharp contrast. The first of the following two selections is Isocrates' *Philippus* 8–9, 16, 30–31, 39–41, 88–92, 128–131, 149–154; the translation is by J. H. Freese. The second selection is abridged from the first of Demosthenes' three *Olynthiac Orations;* the translation is by C. R. Kennedy.

❁❁❁❁❁

Rejoicing then at the resolutions to which you [Philip] had come concerning peace, and thinking that they would be to your advantage, and to that of all the rest of Hellas as well as to ours, I was unable to divert my thoughts from what was connected with it, but was in such a frame of mind that I set to work to consider at once how to give permanence to what we had achieved and to prevent our state from again, after a short interval, desiring other wars; an examination of these questions in my own mind led me to the conclusion that there was no other way for her to live in quiet, except by the determination of the leading states to make up their mutual quarrels and carry the war into Asia, and by their resolving to win from the barbarians the selfish advantages which they now look for at the expense of Hellenes; which was the policy I have already advised in the Panegyric discourse. . . . For my intention is to advise you to take the lead both in securing the harmony of Hellas and in conducting the expedition against the barbarians; and persuasion is expedient with the Greeks, and force useful with the barbarians. Such, then, is the general scope of my discourse. . . .

I will now direct my remarks to my subject itself. I say that, while neglecting none of your private interests, you ought to try to effect a reconciliation between Argos, Sparta, Thebes, and our state; for if you are able to bring these together, you will have no difficulty in causing the other states to agree; for they are all under the influence of those which I have mentioned, and when in fear take refuge with one or other of those states, and draw their succours from thence. So that if you can persuade four states only to be wise, you will release the rest also from many evils. . . .

Now someone will perhaps venture to oppose what I have said, on the ground that I am endeavouring to induce you to undertake an impossible task: "the Argives can never," he may say, "be friends with the Lacedaemonians, or the Lacedaemonians with the Thebans, nor, in a word, can those who have been accustomed always to seek their selfish interests ever cast in their lot with one another."

I think, however, that nothing of this kind could have been effected when our state, or again when Lacedaemon, held the supremacy in Hellas; for either of them could have easily prevented what was going forward; but now I no longer have the same opinion of them. For I know that they have all been brought to a level by their misfortunes, so that I think they will much prefer the benefits of union to the selfish advantages of their former policy.

Then again I admit that there is no one else who could reconcile these states, but to you no such undertaking is hard. For I see that you have accomplished many things which others considered hopeless and beyond expectation, so that it would not be strange if you alone should be capable of effecting this union.

Now men of high aspirations and eminent position should not attempt enterprises which any ordinary man could carry out, but should confine themselves to those which no one would attempt but men of abilities and power like yours. . . .

. . . it is easy to see, in the light of what was not understood at that time, that those who would counsel aright ought not to carry war into the King's country, until someone has reconciled the Hellenes and made them desist from their present folly. And this is just the advice I have given to you.

On this point no sensible man would venture to contradict me, but I think that it would occur to any others who should propose to offer advice concerning the expedition to Asia, to recommend it, by pointing out that all whose lot it has been to undertake war against the barbarians, from obscurity have gained renown, from poverty wealth, and from low estate the ownership of many lands and cities. Now I do not propose to encourage you by means of such instances, but rather by reminding you of the fortune of those who are considered to have been unfortunate, I mean those who accompanied the expedition of Cyrus and Clearchus.[1] It is agreed that they gained as complete a victory over the whole of the King's forces as if they had fought against the Persian women, but that, when they seemed to have the mastery of affairs already within their grasp, they failed owing to the impetuosity of Cyrus; for in his exultation he carried his pursuit beyond the rest, and, falling into the midst of the enemy, met his death.

But, in spite of the great disaster that had befallen his foes, the King had such a contempt for his own power, that he invited Clearchus and the other commanders to a conference, promising to bestow upon them valuable presents, and full pay and release from service to the rest of the soldiers. Having allured them by such expectations and given them the most solemn pledges of the country, he seized and put them to death, preferring to sin against the gods rather than to engage in battle with soldiers who were thus destitute.

What encouragement could be better and more convincing than this? For it is clear that they also would have overthrown the power of the King, had it not been for Cyrus. But for you it is not difficult to avoid the disaster that then occurred, and it is easy for you to equip an army far stronger than that which overthrew his forces. Since, then, you will be able to do both, how can you help undertaking this expedition with the fullest confidence? . . .

Perhaps some of those who are fit to do nothing else may venture to blame me, because I have chosen to exhort you to undertake the campaign against the barbarians and the care of all the Hellenes, and have passed over my own city. Now, if I were undertaking to address myself on these points to others rather than to my own native city, which has thrice freed Hellas, twice from the barbarians, and once from the rule of Lacedaemon, I would allow that I was wrong; but, as it is, it will be seen that I have exhorted Athens before all other cities, with the greatest earnestness of which I was capable, to undertake the task, but, when I perceived that she thought less of what I said than of those who rave upon the platform, I left her alone, but, notwithstanding, did not abandon my efforts. Wherefore all might

1. See Selection 59.

fitly praise me because, as far as the powers I possess permitted me, I have persistently waged war against the barbarians, accused those who did not hold the same opinion as myself, and endeavoured to induce those, whom I hope will be best able to do so, to render some service to the Hellenes, and to deprive the barbarians of their present prosperity. For this reason I now address my words to you, well aware that many will be jealous of them when uttered by me, but that all will rejoice alike at the same undertakings when accomplished by you. For, although no one has taken part in what I have proposed, everyone will think that he is entitled to a share in the advantages that will result from it. . . .

If, in the course of your examination and consideration of the matter, anything of what I have said should appear to be somewhat feeble or in-adequate, lay the blame upon my age, for which all might fairly make excuse; but if this discourse resembles those previously circulated, you must not think that my old age has discovered it, but that the Deity has prompted it, not out of regard for myself, but out of care for Hellas, and from a desire to set it free from its present evils, and to invest you with greater renown than you at present enjoy. And I think you know in what manner the gods conduct the affairs of men. For they do not of their own act bestow the blessings or inflict the evils that befall them, but inspire all of us with such thoughts that each falls to our lot by means of one another. For in-stance, they have assigned to me discourses, while to you they allot the sphere of action, considering that you would best undertake the control of it, and that my discourses would be least wearisome to the audience. But I think that even your earlier undertakings would never have acquired such importance had not one of the gods assisted you to carry them out, not in order that you might be constantly at war only with the barbarians who inhabit Europe, but that, having practised upon them, gained experience, and come to know what manner of man you are, you might be eager for the course I have advocated. It is a disgrace to stay behind when Fortune honourably leads the way, and not to show yourself ready to advance in whatever direction she wishes.

I think that, while you ought to honour all those who speak well of what you have done, you ought to consider that the most honourable eulogy is that of those who consider your talents worthy of still greater deeds than those which you have already accomplished, great as they are, and who express themselves grateful to you, not only in the present, but who will cause posterity to admire your acts beyond those of all who have lived in former times. . . .

It remains to summarize what I have said before, that, in as few words as possible, you may understand the chief point of my advice. I say that you ought to be the benefactor of the Hellenes; the king of Macedonia; and the ruler over as many barbarians as possible. If you succeed in this, all will be grateful to you, the Hellenes by reason of advantages enjoyed, the Macedonians, if you govern them like a king and not like a despot, and the rest of mankind, if they are freed by you from barbarian sway and gain the protection of Hellas.

. . . . .

I believe, men of Athens, you would give much to know, what is the true policy to be adopted in the present matter of inquiry. This being the case, you should be willing to hear with attention those who offer you their counsel. Besides that you will have the benefit of all preconsidered advice, I esteem it part of your good fortune that many fit suggestions will occur to some speakers at the moment, so that from them all you may easily choose what is profitable.

The present juncture, Athenians, all but proclaims aloud that you must yourselves take these affairs in hand, if you care for their success. I know not how we seem disposed in the matter. My own opinion is, vote succour immediately and make the speediest preparations for sending it off from Athens, that you may not incur the same mishap as before; send also ambassadors to announce this, and watch the proceedings. For the danger is that this man [Philip], being unscrupulous and clever at turning events to account, making concessions when it suits him, threatening at other times (his threats may well be believed), slandering us and urging our absence against us, may convert and wrest to his use some of our main resources. Though, strange to say, Athenians, the very cause of Philip's strength is a circumstance favourable to you. His having it in his sole power to publish or conceal his designs, his being at the same time general, sovereign, paymaster, and everywhere accompanying his army, is a great advantage for quick and timely operations in war; but, for a peace with the Olynthians, which he would gladly make, it has a contrary effect. For it is plain to the Olynthians that now they are fighting, not for glory or a slice of territory, but to save their country from destruction and servitude. They know how he treated those Amphipolitans who surrendered to him their city, and those Pydneans who gave him admittance. And generally, I believe, a despotic power is mistrusted by free states, especially if their dominions are adjoining. All this being known to you, Athenians, all else of importance considered,

I say, you must take heart and spirit, and apply yourselves more than ever to the war, contributing promptly, serving personally, leaving nothing undone. No plea or pretence is left you for declining your duty. What you were all so clamorous about, that the Olynthians should be pressed into a war with Philip, has of itself come to pass, and in a way most advantageous to you. For, had they undertaken the war at your instance, they might have been slippery allies, with minds but half resolved perhaps: but since they hate him on a quarrel of their own, their enmity is like to endure on account of their fears and their wrongs. You must not then, Athenians, forego this lucky opportunity, nor commit the error which you have often done heretofore. . . .

Should we abandon these men[2] too, and Philip reduce Olynthus, let any one tell me what is to prevent him marching where he pleases? Does any one of you Athenians compute or consider the means by which Philip, originally weak, has become great? Having first taken Amphipolis, then Pydna, Potidaea next, Methone afterwards, he invaded Thessaly. Having ordered matters at Pherae, Pegasae, Magnesia, everywhere exactly as he pleased, he departed for Thrace; where, after displacing some kings and establishing others, he fell sick; again recovering, he lapsed not into indolence, but instantly attacked the Olynthians. I omit his expeditions to Illyria and Paeonia, that against Arymbas,[3] and some others.

Why, it may be said, do you mention all this now? That you, Athenians, may feel and understand both the folly of continually abandoning one thing after another, and the activity which forms part of Philip's habit and existence, which makes it impossible for him to rest content with his achievements. If it be his principle, ever to do more than he has done, and yours, to apply yourselves vigorously to nothing, see what the end promises to be. Heavens! which of you is so simple as not to know that the war yonder will soon be here, if we are careless? And should this happen, I fear, O Athenians, that as men who thoughtlessly borrow on large interest, after a brief accommodation, lose their estate, so will it be with us: found to have paid dear for our idleness and self-indulgence, we shall be reduced to many hard and unpleasant shifts, and struggle for the salvation of our country.

To censure, I may be told, is easy for any man; to show what measures the case requires, is the part of a counsellor. I am not ignorant, Athenians,

2. Here Demosthenes points to the Olynthian ambassadors.
3. Arymbas was king of the Molossians in Epirus, and uncle of Olympias, Philip's wife.

that frequently, when any disappointment happens, you are angry, not with the parties in fault, but with the last speakers on the subject; yet never, with a view to self-protection, would I suppress what I deem for your interest. I say then, you must give a two-fold assistance here; first, save the Olynthians their towns, and send out troops for that purpose; secondly, annoy the enemy's country with ships and other troops; omit either of these courses, and the expedition will be fruitless. For should he, suffering your incursion, reduce Olynthus, he will easily march to the defence of his kingdom; or, should you only throw succour into Olynthus, and he, seeing things out of danger at home, keep up a close and vigilant blockade, he must in time prevail over the besieged. Your assistance therefore must be effective, and two-fold. . . .

And let not this escape you, Athenians, that you have now the choice, whether you shall fight there, or he in your country. If Olynthus hold out, you will fight there and distress his dominions, enjoying your own home in peace. If Philip take that city, who shall then prevent his marching here? Thebans? I wish it be not too harsh to say, they will be ready to join in the invasion. Phocians? who cannot defend their own country without your assistance. Or some other ally? "But, good sir, he will not desire!" Strange indeed, if, what he is thought fool-hardy for prating now, this he would not accomplish if he might. . . .

# 61  The Last Stand

Demosthenes' urgings fell upon deaf ears. The Athenians of the 340's were not those of a century before. The only thing that could rouse them was a direct threat to the city itself. This came at last. Philip was patient, and his progress in conquering Greece was piecemeal. At last he stood athwart central Greece, and at last the Athenians were convinced that they must either fight or accept Macedonian rule. They joined with Thebes to test the issue in a single battle. It was too late; Philip's army was too strong. In August 338 B.C. the combined Greek armies were crushed by Philip at Chaeronea in Boeotia in the battle that tradition has called "the last stand of Greek freedom."

The following selection is abridged from the third of the orations known as the *Philippics,* in which Demosthenes tried from 344 to 341 to rouse the Athenians to resistance. It is translated by C. R. Kennedy.

Many speeches, men of Athens, are made in almost every assembly about the hostilities of Philip, hostilities which ever since the treaty of peace he has been committing as well against you as against the rest of the Greeks; and all (I am sure) are ready to avow, though they forbear to do so, that our counsels and our measures should be directed to his humiliation and chastisement: nevertheless, so low have our affairs been brought by inattention and negligence, I fear it is a harsh truth to say, that if all the orators had sought to suggest, and you to pass resolutions for the utter ruining of the commonwealth, we could not, methinks, be worse off than we are. A variety of circumstances may have brought us to this state; our affairs have not declined from one or two causes only: but, if you rightly examine, you will find it chiefly owing to the orators, who study to please you rather than advise for the best. Some of whom, Athenians, seeking to maintain the basis of their own power and repute, have no forethought for the future, and therefore think you also ought to have none; others, accusing and calumniating practical statesmen, labour only to make Athens punish Athens, and in such occupation to engage her, that Philip may have liberty to say and do what he pleases. Politics of this kind are common here, but are the causes of your failures and embarrassment.

I beg, Athenians, that you will not resent my plain speaking of the truth. Only consider. You hold liberty of speech in other matters to be the general right of all residents in Athens, insomuch that you allow a measure of it even to foreigners and slaves, and many servants may be seen among you speaking their thoughts more freely than citizens in some other states; and yet you have altogether banished it from your councils. The result has been that in the assembly you give yourselves airs and are flattered at hearing nothing but compliments, in your measures and proceedings you are brought to the utmost peril. If such be your disposition now, I must be silent: if you will listen to good advice without flattery, I am ready to speak. For though our affairs are in a deplorable condition, though many sacrifices have been made, still, if you will choose to perform your duty, it is possible to repair it all. A paradox, and yet a truth, am I about to state. That which is the most lamentable in the past is best for the future. How is this? Because you performed no part of your duty, great or small, and therefore you fared ill: had you done all that became you, and your situation were the same, there would be no hope of amendment. Philip has indeed prevailed over your sloth and negligence, but not over the country; you have not been worsted; you have not even bestirred yourselves.

If now we were all agreed that Philip is at war with Athens and infringing the peace, nothing would a speaker need to urge or advise but the safest and easiest way of resisting him. But since, at the very time when Philip is capturing cities and retaining divers of our dominions and assailing all people, there are men so unreasonable as to listen to repeated declarations in the assembly, that some of us are kindling war, one must be cautious and set this matter right: for whoever moves or advises a measure of defence is in danger of being accused afterwards as author of the war. . . .

But what has caused the mischief? There must be some cause, some good reason, why the Greeks were so eager for liberty then, and now are eager for servitude. There was something, men of Athens, something in the hearts of the multitude then, which there is not now, which overcame the wealth of Persia and maintained the freedom of Greece, and quailed not under any battle by land or sea; the loss whereof has ruined all, and thrown the affairs of Greece into confusion. What was this? Nothing subtle or clever: simply that whoever took money from the aspirants for power or the corruptors of Greece were universally detested: it was dreadful to be convicted of bribery; the severest punishment was inflicted on the guilty, and there was no intercession or pardon. The favourable moments for enterprise, which fortune frequently offers to the careless against the vigilant, to them that will do nothing against those that discharge all their duty, could not be bought from orators or generals; no more could mutual concord, nor distrust of tyrants and barbarians, nor anything of the kind. But now all such principles have been sold as in open market, and those imported in exchange, by which Greece is ruined and diseased. What are they? Envy where a man gets a bribe; laughter if he confesses it; mercy to the convicted; hatred of those that denounce the crime: all the usual attendants upon corruption. For as to ships and men and revenues and abundance of other materials, all that may be reckoned as constituting national strength—assuredly the Greeks of our day are more fully and perfectly supplied with such advantages than Greeks of the olden time. But they are all rendered useless, unavailable, unprofitable, by the agency of these traffickers. . . .

What need of many words? In Oreus Philip's agents were Philistides, Menippus, Socrates, Thoas, and Agapaeus, who now hold the government: that was quite notorious: one Euphraeus, a man that formerly dwelt here among you, was labouring for freedom and independence. How this man was in other respects insulted and trampled on by the people of Oreus were long to tell: but a year before the capture, discovering what Philistides and his accomplices were about, he laid an information against them for treason. A multitude then combining, having Philip for their paymaster, and acting under his direction, take Euphraeus off to prison as a disturber of the public peace. Seeing which, the people of Oreus, instead of assisting the one and beating the others to death, with them were not angry, but said his punishment was just, and rejoiced at it. So the conspirators, having full liberty of action, laid their schemes and took their measures for the surrender of the city; if any of the people observed it, they were silent and intimidated, remembering the treatment of Euphraeus; and so wretched was their condition that on the approach of such a calamity none dared to utter a word, until the enemy drew up before the walls: then some were for defence, others for betrayal. Since the city was thus basely and wickedly taken, the traitors have held despotic rule; people who formerly rescued them, and were ready for any maltreatment of Euphraeus, they have either banished or put to death; Euphraeus killed himself, proving by deed that he had resisted Philip honestly and purely for the good of his countrymen.

What can be the reason—perhaps you wonder—why the Olynthians and Eretrians and Orites were more indulgent to Philip's advocates than to their own? The same which operates with you. They who advise for the best cannot always gratify their audience, though they would; for the safety of the state must be attended to: their opponents by the very counsel which is agreeable advance Philip's interest. One party required contribution; the other said there was no necessity; one were for war and mistrust; the other for peace, until they were ensnared. And so on for everything else (not to dwell on particulars); the one made speeches to please for the moment, and gave no annoyance; the other offered salutary counsel that was offensive. Many rights did the people surrender at last, not from any such motive of indulgence or ignorance, but submitting in the belief that all was lost. Which, by Zeus and Apollo, I fear will be your case, when on calculation you see that nothing can be done. I pray, men of Athens, it may never come to this! Better die a thousand deaths than render homage to Philip, or sacrifice any of your faithful counsellors. A fine recompense have the people of Oreus got for trusting themselves to Philip's friends and spurning Euphraeus! Finely are the Eretrian commons rewarded, for having driven away your ambassadors and yielded to Clitarchus! Yes; they are slaves, exposed to the lash and the torture. Finely he spared the Olynthians, who appointed Lasthenes to command their horse, and expelled Apollonides! It is folly and cowardice to cherish such hopes, and, while you

THE CONQUEST OF GREECE

take evil counsel and shirk every duty, and even listen to those who plead for your enemies, to think you inhabit a city of such magnitude that you cannot suffer any serious misfortune. Yea, and it is disgraceful to exclaim on any occurrence, when it is too late, "Who would have expected it? However—this or that should have been done, the other left undone." Many things could the Olynthians mention now, which, if foreseen at the time, would have prevented their destruction. Many could the Orites mention, many the Phocians, and each of the ruined states. But what would it avail them? As long as the vessel is safe, whether it be great or small, the mariner, the pilot, every man in turn should exert himself, and prevent its being overturned either by accident or design: but when the sea hath rolled over it, their efforts are vain. . . .

Nor is it enough to adopt these resolutions and oppose him by warlike measures: you must on calculation and on principle abhor his advocates here, remembering that it is impossible to overcome your enemies abroad, until you have chastised those who are his ministers within the city. Which, by Zeus and all the gods, you cannot and will not do! You have arrived at such a pitch of folly or madness or—I know not what to call it: I am tempted often to think, that some evil genius is driving you to ruin. . . .

# 62 The League of the Hellenes

The defeat of Athens and Thebes was the signal for the capitulation of the remaining independent Greek states. The Spartans refused to accept Philip's rule, and the conquerer with statesmanlike magnanimity won the regard of those Greeks who were skeptical of his intentions by permitting Sparta to remain independent—for what such independence was worth. In 337 B.C. Philip called for delegates from all the Greek states to attend a congress at Corinth. All—except Sparta—responded, and Philip there declared his intention of honoring the traditional autonomy of the poleis. However, they were no longer to have the privilege of warring on each other. Instead, they were to join in a Hellenic League that would police the stability of the existing governments of the individual states and would prevent wars among them. Philip himself was *hēgemōn* (Leader) of the League, and

SOURCE: Reprinted by permission of the publishers and The Loeb Classical Library from: *Isocrates* Vol. III, tr. LaRue Van Hook, Cambridge, Mass.: Harvard University Press.

he invited the members to vote for the League's first positive action. The response was enthusiastic; the Greek cities voted to send detachments to form a combined Greco-Macedonian army for the invasion of Asia. Philip went back to Pella to complete his preparations. Early in 336 an advance contingent established a beachhead across the Hellespont. Then Philip was assassinated. The events that followed ushered in a new epoch in history.

Isocrates, too, did not live long enough to see his hopes come to fruition. He had died in 338, at the age of ninety-eight, persisting in his crusade to the end. The selection that follows is Isocrates' last work (written after the Battle of Chaeronea), the second *Letter to Philip,* translated by LaRue Van Hook.

❀❀❀❀❀

I have discussed with Antipater[1] the course which is expedient for our city and for you, at sufficient length, I am convinced; but I wished to write to you also regarding the action which I think should be taken after the conclusion of peace, and while this advice is similar to that in my discourse,[2] it is, however, expressed much more concisely.

At that time, you recall, I counselled you that, after you had reconciled our city with Sparta, Thebes, and Argos, you should bring all the Greeks into concord, as I was of opinion that if you should persuade the principal cities to be favourably inclined to such a course, the others also would quickly follow. At that time, however, the state of affairs was different, and now it has come to pass that the need of persuasion no longer exists; for on account of the battle which has taken place,[3] all are compelled to be prudent and to desire that which they surmise you wish to do and to say, namely, that they must desist from the madness and the spirit of aggrandizement, which they were wont to display in their relations with each other, and must carry the war into Asia. Many inquire of me whether I advised you to make the expedition against the barbarians or whether it was your idea and I concurred. I reply that I do not know for certain, since before then I had not been acquainted with you, but that I supposed that you had reached a decision in this matter and that I in my speech had fallen in with your desires. On hearing this, all entreated me to encourage you and to exhort you to hold fast to this same resolution, since they believe that no achievement could be more glorious, more useful to the Greeks, or more timely than this will be.

1.  A high Macedonian official.  2.  See Selection 60.
3.  The battle of Chaeronea.

If I possessed the same vigour which I formerly had and were not utterly spent with years, I should not be speaking with you by letter, but in your presence should myself be spurring and summoning you to undertake these tasks. But even as it is, I do exhort you, as best I can, not to put these matters aside until you bring then to a successful conclusion. To have an insatiate desire for anything else in the world is ignoble—for moderation is generally esteemed—but to set the heart upon a glory that is great and honourable, and never to be satiated with it, befits those men who have far excelled all others. And that is true of you. Be assured that a glory unsurpassable and worthy of the deeds you have done in the past will be yours when you shall compel the barbarians—all but those who have fought on your side—to be serfs of the Greeks, and when you shall force the king who is now called Great to do whatever you command. For then will naught be left for you except to become a god. And to accomplish all this from your present status is much easier for you than it was for you to advance to the power and renown you now possess from the kingship which you had in the beginning.

I am grateful to my old age for this reason alone, because it has prolonged my life to this moment, so that the dreams of my youth, which I attempted to commit to writing both in my Panegyricus and in the discourse which was sent to you, I am now seeing in part already coming to fulfilment through your achievements and in part I have hopes of their future realization.

# IV

## ASPECTS OF CLASSICAL
## GREEK CULTURE

*The cultural flowering that has caused all later periods of history to look back with awe at Greece was spectacular, but it was also brief. The era of Classical Greece spans less than two centuries. The limitation is even more remarkable when it is noted how great a proportion of the achievement emanated from Athens, a "nation" whose total population was never greater than about half a million, whose adult male citizen population numbered no more than forty thousand. The sections that follow are an effort to suggest something of the atmosphere, the way of life both public and private, and the intellectual accomplishments of that distant age. In these sections a prominent place is given to the so-called "Attic orators." Their works are not of the quality of the most celebrated literature, such as the dramas of the tragic poets; but to illustrate the life and the tone of the times, the way things looked and felt, their orations, composed for delivery in the courtroom before a jury of ordinary people, provide an insight into the life of Classical Greece that cannot be surpassed.*

# PUBLIC AND PRIVATE LIFE

I T would be a hopeless task to try to draw up a list of all the details we might like to know about the attitudes, customs, habits, and tastes of the ancient Greeks. Most of them can never be recaptured; but the literature of the period, especially the comedies and the courtroom speeches, is a rich source of graphic insights into the innumerable aspects of daily life in Athens.

# 63 The Law Courts

In Classical Athens the law courts played a role of far greater importance than they do with us. Aristotle places them on a level with the Assembly, as the twin cornerstones of democracy. "The people," he says, "through their votes in the jury courts and in the Assembly made themselves masters of the state." The courts were indeed fundamental to the system of democracy, and an Athenian jury numbering from 201 to 1001 members was a truly democratic body, a piece of the popular assembly. The procedure of the courts was basic to the democracy, too. There was no district attorney nor any professional counsel. Whether a case was in civil or criminal law, public or private, charges had to be brought by a private citizen. The plaintiff himself presented his case, called his witnesses, cited the relevant laws; the defendant was similarly obliged. It was out of this amateur nature of legal procedure that the profession of speech-writer arose. The ordinary man might know little of the law and even less about how to compose a persuasive argument. He could, however, hire an expert who would advise him and write for him the presentation of the case he himself would then make to the jury. The works of Lysias and Isaeus, fourth-century b.c. speech-writers, are speeches written for courtroom delivery, as are the so-called "private orations" of Demosthenes, who before he entered politics had pursued the career of a professional speech-writer.

SOURCE: *The Wasps of Aristophanes,* translated by Benjamin Bickley Rogers (London: George Bell and Sons, various dates). Reprinted by permission of the publisher.

[ 540 ]

Another peculiarity of the democratic, amateur atmosphere of the Athenian courts was the discretion allowed to the jury. The judge was no more than a presiding officer who kept order. He did not, as our judges do, instruct the jury in the law. The individual juror was free to vote on the merits of a case as he saw fit, and a simple majority decided the verdict. The aim of a plea before an Athenian court was purely and simply to persuade the members of the jury. Niceties of evidence or law might go over their heads, but they knew what they liked. The result was that an Athenian trial was likely to be a question not so much of law or fact as of the jury's estimate of the worth and credibility of the two contestants. In short, it was a man's character that was really on trial, and no allegation that might serve to undermine the jury's confidence in one's opponent was irrelevant. Frequently a courtroom plea was little more than a recitation of the speaker's virtues and a parade of slanders about his opponent. A man's political actions and his service to the state were especially subject to scrutiny when he entered the courtroom.

Service on the jury, then, was a conspicuous feature of Athenian life and a basic aspect of democracy. By the fourth century, democratic procedures had proved themselves and were ingrained; but in the fifth century there had still been plenty of opponents to the practices of the democracy, and they availed themselves of the freedom to criticize severely. The jury system received its share of such criticism. The institution of pay was singled out, in particular, as having converted jury duty from a public service to a way of making a living on the part of the aged and infirm, the lazy, the unemployable—in short, the worst elements of the citizenry.

One of the bitterest opponents of the political practices and policies of his time was the comic poet Aristophanes, who throughout the course of the Peloponnesian War put on the stage one antiwar play after another. It is a tribute to the confidence and stability of the Athenian democracy that such freedom under such circumstances was permitted. And Aristophanes also subjected the popular juries to his satirical pen. The *Wasps,* produced in 422 B.C., is a savage attack on the popular leader Cleon, the man who had engineered the victory at Sphacteria (see Selection 54); it is also a lampoon of the jury system and the people who served on the juries. The following selection consists of the *Wasps lines* 211–229, 240–245, 266–269, 273–289, 317–322, 334–347, 379–386, 456–817, 824–850, 860–867, 985–1002. The translation is by Benjamin Bickley Rogers.

❀❀❀❀❀

SOSIAS. Well but at last we have fairly scared him in,
He can't slip out, he can't elude us now,
So why not slumber just a—just a—drop?
BDELYCLEON.[1] Slumber, you rogue! when in a little while
His fellow-justices will come this way
Calling him up.
SOSIAS.                        Why sir, 'tis twilight yet.
BDELYCLEON. Why then, by Zeus, they are very late to-day.
Soon after midnight is their usual time
To come here, carrying lights, and warbling tunes
Sweet-charming-old-Sidono-Phrynichéan
Wherewith they call him out.
SOSIAS.                                    And if they come,
Had we not better pelt them with some stones?
BDELYCLEON. Pelt them, you rogue! you might as well provoke
A nest of wasps as anger these old men.
Each wears beside his loins a deadly sting,
Wherewith they smite, and on with yells and cries
They leap, and strike at you, like sparks of fire.
SOSIAS. Tut, never trouble, give me but some stones,
I'll chase the biggest wasps-nest of them all.

[*The actors retire to their respective posts, and after a short pause the*
CHORUS *make their appearance. They are dressed up to resemble* WASPS,
*and are armed with formidable stings.*]

CHORUS. . . . .
On, on again, with might and main: for Laches' turn is come to-day:
Quick, look alive, a splendid hive of wealth the fellow's got, they say.
And Cleon too, our patron true, enjoined us each betimes to bring
Of anger sore, an ample store, a good three days' provisioning:
On all the man's unrighteous plans a vengeance well-deserved to take.
Come, every dear and tried compeer, come, quickly come, ere morning
    break. . . .
But how is this? Our friend not here! how comes it he's so slack?
By Zeus, he never used to be at all a hanger-back.
He always marched before us all, on legal cares intent,

1.  Bdelycleon (Hater of Cleon) is a young man who is trying to prevent his father
Philocleon (Lover of Cleon) from pursuing the old man's favorite pastime, service
on the jury. Philocleon loves to see the defendant squirm, and makes it a rule
always to vote for a conviction. Sosias is a servant.

[ 542 ]

And some old tune of Phrynichus he warbled as he went. . . .
How is it our friend is not here to receive us?
 Why comes he not forth from his dwelling?
Can it be that he's had the misfortune to lose
  His one pair of shoes;
Or striking his toe in the dark, by the grievous
Contusion is lamed, and his ankle inflamed?
  Or his groin has, it may be, a swelling.
  He of us all, I ween,
Was evermore the austerest, and most keen.
  Alone no prayers he heeded:
  Whene'er for grace they pleaded,
  He bent (like this) his head,
  *You cook a stone,* he said.
Is it all of that yesterday's man who cajoled us,
 And slipped through our hands, the deceiver,
Pretending a lover of Athens to be,
  Pretending that he
Was the first, of the Samian rebellion that told us?
Our friend may be sick with disgust at the trick,
 And be now lying ill of a fever.
 That would be like him quite.
But now up, up, nor gnaw your soul with spite.
 There comes a traitor base,
 A wealthy rogue from Thrace.
 Safe in our toils we've got him,
 Up, up, old friend, and pot him! . . .

PHILOCLEON (*appearing above*). Long my reins have been stirred,
  Long through chinks have I heard,
  Heard your voices below.
  Vain my efforts to sing,
  *These* forbid me to go.
  Vainly my sad heart yearns,
  Yearns to be marching with you,
  On to the judgement urns,
  There some mischief to do. . . .

CHORUS. Who is he that thus detains you?
  Who with bolted door restrains you?
  Tell us, you will speak to friends.

PHILOCLEON. 'Tis my son, but don't be bawling: for he's slumbering now
at ease

There, upon the roof before you: drop your tone a little, please.

CHORUS. What's his object, idle trifler, that he does such things as these?

What's the motive he pretends?

PHILOCLEON. He will let me do no mischief, and no more a lawsuit try.

True it is he'll feast and pet me, but with that I won't comply.

CHORUS. This the Demagogcleon blared

Out against you, since you dared

Truth about the fleet to show.

He must be involved, I see,

In some dark *conspiracy,*

Else he durst not use you so.

It is time some means of escape to find, some novel, ingenious plan,
that so,

Unseen of your son, you may get you down, alighting in safety here
below. . . .

So now to the window lash the cord, and twine it securely your limbs
around.

With all Diopeithes fill your soul, then let yourself cleverly down to
the ground.

PHILOCLEON. But suppose they catch me suspended here, and hoist me up
by the line again,

And angle me into the house once more, say what ye will do to deliver me then.

CHORUS. Our hearts of oak we'll summon to aid, and all give battle at once
for you.

'Twere vain to attempt to detain you more: such wonderful feats we
are going to do.

PHILOCLEON. This then will I do, confiding in you: and if anything happens to me, I implore

That you take me up and bewail my fate, and bury me under the
court-house floor. . . .

[*The old man is caught trying to make his escape.* BDELYCLEON *and the
two slaves issue from the house,* XANTHIAS *armed with a stick,* SOSIAS
*carrying an apparatus for smoking out wasps.*]

BDELYCLEON. Beat them, Xanthias, from the door-way; beat the wasps away
again.

[ 544 ]

XANTHIAS. That I will, sir.

BDELYCLEON.                    Fume them, Sosias, drive the smoke in dense
and thick.
Shoo there, shoo! be off, confound you. At them, Xanthias, with the
stick!
Smoke them, Sosias, smoke, infusing Aeschines, Selartius' son.

SOSIAS. So then we at last were going, as it seems, to make you run.

BDELYCLEON. But you never would have managed thus to beat them off
with ease,
Had it chanced that they had eaten of the songs of Philocles.

CHORUS. Creeping o'er us, creeping o'er us,
    Here at least the poor can see
    Stealthy-creeping *tyranny!*
If you from the laws debar us, which the city has ordained,
You, a curly-haired Amynias, you, a rascal double-grained,
    Not by words of wit persuading,
    Not for weighty reasons shown,
    But because, forsooth, you *will* it,
    Like an autocrat, alone.

BDELYCLEON. Can't we now, without this outcry, and this fierce denunciation,
Come to peaceful terms together, terms of reconciliation?

CHORUS. Terms with *thee,* thou people-hater, and with Brasidas, thou traitor,
Hand and glove!          You who dare          Woolly-fringed
    Clothes to wear,
Yes, and show          Beard and hair          Left to grow
Everywhere.

BDELYCLEON. O, by Zeus, I'd really liefer drop my father altogether
Than endure these daily conflicts, buffeting with waves and weather.

CHORUS. Why, as yet you've hardly entered on the parsley and the rue:
(That we'll just throw in a sample of our three-quart words for you.)
*Now* you care not, wait a little, till the prosecutor trounce you,
Sluicing out these selfsame charges, and *conspirator* denounce you.

BDELYCLEON. O by all the gods I ask you, will ye never go away?
Are ye quite resolved to linger, thwacked and thwacking all the day?

CHORUS. Never more   Will I while   There's a grain   Left of me
Leave your door   Traitor vile   Bent to gain   *Tyranny.*

BDELYCLEON. Ay "Conspiracy" and "Tyrant," these with you are all in all,
Whatsoe'er is brought before you, be the matter great or small.
Everywhere the name of Tyrant, now for fifty years unknown,

Is than cheap salt-fish at Athens commoner and cheaper grown.
Everywhere about the market it is bandied to and fro:
If you wish a bass to purchase, and without a pilchard go,
Straight the man who sells the pilchards grumbles from his stall hard
    by,
*Here is plainly one that caters with a view to Tyranny.*
If a leek, besides, you order, relish for your sprats perchance,
Says the potherb-girl directly, eyeing you with looks askance,
*Leeks indeed! and leeks I prithee! what, with Tyranny in view?*
*Athens must be taxed, you fancy, relish to supply for* YOU!

XANTHIAS. Even so a naughty damsel yesternoon observed to me,
Just because I said her manners were a little bit too free,
She supposed that I was wishing Hippias's Tyranny.

BDELYCLEON. Ay, by charges such as these our litigious friends they
    please.
Now because I'd have my father (quitting all this toil and strife,
This up-early-false-informing-troublesome-litigious life)
Live a life of ease and splendour, live like Morychus, you see
Straight I'm charged with Tyrant leanings, charged with foul con-
    spiracy.

PHILOCLEON. Yes, by Zeus, and very justly. Not for pigeon's milk in store
I the pleasant life would barter which you let me lead no more.
Nought I care for eels and rayfish: daintier food to me would seem
Just a little, tiny lawsuit, dished and stifled in its steam.

BDELYCLEON. Yes, for that's the sort of dainty you, by Zeus, have loved so
    long.
Yet I think I'll soon convince you that your mode of life is wrong,
If you can but once be silent, and to what I say give heed.

PHILOCLEON. I am wrong to be a dicast!²

BDELYCLEON.                         Laughed to utter scorn indeed,
Mocked by men you all but worship, for you can't their treachery see,
You're a slave, and yet don't know it.

PHILOCLEON.                       Name not slavery to me!
I am lord of all, I tell you.

BDELYCLEON.                     You're the veriest drudge, I vow,
Thinking that you're lord of all. For come, my father, teach us now,
If you reap the fruits of Hellas, what's the benefit to you?

PHILOCLEON. Willingly. Let these be umpires.

BDELYCLEON.                       I'll accept their judgement too.

2. A juryman. The court is a dicastery.

Now then all at once release him.

PHILOCLEON.               And besides a sword supply,
If in this dispute I'm worsted, here upon this sword I'll die.

BDELYCLEON. But suppose you won't their final (what's the phrase) award
obey?

PHILOCLEON. May I never drink thereafter, pure and neat, good fortune's
—pay.

CHORUS. Now must the champion, going
    Out of our school, be showing
    Keen wit and genius new.

BDELYCLEON. Bring forth my memorandum-book: bring forth my desk to
write in.

I'll quickly show you what you're like, if that's your style of fighting.

CHORUS. In quite another fashion
    To aught this youth can do.
    Stern is the strife and anxious
    For all our earthly good,
    If he intends to conquer,
    Which Heaven forfend he should.

BDELYCLEON. Now I'll observe his arguments, and take a note of each.

PHILOCLEON. What would you say, if he to-day should make the conquering
speech?

CHORUS. Ah! should that mischance befall us,
    Our old troop were nothing worth:
    In the streets with ribald mirth
    Idle boys would dotards call us,
    Fit for nought but olive-bearing,
    Shrivelled husks of counter swearing.

O friend upon whom it devolves to plead the cause of our Sovereign
Power to-day,

Now show us your best; now bring to the test each trick that an
eloquent tongue can play.

PHILOCLEON. Away, away, like a racer gay, I start at once from the head
of the lists,

To prove that no kinglier power than ours in any part of the world
exists.

Is there any creature on earth more blest, more feared and petted
from day to day,

Or that leads a happier, pleasanter life, than a Justice of Athens,
though old and gray?

For first when rising from bed in the morn, to the criminal Court
betimes I trudge,

Great six-foot fellows are there at the rails, in anxious haste to salute
their Judge.

And the delicate hand, which has dipped so deep in the public purse,
he claps into mine,

And he bows before me, and makes his prayer, and softens his voice
to a pitiful whine:

*O pity me, pity me, Sire,* he cries, *if you ever indulged your longing
for pelf,*

*When you managed the mess on a far campaign, or served some
office of state yourself.*

The man would never have heard my name, if he had not been tried
and acquitted before.

BDELYCLEON (*writing*). I'll take a note of the point you make, that *suppliant fellows your grace implore.*

PHILOCLEON. So when they have begged and implored me enough, and
my angry temper is wiped away

I enter in and I take my seat, and then I do none of the things I say.

I hear them utter all sorts of cries design'd expressly to win my grace,

What won't they utter, what don't they urge, to coax a Justice who
tries their case?

Some vow they are needy and friendless men, and over their poverty
wail and whine,

And reckon up hardships, false with true, till he makes them out to
be equal to mine.

Some tell us a legend of days gone by, or a joke from Aesop witty
and sage,

Or jest and banter, to make me laugh, that so I may doff my terrible
rage.

And if all this fails, and I stand unmoved, he leads by the hand his
little ones near,

He brings his girls and he brings his boys; and I, the Judge, am composed to hear.

They huddle together with piteous bleats: while trembling above them
he prays to me,

Prays as to a God his accounts to pass, to give him a quittance, and
leave him free.

*If thou lovest a bleating male of the flock, O lend thine ear to this boy of mine:*

*Or pity this sweet little delicate girl, if thy soul delights in the squeaking of swine.*

So then we relax the pitch of our wrath, and screw it down to a peg more low.

Is *this* not a fine dominion of mine, a derision of wealth with its pride and show?

BDELYCLEON (*writing*). A second point for my note-book that, *a derision of wealth with its show and its pride.*

Go on to mention the good you get by your empire of Hellas so vast and wide.

PHILOCLEON. 'Tis ours to inspect the Athenian youths, when we enter their names on the rolls of men.

And if ever Oeagrus gets into a suit, be sure that he'll never get out again

Till he give us a speech from his Niobe part, selecting the best and the liveliest one.

And then if a piper gain his cause, he pays us our price for the kindness done,

By piping a tune with his mouth-band on, quick march as out of the Court we go.

And what if a father by will to a friend his daughter and heiress bequeath and bestow,

We care not a rap for the will, or the cap which is there on the seal so grand and sedate,

We bid them begone, and be hanged, and ourselves take charge of the girl and her worthy estate;

And we give her away to whoever we choose, to whoever may chance to persuade us: yet we,

Whilst other officials must pass an account, alone from control and accounting are free.

BDELYCLEON. Ay that, and that only, of all you have said, I own is a privilege lucky and rare,

But uncapping the seal of the heiress's will seems rather a shabby and doubtful affair.

PHILOCLEON. And if ever the Council or People have got a knotty and difficult case to decide,

They pass a decree for the culprits to go to the able and popular Courts to be tried:

Evathlus, and He! the loser of shields, the fawning, the great Cow-
ardonymus say
"They'll always be fighting away for the mob," "the people of Athens
they'll never betray."
And none in the People a measure can pass, unless he propose that
the Courts shall be free,
Dismissed and discharged for the rest of the day when once we have
settled a single decree.
Yea, Cleon the Bawler and Brawler himself, at us, and us only, to
nibble forbears,
And sweeps off the flies that annoy us, and still with a vigilant hand
for our dignity cares.
You never have shown such attention as this, or displayed such a zeal
in your father's affairs.
Yet Theorus, a statesman as noble and grand as lordly Euphemius,
runs at our call
And whips out a sponge from his bottle, and stoops, to black and to
polish the shoes of us all.
Such, such is the glory, the joy, the renown, from which you desire
to retain and withhold me,
And *this* you will show, this Empire of mine, to be bondage and
slavery merely, you told me.

BDELYCLEON. Ay, chatter your fill, you will cease before long: and then
I will show that your boasted success
Is just the success of a tail that is washed, going back to its filth and
its slovenliness.

PHILOCLEON. But the nicest and pleasantest part of it all is this, which I'd
wholly forgotten to say,
'Tis when with my fee in my wallet I come, returning home at the
close of the day,
O then what a welcome I get for its sake; my daughter, the darling,
is foremost of all,
And she washes my feet and anoints them with care, and above them
she stoops, and a kiss lets fall,
Till at last by the pretty Papas of her tongue she angles withal my
three-obol away.
Then my dear little wife, she sets on the board nice manchets of
bread in a tempting array,

And cosily taking a seat by my side, with loving entreaty constrains
    me to feed;
*I beseech you taste this, I implore you try that.* This, this I delight in,
    and ne'er may I need
To look to yourself and your pantler, a scrub who, whenever I ask
    him my breakfast to set,
Keeps grumbling and murmuring under his breath. No! no! if he
    haste not a manchet to get,
Lo here my defence from the evils of life, my armour of proof,
    my impregnable shield.
And what if you pour me no liquor to drink, yet here's an old Ass,
    full of wine, that I wield,
And I tilt him, and pour for myself, and imbibe; whilst sturdy old
    Jack, as a bumper I drain,
Lets fly at your goblet a bray of contempt, a mighty and masterful
    snort of disdain.
    Is *this* not a fine dominion of mine?
    Is it less than the empire of Zeus?
    Why the very same phrases, so grand and divine,
      For me, as for Him, are in use.
    For when we are raging loud and high
      In stormy, tumultuous din,
    *O Lord! O Zeus!* say the passers-by,
      *How thunders the Court within!*
    The wealthy and great, when my lightnings glare,
    Turn pale and sick, and mutter a prayer.
    You fear me too: I protest you do:
    Yes, yes, by Demeter I vow 'tis true.
    But hang me if I am afraid of you.
CHORUS. I never, no, I never
    Have heard so clear and clever
    And eloquent a speech—
PHILOCLEON. Ay, ay, he thought he'd steal my grapes, and pluck them
    undefended,
For well he knew that I'm in this particularly splendid.
CHORUS. No topic he omitted,
    But he duly went through each.
    I waxed in size to hear him
    Till with ecstasy possessed

Methought I sat a-judging
In the Islands of the Blest.

PHILOCLEON. See how uneasily he stands, and gapes, and shifts his ground.
I warrant, sir, before I've done, you'll look like a beaten hound.

CHORUS. You must now, young man, be seeking
Every turn and every twist
Which can your defence assist.
To a youth against me speaking
Mine's a heart 'tis hard to render
(So you'll find it) soft and tender.
And therefore unless you can speak to the point, you must look for
a millstone handy and good,
Fresh hewn from the rock, to shiver and shock the unyielding grit
of my resolute mood.

BDELYCLEON. Hard were the task, and shrewd the intent, for a Comedy-poet
all too great
To attempt to heal an inveterate, old disease engrained in the heart
of the state.
Yet, O dread Cronides, Father and Lord,

PHILOCLEON.                    Stop, stop, don't talk in that father-me way,
Convince me at once that I'm only a slave, or else I protest you shall
die this day,
Albeit I then must ever abstain from the holy flesh of the victims slain.

BDELYCLEON. Then listen my own little pet Papa, and smooth your brow
from its frowns again.
And not with pebbles precisely ranged, but roughly thus on your
fingers count
The tribute paid by the subject States, and just consider its whole
amount;
And then, in addition to this, compute the many taxes and one-per-
cents,
The fees and the fines, and the silver mines, the markets and harbours
and sales and rents.
If you take the total result of the lot, 'twill reach two thousand talents
or near.
And next put down the Justices' pay, and reckon the sums they receive
a year:
Six thousand Justices, count them through, there dwell no more in
the land as yet,

[552]

One hundred and fifty talents a year I think you will find is all
   they get.

PHILOCLEON. Then not one tithe of our income goes to furnish forth the
   Justices' pay.

BDELYCLEON. No, certainly not.

PHILOCLEON.                      And what becomes of all the rest of the
   revenue, pray?

BDELYCLEON. Why, bless you, it goes to the pockets of those, *To the rabble
   of Athens I'll ever be true,*

*I'll always battle away for the mob.* O father, my father, 'tis owing
   to you:

By such small phrases as these cajoled, you lift them over yourselves
   to reign.

And then, believe me, they soon contrive some fifty talents in bribes
   to gain,

Extorting them out of the subject states, by hostile menace and angry
   frown:

*Hand over,* they say, *the tribute-pay, or else my thunders shall crush
   your town.*

You joy the while at the remnants vile, the trotters and tips of your
   power to gnaw.

So when our knowing, acute allies the rest, the scum of the Populace,
   saw

On a vote-box pine, and on nothingness dine, and marked how lanky
   and lean ye grow,

They count you all as a Connas's vote, and ever and ever on these
   bestow

Wines, cheeses, necklaces, sesamè fruit, and jars of pickle and pots
   of honey,

Rugs, cushions, and mantles, and cups, and crowns, and health, and
   vigour, and lots of money.

Whilst *you!* from out of the broad domain for which on the land
   and the wave you toiled,

None gives you so much as a garlic head, to flavour the dish when
   your sprats are boiled.

PHILOCLEON. That's true no doubt, for I just sent out and bought, myself,
   from Eucharides three;

But you wear me away by your long delay in proving my bondage and
   slavery.

[ 553 ]

BDELYCLEON. Why *is* it not slavery pure and neat, when these (themselves
and their parasites too)

Are all in receipt of their pay, God wots, as high officials of state:
whilst you

Must thankful be for your obols three, those obols which ye yourselves
have won

In the battle's roar, by sea and by shore, 'mid sieges and miseries many
a one.

But O what throttles me most of all, is this, that under constraint
you go,

When some young dissolute spark comes in, some son of a Chaereas,
straddling—so

With his legs apart, and his body poised, and a mincing, soft, effeminate air,

And bids you Justices, one and all, betimes in the morn to the Court
repair,

For that any who after the signal come shall lose and forfeit their
obols three.

Yet come as late as he choose himself, he pockets his drachma,
"Counsel's fee."

And then if a culprit give him a bribe, he gets his fellow the job to
share,

And into each other's hands they play, and manage together the suit
to square.

Just like two men at a saw they work, and one keeps pulling, and
one gives way,

While you at the Treasurer stare and gape, and never observe the
tricks they play.

PHILOCLEON. Is *that* what they do! O can it be true! Ah me, the depths of
my being are stirred,

Your statements shake my soul, and I feel, I know not how, at the
things I've heard.

BDELYCLEON. And just consider when you and all might revel in affluence,
free as air,

How these same demagogues wheel you round, and cabin and coop
you, I know not where.

And you, the lord of such countless towns, from Pontus to Sardo,
nought obtain

Save this poor pittance you earn, and this they dole you in driblets,
grain by grain,

As though they were dropping oil from wool, as much forsooth as
will life sustain.

They *mean* you all to be poor and gaunt, and I'll tell you, father,
the reason why.

They want you to know your keeper's hand; and then if he hiss
you on to fly

At some helpless foe, away you go, with eager vehemence ready and
rough,

Since if they wished to maintain you well, the way to do it were plain
enough.

A thousand cities our rule obey, a thousand cities their tribute pay,

Allot them twenty Athenians each, to feed and nourish from day
to day,

And twice ten thousand citizens there, are living immersed in dishes
of hare,

With creams and beestings and sumptuous fare, and garlands and
coronals everywhere,

Enjoying a fate that is worthy the State, and worthy the trophy on
Marathon plain.

Whilst now like gleaners ye all are fain to follow along in the paymaster's train.

PHILOCLEON. O what can this strange sensation mean, this numbness that
over my hand is stealing?

My arm no longer can hold the sword: I yield, unmanned, to a
womanish feeling.

BDELYCLEON. Let a panic possess them, they're ready to give Euboea at
once for the State to divide,

And engage to supply for every man full fifty bushels of wheat
beside.

But five poor bushels of barley each is all that you ever obtained in fact,

And that doled out by the quart, while first they worry you under
the Alien Act.

And therefore it was that I locked you away

To keep you in ease; unwilling that these

With empty mouthings your age should bilk.

And now I offer you here to-day

Without any reserve whatever you please,

Save only a draught of—Treasurer's milk.

CHORUS. 'Twas a very acute and intelligent man, whoever it was, that
happened to say,

*Don't make up your mind till you've heard both sides,* for now I
    protest you have gained the fray.
Our staves of justice, our angry mood, for ever and ever aside we lay,
And we turn to talk to our old compeer, our choir-companion of
    many a day.
    Don't be a fool: give in, give in,
    Nor too perverse and stubborn be;
    I would to Heaven my kith and kin
    Would show the like regard for me.
    Some deity, 'tis plain, befriends
    Your happy lot, believe, believe it;
    With open arms his aid he sends,
    Do you with open arms receive it.
BDELYCLEON. I'll give him whatever his years require,
    A basin of gruel, and soft attire,
    And a good warm rug, and a handmaid fair,
    To chafe and cherish his limbs with care.
    —But I can't like this, that he stands so mute,
    And speaks not a word nor regards my suit.
CHORUS. 'Tis that his soberer thoughts review
    The frenzy he indulged so long,
    And (what he would not yield to you)
    He feels his former life was wrong.
    Perchance he'll now amend his plan,
    Unbend his age to mirth and laughter,
    A better and a wiser man
    By your advice he'll live hereafter.
PHILOCLEON. O misery! O misery!
BDELYCLEON. O father, why that dolorous cry?
PHILOCLEON. Talk not of things like these to me!
    *Those* are my pleasures, *there* would I be
    Where the Usher cries
    *Who has not voted? let him arise.*
    And O that the last of the voting band
    By the verdict-box I could take my stand.
    On, on, my soul! why, where is she gone?
    Hah! by your leave, my shadowy one!
    Zounds, if I catch when in Court I'm sitting
    Cleon again a theft committing!

[ 556 ]

BDELYCLEON. O father, father, by the Gods comply.

PHILOCLEON. Comply with what? name any wish, save one.

BDELYCLEON. Save what, I prithee?

PHILOCLEON.                                Not to judge, but that
Hades shall settle ere my soul comply.

BDELYCLEON. Well but if these are really your delights,
Yet why go *There?* why not remain at home
And sit and judge among your household here?

PHILOCLEON. Folly! judge what?

BDELYCLEON.                                The same as There you do.
Suppose you catch your housemaid on the sly
Opening the door: fine her for that, one drachma.
That's what you did at every sitting There.
And very aptly, if the morning's fine,
You'll fine your culprits, sitting in the sun.
In snow, enter your judgements by the fire
While it rains on: and—though you sleep till midday,
No archon here will close the door against you.

PHILOCLEON. Hah! I like that.

BDELYCLEON.                                And then, however long
An orator proses on, no need to fast,
Worrying yourself (ay, and the prisoner too).

PHILOCLEON. But do you really think that I can judge
As well as now, whilst eating and digesting?

BDELYCLEON. As well? much better. When there's reckless swearing,
Don't people say, what time and thought and trouble
It took the judges to digest the case?

PHILOCLEON. I'm giving in. But you've not told me yet
How I'm to get my pay.

BDELYCLEON.                                I'll pay you.

PHILOCLEON.                                                Good,
Then I shall have mine to myself, alone;
For once Lysistratus, the funny fool,
Played me the scurviest trick. We'd got one drachma
Betwixt us two: he changed it at the fish-stall;
Then laid me down three mullet scales: and I,
I thought them obols, popped them in my mouth;
O the vile smell! O la! I spat them out
And collared him.

[ 557 ]

BDELYCLEON.            And what said he?

PHILOCLEON.                      The rascal!

He said I'd got the stomach of a cock.

*You soon digest hard coin,* he says, says he.

BDELYCLEON. Then there again you'll get a great advantage.

PHILOCLEON. Ay ay, that's something: let's begin at once.

BDELYCLEON. Then stop a moment whilst I fetch the traps.

[BDELYCLEON *goes into the house.*]

PHILOCLEON. See here now, how the oracles come true.

Oft have I heard it said that the Athenians

One day would try their lawsuits in their homes,

That each would have a little Court-let built

For his own use, in his own porch, before

His entrance, like a shrine of Hecate.

BDELYCLEON (*bustles in with a quantity of judicial properties*).

Now then I hope you're satisfied: I've brought

All that I promised, and a lot besides.

See here I'll hang this vessel on a peg,

In case you want it as the suit proceeds.

PHILOCLEON. Now that I call extremely kind and thoughtful,

And wondrous handy for an old man's needs.

BDELYCLEON. And here's a fire, and gruel set beside it,

All ready when you want it.

PHILOCLEON.                    Good again.

Now if I'm feverish I shan't lose my pay,

For here I'll sit, and sip my gruel too.

But why in the world have ye brought me out the cock?

BDELYCLEON. To wake you, father, crowing over head

In case you're dozing whilst a prisoner pleads. . . .

BDELYCLEON. If you got seated sooner, I should sooner

Call a suit on.

PHILOCLEON.          Call on, I've sat for ages.

BDELYCLEON. Let's see: what matter shall I bring on first?

Who's been at mischief of the household here?

That careless Thratta now, she charred the pitcher.

PHILOCLEON. O stop, for goodness sake! you've all but killed me.

What! call a suit on with no railing here,

Always the first of all our sacred things?

[ 558 ]

BDELYCLEON. No more there is, by Zeus.

PHILOCLEON.                              I'll run myself
And forage out whatever comes to hand.

[PHILOCLEON *goes into the house.*]

BDELYCLEON. Heyday! where now? The strange infatuation!

XANTHIAS. Psha! rot the dog! To keep a cur like this!

BDELYCLEON. What's happened now?

XANTHIAS.                              Why, has not Labes here
Got to the kitchen safe, and grabbed a cheese,
A rich Sicilian cheese, and bolted it?

BDELYCLEON. Then that's the first indictment we'll bring on
Before my father: you shall prosecute.

XANTHIAS. Thank you, not I. This other Cur declares
If there's a charge, he'll prosecute with pleasure.

BDELYCLEON. Bring them both here.

XANTHIAS.                              Yes, yes, sir, so I will.

[*Enter* PHILOCLEON, *bearing a little fence.*]

BDELYCLEON (*to* PHILOCLEON). Hallo, what's this?

PHILOCLEON.                              Pigrailings from the hearth.

BDELYCLEON. Sacrilege, eh?

PHILOCLEON.                              No, but I'd trounce some fellow
(As the phrase goes) even from the very hearth.
So call away: I'm keen for passing sentence.

BDELYCLEON. Then now I'll fetch the cause-lists and the pleadings.

PHILOCLEON. O these delays! You weary and wear me out.
I've long been dying to commence my furrows. . . .

BDELYCLEON. . . . .
Ho, there within! some person bring me out
A pan of coals, and frankincense, and myrtle,
That so our business may commence with prayer.

CHORUS. We too, as ye offer the prayer and wine,
    We too will call on the Powers Divine
        To prosper the work begun;
        For the battle is over and done,
    And out of the fray and the strife to-day
    Fair peace ye have nobly won. . . .

[*They proceed to the trial of the dog Labes, accused of stealing a cheese. The evidence is now in:*]

BDELYCLEON. Then will he not get off?

PHILOCLEON.                    'Tis hard to know.

BDELYCLEON. O take, dear father, take the kindlier turn.
Here, hold this vote: then with shut eyes dash by
To the Far Urn. O father, do acquit him.

PHILOCLEON. No, no, my boy. I never learnt the lyre.

BDELYCLEON. Here, let me lead you round the handiest way.

PHILOCLEON. Is this the Nearer?

BDELYCLEON.                    This is.

PHILOCLEON.                            In she goes.

BDELYCLEON (*aside*). Duped, as I live! acquits him by mistake!
(*Aloud*). I'll do the counting.

PHILOCLEON.                    Well, how went the battle?

BDELYCLEON. We shall soon see. O Labes, you're acquitted!
Why, how now, father?

PHILOCLEON (*faintly*).        Water, give me water!

BDELYCLEON. Hold up, sir, do.

PHILOCLEON.                    Just tell me only this,
Is he *indeed* acquitted?

BDELYCLEON.          Yes.

PHILOCLEON.                    I'm done for.

BDELYCLEON. Don't take it so to heart: stand up, sir, pray.

PHILOCLEON. How shall I bear this sin upon my soul?
A man acquitted! What awaits me now?
Yet, O great gods! I pray you pardon me.
Unwilled I did it, not from natural bent. . . .

# 64 The "New Education"

Traditionally, among the Greeks as among other ancient peoples, education was the privilege of a restricted class. The young man of aristocratic

SOURCES: Reprinted from: *The Clouds of Aristophanes* tr. Benjamin Bickley Rogers by permission of George Bell and Sons, London (Eng.).
Reprinted by permission of the publishers and The Loeb Classical Library from: *Minor Attic Orators*, Vol. I, tr. K. J. Maidment, Cambridge, Mass.: Harvard University Press.

family was taught by his father or a private tutor. When democracy was instituted at Athens in the fifth century B.C., a different ideal of education was necessarily a consequence. It is not that the egalitarian spirit was a strong aspect of Athenian democracy, at least in the cultural sphere, but rather that democracy implied the capacity of the ordinary man to take part in public affairs and to make decisions. This does not necessarily require that he *know* anything, but the Athenians, at any rate, thought that some mental cultivation was desirable. The upshot was that in the fifth century education was sought and achieved by an ever-expanding segment of the population. There was still no system of general public education available, and the ordinary working-class citizen was probably barely literate, if that. Nevertheless, in a society in which communication was mainly oral and where the market place, the Assembly, and the theatre provided frequent experience of the discussion of serious matters, the intellectual sophistication of the ordinary Athenian must have been remarkably high.

As for formal education, it underwent a revolution under the impact of democracy. By the end of the fifth century, schools were established institutions, and in what we today would call "higher education" the Sophists had effected a revolution. These men were a combination of philosopher and teacher, that is, independent thinker and instructor. They offered courses of lectures in all the branches of learning that a young society could boast, but in particular they taught that much-sought skill—the key to a successful career in public life—oratory. By this was meant, of course, not merely elocution nor even composition, but the total art of persuasive argument, from the gathering of information to the final delivery of the finished discourse.

It is understandable that the Athenians were much interested in the techniques of persuasive argumentation. A man might remain silent in the Assembly, but if he had any claim to prominence of any kind, he would sooner or later find himself in the courtroom, and there he would have to speak and he would have to persuade. But old-fashioned people were scandalized by the Sophists: they taught for pay, and they taught not "truth" but technique. That is the heart of the case against them and is what Aristophanes had in mind when he mocked the pretensions of the "new education" in his satirical comedy the *Clouds,* produced in 423 B.C. The first of the two selections that follow is a part of the dialogue between Right Logic (old-fashioned common sense) and Wrong Logic (the new casuistical reasoning) from Aristophanes' *Clouds,* lines 1038–1082; the translation is by Benjamin Bickley Rogers. The second selection well illustrates the kind of argument that aroused Aristophanes' anger. The work of the fifth-century B.C. writer Antiphon, it is a set of four speeches forming an exercise in the logical presentation of a hypothetical case at law.

⊛⊛⊛⊛⊛

WRONG LOGIC. I am the Lesser Logic? True: these Schoolmen call me so,
    Simply because I was the first of all mankind to show
    How old established rules and laws might contradicted be:
    And this, as you may guess, is worth a thousand pounds to me,
    To take the feebler cause, and yet to win the disputation.
    And mark me now, how I'll confute his boasted Education!
    You said that always from warm baths the stripling must abstain:
    Why must he? on what grounds do you of these warm baths complain?
RIGHT LOGIC. Why it's the worst thing possible, it quite unstrings a man.
WRONG LOGIC. Hold there: I've got you round the waist: escape me if you
    can.
    And first: of all the sons of Zeus which think you was the best?
    Which was the manliest? which endured more toils than all the rest?
RIGHT LOGIC. Well, I suppose that Heracles was bravest and most bold.
WRONG LOGIC. And are the baths of Heracles so wonderfully cold?
    Aha! you blame warm baths, I think.
RIGHT LOGIC.                     This, this is what they say:
    This is the stuff our precious youths are chattering all the day!
    This is what makes them haunt the baths, and shun the manlier
    Games!
WRONG LOGIC. Well then, we'll take the Forum next: I praise it, and he
    blames.
    But if it *was* so bad, do you think old Homer would have made
    Nestor and all his worthies ply a real forensic trade?
    Well: then he says a stripling's tongue should always idle be:
    I say it should be used of course: so there we disagree.
    And next he says you must be chaste. A most preposterous plan!
    Come, tell me did you ever know one single blessed man
    Gain the least good by chastity? come, prove I'm wrong: make haste.
RIGHT LOGIC. Yes, many, many! Peleus gained a sword by being chaste.
WRONG LOGIC. A sword indeed! a wondrous meed the unlucky fool obtained.
    Hyperbolus the Lamp-maker hath many a talent gained
    By knavish tricks which I have taught: but not a sword, no, no!

RIGHT LOGIC. Then Peleus did to his chaste life the bed of Thetis owe.
WRONG LOGIC. And then she cut and ran away! for nothing so engages
 A woman's heart as forward warmth, old shred of those dark Ages!
 For take this chastity, young man: sift it inside and out:
 Count all the pleasures, all the joys, it bids you live without:
 No kind of dames, no kind of games, no laughing, feasting, drink-
  ing,—
 Why life itself is little worth without these joys, I'm thinking.
 Well I must notice now the wants by Nature's self implanted;
 You love, seduce, you can't help that, you're caught, convicted. Granted.
 You're done for; you can't say one word: while if you follow me
 Indulge your genius, laugh and quaff, hold nothing base to be.
 Why if you're in adultery caught, your pleas will still be ample:
 You've done no wrong, you'll say, and then bring Zeus as your example.
 He fell before the wondrous powers by Love and Beauty wielded:
 And how can you, the Mortal, stand, where He, the Immortal, yielded?

  . . . . .

## 1. PROSECUTION FOR ACCIDENTAL HOMICIDE

Cases in which the facts are agreed upon are settled in advance either
by the law or by the statutes of the Assembly, which between them control every branch of civic life. But should matter for dispute occur, it is
your task, gentlemen, to give a decision. However, I do not imagine that
any dispute will in fact arise between the defendant and myself. My son
was struck in the side by a javelin thrown by yonder lad in the gymnasium,
and died instantly. I accuse him not of killing my son deliberately, but of
killing him by accident—though the loss which I have suffered is not
thereby lessened. But if he has not caused the dead boy himself disquiet, he
has caused disquiet to the living; and I ask you to pity that dead boy's
childless parents: to show your sorrow for his own untimely end: to forbid his slayer to set foot where he is forbidden to set foot by the law: and
to refuse to allow him to defile the whole city.

## 2. REPLY TO A CHARGE OF ACCIDENTAL HOMICIDE

I now see that sheer misfortune and necessity can force those who hate
litigation to appear in court and those who love peace to show boldness

and generally belie their nature in word and deed; for I myself, who, unless I am sorely mistaken, am very far from finding or wanting to find such a task congenial, have to-day been forced by sheer misfortune to depart from my habits and appear as defendant in a case in which I found it hard enough to arrive at the exact truth, but which leaves me still more perplexed when I consider how I should present it to you. I am driven by pitiless necessity: and I, like my opponents, gentlemen of the jury, seek refuge in your sympathy. I beg of you: if my arguments appear more subtle than those generally presented to you, do not allow the circumstances already mentioned so to prejudice you against my defence as to make you base your verdict upon apparent fact instead of upon the truth; apparent fact puts the advantage with the clever speaker, but truth with the man who lives in justice and righteousness.

In training my son in those pursuits from which the state derives most benefit I imagined that both of us would be rewarded; but the result has sadly belied my hopes. For the lad—not from insolence or wantonness, but while at javelin-practice in the gymnasium with his fellows—made a hit, it is true, but killed no one, if one considers his true part in the matter: he accidentally incurred the blame for the error of another which affected that other's own person.

Had the boy been wounded because the javelin had travelled in his direction outside the area appointed for its flight, we should be left unable to show that we had not caused his death. But he ran into the path of the javelin and placed his person in its way. Hence my son was prevented from hitting the target: while the boy, who moved into the javelin's path, was struck, thereby causing us to be blamed for what we did not do. It was because he ran in front of the javelin that the boy was struck. The lad is therefore accused without just cause, as he did not strike anyone standing clear of the target. At the same time, since it is plain to you that the boy was not struck while standing still, but was struck only after deliberately moving into the path of the javelin, you have still clearer proof that his death was due to an error on his own part. Had he stood still and not run across, he would not have been struck.

Both sides are agreed, as you see, that the boy's death was accidental; so by discovering which of the two was guilty of error, we should prove still more conclusively who killed him. For it is those guilty of error in carrying out an intended act who are responsible for accidents: just as it is those who voluntarily do a thing or allow it to be done to them who are responsible for the effects suffered.

Now the lad, on his side, was not guilty of error in respect of anyone: in practising he was not doing what he was forbidden but what he had been told to do, and he was not standing among those engaged in gymnastics when he threw the javelin, but in his place among the other throwers: nor did he hit the boy because he missed the target and sent his javelin instead at those standing clear. He did everything correctly, as he intended; and thus he was not the cause of any accident, but the victim of one, in that he was prevented from hitting the target.

The boy, on the other hand, who wished to run forward, missed the moment at which he could have crossed without being hit, with results which he by no means desired. He was accidentally guilty of an error which affected his own person, and has thus met with a disaster for which he had himself alone to thank. He has punished himself for his error, and is therefore duly requited; not that we rejoice at or approve of it—far from it: we feel both sympathy and sorrow.

It is thus the dead boy who proves to have been guilty of error; so the act which caused his death is to be attributed not to us, but to him, the party guilty of error: just as the recoiling of its effects upon the agent not only absolves us from blame, but has caused the agent to be punished as he deserved directly his error was committed.

Furthermore, our innocence is attested by the law upon which my accuser relies in charging me with the boy's death, the law which forbids the taking of life whether wrongfully or otherwise. For the fact that the victim himself was guilty of error clears the defendant here of having killed him by accident: while his accuser does not even suggest that he killed him deliberately. Thus he is cleared of both charges, of killing the boy by accident and of killing him deliberately.

Not only do the true facts of the case and the law under which he is being prosecuted attest my son's innocence; but our manner of life is equally far from justifying such harsh treatment of us. Not only will it be an outrage, if my son is to bear the blame for errors which he did not commit; but I myself, who am equally innocent, though assuredly not more so, will be visited with woes many times more bitter. Once my son is lost, I shall pass the rest of my days longing for death: once I am left childless, mine will be a life within the tomb.

Have pity, then, on this child, the victim of calamity, though guilty of no error: and have pity on me, an old man in distress, stricken thus suddenly with sorrow. Do not bring a miserable fate upon us by condemning us: but show that you fear God by acquitting us. The dead boy is not unavenged for the calamity which befell him: nor ought we ourselves to share the responsibility for errors due to our accusers. So respect the righteousness which the facts before you have revealed: respect justice: and acquit us as godly and just men should. Do not bring upon a father and a son, two of the most wretched of beings, sorrows which the years of neither can well bear.

## 3. SECOND SPEECH FOR THE PROSECUTION

That sheer necessity can force all men to belie their nature in both word and deed is a fact of which the defendant seems to me to be giving very real proof. Whereas in the past he was the last to show impudence or audacity, his very misfortune has to-day forced him to say things which I for one would never have expected of him. I, in my great folly, imagined that he would not reply; otherwise I would not have deprived myself of half of my opportunities as prosecutor by making only one speech instead of two; and he, but for his audacity, would not have had the twofold advantage over me of using one speech to answer the one speech for the prosecution and making his accusations when they could not be answered.

With his great advantage over us in the matter of the speeches, and with the far greater one which his methods have given him in addition, it is outrageous that the accused should entreat you to listen kindly to his defence. I myself, on the other hand, far from causing any harm, have been the victim of cruel affliction, and am to-day being treated still more cruelly. It is as one who seeks more than a pretended refuge in your sympathy that I make my own request of you. You who take vengeance for unrighteous deeds and determine wherein is righteousness, do not, I beg of you, let worthless subtleties of speech induce you to disregard plain facts and treat the truth as false; for such subtleties result in a tale more plausible than true, whereas the truth, when told, will be less guileful and therefore less convincing.

My faith in justice, then, enables me to despise his defence. Yet my distrust of the pitiless will of fate makes me fear that I may not only lose the benefit of my child, but that I may see him convicted by you of taking his own life in addition. For the defendant has had the audacity and shamelessness to say that he who struck and killed neither wounded nor killed, whereas he who neither touched the javelin nor had any intention of throwing it missed every other point on earth and every other person, and pierced his own side with the javelin. Why, I should myself sound more convincing, I think, were I accusing the lad of wilful murder, than does the defendant in claiming that the lad neither struck nor killed.

My son was bidden at that moment by the master in charge, who was taking the javelins of the throwers into his keeping, to pick them up; but thanks to the wantonness of him who cast it, he was greeted by yonder lad's cruel weapon; though guilty of error in respect of no single person, he died a piteous death. The lad, on the other hand, who mistook the moment at which the javelins were being picked up, was not prevented from making a hit. To my bitter sorrow, he struck a target; and although he did not kill my son deliberately, there are better grounds for maintaining that he did than for asserting that he neither struck nor killed.

Although it was by accident that they killed my son, the effects were the same as those of wilful murder. Yet they deny that they killed him at all, and even maintain that they are not amenable to the law which forbids the taking of life whether wrongfully or otherwise. Then who did throw the javelin? To whom is the boy's death in fact to be attributed? To the spectators or the masters in charge—whom no once accuses at all? The circumstances of my son's death are no mystery: to me, for one, they are only too clear; and I maintain that the law is right when it orders the punishment of those who have taken life; not only is it just that he who killed without meaning to kill should suffer punishment which he did not mean to incur; but it would also be an injustice to the victim, whose injury is not lessened by being accidental, were he deprived of vengeance.

Nor does he deserve acquittal because of his misfortune in committing the error which he did. If, on the one hand, the misfortune is not due to any dispensation of heaven, then, as an error pure and simple, it is right that is should prove disastrous to him who was guilty of it; and if, on the other hand, a defilement from heaven has fallen upon the slayer by reason of some act of sin, then it is wrong for us to impede the visitation of God.

They also maintained that it is wrong for those who have lived as honourably as they to be treated with severity. But what of us? Should we be treated aright, if we are punished with death when our life has been as praiseworthy as theirs?

When he argues that he is not guilty of error and claims that the consequences must be borne by those who are, instead of being diverted to the innocent, he is pleading our case for us. Not only would it be an injustice to my son, who was killed by yonder lad, though guilty of error in respect of no one, were he deprived of vengeance; but it will be an outrage, if I myself, who am even more guiltless than he, fail to obtain from you the recompense which the law assigns me.

Further, the defence's own statements show that the accused cannot be acquitted either of error or of accidentally taking life, but that he and my son are equally guilty of both; I will prove this. Assume that because my son moved into the path of the javelin instead of standing still, he deserves to be treated as his own slayer. Then the lad is not free from blame either; he is only innocent if he was standing still and not throwing his javelin when the boy was killed. The boy's death was therefore due to both of them. Now the boy, whose error affected his own person, has punished himself even more harshly than that error warranted: for he has lost his life. So what right has his accomplice, who joined him in committing his unfortunate error, to escape unpunished?

The accused have themselves proved by their defence that the lad had a share in the slaying. So, as just and godfearing men, you cannot acquit him. If we, who have lost our life through the defendants' error, were found guilty of having taken it ourselves, it would be an act not of righteousness but of wickedness on your part: and if those responsible for our death were not prohibited from setting foot where they should not, it would be an outrage against heaven: you would have acquitted persons stained with guilt.

As the whole of the defilement, upon whomsoever it rests, is extended to you, you must take the greatest care. If you find him guilty and prohibit him from setting foot where the law forbids him to set foot, you will be free of the charges brought to-day; but if you acquit him, you become liable to them. So satisfy the claims of heaven and the laws by taking him and punishing him. Do not share his blood-guilt yourselves: but let me, the parent whom he has sent to a living death, at least appear to have had my sorrow lightened.

## 4. SECOND SPEECH FOR THE DEFENSE

While it is only to be expected that the preoccupation of my opponent with his speech for the prosecution should prevent his understanding my defence, the same is not true of yourselves. You should bear in mind that while we, the interested parties, take a biassed view of the case, each naturally thinking that his own version of it is fair, your duty is to consider the facts conscientiously; and so you must give your attention to me as much as you did to him: as it is in what is said that the true facts are to be sought. For my part, if I have told any falsehoods, I am content that you should treat the truth which I have spoken as itself a piece of equally dishonest pleading. On the other hand, if my arguments have been honest, but close and subtle, it is not I who used them, but he whose conduct made them necessary, upon whom the displeasure which they have caused should properly fall.

I would have you understand to begin with that it requires not mere assertion, but proof, to show that someone has killed someone else. Now our accuser agrees with us as to how the accident happened, but disagrees as to the person responsible; yet it is only from what happened that that person can be determined. He complains bitterly, because, according to him, it is a slur upon his son's memory that he should have been proved a slayer when he neither threw the javelin nor had any intention of so doing. That complaint is not an answer to my arguments. I am not maintaining that his son threw the javelin or struck himself. I am maintaining that since he moved withing range of the javelin, his death was due not to the lad, but to himself; for he was not killed standing in his place. As this running across was his undoing, it follows that if it was at his master's summons that he ran across, the master would be the person responsible for his death; but if he moved into the way of his own accord, his death was due to himself.

Before proceeding to any further argument, I wish to show still more clearly which of the two was responsible for the accident. The lad no more missed the target than any of those practising with him: nor has he rendered himself guilty of any of the acts with which he is charged owing to error on his own part. On the other hand, the boy did not do the same as the other onlookers; he moved into the javelin's path. And this is clear proof that it was through his own error that he met with a disaster which those who stood still did not. The thrower would not have been guilty of an error in any respect, had no one moved into the path of his spear: while the boy would not have been hit, had he remained in his place among the onlookers.

Further, my son was not more concerned in the boy's death than any one of those throwing javelins with him, as I will show. If it was owing to the fact that my son was throwing a javelin that the boy was killed, then all those practising with him must share in the guilt of the deed, as it was not owing to their failure to throw that they did not strike him, but owing to the fact that he did not move into the path of the javelin of any one of them. Similarly the young man, who was no more guilty of error than they, would not have hit the boy any more than they did, had the boy stood still with the onlookers.

Again, not only was the boy guilty of the error committed; he was also to blame for the failure to take due precautions. My son saw no one running across, so how could he have taken precautions against striking anyone? The boy, on the other hand, upon seeing the throwers, might easily have guarded against running across, as he was quite at liberty to remain standing still.

The law which they quote is a praiseworthy one; it is right and fair that it should visit those who have killed without meaning to do so with chastisement which they did not mean to incur. But the lad is not guilty of error; and it would therefore be unjust that he should suffer for him who is. It is enough that he should bear the consequences of his own errors. On the other hand, the boy, who perished through his own error, punished himself as soon as he had committed that error. And as the slayer has been punished, the slaying has not gone unavenged.

The slayer has paid the penalty; so it is not by acquitting us, but by condemning us that you will leave a burden upon your consciences. The boy, who is bearing the consequence of his own error, will leave behind him nothing that calls for atonement from anyone; but if my son, who is innocent, is put to death, the conscience of those who have condemned him will be more heavily burdened than ever.

If the arguments put forward prove the dead boy his own slayer, it is not we who have stated them whom he has to thank, but the fact that the accident happened as it did. Since examination proves beyond doubt that the boy was his own slayer, the law absolves us from blame, and condemns him who was guilty. See, then, that we are not plunged into woes which we do not deserve, and that you yourselves do not defy the powers above by a verdict succouring my opponents in their misfortunes. Remember, as righteousness and justice require you to do, that the accident was caused by him who moved into the javelin's path. Remember, and acquit us; for we are not guilty of his death.

# 65  A Murder Case

*On the Murder of Eratosthenes* is the defense of a man on trial for admittedly having killed the seducer of his wife. His appeal for acquittal is to a law that specifically permitted a private person to administer the death penalty on the spot in such cases. Beyond the intrinsic interest of the speech is its graphic presentation of the domestic arrangements in an Athenian home. It is the work of the fourth-century B.C. speech-writer Lysias; the translation is by W. R. M. Lamb.

⊛⊛⊛⊛⊛

I should be only too pleased, sirs, to have you so disposed towards me in judging this case as you would be to yourselves, if you found yourselves in my plight. For I am sure that, if you had the same feelings about others as about yourselves, not one of you but would be indignant at what has been done; you would all regard the penalties appointed for those who resort to such practices as too mild. And these feelings would be found, not only amongst you, but in the whole of Greece: for in the case of this crime alone, under both democracy and oligarchy, the same requital is accorded to the weakest against the strongest, so that the lowest gets the same treatment as the highest. Thus you see, sirs, how all men abominate this outrage. Well, I conceive that, in regard to the severity of the penalty, you are all of the same mind, and that not one of you is so easy-going as to think it right that men who are guilty of such acts should obtain pardon, or to presume that slight penalties suffice for their deserts. But I take it, sirs, that what I have to show is that Eratosthenes had an intrigue with my wife, and not only corrupted her but inflicted disgrace upon my children and an outrage on myself by entering my house; that this was the one and only enmity between him and me; that I have not acted thus for the sake of money, so as to raise myself from poverty to wealth; and that all I seek to gain is the requital accorded by our laws. I shall therefore set forth to you the whole of my story from the beginning; I shall omit nothing, but will tell the truth. For I consider that my own sole deliverance rests on my telling you, if I am able, the whole of what has occurred.

When I, Athenians, decided to marry, and brought a wife into my house, for some time I was disposed neither to vex her nor to leave her too free to do just as she pleased; I kept a watch on her as far as possible, with such observation of her as was reasonable. But when a child was born to me, thenceforward I began to trust her, and placed all my affairs in her hands, presuming that we were now in perfect intimacy. It is true that in the early days, Athenians, she was the most excellent of wives; she was a

SOURCE: Reprinted by permission of the publishers and The Loeb Classical Library from: *Lysias* tr. W. R. M. Lamb, Cambridge, Mass.: Harvard University Press.

clever, frugal housekeeper, and kept everything in the nicest order. But as soon as I lost my mother, her death became the cause of all my troubles. For it was in attending her funeral that my wife was seen by this man, who in time corrupted her. He looked out for the servant-girl who went to market, and so paid addresses to her mistress by which he wrought her ruin. Now in the first place I must tell you, sirs (for I am obliged to give you these particulars), my dwelling is on two floors, the upper being equal in space to the lower, with the women's quarters above and the men's below.

When the child was born to us, its mother suckled it; and in order that, each time that it had to be washed, she might avoid the risk of descending by the stairs, I used to live above, and the women below. By this time it had become such an habitual thing that my wife would often leave me and go down to sleep with the child, so as to be able to give it the breast and stop its crying. Things went on in this way for a long time, and I never suspected, but was simpleminded enough to suppose that my own was the chastest wife in the city. Time went on, sirs; I came home unexpectedly from the country, and after dinner the child started crying in a peevish way, as the servant-girl was annoying it on purpose to make it so behave; for the man was in the house—I learnt it all later. So I bade my wife go and give the child her breast, to stop its howling. At first she refused, as though delighted to see me home again after so long; but when I began to be angry and bade her go— "Yes, so that you," she said, "may have a try here at the little maid. Once before, too, when you were drunk, you pulled her about." At that I laughed, while she got up, went out of the room, and closed the door, feigning to make fun, and she turned the key in the lock. I, without giving a thought to the matter, or having any suspicion, went to sleep in all content after my return from the country. Towards daytime she came and opened the door. I asked why the doors made a noise in the night; she told me that the child's lamp had gone out, and she had lit it again at our neighbour's. I was silent and believed it was so. But it struck me, sirs, that she had powdered her face, though her brother had died not thirty days before; even so, however, I made no remark on the fact, but left the house in silence.

After this, sirs, an interval occurred in which I was left quite unaware of my own injuries; I was then accosted by a certain old female, who was secretly sent by a woman with whom that man was having an intrigue, as I heard later. This woman was angry with him and felt herself wronged, because he no longer visited her so regularly, and she kept a close watch on him until she discovered what was the cause. So the old creature accosted me where she was on the look-out, near my house, and said—"Euphiletus, do not think it is from any meddlesomeness that I have approached you; for the man who is working both your and your wife's dishonour happens to be our enemy. If, therefore, you take the servant-girl who goes to market and waits on you, and torture her, you will learn all. It is," she said, "Eratosthenes of Oë who is doing this; he has debauched not only your wife, but many others besides; he makes an art of it." With these words, sirs, she took herself off; I was at once perturbed; all that had happened came into my mind, and I was filled with suspicion—reflecting first how I was shut up in my chamber, and then remembering how on that night the inner and outer doors made a noise, which had never occurred before, and how it struck me that my wife had put on powder. All these things came into my mind, and I was filled with suspicion.

Returning home, I bade the servant-girl follow me to the market, and taking her to the house of an intimate friend, I told her I was fully informed of what was going on in my house: "So it is open to you," I said, "to choose as you please between two things—either to be whipped and thrown into a mill, never to have any rest from miseries of that sort, or else to speak out the whole truth and, instead of suffering any harm, obtain my pardon for your transgressions. Tell no lies, but speak the whole truth." The girl at first denied it, and bade me do what I pleased, for she knew nothing; but when I mentioned Eratosthenes to her, and said that he was the man who visited my wife, she was dismayed, supposing that I had exact knowledge of everything. At once she threw herself down at my knees, and having got my pledge that she should suffer no harm, she accused him, first, of approaching her after the funeral, and then told how at last she became his messenger; how my wife in time was persuaded, and by what means she procured his entrances, and how at the Thesmophoria,[1] while I was in the country, she went off to the temple with his mother. And the girl gave an exact account of everything else that had occurred. When her tale was all told, I said—"Well now, see that nobody in the world gets knowledge of this; otherwise, nothing in your arrangement with me will hold good. And I require that you show me their guilt in the very act; I want no words, but manifestation of the fact, if it really is so." She agreed to do this.

1.   A festival in honour of Demeter, celebrated by Athenian matrons in October.

Then came an interval of four or five days . . .[2] as I shall bring strong evidence to show. But first I wish to relate what took place on the last day. I had an intimate friend named Sostratus. After sunset I met him as he came from the country. As I knew that, arriving at that hour, he would find none of his circle at home, I invited him to dine with me; we came to my house, mounted to the upper room, and had dinner. When he had made a good meal, he left me and departed; then I went to bed. Eratosthenes, sirs, entered, and the maid-servant roused me at once, and told me that he was in the house. Bidding her look after the door, I descended and went out in silence; I called on one friend and another, and found some of them at home, while others were out of town. I took with me as many as I could among those who were there, and so came along. Then we got torches from the nearest shop, and went in; the door was open, as the girl had it in readiness. We pushed open the door of the bedroom, and the first of us to enter were in time to see him lying down by my wife; those who followed saw him standing naked on the bed. I gave him a blow, sirs, which knocked him down, and pulling round his two hands behind his back, and tying them, I asked him why he had the insolence to enter my house. He admitted his guilt; then he besought and implored me not to kill him, but to exact a sum of money. To this I replied—"It is not I who am going to kill you, but our city's law, which you have transgressed and regarded as of less account than your pleasures, choosing rather to commit this foul offence against my wife and my children than to obey the laws like a decent person."

Thus it was, sirs, that this man incurred the fate that the laws ordain for those who do such things; he had not been dragged in there from the street, nor had he taken refuge at my hearth as these people say. For how could it be so, when it was in the bedroom that he was struck and fell down then and there, and I pinioned his arms, and so many persons were in the house that he could not escape them, as he had neither steel nor wood nor anything else with which he might have beaten off those who had entered? But, sirs, I think you know as well as I that those whose acts are against justice do not acknowledge that their enemies speak the truth, but lie themselves and use other such devices to foment anger in their hearers against those whose acts are just. So, first read the law.

[*Law*]

He did not dispute it, sirs: he acknowledged his guilt, and besought

2.    There is a lacuna in the text.

[ 574 ]

and implored that he might not be killed, and was ready to pay compensation in money. But I would not agree to his estimate, as I held that our city's law should have higher authority; and I obtained that satisfaction which you deemed most just when you imposed it on those who adopt such courses. Now, let my witnesses come forward in support of these statements.

[*Witnesses*]

Read out also, please, that law from the pillar in the Areopagus.

[*Law*]

You hear, sirs, how the Court of the Areopagus itself, to which has been assigned, in our own as in our fathers' time, the trial of suits for murder, has expressly stated that whoever takes this vengeance on an adulterer caught in the act with his spouse shall not be convicted of murder. And so strongly was the lawgiver convinced of the justice of this in the case of wedded wives, that he even applied the same penalty in the case of mistresses, who are of less account. Now surely it is clear that, if he had had any heavier punishment than this for the case of married women, he would have imposed it. But in fact, as he was unable to devise a severer one for wives, he ordained that it should be the same for that of mistresses also. Please read this law besides.

[*Law*]

You hear, sirs, how it directs that, if anyone forcibly debauches a free adult or child, he shall be liable to double damages; while if he so debauches a woman, in any of the cases where it is permitted to kill him, he is subject to the same rule. Thus the lawgiver, sirs, considered that those who use force deserve a less penalty than those who use persuasion; for the latter he condemned to death, whereas for the former he doubled the damages, considering that those who achieve their ends by force are hated by the persons forced; while those who used persuasion corrupted thereby their victims' souls, thus making the wives of others more closely attached to themselves than to their husbands, and got the whole house into their hands, and caused uncertainty as to whose the children really were, the husbands' or the adulterers'. In view of all this the author of the law made death their penalty. Wherefore I, sirs, not only stand acquitted of wrongdoing by the laws, but am also directed by them to take this satisfaction: it is for you to decide whether they are to be valid or of no account. For to my thinking every city makes its laws in order that on any matter which perplexes us we may resort to them and inquire what we have to do. And so it is they who, in cases like the present, exhort the wronged parties to obtain this kind of satisfaction. I call upon you to support their opinion: otherwise, you will be giving adulterers such licence that you will encourage thieves as well to call themselves adulterers; since they will feel assured that, if they plead this reason in their defence, and allege that they enter other men's houses for this purpose, nobody will touch them. For everyone will know that the laws on adultery are to be dismissed, and that it is your vote that one has to fear, because this has supreme authority over all the city's affairs.

Do not consider, sirs, what they say: they accuse me of ordering the maid-servant on that day to go and fetch the young man. Now I, sirs, could have held myself justified in using any possible means to catch the corrupter of my wife. For if I had bidden the girl fetch him, when words alone had been spoken and no act had been committed, I should have been in the wrong: but if, when once he had compassed all his ends, and had frequently entered my house, I had then used any possible means to catch him, I should have considered myself quite in order. And observe how on this point also they are lying: you will perceive it easily in this way. As I told you, sirs, before, Sostratus was a friend of mine, on intimate terms with me; he met me as he came from the country about sunset, and had dinner with me, and when he had made a good meal he left me and departed. Now in the first place, sirs, you must bear this in mind: if on that night I had designs on Eratosthenes, which was more to my advantage—to go and take my dinner elsewhere, or to bring in my guest to dinner with me? For in the latter case that man would have been less likely to venture on entering my house. And in the second place, do you suppose that I should have let my dinner-guest go and leave me there alone and unsupported, and not rather have bidden him stay, in order that he might stand by me in taking vengeance upon the adulterer? Then again, sirs, do you not think that I should have sent word to my intimate acquaintances in the daytime, and bidden them assemble at the house of one of my friends living nearest to me, rather than have waited till the moment of making my discovery to run round in the night, without knowing whom I should find at home, and who were away? Thus I called on Harmodius, and one other, who were not in town—of this I was not aware—and others, I found, were not in;

[ 576 ]

but those whom I could I took along with me. Yet if I had foreknown this, do you not think that I should have called up servants and passed the word to my friends, in order that I might have gone in myself with all possible safety—for how could I tell whether he too had some weapon? —and so I might have had as many witnesses as possible with me when I took my vengeance? But as in fact I knew nothing of what was to befall on that night, I took with me those whom I could. Now let my witnesses come forward in support of all this.

*[Witnesses]*

You have heard the witnesses, sirs; and consider this affair thus in your own minds, asking yourselves whether any enmity has ever arisen before this between me and Eratosthenes. I say you will discover none. For he had neither subjected me to slanderous impeachment, nor attempted to expel me from the city, nor brought any private suit against me, nor was he privy to any wrongdoing which I was so afraid of being divulged that I was intent on his destruction, nor, should I accomplish this, had I any hope of getting money from anywhere: for there are people who plot each other's death for such purposes. So far, indeed, from either abuse or a drunken brawl or any other quarrel having occurred between us, I had never even seen the man before that night. For what object, then, should I run so grave a risk, unless I had received from him the greatest of injuries? Why, again, did I choose to summon witnesses for my wicked act, when it was open to me, if I was thus criminally intent on his destruction, to have none of them privy to it?

I therefore, sirs, do not regard this requital as having been exacted in my own private interest, but in that of the whole city. For those who behave in that way, when they see the sort of prizes offered for such transgressions, will be less inclined to trespass against their neighbours, if they see that you also take the same view. Otherwise it were better far to erase our established laws, and ordain others which will inflict the penalties on men who keep watch on their own wives, and will allow full immunity to those who would debauch them. This would be a far juster way than to let the citizens be entrapped by the laws; these may bid a man, on catching an adulterer, to deal with him in whatever way he pleases, but the trials are found to be more dangerous to the wronged parties than to those who, in defiance of the laws, dishonour the wives of others. For I am now risking the loss of life, property and all else that I have, because I obeyed the city's laws.

# 66 Profits of Public Service

*On the Property of Aristophanes* (here presented with the final few paragraphs omitted), which dates from about 388 B.C., is significant for the picture it gives of the profits that could be made from public service in the Athenian democracy. The wealthy were expected to contribute to the state, but it was also possible to become wealthy through being active in public life. From this speech, the line between legitimate rewards and graft does not appear to have been clearly drawn. The case at issue is as follows: a certain Nicophemus (friend and associate of Conon, the outstanding Athenian naval commander of the post-Peloponnesian War period) and his son Aristophanes (not the comic poet) were public men of the freebooting adventurer type that became especially common in the fourth century. Following the failure of one of their schemes in 390, they were legally condemned and executed, and their property was confiscated by the state. The property turned out to be disappointingly less than had been expected, and the heirs were accused of holding back some of it. Aristophanes' father-in-law, as legal guardian for his daughter (women could not appear in court but had to be represented by male kin) and her three minor children, was indicted but died before the trial. It is *his* son who then became the legally responsible party and was the speaker in this case. The translation of Lysias' work is by W. R. M. Lamb.

⊛⊛⊛⊛⊛

I find myself greatly embarrassed by this trial, gentlemen of the jury, when I consider that if I fail to speak with effect to-day not only I but my father besides will be held to be guilty, and I shall be deprived of the whole of my possessions. It is necessary therefore, even if I have no natural aptitude for the task, to defend my father and myself as best I can. You see, of course, the artifice and the alacrity of my enemies; of these there is no need to speak; whereas everyone who knows me is aware of my inexperience. I shall therefore beg of you the just and easy favour of hearing us with the same absence of anger as when you listened to our accusers. For the man who speaks in his defence, even if you give

SOURCE: Reprinted by permission of the publishers and The Loeb Classical Library from: *Lysias* tr. W. R. M. Lamb, Cambridge, Mass.: Harvard University Press.

him an impartial hearing, must needs be at a disadvantage: those people
have laid their schemes long before, and without any danger to themselves
have delivered their accusation; whereas we are contending amid fear
and slander and the gravest danger. It is reasonable, therefore, that you
should feel more kindness for those who are making their defence. For
I think you all know that there have been many cases in the past of men
bringing forward a number of formidable accusations, who have been
convicted then and there of lying on such clear evidence that they left
the court detested by all who had been present; while others again, after
bearing false witness and causing people to be unjustly put to death, have
been condemned too late for it to be of any use to their victims. So, when
many cases of this sort have occurred, as I am told, it is reasonable that
you, gentlemen, should wait till we have had our say before you accept
the statements of our accusers as trustworthy. I myself am told, and I
think most of you know also, that slander is the most dangerous thing
on earth. This is especially to be observed when a number of persons are
brought to trial on the same charge. For, as a rule, the last to be judged
are let off, since your anger has then ceased, and as you listen to them
you willingly admit their disproofs.

Reflect therefore that Nicophemus and Aristophanes were put to death
without trial,[1] before anyone could come to their aid as the proof of
their guilt was being made out. For nobody even saw them again after
their arrest, since their bodies were not even delivered for burial: so
awful has their calamity been that, in addition to the rest, they have
suffered this privation also. But from that business I will now pass, as
I can do no good there. Far more miserable, in my opinion, are the children of Aristophanes: for, having done no wrong to anyone in either
private or public affairs, not only have they been bereft of their patrimony
in violation of your laws, but their one remaining hope, of being reared
with the means of their grandfather, has been placed in this serious pre-
dicament. Moreover we, bereft of our kinsfolk, bereft of the dowry, and
compelled to rear three small children, are attacked besides by base informers, and are in danger of losing what our ancestors bequeathed to
us after they had acquired it by honest means. Yet, gentlemen, my father
in all his life spent more on the State than on himself and his family—
twice the amount that we have now, as he often reckoned in my presence.
So you must not rashly convict of guilt the man who spent little on him-

1.   On a summary impeachment allowed in special cases of treason or embezzlement.

self, but a great deal on you each year; you ought rather to condemn all those persons who have made a habit of squandering both their patrimony and whatever they can get from elsewhere on the most disgraceful pleasures. It is difficult indeed, gentlemen, to defend oneself against an impression which some people have received of the property of Nicophemus, and in face of a scarcity of money that is now felt in the city, and when our contention is against the Treasury. Nevertheless, even in these circumstances, you will easily perceive that the accusations are not true; and I request you with all the insistence in my power to give us a kindly hearing to the end, and to deliver the verdict that you may esteem best for you and most agreeable to your oaths.

Now I will inform you, in the first place, of the way in which they became connected with us. Conon, who was in command of operations around the Peloponnese, and who had formed a friendship long before with my father when he equipped a warship, requested him to bestow my sister on her suitor, the son of Nicophemus. My father, finding that these people had been accredited by Conon, and were of proved respectability and—at that time at least—in the good graces of the city, was persuaded to bestow her: he did not know the slander that was to follow. It was a time when anyone among you would have deemed it desirable to be connected with them; for it was not done for the sake of money, as you may readily judge from my father's whole life and conduct. When he was of age, he had the chance of marrying another woman with a great fortune; but he took my mother without a portion, merely because she was a daughter of Xenophon, a son of Euripides,[2] a man not only known for his private virtues but also deemed worthy by you of holding high command, so I am told. Again, my sisters he refused to certain very wealthy men who were willing to take them without dowries, because he judged them to be of inferior birth: he preferred to bestow one upon Philomelus of Paeania, whom most men regard as an honourable rather than a wealthy man, and the other upon a man who was reduced to poverty by no misdemeanour—his nephew, Phaedrus[3] of Myrrhinous—and with her a dowry of forty minae; and he later gave her to Aristophanes with the same sum. Besides doing this, when I could have obtained a great fortune he advised me to take a lesser one, so long as I felt sure of allying myself with people of an orderly and self-respecting character. So now I am married to the daughter of Critodemus of Alopece, who

2. Not the historian; nor the tragic poet.
3. The same person who appears in Plato's *Phaedrus* and *Symposium*.

was killed by the Lacedaemonians after the sea-fight at the Hellespont. Now I submit, gentlemen of the jury, that a man who has himself married a portionless woman, who has bestowed large sums with his two daughters, and who has accepted a small dowry for his son, ought surely in reason to be credited with allying himself to these people without a thought of money.

Nay, more, Aristophanes, although he was now married, must have preferred to be intimate with many people rather than my father, as may readily be conceived. For there was a great difference both in his age and still more in his nature. It was my father's way to mind his own business; whereas Aristophanes sought to concern himself not only with private but also with public affairs, and whatever money he had he spent in the pursuit of glory. You will perceive the truth of what I say from his actual conduct. First, when Conon wanted to send someone to Sicily,[4] he offered himself and went off with Eunomus, who was a friend and guest of Dionysius, and who had rendered a great many services to your people, as I have been told by those who were with him at the Peiraeus. The voyage was undertaken in hopes of persuading Dionysius to connect himself by marriage with Evagoras,[5] and to become an enemy of the Lacedaemonians and a friend and ally of your city. This they set out to do amid many dangers arising from the sea and from the enemy, and they prevailed on Dionysius not to send some warships which he had then prepared for the Lacedaemonians. Next, when the envoys had arrived from Cyprus to procure our assistance, his ardent energy knew no bounds. You had granted them ten warships, and had voted all the material, but they were in need of money for the dispatch of the fleet. They had brought but scanty funds with them, and they required a great deal more: for they had to hire not only men to work the ships but light infantry also, and to purchase arms. Well, it was Aristophanes who personally supplied most of their funds: as he had not enough, he persuaded his friends with entreaties and guarantees, and he took forty minae which he had in deposit at his house for his brother on the father's side, and applied the money to that purpose. The day before he put to sea, he called on my father and pressed him for the loan of such money as he had; for some more was required, he said, to pay the light infantry. We had seven minae in the house: he took these and applied them also. What man,

4. In 393 B.C., to undermine the friendship between Dionysius, despot of Syracuse, and the Spartans, who had helped him to attain his power in 406 B.C.
5. Despot of Salamis in Cyprus, and steady friend of Athens.

think you, who was ambitious of glory, and was receiving letters from his father that told him he would lack for nothing in Cyprus, and had been elected ambassador and was about to sail to Evagoras, would have left behind anything that he possessed, and not have rather gratified that ruler by supplying everything that he could, with a view to a handsome return? Now, to show the truth of all this, please call Eunomus.

[*Testimony*]

Please call the other witnesses also.

[*Witnesses*]

You hear them testify, not only that they lent the money at his request, but also that they have been repaid; for it was conveyed to them in the warship.

Well now, it is easily concluded from my argument that in such emergencies he was not likely to spare his own resources. But the strongest evidence is this: Demus, son of Pyrilampes, who was equipping a warship for Cyprus, requested me to go to Aristophanes; he said he had received a gold cup as a credential from the Great King, and would give it to Aristophanes in pledge for sixteen minae, so as to have means for equipping his warship; when he got to Cyprus, he would redeem it with a payment of twenty minae, since on the strength of that credential he would then obtain plenty of goods and also money all over the continent. Then Aristophanes, on hearing this proposal from Demus and a request from me—although he was to have the gold cup in his hands and receive four minae as interest—said that it was impossible, and he swore that he had already gone elsewhere to borrow more for these foreigners; since, but for that, nobody alive, he declared, would have been more delighted than he to take that credential forthwith and to comply with our request. To show the truth of this, I will produce to you witnesses.

[*Witnesses*]

So then, that Aristophanes did not leave any silver or gold is easily concluded from what I have stated and from these testimonies. Of fine bronze plate he possessed but little: when he was entertaining the envoys of Evagoras, he had to use what he could borrow. The list of the pieces that he left shall be read to you.

[*Inventory of Bronze Plate*]

[ 582 ]

Perhaps to some of you, gentlemen of the jury, they appear few: but bear in mind the fact that before Conon won his victory at sea,[6] Aristophanes had no land except a small plot at Rhamnus. Now the sea-fight occurred in the archonship of Eubulides; and in four or five years it was a difficult thing, gentlemen, when he had no wealth to start with, to be twice a producer of tragedies, on his father's account as well as his own; to equip a warship for three years in succession; to have been a contributor to special levies on many occasions; to purchase a house for fifty minae; and to acquire more than three hundred *plethra* of land. Do you suppose that, besides doing all this, he must have left many personal effects? Why, even people credited with long-established wealth may fail to produce any that are of value: for at times, however much one may desire it, one cannot buy things of the sort that, once acquired, will be a permanent source of pleasure. Again, consider this: in all other cases where you have confiscated the property, not merely have you had no sale of furniture, but even the doors were torn away from the apartments; whereas we, as soon as the confiscation was declared and my sister had left the place, posted a guard in the deserted house, in order that neither door-timber nor utensils nor anything else might be lost. Personal effects were realized to the value of over a thousand drachmae—more than you had received of any previous person. Moreover, we now repeat our former offer to pledge ourselves to the Commissioners, in the most binding terms available to man, that we hold no part of Aristophanes' estate, but are owed from it the dowry of my sister and seven minae which he got from my father at his departure. Could human beings have a more miserable fate than to lose their own property, and then to be supposed to hold that of the mulcted party? And the greatest hardship of all for us will be that, having taken charge of my sister and her many children, we must rear them with no means available even for ourselves, if you deprive us of what we now have.

I adjure you, by the Olympian gods, gentlemen, just consider it in this way: suppose that one of you had happened to bestow his daughter or his sister on Timotheus, son of Conon, and during his absence abroad Conon was involved in some slander and his estate was confiscated, and the city received from the sale of the whole something less than four talents of silver. Would you think it right that his children and relatives should be ruined merely because the property had turned out to be but

6. At Cnidus, 394 B.C. against a Spartan fleet. This event marked the revival of Athenian naval power.

a trifling fraction of the amount at which it stood in your estimation? But of course you are all aware that Conon held the command, and Nicophemus carried out his instructions. Now it is probable that Conon allotted to others but a small proportion of his prizes; so that if it be thought that Nicophemus's gains were great, it must be allowed that Conon's were more than ten times greater. Furthermore, there is no evidence of any dispute having occurred between them; so probably in regard to money they agreed in deciding that each should leave his son with a competence here, while keeping the rest in his own hands. For Conon had a son and a wife in Cyprus, and Nicophemus a wife and a daughter, and they also felt that their property there was just as safe as their property here. Besides, you have to consider that, even if a man had distributed among his sons what he had not acquired but inherited from his father, he would have reserved a goodly share for himself; for everyone would rather be courted by his children as a man of means than beg of them as a needy person.

So, in this case, if you should confiscate the property of Timotheus— which Heaven forbid, unless some great benefit is to accrue to the State —and you should receive a less amount from it than has been derived from that of Aristophanes, would this give you any good reason for thinking that his relatives should lose what belongs to them? No, it is not reasonable, gentlemen of the jury: for Conon's death and the dispositions made under his will in Cyprus have clearly shown that his fortune was but a small fraction of what you were expecting. He dedicated five thousand staters[7] in offerings to Athene and to Apollo at Delphi; to his nephew, who acted as guardian and manager of all his property in Cyprus, he gave about ten thousand drachmae; to his brother three talents; and to his son he left the rest—seventeen talents. The round total of these sums amounts to about forty talents. And nobody can say that there was malversation, or that the accounts were not fairly rendered: for he made his dispositions himself in his illness, while his mind was sound. Please call witnesses to this.

[*Witnesses*]

Why, surely anyone, gentlemen, before the amounts of the two had been revealed, would have thought that the property of Nicophemus was a mere fraction of that of Conon. Now, Aristophanes had acquired a house with land for more than five talents, had produced dramas on his own

7. The Attic stater was a gold coin equal to 20 drachmae.

account and on his father's at a cost of five thousand drachmae, and had spent eighty minae on equipping warships; on account of the two, no less than forty minae have been contributed to special levies; for the Sicilian expedition he spent a hundred minae, and for commissioning the warships, when the Cypriots came and you gave them the ten vessels, he supplied thirty thousand drachmae to pay the light infantry and purchase their arms. The total of all these sums amounts to little short of fifteen talents. Hence you can have no reason to lay blame on us, since the property of Conon, which is admitted to have been fairly accounted for by the owner himself, and was thought to be many times more than that of Aristophanes, is found to be less than thrice the amount of his. And we are omitting from the calculation all that Nicophemus held himself in Cyprus, where he had a wife and a daughter.

I claim, therefore, gentlemen of the jury, that after having produced such an abundance of weighty proofs we ought not to be unjustly ruined. I have been told by my father and other elderly people that you have had similar experiences in the past of being deceived in the fortunes of many men who were supposed to be wealthy while they lived, but whose death showed your supposition to be wide of the mark. For example, Ischomachus during his life was considered by everyone to own more than seventy talents, as I am told: his two sons, on his death, had less than ten talents to divide between them. Stephanus, son of Thallus, was reported to own more than fifty talents; but when he died his fortune was found to be about eleven talents. Again, the estate of Nicias[8] was expected to be not less than a hundred talents—most of it in his house; but when Niceratus was dying, he said that he in his turn was not leaving any silver or gold, and the property that he left to his son is worth no more than fourteen talents. Then Callias, son of Hipponicus, just after his father's death, was thought to have more in his possession than any other Greek, and the story goes that his grandfather valued his own property at two hundred talents; yet his ratable property stands to-day at less than two talents. And you all know how Cleophon for many years had all the affairs of the State in his hands, and was expected to have got a great deal by his office; but when he died this money was nowhere to be found, and moreover his relatives both by blood and by marriage, in whose hands he would have left it, are admittedly poor people.

So it is evident that we have been greatly deceived both in men of hereditary riches and in those who have recently gained a name for

8. The Peloponnesian War general. See Selection 56. Niceratus was his son and heir.

wealth. The cause of this, in my opinion, is that people make light of stating that such an one has got many talents by his office. As to the common statements about dead people, I am not so much surprised, since there is no disproof to fear from them; but what of the lies with which they assail the living? Why, you yourselves were told of late in the Assembly that Diotimus had got forty talents more from the ship-masters and merchants than he himself admitted; and when he rendered an ac‑ count on his return, and was indignant at being slandered in his absence, nobody put that matter to the proof, although the State was in need of money, and he was ready to show his accounts. Just imagine what the position would have been if, after all the Athenians had been told that Diotimus had forty talents, something had then happened to him before he reached our shores. His relatives would then have been in the gravest danger, if they had been obliged to defend themselves against that monstrous slander without any knowledge of the facts of the case. So, for your being deceived in many people even now, and indeed for the ruin that some have unjustly incurred, you have to thank those who make light of telling lies and are bent on bringing malicious charges against their fellows. . . .

# 67 Eligibility for Public Service

Another aspect of public service that brought with it something like a trial was service on the Council (*boulē*). Five hundred individuals were selected by lot each year to serve on the Council, and each of them had to undergo an official inquiry or scrutiny (*dokimasia*) at which his fitness to serve was considered. The following selection illustrates the atmosphere of such inquiries. The speech *In Defense of Mantitheus* dates from about 390 B.C. It sharply illustrates the antiaristocratic bias of democratic Athens in the need felt by the speaker to assert his value as a citizen in spite of his being a member of a noble family. Mantitheus' dignified, unwhimpering description of himself as an aristocrat—and unashamed of it—may seem priggish on its face, but it is courageously impressive in the circumstances. The work is by Lysias, the translation by W. R. M. Lamb.

SOURCE: Reprinted by permission of the publishers and The Loeb Classical Library from: *Lysias* tr. W. R. M. Lamb, Cambridge, Mass.: Harvard University Press.

If I were not conscious, gentlemen of the Council, that my accusers are seeking every possible means of injuring me, I should feel most grateful to them for this accusation; since I consider that the victims of unjust slander have the greatest service rendered to them by anyone who will compel them to undergo an examination of the record of their lives. For I have so strong a confidence in myself that, if there is anyone who is inclined to dislike me, I hope that when he has heard me speak of my conduct in the past he will change his mind, and will think much better of me in the future. Now, gentlemen, I make no claim to special merit, if I merely make plain to you that I am a supporter of the existing constitution and have been compelled to take my own share in your dangers: but if I am found to have lived, in all other respects, a regular life, quite contrary to the opinion and statements of my enemies, I request you to pass me through and to think the worse of these persons. I will begin by showing that I did not serve in the cavalry or reside here under the Thirty, and that I had no hand in the government of that time.

Our father, before the disaster at the Hellespont,[1] had sent us abroad to live at the court of Satyrus, on the Pontus; we were not residing in Athens either when the walls were being demolished or when the constitution was being changed; we came here five days before the people at Phyle returned to the Peiraeus. Surely it was not to be expected that, having arrived at such a moment, we should want to share in dangers that concerned others; while obviously the Thirty were in no mind to share the government with men who were residing abroad and were guilty of no crime: they were rather disfranchising even the men who had helped them to overthrow the democracy. Moreover, to refer to the register for those who served in the cavalry is puerile: for it does not include many of those who admit that they served, while some who were absent abroad are on the list. But the strongest proof lies in the fact that, after you had returned, you voted that the tribal officers should make out a list of those who had served in the cavalry, so that you might recover the allowances from them. Well, nobody will be able to show that I was either put on the list by the tribal officers or reported to the Revenue Commission or made to refund an allowance: yet it is within the knowledge of all that the tribal officers were under the necessity, if they failed

1.   At Aegospotami, 405 B.C.; see Selection 57.

to show who had the allowances, of bearing the loss themselves. Hence you would be far more justified in relying on these lists than on the register: for anyone who wished could easily have his name erased from the latter; but in the former the tribal officers were obliged to record those who had served. Besides, gentlemen, if I had served, I should not deny it as though I had done something monstrous: I should merely claim, after showing that no citizen had suffered injury by my act, to pass the scrutiny. And I see that you also take this view, and that many of those who served then in the cavalry are on the Council, while many others have been elected generals and brigadiers. You must therefore conclude that my only reason for making this defence is that they have dared thus openly to attack me with a falsehood. Mount the daïs, please, and bear witness.

[*Testimony*]

Now, as regards the charge itself, I do not see what more there is to say. But it seems to me, gentlemen, that although in other trials one ought to confine one's defence to the actual points of the accusation, in the case of scrutinies one has a right to render an account of one's whole life. I request you, therefore, to give me a favourable hearing: I will make my defence as briefly as I can.

In the first place, although but little property had been bequeathed to me, owing to the disasters that had befallen both my father and the city, I bestowed two sisters in marriage, with a dowry of thirty minae apiece; to my brother I allowed such a portion as made him acknowledge that he had got a larger share of our patrimony than I had; and towards everyone else my behaviour has been such that never to this day has a single person shown any grievance against me. So much for the tenor of my private life: with regard to public matters, I hold that the strongest proof I can give of my decorous conduct is the fact that all the younger set who are found to take their diversion in dice or drink or the like dissipations are, as you will observe, at feud with me, and are most prolific in lying tales about me. It is obvious, surely, that if we were at one in our desires they would not regard me with such feelings. And moreover, gentlemen, nobody will be able to prove that I have ever been cited in a disgraceful private suit, or in public proceedings, or in a special impeachment; yet you see others frequently involved in such trials. Again, as regards campaigns and dangers in face of the enemy, observe how I discharge my duty to the State. First of all, when you made your alliance with the Boeotians, and we had to go to the relief of Haliartus, I had been enrolled by Orthobulus for service in the cavalry: I saw that it was everyone's opinion that, whereas the cavalry were assured of safety, the infantry would have to face danger; so, while others mounted on horseback illegally, without having passed the scrutiny, I went up to Orthobulus and told him to strike me off the roll, as I thought it shameful, while the majority were to face danger, to take the field with precaution for my own security. Come forward, please, Orthobulus.

*[Testimony]*

Now, when the townsmen had assembled together before their setting out, as I knew that some among them, though true and ardent patriots, lacked means for expenses of service, I said that the well-to-do ought to provide what was necessary for those in needy circumstances. Not only did I recommend this to the others, but I myself gave thirty drachmae each to two men; not as being a person of great possessions, but to set a good example to the others. Come forward, please.

*[Witnesses]*

Then after that, gentlemen, there was the expedition to Corinth;[2] and everyone knew beforehand that it must be a dangerous affair. Some were trying to shirk their duty, but I contrived to have myself posted in the front rank for our battle with the enemy. Our tribe had the worst fortune, and suffered the heaviest losses among its own men: I retired from the field later than the fine fellow of Steiria who has been reproaching everybody with cowardice. Not many days after this event some strong posts in Corinth had been occupied, to prevent the passage of the enemy: when Agesilaus had forced his way into Boeotia, the commanders decided to detach some battalions to the rescue; everyone felt afraid (with some reason, gentlemen; for it was a serious thing, when they had just previously felt the relief of getting off in safety, to face a fresh danger), but I went to the commander and urged him to dispatch our battalion without drawing lots. So if any of you are incensed against those who claim the management of the city's affairs and yet evade its dangers, you can have no right to regard me with any such feeling; for I not only carried out my orders with zeal, but I was also forward to face danger. I acted in this way, not because I did not think it a serious thing to do battle with the Lacedaemonians, but in order that, if ever I should be involved

2. 394 B.C.

in an unjust prosecution, the better opinion that you would form of me on this account might avail to secure me the full measure of my rights. Now let the witnesses to this come forward, please.

[*Witnesses*]

In every other campaign or outpost I have never once failed in my duty, but have adhered throughout to my rule of marching out in the first rank and retreating in the last. Surely it is by such conduct that one ought to judge who are the aspiring and orderly subjects of the State, and not to take the fact of a man's wearing his hair long[3] as a reason for hating him; for such habits as this do no harm either to private persons or to the public weal, while it is from those who are ready to face danger before the enemy that you all derive advantage. Hence it is not fair, gentlemen, to like or dislike any man because of his appearance, but rather to judge him by his actions; for many who gossip little, and are sober in dress have been the cause of grievous mischief, while others who are careless of such things have done you many a valuable service.

I have had occasion to observe, gentlemen, that some people are annoyed with me merely for attempting at too early an age to speak before the people. But, in the first place, I was compelled to speak in public to protect my own interests; and indeed, in the second, I do feel that my tendency has been unduly enterprising: for in reflecting on my ancestors, and how they have continually taken part in the administration, I had you also in my view—I must tell you the truth—as attaching no value to any but men of that stamp. So who, on seeing you so minded, would not be stimulated to work and speak for the benefit of the State? Moreover, how could you be annoyed with such people? For it is you, and none else, who are judges of their worth.

# 68 Social Welfare

Most ancient societies accepted as a matter of course the principle of public responsibility for the basic welfare of individuals. In democratic Athens it is not surprising to find official solicitude for the individual

---

3. An aristocratic fashion among the class of knights.

SOURCE: Reprinted by permission of the publishers and The Loeb Classical Library from: *Lysias* tr. W. R. M. Lamb, Cambridge, Mass.: Harvard University Press.

citizen going far beyond such basic commitment. We are not well informed as to the details of Athenian welfare legislation, and the following
selection by Lysias, the speech *On the Refusal of a Pension to the Invalid,*
is the only information we have that the state provided pensions to disabled citizens. The probable date of the speech is shortly after 403 B.C.
The translation is by W. R. M. Lamb.

@@@@@

I can almost find it in me to be grateful to my accuser, gentlemen
of the Council, for having involved me in these proceedings. For previously I had no excuse for rendering an account of my life; but now,
owing to this man, I have got one. So I will try to show you in my
speech that this man is lying, and that my own life until this day has
been deserving of praise rather than envy; for it is merely from envy,
in my opinion, that he has involved me in this ordeal. But I ask you, if
a man envies those whom other people pity, from what villainy do you
think such a person would refrain? Is it possible that he hopes to get
money by slandering me? And if he makes me out an enemy on whom
he seeks to be avenged, he lies; for his villainy has always kept me from
having any dealings with him either as a friend or as an enemy. So now,
gentlemen, it is clear that he envies me because, although I have to bear
this sore misfortune, I am a better citizen than he is. For indeed I consider, gentlemen, that one ought to remedy the afflictions of the body with
the activities of the spirit; for if I am to keep my thoughts and the general tenor of my life on the level of my misfortune, how shall I be distinguished from this man?

Well, in regard to those matters, let these few words of mine suffice:
I will now speak as briefly as I can on the points with which I am here
concerned. My accuser says that I have no right to receive my civil pension,
because I am able-bodied and not classed as disabled, and because I am
skilled in a trade which would enable me to live without this grant. In
proof of my bodily strength, he instances that I mount on horseback;
of the affluence arising from my trade, that I am able to associate with
people who have means to spend. Now, as to the affluence from my trade
and the nature of my livelihood in general, I think you are all acquainted
with these: I will, however, make some brief remarks of my own. My
father left me nothing, and I have only ceased supporting my mother on
her decease two years ago; while as yet I have no children to take care
of me. I possess a trade that can give me but slight assistance: I already

find difficulty in carrying it on myself, and as yet I am unable to procure someone to relieve me of the work.[1] I have no other income besides this dole, and if you deprive me of it I might be in danger of finding myself in the most grievous plight. Do not, therefore, gentlemen, when you can save me justly, ruin me unjustly; what you granted me when I was younger and stronger, do not take from me when I am growing older and weaker; nor, with your previous reputation for showing the utmost compassion even towards those who are in no trouble, be moved now by this man to deal harshly with those who are objects of pity even to their enemies; nor, by having the heart to wrong me, cause everyone else in my situation to despond. And indeed, how extraordinary the case would be, gentlemen! When my misfortune was but simple, I am found to have been receiving this pension; but now, when old age, diseases, and the ills that attend on them are added to my trouble, I am to be deprived of it! The depth of my poverty, I believe, can be revealed more clearly by my accuser than by anyone else on earth. For if I were charged with the duty of producing tragic drama, and should challenge him to an exchange of property, he would prefer being the producer ten times over to making the exchange once.[2] Surely it is monstrous that he should now accuse me of having such great affluence that I can consort on equal terms with the wealthiest people, while, in the event of such a thing as I have suggested, he should behave as he does. Why, what could be more villainous?

As to my horsemanship, which he has dared to mention to you, feeling neither awe of fortune nor shame before you, there is not much to tell. For I, gentlemen, am of opinion that all who suffer from some affliction make it their single aim and constant study to manage the condition that has befallen them with the least amount of discomfort. I am such an one, and in the misfortune that has stricken me I have devised this facility for myself on the longer journeys that I find necessary. But the strongest proof, gentlemen, of the fact that I mount horses because of my misfortune, and not from insolence, as this man alleges, is this: if I were a man of means, I should ride on a saddled mule, and would not mount

1. He means a slave who would learn the business and carry it on for him.
2. A citizen selected to perform a *leiturgy* could claim lack of personal means. He could challenge another citizen who had never performed the *leiturgy* to an exchange of their respective properties. Both men would then have their properties officially assessed, and exchanged. The man so challenged, presumably being known by the challenger to be by far the wealthier of the two, would prefer to volunteer for the *leiturgy* rather than accept the challenge.

other men's horses. But in fact, as I am unable to acquire anything of the sort, I am compelled, now and again, to use other men's horses. Well, I ask you, gentlemen, is it not extraordinary that, if he saw me riding on a saddled mule, he would hold his peace—for what could he say?—and then, because I mount borrowed horses, he should try to persuade you that I am able-bodied; and that my using two sticks, while others use one, should not be argued by him against me as a sign of being able-bodied, but my mounting horses should be advanced by him as a proof to you that I am able-bodied? For I use both aids for the same reason.

So utterly has he surpassed the whole human race in impudence that he tries with his single voice to persuade you all that I am not classed as disabled. Yet if he should persuade any of you on this point, gentlemen, what hinders me from drawing a lot for election as one of the nine archons, and you from depriving me of my obol as having sound health, and voting it unanimously to this man as being a cripple? For surely, after you have deprived a man of the grant as being able-bodied, the law-officers are not going to debar this same person, as being disabled, from drawing a lot! Nay, indeed, you are not of the same opinion as he is, nor is he either, and rightly so. For he has come here to dispute over my misfortune as if over an heiress, and he tries to persuade you that I am not the sort of man that you all see me to be; but you—as is incumbent on men of good sense—have rather to believe your own eyes than this person's words.

He says that I am insolent, savage, and utterly abandoned in my behaviour, as though he needed the use of terrifying terms to speak the truth, and could not do it in quite gentle language. But I expect you, gentlemen, to distinguish clearly between those people who are at liberty to be insolent and those who are debarred from it. For insolence is not likely to be shown by poor men labouring in the utmost indigence, but by those who possess far more than the neccessaries of life; nor by men disabled in body, but by those who have most reason to rely on their own strength; nor by those already advanced in years, but by those who are still young and have a youthful turn of mind. For the wealthy purchase with their money escape from the risks that they run, whereas the poor are compelled to moderation by the pressure of their want. The young are held to merit indulgence from their elders; but if their elders are guilty of offence, both ages unite in reproaching them. The strong are at liberty to insult whomsoever they will with impunity, but the weak are unable either to beat off their aggressors when insulted, or to get the better of their victims if they choose to insult. Hence it seems to me that my accuser was not serious in speaking of my insolence, but was only jesting: his purpose was, not to persuade you that such is my nature, but to set me in a comic light, as a fine stroke of fancy.

He further asserts that my shop is the meeting place of a number of rogues who have spent their own money and hatch plots against those who wish to preserve theirs. But you must all take note that these statements of his are no more accusations against me than against anyone else who has a trade, nor against those who visit my shop any more than those who frequent other men of business. For each of you is in the habit of paying a call at either a perfumer's or a barber's or a shoemaker's shop, or wherever he may chance to go—in most cases, it is to the tradesmen who have set up nearest the market place, and in fewest, to those who are farthest from it. So if any of you should brand with roguery the men who visit my shop, clearly you must do the same to those who pass their time in the shops of others; and if to them, to all the Athenians: for you are all in the habit of paying a call and passing your time at some shop or other.

But really I see no need for me to be so very particular in rebutting each one of the statements that he has made, and to weary you any longer. For if I have argued the principal points, what need is there to dwell seriously on trifles in the same way as he does? But I beg you all, gentlemen of the Council, to hold the same views concerning me as you have held till now. Do not be led by this man to deprive me of the sole benefit in my country of which fortune has granted me a share, nor let this one person prevail on you to withdraw now what you all agreed to grant me in the past. For, gentlemen, since Heaven had deprived us of the chiefest things, the city voted us this pension, regarding the chances of evil and of good as the same for all alike. Surely I should be the most miserable of creatures if, after being deprived by my misfortune of the fairest and greatest things, the accuser should cause me the loss of that which the city bestowed in her thoughtful care for men in my situation. No, no, gentlemen; you must not vote that way. And why should I find you thus inclined? Because anyone has ever been brought to trial at my instance and lost his fortune? There is nobody who can prove it. Well, is it that I am a busybody, a hothead, a seeker of quarrels? That is not the sort of use I happen to make of such means of subsistence as I have. That I am grossly insolent and savage? Even he would not allege this himself, except he should wish to add one more to the series of his lies. Or that I was in power at the time of the Thirty, and oppressed a great number of the citizens? But I went into exile with your people to Chalcis, and when I was free to live secure as a citizen with those persons[3] I chose to depart and share your perils. I therefore ask you, gentlemen of the Council, not to treat me, a man who has committed no offence, in the same way as those who are guilty of numerous wrongs, but to give the same vote as the other Councils[4] did on my case, remembering that I am neither rendering an account of State moneys placed in my charge, nor undergoing now an inquiry into my past proceedings in any office, but that the subject of this speech of mine is merely an obol.[5] In this way you will all give the decision that is just, while I, in return for that, will feel duly grateful to you; and this man will learn in the future not to scheme against those who are weaker than himself, but only to overreach his equals.

3.  The Thirty.
4.  The Councils of previous years by which he had been certified as infirm.
5.  An obol, the smallest Athenian coin, was traditionally the minimum cost of an adult's daily subsistence.

# FAMILY LIFE AND PROPERTY

A S IN most societies there was a close connection in Classical Athens between family relations and property. The family had its chief importance in the sphere of religion, where its main function was to maintain the necessary rituals at ancestral graves. For this reason the continuance of a family line was crucial. It was crucial also for the maintenance of property, which, although legally disposable, was thought of as a family's possession in perpetuity, an individual's only for his own lifetime. The link between family and property lay at the root of a great deal of very complicated litigation and also of certain peculiarities of Greek law. This is particularly noteworthy in the special position of the heiress. If male heirs were lacking, an entire estate could go to a daughter. Her children, who would eventually inherit the property, would be members of their father's family, and thus the property would leave its original owners. In an effort to prevent this misfortune an heiress (*epiklēros*) was obliged to marry her father's nearest kin—usually his brother, that is, her uncle—if *he* so desired. If the estate was considerable, he usually did so desire. In such instances, he would divorce his own wife in order to marry his niece. Out of this situation resulted some very complicated family relationships.

Legal cases arising out of disputes over inheritance provide us with our best source of information about ordinary relations among ordinary people. The careful provider, the prodigal son, the nasty stepmother, the dutiful daughter; love, hate, greed, anger—these are among the manifold human types and emotions that come to life in the often poignant pages of the speeches written by Isaeus, a professional legal speech-writer in Athens who specialized in inheritance cases. He lived from about 415 to about 340 B.C. and is believed to have been a pupil of Isocrates and a teacher of Demosthenes. The first two selections that follow are the work of Isaeus, translated by Edward S. Forster. The third, by Lysias, is translated by W. R. M. Lamb.

# 69 *An Old Man's Folly*

The picture that emerges from Isaeus' *On the Estate of Philoctemon*, dating from 364 B.C., is that of a wealthy man who in his old age entered upon a life of wasteful folly, to the embarrassment and indignation of his family. The speech is a masterpiece from the point of view of the advocate's goal of discrediting his opponent, which in Athens was simply character assassination as systematically ruthless and reckless as possible. The speech contains, too, a wealth of information on such subjects as forms of wealth and income, the legal and social position of women and of slaves, the importance of religious rites, the persistent prejudice against the rich that existed in Athens.

@@@@@

### ARGUMENT

*Philoctemon, a son of Euctemon, adopted Chaerestratus, the son of one of his two sisters and of Phanostratus, in a will which was deposited with Chaereas, the husband of the other sister, and died during his father's lifetime. When the latter also died, Chaerestratus claimed possession in accordance with the law. When Androcles lodged a protestation that the estate was not adjudicable because Euctemon had a legitimate son, namely, Antidorus, Chaerestratus and his supporters impugned the protestation, declaring that both Antidorus and his sister were illegitimate and that the law ordains that an illegitimate son or daughter cannot inherit as next-of-kin. The question at issue is one of fact; for it is uncertain whether Philoctemon adopted Chaerestratus as his son, and, further, whether Antidorus and the other child are legitimate.*

That I am on terms of very close friendship with Phanostratus and with Chaerestratus here, I think most of you, gentlemen, are aware, but to those who are not aware of it I will give a convincing proof. When Chaerestratus set sail for Sicily in command of a trireme, although, having sailed thither myself before, I knew well all the dangers which I should encounter, yet, at the request of these friends of mine, I sailed with him and shared his misfortune, and we were both made prisoners of war. It would be strange if I endured all this in the face of evident danger because of my friendship and affection for them, and yet were not now to attempt so to plead their cause that you shall pass a sentence in accordance with your oath and that

SOURCE: Reprinted by permission of the publishers and The Loeb Classical Library from: *Isaeus* tr. E. S. Forster, Cambridge, Mass.: Harvard University Press.

justice shall be done to my clients.[1] I entreat you, therefore, to grant me indulgence and to listen to me with goodwill; for the suit is of no slight importance to them, but their most vital interests are at stake.

Philoctemon of Cephisia was a friend of Chaerestratus here, and died, having bequeathed to him his property and having adopted him as his son. Chaerestratus in accordance with the law claimed the estate. But, since it is lawful for any Athenian who wishes to do so to dispute an inheritance by bringing a direct action before you, and if he can establish a better claim, to obtain possession of the estate, Androcles here put in a protestation declaring that the succession was not adjudicable, thus depriving my client of his right to claim the estate and you of your right to decide who ought to be declared heir to Philoctemon's property. He thus thinks by a single verdict and by a single suit to establish, as brothers of the deceased, men who have no sort of connexion with him, to place himself in possession of the estate without further legal procedure, to become legal representative of the sister of the deceased, and to annul the will. Androcles has made a number of extraordinary allegations in his protestation; I will take one point first and prove that Philoctemon made a will and adopted Chaerestratus here as his son. Seeing that Philoctemon had no issue by the woman to whom he was married, and since, as it was war-time, he was running considerable risks, serving in the cavalry and often sailing as trierarch, he resolved to dispose of his property by will, so that he might not leave his house desolate if anything happened to him. He had had two brothers, both of whom died without issue: of his two sisters one, who was the wife of Chaereas, had no son and had never had one, though she had been married for many years; the other, who was wife of Phanostratus here, had two sons. It was the elder of these, Chaerestratus here, whom Philoctemon adopted as his son. Under the terms of his will, if he should have no child by his wife, Chaerestratus inherited his estate. He deposited his will with Chaereas, his brother-in-law, the husband of his other sister. This will shall now be read to you, and those who were present at its execution shall give evidence. Please read it.

[*Will. Witnesses*]

You have now heard that Philoctemon made a will, and on what con-

1. The word "clients" is used simply as a manner of speaking, since a professional advocate had no place in an Athenian court. It is the "close friendship" of the opening words of the speech that gave the speaker the right to plead as a "representative" of the interested parties who, presumably, availed themselves of this device because they were ineffective orators.

ditions he adopted Chaerestratus as his son. To prove that he had a right to do so, I will produce the text of the law which is in my opinion the best source of information in such matters. Please read it.

[*Law*]

This law, gentlemen, holds good for all men alike, permitting anyone to dispose of his property in default of male issue, providing that, at the time of doing so, he is not insane or mentally incapacitated by old age or any other of the causes mentioned in the law. That Philoctemon did not fall under any of these exceptions, I will prove to you in a few words. For how could anyone dare to say that a man was not in full possession of his faculties, who all his life showed himself so good a citizen, that, owing to your esteem for him, he was considered worthy to hold command, and who died fighting against the enemy?

That he made a will and adopted a son when he was in full possession of his faculties, as he was entitled to do, has been proved to you; it follows from this that Androcles has been proved to have committed perjury. But since he has further stated in his protestation that my opponent is a legitimate son of Euctemon, I will prove this also to be false. The real sons of Euctemon, the father of Philoctemon, namely, Philoctemon himself, Ergamenes, and Hegemon, and his two daughters and their mother, Euctemon's wife, the daughter of Meixiades of Cephisia, are well known to all their relatives and to the members of the ward and to most of the demesmen, and they shall testify to you; but no one is aware or ever heard a word during Euctemon's lifetime of his having married any other wife who became mother by him of our opponents. Yet it is only natural that these should be thought most trustworthy witnesses; for relatives ought to know about such matters. Please call them first and read the depositions.

[*Depositions*]

Further, I will prove that our adversaries have actually given evidence in support of these facts. When the interrogations took place before the archon, and my opponents paid money into court in support of their claim that these young men were the legitimate sons of Euctemon, on being asked by us who, and whose daughter, their mother was, they could not supply the information, although we protested and the archon ordered them to reply in accordance with the law. It was surely a strange proceeding, gentlemen, to make a claim on their behalf as legitimate and to lodge a protestation, and yet not be able to state who was their mother or name any of their relatives. At the time they alleged that she was a Lemnian and so secured a delay; subsequently, when they appeared at the interrogation, without giving time for anyone to ask a question, they immediately declared that the mother was Callippe and that she was the daughter of Pistoxenus, as though it was enough for them merely to produce the name of Pistoxenus. When we asked who he was and whether he was alive or not, they said that he had died on military service in Sicily, leaving a daughter, this Callippe, in the house of Euctemon, and that these two sons were born to her while she was under his guardianship, thus inventing a story surpassing the limits of impudence and quite untrue, as I will prove to you first of all from the answers which they themselves gave. Fifty-two years have passed since the Sicilian expedition, reckoning from the date of its departure in the archonship of Arimnestus; yet the elder of these two alleged sons of Callippe and Euctemon has not yet passed his twentieth year. If these years are deducted, more than thirty years still remain since the Sicilian expedition; so that Callippe, if she were thirty years of age, ought to have been no longer under a guardian, nor unmarried and childless, but long ago married, given in marriage either by her guardian, according to the law, or else by an adjudication of the court. Furthermore, she must necessarily have been known to the relatives and to the slaves of Euctemon if she had really been married to him and lived so long in the house. It is not enough merely to produce such statements at the interrogation, but it must be proved that the alleged events really took place and they must be supported by the testimony of the relatives. When we insisted that they should indicate one of Euctemon's family who knew of anyone of the name of Callippe as having been either married to him or under his guardianship, and that they should make an inquiry from our slaves, or hand over to us for examination any of their slaves who said they had knowledge of these facts, they refused to take any of our slaves for examination or to hand over any of their own to us. Now please read their answer to the interrogation and our depositions and challenges.

[*Answer to Interrogation, Depositions, Challenges*]

My opponents, then, avoided a mode of proof so vital to their case; but I will show you the origin and position of these men whom my opponents testified to be legitimate and are seeking to establish as heirs of Euctemon's property. It is perhaps painful, gentlemen, to Phanostratus to bring to light the misfortunes of Euctemon; but it is essential that a few facts should be given, so that, knowing the truth, you may more easily give your verdict aright. Euctemon lived for ninety-six years, and for most of this period had the reputation of being a fortunate man; he possessed considerable property and had children and a wife, and in all other respects enjoyed a reasonable degree of prosperity. In his old age, however, a serious misfortune befell him, which brought ruin to his house, caused him great financial loss, and set him at variance with his nearest relatives. The cause and manner of it I will set forth in the fewest possible words.

He had a freedwoman, gentlemen, who managed a tenement-house of his at the Peiraeus and kept prostitutes. As one of these she acquired a woman of the name of Alce, whom I think many of you know. This Alce, after her purchase, lived the life of a prostitute for many years but gave it up when she became too old. While she was still living in the tenement-house, she had relations with a freedman whose name was Dion, whom she declared to be the father of these young men; and Dion did, in fact, bring them up as his own children. Some time later Dion, having committed a misdemeanour and being afraid of the consequences, withdrew to Sicyon. The woman Alce was then installed by Euctemon to look after his tenement-house in the Cerameicus,[2] near the postern gate, where wine is sold. Her establishment there, gentlemen, had many evil consequences. Euctemon, going there constantly to collect the rent, used to spend most of his time in the tenement-house, and sometimes took his meals with the woman, leaving his wife and children and his own home. In spite of the protests of his wife and sons, not only did he not cease to go there but eventually lived there entirely, and was reduced to such a condition by drugs or disease or some other cause, that he was persuaded by the woman to introduce the elder of the two boys to the members of his ward under his own name. When, however, his son Philoctemon refused to agree to this, and the members of the ward would not admit the boy, and the victim for the sacrifice of admission was removed from the altar, Euctemon, being enraged against his son and wishing to insult him, announced his intention of marrying a sister of Democrates of Aphidna and recognizing any children who should be born to her and bringing them into the family, unless he consented to allow Alce's son to be introduced. His relatives, knowing that no more children would be born to him at his time of life but that they would be forthcoming in some other manner, and that, as a result, still more serious quarrels would arise, advised Philoctemon, gentlemen, to allow him to introduce this child on the conditions which he demanded, giving him a single farm. And Philoctemon, ashamed at his father's folly but at a loss

2.   The Potters' Quarter in Athens.

how to deal with the embarrassment of the moment, made no objection. An agreement having been thus concluded, and the child having been introduced on these terms, Euctemon gave up his project of marriage, proving thereby that the object of his threatened marriage was not to procure children but to obtain the introduction of this child into the ward. For what need had he to marry, Androcles, if these children had been born to him from a marriage with an Athenian citizen, as you have affirmed them to have been in your evidence? If they were legitimate, who could prevent him from introducing them? And why did he introduce them on special terms, when the law ordains that all the legitimate sons have an equal right to share in their father's property? And why did he introduce the elder of the two children on special terms, but said not a word about the younger, though already born, during the lifetime of Philoctemon either to Philoctemon or to his other relatives? Yet you have explicitly borne witness that they are legitimate and heirs to the property of Euctemon. In proof of the truth of these assertions, read the depositions.

[*Depositions*]

It was after this, then, that Philoctemon died by the enemy's hands while commanding a trireme off Chios. Some time later Euctemon informed his sons-in-law that he wished to make a written record of his arrangement with his son and place it in safe keeping. Phanostratus was on the point of setting out with Timotheus in command of a trireme, and his ship lying at anchor at Munychia, and his brother-in-law Chaereas was there bidding him farewell. Euctemon, taking certain persons with him, came to where the ship was anchored, and having drawn up a document detailing the conditions under which he introduced the child, deposited it in the presence of those men with his relative Pythodorus of Cephisia. The very fact that he acted thus is a sufficient proof, gentlemen, that Euctemon was not dealing with them as legitimate children, as Androcles has declared in his evidence; for no one ever makes a gift by will of anything to the sons of his own body, because the law of itself gives his father's estate to the son and does not even allow anyone who has legitimate children to dispose of his property.

When the document had remained deposited for almost two years and Chaereas had died, my opponents, having come under the influence of Alce and seeing that the property was going to ruin and that the old age and imbecility of Euctemon gave them an excellent opportunity, made a combined plan of attack. They first urged Euctemon to cancel the will on the ground that it was not to the boys' advantage; for no one would have any claim to the real estate on Euctemon's death except the daughters and their issue; whereas, if he sold part of the property and left it in cash, they would get secure possession of it. Euctemon listened to them and immediately demanded the document back from Pythodorus and served upon him a summons to produce it. When Pythodorus appeared before the archon, Euctemon stated that he wished to annul the will. Pythodorus was prepared to agreee with Euctemon and Phanostratus, who was present, that the document should be destroyed; but, as Chaereas, who had been a party to its deposition, had left an only daughter, he suggested that it should be destroyed only after appointment of her legal representative, and the archon decided in favour of this course. Euctemon, after agreeing to this in the presence of the archon and his assessors, called many persons to witness that the will deposited by him no longer existed and then went his way. In a very short time—and this was the object of their advice to Euctemon to annul the will—he sold a farm at Athmonon to Antiphanes for seventy-five minas and the bath-house at Serangion to Aristolochus for 3000 drachmas; and he realized a mortgage of forty-four minas on a house in Athens from the hierophant.[3] Further, he sold some goats with their goat-herd for thirteen minas, and two pairs of mules, one for eight minas and the other for five hundred and fifty drachmas, and all the slaves he had that were craftsmen. In all, the value of the property which he hurriedly sold after Philoctemon's death, was more than three talents. And to prove that I am speaking the truth, I will first call witnesses in support of each of my statements.

[*Witnesses*]

So much for these transactions. They then immediately began scheming to obtain the rest of the property and planned the most outrageous plot of all, which merits your careful attention. Seeing that Euctemon was completely incapacitated by old age and could not even leave his bed, they began to look about for a means whereby all his property should be under their control after his death. And what did they do? They inscribed these two boys before the archon as adopted children of the sons of Euctemon who had died,[4] inscribing themselves as guardians, and requested the archon to grant a lease of the house-property as being the property of orphans, in order that part of the property might be leased and part might be used as a security, and mortgage notices adfixed to it in the children's names during

3.   The official who displayed the sacred emblems at the Eleusinian mysteries.
4.   Philoctemon and Ergamenes.

the lifetime of Euctemon, and they themselves might become lessees and receive the income. On the first day that the courts met, the archon put the lease up for auction and they offered to lease the property. Certain persons, however, who were present, denounced the plot to the relatives, and they came and informed the judges of the real state of affairs. The result was that the judges voted against allowing the houses to be leased. If the plot had not been detected, the whole property would have been lost. Please call as witnesses those who were present.

[*Witnesses*]

Before my opponents had made the woman's acquaintance and plotted with her against Euctemon, he and his son Philoctemon possessed so large a fortune that both of them were able to undertake the most costly public offices without realizing any of their capital, and at the same time to save out of their income, so that they continually grew richer. After the death of Philoctemon, on the other hand, the property was reduced to such a condition that less than half the capital remains and all the revenues have disappeared. And they were not even content, sirs, with this misappropriation; but, when Euctemon also died, they had the impudence, while he was lying dead in the house, to shut up the slaves, so that none of them might take the news to his two daughters or to his wife or to any of his relatives. Meanwhile, with the aid of the woman they conveyed the furniture from within to the adjoining house, which was leased and occupied by one of their gang, the infamous Antidorus. When Euctemon's daughters and wife arrived, having learnt the news from others, even then they refused them admittance and shut the door in their faces, declaring that it was not their business to bury Euctemon. They only obtained admittance with difficulty about sunset. When they entered, they found that he had been dead in the house for two days, as the slaves declared, and that everything in the house had been carried off by these people. While the women, as was right, were attending to the deceased, my clients here immediately called the attention of those who had accompanied them to the state of affairs in the house, and began by asking the slaves in their presence to what place the furniture had been removed. When they replied that our opponents had conveyed it away to the next house, and my clients immediately claimed the right to search the house in the proper legal manner, and requested that the slaves who had removed it should be produced, our opponents refused to accede to any of their just demands. And to prove that I am speaking the truth, take and read these documents.

[*Depositions*]

Having removed all this furniture from the house, and sold so much property and kept the proceeds, and having further made away with the revenue which accrued during that period, they yet expect to obtain possession of what remains; and their impudence is such that, not daring to bring a direct action, they lodged a protestation—as though it were a question of legitimate children—which is at once false and in contradiction to their own previous action. For, whereas they had inscribed the children before the archon, one as the son of Philoctemon and the other as the son of Ergamenes, they have now stated in their protestation that they are the sons of Euctemon. Yet if they were Euctemon's legitimate sons and had afterwards been adopted, as our opponent states, even so they cannot be described as the sons of Euctemon: for the law does not allow the return of an adopted son to his original family, unless he leaves a legitimate son in the family which he quits. So that in view even of their own acts their evidence is necessarily untrue. If our opponents had then so contrived that the houses were leased, my clients would no longer have been able to claim them; but, as it is, since the judges decided against them as having no right, they have not dared to put in a claim, but, to put the finishing touch to their impudence, they have submitted additional evidence to the effect that these young men, whom you excluded by your verdict, are heirs.

Further, mark the effrontery and impudence of the witness himself, who has claimed for himself Euctemon's daughter as being an heiress and a fifth of Euctemon's estate itself as being adjudicable, while he has given evidence that Euctemon has a legitimate son. In doing so does he not clearly convict himself of having given false evidence? For obviously, if Euctemon had a legitimate son, his daughter could not be heiress or the estate adjudicable. To prove, then, that he made these claims, the clerk shall read you the depositions.

[*Depositions*]

Thus the contrary has been done of that which the law has prescribed; for according to the law no male or female bastard has any right, based on kinship, to participate in the cults or property of a family since the archonship of Eucleides;[5] yet Androcles and Antidorus consider themselves entitled to rob the legitimate daughters of Euctemon and their issue, and to possess the property both of Euctemon and of Philoctemon. And the woman who

5.  403–402 B.C.

destroyed Euctemon's reason and laid hold of so much property is so insolent, that relying on the help of our opponents, she shows her contempt not only for the members of Euctemon's family but for the whole city. When you have heard a single instance, you will easily realize the lawlessness of her conduct. Please take and read this law.

[*Law*]

Such are the solemn and pious terms in which you gave legal expression to the importance which you attach to piety towards these goddesses and all the other deities. Yet the mother of these young men, being admittedly a slave, and having always lived a scandalous life, who ought never to have entered the temple and seen any of the rites performed there, had the effrontery to join in the procession when a sacrifice was being made in honour of these goddesses and to enter the temple and see what she had no right to see. That I am speaking the truth you will learn from the decrees which the Council passed concerning her. Take this decree.

[*Decree*]

You have, therefore, gentlemen, to consider whether this woman's son ought to be heir to Philoctemon's property and go to the family tombs to offer libations and sacrifices, or my client, Philoctemon's sister's son, whom he himself adopted; and whether Philoctemon's sister, formerly the wife of Chaereas and now a widow, ought to pass into the power of our opponents and be married to anyone they choose or else be allowed to grow old in widowhood, or whether, as a legitimate daughter, she ought to be subject to your decision as to whom she ought to marry. These are the points which you have now to decide by your verdict; for the purpose of their protestation is to throw all the risk upon my clients, and that our opponents, even if they lose their case on this occasion and the estate is held to be adjudicable, may, by bringing forward a competing claim, fight a second action about the same property. Yet if Philoctemon disposed of his property by will when he was not entitled to do so, the point against which they ought to have protested is that he was not legally capable of adopting my client as his son; but if it is lawful to make a will, and our opponent claims on the ground that Philoctemon made no donation or will, he ought not to have hindered proceedings by a protestation, but to have proceeded by means of a direct action. As it is, what clearer method is there of convicting him of perjury than by putting the following question to him: "How do you know, Androcles, that Philoctemon neither made a will nor adopted

Chaerestratus as his son?" For when a man has been present, gentlemen, it is just that he should give evidence of what he has seen, and when he has not been present but has heard someone else describe what happened, he can give evidence by hearsay; but you, though you were not present, have given explicit evidence that Philoctemon made no will and died childless. How, gentlemen, can he possibly know this? It is as though he were to say, not having been present, that he knows about all the acts of you all. Impudent as he is, he will scarcely assert that he was present at and is acquainted with all the acts of Philoctemon's life; for Philoctemon regarded him as his bitterest enemy, both because of his general bad character, and because he was the only one of his kinsmen who, in league with the infamous Alce, plotted with this friend of his and his other accomplices against the property of Euctemon, and committed the acts which I have described to you.

But what calls for the greatest indignation is the wicked use which our opponents make of the name of Euctemon, my client's grandfather. For if, as they assert, Philoctemon had no right to make a will, and the estate was Euctemon's, who have a better right to inherit Euctemon's property? His daughters, who are admittedly legitimate, and we who are their sons? Or men who bear no relation to him, and whose claims are refuted not only by us but also by the acts which they have themselves committed as guardians? For I beg and earnestly beseech you, gentlemen, to remember the point which I put before you a short while ago, that Androcles here declares that he is guardian of the claimants as being the legitimate sons of Euctemon, and has also himself claimed for himself the estate of Euctemon and his daughter as heiress; and evidence of this has been placed before you. By the gods of Olympus, is it not extraordinary, gentlemen, that, if the children are legitimate, their guardian should claim for himself the estate of Euctemon and his daughter as an heiress, and, if they are not legitimate, that he should have given evidence now in support of their legitimacy? For these acts are the very contrary of one another; so that he is convicted of perjury not only by us but by his own acts. No one is putting in a protestation that the estate is not adjudicable, and Androcles was at liberty to proceed by means of a direct action; now he is depriving everyone else of their right to claim. Having explicitly stated in his evidence that the children are legitimate, he thinks that you will be satisfied with rhetorical digressions, and that if he does not attempt to prove his point or dwells only very lightly upon it, but rails against us in a loud voice and says that my clients are rich, while he is poor—all this will make it appear that the children are legitimate. Now the fortune of my clients, sirs, is being spent rather upon the city than upon these clients themselves. Phanostratus has already been trierarch seven times, and he has performed all the public services and has generally been victorious. Chaerestratus here, young as he is, has been trierarch; he has been *choregus* in the tragic competitions; he has been gymnasiarch at the torch-races. Both of them have paid all the special war-taxes, being numbered among the three hundred.[6] Formerly only these two members of the family contributed, but now the younger son here is *choregus* in the tragic competitions and has been enrolled among the three hundred and pays the war-tax. No grudge ought, therefore, to be felt against them, but rather, by Zeus and Apollo, against our opponents, if they obtain what does not belong to them. If the estate of Philoctemon is adjudicated to my client, he will hold it in trust for you, performing all the public services which you lay upon him, as he has done hitherto, and with even greater generosity. If, on the other hand, our opponents receive it, they will squander it and then seek other victims.

I beseech you, therefore, gentlemen, in order that you may not be misled, to give your careful attention to the protestation about which you are going to give your verdict. Instruct him to make that the subject of his defence, just as it has been the subject of our accusation. The text of the protestation has stated that Philoctemon made no gift of property or will; this has been proved to be false, for those who were present are witnesses that he did so. What further do they say? That Philoctemon died childless. How could he be childless, when he adopted and was survived by his own nephew, to whom the law gives the right of inheritance just as much as to children of his own body? Indeed, it is expressly stated in the law that, if children are born subsequently to one who has adopted a son, each child takes his share of the estate and both classes of children alike inherit. Let Androcles, therefore, prove that the children are legitimate, as any one of you would have to do in similar circumstances. His mere mention of a mother's name does not suffice to make them legitimate, but he must prove that he is speaking the truth by producing the relatives who know that she was married to Euctemon, and the members of the deme and of the ward, if they have ever heard or have any knowledge that Euctemon performed any public services on her behalf. We must know where she is buried and in what sort of tomb, and who has ever seen Euctemon performing the customary rites over her, and whither her sons still go to offer sacrifices and libations, and who of the citizens or of the slaves of Euctemon has ever seen these rites being

6. The richest class.

performed. It is all these details, and not mere invective, which constitute a proof. If you bid him prove the actual contention which is the subject of his protestation, you will give a verdict which accords with your oath and with the laws, and justice will be done to my clients.

# 70 A Childless Marriage

Isaeus' *On the Estate of Menecles,* dated about 355 B.C., contains a touching allusion to a warm and mutually respectful relation between a husband and wife. This is particularly interesting in the light of the commonly held view that Athenian women were held in very low regard by their husbands. The story that emerges from the speech is that of a conflict between personal affection and the overriding economic and religious necessity to have a son, which is emphasized again and again.

◎◎◎◎◎

ARGUMENT

*Menecles adopted a son and lived for twenty-three years after the date of the adoption. When his brothers claimed his estate, a certain Philonides attested that the estate was not adjudicable, because Menecles had left a son. The brothers then brought an action for perjury against Philonides, and it is against them that the son undertakes the defence of Philonides. . . . The discussion concerns a point of law with a controversy on a point of fact; for the speaker affirms that the deceased had the right to adopt a son, and then deals with the point of fact, saying, "It was not under the influence of a woman that he adopted me."*

I think, gentlemen, that, if any adoption was ever made in accordance with the laws, mine was, and no one could ever dare to say that Menecles adopted me in a moment of insanity or under the influence of a woman. But since my uncle, acting, as I assert, under a misapprehension, is trying by every means in his power to deprive his dead brother of descendants,

SOURCE: Reprinted by permission of the publishers and The Loeb Classical Library from: *Isaeus* tr. E. S. Forster, Cambridge, Mass.: Harvard University Press.

showing no respect for the gods of his family or for any of you, I feel constrained to come to the aid of the father who adopted me, and to my own aid. I intend, therefore, first to show you that my adoption was appropriate and legal, and that there is no question of adjudicating the estate of Menecles, since he had a son, namely, myself, and that the evidence of the witness was true. I beg and entreat and beseech you all to listen with favour to what I have to say.

My father, gentlemen, Eponymus of Acharnae, was a friend and close acquaintance of Menecles and lived on terms of intimacy with him; there were four of us children, two sons and two daughters. After my father's death we married our elder sister, when she reached a suitable age, to Leucolophus, giving her a dowry of twenty minae. Four or five years later, when our younger sister was almost of marriageable age, Menecles lost his first wife. When he had carried out the customary rites over her, he asked for our sister in marriage, reminding us of the friendship which had existed between our father and himself and of his friendly disposition towards ourselves. Knowing that our father would have given her to no one with greater pleasure, we gave her to him in marriage—not dowerless, as my opponent asserts on every possible occasion, but with the same portion as we gave to our elder sister. In this manner, having been formerly his friends, we became his kinsmen. I should like first to produce evidence that Menecles received a dowry of twenty minae with my sister.

*[Evidence]*

Having thus settled our sisters, gentlemen, and, being ourselves of military age, we adopted the career of a soldier and went abroad with Iphicrates to Thrace. Having proved our worth there, we returned hither after saving a little money; and we found that our elder sister had two children, but that the younger, the wife of Menecles, was childless. A month or two later Menecles, with many expressions of praise for our sister, approached us and said that he viewed with apprehension his increasing age and childlessness: she ought not, he said, to be rewarded for her virtues by having to grow old with him without bearing children; it was enough that he himself was unfortunate. His words clearly prove that he loved her when he put her away; for no one utters supplications for one whom he hates. He, therefore, begged us to do him the favour of marrying her to someone else with his consent. We told him that it was for him to persuade her in the matter, for we would do whatever she agreed. At first she would not even listen to his suggestion, but in course of time she with difficulty consented. So we gave

[ 610 ]

her in marriage to Elius of Sphettus, and Menecles handed over her dowry to him—for he had become part-lessee of the estate of the children of Nicias —and he gave her the garments which she had brought with her to his house and the jewelry which there was. Some time after this Menecles began to consider how he could put an end to his childless condition and have someone to tend his old age and bury him when he died and there-after carry out the customary rites over him. He saw that my opponent had only one son; so he thought it wrong to ask him to give him his son to adopt and so deprive him of male offspring. Thus he could find no nearer relative than us; he, therefore, approached us and said that he thought it right, since fate had decreed that he should have no children by our sister, that he should adopt a son out of the family from which he would have wished to have a son of his own in the course of nature; "I should like, therefore," he said, "to adopt one of you two, whichever is willing." My brother, on hearing this, expressed his approval of Menecles' proposal and agreed that his age and solitary condition required someone who would look after him, and remain at home; "I," he said, "as you know, go abroad; but my brother here" (meaning me) "will look after your affairs as well as mine, if you wish to adopt him." Menecles approved of his suggestion and thus adopted me.

I wish next to prove to you that the adoption was carried out in the proper legal manner. So please read me the law which ordains that a man can dis-pose as he likes of his own property, if he does not possess legitimate male issue. The lawgiver, gentlemen, legislated thus, because he saw that for childless persons the only refuge for their solitary condition, and the only possible comfort in life, lay in the possibility of adopting whomsoever they wished. The law thus allowing Menecles, because he was childless, to adopt a son, he adopted me, sirs, not by will made at point of death, as other citizens have done, nor during illness; but when he was sound in body and mind, and fully aware of what he was doing, he adopted me and introduced me to his fellow-wardsmen in the presence of my opponents and enrolled me among the demesmen and the members of his confraternity.[1] At the time my opponents raised no objection to his action on the ground that he was not in his right mind, although it would have been much better to have tried to win him over to their point of view during his lifetime rather than insult him now that he is dead and try to desolate his house. For he lived on after the adoption, not one or two years, but twenty-three, and during all this period he never regretted what he had done, because it was

1.   A private religious association.

universally acknowledged that he had been well advised in what he did. To prove the truth of these statements, I will produce before you, as witnesses of the transaction, the wardsmen, the members of the confraternity, and the demesmen, and, to prove that Menecles was at liberty to adopt me, the clerk of the court shall read you the text of the law in accordance with which the adoption was made. Please read these depositions and the law.

[*Depositions. Law*]

The law itself makes it clear that Menecles was free to adopt anyone he liked as his son; that he did adopt a son, the wardsmen, the demesmen, and the members of the confraternity have provided evidence. Thus we have clearly proved it, gentlemen, the witness[2] has attested the truth of it, and my opponents cannot say a word against the actual fact of the adoption.

After this, Menecles began to look about for a wife for me, and said I ought to marry. So I married the daughter of Philonides. Menecles exercised the forethought on my behalf which a father would naturally exercise for his son, and I tended him and respected him as though he were my true father, as also did my wife, so that he praised us to all his fellow-demesmen.

That Menecles was not insane or under the influence of a woman but in his right mind when he adopted me, you can easily understand from the following facts. In the first place, my sister, with whom most of my opponent's argument has been concerned, and under whose influence he alleges that Menecles adopted me, had remarried long before the adoption took place, so that, if it had been under her influence that he was adopting his son, he would have adopted one of her boys; for she has two. But, gentlemen, it was not under her influence that he adopted me as his son; his chief motive was his loneliness, and, secondly, the other causes I have mentioned, and the goodwill which he felt towards my father, and, thirdly, because he had no other relative from whose family he might have adopted a son. These were the motives which at the time induced him to adopt me; so that it is quite clear that he was not insane or under the influence of a woman, unless, indeed, my opponent wishes to describe his loneliness and childlessness in these terms.

I feel that I should like my opponent, who thinks himself so wise, to tell me whom of his relatives Menecles ought to have adopted? Ought he to have adopted my opponent's son? But he would never have given him up and so rendered himself childless; he is not so avaricious as all that. Well

2. Philonides.

then, the son of his sister or of his male or female cousin? But he had no such relative at all. He was, therefore, obliged to adopt someone else, or, failing that, grow old in childlessness, as my opponent now thinks he ought to have done. I think, therefore, that you would all admit that, when he adopted a son, he could not have adopted anyone who was more closely connected with him than I was. Otherwise, let my opponent indicate such a person. He cannot possibly do so; for he had no other kinsman than those whom I have mentioned.

But my opponent is now clearly blaming Menecles not for failing to adopt his own son but for adopting any son at all and not dying childless. It is for this that he blames him, a proceeding which is as spiteful as it is unjust; for while he has children of his own, he is obviously blaming Menecles for being childless and unfortunate. All other men, whether Greek or barbarians, regard this law about adoption as a good one and therefore all make use of it; but my uncle here is not ashamed to deprive his own brother of this right to adopt a son, the enjoyment of which no one has ever grudged even those who were no relatives at all. I think that my opponent, if anyone were to ask him what he would have done in the same circumstances as Menecles, would have nothing to say except that he would have adopted someone who was likely to look after him while he lived and bury him when he died; and it is obvious that the adoption would have been carried out under the same law as mine was. He himself, then, if he had been childless, would have adopted a son; but when Menecles acted in the same manner, he declares that he was insane and under the influence of a woman when he adopted me. Is it not clear that he is talking in an abominable manner? I am of opinion that it is much rather my opponent who is insane by reason of the line of argument which he employs and the things which he does. For he is clearly arguing the contrary of the laws and of justice and of what he himself would have done, and is not ashamed of making the law about adoption valid for himself, while he seeks to render this same law of no effect for his brother. . . .[3]

Thus it is my uncle here, gentlemen, who has inherited the property of Menecles—really and not merely nominally, as I have—and has a much larger share than I have; for I received only the three hundred drachmae which remained over out of the proceeds of the sale and a small house not worth three minae. My opponent, on the other hand, being in possession

3. The omitted passage contains an account of a legal dispute over property that occurred some years earlier between Menecles and his brothers. The dispute had finally been settled by Menecles' cession of a portion of his property to his brothers.

of land worth more than ten minae, has now, moreover, come into court with the object of rendering desolate the house of the deceased. I, the adopted son, with the aid of my wife, the daughter of Philonides here, tended Menecles while he lived and gave his name to my little son, in order that his family might not lack a representative. On his death, I buried him in a manner befitting both him and myself, and I erected a fine monument to him and celebrated the commemorative ceremony on the ninth day and performed all the other rites at the tomb in the best manner possible, so that I won the praise of all the members of my deme. But my opponent, his kinsman, who blames him for having adopted a son, during his lifetime deprived him of the landed property which remained to him, and, now that he is dead, wishes to render him childless and wipe out his very name; that is the kind of man he is. In proof that I buried Menecles and performed the ceremonies on the third and ninth days and all the other rites connected with the burial, the clerk shall read you the depositions of those who are acquainted with the facts.

[*Evidence*]

In support of the truth of my assertion, gentlemen, that Menecles, when he adopted me, was not insane or under the influence of a woman, I wish to bring before you my opponents themselves as witnesses, not in word but in deed, by their own conduct. For it is notorious that both of them went through the process of reconciliation with me and not with Menecles, and swore an oath to me, as I did to them. Yet if the adoption had not been carried out in proper legal form and I had not been recognized as heir to Menecles' property by my opponents themselves, what need was there for them to swear to me and to receive an oath from me? Surely none. By so acting then they themselves clearly bear witness that I was legally adopted and am the rightful heir of Menecles. It is clear, I think, to you all that it was acknowledged even by my opponents themselves that Menecles was not insane but that it is much rather my opponent who is insane now, seeing that, after having effected a settlement of his quarrel with us and having sworn oaths, he has now again come forward in violation of his acknowledgements and oaths, and demands that I shall be deprived of these poor remnants of the estate. Were it not that I think it an altogether base and shameful act to betray him whose son I was called and who adopted me, I would have readily abandoned the right of succession to his estate in favour of my opponent; for there is nothing at all left, as I think you realize. But, in the circumstances, I consider it terrible and disgraceful that, when

Menecles possessed property, I accepted adoption as his son and out of his property, before the land was sold, acted as gymnasiarch in his deme and won credit as his son, and served in his tribe and deme on all the campaigns which took place during that period; and, now that he is dead, if I shall betray him and go off leaving his house desolate, would it not seem a strange and ridiculous proceeding, and give those who wish to do so a good occasion to speak evil of me? And these are not the only motives which induce me to fight this case; but what grieves me is the possibility of being thought so worthless and good-for-nothing as not to be able to find a friend in his right senses, but only a madman, to adopt me.

I beg you all therefore, gentlemen, and beseech and entreat you to pity me and to acquit the witness here. I have shown you that, in the first place, I was adopted by Menecles with the strictest possible legality, and that the form of adoption was not merely verbal or by will but by very act and deed; and of these things I produced before you the evidence of the wardsmen, the demesmen, and the members of the confraternity. I further showed that Menecles lived for twenty-three years after he had adopted me. Further, I placed before you the laws which permit those who are childless to adopt sons. In addition to this I am shown to have tended him in his lifetime and to have buried him when he died. My opponent wishes now to deprive me of my father's estate, whether it be large or small, and to render the deceased childless and nameless, so that there may be no one to honour in his place the family cults and perform for him the annual rites, but that he may be robbed of all his due honours. It was to provide against this that Menecles, being master of his own property, adopted a son, so that he might secure all these advantages.

Do not therefore, gentlemen, listen to my opponents and deprive me of my name, the sole remnant of my inheritance, and annul Menecles' adoption of me; but since the matter has come before you for judgement and you have the sovereign right of decision, come to the aid both of us and of him who is in the other world, and do not allow Menecles, by the gods and deities I beseech you, to be insulted by my opponents, but mindful of the law and of the oath which you have sworn and of the arguments which have been used in support of my plea, pass in accordance with the laws the verdict which is just and in conformity with your oath.

# 71  A Swindling Guardian

It is a pity that Lysias' speech *Against Diogeiton,* dating from about 400 B.C., is incomplete. It was much admired in antiquity and rightly so. Its arguments are well organized and clearly presented, and the low-keyed tone of the speeech, even in its appeals to the jurors' emotions, is a relief from the frequent stridency found in Lysias' work. The case is that favorite of old-fashioned melodrama, the guardian who swindles the estate of his orphaned wards. From it emerges all manner of interesting details about the costs of bringing up children, the items upon which money is spent, the ways of investing ready cash and the size of the returns that could be expected. The family relationship is in itself intense, for the children's father had married his own niece. The alleged swindler was both their grandfather (their mother's father) and their uncle (their father's brother). Especially striking is the mother's forceful speech against her own father. Women could not be parties themselves in court actions and had to be represented by male relatives, but the speaker quotes the mother's accusations at length.

❀❀❀❀❀

. . . Diodotus and Diogeiton, gentlemen of the jury, were brothers born of the same father and mother, and they had divided between them the personal estate, but held the real property in partnership. When Diodotus had made a large fortune in the shipping business, Diogeiton induced him to marry the one daughter that he had, and two sons and a daughter were born to him. Some time later, when Diodotus was enrolled for infantry service, he summoned his wife, who was his niece, and her father, who was also his father-in-law and his brother, and grandfather and uncle of the little ones, as he felt that owing to these connexions there was nobody more bound to act justly by his children: he then gave him a will and five talents of silver in deposit; and he also produced an account of his loans on bottomry, amounting to seven talents and forty minae . . .[1] and two thousand drachmae invested in the Chersonese. He charged him, in case anything should happen to himself, to dower his wife and his daughter with a talent each, and to give his wife the contents of the room; he also bequeathed to his wife twenty minae and thirty staters of Cyzicus. Having made these arrangements and left duplicate deeds in his house, he went to serve abroad

1.  There is a lacuna in the text.
SOURCE: Reprinted by permission of the publishers and The Loeb Classical Library from: *Lysias* tr. W. R. M. Lamb, Cambridge, Mass.: Harvard University Press.

with Thrasyllus. He was killed at Ephesus: for a time Diogeiton concealed from his daughter the death of her husband, and took possession of the deeds which he had left under seal, alleging that these documents were needed for recovering the sums lent on bottomry. When at length he informed them of the death, and they had done what is customary they lived for the first year in the Peiraeus, as all their provisions had been left there. But when these began to give out, he sent up the children to the city, and gave their mother in marriage with a dowry of five thousand drachmae—a thousand less than her husband had given her. Seven years later the elder of the boys was certified to be of age;[2] when Diogeiton summoned them, and said that their father had left them twenty minae of silver and thirty staters, adding—"Now I have spent a great deal of my own money on your support: so long as I had the means, I did not mind; but at this moment I too am in difficulties myself. You, therefore, since you have been certified and have attained manhood, must henceforth contrive to provide for yourself." On hearing these words they went away, aghast and weeping, to their mother, and brought her along with them to me.[3] It was pitiful to see how they suffered from the blow: the poor wretches, turned out of doors, wept aloud and besought me not to allow them to be deprived of their patrimony and reduced to beggary by the last persons who ought to have committed this outrage upon them, but to give my best aid, for their sister's sake as well as their own.

Of the mourning that filled my house at that time it would take long to tell. In the end, their mother implored and entreated me to assemble her father and friends together, saying that even though she had not before been accustomed to speak in the presence of men, the severity of their misfortunes would compel her to give us a full account of their hardships. I went first and expressed my indignation to Hegemon, the husband of this man's daughter; I then discussed the matter with the other relations; and I called upon this man to allow his handling of the money to be investigated. Diogeiton at first refused, but finally he was compelled by his friends. When we held our meeting, the mother asked him what heart he could have, that he thought fit to take such measures with the children, "when you are their father's brother," she said, "and my father, and their uncle and grandfather. Even if you felt no shame before any man, you ought to have feared the gods. For you received from him, when he went on the expedition, five talents in deposit. I offer to swear to the truth of this on the lives of my children, both these and those since born to me, in any

2. That is, in his eighteenth year.
3. The speaker is the boys' brother-in-law, the husband of their only sister.

place that you yourself may name. Yet I am not so abject, or so fond of money, as to take leave of life after perjuring myself on the lives of my own children, and to appropriate unjustly my father's estate." And she convicted him further of having recovered seven talents and four thousand drachmae of bottomry loans, and she produced the record of these; for she showed that in the course of his removal from Collytus to the house of Phaedrus the children had happened upon the register, which had been mislaid, and had brought it to her. She also proved that he had recovered a hundred minae which had been lent at interest on land mortgages, besides two thousand drachmae and some furniture of great value; and that corn came in to them every year from the Chersonese. "After that," she said, "you had the audacity to state, when you had so much money in your possession, that their father bequeathed them two thousand drachmae and thirty staters—just the amount that was bequeathed to me, and that I gave you after his decease! And you thought fit to turn these, the children of your daughter, out of their own house, in worn-out clothes, without shoes or attendant or bedding or cloaks; without the furniture which their father bequeathed to them, and without the money which he had deposited with you. And now you are bringing up the children you have had by my stepmother in all the comforts of affluence; and you are quite right in that: but you are wronging mine, whom you ejected from the house in dishonour, and whom you are intent on turning from persons of ample means into beggars. And over proceedings of this sort you feel neither fear of the gods nor shame before me who am cognizant of the facts, nor are you mindful of your brother, but you put money before us all." Thereupon, gentlemen of the jury, after hearing all the severe things spoken by the mother, the whole company of us there were so affected by this man's conduct and by her statements—when we saw how the children had been treated, and recalled the dead man to mind and how unworthy was the guardian he had left in charge of his estate, and reflected how hard it is to find a person who can be trusted with one's affairs—that nobody, gentlemen, among us there was able to utter a word: we could only weep as sadly as the sufferers, and go our ways in silence.

Now, first, will you come forward, witnesses, to support what I say.

[*Witnesses*]

Well, gentlemen of the jury, I ask that due attention be given to this reckoning, in order that you may take pity on the young people for the depth of their misfortune, and may consider that this man deserves the anger of everyone in the city. For Diogeiton is reducing all men to such a state of suspicion towards their fellows that neither living nor dying can they place any more confidence in their nearest relations than in their bitterest enemies; since he has had the face to deny one part of his debt and, after finally confessing to the rest, to make out a sum of seven talents of silver and seven thousand drachmae as receipts and expenses on account of two boys and their sister during eight years. So gross is his impudence that, not knowing under what headings to enter the sums spent, he reckoned for the viands of the two young boys and their sister five obols a day; for shoes, laundry and hairdressing he kept no monthly or yearly account, but he shows it inclusively, for the whole period, as more than a talent of silver. For the father's tomb, though he did not spend twenty-five minae of the five thousand drachmae shown, he charges half this sum to himself, and has entered half against them. Then for the Dionysia, gentlemen of the jury—I do not think it irrelevant to mention this also—he showed sixteen drachmae as the price of a lamb, and charged eight of these drachmae to the children: this entry especially roused our anger. And so it is, gentlemen: in the midst of heavy losses the sufferers of wrong are sometimes wounded as much by little things; for these expose in so very clear a light the wickedness of the wrongdoer. Then for the other festivals and sacrifices he charged to their account an expenditure of more than four thousand drachmae; and he added a multitude of things which he counted in to make up his total, as though he had been named in the will as guardian of the children merely in order that he might show them figures instead of the money, and reduce them from wealth to utter poverty, and that they might forget whatever ancestral enemy they might have, to wage war on their guardian for stripping them of their patrimony!

But yet, had he wished to act justly by the children, he was free to act in accordance with the laws which deal with orphans for the guidance of incapable as well as capable guardians: he might have farmed out the estate and so got rid of a load of cares, or have purchased land and used the income for the children's support; whichever course he had taken, they would have been as rich as anyone in Athens. But the fact is, in my opinion, that at no time has he had any notion of turning their fortune into real estate, but has meant to keep their property for himself,[4] assuming that his own wickedness ought to be heir of the wealth of the deceased. Most monstrous of all, gentlemen of the jury, he asserts that in sharing with Alexis, son of Aristodicus, the service of equipping a warship, he paid a contribution of

---

4. The insinuation is that by keeping the estate liquid the guardian was easily able to falsify the accounts; if he had had the inheritance in real property, it would have been much more difficult to mask his juggling.

forty-eight minae, and has entered half of this against these orphan children, whom the State has not only exempted during their childhood, but has freed from all public services for a year after they have been certified to be of age. Yet he, their grandfather, illegally exacts from his daughter's children one half of his expenses in equipping a warship! Again, he dispatched to the Adriatic a cargo of two talents' value, and told their mother, at the moment of its sailing, that it was at the risk of the children; but when it went safely through and the value was doubled,[5] he declared that the venture was his. But if he is to lay the losses to their charge, and keep the successful gains for himself, he will have no difficulty in making the account show on what the money has been spent, while he will find it easy to enrich himself from the money of others. To set the reckoning before you in detail, gentlemen of the jury, would be a lengthy affair; but when with some trouble I had got him to hand over the balance-sheet, in the presence of witnesses I asked Aristodicus, brother of Alexis—the latter being now dead—whether he had the account for the equipment of a warship. He told me that he had, and we went to his house and found that Diogeiton had paid Alexis a contribution of twenty-four minae towards equipping the warship. But the expenditure that he showed was forty-eight minae, so that the children have been charged exactly the total of what he has spent. Now, what do you suppose he has done in cases of which nobody else has had cognizance, and where he managed the business alone, when in those which were conducted through others and of which information could easily be obtained he did not shrink from falsehood in mulcting his own daughter's children to an amount of twenty-four minae? Please come forward, witnesses, in support of this.

*[Witnesses]*

You have heard the witnesses, gentlemen of the jury. I will now base my reckoning against him on the sum which he did eventually confess to holding—seven talents and forty minae: not counting in any income, I will put down, as spent out of capital, a larger amount than anyone in the city has ever spent—for two boys and their sister, an attendant and a maid, a thousand drachmae a year, a little less than three drachmae a day. For eight years, that amounts to eight thousand drachmae; and we can show a balance of six talents and twenty minae. For he will not be able to show that he has either had losses by pirates, or met with failure or paid off debts. . . . [*The text breaks off here.*]

5. A 100 per cent return on an investment of this kind was not unusual.

# BUSINESS AND FINANCE

IMPERIAL Athens in the fifth century B.C. was a thriving center of world trade, where the state grew wealthy from the taxes—euphemistically called contributions—levied upon its subject states. Individuals could prosper from the trade that passed through Athens' port or from supplying her growing population with the necessities and luxuries it craved.

In the fourth century the state, with its imperial revenues gone, no longer prospered; but private business activity increased. Financial and business transactions were sometimes on an impressively large scale (as can be seen from some of the disputes over property in preceding selections). Nevertheless, the techniques of business enterprise were surprisingly crude. It is worth noting that the Greek civilization that achieved such subtlety and profundity in philosophy, art, and literature remained on a relatively primitive level in its economic institutions.

## 72 *Athenian Bankers*

The banking business that developed in Athens in the fourth century did not progress beyond simple moneylending and deposit banking. Instruments of credit were unknown, as was the concept of limited liability. It is only by courtesy that the temporary partnerships set up to finance occasional large-scale trading operations can be thought of as representative of corporate finance.

The most famous and wealthy financial house in Athens was the banking business of Pasion and Phormion. A picture of the bankers and of the nature of their operations emerges from the following selection. It is a courtroom oration in a dispute over money between Pasion's son Apollodorus and the young man's stepfather Phormion, who was also Pasion's successor

SOURCE: G. W. Botsford and E. G. Sihler, eds., *Hellenic Civilization* (Columbia University Records of Civilization, Vol. I) (New York: Columbia University Press, 1929). Reprinted by permission of the publisher.

in managing the bank. The speech is dated 350–349 B.C. As so frequently in the courtroom pleas in previous selections, the merits of the case are not clear; what does become evident is the magnitude of the sums involved in comparison with the private fortunes of wealthy citizen families that appear in several of the foregoing selections. On the evidence here presented it is also clear that the banking business was pre-eminently in the hands of slaves and that these men were able by means of their business acumen to acquire their freedom, Athenian citizenship, and lofty positions in society.

The speech *In Behalf of Phormion* has come down to us among the works of Demosthenes, but most modern scholars are agreed that it is not by the famous orator. The translation is that of G. W. Botsford and is abridged, containing only the passages that relate to the banking business and to the personal characters of Pasion and Phormion.

⊕⊕⊕⊕⊕

Phormion's lack of ability in speaking because of inexperience all of you know, gentlemen of the jury. It is necessary, therefore, for us, his friends, to relate for your information what we know, having often heard him recount these matters. Our object is that you with full knowledge, after correctly ascertaining the facts from us, may vote whatever is just and in accordance with your oaths. We have adopted the paragraphê[1] as our form of procedure, not with a view to confusing the issue by urging the statute of limitations, but that if the defendant can prove that he has committed no wrong whatever, a cessation from trouble may be validated for him by you. Everything that with other people arranges and settles disputes without bringing them to trial before you Phormion has done. He has conferred great benefits on the plaintiff Apollodorus and has justly paid for, or handed over, everything of which he was left manager for the plaintiff, and afterward was released from all claims. Nevertheless, as you see, since the defendant is unable to endure this man's treatment, the latter has maliciously brought against him this suit for twenty talents. I shall endeavor therefore to narrate from the beginning all the transactions of the defendant with Pasion and Apollodorus in the briefest terms. From these facts I know well that the plaintiff's conduct will appear malicious, and that you, having heard these statements, will decide that the case is not actionable.

In the first place you will hear read the articles of agreement, in accordance with which Pasion leased the bank and the shield-factory to the de-

1. A particular procedural formula in Athenian law.

fendant. Take therefore the agreement and the challenge and the testimonies.

[*Articles of Agreement. Challenges. Testimonies*]

These, then, are the articles of agreement by which Pasion leased the bank and the shield-factory to the defendant when the latter became his own master, men of Athens. It is necessary also for you to hear and learn in what way Pasion came to owe eleven talents to the bank. It was not through want that he owed it but because of his enterprise in business; for the landed property of Pasion was worth about twenty talents, and in addition to this amount he had lent out more than fifty talents of his own. Among these fifty talents there were eleven talents from the bank deposits productively invested. The defendant accordingly when he took in lease this business of the bank and received the deposits, seeing that he had not yet been made a citizen by you, and would therefore be unable to recover the amounts lent by Pasion on lands and tenements,[2]—for these reasons he chose to have Pasion debtor to him for this sum rather than the others to whom the loans had been made. Hence it was that Pasion was recorded in the lease as owing the defendant eleven talents, just as the witnesses have testified before you.

In what way the lease was made has been testified before you by the manager of the bank. Afterward, when Pasion fell ill, consider the terms of the will that he made. Take the copy of the will and this challenge and these testimonies made by the persons with whom the will has been deposited.

[*Will. Challenge. Testimonies*]

After Pasion had died, having left this will, Phormion the defendant married the widow as the will directed[3] and became guardian of the minor son. As the plaintiff, however, kept appropriating moneys belonging to the common estate, and thought it proper to spend these sums, the guardians reasoned among themselves that, if it should be necessary according to the will to deduct whatever he should spend from the common estate and then divide the remainder, there would in fact be nothing left to divide. For this reason they concluded in behalf of the boy to divide the property

---

2. An alien could not acquire real estate in Attica, unless granted the right as a special favor. For that reason Phormion, before he became a citizen, could not force the collection of debts on the security of real estate.
3. It was a common custom for a man in his will to provide for the remarriage of his wife.

forthwith. They made a division, accordingly, of all the estate except the part of which the defendant had taken a lease; and half the revenue from this amount they rendered regularly to the plaintiff. Up to this point how is it possible for him to make any complaint regarding the lease? He ought not to have waited till now but should have expressed his dissatisfaction at the very time. In fact it is impossible for him to deny that he received the rents which afterwards became due. When Pasicles became of age and the defendant was discharged from the lease, the plaintiff would not have given him a quittance of all claims, but would at that very time have made his demand, if the defendant owed anything further. To prove that I am speaking the truth, and that the plaintiff divided the estate with his brother when a minor, and that they gave the defendant a quittance of the lease and of all other claims, take this testimony.

[*Testimony*]

Immediately after they had discharged the defendant from the lease, men of Athens, they divided between them the bank and the shield-factory; and Apollodorus, making choice, preferred the shield-factory to the bank. Yet if he had had any private capital in the bank, why would he ever have chosen the factory rather than the bank? Certainly the revenue was not greater but less (the one brought in a talent, the other a hundred minas); nor was the business more agreeable, if indeed he had private capital in the bank. But he did not have it. Therefore he prudently chose the shield-factory; for one was without risk, the other brought a precarious income from other people's property.

Many proofs could be brought forward in evidence that the claim of the plaintiff to banking stock is fraudulent; but in my opinion the most cogent of all evidence of his having received no banking stock is the fact that in the lease Pasion is recorded as owing money to the bank and not as having invested in banking stock, secondly the fact that at the division of the estate the plaintiff made no claim for such a thing, and thirdly, that when he afterward lent the same business to other persons for the same amount of money, it will be proved that he did not let in addition any private banking stock. But surely if he had been deprived by the defendant of anything left by his father, it was his business to provide it from some other source and to hand it over to the lessees. To prove that I am telling the truth, and that he afterward leased the bank to Xenon, Euphraeus, Euphron, and Callistratus, and that he delivered to them no private banking stock, but leased to them the deposits and the business connected with them,[4] read for me the deposition as to these matters and also as to the fact that he chose the shield-factory. . . .

For my part I wonder, gentlemen of the jury, what in the world the plaintiff Apollodorus will attempt to say in reply to these arguments. Surely he has not supposed that you, seeing him altogether unharmed in property rights, will be angry because Phormion married his mother; for he is not unaware of the fact, nor has it escaped the attention either of him or of many of your number that Socrates the banker,[5] when liberated from his masters, just as this man's father, gave his own wife to Satyrus, who had formerly been his slave. Socles another banker gave his wife to Timodemus, who is still living but who was once his slave. Not only in our state, men of Athens, do persons engaged in this business follow this policy, but also in Aegina Strymodorus gave his wife to Hermaeus, his own domestic, and after her death he gave his own daughter to the same person. In fact one would be able to mention many such cases. But to you, men of Athens, who are citizens by descent, it is fitting to prefer no sum of money however great to respectable birth, whereas men who receive the gift of citizenship from you or from other states, and who have been deemed worthy of these honors from their original good fortune in the transaction of business and in their acquisition of properties above the average, must hold to these advantages. Pasion your father, therefore, was not the first and only man to do such a thing, nor did he thereby do violence either to himself or to you his sons, but seeing that the only security to his business lay in his attaching the defendant to you by close ties, he gave the defendant his own wife and your mother. . . .

Regarding the prosperity of Phormion and the idea that he got it from your father and all the matters on which you say you will make inquiry of him, you alone of all men that are, have the least right to call Phormion to account for the source of his possessions. The reason is that not even your father Pasion acquired his wealth by his own invention, nor received it as a heritage from his father, but while he was still with his masters, Antisthenes and Archestratus, in the banking business he gave proof of honesty

4. Here is an example of a partnership of four persons for taking a banking business in lease. Rarely were partnerships made for any other kind of business except for commercial enterprises. In the latter line of business they were usually for a single voyage out and return, whereas in banking they were necessarily of longer duration.
5. Not the philosopher.

and uprightness, and therefore won confidence. To men occupied with merchandise and money-making it seems a wonderful thing that the same person should be diligent and honest. Now his masters did not hand over this quality to him but he was himself honest by nature. Nor did your father give this virtue to the defendant, for he would have preferred to make you honest instead, had it been in his power. If you are ignorant of this fact that trustworthiness is the greatest asset in business life, you must be ignorant of everything. Apart from these considerations Phormion has in many ways proved useful to your father and to you and to your business generally. . . .

# 73 Public Revenues

Without her imperial revenues Athens was hard put in the fourth century to meet the ordinary financial obligations of a state, let alone to find money for the military enterprises that any self-respecting power among the Greek cities had to pursue. One of the rare instances we have of a Greek writer turning his attention to the problems of public finance is the pamphlet of Xenophon known as *On Revenues* (or *Ways and Means*). It consists of a number of suggestions, some of them ingenious, as to how the state can raise money. The essay is as valuable for what it does not say as for what it does contain, for a great deal is implied in it about the limits—both of imagination and of custom—to what the state could do in ancient Greece in its search for money. The translation is that of H. G. Dakyns.

❀❀❀❀❀

For myself I hold to the opinion that the qualities of the leading statesmen in a state, whatever they be, are reproduced in the character of the constitution itself.

As, however, it has been maintained by certain leading statesmen in Athens that the recognised standard of right and wrong is as high at Athens as elsewhere, but that, owing to the pressure of poverty on the masses, a certain measure of injustice in their dealing with the allied states could not be avoided; I set myself to discover whether by any manner of means it were possible for the citizens of Athens to be supported solely from the soil of Attica itself, which was obviously the most equitable solution. For if so, herein lay, as I believed, the antidote at once to their own poverty and to the feeling of suspicion with which they are regarded by the rest of Hellas.

I had no sooner begun my investigation than one fact presented itself clearly to my mind, which is that the country itself is made by nature to provide the amplest resources. And with a view to establishing the truth of this inital proposition I will describe the physical features of Attica.

In the first place, the extraordinary mildness of the climate is proved by the actual products of the soil. Numerous plants which in many parts of the world appear as stunted leafless growths are here fruit-bearing. And as with the soil so with the sea indenting our coasts, the varied productivity of which is exceptionally great. Again with regard to those kindly fruits of earth which Providence bestows on man season by season, one and all they commence earlier and end later in this land. Nor is the supremacy of Attica shown only in those products which year after year flourish and grow old, but the land contains treasures of a more perennial kind. Within its folds lies imbedded by nature an unstinted store of marble, out of which are chiselled temples and altars of rarest beauty and the glittering splendour of images sacred to the gods. This marble, moreover, is an object of desire to many foreigners, Hellenes and barbarians alike. Then there is land which, although it yields no fruit to the sower, needs only to be quarried in order to feed many times more mouths than it could as corn-land. Doubtless we owe it to a divine dispensation that our land is veined with silver; if we consider how many neighbouring states lie round us by land and sea and yet into none of them does a single thinnest vein of silver penetrate.

Indeed it would be scarcely irrational to maintain that the city of Athens lies at the navel, not of Hellas merely, but of the habitable world. So true is it, that the farther we remove from Athens the greater the extreme of heat or cold to be encountered; or to use another illustration, the traveller who desires to traverse the confines of Hellas from end to end will find that, whether he voyages by sea or by land, he is describing a circle, the center of which is Athens.

Once more, this land though not literally sea-girt has all the advantages of an island, being accessible to every wind that blows, and can invite to its bosom or waft from its shore all products, since it is peninsular; whilst by land it is the emporium of many markets, as being a portion of the continent.

Lastly, whilst the majority of states have barbarian neighbours, the source of many troubles, Athens has as her next-door neighbours civilised states which are themselves far remote from the barbarians.

All these advantages, to repeat what I have said, may, I believe, be traced primarily to the soil and position of Attica itself. But these natural blessings may be added to: in the first place, by a careful handling of our resident alien population. And, for my part, I can hardly conceive of a more splendid source of revenue than lies open in this direction. Here you have a self-supporting class of residents conferring large benefits upon the state, and instead of receiving payment themselves, contributing on the contrary to the gain of the exchequer by the sojourners' tax. Nor, under the term careful handling, do I demand more than the removal of obligations which, whilst they confer no benefit on the state, have an air of inflicting various disabilities on the resident aliens. And I would further relieve them from the obligation of serving as hoplites side by side with the citizen proper; since, beside the personal risk, which is great, the trouble of quitting trades and homesteads is no trifle. Incidentally the state itself would be benefited by this exemption, if the citizens were more in the habit of campaigning with one another, rather than shoulder to shoulder with Lydians, Phrygians, Syrians, and barbarians from all quarters of the world, who form the staple of our resident alien class. Besides the advantage of so weeding the ranks, it would add a positive lustre to our city, were it admitted that the men of Athens, her sons, have reliance on themselves rather than on foreigners to fight her battles. And further, supposing we offered our resident aliens a share in various other honourable duties, including the cavalry service, I shall be surprised if we do not increase the goodwill of the aliens themselves, whilst at the same time we add distinctly to the strength and grandeur of our city.

In the next place, seeing that there are at present numerous building sites within the city walls as yet devoid of houses, supposing the state were to make free grants of such land to foreigners for building purposes in cases where there could be no doubt as to the respectability of the applicant, if I am not mistaken, the result of such a measure will be that a large number of persons, and of a better class, will be attracted to Athens as a place of residence.

Lastly, if we could bring ourselves to appoint, as a new government office, a board of guardians of foreign residents like our Guardians of Orphans, with special privileges assigned to those guardians who should show on their books the greatest number of resident aliens,—such a measure would tend to improve the goodwill of the class in question, and in all probability all people without a city of their own would aspire to the status of foreign residents in Athens, and so further increase the revenues of the city.

[ 628 ]

At this point I propose to offer some remarks in proof of the attractions and advantages of Athens as a centre of commercial enterprise. In the first place, it will hardly be denied that we possess the finest and safest harbourage for shipping, where vessels of all sorts can come to moorings and be laid up in absolute security as far as stress of weather is concerned. But further than that, in most states the trader is under the necessity of lading his vessel with some merchandise or other in exchange for his cargo, since the current coin has no circulation beyond the frontier. But at Athens he has a choice: he can either in return for his wares export a variety of goods, such as human beings seek after, or, if he does not desire to take goods in exchange for goods, he has simply to export silver, and he cannot have a more excellent freight to export, since wherever he likes to sell it he may look to realise a large percentage on his capital.

Or again, supposing prizes were offered to the magistrates in charge of the market for equitable and speedy settlements of points in dispute to enable any one so wishing to proceed on his voyage without hindrance, the result would be that far more traders would trade with us and with greater satisfaction.

It would indeed be a good and noble institution to pay special marks of honour, such as the privilege of the front seat, to merchants and ship-owners, and on occasion to invite to hospitable entertainment those who, through something notable in the quality of ship or merchandise, may claim to have done the state a service. The recipients of these honours will rush into our arms as friends, not only under the incentive of gain, but of distinction also.

Now the greater the number of people attracted to Athens either as visitors or as residents, clearly the greater the development of imports and exports. More goods will be sent out of the country, there will be more buying and selling, with a consequent influx of money in the shape of rents to individuals and dues and customs to the state exchequer. And to secure this augmentation of the revenues, mark you, not the outlay of one single penny; nothing needed beyond one or two philanthropic measures and certain details of supervision.

With regard to the other sources of revenue which I contemplate, I admit, it is different. For these I recognise the necessity of a capital to begin with. I am not, however, without good hope that the citizens of this state will contribute heartily to such an object, when I reflect on the large sums subscribed by the state on various late occasions, as, for instance, when rein-forcements were sent to the Arcadians under the command of Lysistratus, and again at the date of the generalship of Hegesileos. I am well aware that ships of war are frequently despatched and that too although it is uncertain whether the venture will be for the better or for the worse, and the only certainty is that the contributor will not recover the sum subscribed nor have any further share in the object for which he gave his contribution.

But for a sound investment I know of nothing comparable with the initial outlay to form this fund. Any one whose contribution amounts to ten minae may look forward to a return as high as he would get on bottomry, of nearly one-fifth, as the recipient of three obols a day. The contributor of five minae will on the same principle get more than a third while the majority of Athenians will get more than cent per cent on their contribution. That is to say, a subscription of one mina will put the subscriber in possession of nearly double that sum, and that, moreover, without setting foot outside Athens, which, as far as human affairs go, is as sound and durable a security as possible.

Moreover, I am of opinion that if the names of contributors were to be inscribed as benefactors for all time, many foreigners would be induced to contribute, and possibly not a few states, in their desire to obtain the right of inscription; indeed I anticipate that some kings, tyrants, and satraps will display a keen desire to share in such a favour.

To come to the point. Were such a capital once furnished, it would be a magnificent plan to build lodging-houses for the benefit of shipmasters in the neighbourhood of the harbours, in addition to those which exist; and again, on the same principle, suitable places of meeting for merchants, for the purposes of buying and selling; and thirdly, public lodging-houses for persons visiting the city. Again, supposing dwelling-houses and stores for vending goods were fitted up for retail dealers in Piraeus and the city, they would at once be an ornament to the state and a fertile source of revenue. Also it seems to me it would be a good thing to try to see if, on the principle on which at present the state possesses public warships, it would not be possible to secure public merchant vessels, to be let out on the security of guarantors just like any other public property. If the plan were found feasible this public merchant navy would be a large source of extra revenue.

I come to a new topic. I am persuaded that the establishment of the silver mines on a proper footing would be followed by a large increase of wealth apart from the other sources of revenue. And I would like, for the benefit of those who may be ignorant, to point out what the capacity of these mines really is. You will then be in a position to decide how to turn them to better account. It is clear, I presume, to every one that these mines have for a very long time been in active operation; at any rate no one will venture to fix the date at which they first began to be worked. Now in spite of the fact that the silver ore has been dug and carried out for so long a time, I would ask you to note that the mounds of rubbish so shovelled out are but a fractional portion of the series of hillocks containing veins of silver, and as yet unquarried. Nor is the silver-bearing region gradually becoming circumscribed. On the contrary it is evidently extending in wider area from year to year. That is to say, during the period in which thousands of workers have been employed within the mines no hand was ever stopped for want of work to do. Rather, at any given moment, the work to be done was more than enough for the hands employed. And so it is to-day with the owners of slaves working in the mines; no one dreams of reducing the number of his hands. On the contrary, the object is perpetually to acquire as many additional hands as the owner possibly can. The fact is that with few hands to dig and search, the find of treasure will be small, but with an increase of labour the discovery of the ore itself is more than proportionally increased. So much so, that of all operations with which I am acquainted, this is the only one in which no sort of jealousy is felt at a further development of the industry. I may go a step farther; every proprietor of a farm will be able to tell you exactly how many yoke of oxen are sufficient for the estate, and how many farm hands. To send into the field more than the exact number requisite every farmer would consider a dead loss. But in silver mining operations the universal complaint is the want of hands. Indeed there is no analogy between this and other industries. With an increase in the number of bronze-workers articles of bronze may become so cheap that the bronze-worker has to retire from the field. And so again with ironfounders. Or again, in a plethoric condition of the corn and wine market these fruits of the soil will be so depreciated in value that the particular husbandries cease to be remunerative, and many a farmer will give up his tillage of the soil and betake himself to the business of a merchant, or of a shopkeeper, to banking or money-lending. But the converse is the case in the working of silver; there the larger the quantity of ore discovered and the greater the amount of silver extracted, the greater the number of persons ready to engage in the operation. One more illustration: take the case of movable property. No one when he has got sufficient furniture for his house dreams of making further purchases on his head, but of silver no one ever yet possessed so much that he was forced to cry "enough." On the contrary, if ever anybody does become possessed of an immoderate amount he finds as much pleasure in digging a hole in the ground and hoarding it as in the actual employment of it. And from a wider point of view: when a state is prosperous there is nothing which people so much desire as silver. The men want money to expend on beautiful armour and fine horses, and houses, and sumptuous paraphernalia of all sorts. The women betake themselves to expensive apparel and ornaments of gold. Or when states are sick, either through barrenness of corn and other fruits, or through war, the demand for current coin is even more imperative (whilst the ground lies unproductive), to pay for necessaries or military aid.

And if it be asserted that gold is after all just as useful as silver, without gainsaying the proposition I may note this fact about gold, that, with a sudden influx of this metal, it is the gold itself which is depreciated whilst causing at the same time a rise in the value of silver.

The above facts are, I think, conclusive. They encourage us not only to introduce as much human labour as possible into the mines, but to extend the scale of operations within, by increase of plant, etc., in full assurance that there is no danger either of the ore itself being exhausted or of silver becoming depreciated. And in advancing these views I am merely following a precedent set me by the state herself. So it seems to me, since the state permits any foreigner who desires it to undertake mining operations on a footing of equality with her own citizens.

But, to make my meaning clearer on the question of maintenance, I will at this point explain in detail how the silver mines may be furnished and extended so as to render them much more useful to the state. Only I would premise that I claim no sort of admiration for anything which I am about to say, as though I had hit upon some recondite discovery. Since half of what I have to say is at the present moment still patent to the eyes of all of us, and as to what belongs to past history, if we are to believe the testimony of our fathers, things were then much of a piece with what is going on now. No, what is really marvellous is that the state, with the fact of so many private persons growing wealthy at her expense, and under her very eyes, should have failed to imitate them. It is an old story, trite enough to those of us who have cared to attend to it, how once on a time Nicias,[1] the son of Niceratus, owned a thousand men in the silver mines, whom he let out to Sosias, a Thracian, on the following terms. Sosias was to pay him a net obol a day, without charge or deduction, for every slave of the thousand, and be responsible for keeping up the number perpetually at that figure. So again Hipponicus had six hundred slaves let out on the same principle, which brought him in a net mina a day without charge or

1.  The Peloponnesian War general, legendary for his wealth; see Selection 66, n. 8.

deduction. Then there was Philemonides, with three hundred, bringing him in half a mina, and others, I make no doubt there were, making profits in proportion to their respective resources and capital. But there is no need to revert to ancient history. At the present moment there are hundreds of human beings in the mines let out on the same principle. And given that my proposal were carried into effect, the only novelty in it is that, just as the individual in acquiring the ownership of a gang of slaves finds himself at once provided with a permanent source of income, so the state, in like fashion, should possess herself of a body of public slaves, to the number, say, of three for every Athenian citizen. As to the feasibility of our proposals, I challenge any one whom it may concern to test the scheme point by point, and to give his verdict.

With regard to the price then of the men themselves, it is obvious that the public treasury is in a better position to provide funds than any private individuals. What can be easier than for the Council to invite by public proclamation all whom it may concern to bring their slaves, and to buy up those produced? Assuming the purchase to be effected, is it credible that people will hesitate to hire from the state rather than from the private owner, and actually on the same terms? People have at all events no hesitation at present in hiring consecrated grounds, sacred victims, houses, etc., or in purchasing the right of farming taxes from the state. To ensure the preservation of the purchased property, the treasury can take the same securities precisely from the lessee as it does from those who purchase the right of farming its taxes. Indeed, fraudulent dealing is easier on the part of the man who has purchased such a right than of the man who hires slaves. Since it is not easy to see how the exportation of public money is to be detected, when it differs in no way from private money. Whereas it will take a clever thief to make off with these slaves, marked as they will be with the public stamp, and in face of a heavy penalty attached at once to the sale and exportation of them. Up to this point then it would appear feasible enough for the state to acquire property in men and to keep a safe watch over them.

But with reference to an opposite objection which may present itself to the mind of some one: what guarantee is there that, along with the increase in the supply of labourers, there will be a corresponding demand for their services on the part of contractors? It may be reassuring to note, first of all, that many of those who have already embarked on mining operations will be anxious to increase their staff of labourers by hiring some of these public slaves (remember, they have a large capital at stake; and again, many of the actual labourers now engaged are growing old); and secondly, there are many others, Athenians and foreigners alike, who, though unwilling and indeed incapable of working physically in the mines, will be glad enough to earn a livelihood by their wits as superintendents.

Let it be granted, however, that at first a nucleus of twelve hundred slaves is formed. It is hardly too sanguine a supposition that out of the profits alone, within five or six years this number may be increased to at least six thousand. Again, out of that number of six thousand—supposing each slave to bring in an obol a day clear of all expenses—we get a revenue of sixty talents a year. And supposing twenty talents out of this sum laid out on the purchase of more slaves, there will be forty talents left for the state to apply to any other purpose it may find advisable. By the time the round number of ten thousand is reached the yearly income will amount to a hundred talents.

As a matter of fact, the state will receive much more than these figures represent, as any one here will bear me witness who can remember what the dues derived from slaves realised before the troubles at Decelea. Testimony to the same effect is borne by the fact, that in spite of the countless number of human beings employed in the silver mines within the whole period, the mines present exactly the same appearance to-day as they did within the recollection of our forefathers. And once more everything that is taking place to-day tends to prove that, whatever the number of slaves employed, you will never have more than the works can easily absorb. The miners find no limit of depth in sinking shafts or laterally in piercing galleries. To open cuttings in new directions to-day is just as possible as it was in former times. In fact no one can take on himself to say whether there is more ore in the regions already cut into, or in those where the pick has not yet struck. Well then, it may be asked, why is it that there is not the same rush to make new cuttings now as in former times? The answer is, because the people concerned with the mines are poorer nowadays. The attempt to restart operations, renew plant, etc., is of recent date, and any one who ventures to open up a new area runs a considerable risk. Supposing he hits upon a productive field, he becomes a rich man, but supposing he draws a blank, he loses the whole of his outlay; and that is a danger which people of the present time are shy of facing.

It is a difficulty, but it is one on which, I believe, I can offer some practical advice. I have a plan to suggest which will reduce the risk of opening up new cuttings to a minimum.

The citizens of Athens are divided, as we all know, into ten tribes. Let the state then assign to each of these ten tribes an equal number of slaves, and let the tribes agree to associate their fortunes and proceed to open new cuttings. What will happen? Any single tribe hitting upon a productive lode will be the means of discovering what is advantageous to all. Or, supposing two or three, or possibly the half of them, hit upon a lode, clearly these several operations will proportionally be more remunerative still. That the whole ten will fail is not at all in accordance with what we should expect from the history of the past. It is possible, of course, for private persons to combine in the same way, and share their fortunes and minimise their risks. Nor need you apprehend, sirs, that a state mining company, established on this principle, will prove a thorn in the side of the private owner, or the private owner prove injurious to the state. But rather like allies who render each other stronger the more they combine so in these silver mines, the greater number of companies at work the larger the riches they will discover and disinter.

This then is a statement, as far as I can make it clear, of the method by which, with the proper state organisation, every Athenian may be supplied with ample maintenance at the public expense. Possibly some of you may be calculating that the capital requisite will be enormous. They may doubt if a sufficient sum will ever be subscribed to meet all the needs. All I can say is, even so, do not despond. It is not as if it were necessary that every feature of the scheme should be carried out at once, or else there is to be no advantage in it at all. On the contrary, whatever number of houses are erected, or ships built, or slaves purchased, etc., these portions will begin to pay at once. In fact, the bit-by-bit method of proceeding will be more advantageous than a simultaneous carrying into effect of the whole plan, to this extent: if we set about erecting buildings wholesale we shall make a more expensive and worse job of it than if we finish them off gradually. Again, if we set about bidding for hundreds of slaves at once we shall be forced to purchase an inferior type at a higher cost. Whereas, if we proceed tentatively, as we find ourselves able, we can complete any well-devised attempt at our leisure, and, in case of any obvious failure, take warning and not repeat it. Again, if everything were to be carried out at once, it is we, sirs, who must make the whole provision at our expense. Whereas, if part were proceeded with and part stood over, the portion of revenue in hand will help to furnish what is necessary to go on with. But to come now to what every one probably will regard as a really grave danger, lest the state may become possessed of an over large number of slaves, with the result that the works will be overstocked. That again is an apprehension which we may escape if we are careful not to put into the works more hands from year to year than the works themselves demand. Thus I am persuaded that the easiest method of carrying out this scheme, as a whole, is also the best. If, however, you are persuaded that, owing to the extraordinary property taxes to which you have been subjected during the present war, you will not be equal to any further contributions at present, what you should do is this: during the current year resolve to carry on the financial administration of the state within the limits of a sum equivalent to that which your dues realised before the peace. That done, you are at liberty to take any surplus sum, whether directly traceable to the peace itself, or to the more courteous treatment of our resident aliens and traders, or to the growth of the imports and exports, coincident with the collecting together of larger masses of human beings, or to an augmentation of harbour and market dues: this surplus, I say, however derived, you should take and invest so as to bring in the greatest revenue.

Again, if there is an apprehension on the part of any that the whole scheme will crumble into nothing on the first outbreak of war, I would only beg these alarmists to note that, under the condition of things which we propose to bring about, war will have more terrors for the attacking party than for this state. Since what possesion I should like to know can be more serviceable for war than that of men? Think of the many ships which they will be capable of manning on public service. Think of the number who will serve on land as infantry in the public service and will bear hard upon the enemy. Only we must treat them with courtesy. For myself, my calculation is, that even in the event of war we shall be quite able to keep a firm hold of the silver mines. I may take it, we have in the neighbourhood of the mines certain fortresses—one on the southern slope in Anaphlystus; and we have another on the northern side in Thoricus, the two being about seven and a half miles apart. Suppose then a third breastwork were to be placed between these, on the highest point of Besa, that would enable the operatives to collect into one out of all the fortresses, and at the first perception of a hostile movement it would only be a short distance for each to retire into safety. In the event of an enemy advancing in large numbers they might certainly make off with whatever corn or wine or cattle they found outside. But even if they did get hold of the silver ore, it would be little better to them than a heap of stones. But how is an enemy ever to march upon the mines in force? The nearest state, Megara, is distant, I take it, a good deal over sixty miles; and the next closest, Thebes, a good deal nearer seventy. Supposing then an enemy to advance from some such point to attack the mines, he cannot avoid passing Athens; and presuming his force to be small, we may expect him to be annihilated by our cavalry and frontier police. I say, presuming his force to be small, since to march with anything like a large force, and thereby leave his own territory denuded of troops, would be a startling achievement. Why, the fortified city of Athens will be much closer the states of the attacking parties than they themselves will be by the time they have got to the mines. But, for the sake of argument, let us suppose an enemy to have arrived in the neighbourhood of Laurium; how is he going to stop there without provisions? To go out in search of supplies with a detachment of his force would imply risk, both for the foraging party and for those who have to do the fighting; whilst, if they are driven to do so in force each time, they may call themselves besiegers, but they will be practically in a state of siege themselves.

But it is not the income derived from the slaves alone to which we look to help the state towards the effective maintenance of her citizens, but with the growth and concentration of a thick population in the mining district various sources of revenue will accrue, whether from the market at Sunium, or from the various state buildings in connection with the silver mines, from furnaces and all the rest. Since we must expect a thickly populated city to spring up here, if organised in the way proposed, and plots of land will become as valuable to owners out there as they are to those who possess them in the neighbourhood of the capital.

If, at this point, I may assume my proposals to have been carried into effect, I think I can promise, not only that our city shall be relieved from a financial strain, but that she shall make a great stride in orderliness and in tactical organisation, she shall grow in martial spirit and readiness for war. I anticipate that those who are under orders to go through gymnastic training will devote themselves with a new zeal to the details of the training school, now that they will receive a larger maintenance whilst under the orders of the trainer in the torch race. So again those on garrison duty in the various fortresses, those enrolled as peltasts, or again as frontier police to protect the rural districts, one and all will carry out their respective duties more ardently when the maintenance appropriate to these several functions is duly forthcoming.

But now, if it is evident that, in order to get the full benefit of all these sources of revenue, peace is an indispensable condition—if that is plain, I say, the question suggests itself, would it not be worth while to appoint a board to act as guardians of peace? Since no doubt the election of such a magistracy would enhance the charm of this city in the eyes of the whole world, and add largely to the number of our visitors. But if any one is disposed to take the view, that by adopting a persistent peace policy, this city will be shorn of her power, that her glory will dwindle and her good name be forgotten throughout the length and breadth of Hellas, the view so taken by our friends here is in my poor judgment somewhat unreasonable. For they are surely the happy states, they, in popular language, are most fortune-favoured, which endure in peace the longest season. And of all states Athens is pre-eminently adapted by nature to flourish and wax strong in peace. The while she abides in peace she cannot fail to exercise an attractive force on all. From the mariner and the merchant upwards, all seek her, flocking they come; the wealthy dealers in corn and wine and oil, the owner of many cattle. And not these only, but the man who depends upon his wits, whose skill is to do business and make gain out of money and its employment. And here another crowd, artificers of all sorts, artists and artisans, professors of wisdom, philosophers, and poets, with those who exhibit and popularise their works. And next a new train of pleasure-seekers, eager to feast on everything sacred or secular, which may captivate and charm eye and ear. Or once again, where are all those who seek to effect a rapid sale or purchase of a thousand commodities, to find what they want, if not at Athens?

But if there is no desire to gainsay these views—only that certain people, in their wish to recover that headship which was once the pride of our city, are persuaded that the accomplishment of their hopes is to be found, not in peace but in war, I beg them to reflect on some matters of history, and to begin at the beginning, the Median war. Was it by high-handed violence, or as benefactors of Hellenes, that we obtained the headship of the naval forces, and the trusteeship of the treasury of Hellas? Again, when through the too cruel exercise of her presidency, as men thought, Athens was deprived of her empire, is it not the case that even in those days, as soon as we held aloof from injustice we were once more reinstated by the islanders, of their own free will, as presidents of the naval force? Nay, did not the very Thebans, in return for certain benefits, grant to us Athenians to exercise leadership over them? And at another date the Lacedaemonians suffered us Athenians to arrange the terms of hegemony at our discretion, not as driven to such submission, but in requital of kindly treatment. And to-day, owing to the chaos which reigns in Hellas, if I mistake not, an opportunity has fallen to this city of winning back our fellow-Hellenes without pain or peril or expense of any sort. It is given to us to try to harmonise states which are at war with one another: it is given to us to reconcile the differences of rival factions within those states themselves, wherever existing.

Make it but evident that we are minded to preserve the independence of the Delphic shrine in its primitive integrity, not by joining in any war but by the moral force of embassies throughout the length and breadth of Hellas—and I for one shall not be astonished if you find our brother Hellenes of one sentiment and eager under seal of solemn oaths to proceed against those, whoever they may be, who shall seek to step into the place vacated by the Phocians and to occupy the sacred shrine. Make it but evident that you intend to establish a general peace by land and sea, and, if I mistake not, your efforts will find a response in the hearts of all. There is no man but will pray for the salvation of Athens next to that of his own fatherland.

Again, is any one persuaded that, looking solely to riches and money-making, the state may find war more profitable than peace? If so, I cannot conceive a better method to decide that question than to allow the mind to revert to the past history of the state and to note well the sequence of events. He will discover that in times long gone by during a period of peace vast wealth was stored up in the acropolis, the whole of which was lavishly expended during a subsequent period of war. He will perceive, if he examines closely, that even at the present time we are suffering from its ill effects. Countless sources of revenues have failed, or if they have still flowed in, been lavishly expended on a multiplicity of things. Whereas, now that peace is established by sea, our revenues have expanded and the citizens of Athens have it in their power to turn these to account as they like best.

But if you turn on me with the question, "Do you really mean that even in the event of unjust attacks upon our city on the part of any, we are still resolutely to observe peace towards that offender?" I answer distinctly, No! But, on the contrary, I maintain that we shall all the more promptly retaliate on such aggression in proportion as we have done no wrong to any one ourselves. Since that will be to rob the aggressor of his allies.

But now if none of these proposals be impracticable or even difficult of execution; if rather by giving them effect we may conciliate further the friendship of Hellas, whilst we strengthen our own administration and increase our fame; if by the same means the people shall be provided with the necessaries of life, and our rich men be relieved of expenditure on war; if with the large surplus to be counted on, we are in a position to conduct our festivals on an even grander scale than heretofore, to restore our temples, to rebuild our forts and docks, and to reinstate in their ancient privileges our priests, our senators, our magistrates, and our knights—surely it were but reasonable to enter upon this project speedily, so that we too, even in our own day, may witness the unclouded dawn of prosperity in store for our city.

But if you are agreed to carry out this plan, there is one further counsel which I would urge upon you. Send to Dodona and to Delphi, I would beg you, and consult the will of Heaven whether such provision and such a policy on our part be truly to the interest of Athens both for the present and for the time to come. If the consent of Heaven be thus obtained, we ought then, I say, to put a further question: whose special favour among the gods shall we seek to secure with a view to the happier execution of these measures?

And in accordance with that answer, let us offer a sacrifice of happy omen to the deities so named, and commence the work; since if these transactions be so carried out with the will of God, have we not the right to prognosticate some further advance in the path of political progress for this whole state?

# RELIGION

THE religion of Classical Greece is a subject of great complexity, and we are frustratingly poorly informed on many of the most interesting facets of it. From one point of view—that of ritual forms and ritual objects —Greek religion is a weird hodge-podge of elements ranging from the crudely primitive to the delicately abstract. From the point of view of organization it similarly shows wide variety. It is in the sphere of theology, of ideas, however, that the single most important observation can be made in regard to Greek religion: it had none. The significance of this merits the greatest emphasis. Theology was the business of the philosopher and the poet, not the priest. In other words, whatever it was that the worshiper sought in a Greek temple, it was not instruction, it was not ideas.

## 74 Sacrilege

Formal Greek religion is most familiarly seen in the cults of the Olympian gods. These were indeed to be found everywhere, and their universality and that of their cult practices justify the general statement that among the cultural phenomena that served to unify the divided world of the independent city-states was religion. Nevertheless, it is necessary to understand that it is only in similarity and familiarity that the unifying stimulus is to be found, for the actual cults were as exclusive as the cities of which they were a part. The worshiper of Athena Polias at Athens was directing his prayers to the same goddess worshiped under the name of Athena elsewhere, but he was worshiping Athena in her specific role as guardian deity of Athens, not as the generalized goddess of the Homeric poems and the myths. The cult was an Athenian cult, open only to citizens. The worshiper at a temple to Athena in, say, Corinth would not be admissible to the temple in Athens. That is what it means to speak of a "state cult" in Classical Greece. Indeed, formal religion has been described as being essentially "patriotic pageantry." The close connection between the state and religion is thus an outstanding feature, and a crime against religion is easily construed as a crime against the state. Accusations of sacrilege are by no means unfamiliar in Classical Athens and it is worthy of note that an accusation of atheism, for example, should be understood not as an effort to require uniformity of religious thought but rather as an attempt to protect the state from the calamity of indifference to its rituals.

During the later years of the Peloponnesian War when Athens was increasingly under attack from within by opponents of the democracy, sacrilegious acts, the desecration of shrines and of rituals, became familiar and frightening tokens of subversion. A famous incident was the profanation of the cult of the Eleusinian Mysteries in 415 B.C. (see Selection 56). It produced a major scandal. One of the men convicted of the crime, Andocides, after imprisonment and exile, was finally restored to citizenship under the amnesty of 403. In 399 he was again indicted for impiety on a charge of having taken part in the Mysteries although now legally disqualified on account of his previous guilt. His defense, which was successful, has come down to us under the title *On the Mysteries*. In it he once again went into detail about the events of 415. The following selection is from *On the Mysteries* 10-30 (abridged). The translation was made in 1896 by a committee of undergraduate members of the Philomathean Society at the University of Pennsylvania.

❁❁❁❁❁

As I have said before, I shall make my defence from the beginning of the affair, first explaining the charge itself, whence the information came on account of which I am brought to trial; secondly, showing that I have neither committed any impiety in regard to the Mysteries, nor given information, nor made a confession; and I do not know whether those who preferred the charges made false revelations or not. These assertions I shall clearly prove.

There was held a meeting of the generals, Nicias, Lamachus and Alcibiades, previous to their departure for Sicily, and the trireme of Lamachus rode at anchor outside the port. When the assembly came to order, Pythonicus, the Athenian, rose and said: "Athenians, you are about to dispatch a large force and to incur great danger at a moment when I am prepared to show you that your general, Alcibiades and others have profaned the Sacred Mysteries in a private house. If you will pass a vote of immunity from punishment for the person whom I shall call, I shall produce before you a slave belonging to a man present at the time, who, although

[ 642 ]

he is not initiated into the Mysteries himself, will tell you what happened. You may deal with me in any manner you please, shall my statements prove false."

Although Alcibiades strenuously denied the charge, the council thought it best to order the uninitiated to withdraw[1] and to go in person for the slave mentioned by Pythonicus. So they went out and returned with a slave of Polemarchus, named Andromachus. When they had promised him free pardon, he said that the Mysteries were performed in the house of Pulition, that Alcibiades, Nicias and Meletus witnessed the profanation and even took part themselves, and that there were some slaves present, himself, his brother, Icesius, the flute player and a slave of Meletus. This slave was the first to testify about the affair and to denounce the criminals, some of whom were captured by Polystratus and put to death, while others took refuge in flight and were condemned by you. . . .

But another source of information has arisen. A foreigner, Teucer, who was living here, fled to Megara and from there made the following offer to the Senate[2]—if they would promise him pardon, he would give an account of the Profanation of the Mysteries, since he himself had been a participant; he would reveal the names of the others who had assisted him, and would tell all he knew about the Mutilation of the Hermae. When the Senate had promised him immunity, for it had full power to do so, a number of the members visited him at Megara. Teucer, having returned in safety, informed against his companions, and they fled as soon as he had made his statement. . . .

Remember, gentlemen, that the charges against all these men have been proved true by their own confession.

There is a third source of information. The wife of Almaeonides, who had formerly been the wife of Damon—Agariste was her name—testified that Alcibiades, Axiochus and Adimantus had celebrated the Mysteries at the house of Charmides, near the Temple of Zeus. At this charge all of them fled.

And yet there has been other information given. Lydus, a slave of Pherecles of Themacus, swore that the Mysteries had been profaned at the house of his master, Pherecles, in Themacus. He gave the names of many and said that my father was there, but that during the performance he was

1. Membership in the cult of the Mysteries was not simply by virtue of citizenship, but by individual rites of initiation. It was forbidden to the uninitiated to know anything of the ritual.
2. The Council (*boulē*) is meant.

asleep, wrapped in his cloak. Speusippus, a member of the Senate, handed the accused over to the court. Then my father, having obtained bail, brought action against Speusippus before the Six Thousand on the ground that he had violated the law, and when the verdict was delivered Speusippus received scarcely two hundred votes from so large a number of jurymen. On this account my father's relations and I urged him to remain in the city. . . .

You have heard, gentlemen of the jury, what took place, and the witnesses have testified before you; now consider what my accusers have dared to say, for justice demands that I should make my defence by calling to your minds the statements of my foes and by confuting them. They said that I made disclosures about the profanation of the Mysteries, and, in addition, that I informed against my own father, a charge which I consider the most unnatural and wicked that could possibly be devised. The man who indicted him was Lydus, the slave of Pherecles; I implored him to stay here and not to seek refuge in flight, going even so far as to embrace his knees. For why should I, if I had betrayed my father, as these men assert, beseech him to remain, that he might die at my hands? And would my father likely have been persuaded to face a trial in which he would surely be confronted with one of two calamities: either to be put to death through my agency, or, if he himself were saved, to be the cause of my death? For the law is as follows:

If anyone bring forward a true accusation, he need fear nothing; if the charge be false, he shall die. . . .

In this way the four accusations concerning the Profanation of the Mysteries were made. I have read you the names of those who fled at each indictment and witnesses have given testimony regarding the facts of the case. But in order to convince you more thoroughly, gentlemen of the jury, I shall in addition do as follows. (For of those who took to flight in consequence of the violation of the Mysteries some have died in exile, while others are present in this court, summoned by me.) I shall grant permission to anyone (occupying part of the time allotted to me for my speech) to prove, if he wishes, that any of these men fled through fear of me, or that I brought forward a charge against anyone, or that they all did not take to flight on account of the accusations made by others which I have described to you. If any one is able to prove that I have lied, you, gentlemen, may treat me as you think I deserve. I am willing to stand aside and to keep silent, if anyone wishes to speak against me from the rostrum.

And now let us see what happened after these revelations about which I have spoken. At the time when they were made there were two rewards open to the informers—one of a thousand drachmae, by the Decree of Cleonymus, and one of ten thousand, by the Decree of Pisander. The informers and Pythonicus quarreled over these rewards, he (Pythonicus) claiming that he had been the first to give information concerning the affair, while Androcles asserted that the rewards should be conferred upon the Senate. To settle this dispute, it was resolved at a public meeting that those of the Senate who had been initiated into the Mysteries, after hearing the information which each claimant had given, should pass judgment upon the case. The Senators awarded the larger sum to Andromachus and the other to Teucer; so Andromachus received ten thousand drachmae and Teucer one thousand at the All-Athenians' Festival. Please call the witnesses to testify to these facts.

*[Examination of Witnesses]*

I have proved, gentlemen of the jury, that concerning the profanation of the Mysteries, on account of which this investigation has arisen and you who are initiated have come into court, I have proved, I say, that I have neither acted in a sacrilegious manner, given information about anyone, made any confession in regard to the Mysteries nor incurred the anger of the two Goddesses to the very slightest degree. And it is of the greatest importance to me that I should have proved it to you. For the speeches of my accusers, who have painted in vivid colors these awful deeds, have plainly shown you what terrible sufferings and punishments were undergone by others who committed offences and acts of impiety toward the Goddesses; but why should their words or actions concern me? I should much rather accuse them and say that they ought to be put to death on account of their impiety and I myself set free, since I have committed no crime. . . .

# 75 *A Sacred Object*

In ancient Greece objects might be sacred because of their location or because of some mythical association or by virtue of some other peculiarity.

SOURCE: Reprinted by permission of the publishers and The Loeb Classical Library from: *Lysias* tr. W. R. M. Lamb, Cambridge, Mass.: Harvard University Press.

In any case, the protection of the sacred object was a matter of public law. The kind of legal problems that could result from situations involving sacred objects can be envisaged by suggesting the analogy of an American Revolutionary War cemetery that happened to be on the proposed site of a runway for an Air Force base. Since, strictly speaking, no material object is actually sacred for us in the way that the ancient world understood such things, the analogy is only a pale suggestion of the intensity with which a Greek viewed such things.

Lysias' speech for the defendant in the case of *The Sacred Olive Tree* is a vivid presentation of the attitudes held by Athenians in such matters and of the atmosphere of the courtroom in such a proceeding. The olive tree, or rather stump, in question was one of those designated as sacred by virtue of their being (allegedly) offshoots of the tree originally planted on the Acropolis by the goddess Athena herself. The seriousness of the case can be bluntly stated by noting that the punishment for its removal would once have been death but was now (early fourth century B.C.) somewhat lightened—exile and confiscation of the condemned man's property. The translation is by W. R. M. Lamb.

❀❀❀❀❀

Heretofore, gentlemen of the Council, I thought it possible for a person who so desired to avoid both law-suits and anxieties by leading a quiet life; but now I find myself so unexpectedly embarrassed with accusations and with nefarious slanderers that, if such a thing could be, I conceive that even those who are yet unborn ought now to be feeling alarmed for what is in store for them, since the conduct of these men brings as great a share of danger upon those who have done no wrong as upon those who are guilty of many offences. And this trial has been made specially perplexing for me, because at first I was indicted for clearing away an olive-tree from my land, and they went and made inquiry of the men who had bought the produce of the sacred olives; but having failed by this method to find that I have done anything wrong, they now say it is an olive-stump that I cleared away, judging that for me this is a most difficult accusation to refute, while to them it allows more freedom to make any statement that they please. So I am obliged, on a charge which this man has carefully planned against me before coming here, and which I have only heard at the same moment as you who are to decide on the case, to defend myself against the loss of my native land and my possessions. Nevertheless I will try to explain the affair to you from the beginning.

This plot of ground belonged to Peisander; but when his property was confiscated, Apollodorus of Megara had it as a gift from the people and cultivated it for some time, until, shortly before the Thirty, Anticles bought it from him and let it out. I bought it from Anticles when peace had been made. So I consider, gentlemen, that my business is to show that, when I acquired the plot, there was neither olive-tree nor stump upon it. For I conceive that in respect of the previous time, even had there been sacred olives of old upon it, I could not with justice be penalized; since if we have had no hand in their clearance, there is no relevance in our being charged as guilty of the offences of others. For you are all aware that, among the numerous troubles that have been caused by the war, the outlying districts were ravaged by the Lacedaemonians, while the nearer were plundered by our friends; so how can it be just that I should be punished now for the disasters that then befell the city? And in particular, this plot of land, as having been confiscated during the war, was unsold for over three years: it is not surprising if they uprooted the sacred olives at a time in which we were unable to safeguard even our personal property. You are aware, gentlemen—especially those of you who have the supervision of such matters,— that many plots at that time were thick with private and sacred olive-trees which have now for the most part been uprooted, so that the land has become bare; and although the same people have owned these plots in the peace as in the war, you do not think fit to punish them for the uprooting done by others. And yet, if you exculpate those who have cultivated the land throughout the whole period, surely those who bought it in the time of the peace ought to leave your court unpunished.

Well now, gentlemen, although I might speak at length on what had previously occurred, I think these remarks will suffice: but when I took over the plot, after an interval of five days I let it out to Callistratus, in the archonship of Pythodorus;[1] he cultivated it for two years, and had taken over no olive-tree, either private or sacred, nor any olive-stump. In the third year it was worked by Demetrius here for a twelvemonth; in the fourth I let it to Alcias, a freedman of Antisthenes, who is dead. After that Proteas too hired it in the same state during three years. Now, please step this way, witnesses.

[*Witnesses*]

Well now, since the termination of that time I have cultivated it myself.

1.   404–403 B.C.

My accuser says that in the archonship of Souniades[2] an olive-stump was uprooted by me. And the previous cultivators, who rented it from me for a number of years, have testified to you that there was no stump on the plot. I ask you, how could one convict the accuser more patently of lying? For it is not possible that the cultivator who came after cleared away what was not there before.

Now formerly, gentlemen, whenever people declared me to be a shrewd, exact man who would do nothing at random or without calculation, I would take it hard, feeling that these terms were wide of my true character; but now I should be glad if you all held this opinion of me, so that you should expect me, if I did set about such an act as this, to consider what profit I stood to get by clearing away the stump, and what loss by preserving it, what I should have achieved if I went undetected, and what I should suffer at your hands if I were exposed. For in every case such acts are done, not for mere mischief, but for profit; and that is the proper direction for your inquiry, and the prosecution should make that the basis of their accusation, by showing what benefit accrued to the wrongdoers. Yet this man is quite unable to show either that I was compelled by poverty to venture on such an act, or that the plot was declining in value to me while the stump existed, or that it was obstructing vines or close to a building, or that I was un-apprised of the dangers awaiting me in your court. And I would make it obvious that many great penalties were my lot if I attempted anything of the kind; for in the first place, it was daylight when I uprooted the stump —as though I had not to do it unseen by all, but must let all the Athenians know! If the act had been merely disgraceful, one might perhaps have disregarded the passers-by; but the case was one of my risking, not disgrace, but the severest penalty. And surely I must have been the most wretched of human creatures if my own servants were to be no longer my slaves, but my masters for the rest of my life, since they would be privy to that act of mine; so that, however great might be their offences against me, I should have been unable to get them punished. For I should have been fully aware that it was in their power at once to be avenged on me and to win their own freedom by informing against me. Furthermore, supposing I had been of a mind to be heedless of my domestics, how should I have dared, when so many persons had rented the plot, and all were acquainted with the facts, to clear away the stump for the sake of a petty profit, while there was no statute of limitations to protect them, so that all who had worked the plot were alike concerned in the preservation of the stump, and hence they would

2.  397–396 B.C.

be able, if anyone accused them, to transfer the blame to their successor? But as it is, they have manifestly absolved me, and have thus taken upon themselves a share of the charge in case they are lying. Again, if I had settled this matter by arrangement, how could I have prevailed on all the passers-by, or the neighbours who not only know of each other what is open for all to see, but even get information of what we try to keep hidden from the knowledge of anyone? Now, some of those people are my friends, but others are at feud with me about my property: these persons he ought to have produced as witnesses, instead of merely bringing these hazardous accusations; for he says I stood by while my domestics hewed down the stems and the wagoner loaded up the wood and took it right away.

But surely, Nicomachus, you ought, at the time, both to have called up those who were present as witnesses, and to have exposed the affair: you would then have left me without any defence, while on your own part, if I was your enemy, you would have achieved by this means your vengeance upon me; while if you were acting in the interest of the State, you would in this way have convicted me without being regarded as a slanderer. If you were looking for profit, you would have made the largest then; for, the fact being exposed, I should have decided that my sole deliverance lay in seducing you. Well, you did nothing of the sort, and you expect that your statements will effect my ruin: you put in the plea that owing to my influence and my means there is no one willing to bear you witness. Yet if, when you saw me—as you say—clearing away the sacred olive, you had brought the nine archons on the scene, or some other members of the Areopagus, you would not have had to seek witnesses elsewhere; for then the truth of your statements would have been ascertained by the very persons who were to decide upon the matter.

So he makes my situation most perplexing; for if he had produced witnesses, he would have expected you to believe them, but as he has none, he thinks that this also should count to my detriment. And I am not surprised —at him; for, to be sure, in his slanderous proceedings he is not going to be as hard up for statements of this sort as he is for witnesses; but you, I trust, will not be in agreement with this man. For you understand that in the plain there are many sacred olives and burnt stumps on my other plots which, had I so desired, it would have been much safer to clear away or cut down or encroach on inasmuch as among so many of them the wrongful act was likely to be less evident.

But the fact is that I have as great a regard for them as for my native land and my whole property, realizing that it is the loss of both of these that I have at stake. And you yourselves I shall produce as witnesses to that fact; for you supervise the matter every month, and also send assessors every year, none of whom has ever penalized me for working the ground about the sacred olives. Now surely, when I pay so much regard to those small penalties, I cannot so utterly disregard the perils involved for my person. You find me taking all this care of the many olive-trees upon which I could more freely commit the offence, and I am on my trial to-day for clearing away the sacred olive which it was impossible to dig up unobserved!

And under which government was I better placed for breaking the law, gentlemen—that of the democracy, or that of the Thirty? I do not mean that I was influential then, or that I am in bad odour now, but that there was a better chance for anyone who wished to commit a crime then than there is at present. Well, you will find that not even in that time did I do anything wrong, either in this or in any other way. And how—except in all the world I were my own most malignant enemy—could I have attempted, with you supervising as you do, to clear away the sacred olive from this plot; in which there is not a single tree, but there was, as he says, a stump of one olive; where a road skirts the plot all round, and neighbours live about it on both sides, and it is unfenced and open to view from every point? So who would have been so foolhardy, in these circumstances, as to attempt such a proceeding? And I feel it is extraordinary that you, whom the city has charged with the perpetual supervision of the sacred olives, have never either punished me for encroaching on one of them nor brought me to trial for having cleared one away, and that now this man, who, as it happens, is neither farming near me nor has been appointed a supervisor nor is of an age to know about such matters, should have indicted me for clearing away a sacred olive from the land.

I beg you, therefore, not to consider such statements more credible than the facts, nor to tolerate such assertions from my enemies about matters of which you are personally cognizant: let your reflections be guided by what I have told you and by the whole tenor of my citizenship. For I have performed all the duties laid upon me with greater zeal than the State required: alike in equipping a warship, in contributing to war funds, in producing drama, and in the rest of my public services, my munificence was equal to that of any other citizen. Yet, if I had done these things but moderately and without that zeal, I should not be struggling to save myself at once from exile and from the loss of all my property, but should have increased my possessions without incurring guilt or imperilling my life: whereas, had I done what this man accuses me of doing, I stood to make no profit, but

[ 650 ]

only to endanger myself. Surely you will all acknowledge that it is fairer to judge important issues by important proofs, and to give more credit to the testimony of the whole city than to the accusations of this single person.

And further, gentlemen, take note of the other events in the case. I went with witnesses to see him, and said that I still had the servants that I owned when I took over the plot, and was ready to deliver any that he wished to the torture,[3] thinking that this would put his statements and my acts to stronger test. But he declined, asserting that no credit could be given to servants. To my mind it is surprising that, when put to the torture on their own account, they accuse themselves, in the certain knowledge that they will be executed, but when it is on account of their masters, to whom they naturally have most animosity, they can choose rather to endure the torture than to get release from their present ills by an incrimination! Nay, in truth, gentlemen, I think it is manifest to all that, had I refused to deliver the men at Nichomachus's request, I should be considered conscious of my guilt; so, since he declined to accept them when I offered to deliver them, it is fair to form the same opinion regarding him, especially as the danger is not equal for us both. For if they had made the statements about me that he desired, I should not even have had a chance of defending myself; while if they had not supported his statements, he was liable to no penalty. It behoved him, therefore, much rather to take them than it suited me to deliver them. For my part, I was so solicitous in the matter, because I felt it was in my favour to have you informed of the truth regarding this matter, at once by torture, by witnesses, and by evidence. And you should consider, gentlemen, which side you ought rather to credit, those for whom many have borne witness, or one for whom nobody has ventured to do so; whether it is more likely that this man is lying, as he can without danger,[4] or that in face of so grave a danger I committed such an act; and whether you think that he is vindicating the cause of the State, or has been plying the slanderer's trade in his accusation.

For I believe it is your opinion that Nicomachus has been prevailed upon by my enemies to conduct this prosecution, not as hoping to establish my guilt, but as expecting to obtain money from me. For precisely as such actions at law are most damaging and perplexing, so everyone is most anxious to avoid them.

3. Great credit was given in Athenian courts to the testimony given by slaves under torture.

4. In prosecutions for impiety the accuser was not subject to the rule that he forfeit 1000 drachmae and some of his civic rights if he failed to get a fifth of the votes of the judges.

But I, gentlemen, disdained that: as soon as he charged me, I placed myself entirely at your disposal, and came to terms with none of my enemies on account of this ordeal, though they take more pleasure in vilifying me than in commending themselves. Not one of them has ever attempted, openly and in his own person, to do me a single hurt; they prefer to set upon me men of this stamp, whom you cannot honestly believe. For I shall be the most miserable of creatures if I am to be unjustly declared an exile: I am childless and alone, my house would be abandoned, my mother would be in utter penury, and I should be deprived of a native land, that is so much to me, on the most disgraceful of charges—I, who in her defence have engaged in many sea-fights and fought many battles on land, and have shown myself an orderly person under both democracy and oligarchy.

But on these matters, gentlemen, I do not know what call I have to speak in this place. However, I have proved to you that there was no stump on the plot, and I have produced witnesses and evidence: these you should bear in mind when you make your decision on the case, and require this man to inform you why it was that, neglecting to convict me as taken in the act, he has delayed so long in bringing so serious an action against me; why he seeks to be credited on the strength of his statements, unsupported by a single witness, when the bare facts would have sufficed to establish my guilt; and why, on my offering all the servants whom he asserts to have been then present, he declined to accept them.

# 76 The Delphic Oracle

One of the most celebrated aspects of the Greek gods and their cults was prophecy. The ability to foretell the future is inevitably associated with deity. Persons who had the peculiar skill were thought of as being invaded by a god; and while in the actual throes of prophecy at the behest of the god who was speaking through them, they were thought to be suffering a kind of madness. Certain deities were especially reputed for the prophetic power, and specific shrines enjoyed world-wide fame as the sites of prophetic oracles. The most celebrated of all was the temple of Apollo at Delphi. Advice was sought from the Delphic Oracle by kings and commoners, Greeks and barbarians. The actual seer was a woman trained for her position and dedicated to it. At stated times she received suppliants, who found her seated in a bowl on a tripod set over a natural chasm whence emanated smoke and fumes from the bowels of the earth. In her trance, seized by the inspiration of the god, she would utter incomprehensible babblings in answer to the questions asked. The priests of the temple translated these sounds into Greek verses, which became famous as masterpieces of ambiguity. The prestige of the Delphic Oracle was immense, but although the oracle lasted until the latter half of the fourth century A.D., it never really regained its traditional reputation after apparently guessing wrong on the crucial event that launched Classical Greece—the outcome of the Persian Wars.

Two opposed attitudes toward oracular utterance are displayed by the fifth-century B.C. historians Herodotus and Thucydides. The first of the passages that follow contains Herodotus' famous account (1.46–48) of the prophecy given by Delphi in response to a "test question" asked by King Croesus of Lydia prior to his war against the Persian king Cyrus the Great. It is translated by George Rawlinson. The second passage contains Thucydides' succinct view of oracles (2.54), which he presents at the conclusion of his account of the plague at Athens in 430 B.C. (see Selection 78). It is translated by R. Crawley.

❁❁❁❁❁

At the end of this time the grief of Croesus was interrupted by intelligence from abroad. He learned that Cyrus, the son of Cambyses, had destroyed the empire of Astyages, the son of Cyaxares; and that the Persians were becoming daily more powerful. This led him to consider with himself whether it were possible to check the growing power of that people before it came to a head. With this design he resolved to make instant trial of the several oracles in Greece, and of the one in Libya. So he sent his messengers in different directions, some to Delphi, some to Abae in Phocis, and some to Dodona; others to the oracle of Amphiaraus; others to that of Trophonius; others, again, to Branchidae in Milesia. These were the Greek oracles which he consulted. To Libya he sent another embassy, to consult the oracle of Ammon. These messengers were sent to test the knowledge of the oracles, that, if they were found really to return true answers, he might send a second time, and inquire if he ought to attack the Persians.

The messengers who were despatched to make trial of the oracles were given the following instructions: they were to keep count of the days from the time of their leaving Sardis, and, reckoning from that date, on the hundredth day they were to consult the oracles, and to inquire of them what Croesus the son of Alyattes, king of Lydia, was doing at that moment. The answers given them were to be taken down in writing, and brought back to him. None of the replies remain on record except that of the oracle at Delphi. There, the moment that the Lydians entered the sanctuary, and before they put their questions, the priestess thus answered them in hexameter verse:

> I can count the sands, and I can measure the ocean;
> I have ears for the silent, and know what the dumb man meaneth;
> Lo! on my sense there striketh the smell of a shell-covered tortoise,
> Boiling now on a fire, with the flesh of a lamb, in a cauldron,
> Brass is the vessel below, and brass the cover above it.

These words the Lydians wrote down at the mouth of the priestess as she prophesied, and then set off on their return to Sardis. When all the messengers had come back with the answers which they had received, Croesus undid the rolls, and read what was written in each. Only one approved itself to him, that of the Delphic oracle. This he had no sooner heard than he instantly made an act of adoration, and accepted it as true, declaring that the Delphic was the only really oracular shrine, the only one that had discovered in what way he was in fact employed. For on the departure of his messengers he had set himself to think what was most impossible for any one to conceive of his doing, and then, waiting till the day agreed on came, he acted as he had determined. He took a tortoise and a lamb, and cutting them in pieces with his own hands, boiled them both together in a brazen cauldron, covered over with a lid which was also of brass.

. . . . .

Such was the nature of the calamity, and heavily did it weigh on the Athenians; death raging within the city and devastation without. Among other things which they remembered in their distress was, very naturally, the following verse which the old men said had long ago been uttered:

> A Dorian war shall come and with it death.

So a dispute arose as to whether dearth and not death[1] had not been the word in the verse; but at the present juncture, it was of course decided in favour of the latter; for the people made their recollection fit in with their sufferings. I fancy, however, that if another Dorian war should ever afterwards come upon us, and a dearth should happen to accompany it, the

---

1. The play on words in the Greek is ingeniously captured by the translator.

verse will probably be read accordingly. The oracle also which had been given to the Lacedaemonians was now remembered by those who knew of it. When the God was asked whether they should go to war, he answered that if they put their might into it, victory would be theirs, and that he would himself be with them. With this oracle events were supposed to tally. For the plague broke out so soon as the Peloponnesians invaded Attica, and never entering Peloponnese (not at least to an extent worth noticing), committed its worst ravages at Athens, and next to Athens, at the most populous of the other towns.

# MEDICAL SCIENCE

PHILOSOPHY—the investigation of the world of nature—tended among the Classical Greeks to become abstract and deliberately divorced from the sphere of concrete, everyday sense experience. The combination of abstract thought and concrete observation that we think of as lying at the core of the natural sciences did not occur in most philosophical inquiry. The philosopher, in principle, at any rate, dealt with the timeless, the unchanging, the general. One who worked with specific objects, with the phenomena of the changing world of daily experience, was considered not a philosopher but a *technitēs* (craftsman), whether he be actor or shoemaker or speech-writer or any other of dozens of trades and professions. In one craft, however, the foundations were laid for a bridge between philosophy and technique. It was in medicine that a development occurred in the fifth century B.C. which was ultimately to prove immensely fruitful: the creation of a "scientific medicine." It was a medical practice that combined traditional healing "technique" with cumulative "knowledge" of illness and its treatment, together with philosophical "concepts" about such things as the nature of health and the cause of disease. The chief monument of this medical science is the so-called "Hippocratic Corpus," a large collection of writings on various aspects of medicine. Tradition assigned them all to the authorship of a fifth-century B.C. physician, Hippocrates of Cos, about whose life and work one modern scholar has written that there is no single fact beyond dispute—except that there was such a person. Actually the essays are by different—and unknown—authors, from different periods and different schools of medical thought and practice reaching over hundreds of years. Minute study of the separate essays has now dated a number of them with reasonable certainty in the latter part of the fifth century B.C., the epoch when scientific, "Hippocratic" medicine was being developed.

# 77 *Environment and Health*

As with so much of the Greek intellectual achievement, one very significant facet of Hippocratic medicine was its firm refusal to admit into its range of inquiry the supernatural, the occult, and the arbitrary. It assumed that the world was "divine" but that the nature of the divine governance of the universe lay in consistency and rationality, not whimsicality and miraculous intervention. Thus in the essay on *The Sacred Disease* (epilepsy) the author insists that this malady is no more and no less "sacred" than any other, that its nature, its causes, and its treatment are to be discussed with the same attention to observation, experience, and reason as would be applied to the treatment of, say, a broken arm. The Greek physicians, then, understood health and disease to be rationally explicable events. In their efforts to find the keys to a rational explanation they were aware of the general fact of heredity as a contributing factor in the development of physical types and in the incidence of various kinds of ailment. They placed the greater emphasis, however, upon the environment in their search for a causal explanation.

The fifth-century B.C. essay *Airs, Waters, Places* is an effort to explain susceptibility to diseases and the actual occurrence of illness by reference to the basic climatic and topographical features of the natural environment and also to the man-made features of the social environment. To the modern reader it appears as a curious mixture of acute observation and shrewd deduction combined with mistaken hypotheses and quaintly legendary misinformation. The translation (here abridged) of the Hippocratic *Airs, Waters, Places* is by Francis Adams.

❀❀❀❀❀

Whoever wishes to investigate medicine properly, should proceed thus: in the first place to consider the seasons of the year, and what effects each of them produces (for they are not at all alike, but differ much from themselves in regard to their changes). Then the winds, the hot and the cold, especially such as are common to all countries, and then such as are peculiar to each locality. We must also consider the qualities of the waters, for as they differ from one another in taste and weight, so also do they differ much in their qualities. In the same manner, when one comes into a city to which he is a stranger, he ought to consider its situation, how it lies as to the winds and the rising of the sun; for its influence is not the same whether it lies to the north or the south, to the rising or to the setting sun. These things one ought to consider most attentively, and concerning the waters which the inhabitants use, whether they be marshy and soft, or hard, and running from elevated and rocky situations, and then if saltish and unfit for cooking; and the ground, whether it be naked and deficient in water, or wooded and well watered, and whether it lies in a hollow, confined situation, or is elevated and cold; and the mode in which the inhabitants live, and what are their pursuits, whether they are fond of drinking and eating to excess, and given to indolence, or are fond of exercise and labor, and not given to excess in eating and drinking.

From these things he must proceed to investigate everything else. For if one knows all these things well, or at least the greater part of them, he cannot miss knowing, when he comes into a strange city, either the diseases peculiar to the place, or the particular nature of common diseases, so that he will not be in doubt as to the treatment of the diseases, or commit mistakes, as is likely to be the case provided one had not previously considered these matters. And in particular, as the season and the year advances, he can tell what epidemic diseases will attack the city, either in summer or in winter, and what each individual will be in danger of experiencing from the change of regimen. For knowing the changes of the seasons, the risings and settings of the stars, how each of them takes place, he will be able to know beforehand what sort of a year is going to ensue. Having made these investigations, and knowing beforehand the seasons, such a one must be acquainted with each particular, and must succeed in the preservation of health, and be by no means unsuccessful in the practice of his art. And if it shall be thought that these things belong rather to meteorology, it will be admitted, on second thoughts, that astronomy contributes not a little, but a very great deal, indeed, to medicine. For with the seasons the digestive organs of men undergo a change.

But how each of the aforementioned things should be investigated and explained, I will now declare in a clear manner. A city that is exposed to hot winds (these are between the wintry rising, and the wintry setting of the sun), and to which these are peculiar, but which is sheltered from the north winds; in such a city the waters will be plenteous and saltish, and as they run from an elevated source, they are necessarily hot in summer, and cold in winter; the heads of the inhabitants are of a humid and pituitous constitution, and their bellies subject to frequent disorders, owing to the phlegm running down from the head; the forms of their bodies, for the most part, are rather flabby; they do not eat nor drink much; drinking wine in particular, and more especially if carried to intoxication, is oppressive to them; and the following diseases are peculiar to the district: in the first place, the women are sickly and subject to excessive menstruation; then many are unfruitful from disease, and not from nature, and they have frequent miscarriages; infants are subject to attacks of convulsions and asthma, which they consider to be connected with infancy, and hold to be a sacred disease (epilepsy). The men are subject to attacks of dysentery, diarrhea, hepialus,[1] chronic fevers in winter, of epinyctis,[2] frequently, and of hemorrhoids about the anus. Pleurisies, peripneumonies, ardent fevers, and whatever diseases are reckoned acute, do not often occur, for such diseases are not apt to prevail where the bowels are loose. Ophthalmies occur of a humid character, but not of a serious nature, and of short duration, unless they attack epidemically from the change of the seasons. And when they pass their fiftieth year, defluxions supervening from the brain, render them paralytic when exposed suddenly to strokes of the sun, or to cold. These diseases are endemic to them, and, moreover, if any epidemic disease connected with the change of the seasons, prevail, they are also liable to it.

But the following is the condition of cities which have the opposite exposure, namely, to cold winds, between the summer settings and the summer risings of the sun, and to which these winds are peculiar, and which are sheltered from the south and the hot breezes. In the first place the waters are, for the most part, hard and cold. The men must necessarily be well braced and slender, and they must have the discharges downwards of the alimentary canal hard, and of difficult evacuation, while those upwards are more fluid, and rather bilious than pituitous. Their heads are sound and hard, and they are liable to burstings (of vessels?) for the most part. The diseases which prevail epidemically with them, are pleurisies, and those which are called acute diseases. This must be the case when the bowels are bound; and from any causes, many become affected with suppurations in the lungs, the cause of which is the tension of the body, and hardness of the bowels; for their dryness and the coldness of the water dispose them to ruptures (of vessels?). Such constitutions must be given to excess of eating, but not of drinking; for it is not possible to be gourmands and drunkards at the same time. Ophthalmies, too, at length supervene; these being of a hard and violent nature, and soon ending in rupture of the eyes; persons under thirty years of age are liable to severe bleedings at the nose in summer;

1. Hepialus is a species of intermittent fever, very common in warm climates.
2. A disease of the skin.

attacks of epilepsy are rare but severe. Such people are likely to be rather long-lived; their ulcers are not attended with serous discharges, nor of a malignant character; in disposition they are rather ferocious than gentle. The diseases I have mentioned are peculiar to the men, and besides they are liable to any common complaint which may be prevailing from the changes of the seasons. But the women, in the first place, are of a hard constitution, from the waters being hard, indigestible, and cold; and their menstrual discharges are not regular, but in small quantity, and painful. Then they have difficult parturition, but are not very subject to abortions. And when they do bring forth children, they are unable to nurse them; for the hardness and indigestible nature of the water puts away their milk. Phthisis frequently supervenes after childbirth, for the efforts of it frequently bring on ruptures and strains. Children while still little are subject to dropsies in the testicle, which disappear as they grow older; in such a town they are late in attaining manhood. It is, as I have now stated, with regard to hot and cold winds and cities thus exposed. . . .

Whoever studies and observes these things may be able to foresee most of the effects which will result from the changes of the seasons; and one ought to be particularly guarded during the greatest changes of the seasons, and neither willingly give medicines, nor apply the cautery to the belly, nor make incisions there until ten or more days be past. Now, the greatest and most dangerous are the two solstices, and especially the summer, and also the two equinoxes, but especially the autumnal. One ought also to be guarded about the rising of the stars, especially of the Dogstar, then of Arcturus, and then the setting of the Pleiades; for diseases are especially apt to prove critical in those days, and some prove fatal, some pass off, and all others change to another form and another constitution. So it is with regard to them.

I wish to show, respecting Asia and Europe, how, in all respects, they differ from one another, and concerning the figure of the inhabitants, for they are different, and do not at all resemble one another. To treat of all would be a long story, but I will tell you how I think it is with regard to the greatest and most marked differences. I say, then, that Asia differs very much from Europe as to the nature of all things, both with regard to the productions of the earth and the inhabitants, for everything is produced much more beautiful and large in Asia; the country is milder, and the dispositions of the inhabitants also are more gentle and affectionate. The cause of this is the temperature of the seasons, because it lies in the middle of the risings of the sun towards the east, and removed from the cold (and heat), for nothing tends to growth and mildness so much as when the climate has no predominant quality, but a general equality of temperature prevails. It is not everywhere the same with regard to Asia, but such parts of the country as lie intermediate between the heat and the cold, are the best supplied with fruits and trees, and have the most genial climate, and enjoy the purest waters, both celestial and terrestrial. For neither are they much burnt up by the heat, nor dried up by the drought and want of rain, nor do they suffer from the cold; since they are well watered from abundant showers and snow, and the fruits of the season, as might be supposed, grow in abundance, both such as are raised from seed that has been sown, and such plants as the earth produces of its own accord, the fruits of which the inhabitants make use of, training them from their wild state and transplanting them to a suitable soil; the cattle also which are reared there are vigorous, particularly prolific, and bring up young of the fairest description; the inhabitants too, are well fed, most beautiful in shape, of large stature, and differ little from one another either as to figure or size; and the country itself, both as regards its constitution and mildness of the seasons, may be said to bear a close resemblance to the spring. Manly courage, endurance of suffering, laborious enterprise, and high spirit, could not be produced in such a state of things either among the native inhabitants or those of a different country, for there pleasure necessarily reigns. For this reason, also, the forms of wild beasts there are much varied. Thus it is, as I think, with the Egyptians and Libyans. . . .

I will pass over the smaller differences among the nations, but will now treat of such as are great either from nature, or custom; and, first, concerning the Macrocephali. There is no other race of men which have heads in the least resembling theirs. At first, usage was the principal cause of the length of their head, but now nature cooperates with usage. They think those the most noble who have the longest heads. It is thus with regard to the usage: immediately after the child is born, and while its head is still tender, they fashion it with their hands, and constrain it to assume a lengthened shape by applying bandages and other suitable contrivances whereby the spherical form of the head is destroyed, and it is made to increase in length. Thus, at first, usage operated, so that this constitution was the result of force: but, in the course of time, it was formed naturally; so that usage had nothing to do with it; for the semen comes from all parts of the body, sound from the sound parts, and unhealthy from the unhealthy parts. If, then, children with bald heads are born to parents with bald heads; and children with blue eyes to parents who have blue eyes; and if the children of parents having distorted eyes squint also for the most part; and if the same may be said of other forms of the body, what is to prevent it from happening that a child with a long head should be produced by a parent having a long head? But now these things do not happen as they did formerly, for the custom no longer prevails owing to their intercourse with other men. Thus it appears to me to be with regard to them. . . .

And with regard to the pusillanimity and cowardice of the inhabitants, the principal reason why the Asiatics are more unwarlike and of more gentle disposition than the Europeans is, the nature of the seasons, which do not undergo any great changes either to heat or cold, or the like; for there is neither excitement of the understanding nor any strong change of the body by which the temper might be ruffled, and they be roused to inconsiderate emotion and passion, rather than living as they do always in the same state. It is changes of all kinds which arouse the understanding of mankind, and do not allow them to get into a torpid condition. For these reasons, it appears to me, the Asiatic race is feeble, and further, owing to their laws; for monarchy prevails in the greater part of Asia, and where men are not their own masters nor independent, but are the slaves of others, it is not a matter of consideration with them how they may acquire military discipline, but how they may seem not to be warlike, for the dangers are not equally shared, since they must serve as soldiers, perhaps endure fatigue, and die for their masters, far from their children, their wives, and other friends; and whatever noble and manly actions they may perform lead only to the aggrandizement of their masters, whilst the fruits which they reap are dangers and death; and, in addition to all this, the lands of such persons must be laid waste by the enemy and want of culture. Thus, then, if any one be naturally warlike and courageous, his disposition will be changed by the institutions. As a strong proof of all this, such Greeks or barbarians in Asia as are not under a despotic form of government, but are independent, and enjoy the fruits of their own labors, are of all others the most warlike; for these encounter dangers on their own account, bear the prizes of their own valor, and in like manner endure the punishment of their own cowardice. And you will find the Asiatics differing from one another, for some are better and others more dastardly; of these differences, as I stated before, the changes of the seasons are the cause. Thus it is with Asia.

In Europe there is a Scythian[3] race, called Sauromatae, which inhabits the confines of the Palus Maeotis, and is different from all other races. Their women mount on horseback, use the bow, and throw the javelin from

3.   Scythia is the south Russian steppe.

their horses, and fight with their enemies as long as they are virgins; and they do not lay aside their virginity until they kill three of their enemies, nor have any connection with men until they perform the sacrifices according to law. Whoever takes to herself a husband, gives up riding on horseback unless the necessity of a general expedition obliges her. They have no right breast; for while still of a tender age their mothers heat strongly a copper instrument constructed for this very purpose, and apply it to the right breast, which is burnt up, and its development being arrested, all the strength and fullness are determined to the right shoulder and arm. . . .

In respect of the seasons and figure of body, the Scythian race, like the Egyptian, have a uniformity of resemblance, different from all other nations; they are by no means prolific, and the wild beasts which are indigenous there are small in size and few in number, for the country lies under the Northern Bears, and the Rhiphaean mountains, whence the north wind blows; the sun comes very near to them only when in the summer solstice, and warms them but for a short period, and not strongly; and the winds blowing from the hot regions of the earth do not reach them, or but seldom, and with little force; but the winds from the north always blow, congealed, as they are, by the snow, the ice, and much water, for these never leave the mountains, which are thereby rendered uninhabitable. A thick fog covers the plains during the day, and amidst it they live, so that winter may be said to be always present with them; or, if they have summer, it is only for a few days, and the heat is not very strong. Their plains are high-lying and naked, not crowned with mountains, but extending upwards under the Northern Bears. The wild beasts there are not large, but such as can be sheltered underground; for the cold of winter and the barrenness of the country prevent their growth, and because they have no covert nor shelter. The changes of the seasons, too, are not great nor violent, for, in fact, they change gradually; and therefore their figures resemble one another, as they all equally use the same food, and the same clothing summer and winter, respiring a humid and dense atmosphere, and drinking water from snow and ice; neither do they make any laborious exertions, for neither body nor mind is capable of enduring fatigue when the changes of the seasons are not great. For these reasons their shapes are gross and fleshy, with ill-marked joints, of a humid temperament, and deficient in tone: the internal cavities, and especially those of the intestines, are full of humors; for the belly cannot possibly be dry in such a country, with such a constitution and in such a climate; but owing to their fat, and the absence of hairs from their bodies, their shapes resemble one another, the males being all alike, and so also with the women; for the seasons being of a uniform temperature, no corruption or deterioration takes place in the concretion of the semen, unless from some violent cause, or from disease. . . .

It is impossible that persons of such a constitution could be prolific, for, with the man, the sexual desires are not strong, owing to the laxity of his constitution, the softness and coldness of his belly, from all which causes it is little likely that a man should be given to venery; and besides, from being jaded by exercise on horseback, the men become weak in their desires. On the part of the men these are the causes; but on that of the women, they are embonpoint and humidity; for the womb cannot take in the semen, nor is the menstrual discharge such as it should be, but scanty and at too long intervals; and the mouth of the womb is shut up by fat and does not admit the semen; and, moreover, they themselves are indolent and fat, and their bellies cold and soft. From these causes the Scythian race is not prolific. Their female servants furnish a strong proof of this; for they no sooner have connection with a man than they prove with child, owing to their active course of life and the slenderness of body.

And, in addition to these, there are many eunuchs among the Scythians, who perform female work, and speak like women. Such persons are called effeminates. The inhabitants of the country attribute the cause of their impotence to a god, and venerate and worship such persons, every one dreading that the like might befall himself; but to me it appears that such affections are just as much divine as all others are, and that no one disease is either more divine or more human than another, but that all are alike divine, for that each has its own nature, and that no one arises without a natural cause. But I will explain how I think that the affection takes its rise. From continued exercise on horseback they are seized with chronic defluxions in their joints owing to their legs always hanging down below their horses; they afterwards become lame and stiff at the hip-joint, such of them, at least, as are severely attacked with it. They treat themselves in this way: when the disease is commencing, they open the vein behind either ear, and when the blood flows, sleep, from feebleness, seizes them, and afterwards they awaken, some in good health and others not. To me it appears that the semen is altered by this treatment, for there are veins behind the ears which, if cut, induce impotence; now, these veins would appear to me to be cut. Such persons afterwards, when they go in to women and cannot have connection with them, at first do not think much about it, but remain quiet; but when, after making the attempt two, three, or more times, they succeed

[ 664 ]

no better, fancying they have committed some offence against the god whom they blame for the affection, they put on female attire, reproach themselves for effeminacy, play the part of women, and perform the same work as women do. This the rich among the Scythians endure, not the basest, but the most noble and powerful, owing to their riding on horseback; for the poor are less affected, as they do not ride on horses. And yet, if this disease had been more divine than the others, it ought not to have befallen the most noble and the richest of the Scythians alone, but all alike, or rather those who have little, as not being able to pay honors to the gods, if, indeed, they delight in being thus rewarded by men, and grant favours in return; for it is likely that the rich sacrifice more to the gods, and dedicate more votive offerings, inasmuch as they have wealth, and worship the gods; whereas the poor, from want, do less in this way, and, moreover, upbraid the gods for not giving them wealth, so that those who have few possessions were more likely to bear the punishments of these offences than the rich. But, as I formerly said, these affections are divine just as much as others, for each springs from a natural cause, and this disease arises among the Scythians from such a cause as I have stated. But it attacks other men in like manner, for whenever men ride much and very frequently on horseback, then many are affected with rheums in the joints, sciatica, and gout, and they are inept at venery. But these complaints befall the Scythians, and they are the most impotent of men for the aforesaid causes, and because they always wear breeches, and spend the most of their time on horseback, so as not to touch their privy parts with the hands, and from the cold and fatigue they forget the sexual desire, and do not make the attempt until after they have lost their virility. Thus it is with the race of the Scythians.

The other races in Europe differ from one another, both as to stature and shape, owing to the changes of the seasons, which are very great and frequent, and because the heat is strong, the winters severe, and there are frequent rains, and again protracted droughts, and winds, from which many and diversified changes are induced. These changes are likely to have an effect upon generation in the coagulation of the semen, as this process cannot be the same in summer as in winter, nor in rainy as in dry weather; wherefore, I think, that the figures of Europeans differ more than those of Asiatics; and they differ very much from one another as to stature in the same city; for vitiations of the semen occur in its coagulation more frequently during frequent changes of the seasons, than where they are alike and equable. And the same may be said of their dispositions, for the wild, and unsociable, and the passionate occur in such a constitution; for frequent excitement of the mind induces wildness, and extinguishes sociableness and mildness of disposition, and therefore I think the inhabitants of Europe more courageous than those of Asia; for a climate which is always the same induces indolence, but a changeable climate, laborious exertions both of body and mind; and from rest and indolence cowardice is engendered, and from laborious exertions and pains, courage. On this account the inhabitants of Europe are more warlike than the Asiatics, and also owing to their institutions, because they are not governed by kings like the latter, for where men are governed by kings there they must be very cowardly, as I have stated before; for their souls are enslaved, and they will not willingly, or readily undergo dangers in order to promote the power of another; but those that are free undertake dangers on their own account, and not for the sake of others; they court hazard and go out to meet it, for they themselves bear off the rewards of victory, and thus their institutions contribute not a little to their courage.

Such is the general character of Europe and Asia. . . .

# 78 Disease and Its Treatment

In the actual treatment of disease the Greek physicians were severely limited, and there were many ailments with which they were powerless to cope. But in their conscious desire to learn from their experiences, to carefully record and to share their knowledge, they were on the track that ultimately has led to the spectacular achievements of modern science and of modern medical science in particular. It is for this reason that ancient Greek descriptions of disease, case histories, have received from modern scholars a praise that may at first glance seem exorbitant.

The first of the following two selections consists of passages from Book I of the fifth-century B.C. Hippocratic work *Epidēmiai* (signifying "visits to the sick"). These very unliterary, unbeautiful notes of a practicing physician have been called the "most golden of all the achievements of the Golden Age of Greece." It is interesting to compare them with the Egyptian "Book of Surgery" (Selection 14). The translation is by Francis Adams. The second selection is perhaps the most famous of all descriptions of disease: Thucydides' account (2.47-53) of the plague that broke out in Athens in the second year of the Peloponnesian War. It is translated by R. Crawley.

❀❀❀❀❀

## Case 2

Silenus lived on the Broad-way, near the house of Evalcidas. From fatigue, drinking, and unseasonable exercises, he was seized with fever. He began with having pain in the loins; he had heaviness of the head, and there was stiffness of the neck. On the first day the alvine discharges were bilious, unmixed, frothy, high colored, and copious; urine black, having a black sediment; he was thirsty, tongue dry; no sleep at night. On the second, acute fever, stools more copious, thinner, frothy; urine black, an uncomfortable night, slight delirium. On the third, all the symptoms exacerbated; an oblong distention, of a softish nature, from both sides of the hypochondrium to the navel; stools thin, and darkish; urine muddy, and darkish; no sleep at night; much talking, laughter, singing, he could not restrain himself. On the fourth, in the same state. On the fifth, stools bilious, unmixed, smooth, greasy; urine thin, and transparent; slight absence of delirium. On the sixth, slight perspiration about the head; extremities cold and livid; much tossing about; no passage from the bowels, urine suppressed, acute fever. On the seventh, loss of speech; extremities could no longer be kept warm; no discharge of urine. On the eighth, a cold sweat all over; red rashes with sweat, of a round figure, small, like *vari,* persistent, not subsiding; by means of a slight stimulus, a copious discharge from the bowels, of a thin and undigested character, with pain; urine acrid, and passed with pain; extremities slightly heated; sleep slight, and comatose; speechless; urine thin, and transparent. On the ninth, in the same state. On the tenth, no drink taken; comatose, sleep slight; alvine discharges the same; urine abundant, and thickish; when allowed to stand, the sediment farinaceous and white; extremities again cold. On the eleventh, he died. At the commencement, and throughout, the respiration was slow and large; there was a constant throbbing in the hypochondrium; his age was about twenty.

## Case 3

Herophon was seized with an acute fever; alvine discharges at first were scanty, and attended with tenesmus; but afterwards they were passed of a thin, bilious character, and frequent; there was no sleep; urine black, and thin. On the fifth, in the morning, deafness; all the symptoms exacerbated;

spleen swollen; distension of the hypochondrium; alvine discharges scanty, and black; he became delirious. On the sixth, delirious; at night, sweating, coldness; the delirium continued. On the seventh, he became cold, thirsty, was disordered in mind; at night recovered his senses; slept. On the eighth, was feverish; the spleen diminished in size; quite collected; had pain at first about the groin, on the same side as the spleen; had pains in both legs; night comfortable; urine better colored, had a scanty sediment. On the ninth, sweated; the crisis took place; fever remitted. On the fifth day afterwards, fever relapsed, spleen immediately became swollen; acute fever; deafness again. On the third day after the relapse, the spleen diminished; deafness less; legs painful; sweated during the night; crisis took place on the seventeenth day; had no disorder of the senses during the relapse.

## Case 5

The wife of Epicrates, who was lodged at the house of Archigetes, being near the term of delivery, was seized with a violent rigor, and, as was said, she did not become heated; next day the same. On the third, she was delivered of a daughter, and everything went on properly. On the day following her delivery, she was seized with acute fever, pain in the cardiac region of the stomach, and in the genital parts. Having had a suppository, was in so far relieved; pain in the head, neck, and loins; no sleep; alvine discharges scanty, bilious, thin, and unmixed; urine thin, and blackish. Towards the night of the sixth day from the time she was seized with the fever, became delirious. On the seventh, all the symptoms exacerbated; insomnolency, delirium, thirst; stools bilious, and high colored. On the eighth, had a rigor; slept more. On the ninth, the same. On the tenth, her limbs painfully affected; pain again of the cardiac region of the stomach; heaviness of the head; no delirium; slept more; bowels constipated. On the eleventh, passed urine of a better color, and having an abundant sediment; felt lighter. On the fourteenth had a rigor; acute fever. On the fifteenth, had a copious vomiting of bilious and yellow matters; sweated; fever gone; at night acute fever; urine thick, sediment white. On the seventeenth, an exacerbation; night uncomfortable; no sleep; delirium. On the eighteenth, thirsty; tongue parched; no sleep; much delirium; legs painfully affected. About the twentieth, in the morning, had a slight rigor; was comatose; slept tranquilly; had slight vomiting of bilious and black matters; towards night deafness. About the twenty-first, weight generally in the left side, with pain; slight cough; urine thick, muddy, and reddish; when allowed to stand, had no sediment; in other respects felt lighter; fever not gone; fauces painful from the commencement, and red; uvula retracted; defluxion remained acrid, pungent, and saltish throughout. About the twenty-seventh, free of fever; sediment in the urine; pain in the side. About the thirty-first, was attacked with fever, bilious diarrhœa; slight bilious vomiting on the fortieth. Had a complete crisis, and was freed from the fever on the eightieth day.

## Case 8

Erasinus, who lived near the Canal of Bootes, was seized with fever after supper; passed the night in an agitated state. During the first day quiet, but in pain at night. On the second, symptoms all exacerbated; at night delirious. On the third, was in a painful condition; great incoherence. On the fourth, in a most uncomfortable state; had no sound sleep at night, but dreaming and talking; then all the appearances worse, of a formidable and alarming character; fear, impatience. On the morning of the fifth, was composed, and quite coherent, but long before noon was furiously mad, so that he could not constrain himself; extremities cold, and somewhat livid; urine without sediment; died about sunset. The fever in this case was accompanied by sweats throughout; the hypochondria were in a state of meteorism, with distention and pain; the urine was black, had round substances floating in it, which did not subside; the alvine evacuations were not stopped; thirst throughout not great; much spasms with sweats about the time of death.

## Case 11

The wife of Dromeades having been delivered of a female child, and all other matters going on properly, on the second day after was seized with rigor and acute fever. Began to have pain about the hypochondrium on the first day; had nausea and incoherence, and for some hours afterwards had no sleep; respiration rare, large, and suddenly interrupted. On the day following that on which she had the rigor, alvine discharges proper; urine thick, white, muddy, like urine which has been shaken after standing for some time, until the sediment had fallen to the bottom; it had no sediment; she did not sleep during the night. On the third day, about noon, had a rigor, acute fever; urine the same; pain of the hypochondria, nausea, an uncomfortable night, no sleep; a coldish sweat all over, but heat quickly restored. On the fourth, slight alleviation of the symptoms about the hypochondria; heaviness of the head, with pain; somewhat comatose; slight epistaxis, tongue dry, thirst, urine thin and oily; slept a little, upon awakening was somewhat comatose; slight coldness, slept during the night, was delirious. On the morning of the sixth had a rigor, but soon recovered her heat, sweated all over; extremities cold, was delirious, respiration rare and large. Shortly afterwards spasms from the head began, and she immediately expired.

．．．．．

In the first days of summer the Lacedaemonians and their allies, with two-thirds of their forces as before, invaded Attica, under the command of Archidamus, son of Zeuxidamus, king of Lacedaemon, and sat down and laid waste the country. Not many days after their arrival in Attica the plague first began to show itself among the Athenians. It was said that it had broken out in many places previously in the neighbourhood of Lemnos and elsewhere; but a pestilence of such extent and mortality was nowhere remembered. Neither were the physicians at first of any service, ignorant as they were of the proper way to treat it, but they died themselves the most thickly, as they visited the sick most often; nor did any human art succeed any better. Supplications in the temples, divinations, and so forth were found equally futile, till the overwhelming nature of the disaster at last put a stop to them altogether.

It first began, it is said, in the parts of Ethiopia above Egypt, and thence descended into Egypt and Libya and into most of the king's country. Suddenly falling upon Athens, it first attacked the population in Piraeus—which was the occasion of their saying that the Peloponnesians had poisoned the reservoirs, there being as yet no wells there—and afterwards appeared in the upper city, when the deaths became much more frequent. All speculation as to its origin and its causes, if causes can be found adequate to produce so great a disturbance, I leave to other writers, whether lay or professional; for myself, I shall simply set down its nature, and explain the symptoms by which perhaps it may be recognised by the student, if it should ever break out again. This I can the better do, as I had the disease myself, and watched its operation in the case of others.

That year then is admitted to have been otherwise unprecedentedly free from sickness; and such few cases as occurred, all determined in this. As a rule, however, there was no ostensible cause; but people in good health were all of a sudden attacked by violent heats in the head, and redness and inflammation in the eyes, the inward parts, such as the throat or tongue, becoming bloody and emitting an unnatural and fetid breath. These symptoms were followed by sneezing and hoarseness, after which the pain soon reached the chest, and produced a hard cough. When it fixed in the stomach, it upset it; and discharges of bile of every kind named by physicians ensued, accompanied by very great distress. In most cases also an ineffectual retching followed, producing violent spasms, which in some cases ceased soon after, in others much later. Externally the body was not very hot to the touch, nor pale in its appearance, but reddish, livid, and breaking out into small pustules and ulcers. But internally it burned so that the patient could not bear to have on him clothing or linen even of the very lightest description; or indeed to be otherwise than stark naked. What they would have liked best would have been to throw themselves into cold water; as indeed was done by some of the neglected sick, who plunged into the rain-tanks in their agonies of unquenchable thirst; though it made no difference whether they drank little or much. Besides this, the miserable feeling of not being able to rest or sleep never ceased to torment them. The body meanwhile did not waste away so long as the distemper was at its height, but held out to a marvel against its ravages; so that when they succumbed, as in most cases, on the seventh or eighth day to the internal inflammation, they had still some strength in them. But if they passed this stage, and the disease descended further into the bowels, inducing a violent ulceration there accompanied by severe diarrhoea, this brought on a weakness which was generally fatal. For the disorder first settled in the head, ran its course from thence through the whole of the body, and even where it did not prove mortal, it still left its mark on the extremities; for it settled in the privy parts, the fingers and the toes, and many escaped with the loss of these, some too with that of their eyes. Others again were seized with an entire loss of memory on their first recovery, and did not know either themselves or their friends.

But while the nature of the distemper was such as to baffle all description, and its attacks almost too grievous for human nature to endure, it was still in the following circumstance that its difference from all ordinary disorders was most clearly shown. All the birds and beasts that prey upon human bodies, either abstained from touching them (though there were many lying unburied), or died after tasting them. In proof of this, it was noticed that birds of this kind actually disappeared; they were not about the bodies, or indeed to be seen at all. But of course the effects which I have mentioned could best be studied in a domestic animal like the dog.

Such then, if we pass over the varieties of particular cases, which were many and peculiar, were the general features of the distemper. Meanwhile the town enjoyed an immunity from all the ordinary disorders; or if any case occurred, it ended in this. Some died in neglect, others in the midst of every attention. No remedy was found that could be used as a specific; for what did good in one case, did harm in another. Strong and weak constitutions proved equally incapable of resistance, all alike being swept away, although dieted with the utmost precaution. By far the most terrible feature in the malady was the dejection which ensued when any one felt himself sickening, for the despair into which they instantly fell took away their power of resistance, and left them a much easier prey to the disorder; besides which, there was the awful spectacle of men dying like sheep, through having caught the infection in nursing each other. This caused the greatest mortality. On the one hand, if they were afraid to visit each other, they perished from neglect; indeed many houses were emptied of their inmates for want of a nurse: on the other, if they ventured to do so, death was the consequence. This was especially the case with such as made any pretensions to goodness: honour made them unsparing of themselves in their attendance in their friends' houses, where even the members of the family were at last worn out by the moans of the dying, and succumbed to the force of the disaster. Yet it was with those who had recovered from the disease that the sick and the dying found most compassion. These knew what it was from experience, and had now no fear for themselves; for the same man was never attacked twice—never at least fatally. And such persons not only received the congratulations of others, but themselves also, in the elation of the moment, half entertained the vain hope that they were for the future safe from any disease whatsoever.

An aggravation of the existing calamity was the influx from the country into the city, and this was especially felt by the new arrivals. As there were no houses to receive them, they had to be lodged at the hot season of the year in stifling cabins, where the mortality raged without restraint. The bodies of dying men lay one upon another, and half-dead creatures reeled about the streets and gathered round all the fountains in their longing for water. The sacred places also in which they had quartered themselves were full of corpses of persons that had died there, just as they were; for as the disaster passed all bounds, men, not knowing what was to become of them, became utterly careless of everything, whether sacred or profane. All the burial rites before in use were entirely upset, and they buried the bodies as best they could. Many from want of the proper appliances, through so many of their friends having died already, had recourse to the most shameless sepultures: sometimes getting the start of those who had raised a pile, they threw their own dead body upon the stranger's pyre and ignited it; sometimes they tossed the corpse which they were carrying on the top of another that was burning, and so went off.

Nor was this the only form of lawless extravagance which owed its origin to the plague. Men now coolly ventured on what they had formerly done in a corner and not just as they pleased, seeing the rapid transitions produced by persons in prosperity suddenly dying and those who before had nothing succeeding to their property. So they resolved to spend quickly and enjoy themselves, regarding their lives and riches as alike things of a day. Perseverance in what men called honour was popular with none, it was so uncertain whether they would be spared to attain the object; but it was settled that present enjoyment, and all that contributed to it, was both honourable and useful. Fear of gods or law of man there was none to restrain them. As for the first, they judged it to be just the same whether they worshipped them or not, as they saw all alike perishing; and for the last, no one expected to live to be brought to trial for his offences, but each felt that a far severer sentence had been already passed upon them all and hung ever over their heads, and before this fell it was only reasonable to enjoy life a little.

# THE NATURE OF MAN

NO ONE who has occasion to discuss the ancient Greeks ever fails to take note of their "discovery of man." The intense preoccupation of the Greeks with man—his nature, his destiny, his virtues and his defects, his relation to the world, to his fellow man, and to himself—is perhaps the most Greek of all the characteristics we are taught to think of as especially Greek. The Greek's fascination with his own species is most familiarly and convincingly observed in Greek art, where the depiction of the human form is the chief subject-matter. It is found also in every facet of Greek life and thought. The Greeks have been praised to the skies for their anticipation of the formula that the "proper study of mankind is man." And they have been as fiercely condemned. They have been condemned often—most recently by Arnold J. Toynbee in *Hellenism* (1959)—for an infatuation that cost them a true perspective on a world in which man is not in any sense a measure, for a vainglorious adventure that turned them away from reverence for God and turned them toward a blasphemous idolizing of man. As the readings on other elements of Greek history and civilization suggest, the most immediately striking aspect of the Greek interest in man is the sheer variety of treatment and approach. The passages in this section have been chosen from almost innumerable possible selections to illustrate the Greek interest in the nature of man and in the quality of human experience.

# *79 What Is Happiness?*

An awareness of the ephemeral nature of human life with its triumphs and its failures is a part of the tragic concept that can be found as far back as Homer with his observation that:

> As is the generation of leaves, so is that of humanity.
> The wind scatters the leaves on the ground, but the live timber

Burgeons with leaves again in the season of spring returning.
So one generation of men will grow while another dies. . . .*

In the light of this view the series of anecdotes with which Herodotus presents his definition of happiness is especially revealing. The translation is by George Rawlinson of Herodotus 1.29–33.

❀❀❀❀❀

When all these conquests had been added to the Lydian empire, and the prosperity of Sardis was now at its height, there came thither, one after another, all the sages of Greece living at the time, and among them Solon, the Athenian. He was on his travels, having left Athens to be absent ten years, under the pretence of wishing to see the world, but really to avoid being forced to repeal any of the laws which, at the request of the Athenians, he had made for them. Without his sanction the Athenians could not repeal them, as they had bound themselves under a heavy curse to be governed for ten years by the laws which should be imposed on them by Solon.[1]

On this account, as well as to see the world, Solon set out upon his travels, in the course of which he went to Egypt to the court of Amasis, and also came on a visit to Croesus at Sardis. Croesus received him as his guest, and lodged him in the royal palace. On the third or fourth day after, he bade his servants conduct Solon over his treasuries, and show him all their greatness and magnificence. When he had seen them all, and, so far as time allowed, inspected them, Croesus addressed this question to him, "Stranger of Athens, we have heard much of your wisdom and of your travels through many lands, from love of knowledge and a wish to see the world. I am curious therefore to inquire of you, whom, of all the men that you have seen, you consider the most happy?" This he asked because he thought himself the happiest of mortals: but Solon answered him without flattery, according to his true sentiments, "Tellus of Athens, sire." Full of astonishment at what he heard, Croesus demanded sharply, "And wherefore do you deem Tellus happiest?" To which the other replied, "First, because his country was flourishing in his days, and he himself had sons both beautiful and good, and he lived to see children born to each of them, and these children all grew up; and further because,

---

* Reprinted from *The Iliad of Homer* (6. 146–150) tr. Richmond Lattimore by permission of The University of Chicago Press. Copyright 1951 by The University of Chicago.

1.   See Selection 45.

after a life spent in what our people look upon as comfort, his end was surpassingly glorious. In a battle between the Athenians and their neighbours near Eleusis, he came to the assistance of his countrymen, routed the foe, and died upon the field most gallantly. The Athenians gave him a public funeral on the spot where he fell, and paid him the highest honours."

Thus did Solon admonish Croesus by the example of Tellus, enumerating the manifold particulars of his happiness. When he had ended, Croesus inquired a second time, who after Tellus seemed to him the happiest, expecting that, at any rate, he would be given the second place. "Cleobis and Bito," Solon answered, "they were of Argive race: their fortune was enough for their wants, and they were besides endowed with so much bodily strength that they had both gained prizes at the Games. Also this tale is told of them: There was a great festival in honour of the goddess Hera at Argos, to which their mother must needs be taken in a car. Now the oxen did not come home from the field in time: so the youths, fearful of being too late, put the yoke on their own necks, and themselves drew the car in which their mother rode. Five miles they drew her, and stopped before the temple. This deed of theirs was witnessed by the whole assembly of worshippers, and then their life closed in the best possible way. Herein, too, God showed forth most evidently, how much better a thing for man death is than life. For the Argive men stood thick around the car and extolled the vast strength of the youths; and the Argive women extolled the mother who was blessed with such a pair of sons; and the mother herself, overjoyed at the deed and at the praises it had won, standing straight before the image, besought the goddess to bestow on Cleobis and Bito, the sons who had so mightily honoured her, the highest blessing to which mortals can attain. Her prayer ended, they offered sacrifice, and partook of the holy banquet, after which the two youths fell asleep in the temple. They never woke more, but so passed from the earth. The Argives, looking on them as among the best of men, caused statues of them to be made, which they gave to the shrine at Delphi."

When Solon had thus assigned these youths the second place, Croesus broke in angrily, "What, stranger of Athens, is my happiness, then, valued so little by you, that you do not even put me on a level with private men?"

"Croesus," replied the other, "you asked a question concerning the condition of man, of one who knows that the power above us is full of jealousy, and fond of troubling our lot. A long life gives one to witness much, and experience much oneself, that one would not choose. Seventy years I regard as the limit of the life of man. In these seventy years are contained, without reckoning intercalary months, 25,200 days. Add an intercalary month to every other year, that the seasons may come round at the right time, and there will be, besides the seventy years, thirty-five such months, making an addition of 1,050 days. The whole number of the days contained in the seventy years will thus be 26,250, whereof not one but will produce events unlike the rest. Hence man is wholly accident. For yourself, Croesus, I see that you are wonderfully rich, and the lord of many nations; but with respect to your question, I have no answer to give, until I hear that you have closed your life happily. For assuredly he who possesses great store of riches is no nearer happiness than he who has what suffices for his daily needs, unless luck attend upon him, and so he continue in the enjoyment of all his good things to the end of life. For many of the wealthiest men have been unfavoured of fortune, and many whose means were moderate, have had excellent luck. Men of the former class excel those of the latter but in two respects; these last excel the former in many. The wealthy man is better able to content his desires, and to bear up against a sudden buffet of calamity. The other has less ability to withstand these evils (from which, however, his good luck keeps him clear), but he enjoys all these following blessings: he is whole of limb, a stranger to disease, free from misfortune, happy in his children, and comely to look upon. If, in addition to all this, he end his life well, he is of a truth the man of whom you are in search, the man who may rightly be termed happy. Call him, however, until he die, not happy but fortunate. Scarcely, indeed, can any man unite all these advantages: as there is no country which contains within it all that it needs, but each, while it possesses some things, lacks others, and the best country is that which contains the most; so no single human being is complete in every respect—something is always lacking. He who unites the greatest number of advantages, and retaining them to the day of his death, then dies peaceably, that man alone, sire, is, in my judgment, entitled to bear the name of 'happy.' But in every matter we must mark well the end; for oftentimes God gives men a gleam of happiness, and then plunges them into ruin."

Such was the speech which Solon addressed to Croesus, a speech which brought him neither largess nor honour. The king saw him depart with much indifference, since he thought that a man must be an arrant fool who made no account of present good, but bade men always wait and mark the end.

# 80 Individual, Family, and State in an Ideal World

In Athens in the fourth century B.C. there lived, wrote, and taught two of the most celebrated thinkers of all time, Plato (c. 429–347 B.C.) and Aristotle (384–322 B.C.). For some twenty years Aristotle studied at Plato's school, the Academy. He left after Plato's death and taught and worked in other places, including a stint from 343 to 340 at Philip of Macedon's court as private tutor to the young Alexander. In 335 he returned to Athens to establish his own school, the Lyceum.

Both Plato and Aristotle are represented by a large quantity of extant writings. The works of Plato are polished literary pieces, almost all of them cast in the form of dialogues in which the principal speaker, Socrates, leads his interlocutors by question and answer through an exposition of his views on a stated subject. The works of Aristotle have come down to us in the form of summaries and extensive notes of the lectures he delivered to his students. Both philosophers dealt with a vast range of subject-matter. One of the topics in the surviving works of both is concerned with these questions: What would constitute the ideal or perfect state? What sort of people would live in it? How would they be educated? Plato's inquiry is contained in a very long dialogue known to us as *The Republic;* Aristotle's is in part found in a major work known as *The Politics.* The first of the two selections that follow consists of excerpts from Aristotle's *Politics* (1252b28–1253a39, 1332a39–1332b11, 1334b7–1336b23, 1337a3–33). The second selection is abridged from Book V of Plato's *Republic.* Both are translated by the nineteenth-century English classical scholar Benjamin Jowett.

⚜⚜⚜⚜⚜

When several villages are united in a single complete community, large enough to be nearly or quite self-sufficing, the State comes into existence, originating in the bare needs of life, and continuing in existence for the sake of a good life. And therefore, if the earlier forms of society are natural, so is the State, for it is the end of them, and the nature of a thing is its end. For what each thing is when fully developed, we call its nature,

[ 678 ]

whether we are speaking of a man, a horse, or a family. Besides, the final cause and end of a thing is the best, and to be self-sufficing is the end and the best.

Hence it is evident that the State is a creation of nature, and that man is by nature a political animal. And he who by nature and not by mere accident is without a State, is either a bad man or above humanity; he is like the

## Tribeless, lawless, hearthless one

whom Homer denounces—the natural outcast is forthwith a lover of war; he may be compared to an isolated piece at draughts.

Now, that man is more of a political animal than bees or any other gregarious animals is evident. Nature, as we often say, makes nothing in vain, and man is the only animal whom she has endowed with the gift of speech. And whereas mere voice is but an indication of pleasure or pain, and is therefore found in other animals (for their nature attains to the perception of pleasure and pain and the intimation of them to one another, and no further), the power of speech is intended to set forth the expedient and inexpedient, and therefore likewise the just and the unjust. And it is a characteristic of man that he alone has any sense of good and evil, of just and unjust, and the like, and the association of living beings who have this sense makes a family and a State.

Further, the State is by nature clearly prior to the family and to the individual, since the whole is of necessity prior to the part; for example, if the whole body be destroyed, there will be no foot or hand, except in an equivocal sense, as we might speak of a stone hand; for when destroyed the hand will be no better than that. But things are defined by their working and power; and we ought not to say that they are the same when they no longer have their proper quality, but only that they have the same name. The proof that the State is a creation of nature and prior to the individual is that the individual, when isolated, is not self-sufficing; and therefore he is like a part in relation to the whole. But he who is unable to live in society, or who has no need because he is sufficient for himself, must be either a beast or a god: he is no part of a State. A social instinct is implanted in all men by nature, and yet he who first founded the State was the greatest of benefactors. For man, when perfected, is the best of animals, but, when separated from law and justice, he is the worst of all; since armed injustice is the more dangerous, and he is equipped at birth with arms, meant to be used by intelligence and virtue, which he may use for the worst ends. Wherefore, if he have not virtue, he is the most unholy and the most savage of animals, and the most full of lust and gluttony. But justice is the bond of men in States, for the administration of justice, which is the determination of what is just, is the principle of order in political society. . . .

There are three things which make men good and virtuous; these are nature, habit, rational principle. In the first place, every one must be born a man and not some other animal; so, too, he must have a certain character, both of body and soul. But some qualities there is no use in having at birth, for they are altered by habit, and there are some gifts which by nature are made to be turned by habit to good or bad. Animals lead for the most part a life of nature, although in lesser particulars some are influenced by habit as well. Man has rational principle, in addition, and man only. Wherefore nature, habit, rational principle must be in harmony with one another; for they do not always agree; men do many things against habit and nature, if rational principle persuades them that they ought. We have already determined what natures are likely to be most easily moulded by the hands of the legislator. All else is the work of education; we learn some things by habit and some by instruction. . . .

We have already determined that nature and habit and rational principle are required, and, of these, the proper *nature* of the citizens has also been defined by us. But we have still to consider whether the training of early life is to be that of rational principle or habit, for these two must accord, and when in accord they will then form the best of harmonies. The rational principle may be mistaken and fail in attaining the highest ideal of life, and there may be a like evil influence of habit. Thus much is clear in the first place, that, as in all other things, birth implies an antecedent beginning,[1] and that there are beginnings whose end is relative to a further end. Now, in men rational principle and mind are the end towards which nature strives, so that the birth and moral discipline of the citizens ought to be ordered with a view to them. In the second place, as the soul and body are two, we see also that there are two parts of the soul, the rational and the irrational, and two corresponding states—reason and appetite. And as the body is prior in order of generation to the soul, so the irrational is prior to the rational. The proof is that anger and wishing and desire are implanted in children from their very birth, but reason and understanding are developed as they grow older. Wherefore, the care of the body ought to precede that of the soul, and the training of the

1.   That is, the union of the parents.

appetitive part should follow: none the less our care of it must be for the sake of the reason, and our care of the body for the sake of the soul.

Since the legislator should begin by considering how the frames of the children whom he is rearing may be as good as possible, his first care will be about marriage—at what age should his citizens marry, and who are fit to marry? In legislating on this subject he ought to consider the persons and the length of their life, that their procreative life may terminate at the same period, and that they may not differ in their bodily powers, as will be the case if the man is still able to beget children while the woman is unable to bear them, or the woman able to bear while the man is unable to beget, for from these causes arise quarrels and differences between married persons. Secondly, he must consider the time at which the children will succeed to their parents; there ought not to be too great an interval of age, for then the parents will be too old to derive any pleasure from their affection, or to be of any use to them. Nor ought they to be too nearly of an age; to youthful marriages there are many objections—the children will be wanting in respect to the parents, who will seem to be their contemporaries, and disputes will arise in the management of the household. Thirdly, and this is the point from which we digressed, the legislator must mould to his will the frames of newly-born children. Almost all these objects may be secured by attention to one point. Since the time of generation is commonly limited within the age of seventy years in the case of a man, and of fifty in the case of a woman, the commencement of the union should conform to these periods. The union of male and female when too young is bad for the procreation of children; in all other animals the offspring of the young are small and ill-developed, and with a tendency to produce female children, and therefore also in man, as is proved by the fact that in those cities in which men and women are accustomed to marry young, the people are small and weak; in childbirth also younger women suffer more, and more of them die; some persons say that this was the meaning of the response once given to the Troezenians—the oracle really meant that many died because they married too young; it had nothing to do with the ingathering of the harvest.[2] It also conduces to temperance not to marry too soon; for women who marry early are apt to be wanton; and in men too the bodily frame is stunted if they marry while the seed is growing (for there is a time when the growth of the seed, also, ceases, or continues to but a slight extent). Women should marry when they are about eighteen years of age, and

2.  The oracular advice was: "Plough not the young field."

men at seven and thirty; then they are in the prime of life, and the decline in the powers of both will coincide. Further, the children, if their birth takes place soon, as may reasonably be expected, will succeed in the beginning of their prime, when the fathers are already in the decline of life, and have nearly reached their term of three-score years and ten.

Thus much of the age proper for marriage: the season of the year should also be considered; according to our present custom, people generally limit marriage to the season of winter, and they are right. The precepts of physicians and natural philosophers about generation should also be studied by the parents themselves; the physicians give good advice about the favourable conditions of the body, and the natural philosophers about the winds; of which they prefer the north to the south.

What constitution in the parent is most advantageous to the offspring is a subject which we will consider more carefully when we speak of the education of children, and we will only make a few general remarks at present. The constitution of an athlete is not suited to the life of a citizen, or to health, or to the procreation of children, any more than the valetudinarian or exhausted constitution, but one which is in a mean between them. A man's constitution should be inured to labor, but not to labor which is excessive or of one sort only, such as is practised by athletes; he should be capable of all the actions of a freeman. These remarks apply equally to both parents.

Women who are with child should be careful of themselves; they should take exercise and have a nourishing diet. The first of these prescriptions the legislator will easily carry into effect by requiring that they shall take a walk daily to some temple, where they can worship the gods who preside over birth. Their minds, however, unlike their bodies, they ought to keep quiet, for the offspring derive their natures from their mothers as plants do from the earth.

As to the exposure and rearing of children, let there be a law that no *deformed* child shall live, but that on the ground of an *excess* in the number of children, if the established customs of the State forbid this (for in our State population has a limit), no child is to be exposed, but when couples have children in excess, let abortion be procured before sense and life have begun; what may or may not be lawfully done in these cases depends on the question of life and sensation.

And now, having determined at what ages men and women are to begin their union, let us also determine how long they shall continue to beget and bear offspring for the State; men who are too old, like men who are too young, produce children who are defective in body and mind; the children of very old men are weakly. The limit, then, should be the age which is the prime of their intelligence, and this in most persons, according to the notion of some poets who measure life by periods of seven years, is about fifty; at four or five years later, they should cease from having families; and from that time forward only cohabit with one another for the sake of health; or for some similar reason.

As to adultery, let it be held disgraceful, in general, for any man or woman to be found in any way unfaithful when they are married, and called husband and wife. If during the time of bearing children anything of the sort occur, let the guilty person be punished with a loss of privileges in proportion to the offence.

After the children have been born, the manner of rearing them may be supposed to have a great effect on their bodily strength. It would appear from the example of animals, and of those nations who desire to create the military habit, that the food which has most milk in it is best suited to human beings; but the less wine the better, if they would escape diseases. Also all the motions to which children can be subjected at their early age are very useful. But in order to preserve their tender limbs from distortion, some nations have had recourse to mechanical appliances which straighten their bodies. To accustom children to the cold from their earliest years is also an excellent practice, which greatly conduces to health, and hardens them for military service. Hence many barbarians have a custom of plunging their children at birth into a cold stream; others, like the Celts, clothe them in a light wrapper only. For human nature should be early habituated to endure all which by habit it can be made to endure; but the process must be gradual. And children, from their natural warmth, may be easily trained to bear cold. Such care should attend them in the first stage of life.

The next period lasts to the age of five; during this no demand should be made upon the child for study or labor, lest its growth be impeded; and there should be sufficient motion to prevent the limbs from being inactive. This can be secured, among other ways, by amusement, but the amusement should not be vulgar or tiring or effeminate. The Directors of Education, as they are termed, should be careful what tales or stories the children hear, for all such things are designed to prepare the way for the business of later life, and should be for the most part imitations of the occupations which they will hereafter pursue in earnest. Those are wrong who in their laws attempt to check the loud crying and screaming of children, for these contribute towards their growth, and, in a manner, exercise their bodies. Straining the voice has a strengthening effect similar to that produced by the retention of the breath in violent exertions. The Directors of Education should have an eye to their bringing up, and in particular should take care that they are left as little as possible with slaves. For until they are seven years old they must live at home; and therefore, even at this early age, it is to be expected that they should acquire a taint of meanness from what they hear and see. Indeed, there is nothing which the legislator should be more careful to drive away than indecency of speech; for the light utterance of shameful words leads soon to shameful actions. The young especially should never be allowed to repeat or hear anything of the sort. A freeman who is found saying or doing what is forbidden, if he be too young as yet to have the privilege of reclining at the public tables, should be disgraced and beaten, and an elder person degraded as his slavish conduct deserves. And since we do not allow improper language, clearly we should also banish pictures or speeches from the stage which are indecent. Let the rulers take care that there be no image or picture representing unseemly actions, except in the temples of those Gods at whose festivals the law permits even ribaldry, and whom the law also permits to be worshipped by persons of mature age on behalf of themselves, their children, and their wives. But the legislator should not allow youth to be spectators of iambi or of comedy until they are of an age to sit at the public tables and to drink strong wine; by that time education will have armed them against the evil influences of such representations. . . .

Let us then first inquire if any regulations are to be laid down about children, and secondly, whether the care of them should be the concern of the State or of private individuals, which latter is in our own day the common custom, and in the third place, what these regulations should be.

No one will doubt that the legislator should direct his attention above all to the education of youth; for the neglect of education does harm to the constitution. The citizen should be moulded to suit the form of government under which he lives. For each government has a peculiar character which originally formed and which continues to preserve it. The character of democracy creates democracy, and the character of oligarchy creates oligarchy; and always the better the character, the better the government.

Again, for the exercise of any faculty or art a previous training and habituation are required; clearly therefore for the practice of virtue. And since the whole city has one end, it is manifest that education should be one and the same for all, and that it should be public, and not private —not as at present, when every one looks after his own children separately, and gives them separate instruction of the sort which he thinks best; the training in things which are of common interest should be the same for all. Neither must we suppose that any one of the citizens belongs to himself, for they all belong to the State, and are each of them a part of the State, and the care of each part is inseparable from the care of the whole. In this particular as in some others the Lacedaemonians are to be praised, for they take the greatest pains about their children, and make education the business of the State.

. . . . .

[*Socrates is the principal speaker. He is here represented as recounting a dialogue that occurred previously, and is identified frequently with the phrase, "I said."*]

Here, then, is one difficulty in our law about women, which we may say that we have now escaped; the wave has not swallowed us up alive for enacting that the guardians[3] of either sex should have all their pursuits in common; to the utility and also to the possibility of this arrangement the consistency of the argument with itself bears witness.

Yes, that was a mighty wave which you have escaped.

Yes, I said, but a greater is coming; you will not think much of this when you see the next.

Go on; let me see.

The law, I said, which is the sequel of this and of all that has preceded, is to the following effect—"that the wives of our guardians are to be common, and their children are to be common, and no parent is to know his own child, nor any child his parent."

Yes, he said, that is a much greater wave than the other; and the possibility as well as the utility of such a law are far more questionable.

I do not think, I said, that there can be any dispute about the very great utility of having wives and children in common; the possibility is quite another matter, and will be very much disputed. . . .

Now I myself am beginning to lose heart, and I should like, with your permission, to pass over the question of possibility at present. Assuming therefore the possibility of the proposal, I shall now proceed to inquire how the rulers will carry out these arrangements, and I shall demonstrate

3. The "guardians" are the warrior class in Plato's Ideal State.

that our plan, if executed, will be of the greatest benefit to the State and to the guardians. First of all, then, if you have no objection, I will endeavor with your help to consider the advantages of the measure; and hereafter the question of possibility.

I have no objection; proceed.

First, I think that if our rulers and their auxiliaries are to be worthy of the name which they bear, there must be willingness to obey in the one and the power of command in the other; the guardians must themselves obey the laws, and they must also imitate the spirit of them in any details which are entrusted to their care.

That is right, he said.

You, I said, who are their legislator, having selected the men, will now select the women and give them to them;—they must be as far as possible of like natures with them; and they must live in common houses and meet at common meals. None of them will have anything specially his or her own; they will be together, and will be brought up together, and will associate at gymnastic exercises. And so they will be drawn by a necessity of their natures to have intercourse with each other—necessity is not too strong a word, I think?

Yes, he said; necessity, not geometrical, but another sort of necessity which lovers know, and which is far more convincing and constraining to the mass of mankind.

True, I said; and this, Glaucon, like all the rest, must proceed after an orderly fashion; in a city of the blessed, licentiousness is an unholy thing which the rulers will forbid.

Yes, he said, and it ought not to be permitted.

Then clearly the next thing will be to make matrimony sacred in the highest degree, and what is most beneficial will be deemed sacred?

Exactly.

And how can marriages be made most beneficial? That is a question which I put to you, because I see in your house dogs for hunting, and of the nobler sort of birds not a few. Now, I beseech you, do tell me, have you ever attended to their pairing and breeding?

In what particulars?

Why, in the first place, although they are all of a good sort, are not some better than others?

True.

And do you breed from them all indifferently, or do you take care to breed from the best only?

From the best.

And do you take the oldest or the youngest, or only those of ripe age? I choose only those of ripe age.

And if care was not taken in the breeding, your dogs and birds would greatly deteriorate?

Certainly.

And the same of horses and animals in general?

Undoubtedly.

Good heavens! my dear friend, I said, what consummate skill will our rulers need if the same principle holds of the human species!

Certainly, the same principle holds; but why does this involve any particular skill?

Because, I said, our rulers will often have to practise upon the body corporate with medicines. Now you know that when patients do not require medicines, but have only to be put under a regimen, the inferior sort of practitioner is deemed to be good enough; but when medicine has to be given, then the doctor should be more of a man.

That is quite true, he said; but to what are you alluding?

I mean, I replied, that our rulers will find a considerable dose of falsehood and deceit necessary for the good of their subjects: we were saying that the use of all these things regarded as medicines might be of advantage.

And we were very right.

And this lawful use of them seems likely to be often needed in the regulations of marriages and births.

How so?

Why, I said, the principle has been already laid down that the best of either sex should be united with the best as often, and the inferior with the inferior, as seldom as possible; and that they should rear the offspring of the one sort of union, but not of the other, if the flock is to be maintained in first-rate condition. Now these goings on must be a secret which the rulers only know, or there will be a further danger of our herd, as the guardians may be termed, breaking out into rebellion.

Very true.

Had we not better appoint certain festivals at which we will bring together the brides and bridegrooms, and sacrifices will be offered and suitable hymeneal songs composed by our poets: the number of weddings is a matter which must be left to the discretion of the rulers, whose aim will be to preserve the average of population? There are many other things which they will have to consider, such as the effects of wars and diseases and any similar agencies, in order as far as this is possible to prevent the State from becoming either too large or too small.

Certainly, he replied.

We shall have to invent some ingenious kind of lots which the less worthy may draw on each occasion of our bringing them together, and then they will accuse their own ill-luck and not the rulers.

To be sure, he said.

And I think that our braver and better youth, besides their other honors and rewards, might have greater facilities of intercourse with women given them; their bravery will be a reason, and such fathers ought to have as many sons as possible.

True.

And the proper officers, whether male or female or both, for offices are to be held by women as well as by men—

Yes—

The proper officers will take the offspring of the good parents to the pen or fold, and there they will deposit them with certain nurses who dwell in a separate quarter; but the offspring of the inferior, or of the better when they chance to be deformed, will be put away in some mysterious, unknown place, as they should be.

Yes, he said, that must be done if the breed of the guardians is to be kept pure.

They will provide for their nurture, and will bring the mothers to the fold when they are full of milk, taking the greatest possible care that no mother recognizes her own child; and other wet-nurses may be engaged if more are required. Care will also be taken that the process of suckling shall not be protracted too long; and the mothers will have no getting up at night or other trouble, but will hand over all this sort of thing to the nurses and attendants.

You suppose the wives of our guardians to have a fine easy time of it when they are having children.

Why, said I, and so they ought. Let us, however, proceed with our scheme. We were saying that the parents should be in the prime of life?

Very true.

And what is the prime of life? May it not be defined as a period of about twenty years in a woman's life, and thirty in a man's?

Which years do you mean to include?

A woman, I said, at twenty years of age may begin to bear children to the State, and continue to bear them until forty; a man may begin at five-

and twenty, when he has passed the point at which the pulse of life beats quickest, and continue to beget children until he be fifty-five.

Certainly, he said, both in men and women those years are the prime of physical as well as of intellectual vigor.

Any one above or below the prescribed ages who takes part in the public hymeneals shall be said to have done an unholy and unrighteous thing; the child of which he is the father, if it steals into life, will have been conceived under auspices very unlike the sacrifices and prayers, which at each hymeneal priestesses and priests and the whole city will offer, that the new generation may be better and more useful than their good and useful parents, whereas his child will be the offspring of darkness and strange lust.

Very true, he replied.

And the same law will apply to any one of those within the prescribed age who forms a connection with any woman in the prime of life without the sanction of the rulers; for we shall say that he is raising up a bastard to the State, uncertified and unconsecrated.

Very true, he replied.

This applies, however, only to those who are within the specified age: after that we allow them to range at will, except that a man may not marry his daughter or his daughter's daughter, or his mother or his mother's mother; and women, on the other hand, are prohibited from marrying their sons or fathers, or son's son or father's father, and so on in either direction. And we grant all this, accompanying the permission with strict orders to prevent any embryo which may come into being from seeing the light; and if any force a way to the birth, the parents must understand that the offspring of such an union can not be maintained, and arrange accordingly.

That also, he said, is a reasonable proposition. But how will they know who are fathers and daughters, and so on?

They will never know. The way will be this: dating from the day of the hymeneal, the bridegroom who was then married will call all the male children who are born in the seventh and the tenth month afterwards his sons, and the female children his daughters, and they will call him father, and he will call their children his grandchildren, and they will call the elder generation grandfathers and grandmothers. All who were begotten at the time when their fathers and mothers came together will be called their brothers and sisters, and these, as I was saying, will be forbidden to intermarry. This, however, is not to be understood as an absolute prohibition of the marriage of brothers and sisters; if the lot favors them, and they receive the sanction of the Pythian oracle, the law will allow them.

Quite right, he replied.

Such is the scheme, Glaucon, according to which the guardians of our State are to have their wives and families in common. . . .

The inquiry, I said, has yet to be made, whether such a community will be found possible—as among other animals, so also among men—and if possible, in what way possible? . . .

Let me begin by reminding you that we found our way hither in the search after justice and injustice.

True, he replied; but what of that?

I was only going to ask whether, if we have discovered them, we are to require that the just man should in nothing fail of absolute justice; or may we be satisfied with an approximation, and the attainment in him of a higher degree of justice than is to be found in other men?

The approximation will be enough.

We were inquiring into the nature of absolute justice and into the character of the perfectly just, and into injustice and the perfectly unjust, that we might have an ideal. We were to look at these in order that we might judge of our own happiness and unhappiness according to the standard which they exhibited and the degree in which we resembled them, but not with any view of showing that they could exist in fact.

True, he said.

Would a painter be any the worse because, after having delineated with consummate art an ideal of a perfectly beautiful man, he was unable to show that any such man could ever have existed?

He would be none the worse.

Well, and were we not creating an ideal of a perfect State?

To be sure.

And is our theory a worse theory because we are unable to prove the possibility of a city being ordered in the manner described?

Surely not, he replied.

That is the truth, I said. But if, at your request, I am to try and show how and under what conditions the possibility is highest, I must ask you, having this in view, to repeat your former admissions.

What admissions?

I want to know whether ideals are ever fully realized in language? Does not the word express more than the fact, and must not the actual, whatever a man may think, always, in the nature of things, fall short of the truth?

What do you say?

I agree.

Then you must not insist on my proving that the actual State will in every respect coincide with the ideal: if we are only able to discover how a city may be governed nearly as we proposed, you will admit that we have discovered the possibility which you demand; and will be contented. I am sure that I should be contented—will not you?

Yes, I will.

Let me next endeavor to show what is that fault in States which is the cause of their present maladministration, and what is the least change which will enable a State to pass into the truer form; and let the change, if possible, be of one thing only, or, if not, of two; at any rate, let the changes be as few and slight as possible.

Certainly, he replied.

I think, I said, that there might be a reform of the State if only one change were made, which is not a slight or easy though still a possible one.

What is it? he said.

Now then, I said, I go to meet that which I liken to the greatest of the waves; yet shall the word be spoken, even though the wave break and drown me in laughter and dishonor; and do you mark my words.

Proceed.

I said: *Until philosophers are kings, or the kings and princes of this world have the spirit and power of philosophy, and political greatness and wisdom meet in one, and those commoner natures who pursue either to the exclusion of the other are compelled to stand aside, cities will never have rest from their evils—no, nor the human race, as I believe—and then only will this our State have a possibility of life and behold the light of day.*

# 81 *The Best Man in This World*

The Socrates whom Plato made the spokesman of his thought was in life an Athenian, a stonecutter by trade, who gave up his craft to spend his life in philosophical inquiry. His method appears actually to have been the dialetic (question-and-answer) form in which Plato cast his own writings. Socrates left nothing in writing himself and is know to us only from the works of two of his followers, Plato and the energetic Xenophon, among whose varied writings are found some which contain information about the historical Socrates.

In 399 B.C. Socrates, at the age of seventy, was brought to trial at Athens, condemned, and executed by the public executioner. The charges were "corruption of the youth" and "belief in gods other than those of the State," but the trial was not without political implications (see the introduction to Selection 58). The trial and death of Socrates left an indelible mark in the mind of Plato, who was about thirty years old at the time and who saw in the death of his revered teacher the vicious and ungrateful nature of his fellow citizens. The following selections are taken from a group of Platonic works that deal with the trial and death of Socrates. These works are thought to mirror something of the historical actuality of Socrates' last days, even though they cannot be taken as historical reporting but must be looked upon as literary art created by Plato from the raw material of the actual events. The first selection is the *Apology* (slightly abridged), the speech that Socrates made in his defense at the trial. The second is from the *Phaedo,* in which the last hours of Socrates' life are described. The passage presented here consists of the final pages, recounting Socrates' death in his prison cell while surrounded by his intimate friends. The translations are by Benjamin Jowett.

⊛⊛⊛⊛⊛

How you, O Athenians, have been affected by my accusers, I cannot tell; but I know that they almost made me forget who I was—so persuasively did they speak; and yet they have hardly uttered a word of truth. But of the many falsehoods told by them, there was one which quite amazed me— I mean when they said that you should be upon your guard and not allow yourselves to be deceived by the force of my eloquence. To say this, when they were certain to be detected as soon as I opened my lips and proved myself to be anything but a great speaker, did indeed appear to me most shameless—unless by the force of eloquence they mean the force of truth; for if such is their meaning, I admit that I am eloquent. But in how different a way from theirs! Well, as I was saying, they have scarcely spoken the truth at all; but from me you shall hear the whole truth: not, however, delivered after their manner in a set oration duly ornamented with words and phrases. No, by heaven! but I shall use the words and arguments which occur to me at the moment; for I am confident in the justice of my cause: at my time of life I ought not to be appearing before you, O men of Athens, in the character of a juvenile orator—let no one expect it of me. And I must beg of you to grant me a favour: If I defend myself in my accustomed manner, and you hear me using the words which I have been in the habit of using in the agora, at the tables of the money-changers, or anywhere else, I would ask you not to be surprised, and not to interrupt me on this account. For I am more than seventy years of age, and appearing now for the first time in a court of law, I am quite a stranger to the language of the place; and therefore I would have you regard me as if I were really a stranger, whom you would excuse if he spoke in his native tongue, and after the fashion of his country: Am I making an unfair request of you? Never mind the manner, which may or may not be good; but think only of the truth of my words, and give heed to that: let the speaker speak truly and the judge decide justly.

And first, I have to reply to the older charges and to my first accusers, and then I will go on to the later ones. For of old I have had many accusers, who have accused me falsely to you during many years; and I am more afraid of them than of Anytus and his associates,[1] who are dangerous, too, in their own way. But far more dangerous are the others, who began when you were children, and took possession of your minds with their falsehoods, telling of one Socrates, a wise man, who speculated about the heaven above, and searched into the earth beneath, and made the worse appear the better cause. . . .

I dare say, Athenians, that some one among you will reply, "Yes, Socrates, but what is the origin of these accusations which are brought against you; there must have been something strange which you have been doing? All these rumours and this talk about you would never have arisen if you had been like other men: tell us, then, what is the cause of them, for we should be sorry to judge hastily of you." Now, I regard this as a fair challenge, and I will endeavour to explain to you the reason why I am called wise and have such an evil fame. Please to attend then. And although some of you may think that I am joking, I declare that I will tell you the entire truth. Men of Athens, this reputation of mine has come of a certain sort of wisdom which I possess. If you ask me what kind of wisdom, I reply, wisdom such as may perhaps be attained by man, for to that extent I am inclined to believe that I am wise; whereas the persons of whom I was speaking have a superhuman wisdom, which I may fail to describe, because I have it not myself; and he who says that I have, speaks falsely, and is taking

1.  The men who brought the charges on which Socrates is now on trial.

away my character. And here, O men of Athens, I must beg you not to interrupt me, even if I seem to say something extravagant. For the word which I will speak is not mine. I will refer you to a witness who is worthy of credit; that witness shall be the God of Delphi—he will tell you about my wisdom, if I have any, and of what sort it is. You must have known Chaerephon; he was early a friend of mine, and also a friend of yours, for he shared in the recent exile of the people, and returned with you. Well, Chaerephon, as you know, was very impetuous in all his doings, and he went to Delphi and boldly asked the oracle to tell him whether—as I was saying, I must beg you not to interrupt—he asked the oracle to tell him whether any one was wiser than I was, and the Pythian prophetess answered, that there was no man wiser. Chaerephon is dead himself; but his brother, who is in court, will confirm the truth of what I am saying.

Why do I mention this? Because I am going to explain to you why I have such an evil name. When I heard the answer, I said to myself, What can the God mean? and what is the interpretation of his riddle? for I know that I have no wisdom, small or great. What then can he mean when he says that I am the wisest of men? And yet he is a god, and cannot lie; that would be against his nature. After long consideration, I thought of a method of trying the question. I reflected that if I could only find a man wiser than myself, then I might go to the god with a refutation in my hand. I should say to him, "Here is a man who is wiser than I am; but you said that I was the wisest." Accordingly I went to one who had the reputation of wisdom, and observed him—his name I need not mention; he was a politician whom I selected for examination—and the result was as follows: When I began to talk with him, I could not help thinking that he was not really wise, although he was thought wise by many, and still wiser by himself; and thereupon I tried to explain to him that he thought himself wise, but was not really wise; and the consequence was that he hated me, and his enmity was shared by several who were present and heard me. So I left him, saying to myself, as I went away: Well, although I do not suppose that either of us knows anything really beautiful and good, I am better off than he is—for he knows nothing, and thinks that he knows; I neither know nor think that I know. In this latter particular, then, I seem to have slightly the advantage of him. Then I went to another who had still higher pretensions to wisdom, and my conclusion was exactly the same. Whereupon I made another enemy of him, and of many others besides him.

Then I went to one man after another, being not unconscious of the enmity which I provoked, and I lamented and feared this: but necessity was laid upon me—the word of God, I thought, ought to be considered first. And I said to myself, Go I must to all who appear to know, and find out the meaning of the oracle. And I swear to you, Athenians, by the dog I swear!—for I must tell you the truth—the result of my mission was just this: I found that the men most in repute were all but the most foolish; and that others less esteemed were really wiser and better. I will tell you the tale of my wanderings and of the "Herculean" labours, as I may call them, which I endured only to find at last the oracle irrefutable. After the politicians, I went to the poets; tragic, dithyrambic, and all sorts. And there, I said to myself, you will be instantly detected; now you will find out that you are more ignorant than they are. Accordingly I took them some of the most elaborate passages in their own writings, and asked what was the meaning of them—thinking that they would teach me something. Will you believe me? I am almost ashamed to confess the truth, but I must say that there is hardly a person present who would not have talked better about their poetry than they did themselves. Then I knew that not by wisdom do poets write poetry, but by a sort of genius and inspiration; they are like diviners or soothsayers who also say many fine things, but do not understand the meaning of them. The poets appeared to me to be much in the same case; and I further observed that upon the strength of their poetry they believed themselves to be the wisest of men in other things in which they were not wise. So I departed, conceiving myself to be superior to them for the same reason that I was superior to the politicians.

At last I went to the artisans, I was conscious that I knew nothing at all, as I may say, and I was sure that they knew many fine things; and here I was not mistaken, for they did know many things of which I was ignorant, and in this they certainly were wiser than I was. But I observed that even the good artisans fell into the same error as the poets—because they were good workmen they thought that they also knew all sorts of high matters, and this defect in them overshadowed their wisdom; and therefore I asked myself on behalf of the oracle, whether I would like to be as I was, neither having their knowledge nor their ignorance, or like them in both; and I made answer to myself and to the oracle that I was better off as I was.

This inquisition has led to my having many enemies of the worst and most dangerous kind, and has given occasion also to many calumnies. And I am called wise, for my hearers always imagine that I myself possess the wisdom which I find wanting in others: but the truth is, O men of

Athens, that God only is wise; and by his answer he intends to show
that the wisdom of men is worth little or nothing; he is not speaking of
Socrates, he is only using my name by way of illustration, as if he said,
He, O men, is the wisest, who, like Socrates, knows that his wisdom is
in truth worth nothing. And so I go about the world obedient to the god,
and search and make enquiry into the wisdom of any one, whether citizen
or stranger, who appears to be wise; and if he is not wise, then in vindi-
cation of the oracle I show him that he is not wise; and my occupation
quite absorbs me, and I have no time to give either to any public matter
of interest or to any concern of my own, but I am in utter poverty by
reason of my devotion to the god.

There is another thing: young men of the richer classes, who have not
much to do, come about me of their own accord; they like to hear the
pretenders examined, and they often imitate me, and proceed to examine
others; there are plenty of persons, as they quickly discover, who think
that they know something, but really know little or nothing; and then
those who are examined by them instead of being angry with themselves
are angry with me: This confounded Socrates, they say; this villainous
misleader of youth!—and then if somebody asks them, Why, what evil
does he practise or teach? they do not know, and cannot tell; but in order
that they may not appear to be at a loss, they repeat the ready-made charges
which are used against all philosophers about teaching things up in the
clouds and under the earth, and having no gods, and making the worse
appear the better cause; for they do not like to confess that their pretence
of knowledge has been detected—which is the truth; and as they are
numerous and ambitious and energetic, and are drawn up in battle array
and have persuasive tongues, they have filled your ears with their loud
and inveterate calumnies. And this is the reason why my three accusers,
Meletus and Anytus and Lycon, have set upon me; Meletus, who has a
quarrel with me on behalf of the poets; Anytus, on behalf of the craftsmen and politicians; Lycon, on behalf of the rhetoricians: and, as I said
at the beginning, I cannot expect to get rid of such a mass of calumny
all in a moment. And this, O men of Athens, is the truth and the whole
truth; I have concealed nothing, I have dissembled nothing. And yet, I
know that my plainness of speech makes them hate me, and what is their
hatred but a proof that I am speaking the truth? Hence has arisen the
prejudice against me; and this is the reason of it, as you will find out
either in this or in any future enquiry.

I have said enough in my defence against the first class of my accusers;

I turn to the second class. They are headed by Meletus, that good man and true lover of his country, as he calls himself. Against these, too, I must try to make a defence: Let their affidavit be read: it contains something of this kind: It says that Socrates is a doer of evil, who corrupts the youth; and who does not believe in the gods of the State, but has other new divinities of his own. Such is the charge; and now let us examine the particular counts. He says that I am a doer of evil, and corrupt the youth; but I say, O men of Athens, that Meletus is a doer of evil, in that he pretends to be in earnest when he is only in jest, and is so eager to bring men to trial from a pretended zeal and interest about matters in which he really never had the smallest interest. And the truth of this I will endeavour to prove to you. . . .

I have said enough in answer to the charge of Meletus: any elaborate defence is unnecessary; but I know only too well how many are the enmities which I have incurred, and this is what will be my destruction if I am destroyed—not Meletus, nor yet Anytus, but the envy and detraction of the world, which has been the death of many good men, and will probably be the death of many more; there is no danger of my being the last of them.

Some one will say: And are you not ashamed, Socrates, of a course of life which is likely to bring you to an untimely end? To him I may fairly answer: There you are mistaken: a man who is good for anything ought not to calculate the chance of living or dying; he ought only to consider whether in doing anything he is doing right or wrong—acting the part of a good man or of a bad. Whereas, upon your view, the heroes who fell at Troy were not good for much, and the son of Thetis above all, who altogether despised danger in comparison with disgrace; and when he was so eager to slay Hector, his goddess mother said to him, that if he avenged his companion Patroclus, and slew Hector, he would die himself —"Fate," she said, in these or the like words, "waits for you next after Hector"; he, receiving this warning, utterly despised danger and death, and instead of fearing them, feared rather to live in dishonour, and not to avenge his friend. "Let me die forthwith," he replies, "and be avenged of my enemy, rather than abide here by the beaked ships, a laughing-stock and a burden of the earth." Had Achilles any thought of death and danger? For wherever a man's place is, whether the place which he has chosen or that in which he has been placed by a commander, there he ought to remain in the hour of danger; he should not think of death or of anything but of disgrace. And this, O men of Athens, is a true saying.

Strange, indeed, would be my conduct, O men of Athens, if I, who, when I was ordered by the generals whom you chose to command me at Potidaea and Amphipolis and Delium,[2] remained where they placed me, like any other man, facing death—if now, when, as I conceive and imagine, God orders me to fulfil the philosopher's mission of searching into myself and other men, I were to desert my post through fear of death, or any other fear; that would indeed be strange, and I might justly be arraigned in court for denying the existence of the gods, if I disobeyed the oracle because I was afraid of death, fancying that I was wise when I was not wise. For the fear of death is indeed the pretence of wisdom, and not real wisdom, being a pretence of knowing the unknown; and no one knows whether death, which men in their fear apprehend to be the greatest evil, may not be the greatest good. Is not this ignorance of a disgraceful sort, the ignorance which is the conceit that a man knows what he does not know? And in this respect only I believe myself to differ from men in general, and may perhaps claim to be wiser than they are: that whereas I know but little of the world below, I do not suppose that I know: but I do know that injustice and disobedience to a better, whether God or man, is evil and dishonourable, and I will never fear or avoid a possible good rather than a certain evil.

And therefore if you let me go now, and are not convinced by Anytus, who said that since I had been prosecuted I must be put to death; (or if not that I ought never to have been prosecuted at all); and that if I escape now, your sons will all be utterly ruined by listening to my words —if you say to me, Socrates, this time we will not mind Anytus, and you shall be let off, but upon one condition, that you are not to enquire and speculate in this way any more, and that if you are caught doing so again you shall die; if this was the condition on which you let me go, I should reply: Men of Athens, I honour and love you; but I shall obey God rather than you, and while I have life and strength I shall never cease from the practice and teaching of philosophy, exhorting any one whom I meet and saying to him after my manner: You, my friend—a citizen of the great and mighty and wise city of Athens—are you not ashamed of heaping up the greatest amount of money and honour and reputation, and caring so little about wisdom and truth and the greatest improvement of the soul, which you never regard or heed at all? And if the person with whom I am arguing, says: Yes, but I do care; then I do not leave him or let him go at once; but I proceed to interrogate and examine and

2.   The references are to campaigns of the Peloponnesian War in which Socrates saw active service.

cross-examine him, and if I think that he has no virtue in him, but only says that he has, I reproach him with undervaluing the greater, and overvaluing the less. And I shall repeat the same words to every one whom I meet, young and old, citizen and alien, but especially to the citizens, inasmuch as they are my brethren. For know that this is the command of God; and I believe that no greater good has ever happened in the State than my service to the God. For I do nothing but go about persuading you all, old and young alike, not to take thought for your persons or your properties, but first and chiefly to care about the greatest improvement of the soul. I tell you that virtue is not given by money, but that from virtue comes money and every other good of man, public as well as private. This is my teaching, and if this is the doctrine which corrupts the youth, I am a mischievous person. But if any one says that this is not my teaching, he is speaking an untruth. Wherefore, O men of Athens, I say to you, do as Anytus bids or not as Anytus bids, and either acquit me or not; but whichever you do, understand that I shall never alter my ways, not even if I have to die many times.

Men of Athens, do not interrupt, but hear me; there was an understanding between us that you should hear me to the end: I have something more to say, at which you may be inclined to cry out; but I believe that to hear me will be good for you, and therefore I beg that you will not cry out. I would have you know, that if you kill such an one as I am, you will injure yourselves more than you will injure me. Nothing will injure me, not Meletus nor yet Anytus—they cannot, for a bad man is not permitted to injure a better than himself. I do not deny that Anytus may, perhaps, kill him, or drive him into exile, or deprive him of civil rights; and he may imagine, and others may imagine, that he is inflicting a great injury upon him: but there I do not agree. For the evil of doing as he is doing—the evil of unjustly taking away the life of another—is greater far.

And now, Athenians, I am not going to argue for my own sake, as you may think, but for yours, that you may not sin against the God by condemning me, who am his gift to you. For if you kill me you will not easily find a successor to me, who, if I may use such a ludicrous figure of speech, am a sort of gadfly, given to the State by God; and the State is a great and noble steed who is tardy in his motions owing to his very size, and requires to be stirred into life. I am that gadfly which God has attached to the State, and all day long and in all places am always fastening upon you, arousing and persuading and reproaching you. You will not easily find another like me, and therefore I would advise you to spare me. I dare say that you may feel out of temper (like a person who is suddenly awakened from sleep), and you think that you might easily strike me dead as Anytus advises, and then you would sleep on for the remainder of your lives, unless God in his care of you sent you another gadfly. When I say that I am given to you by God, the proof of my mission is this: if I had been like other men, I should not have neglected all my own concerns or patiently seen the neglect of them during all these years, and have been doing yours, coming to you individually like a father or elder brother, exhorting you to regard virtue; such conduct, I say, would be unlike human nature. If I had gained anything, or if my exhortations had been paid, there would have been some sense in my doing so; but now, as you will perceive, not even the impudence of my accusers dares to say that I have ever exacted or sought pay of any one; of that they have no witness. And I have a sufficient witness to the truth of what I say—my poverty.

Someone may wonder why I go about in private giving advice and busying myself with the concerns of others, but do not venture to come forward in public and advise the State. I will tell you why. You have heard me speak at sundry times and in divers places of an oracle or sign which comes to me, and is the divinity which Meletus ridicules in the indictment. This sign, which is a kind of voice, first began to come to me when I was a child; it always forbids but never commands me to do anything which I am going to do. This is what deters me from being a politician. And rightly, as I think. For I am certain, O men of Athens, that if I had engaged in politics, I should have perished long ago, and done no good either to you or to myself. And do not be offended at my telling you the truth: for the truth is, that no man who goes to war with you or any other multitude, honestly striving against the many lawless and unrighteous deeds which are done in a state, will save his life; he who will fight for the right, if he would live even for a brief space, must have a private station and not a public one.

I can give you convincing evidence of what I say, not words only, but what you value far more—actions. Let me relate to you a passage of my own life which will prove to you that I should never have yielded to injustice from any fear of death and that "as I should have refused to yield" I must have died at once. I will tell you a tale of the courts, not very interesting perhaps, but nevertheless true. The only office of State which I ever held, O men of Athens, was that of senator:[3] the tribe Antiochis, which is my tribe, had the presidency at the trial of the generals who had

3.  Member of the Council (*boulē*).

not taken up the bodies of the slain after the battle of Arginusae,[4] and you proposed to try them in a body, contrary to law, as you all thought afterwards; but at the time I was the only one of the Prytanes[5] who was opposed to the illegality, and I gave my vote against you; and when the orators threatened to impeach and arrest me, and you called and shouted, I made up my mind that I would run the risk, having law and justice with me, rather than take part in your injustice because I feared imprisonment and death. This happened in the days of the democracy. But when the oligarchy of the Thirty was in power, they sent for me and four others into the rotunda, and bade us bring Leon the Salaminian from Salamis, as they wanted to put him to death. This was a specimen of the sort of commands which they were always giving with the view of implicating as many as possible in their crimes; and then I showed, not in word only but in deed, that, if I may be allowed to use such an expression, I cared not a straw for death, and that my great and only care was lest I should do an unrighteous or unholy thing. For the strong arm of that oppressive power did not frighten me into doing wrong; and when we came out of the rotunda the other four went to Salamis and fetched Leon, but I went quietly home. For which I might have lost my life, had not the power of the Thirty shortly afterwards come to an end. And many will witness to my words.

Now, do you really imagine that I could have survived all these years, if I had led a public life, supposing that like a good man I had always maintained the right and had made justice, as I ought, the first thing? No, indeed, men of Athens, neither I nor any other man. But I have been always the same in all my actions, public as well as private, and never have I yielded any base compliance to those who are slanderously termed my disciples, or to any other. Not that I have any regular disciples. But if any one likes to come and hear me while I am pursuing my mission, whether he be young or old, he is not excluded. Nor do I converse only with those who pay; but any one, whether he be rich or poor, may ask and answer me and listen to my words; and whether he turns out to be a bad man or a good one, neither result can be justly imputed to me; for I never taught or professed to teach him anything. And if any one says that he has ever learned or heard anything from me in private which all the world has not heard, let me tell you that he is lying.

4. 406 B.C.
5. Members of the Committee of the Council that was in actual session at any given time.

But I shall be asked, Why do people delight in continually conversing with you? I have told you already, Athenians, the whole truth about this matter: they like to hear the cross-examination of the pretenders to wisdom; there is amusement in it. Now, this duty of cross-examining other men has been imposed upon me by God; and has been signified to me by oracles, visions, and in every way in which the will of divine power was ever intimated to any one. This is true, O Athenians; or, if not true, would be soon refuted. If I am or have been corrupting the youth, those of them who are now grown up and have become sensible that I gave them bad advice in the days of their youth should come forward as accusers, and take their revenge; or if they do not like to come themselves, some of their relatives, fathers, brothers, or other kinsmen, should say what evil their families have suffered at my hands. Now is their time. Many of them I see in the court. There is Crito, who is of the same age and of the same deme with myself, and there is Critobulus his son, whom I also see. Then again there is Lysanias of Sphettus, who is the father of Aeschines—he is present; and also there is Antiphon of Cephisus, who is the father of Epigenes; and there are the brothers of several who have associated with me. There is Nicostratus the son of Theodotides, and the brother of Theodotus (now Theodotus himself is dead, and therefore he, at any rate, will not seek to stop him); and there is Paralus the son of Demodocus, who had a brother Theages; and Adeimantus the son of Ariston, whose brother Plato is present; and Aeantodorus, who is the brother of Apollodorus, whom I also see. I might mention a great many others, some of whom Meletus should have produced as witnesses in the course of his speech; and let him still produce them, if he has forgotten— I will make way for him. And let him say, if he has any testimony of the sort which he can produce. Nay, Athenians, the very opposite is the truth. For all these are ready to witness on behalf of the corrupter, of the injurer of their kindred, as Meletus and Anytus call me; not the corrupted youth only—there might have been a motive for that—but their uncorrupted elder relatives. Why should they too support me with their testimony? Why, indeed, except for the sake of truth and justice, and because they know that I am speaking the truth, and that Meletus is a liar.

Well, Athenians, this and the like of this is all the defence which I have to offer. Yet a word more. Perhaps there may be some one who is offended at me, when he calls to mind how he himself on a similar, or even a less serious occasion, prayed and entreated the judges with many tears, and how he produced his children in court, which was a moving spectacle, together with a host of relations and friends; whereas I, who am probably in danger of my life, will do none of these things. The contrast may occur to his mind, and he may be set against me, and vote in anger because he is displeased at me on this account. Now, if there be such a person among you—mind, I do not say that there is—to him I may fairly reply: My friend, I am a man, and like other men, a creature of flesh and blood, and not "of wood or stone," as Homer says; and I have a family, yes, and sons, O Athenians, three in number, one almost a man, and two others who are still young; and yet I will not bring any of them hither in order to petition you for an acquittal. And why not? Not from any self-assertion or want of respect for you. Whether I am or am not afraid of death is another question, of which I will not now speak. But, having regard to public opinion, I feel that such conduct would be discreditable to myself, and to you, and to the whole State. One who has reached my years, and who has a name for wisdom, ought not to demean himself. Whether this opinion of me be deserved or not, at any rate the world has decided that Socrates is in some way superior to other men. And if those among you who are said to be superior in wisdom and courage, and any other virtue, demean themselves in this way, how shameful is their conduct! I have seen men of reputation, when they have been condemned, behaving in the strangest manner: they seemed to fancy that they were going to suffer something dreadful if they died, and that they could be immortal if you only allowed them to live; and I think that such are a dishonour to the State, and that any stranger coming in would have said of them that the most eminent men of Athens, to whom the Athenians themselves give honour and command, are no better than women. And I say that these things ought not to be done by those of us who have a reputation; and if they are done, you ought not to permit them; you ought rather to show that you are far more disposed to condemn the man who gets up a doleful scene and makes the city ridiculous, than him who holds his peace.

But, setting aside the question of public opinion, there seems to be something wrong in asking a favour of a judge, and thus procuring an acquittal, instead of informing and convincing him. For his duty is, not to make a present of justice, but to give judgment; and he has sworn that he will judge according to the laws, and not according to his own good pleasure; and we ought not to encourage you, nor should you allow yourselves to be encouraged, in this habit of perjury—there can be no piety in that. Do not then require me to do what I consider dishonourable and impious and wrong, especially now, when I am being tried for impiety on the indictment of Meletus. For if, O men of Athens, by force of persuasion and entreaty I could overpower your oaths, then I should be teaching you to believe that there are no gods, and in defending should simply convict myself of the charge of not believing in them. But that is not so—far otherwise. For I do believe that there are gods, and in a sense higher than that in which any of my accusers believe in them. And to you and to God I commit my cause, to be determined by you as is best for you and me.

[*The jury voted Socrates' conviction. In a case in which the penalty was not strictly prescribed in the law, the prosecution and then the defense might propose what each side considered a suitable punishment. The jury then voted on these proposals. The prosecution has requested the death penalty; it is now Socrates' turn to speak:*]

There are many reasons why I am not grieved, O men of Athens, at the vote of condemnation. I expected it, and am only surprised that the votes are so nearly equal; for I had thought that the majority against me would have been far larger; but now, had thirty votes gone over to the other side, I should have been acquitted. And I may say, I think, that I have escaped Meletus. I may say more; for without the assistance of Anytus and Lycon, any one may see that he would not have had a fifth part of the votes, as the law requires, in which case he would have incurred a fine of a thousand drachmae.

And so he proposes death as the penalty. And what shall I propose on my part, O men of Athens? Clearly that which is my due. And what is my due? What returns shall be made to the man who has never had the wit to be idle during his whole life; but has been careless of what the many care for—wealth, and family interests, and military offices, and speaking in the assembly, and magistracies, and plots, and parties. Reflecting that I was really too honest a man to be a politician and live, I did not go where I could do no good to you or to myself; but where I could do the greatest good privately to every one of you, thither I went, and sought to persuade every man among you that he must look to himself, and seek virtue and wisdom before he looks to his private interests, and look to the State before he looks to the interests of the State; and that this should be the order which he observes in all his actions. What shall be done to such an one? Doubtless some good thing, O men of Athens, if he has his reward; and the good should be of a kind suitable to him. What would be a reward suitable to a poor man who is your benefactor, and who desires leisure that he may instruct you? There can be no reward so fitting as maintenance in the Prytaneum, O men of Athens, a reward which he deserves far more than the citizen who has won the prize at Olympia in the horse or chariot race, whether the chariots were drawn by two horses or by many. For I am in want, and he has enough; and he only gives you the appearance of happiness, and I give you the reality. And if I am to estimate the penalty fairly, I should say that maintenance in the Prytaneum is the just return.[6]

Perhaps you think that I am braving you in what I am saying now, as in what I said before about the tears and prayers. But this is not so. I speak rather because I am convinced that I never intentionally wronged any one, although I cannot convince you—the time has been too short; if there were a law at Athens, as there is in other cities, that a capital cause should not be decided in one day, then I believe that I should have convinced you. But I cannot in a moment refute great slanders; and, as I am convinced that I never wronged another, I will assuredly not wrong myself. I will not say to myself that I deserve any evil, or propose any penalty. Why should I? Because I am afraid of the penalty of death which Meletus proposes? When I do not know whether death is a good or an evil, why should I propose a penalty which would certainly be an evil? Shall I say imprisonment? And why should I live in prison, and be the slave of the magistrate of the year—of the Eleven? Or shall the penalty be a fine, and imprisonment until the fine is paid? There is the same objection. I should have to lie in prison, for money I have none, and cannot pay. And if I say exile (and this may possibly be the penalty which you will affix), I must indeed be blinded by the love of life, if I am so irrational as to expect that when you, who are my own citizens, cannot endure my discourses and words, and have found them so grievous and odious that you will have no more of them, others are likely to endure me. No, indeed, men of Athens, that is not very likely. And what a life should I lead, at my age, wandering from city to city, ever changing my place of exile, and always being driven out! For I am quite sure that wherever I go, there as here, the young men will flock to me; and if I drive them away, their elders will drive me out at their request; and if I let them come, their fathers and friends will drive me out for their sakes.

Some one will say: Yes, Socrates, but cannot you hold your tongue, and then you may go into a foreign city, and no one will interfere with you? Now, I have great difficulty in making you understand my answer to this.

6. To take their meals at the public expense in the town hall was a reward given to public benefactors, among whom were included winners in the Olympian games.

For if I tell you that to do as you say would be a disobedience to the God, and therefore that I cannot hold my tongue, you will not believe that I am serious; and if I say again that daily to discourse about virtue, and of those other things about which you hear me examining myself and others, is the greatest good of man, and that the unexamined life is not worth living, you are still less likely to believe me. Yet I say what is true, although a thing of which it is hard for me to persuade you. Also, I have never been accustomed to think that I deserve to suffer any harm. Had I money I might have estimated the offence at what I was able to pay, and not have been much the worse. But I have none, and therefore I must ask you to proportion the fine to my means. Well, perhaps I could afford a mina, and therefore I propose that penalty: Plato, Crito, Critobulus, and Apollodorus, my friends here, bid me say thirty minae, and they will be the sureties. Let thirty minae be the penalty; for which sum they will be ample security to you.

[*The jury votes; he is condemned to death. Socrates addresses the court:*]

Not much time will be gained, O Athenians, in return for the evil name which you will get from the detractors of the city, who will say that you killed Socrates, a wise man; for they will call me wise, even although I am not wise, when they want to reproach you. If you had waited a little while, your desire would have been fulfilled in the course of nature. For I am far advanced in years, as you may perceive, and not far from death. I am speaking now not to all of you, but only to those who have condemned me to death. And I have another thing to say to them: You think that I was convicted because I had no words of the sort which would have procured my acquittal—I mean, if I had thought fit to leave nothing undone or unsaid. Not so; the deficiency which led to my conviction was not of words—certainly not. But I had not the boldness or impudence or inclination to address you as you would have liked me to do, weeping and wailing and lamenting, and saying and doing many things which you have been accustomed to hear from others, and which, as I maintain, are unworthy of me. I thought at the time that I ought not to do anything common or mean when in danger: nor do I now repent of the style of my defence; I would rather die having spoken after my manner, than speak in your manner and live. For neither in war nor yet at law ought I or any man to use every way of escaping death. Often in battle there can be no doubt that if a man will throw away his arms, and fall on his knees before his pursuers, he may escape death; and in other dangers there are other ways of escaping death, if a man is willing to say and do anything. The difficulty, my friends, is not to avoid death, but to avoid unrighteousness; for that runs faster than death. I am old and move slowly, and the slower runner has overtaken me, and my accusers are keen and quick, and the faster runner, who is unrighteousness, has overtaken them. And now I depart hence condemned by you to suffer the penalty of death —they too go their ways condemned by the truth to suffer the penalty of villainy and wrong; and I must abide by my award—let them abide by theirs. I suppose that these things may be regarded as fated—and I think that they are well.

And now, O men who have condemned me, I would fain prophesy to you; for I am about to die, and in the hour of death men are gifted with prophetic power. And I prophesy to you who are my murderers, that immediately after my departure punishment far heavier than you have inflicted on me will surely await you. Me you have killed because you wanted to escape the accuser, and not to give an account of your lives. But that will not be as you suppose: far otherwise. For I say that there will be more accusers of you than there are now; accusers whom hitherto I have restrained: and as they are younger they will be more inconsiderate with you, and you will be more offended at them. If you think that by killing men you can prevent some one from censuring your evil lives, you are mistaken; that is not a way of escape which is either possible or honourable; the easiest and the noblest way is not to be disabling others, but to be improving yourselves. This is the prophecy which I utter before my departure to the judges who have condemned me.

Friends, who would have acquitted me, I would like also to talk with you about the thing which has come to pass, while the magistrates are busy, and before I go to the place at which I must die. Stay then a little, for we may as well talk with one another while there is time. You are my friends, and I should like to show you the meaning of this event which has happened to me. O my judges—for you I may truly call judges —I should like to tell you of a wonderful circumstance. Hitherto the divine faculty of which the internal oracle is the source has constantly been in the habit of opposing me even about trifles, if I was going to make a slip or error in any matter; and now as you see there has come upon me that which may be thought, and is generally believed to be, the last and worst evil. But the oracle made no sign of opposition, either when I was leaving my house in the morning, or when I was on my way to the court, or while I was speaking, at anything which I was going to say; and yet I have often been stopped in the middle of a speech, but now in nothing I either said or did touching the matter in hand has the oracle opposed me. What do I take to be the explanation of this silence? I will tell you. It is an intimation that what has happened to me is a good, and that those of us who think that death is an evil are in error. For the customary sign would surely have opposed me had I been going to evil and not to good.

Let us reflect in another way, and we shall see that there is great reason to hope that death is a good; for one of two things—either death is a state of nothingness and utter unconsciousness, or, as men say, there is a change and migration of the soul from this world to another. Now, if you suppose that there is no consciousness, but a sleep like the sleep of him who is undisturbed even by dreams, death will be an unspeakable gain. For if a person were to select the night in which his sleep was undisturbed even by dreams, and were to compare with this the other days and nights of his life, and then were to tell us how many days and nights he had passed in the course of his life better and more pleasantly than this one, I think that any man, I will not say a private man, but even the great king will not find many such days or nights, when compared with the others. Now, if death be of such a nature, I say that to die is gain; for eternity is then only a single night. But if death is the journey to another place, and there, as men say, all the dead abide, what good, O my friends and judges, can be greater than this? If, indeed, when the pilgrim arrives in the world below, he is delivered from the professors of justice in this world, and finds the true judges who are said to give judgment there, Minos and Rhadamanthus and Aeacus and Triptolemus, and other sons of God who were righteous in their own life, that pilgrimage will be worth making. What would not a man give if he might converse with Orpheus and Musaeus and Hesiod and Homer? Nay, if this be true, let me die again and again. I myself, too, shall have a wonderful interest in there meeting and conversing with Palamedes, and Ajax the son of Telamon, and any other ancient hero who has suffered death through an unjust judgment; and there will be no small pleasure, as I think, in comparing my own sufferings with theirs. Above all, I shall then be able to continue my search into true and false knowledge; as in this world, so also in the next; and I shall find out who is wise, and who pretends to be wise, and is not. What would not a man give, O judges, to be able to examine the leader of the great Trojan expedition; or

Odysseus or Sisyphus, or numberless others, men and women too! What infinite delight would there be in conversing with them and asking them questions! In another world they do not put a man to death for asking questions: assuredly not. For besides being happier than we are, they will be immortal, if what is said is true.

Wherefore, O judges, be of good cheer about death, and know of a certainty, that no evil can happen to a good man, either in life or after death. He and his are not neglected by the gods; nor has my own approaching end happened by mere chance. But I see clearly that the time had arrived when it was better for me to die and be released from trouble; wherefore the oracle gave no sign. For which reason, also, I am not angry with my condemners, or with my accusers; they have done me no harm, although they did not mean to do me any good; and for this I may gently blame them.

Still, I have a favour to ask of them. When my sons are grown up, I would ask you, O my friends, to punish them; and I would have you trouble them, as I have troubled you, if they seem to care about riches, or anything, more than about virtue; or if they pretend to be something when they are really nothing, then reprove them, as I have reproved you, for not caring about that for which they ought to care, and thinking that they are something when they are really nothing. And if you do this, both I and my sons will have received justice at your hands.

The hour of departure has arrived, and we go our ways—I to die, and you to live. Which is better God only knows.

. . . . .

. . . When he had done speaking, Crito said: And have you any commands for us, Socrates—anything to say about your children, or any other matter in which we can serve you?

Nothing particular, Crito, he replied: only, as I have always told you, take care of yourselves; that is a service which you may be ever rendering to me and mine and to all of us, whether you promise to do so or not. But if you have no thought for yourselves, and care not to walk according to the rule which I have prescribed for you, not now for the first time, however much you may profess or promise at the moment, it will be of no avail.

We will do our best, said Crito: And in what way shall we bury you?

In any way that you like; but you must get hold of me, and take care that I do not run away from you. Then he turned to us, and added with a smile: I cannot make Crito believe that I am the same Socrates who has been talking and conducting the argument; he fancies that I am the other Socrates whom he will soon see, a dead body—and he asks, How shall he bury me? And though I have spoken many words in the endeavour to show that when I have drunk the poison I shall leave you and go to the joys of the blessed—these words of mine, with which I was comforting you and myself, have had, as I perceive, no effect upon Crito. And therefore I want you to be surety for me to him now, as at the trial he was surety to the judges for me: but let the promise be of another sort; for he was surety for me to the judges that I would remain, and you must be my surety to him that I shall not remain, but go away and depart; and then he will suffer less at my death, and not be grieved when he sees my body being burned or buried. I would not have him sorrow at my hard lot, or say at the burial, Thus we lay out Socrates, or, Thus we follow him to the grave or bury him; for false words are not only evil in themselves, but they inflict the soul with evil. Be of good cheer then, my dear Crito, and say that you are burying my body only, and do with that whatever is usual, and what you think best.

When he had spoken these words, he arose and went into a chamber to bathe; Crito followed him and told us to wait. So we remained behind, talking and thinking of the subject of discourse, and also of the greatness of our sorrow; he was like a father of whom we were being bereaved, and we were about to pass the rest of our lives as orphans. When he had taken the bath his children were brought to him (he had two young sons and an elder one); and the women of his family also came, and he talked to them and gave them a few directions in the presence of Crito; then he dismissed them and returned to us.

Now the hour of sunset was near, for a good deal of time had passed while he was within. When he came out, he sat down with us again after his bath, but not much was said. Soon the jailer, who was the servant of the Eleven, entered and stood by him, saying: To you, Socrates, whom I know to be the noblest and gentlest and best of all who ever came to this place, I will not impute the angry feeling of other men, who rage and swear at me, when, in obedience to the authorities, I bid them drink the poison—indeed, I am sure that you will not be angry with me; for others, as you are aware, and not I, are to blame. And so fare you well, and try to bear lightly what must needs be—you know my errand. Then bursting into tears he turned away and went out.

Socrates looked at him and said: I return your good wishes, and will do as you bid. Then turning to us, he said, How charming the man is: since I have been in prison he has always been coming to see me, and at times he would talk to me, and was as good to me as could be, and now see how generously he sorrows on my account. We must do as he says, Crito; and therefore let the cup be brought, if the poison is prepared: if not, let the attendant prepare some.

Yet, said Crito, the sun is still upon the hill-tops, and I know that many a one has taken the draught late, and after the announcement has been made to him, he has eaten and drunk, and enjoyed the society of his beloved: do not hurry—there is time enough.

Socrates said: Yes, Crito, and they of whom you speak are right in so acting, for they think that they will be gainers by the delay; but I am right in not following their example, for I do not think that I should gain anything by drinking the poison a little later; I should only be ridiculous in my own eyes for sparing and saving a life which is already forfeit. Please then to do as I say, and not to refuse me.

Crito made a sign to the servant, who was standing by; and he went out, and having been absent for some time, returned with the jailer carrying the cup of poison. Socrates said: You, my good friend, who are experienced in these matters, shall give me directions how I am to proceed. The man answered: You have only to walk about until your legs are heavy, and then to lie down, and the poison will act. At the same time he handed the cup to Socrates, who in the easiest and gentlest manner, without the least fear or change of colour or feature, looking at the man with all his eyes, as his manner was, took the cup and said: What do you say about making a libation out of this cup to any god? May I, or not? The man answered: We only prepare, Socrates, just so much as we deem enough. I understand, he said: but I may and must ask the gods to prosper my journey from this to the other world—even so—and so be it according to my prayer. Then raising the cup to his lips, quite readily and cheerfully he drank off the poison. And hitherto most of us had been able to control our sorrow; but now when we saw him drinking, and saw too that he had finished the draught, we could no longer forbear, and in spite of myself my own tears were flowing fast; so that I covered my face and wept, not for him, but at the thought of my own calamity in having to part from such a friend. Nor was I the first; for Crito, when he found himself unable to restrain his tears, had got up, and I followed; and at that moment, Apollodorus, who had been weeping all the time, broke out in a loud and passionate cry which made cowards of us all.

Socrates alone retained his calmness: What is this strange outcry? he said. I sent away the women mainly in order that they might not misbehave in this way, for I have been told that a man should die in peace. Be quiet then, and have patience. When we heard his words we were ashamed, and refrained our tears; and he walked about until, as he said, his legs began to fail, and then he lay on his back, according to directions, and the man who gave him the poison now and then looked at his feet and legs; and after a while he pressed his foot hard, and asked him if he could feel; and he said, No; and then his leg, and so upwards and upwards, and showed us that he was cold and stiff. And he felt them himself, and said: When the poison reaches the heart, that will be the end. He was beginning to grow cold about the groin, when he uncovered his face, for he had covered himself up, and said—they were his last words—he said: Crito, I owe a cock to Asclepius; will you remember to pay the debt? The debt shall be paid, said Crito; is there anything else? There was no answer to this question; but in a minute or two a movement was heard, and the attendants uncovered him; his eyes were set, and Crito closed his eyes and mouth.

Such was the end of our friend; concerning whom I may truly say, that of all men of his time whom I have known, he was the wisest and justest and best.

# 82  The Wonder of Man

The Greek was filled with a sense of pride and wonder at the qualities he found in man. The best-known expression of this enthusiasm—with all of its overtones of irony and sadness—is a chorus (lines 332–368) from Sophocles' tragic drama *Antigone*. The translation is by Lewis Campbell.

Many a wonder lives and moves, but the wonder of all is man,
That courseth over the grey ocean, carried of Southern gale;
Faring amidst high-swelling seas that rudely surge around,
And Earth, supreme of mighty Gods, eldest, imperishable,
Eternal, he with patient furrow wears and wears away
    As year by year the plough-shares turn and turn—
Subduing her unwearied strength with children of the steed.

And wound in woven coils of nets he seizeth for his prey
The aëry tribe of birds and wilding armies of the chase,
And sea-born millions of the deep—man is so crafty-wise.
And now with engine of his wit he tameth to his will
The mountain-ranging beast whose lair is in the country wild;
    And now his yoke hath passed upon the mane
Of horse with proudly crested neck and tireless mountain bull.

Wise utterance and wind-swift thought, and city moulding mind,
And shelter from the clear-eyed power of biting frost,
He hath taught him, and to shun the sharp, roof-penetrating rain,—
Full of resource, without device he meets no coming time;
    From Death alone he shall not find reprieve;
No league may gain him that relief; but even for fell disease,
That long hath baffled wisest leech, he hath contrived a cure.

Inventive beyond wildest hope, endowed with boundless skill,
One while he moves toward evil, and one while toward good,
According as he loves his land and fears the Gods above. . . .

# GLOSSARY

*A few technical terms that occur in the source readings are not contained in the following list either because the meanings are unknown or because the context gives a sufficient indication of the usage.*

ABBUTTUM. Type of branding used to identify slaves in Sumer.

ACROPOLIS. Literally, "the high city"; Greek cities were often built around a hill, on top of which were the temples of the gods, and which in time of war served as a citadel of last-ditch defense.

AGORA. The market-place of a Greek city, where citizens met to shop, stroll, and talk.

ARCHON. One of a board of nine (originally three: see basileus, polemarch, eponymos) chief administrative officials in Athens; under the democracy the archons were elected annually by lot and had little power.

AREOPAGUS. The original Athenian Council, composed of ex-archons; under the democracy it was maintained but relegated to an insignificant position in the political structure.

BASILEUS. The Greek word for a king; in Athens the basileus was an archon (*q.v.*) who in Classical times was a purely religious functionary.

BOULĒ. The Athenian Council of Five Hundred, annually elected, with fifty members from each of the ten tribes.

CHOREGIA. One of the Athenian leiturgies (*q.v.*); the staging of a play at one of the dramatic festivals, the chief expense of which was the training of the chorus.

COINAGE, GREEK. In Attic (Athenian) currency, which from the fifth century B.C. became more or less standard in Greece, the monetary units were: 6 obols equal one drachma; 20 drachmae equal one stater (a gold coin); 100 drachmae equal one mina; 60 minae equal one talent.

CORN. Cereal grain, normally wheat; many translations in this volume are by English translators who use "corn" where in America one would say "grain" or "wheat."

CRISIS. A technical term in Greek medicine; the turning point in the progress of a severe disease, at which eventual recovery might be foreseen.

CUBIT. A measure of length equal to about 18 inches.

DARIC. A Persian gold coin.

DEBEN. An Egyptian unit of metallic weight used as a standard of value; in monetary transactions between Egypt and the Near East, one deben equals 10 shekels (*q.v.*).

DEMOS. The citizen body of Athens; "the people."

DEME. A voting district, the basic political division of the Athenian democracy.

DICAST. A juryman in an Athenian court; frequently translated as "judge."

DOKIMASIA. Official examination into the eligibility for service of persons elected to the Athenian boulē (*q.v.*).

DRACHMA. The commonest Greek coin, traditionally the daily wage of a skilled worker; see coinage, Greek.

ENSI. The administrative head of a Sumerian city-state, sometimes king, sometimes administrator of the main temple estate; also called patesi.

EPARCH. Greek word for a provincial military official.

EPHOR. One of a board (the ephorate) of five men, the highest administrative officials in Sparta.

EPIKLEROS. An heiress, whose position was a special one in Athenian law.

EPONYMOS. An Athenian archon (*q.v.*); nominally the highest official in the state, the eponymos is meant in any reference simply to "the archon."

GAN. A Mesopotamian land measure; one gan equals about 1½ acres.

GUR. A Mesopotamian dry measure; one gur equals 7.2 bushels; also called kor and kur.

GYMNASIARCHIA. An office the duty of which was the undertaking of the expense of the torch races at certain Athenian festivals; one of the Athenian leiturgies (*q.v.*).

HEKET. An Egyptian dry measure; slightly more than half a bushel.

HELOT. An agricultural laborer at Sparta; the helots were the economic foundation of the Spartan military state; they were bound to the land, and their status is frequently likened to that of the medieval European serf.

HOPLITE. A heavy-armed Greek infantryman.

HYPARCH. Greek word for a provincial governor.

KA. 1. In Egypt, the soul or vital spirit of an individual. 2. In Mesopotamia, a measure of volume, both liquid and dry; one ka equals about ¾ of a quart; also called qa and qu.

KANNUM. Type of branding used to identify slaves in Sumer.

KASBU. A Mesopotamian measure of length (distance of considerable magnitude), also of area.

KIDET. An Egyptian unit of metallic weight used as a standard of value; a fractional part of a deben (*q.v.*).

KOR. See gur.

KUR. See gur.

LACEDAEMON. Sparta.

LEITURGY. In Athens, a public service the expense for which was required to be borne by a wealthy citizen; see Choregia, Gymnasiarchia, Trierarchia.

MASKANUM. Type of branding used to identify slaves in Sumer.

MASSIKTUM. A Mesopotamian measure of volume, both liquid and dry; a multiple of the seah (*q.v.*).

METIC. A resident alien in Athens.

MINA. In the Near East a monetary unit of metal by weight; 60 shekels (*q.v.*) equal one mina; adopted also by the Greeks: see coinage, Greek.

MUDUM. A member of a social class in Sumer.

NAPTARUM. A member of a social class in Sumer.

NOMARCH. The governor of a nome.

NOME. The basic regional administrative division in Egypt.

OBOL. The smallest Greek coin; traditionally the minimum daily cost of an adult's bare subsistence; see coinage, Greek.

PATESI. See ensi.

PELTAST. A light-armed spearman in a Greek army.

PLETHRON. A Greek land measure (plural, plethra); about $3\frac{3}{4}$ plethra equal one acre.

POLEMARCH. An Athenian archon (*q.v.*); the polemarch in Classical times was nominally the highest military official of the state, a function he had originally fulfilled in actuality.

POLIS. The Greek city-state (plural, poleis).

QA. See ka.

QU. See ka.

SABITUM. A licensed woman liquor-dealer in Sumer.

SAKANAKKU. A Sumerian public official.

SAR. A Mesopotamian measure of area; one sar equals slightly over 42 square yards (of floor space).

SATRAP. Regional or provincial governor in the Persian empire; the district for which he was responsible was a satrapy.

SEAH. A Mesopotamian measure of volume, both liquid and dry; a multiple of the ka (2) (*q.v.*) and a fractional part of the massiktum.

SHE. The smallest Mesopotamian unit of metallic weight used in exchange; 180 she equal one shekel (*q.v.*).

SHEKEL. The basic Mesopotamian unit of metallic weight used as a standard of exchange value throughout the Near East; see also mina, she.

SILA. A Mesopotamian dry measure; 500 sila equal one gur (*q.v.*); used in calculating interest payment in kind: a convenient fractional part of the gur, inasmuch as the normal annual interest rate was 20 per cent.

SIPPU. Part of a Mesopotamian house near the entrance.

STADE. A Greek measure of length, approximately equal to 600 feet.

STATER. A Greek monetary unit; see coinage, Greek.

STRATEGUS. An Athenian general; under the democracy, one of ten annually elected officials who were in charge of military affairs.

TALENT. A Greek monetary unit; see coinage, Greek.

TAMKARRUM. A Mesopotamian state finance official.

TRIERARCHIA. The undertaking of the expense of outfitting a warship, one of the Athenian leiturgies (*q.v.*); elsewhere in Greece the trierarchy was simply the command of a warship.

TRIREME. A warship; the standard craft in Classical Greek navies.

UBARUM. A member of a social class in Sumer.

# INDEX OF SOURCES

[ 719 ]